AN ILLUSTRATED AND COMPREHENSIVE
CATHOLIC BIBLE DICTIONARY

AND

A COMPREHENSIVE HISTORY

OF THE BOOKS OF

THE HOLY CATHOLIC BIBLE

BY

REV. BERNARD O'REILLY, L.D. (LAVAL.)

Catholic Treasures
626 Montana Street
Monrovia, California
91016

D1599756

Approbations of the Archbishops and Bishops of the Holy Catholic Church in America and England to the E.W. Sawyer and Co. 1881 reprint edition of *An Illustrated and Comprehensive Catholic Bible Dictionary and A Comprehensive History of the Books of the Holy Catholic Bible* by Rev. Bernard O'Reilly, L.D. (Laval).

+ Cardinal Mc Closkey, Archbishop of New York.
+ Late Archbishop Hughes, of New York.
+ Archbishop Purcell, of Cincinnati.
+ Archbishop Blanc, of New Orleans.
+ Archbishop Kenrick, of St. Louis.
+ Bishop Wood, of Philadelphia.
+ Bishop Lefevre, of Detroit.
+ Bishop Shanahan, of Harrisburg.
+ Bishop Loughin, of Brooklyn.
+ Bishop Wigger, of Newark.
+ Bishop O'Farrell, of Trenton.
+ Bishop Fitzpatrick, of Boston.
+ Bishop Rappe, of Cleveland.
+ Bishop Miles, of Nashville.
+ Bishop Chanche, of Natchez.
+ Bishop O'Reilly, of Hartford.
+ Bishop O'Regan, of Chicago.
+ Bishop Spalding, of Baltimore.
+ Cardinal Wiseman, Archbishop of Westminster.
+ Bishop Brown, of the Lancashire District.
+ Bishop Brown, of the Welsh District.
+ Bishop Briggs, of the Yorkshire District.
+ Bishop Wareing, of the Eastern District.

This book is photographically reproduced from an unabridged edition of the Holy Bible containing the entire canonical scriptures according to the decree of the council or trent translated from the Latin Vulgate. Printed in 1881 by E.W. Sawyer & Company of Boston, Massachusetts

© Copyright 1991 by Catholic Treasures. All rights reserved.

Library of Congress Catalog Card No.# 9 1-0 7 7 1 6 9

ISBN 0-9620994-2-2

Printed in the United States of America.

Published by: Catholic Treasures
                   626 Montana Street
                   Monrovia, California 91016

AN ILLUSTRATED AND COMPREHENSIVE
CATHOLIC BIBLE DICTIONARY,

BASED ON THE

WORKS OF CALMET, DIXON, AND OTHER CATHOLIC AUTHORS,

AND ADAPTED TO

THE ENGLISH VERSION FIRST PUBLISHED AT RHEIMS AND DOUAY,

AS REVISED

BY THE VEN. RICHARD CHALLONER.

AND GENERALLY APPROVED BY THE CATHOLIC HIERARCHY.

EMBELLISHED WITH APPROPRIATE ILLUSTRATIONS AND MAPS.

Entered according to Act of Congress, in the year 1882, by JOSHUA RILEY JONES, in the Office of the Librarian of Congress, at Washington, D. C.

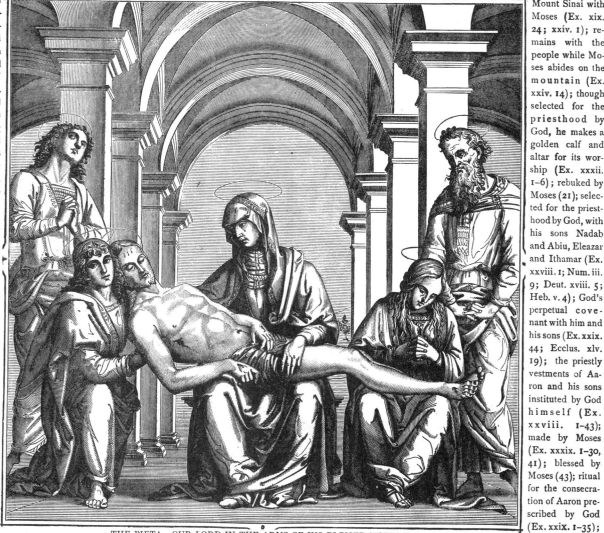

THE PIETA. OUR LORD IN THE ARMS OF HIS BLESSED MOTHER.

AARON, son of Amram and Jochabed, and great-grandson of Levi (Ex. vi. 20); born 1570 B. C., and older brother of Moses (Ex. vii. 7). When God appeared to Moses in the burning bush, he directed him to put his words in the mouth of Aaron, who had come to meet him (Ex. iv. 15; vii. 1); he goes with Moses to Pharao, and is associated with him in delivering the children of Israel (Ex. v. 1; vi. 13; Mich. vi. 4); works signs before the people (Ex. iv. 30); casts his rod before Pharao, and it is turned into a serpent (Ex. vii. 9, 10); which devours those of the magicians (12); turns water into blood (Ex. vii. 20); brings the plague of frogs upon Egypt (Ex. viii. 8); brings the sciniphs upon Egypt (17); associated with Moses in freeing the people (Ex. vii. 11); the ministry in Aaron (Ex. vi. 16, 30; vii. 1, 2); receives with Moses the order to institute the Pasch (Ex. xii.); preserves some of the manna in a vessel (Ex. xvi. 34); holds up the arms of Moses, during the battle with Amalec (Ex. xvii. 12); ordered to go up Mount Sinai with Moses (Ex. xix. 24; xxiv. 1); remains with the people while Moses abides on the mountain (Ex. xxiv. 14); though selected for the priesthood by God, he makes a golden calf and altar for its worship (Ex. xxxii. 1–6); rebuked by Moses (21); selected for the priesthood by God, with his sons Nadab and Abiu, Eleazar and Ithamar (Ex. xxviii. 1; Num. iii. 9; Deut. xviii. 5; Heb. v. 4); God's perpetual covenant with him and his sons (Ex. xxix. 44; Ecclus. xlv. 19); the priestly vestments of Aaron and his sons instituted by God himself (Ex. xxviii. 1–43); made by Moses (Ex. xxxix. 1–30, 41); blessed by Moses (43); ritual for the consecration of Aaron prescribed by God (Ex. xxix. 1–35); consecrated by Moses (Levit. viii.); offers sacrifices for the people and blesses them, (ix;) Nadab and Abiu for offering incense when not commanded destroyed by fire

(1)

(Lev. x. 1, 2); Aaron forbidden to mourn for his sons (6); Core, Dathan, Abiron and Hon, swallowed up for attempting to usurp the priesthood (Num. xvi.); the priesthood confirmed to Aaron by the blooming of his rod (xvii. 1–8); the miraculous rod preserved in the tabernacle by God's order (10);

THE HIGH-PRIEST IN HIS VESTMENTS.

commanded to abstain from wine (Lev. x. 9); share of Aaron and the other priests and Levites in the sacrifices (12); Levites give tithes to the priests (Num. xviii.); incredulity of Aaron at the waters of contradiction, for which God excludes him from the promised land (Num. xx. 12, 24); Moses by command of God takes the insignia of the high-priesthood from Aaron at Mount Hor, and vests Eleazar with them (26, 28); Aaron dies on Mount Hor, aged 123 (xx. 24–30; xxxiii. 38); praised (Ecclus. xlv. 7); the priesthood not to be assumed by any man unless he is called by God as Aaron was (Heb. v. 4).

AARONITES, the descendants of Aaron (1 Paral. xxvii. 17).

ABAD'DON (the Destroyer), the Hebrew name of the king, the angel of the bottomless pit, who was over the locusts, after the fifth angel sounded his trumpet (Apoc. ix. 10, 11).

ABA'NA, one of the rivers of Damascus (4 Kings v. 12), apparently the Barrady, which rises in Mount Libanus, runs through Damascus and is lost in a marsh in the desert.

AB'ARON, a surname of Eleazar, brother of Judas Machabeus (1 Mac. ii. 5).

AB'ARIM, a mountain in Moab, facing Jericho, from which Moses beheld the promised land just before his death (Num. xxvii. 12, 14; Deut. xxxii. 49–52).

AB'BA, the Syriac word for Father; used by our

Lord in the prayer in the garden (Mark xiv. 36); St. Paul says we utter it by the spirit of Christ in our hearts to show our adoption as sons (Rom. viii. 15; Gal. iv. 6).

AB'BITAL, one of the wives of David, and mother of Saphathia (2 Kings iii. 4).

AB'DEME'LECH, an Ethiopian eunuch in the palace of king Sedecias. He speaks to the king in favor of Jeremias, and delivers the prophet from the pit (Jerem. xxxviii. 7–13); God rewards his work of mercy by announcing that he shall be delivered from the hands of the Chaldees (Jerem. xxxix. 16–18).

ABDENA'GO, the Chaldean name given by the master of the Eunuchs to Azarias, the companion of the prophet Daniel (Dan. i. 7). One of the youths of royal or princely race selected as attendants of king Nabuchodonosor (Dan. i. 3); abstained from forbidden food (14, 15); his wisdom (19, 20); set over the works of the province of Babylon (ii. 49; iii. 12); refuses to worship the heathen gods, or the statue of the king (iii. 12); his reply to the king (16–18); condemned to be thrown into the furnace (20); his prayer in the midst of the fire (25–45); saved by an angel (49); the canticle of the three (52–90); ordered by Nabuchodonosor to come forth (93); not a hair singed or garments altered (94); promoted by the king (97).

ABDI'AS, governor of king Achab's house, and a man who feared God (3 Kings xviii. 3). In the time of Jezabel he concealed one hundred prophets in caves, and fed them on bread and water (4); sent by Achab to seek pasture, meets Elias, and bears his message to the king (7–16).

ABDI'AS (the servant of the Lord), the fourth of the twelve minor prophets (called in the King James' Bible and by Protestants generally Obadi'ah). He is believed to have prophesied in the time of Osee, Joel and Amos (588–583 B. C.) His prophecy contains only one chapter, and foretells the de-

THE ALTAR OF INCENSE.

struction of Edom, and the return of the Jews from captivity. Abd.

AB'DON, son of Illel of the tribe of Ephraim, was the tenth of the Judges of Israel (Judg. xii. 13). He succeeded Ahialon (2840 B. C.), and judged Israel eight years. He was buried at Pharathon (15).

AB'DON. See ACHOBOR.

AB'DON, a city in the tribe of Aser (Jos. xxi. 30); allotted to the Levites of the family of Gerson (1 Par. vi. 74).

A'BEL, second son of Adam and Eve. Cain tilled the earth, and Abel had flocks of sheep. Each offered sacrifice to God. The Almighty accepted the sacrifice of Abel, a lamb of his flock, which was offered with a lively faith (Heb. xi. 4) and ardent charity, but he rejected that of Cain. Abel was then persuaded to go into the fields by Cain, who rose up

THE SACRIFICE OF ABEL.

against him and slew him (Gen. iv. 2–8). Our Lord calls Abel *the just*, and places him as the first of the martyrs (Matt. xxiii. 35; Luke xi. 51). His blood cried to heaven for vengeance (Gen. iv. 10); and St. Paul makes a comparison between it and that of Jesus (Heb. xii. 24).

A'BEL or **ABELA,** a town east of the Jordan in the half tribe of Manasses (Judg. xi. 33).

A'BEL, house of Ma'acha or Abela and Beth Ma'acha, a town in the tribe of Nephthali north of Damascus, between Libanus and Anti-Libanus; besieged by Joab (2 Kings xx. 14–18); taken by Benadad, king of Syria (3 Kings xv. 20); and by Theglathphalasar (4 Kings xv. 29). Called also Abel-maim (2 Paral. xvi. 4), and Abilina (Luke iii. 1).

A'BELME'HULA or **A'BELME'ULA,** a town in the valley of the Jordan. Near it Gedeon defeated the Madianites (Judg. vii. 23); placed by Solomon under the government of Bana (3 Kings iv. 12); the birthplace of the prophet Eliseus (3 Kings xix. 16).

A'BELSATIM, a place in the plains of the Moabites, to which the camp of Israel extended (Num. xxxiii. 49). Here the Israelites fell into fornication and idolatry (xxv. 1).

A'BENBOEN (the Stone of Boen), an enormous rock between Juda and Benjamin (Jos. xviii. 18).

ABES'ALOM, ambassador of Judas Machabeus to Lysias, general of the army of Antiochus Eupator (2 Mac. xi. 17).

AB'ESAN, of the tribe of Juda, the eighth of the Judges of Israel. He was of Bethlehem; he succeeded Jephte, governed seven years and was buried in Bethlehem (1170 B. C.; Judges xii. 8, 9).

ABI or **ABI'A,** daughter of Zacharias, the high-priest, and mother of Ezechias, king of Juda (4 Kings xviii. 2; 2 Paral. xxix. 1).

ABI'A, second son of Samuel, abuses his power so that the people asked for a king (1 Kings viii. 1–6).

ABI'A, ABI'AM or ABI'AS, son of Roboam, king of Juda, by Maacha. He succeeded his father (958 B. C.) He marched against Jeroboam, and was nearly defeated by him but delivered by God. He wrested several cities from Jeroboam. Abia reigned three years, and imitated the wickedness of his father (3 Kings xiv. 31; xv. 1–8; 2 Paral. xiii. 1–22; 1 Paral. iii. 10; Matt. i. 7).

ABI'A, a descendant of Eleazar, son of Aaron, and prince or head of the eighth of the twenty-four courses into which David divided the priests (1 Paral. xxiv. 10); Zachary, father of St. John the Baptist, belonged to this course (Luke i. 5).

ABI'ATHAR or ACHIM'ELECH, tenth high-priest of the Jews. He escapes from the massacre of the priests under Saul and joined David (1 Kings xxii. 20; xxiii. 6). He remained with him as high-priest, while Saul schismatically set up Sadoc (1 Paral. vi. 53). In the reign of Solomon Abiathar espoused the cause of Adonias (3 Kings i. 7); and was deprived of the high priesthood and banished to Anathoth by Solomon (3 Kings ii. 26); as had been foretold by the high-priest Heli (1 Kings ii. 32).

AB'IDAN, prince of the tribe of Benjamin when the Israelites left Egypt (Num. i. 11; x. 24); like the other princes he made offerings for the tabernacle (vii. 60–65).

A'BIEL, grandfather of Saul (1 Kings ix. 1).

ABIE'ZER, of the tribe of Benjamin, one of David's bravest champions, commanding 24,000 men (1 Paral. xi. 28; xxvii. 12).

ABIE'ZER, son of Galaad, and also called Jeser (Num. xxvi. 30; Jos. xvii. 2); his house was the first to join Gedeon, when he sounded the trumpet for the war against the Madianites (Judg. vi. 34).

AB'IGAIL, wife of the impious Nabal of Carmel, appeases David (1 Kings xxv. 14–36); becomes his wife after Nabal's death (40–42); and bore him a son, Cheleab or Daniel (2 Kings iii. 3; 1 Paral. iii. 1).

AB'IGAIL, sister of David, wife of Jether and mother of Amasa (1 Par. ii. 16, 17; 2 Kings xvii. 25).

ABILI'NA, a little province in Cœlo-Syria, between Libanus and Anti-Libanus, of which Lysinias was tetrarch (Luke iii. 1).

ABIM'AEL, son of Jectan (Gen. x. 28; 1 Paral. i. 22); generally regarded as the progenitor of an Arabian race.

ABIM'ELECH, king of Gerara, in the country of the Philistines, struck by the beauty of Sara, whom Abraham had represented as his sister, sought to marry her, but God threatened him with death, and

struck his house with sterility, but cured them at the prayer of Abraham. Abimelech gave Sara a thousand pieces of silver for a veil, and allowed Abraham to settle many parts of his kingdom (Gen. xx.); he subsequently formed an alliance with Abraham (xxi. 22–34), 1801 B. C.

ABIM'ELECH, king of the Palestines at Gerara (Gen. xxvi. 1); receives Isaac, but finding that he grew too powerful asked him to depart 16); he afterwards makes an alliance with him (26–31).

ABIM'ELECH, son of Gedeon by a concubine, seized the government on his father's death, and was recognized at Sichem as king (Judg. ix. 6) or judge of Israel. He reigned three years over Israel (ix. 22); he put sixty-nine of his brothers to death

THE BLESSED VIRGIN AND THE INFANT SAVIOUR.

(ix. 5); he defeated Gaal and destroyed the town of Sichem (ix. 39–45); but was killed under the tower of Thebes by a woman who threw a millstone down on his head (53; 2 Kings xi. 21).

ABIN'ADAB, a Levite, receives the ark of the covenant from the hands of the Philistines (1 Kings vii. 1); it remained in his house at Gabaa, a height near Cariathiarim, till David removed it (2 Kings vi. 3).

ABI'RAM, son of Hiel of Bethel, who attempted to rebuild Jericho, notwithstanding Josue's curse (Jos. vi. 26); he lost his eldest son Abiram when he laid the foundation, and his youngest Segub when he set up the gates (3 Kings xvi. 34).

ABI'RON, son of Eliab, of the tribe of Ruben, conspires with Core and Dathan against Moses and Aaron to usurp the priesthood, and is swallowed up by the earth with all his accomplices (Num. xvi.; xxvi. 8–11; Deut. xi. 6; Ps. cv. 17, 18; Ecclus. xlv. 22–24).

AB'ISAG, a native of Sunam in the tribe of Issachar, and exceedingly beautiful. David marries her, but does not know her (3 Kings i. 3, 4); after David's death Adonias asked her for his wife, on which account Solomon put him to death (ii. 17).

ABISA'I, son of Sarvia, sister of David. He was one of the bravest men of his time, and one of the highest generals of David's armies. He saved David's life by killing Jesbibenob, a giant of the race of the Rephaim (2 Kings xxi. 16); David prevented his killing Saul when they were in his tent (1 Kings xxvi. 9); he would have killed Semei, but for David (2 Kings xvi. 9–12); he aided in overthrowing Isboseth (2 Kings ii. 18, 24); defeated the Edomites in the valley of the salt-pits, killing 18,000 and making them tributary to David (2 Kings viii. 13, 14; 1 Paral. xviii. 12, 13); was sent against the Ammonites (2 Kings x. 10; 2 Paral. xix. 11); he commanded a division of David's army against Absalom (2 Kings xviii. 2); and was sent against Seba (xx. 6); he is said to have killed 300 enemies with his lance (2 Kings xxiii. 18, 19; 1 Paral. xi. 20, 21).

ABISU'E, son of Phinees (1 Paral. vi. 4, 50; Esd. vii. 5), and fourth high-priest.

ABI'U, son of the high-priest Aaron and Elizabeth was destroyed with his brother Nadab by fire coming out from the Lord, for offering strange fire before the Lord (Levit. x. 1, 2; xvi. 1; Num. iii. 4; xxvi. 61).

ABI'UD, son of Zorobabel, one of the ancestors of Christ according to the flesh (Matt. i. 13).

AB'NER, son of Ner, general of Saul's armies, preserved the crown for Isboseth and maintained him for seven years over eleven tribes against David, who reigned at Hebron (2 Kings ii. 8); defeated at the Pool of Gabaon by Joab (17); kills Asael, brother of Joab (23); Isboseth having offended him (iii. 7, 8) he went over to David (12–21); but was treacherously slain by Joab (27); David showed great grief, and made a touching lamentation over him (33).

ABOM'INATION. Shepherds were an abomination to the Egyptians (Gen. xlvi. 34); and Moses calls cattle and sheep abominations of the Egyptians (Ex. viii. 26).

ABOM'INATION means also all criminal

actions (Lev. xviii. 22, 25, 29; Isai. xli. 24; lxvi. 3; Jerem. vi. 15; vii. 10; Ezech. v., viii.; Mal. ii. 11; 1 Mac. i. 51; Apoc. xxi. 27); idolatry (Deut. xii. 31; 2 Paral. xxxiii. 2; Apoc. xvii. 4, 5; an idol, or false god (Deut. xxix. 17; 4 Kings xxiii. 13; Ezec. vii. 20; Ecclus xlix. 3; Zach. ix. 7).

ABOM′INATION of Desolation, foretold by Daniel (xi. 31), means according to the best commentators the idol of Jupiter Olympius placed in the temple of Jerusalem by Antiochus Epiphanes (1 Mac.

ABRAHAM'S OAK AT HEBRON.

vi. 7; 2 Mac. vi. 2); that in Dan. ix. 27 refers to the profanation of the temple before the capture by Titus (see Matt. xxiv. 15); that in Dan. xii. 11, to the time of antichrist.

A′BRAM, afterwards called A′braham, called by God to be the founder of his chosen people. He was a descendant of Sem and son of Thare (Gen. xi. 10–32); he was born in Ur of the Chaldees (xi. 26–31); he was called by God to leave his country and kindred and go into Chanaan, God promising that in him all the kindreds of the earth should be blessed (Gen. xii. 1–3); he set out with his wife Sarai and his nephew Lot, and entered Chanaan, but was forced by a famine to go into Egypt (xii. 10); but returned to Chanaan (xiii.); he rescued Lot and his flocks from the four kings (xiv. 14–16); and was blessed by Melchisedech, king of Salem, priest of the Most High God, to whom he paid tithes (xiv. 18–20); his wife had been barren, but God promised him seed more numerous than the stars (Gen. xv. 5); and God made a covenant with him (xv. 18; xvii. 2); and changed his name to Abraham, establishing circumcision as a sign of the covenant (10–14); the birth of his son Isaac by Sara was foretold, and the prophecy was renewed by three angels who visited him in the vale of Mambre (xvii. 19; xviii. 10); when they announced the destruction of Sodom and Gomorrah Abraham interceded for the guilty cities (Gen. xviii. 17–33); he then removed to Gerara, where Abimelech, the king, wished to take Sara as a wife (Gen. xx.); after the birth of Isaac, he sent off Agar and Ismael his son by her (Gen. xxi.); he made a league with Abimelech and sojourned for a long time in the land of the Palestines (Gen. xxi. 22–34); his faith and obedience were proved by his readiness to sacrifice his son Isaac at the command of God. As he put forth his hand to sacrifice his son, his hand was stayed by an angel. God again blessed him and renewed the promise that in his seed all the nations of the earth should be blessed (Gen. xxii. 1–19; 1 Mac. ii. 52); his wife Sara died at Arbee or Hebron, and he buried her in

a cave which he purchased of the children of Heth (Gen. xxiii.); not wishing Isaac to marry any of the Chanaanites, he sent his servant to Mesopotamia to obtain Rebecca, granddaughter of his brother Nachor (Gen. xxiv.) He died at the age of 175, and was buried by his sons in the cave beside Sara (Gen. xxv. 9); Abraham had children by Cetura, whom he married after Sara's death (Gen. xxv. 1–4). Abraham is proposed as a model (Ecclus. xliv. 20; Isai. li. 2); called the friend of God (2 Paral. xx. 7; Isai. xli. 8; James ii. 23); called the father of many nations and of all who believe (Gen. xvii. 5; Matt. iii. 9; Luke xix. 9; John viii. 39; Rom. iv. 11, 17); as to his posterity, see Jos. xxiv. 3; Isai. xli. 8; Ezech. xxxiii. 24; 2 Esd. ix. 7; Matt. viii. 11; Acts vii. 2, 16; Heb. xi. 17; who are his true children (John viii. 33; Rom. ix. 9; Gal. iii. 7). Jesus Christ the seed of Abraham in whom all the nations are blessed (Matt. i. 1, 2).

AB′SALOM, son of David by Maacha, daughter of Tholomaï, king of Gessur. He had a sister Thamar, who was violated by her half-brother Amnon (2 Kings xiii. 1–19); in revenge Absalom caused Amnon to be killed by his servants at a sheep-shearing in Baalhasor, after which he fled to Gessur, where he remained three years (2 Kings xiii. 22–38), till Joab procured his pardon from David, when he returned, but for two years David would not see him (2 Kings xiv.) Immediately after his reconciliation he sought to ingratiate himself with

THE PORT OF ACRE.

the people, and acquired popularity by his beauty and pomp. At last he asked his father's permission to go and fulfil a vow in Hebron (xv. 7), and immediately set up a revolt, proclaiming himself king (10–13); David fled from Jerusalem, which Absalom entered, taking possession of his father's harem (xv., xvi.); after being solemnly anointed king (xix. 10) he marched across the Jordan to attack his father, but was defeated in the forest of Ephraim in a battle in

which twenty thousand were slain (xviii. 7); Absalom fleeing from the field, caught by his head in a tree and was slain by Joab (14), contrary to David's orders (5); Absalom was buried in a pit, although he had erected a tomb for himself (17, 18); David mourned bitterly for his rebellious son (xviii. 33; xix. 4).

ABSTINENCE from articles of food is repeatedly enjoined in the Bible. God forbade Adam and Eve to eat the fruit of the tree of the knowledge of good and evil (Gen. ii. 17; iii. 11); the eating of flesh with its blood is forbidden in Gen. ix. 4; Deut. xii. 16, and in Acts xv. 29; the paschal lamb was not to be eaten raw or boiled (Ex. xii. 9); the use of leaven was forbidden during the pasch (xiii. 7); the flesh of an ox that had killed a man was not to be eaten (xxi. 28); no animal which had been partly eaten by wild beasts could be used (xxii. 31); the flesh of animals dying of themselves was forbidden (Lev. xxii. 8; Deut. xiv. 21); the flesh of a sacrifice or the bread offered with it could not be eaten on the following day (Ex. xxix. 34; Levit. vii. 18; xix. 7); nor sin-offerings (vi. 30); the flesh of all animals that had not the hoof cloven and that did not chew the cud was forbidden (Lev. xi.; Deut. xiv. 7); certain fish and birds forbidden (Deut. xiv. 9–18); consecrated things were not to be eaten by a person legally unclean (Lev. xxii. 3); nor out of the holy place (Num. xviii. 10); certain loaves were not to be eaten except by the priests (Lev. xxiv. 9; Matt. xii. 4); Nazarites could not drink wine or eat any product of the vineyard (Num. vi. 1–3); priests were forbidden to drink wine (Lev. x. 9; Ezech. xliv. 21); also the Rechabites (Jer. xxxv. 6); Tobias would eat nothing defiled (Tob. i. 12); nor Judith (Jud. xii. 2); nor Daniel and his companions (Dan. i. 8); nor the Machabees (2 Mac. vii. 1); Eleazar preferred to die rather than seem to violate the law (2 Mac. vi. 18); the abstinence of St. John the Baptist (Luke i. 15); lawful food to be abstained from, so as not to scandalize others (2 Mac. vi. 24; vii. 1, 2; Rom. xiv. 20, 21; 1 Cor. viii. 13).

AC′CARON, a town of the Philistines, refuses to receive the ark (1 Kings v. 10); Beelzebub worshipped there (4 Kings i. 2, 3); its destruction foretold (Jerem. xxv. 20; Amos i. 8; Soph. ii. 4); given to Jonathan Machabeus by Alexander Bales (1 Mac. x. 89).

AC'CHO, a seaport in the tribe of Aser, north of Carmel and near the mouth of the river Belus (Judg. i. 31); it was captured, but the inhabitants were spared. Some identify it with Axaph (Jos. xix. 25); in the time of the Machabees it was called Ptolemais (1 Mac. v.; 2 Mac. xiii.) It is the modern Acre.

AC'COS, the prince or chief of the seventh course of priests established by David (1 Paral. xxiv. 10); his descendants unable to prove their genealogy were excluded by Esdras (1 Esd. ii. 61, 62; 2 Esd. vii. 63).

AC'CUB, a Levite (1 Paral. iii. 24); one of the porters of the temple appointed by David (1 Paral. ix. 17); one of his descendants who returned from the captivity with Zorobabel (1 Esd. ii. 42; 2 Esd. vii. 46), was also called Ac'cub, who was chief porter (2 Esd. xi. 19); who read the scriptures to the people (2 Esd. viii. 7–9).

A'CHAB, son of Amri, seventh king of Israel, reigned B. C. 918–896; he married Jezabel, daughter of Ethbaal, king of Sidon, and built a temple to Baal, where he worshipped that false god (3 Kings xvi. 28–33); he permits Jezabel to slay the prophets (xviii. 4); his kingdom is punished by a drought, from which the prophet Elias delivered it after confounding the priests of Baal by a miracle (xviii. 5–46); he twice defeated and at last captured Benadad, king of Syria, who had besieged Samaria (xx.); in order to obtain the vineyard of Naboth as grounds for his ivory palace (3 Kings xxii. 39) he countenanced Jezabel's murdering him and his sons (3 Kings xxi.; 4 Kings ix. 26), for which Elias denounced against him the vengeance of God (3 Kings xxi. 18–24); on his repentance the execution of the sentence was deferred (29); believing the false prophets rather than Micheas, he with Josaphat, king of Juda, attacked Ramoth-Galaad, then held by the Syrians (3 Kings xxii. 1–29); although he disguised himself, a chance arrow gave him a mortal wound, of which he died that day (30–35); his blood ran down into his chariot, and was licked up by dogs as the prophet Elias had foretold (3 Kings xxii. 38; xxi. 19).

A'CHAB, a false prophet who seduced the Israelites at Babylon (Jerem. xxix. 21, 22).

A'CHAD, a city built by Nemrod (Gen. x. 10).

ACHA'IA, a Roman province including the Peloponnesus and most of Hellas. This province and that of Macedonia in the New Testament comprise the whole of Greece. In the reign of Claudius it was governed by Gallio as proconsul (Acts xviii. 12). St. Paul preached in this province at Corinth, and was opposed by the Jews (Acts xviii. 12, 27); a fervent church was formed (Rom. xv. 26; 2 Cor. ix. 2); St. Paul took nothing from them for his support (xi. 9, 10); he addresses his second epistle to the Corinthians to all the faithful in Achaia (i. 1).

ACHA'ICUS, a disciple of St. Paul, whom the apostle commends to the Corinthians. He was one of those who carried the first Epistle of St. Paul to them A. D. 56 (1 Cor. xvi. 15, 17).

A'CHAN (or A'char, 1 Paral. ii. 7), son of Charmi of the tribe of Juda, through covetousness kept some of the spoils of Jericho contrary to the commandment of God (Jos. vi. 17; vii. 1). In consequence the Israelites were defeated at Hai (vii. 5). The sin was traced to Achan (18); who confessed his sin (20, 21); and was stoned with all his family, and all his possessions burned up in the valley of Achor.

A'CHAZ, eleventh king of Juda, son of Joatham,

reigned 742–726 B. C. He was besieged in Jerusalem by Rasin, king of Syria, and Phacee, king of Israel (4 Kings xvi. 5; 2 Paral. xxviii.; Isai. vii. 1), and lost the port of Aila, on the Red Sea, and 200,000 of his people (2 Paral. xxviii. 8). In his distress he invoked the aid of Theglathphalasar, king of Assyria, sending him a large amount of treasure (2 Paral. xxviii. 21). Theglathphalasar took Damascus, killed Rasin, and carried off the people as captives. Achaz went to meet the conqueror in Damascus. Although the prophet Isaias foretold him from God the destruction of his enemies, and announced the birth of Emmanuel by a virgin mother (Isai. vii.), Achaz destroyed the sacred vessels, closed the temple (2 Paral. xxviii. 24, 25; 4 Kings xvi. 14, 17), and set up heathen altars, where he offered sacrifice (4 Kings xvi. 10, 15; 2 Paral. xxviii. 22, 23, 25). He died in Jerusalem, but was not buried in the sepulchre of the kings (2 Paral. xxviii. 27).

ACH'AZIB, a town in the tribe of Aser, and spared by that tribe (Judg. i. 31).

ACHI'AS, son of the high-priest Achitob, and his successor (1 Kings xiv. 3). During a battle with the Philistines he was ordered by Saul to bring forth the Ark of the Lord (18).

ACH'IMAAS, son of the high-priest Sadoc, announces to David the defeat of Absalom (2 Kings xviii. 19).

ACH'IMAAS, husband of Basemath, Solomon's daughter, was governor over Nephtha'li (3 Kings iv. 15).

ACH'IMAN, a giant of the race of Enac, lived at Hebron when the spies were sent into the land of Chanaan (Num. xiii. 23).

ACHIM'ELECH, son of Achitob, succeeded his brother Achias as high-priest. He resided at Nobe, where the tabernacle then was. When David fled from Saul, Achimelech gave him the loaves of proposition and the sword of Goliath (1 Kings xxi. 1–9); Saul summoned Achimelech before him, and though the high-priest averred that he supposed David to be a faithful servant of the king, Saul ordered him and all his father's house to be put to death. As the Israelites would not slay the priests, Doeg the Edomite killed eighty-five priests and destroyed Nobe (xxii. 9–19). His son Abi'athar escaped (20); Achim'elech himself is called Abi'athar (Mark ii. 26).

ACHIM'ELECH, a Hethite, one of David's officers (1 Kings xxvi. 6).

ACHINO'AM, a Jezraelitess, wife of David, and mother of Amnon, his first-born (1 Kings xxv. 43; 2 Kings iii. 2; 1 Paral. iii. 1). She was with him at Geth (1 Kings xxvii. 3); and at Hebron (2 Kings ii. 2). She was captured by the Amalecites in Siceleg (1 Kings xxx. 1–5); but was rescued by David (18).

A'CHIOR, of the tribe of Nephthali, captive in Ninive, relative of Tobias (Tob. xi. 20).

A'CHIOR, chief of the Ammonites, warns Holofernes not to attack the Israelites unless they had offended God (Jud. v. 5–25); but was by orders of that general bound hand and foot to a tree near Bethulia (vi. 9); he was taken into the town by the Israelites, and told them of the threats of Holofernes (12, 13); when Judith returned with the head of Holofernes, he blessed her (xiii. 31); and renouncing his idolatry, believed in God (xiv. 6).

A'CHIS, son of Ma'och, king of Geth. David fled to him from the anger of Saul, but as the king's officers menaced him he feigned madness and

fled (1 Kings xxi. 10); three or four years after Achis received David with the troops under him (xxvii. 2); and gave him the town of Siceleg (6); David with his troops marched under Achis, against Saul, but the princes of the Philistines compelled Achis to send him back (xxix.); Achis is called Achimelech (Ps. xxxiii. 1).

A'CHIS, son of Maacha, king of Geth, to whom the servants of Semei fled (3 Kings ii. 39–41).

ACH'ITOB I., son of Phinees II., succeeded Heli as high-priest (1 Kings xxii. 9; xiv. 3).

ACH'ITOB II., son of Amarias, of the race of Eleazar (1 Paral. vi. 7; 2 Kings viii. 17).

ACH'ITOB III., son of Amarias, prince of the house of God (1 Paral. vi. 11, 12; 1 Esd. vii. 2; 2 Esd. xi. 11).

ACHIT'OPHEL, a native of Gilo (2 Kings xv. 12). He was a counsellor of David and highly esteemed for his wisdom (xvi. 23); he deserted David and joined Absalom in Hebron (xv. 12); and accompanied him to Jerusalem (xvi. 15); where he gave Absalom the most shameful advice (21); David prayed to God to infatuate his counsels (xv. 31); and refers to his treachery in Ps. xl. 10; liv. 13, 14. When Achitophel saw that Absalom would not take his advice, but delayed in pursuing David, he lost all hope, and going home hanged himself (xvii. 23).

ACHO'BOR, son of Micha, an officer of king Josias, sent to consult Holda the prophetess in regard to the book of the law found by Helcias (4 Kings xxii. 12, 14). His son Elnathan was sent into Egypt by king Joakim (Jerem. xxvi. 22).

A'CHOR, a valley in the territory of Jericho, where Achan and his house were stoned (Jos. vii. 24).

ACH'SAPH, a city of Chanaan; its king defeated by Josue at the Waters of Merom (Jos. xi. 1–9; xii. 20); it fell to the tribe of Aser (xix. 25).

ACH'ZIB, a town in the tribe of Juda (Jos. xv. 44).

ACH'ZIBA (Jos. xix. 29) or Achazib (Judg. i. 31), a Phœnician city.

A'CRABA'THANE, a place near Edom, in what was called The Ascent of the Scorpion (Num. xxxiv. 4). Judas Machabeus defeats its inhabitants (1 Mac. v. 3).

ACTS of the APOSTLES, the, a canonical book of the New Testament written by St. Luke after his gospel. It embraces the earliest history of the church, and much of the ministry of St. Peter and St. Paul from the Ascension of our Lord till St. Paul's arrival in Rome, on his appeal to Cæsar, a period of twenty-eight or thirty years. It gives the acts of the Council of Jerusalem, held by the apostles, and many details of the journeys of St. Paul, whom St. Luke accompanied for some time. It was written in Greek, apparently at Rome, about A. D. 62, 63. From chapter xx. to xxv. the writer speaks as an eyewitness, so that he apparently joined St. Paul after his wintering at Corinth. The book is addressed to Theophilus (Acts i. 1).

A'DA, wife of Lamech and mother of Jabel and Jubal (Gen. iv. 19).

A'DA, daughter of Elon the Hethite, and wife of Esau, to whom she bore Eliphaz (Gen. xxxvi. 2, 4, 10, 16). She is called also Basemath (Gen. xxvi. 34).

A'DAD, son of Badad, king of Edom, defeated the Madianites. His capital was Avith (Gen. xxxvi. 35; 1 Paral. i. 46).

A'DAD II. (or A'dar, Gen. xxxvi. 39), succeeded Balanan as king of Edon. His royal city was Phau (1 Paral. i. 50).

A'DAD, king of Edom, was saved when a child from Joab's slaughter of the royal family and people, and carried into Egypt, when Pharao gave him the queen's sister for a wife. On the death of David, he returned to his country with an army and harassed Solomon during his whole reign (3 Kings xi. 14–25).

AD'ADREM'MON, a place near Mageddo in the half tribe of Manasses, where the good king Josias of Juda was mortally wounded (4 Kings xxiii. 29; 2 Paral. xxxv. 22.) From this circumstance " The Lamentation of Adadremmon "·became proverbial (Zach. xii. 11).

AD'AM (Gen. ii. 19), the first man created by God (Gen. i. 26, 27). As Adam in Hebrew means *red*, it is supposed by some that he was called so from the red earth of which he was made (ii. 7). The name also signifies man in general (Gen. v. 2). God breathed into his face the breath of life (ii. 7), and placed him in a paradise of pleasure (ii. 8); he gave him dominion over all animals, and brought them to Adam to name (ii. 19); he forbade Adam to eat of the tree of the knowledge of good and evil (ii. 17). Then God created Eve out of one of the ribs of Adam (21–24). Although in a state of perfect happiness, and in direct communion with God, Adam and Eve were led to transgress the only pro-

CERASTES, THE HORNED ADDER.

hibition made. Eve, tempted by the serpent, who assured her that if they ate the fruit of the forbidden tree they should not die, but should become as gods, knowing good and evil, ate of the fruit and gave to Adam, who ate also (Gen. iii. 1–6); they felt at once a sense of shame of their nakedness, and made aprons of fig-leaves, and endeavored to hide from the presence of God (7, 8); Adam threw the blame of his transgression on Eve, who confessed: " The serpent deceived me and I did eat " (9–13); God cursed the serpent and promised to put enmities between it and the woman: "she shall crush thy head, and thou shalt be in wait for her heel" (15); woman was condemned to the pains of childbirth, and the earth was cursed, so that man should derive his sustenance from it only by toil, and the sweat of his face (16–19); Adam and Eve were cast out of paradise (23, 24). Adam lived to the age of 930 (Gen. v. 5); having begotten Cain, Abel, Seth, and other "sons and

daughters" (Gen. iv.; v. 4). The serpent is regarded as the devil (John viii. 44; 2 Cor. xi. 3; Apoc. xii. 9).

AD'AM, the greatest among the Enacim, buried at Hebron (Jos. xiv. 15).

ADAM'A, one of the five cities of the plain, Sennaab being its king in the time of Abraham (Gen. xiv. 1, 8). It was destroyed with Sodom and Gomorrha (Deut. xxix. 23; Osee xi. 8).

AD'AMANT, used by the prophets as a symbol of hardness (Ezec. iii. 9; Zach. vii. 12); supposed to be corundum.

AD'AMI, a town in Nephthali (Jos. xix. 33).

A'DAR, king of Edom. See ADAD.

A'DAR, the twelfth of the Jewish months (1 Esd. vi. 15; Esth. iii. 7; viii. 12; 1 Mac. vii. 43; 2 Mac. xv. 37). The Phurim or feast of the deliverance from Haman occurred in this month.

A'DAR or **ADDAR,** a town in Juda (Num. xxxiv. 4; Jos. xv. 3).

ADARE'ZER, son of Rohob, and king of Soba, defeated by David, who took 21,700 prisoners (2 Kings viii. 3, 4) and great spoils (8); 1044 B. C. Seven years after Adarezer incited several princes to make war on David. David took the field against them, and crossing the Jordan defeated them at Helam, killing Sobach or Sophach, the general, and 40,700 men (2 Kings x. 16–18; 1 Paral. xix. 16–18). The subjects of Adarezer then submitted.

ADAR'SA or **ADAZER,** a place in the tribe of Ephraim near which Judas Machabeus defeated and killed Nicanor (161 B. C.; 1 Mac. vii. 40–45).

AD'BEEL, third son of Ismael and head of a tribe of Ismaelites (Gen. xxv. 13).

AD'DI, son of Cosan and father of Melchi, one of the ancestors of Christ according to the flesh (Luke iii. 28).

AD'DO, a prophet of the kingdom of Juda who wrote the history of the reigns of Roboam and Abia (2 Paral. xii. 15; xiii. 22); and prophecies against Jeroboam which contained part of the reign of Solomon (ix. 29).

AD'DO, one of the priests who returned from the captivity (2 Esd. xii. 4).

AD'DO, father or grandfather of the prophet of Zacharias (1 Esd. v. 1; vi. 14; 1 Zac. i. 1).

AD'DON (2 Esd. vii. 61) or **ADON** (1 Esd. ii. 59). The Jews who returned from captivity at, could not prove their genealogies.

AD'DUS, a city in Juda where Simon encamped to await Tryphon (1 Mac. xiii. 13).

A'DE'ODA'TUS (Elchanan), son of Forest (of Saltus), an embroiderer of Bethlehem, slew at

ATTITUDES OF PRAYER.

Gob Goliath the Gethite, or his brother, the shaft of whose spear was like a weaver's beam (2 Kings xxi. 19; 1 Paral. xx. 5; 2 Kings xxiii. 24).

ADIA'DA, a town built and fortified by Simon Machabeus in Sephela (1 Mac. xii. 38).

A'DIN, head of house of which 454 or 655 descendants returned from the captivity (1 Esd. ii. 15; 2 Esd. vii. 20; x. 16).

ADI'NA, prince of the Rubenites, one of David's heroes (1 Paral. xi. 42).

AD'ITHAIM, a city of Juda (Jos. xv. 36).

ADMA'THA, an officer of king Assuerus (Esth. i. 14).

ADOM'MIM, a mountain in the tribe of Benjamin (Jos. xv. 7; xviii. 18).

ADON'A-I, one of the names of God (Ex. vi. 3; Judith xvi. 16). The Jews employ it in all cases for the unpronounceable name.

ADONI'AS, David's fourth son by Haggith, was born at Hebron (2 Kings iii. 4); aimed at the crown (3 Kings i. 5–25); in consequence of which David, at Bethsabee's prayer, caused Solomon to be anointed king (39; 1 Paral. xxiii. 1); Adonias fled to the temple and took hold of the altar till Solomon promised not to kill him (3 Kings i. 50–52); after David's death he asked for Abisag the Sunamitess as his wife, for which Solomon ordered him to be put to death (3 Kings ii. 13–25).

ADONI'AS, a Levite, appointed by Josaphat, king of Juda, to instruct the people (2 Par. xvii. 8, 9).

ADONIBE'ZEC, king of Bezec, in the land of Chanaan. He had conquered seventy kings, cut off their fingers and toes, and made them gather their food under his table. The tribes of Juda and Simeon attacked him in Bezec, and when he fled overtook him, and treated him as he had treated others. He died in Jerusalem (Judg. i. 3–7).

ADONI'RAM, Solomon's superintendent over the workmen in Libanus (3 Kings v. 14).

ADO'NIS (in Hebrew Thammuz). Ezechiel in a vision sees women seated in the temple mourning for Adonis (Ezech. viii. 14).

ADONISE'DEC, king of Sedec or Jerusalem, hearing that the Gabaonites had made terms with the children of Israel, who had taken Jericho and Hai, excited several kings to join him in attacking Gabaon. Josue marched against them, cut them to pieces, and pursued them to Bethhoron (Jos. x. 1–10). It was in this battle that God sent down great stones from heaven on the enemy, and that Josue caused the sun and moon to stand still (11, 12). Adonisedec and four other kings fled to a cave in Maceda, but were taken by Josue, who set his foot on their necks, slew them, and hung them on gibbets (16–26).

A'DOR, a town in the tribe of Juda (1 Mac. xiii. 20).

ADO'RAM or Adu'ram, son of Jectan, son of Heber, is supposed to have settled near the Persian gulf (Gen. x. 27; 1 Paral. i. 21).

ADO'RAM, son of Thou, king of Emath, sent to congratulate David on his victory over Aderezer (1 Paral. xviii. 10). In 2 Kings viii. 10 he is called Joram.

ADORE', originally meant to raise the hand to the mouth in order to kiss it in token of reverence (Job xxxi. 26, 27; 3 Kings·xix. 18). Used to mean *bow* (Gen. xviii. 2); to pay divine honors (Ex. xxxiv. 14); hence the prohibition to adore idols or false gods (Ex. xx. 5);˙ and the command, The Lord thy God thou shalt adore (Luke iv. 8.)

ADRAME'LECH, a god to whom the Sepharvaim who colonized Samaria burned their own children (4 Kings xvii. 31).

ADRAME'LECH, son of Sennacherib, king of Assyria (Isai. xxxvii. 38; 4 Kings xix.); killed his father in the temple of Nes-roch and fled to Armenia (4 Kings xix. 37; B. C.·710).

A'DRIA, the Sicilian and Ionian sea (Acts xxvii. 27).

ADRUME'TUM, a city of Libya in Africa (Acts xxvii. 2).

ADUL'LAM or Odollam, a city in the tribe of Juda (Gen. xxxviii. 1, 12, 20; Jos. xv. 35; xii. 15); restored and fortified by Roboam (2 Paral. xi. 7); reoccupied by the Jews after the captivity (2 Esd. xi. 30); Judas Machabeus encamped near it (2 Mac. xii. 38). The caves near it were the refuge of David (1 Kings xxii. 1; 2 Kings xxiii. 13; 1 Paral. xi. 15).

ADUL'TERY, a crime forbidden (Gen. xx. 2; xxvi. 11; Exod. xx. 14; Levit. xviii. 8; Deut. v. 18; Prov. v. 3, 8, 20; vii. 24–27; Matt. v. 27; xix. 9; 1 Cor. vi. 9; 1 Thess. iv. 3; Heb. xiii. 4); it was punished by death under the patriarchs (Gen. xxxviii. 24); by the Mosaic law (Lev. xx. 10; Deut. xxii. 22; Ps. lxxii. 27; Prov. vi. 32); it is punished on the offspring (Wisd. iii. 16; iv. 3); adultery seeks darkness (Job xxiv. 15); he who marries a divorced woman commits adultery (Matt. v. 32); Susanna falsely accused of adultery (Dan. xiii. 1–63); he who looks on a woman to lust after her commits adultery in heart (Matt. v. 28).

ADU'RAM, superintendent of the tributes under David (2 Kings xx. 24).

ADU'RAM, Roboam's treasurer, stoned by the people, exasperated at the exactions (3 Kings xii. 18).

ADU'RAM, a city in Juda fortified by Roboam (2 Paral. xi. 9).

AEN or Ain, a priestly city (Jos. xxi. 16; xv. 32; 1 Paral. iv. 32).

AFFLICTION, the lot of the children of God (Prov. iii. 11, 12; Wisd. xi. 10; Job i. 11; Matt. v. 10, 12); not a mark of sin (Eccles. viii. 14); should be borne patiently (Eccles. ii. 3; Isai. xxv. 9); afflictions come from God (Isai. xlv. 7; Osee vi. 2; Amos iii. 6; Judith viii. 21–27); there is no

proportion between the afflictions of this life, and the glory to come (Rom. viii. 18).

AG'ABUS, a prophet among the primitive Christians in the time of the apostles, foretold a great famine over the whole earth (Acts xi. 28), which came to pass in the fourth year of the reign of Claudius (A. D. 44). In the year 58, when St. Paul landed at Cesarea in Palestine on his way to Jerusalem, Agabus bound the apostle's feet and hands with his girdle, and foretold that he should be thus bound by the Jews of Jerusalem, and delivered up to the Gentiles (Acts xxi. 10).

A'GAG, a king (Num. xxiv. 7).

"ADORE HIM ALL YOU HIS ANGELS."—Ps. xcvi. 8.

A'GAG, king of the Amalecites, spared by Saul with the best of his spoil (1 Kings xv. 8, 9, 20, 32); although he knew the destruction of the Amalecites was commanded (Exod. xvii. 14; Deut. xxv. 19). For this disobedience Samuel announced to Saul that he was rejected by God, and he hewed Agag to pieces (1 Kings xv. 8–33).

A'GAR, an Egyptian handmaid of Sarai, despises her mistress, and being afflicted ran away (Gen. xvi. 1–6); is directed to return by an angel who says that she shall bear a son, Ismael, who should be the father of a people in tents, whose hand should

be against every man (7–14); she bore Ismael (A. C. 1911); Sara demands that she and her son be cast out (Gen. xxi. 10); she is sent away by Abraham, and is relieved by an angel in the desert of Bersabee. When Ismael grew up she took a wife for him from Egypt (14–21). Agar declared by St. Paul to be a figure of the Jews (Gal. iv. 24).

AG'ARENS (Ps. lxxxii. 7). Ag'arites (1 Paral. v. 10); the Ismaelites, defeated by the tribe of Ruben, Gad and Manasses during the reign of Saul, and driven out of the country east of Galaad (1 Paral. v. 18–20).

AG'ATE, a precious stone in the rational of judgment (Ex. xxviii. 19; xxxix. 12).

AGGEUS, the tenth of the lesser prophets, was born apparently at Babylon, and returned from thence with Zorobabel. The rebuilding of the temple was begun (1 Esd. iii. 8); but at the instigation of the enemies of the Jews was suspended by order of Cyrus and Cambyses. When Darius ascended the throne, God raised up Aggeus (1 Esd. v. 1, 2; Agg. i.), to exhort Zorobabel, prince of Juda, and the high-priest Jesus, son of Josedech, to resume the building of the temple. His reproaches were effectual; work was begun again (520 B. C.), sixteen years after their return from captivity (Agg. i. 14; ii. 1). Soon after the resumption of the building, Aggeus inspired by God announced to those who had seen the glory of the former temple, and might look with less reverence on this, what honor awaited it. "The desired of all nations shall come : and I will fill this house with glory, saith the Lord of hosts." "Great shall be the glory of this last house, more than of the first, saith the Lord of hosts" (Agg. ii. 8, 10). The name of this prophet with that of Zacharias occurs in the title of Psalms cxi., cxlv.

AG'GI, second son of Gad, head of the Aggites (Num. xxvi. 15).

AG'ONY of our Lord in the garden of Gethsemani is described (Matt. xxvi. 38; Mark xiv. 34; Luke xxii. 42).

AG'RICULTURE. As the earth was cursed after the fall of our first parents, and man was condemned to make the earth fruitful by his labor, agriculture became the lot of a large part of the human race. It was practised by Adam (Gen. iii. 23); by Cain (iv. 2); by Noe (ix. 20); by the Egyptians (xlvii. 24). For the Mosaic laws in regard to agriculture see Exod. xxii. 5; xxiii.; xxxiv.; Deut. xiv. –xvi. Among the Jews land remained in the family, and if sold reverted to them in the year of the jubilee (Lev. xxv. 8, 16; 23–35). The grains raised by the Israelites were chiefly wheat (Gen. xxx. 14; Deut. viii. 8; Ps. lxxx. 17; Isai. xxviii. 25; Ezech. iv. 9); barley (Isai. xxviii. 25; Levit. xxvii. 16; Deut. viii. 8; Ruth ii. 17; ˙2 Kings xxi. 9; Judg. vii. 13; John vi. 9); millet (Isai. xxviii. 25; Ezech. iv. 9); they cultivated also beans, vetches, lentils, cummin, gith (Isai. xxviii. 25; Ez. iv. 9); cucumbers (Isai. i. 8); and had apple trees (Cant. ii. 3; viii. 5; Joel i. 12); olive, fig, pomegranate trees (Deut. viii. 8); the vine (Num. xiii. 24).

AGRIP'PA (Acts xxv. 13; xxvi.); see Herod Agrippa II.

AHA'RA or **AHI'RAM,** third son of Benjamin (1 Paral. viii. 1; Num. xxvi. 38).

AHA'VA, a river and locality in Babylonia where Esdras collected his companions before they set out for Jerusalem (1 Esd. viii. 15, 21, 31).

AHI'AM, the name of one of David's champions (2 Kings xxiii. 33; 1 Paral. xi. 34).

AHI'A, one of Solomon's scribes (3 Kings iv. 3).

ALABASTER VESSELS. (From the British Museum.)

AHI'ALON, of the tribe of Zabulon, one of the judges of Israel. He succeeded Abe'san. He judged Israel for ten years and was buried at Zabulon (1164 B. C.; Judges xii. 11, 12).

AHI'AS, a prophet of the Lord dwelling at Silo. He wrote the acts of Solomon's reign (2 Paral. ix. 29); he foretold to Jeroboam that God would give him ten of the twelve tribes (3 Kings xi. 29–31); and declared what God would do for his house if he proved faithful (38). When the son of Jeroboam fell ill, he sent his wife to Ahias, who declared that the house of Jeroboam should be destroyed (xiv. 1–16).

A'HICAM, the son of Saphan, was sent by Josias to consult Holda the prophetess in regard to the book of the law (4 Kings xxii. 11, 12). He saved the prophet Jeremias (Jere. xxvi. 24).

AHIE'ZER, son of Ammisadai, prince of the tribe of Dan, led 62,700 men of his tribe out of Egypt (Num. i. 38; ii. 25; x. 25). For his offering towards the tabernacle, see Num. vii. 66–71.

AHIMAN, of the race of Enac, driven from Hebron by Caleb (Jos. xv. 14; Judg. i. 10).

AHI'O, with his brother Oza, appointed to bring the ark from the house of Abinadab to the tabernacle in Jerusalem (2 Kings vi. 3, 4).

AHI'ON, city of Nephthali, taken from Baasa, king of Israel, by Benadad (3 Kings xv. 20; 2 Paral. xvi. 4).

AHI'RA, prince of the tribe of Nephthali, led 53,400 men of his tribe out of Egypt (Num. i. 15, 42; ii. 29; x. 27). For his offerings to the tabernacle, see Num. vii. 78.

AHI'UD, son of Salomi, of the tribe of Aser, appointed by Moses to partition the land of Chanaan (Num. xxxiv. 27).

A'HOD, third son of Simeon, went into Egypt (Gen. xlvi. 10).

A'HOD, of the tribe of Benjamin (1 Paral. viii. 6).

AHO'E, grandson of Benjamin (1 Paral. viii. 3, 4).

AHOHI'TE (2 Kings xxiii. 9, 28; 1 Paral. xi. 12, 29; xxvii. 4); according to Calmet, a descendant of Ahoe.

AI'ON, a town taken by Theglathphalasar, king of Assyria (4 Kings xv. 29).

AJALON, a city in tribe of Dan (Jos. xix. 42); assigned to the Levites of the family of Caath (Jos. xxi. 24). It lay between Bethsames and Thamnan (2 Paral. xxviii. 18); near it Josue defeated the five kings and arrested the sun (Jos. x. 12); Jonathan defeated the Philistines (1 Kings xiv. 31); it was fortified by Roboam (2 Paral. xi. 10); it was, however, taken by the Philistines in the time of Achaz (xxviii. 18). Being on the border, it is sometimes spoken of as in Dan, and at other times as in Ephraim, or Benjamin.

AL'ABAS'TER. When our Lord was at the house of Simon the leper in Bethany, a woman, generally regarded as identical with Mary Magdalene, came with an alabaster box of precious ointment, and poured it on his head (Matt. xxvi. 7; Mark xiv. 3); and his feet (Luke vii. 37). The breaking is supposed to be the breaking of the seal.

AL'CIMUS obtained the high-priesthood by the aid of Demetrius, son of Antiochus Epiphanes (1 Mac. vii. 20; 2 Mac. xiv. 3, 4); by presents (4); he had wilfully defiled himself by idolatrous acts (3); and gathered a force of apostates to oppose the Machabees (1 Mac. vii. 22–25; 2 Mac. xiv. 26). Judas for a time compelled him to retire, but he returned with the army under Bacchides (1 Mac. ix. 1); which defeated and killed Judas. In the year 160 B. C. Alcimus threw down the interior walls of the sanctuary and destroyed the works of the prophets, but was smitten with paralysis and died in great torment (1 Mac. ix. 54–56).

A'LEPH, the first letter of the Hebrew alphabet, used like the other letters as a numeral (Ps. cxviii. 1–8; Lament. i. 1; ii. 1; iii. 1; iv. 1).

ALEXAN'DER BA'LES claimed the throne of Syria 152 B. C.; obtained aid of Jonathan Machabeus against Demetrius (1 Mac. x. 18, 22, etc.; x. 48); he married the daughter of Ptolemy Philometor (1 Mac. x. 57); Jonathan and Simon defeated Demetrius Nicator (1 Mac. x. 69); Ptolemy, however, overran Syria; Alexander retired to Cilicia and raised an army, but was defeated, and fleeing to Arabia, was killed by Zabdiel, a prince, who sent his head to Ptolemy (1 Mac. xi. 4–17).

ALEXAN'DER, son of Simon the Cyrenian (Mark xv. 21).

ALEXAN'DER, a Jew of Ephesus who endeavored to appease the idolatrous mob (Acts xix. 33).

ALEXAN'DER, the coppersmith, excommunicated by St. Paul (1 Tim. i. 19, 20; 2 Tim. iv. 14).

ALEXAN'DRIA, a celebrated city of Egypt, founded by Alexander the Great, 331 B. C. It is mentioned, Nahum iii. 8; Jerem. xlvi. 25; Ezech. xxx. 14–16.

ALLELU'IA, a Hebrew expression, meaning Praise the Lord. It was chanted on occasions of joy. It opens many of the Psalms (civ.–cvi., cx.–cxviii., cxxxiv., cxxxv., cxlv.–cl.); Tobias foretold that it should be chanted again in the streets of Jerusalem (xiii. 22); St. John in the Apocalypse heard it chanted in heaven (Apoc. xix. 1–6).

ALLIANCE of the Lacedemonians and Romans with the Machabees (1 Mac. xii., xiv.); alliances with the enemies of God are hateful to him (3 Kings xi. 4).

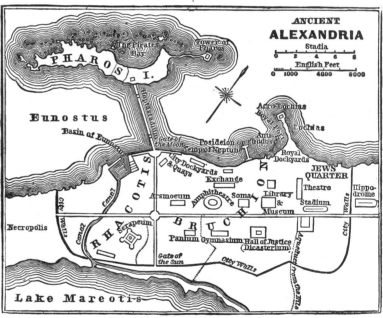

PLAN OF ALEXANDRIA. (From Ebn.)

ALEXANDER THE GREAT, son of Philip, king of Macedon. He is designated in the prophecy of Daniel by a four-winged leopard (vii. 6); and by a goat which attacks and overcomes a ram (Darius), (viii. 4–7). His monarchy is the belly of brass in Nabuchodonosor's statue (Dan. ii. 39). After defeating Darius he overran Syria, and while besieging Tyre wrote to Jannus the high-priest to demand his submission. On his refusal Alexander marched against Jerusalem, but was appeased by the high-priest, who went out to meet him. His career is briefly sketched in 1 Mac. i. 1–8; and the division of his kingdom among his generals (7), as foretold by Daniel xi. 4.

ALMATH, a city of refuge in the tribe of Benjamin (1 Paral. vi. 60; vii. 8).

ALM'OND, a fruit (Gen. xliii. 11; Num. xvii. 8; Eccles. xii. 5).

ALMS; the obligation of giving alms is declared in many parts of the Scriptures (Ex. xxiii. 11; Lev. xxiii. 22; Deut. xv. 7–10; Tob. iv. 7–17; xii. 9; Job xxx. 25; Ps. xl. 1; lxxxi. 4; Prov. iii. 28; xi. 24; xxi. 13; xxii. 9; xxviii. 27; Ecclus. iv. 2; vii. 36; xii. 3; xxix. 12; Isaias lviii. 7; Ezech. xvi. 49; Amos viii. 4; Matt. x. 42; xix. 21; Luke iii. 11; vi. 35; xi. 41; xii. 33; xiv. 13; xvi. 9; Acts ix. 36; xi. 29; xx. 35; Rom. xii. 8, 22; 1 Cor. xvi.; 2 Cor. viii. 11; ix. 7–11; Eph. iv. 28; Heb. xiii. 16;

1 John iii. 17); a blessing pronounced on those who give alms (Prov. xiv. 21, 31; xxii. 9); alms given to the poor are lent to the Lord (Prov. xix. 17); alms-giving recommended (Prov. xvii. 5; Ecclus. vii. 36; 3 Kings xvii. 19). Its reward (Ecclus. xxix. 15; Tobias iv. 10; xii. 9). Alms-giving practised by the primitive Christians (Acts xi. 29, 30).

AL′OES, used by the Jews as a perfume (Prov. vii. 17; Cant. iv. 14); it was used also in embalming (John xix. 39).

ters are of Chaldee origin, and came into use after the captivity. In writing, most of the vowels were omitted. After the fall of Jerusalem and the revival of Jewish learning, the school of Masora introduced vowel points, hence called Masoretic. At this time the language was no longer generally spoken, and these rabbis read the Hebrew differently from those who had translated the Hebrew into Greek while the language was still a living tongue. Catholics have followed the Septuagint, which is older, and would

him with Cleophas (Luke xxiv. 18), believing that to be his Syriac and Alpheus his Greek name.

AL′PHEUS, father of Levi or St. Matthew (Mark ii. 14).

AL′TAR, essentially connected with the worship of Almighty God, from the days of the patriarchs (Gen. viii. 20); the Mosaic law (Ex. xx. 24); the Christian law (Heb. xiii. 10); in heaven (Apoc. vi. 9; viii. 3). The first altar named is that erected by Noe on leaving the ark (Gen. viii. 20); the first

ANCIENT ALPHABETS.

AL′PHA and OMEGA, the first and last letters of the Greek alphabet, used by our Lord in the Apocalypse to signify the beginning and the end (Apoc. i. 8, 17; ii. 8; xxi. 6; xxii. 13).

AL′PHABET. The Hebrew alphabet consists of twenty-two letters. The original Hebrew characters are those now called Samaritan, or which appear on Jewish coins. The present square charac-

seem to be more correct; Protestants follow the later Jewish rendering. The letters of the Hebrew alphabet are used to mark divisions in Ps. cxviii.; Lament. i.–iv.

AL′PHEUS, father of St. James the Less, and husband of Mary, apparently sister of the Blessed Virgin (Matt. x. 3; Luke vi. 15); whence St. James is called the Brother of the Lord. Some identify

altars were apparently of undressed stone or earth. God so directed Moses to build them (Ex. xx. 24–26; Deut. xxvii. 5); Elias erected such an altar (3 Kings xviii. 32). When God gave the law to Moses, he directed two altars to be made, (1) the Altar of Holocausts, in the Tabernacle, was five cubits square and three high, hollow, made of planks of setim wood, with horns at the corners, all overlaid with brass. It was carried by means of bars of setim wood, covered with brass, running through rings at the sides (Exod. xxvii., xxviii.; Num. vii.) The altar of holocausts in Solomon's temple was twenty cubits square and ten high, and all of brass (3 Kings viii. 64; 2 Paral. iv. 1; vii. 7). It was restored by Asa (2 Paral.

GROUP OF ANCIENT ALTARS.

xv. 8); profaned by Achaz (4 Kings xvi. 14). Of that in the second temple (1 Esd. iii. 2; vi. 16) there is no description. It was restored by Judas Machabeus (1 Mac. iv. 47, 53). A perpetual fire was kept on this altar by command of God (Levit. vi. 12, 13). (2) The Altar of Incense in the Tabernacle was a cubit square and two cubits high; also with horns, all of setim wood overlaid with gold (Ex. xxx. 1–6; xxxviii. 25; xl. 5); that in the temple was of cedar, overlaid with gold (3 Kings vii. 48; 1 Paral. xxviii. 18). Antiochus Epiphanes removed the altar of incense from the second temple, but Judas Machabeus restored it (1 Mach. i. 23; iv. 49). On this the incense was offered every morning and evening (Ex. xxx. 7, 8; Luke i. 9–11).

ALTAR to an unknown god erected at Athens (Acts xvii. 22, 23).

A'LUS, one of the encampments of the Israelites (Num. xxxiii. 13).

AMA'AD, a town of the tribe of Aser (Jos. xix. 26).

AM'ALEC, son of Eliphaz and Thamna, and grandson of Esau (Gen. xxxvi. 12, 16; 1 Paral. i. 36).

AMAL'ECITES, descendants of Amalec, occupied the country between the Dead and Red Seas, or between Hevila and Sur (1 Kings xv. 7). They attacked the Israelites in the desert of Raphidim and killed the stragglers (Ex. xvii. 8–14; Num. xiv. 43–45). Josue gave them battle and defeated them by the aid of the prayers of Moses (Ex. xvii. 8–14); 1491 B. C. In the days of the Judges the Amalecites joined the Moabites against the Israelites, and made them tributaries, till they were delivered by Aod (Judges iii. 13–30). They also aided the Madianites against the Israelites, but they were utterly defeated by Gedeon (Judges vi.; vii.); Saul also defeated them (1 Kings xiv. 48); and they were utterly destroyed with their king Agag (1 Kings xv.), as it had been foretold (Ex. xvii. 14; Num. xxiv. 20; Deut. xxv. 19). A part of the tribe captured Siceleg from David, but he pursued and cut them to pieces, except four hundred, who escaped (1 Kings xviii. 8; xxx. 1, 9, 17).

AM'ALEC, a mountain in Ephraim where

Abdon, one of the judges, was buried (Judges xii. 15).

A'MAM, a city of Juda (Jos. xv. 26).

AMAN, son of Amadathi, an Amalecite of the race of Agag (Esth. iii. 1); called also a Macedonian (xvi. 10); he was the favorite minister of Assuerus, but not receiving homage from Mardocheus, a Jew, sought to destroy him and his nation; Assuerus gave him power to do as he chose in regard to the Jews, and Aman appointed the thirteenth day of the month Adar for a general massacre. Esther, queen of Assuerus, who was a Jewess, after praying to God, ventured into the king's presence and pleaded for her own life, and the lives of her people. Assuerus asked who dared menace her life, and when she indicated Aman, his doom was sealed, and he was hanged on a gibbet which he had erected for Mardocheus (Esther i.–xvi.)

AMA'NA, a mountain near Libanus (Cant. iv. 8).

AMARI'A, one of the priests and Levites who returned from the captivity (2 Esd. xii. 2).

AMARI'AS, the name of several high-priests: (1) son of Meraioth (1 Paral. vi. 7); (2) a high-priest in the reign of Josaphat (2 Paral. xix. 11); (3) son of Azarias (1 Paral. vi. 11); and supposed to be the high-priest who resisted king Ozias when he wished to offer incense, for which he was struck with leprosy (2 Paral. xxvi. 16–21).

AMA'SA, son of Jether and of Abigail, David's sister. He commanded the army of Absalom, and was pardoned by David after the defeat by Joab (2 Kings xvii. 25; xix. 13); David sent him against Seba, but he was treacherously slain by Joab at Gabaon (xx. 4–12).

AMASA'I, a brave man who moved by the Spirit joined David in Hebron with thirty men (1 Paral. xii. 18).

AMASA'I, a priest and musician in the time of David (1 Paral. xv. 24).

AMASI'AS, eighth king of Juda, son of Joas (2 Paral. xxiv. 27; xxv. 1; 4 Kings xiv.) He ascended the throne at the age of 25, 839 B. C., and reigned twenty-nine years. He was one of the good kings, but did not abolish the high-places. He punished his father's murderers, and took a census of his people. He hired troops from the king of Israel, but on being reproved by a prophet sent them back (2 Paral. xxv. 7). He defeated the Edomites in the valley of the salt-pits (4 Kings xiv. 7). He then fell into idolatry and worshipped the gods of Edom, and though reproved by a prophet remained

impenitent (2 Paral. xxv. 14). He made war on Joas, king of Israel, but was defeated at Bethsames, and fell into the hands of Joas, who then dismantled Jerusalem and plundered the temple. He reigned fifteen years more, but did not repent. A conspiracy being formed against him he fled to Lachis, but was pursued and assassinated, 810 B. C. He was buried in the city of David (17–28).

AMASI'AS, priest of the golden calves at Bethel in the reign of Jeroboam, opposed the prophet Amos, about 789 B. C. (Amos vii. 10–17).

AM'ATHITE, descendants of Amath, son of Chanaan (Gen. x. 18; see 1 Mac. xii. 25).

AMBIT'ION ruins many (Ecclus. ix. 16).

A'MEN' in Hebrew signifies true, faithful, certain. It was also used to affirm by our Lord. Amen, Amen, I say to you (John i. 51, etc.) It was also used for assent. "Be it so" (Num. v. 22; Deut. xxvii. 15); and to express belief (1 Cor. xiv. 16). The Greek and Latin churches retain the word to conclude their prayers, as in Tobias xiii. 23; Matt. vi. 13.

AM'ETHYST, a precious stone. It was in the third row in Aaron's Rational of Judgment (Exod. xxviii. 19; xxxix. 12). It bore the name of Issachar.

AMIN'ADAB, of the tribe of Juda, and son of Aram (Ex. vi. 23; Num. i. 7; Ruth iv. 19; 1 Paral. ii. 10; Matt. i. 4; Luke iii. 33).

AMIN'ADAB. His chariots are referred to, Cant. vi. 11.

AMIN'ADAB, a priest, chief of the sons of Oziel, selected to carry the ark (1 Paral. xv. 10); a Levite also selected (11).

AM'ITAL, wife of king Josias, and mother of Joachas and Sedecias, kings of Juda (4 Kings xxiii. 31).

ALTAR OF HOLOCAUSTS.

AM'MAUS or Emmaus, a town near the mountains of Juda, where Judas Machabeus defeated Gorgias and Nicanor (1 Mac. iii. 57; iv. 3; ix. 50).

AM'MIEL, son of Gemalli of the tribe of Dan, one of the spies sent by Moses into the land of Chanaan (Num. xiii. 13).

AM'MIEL, son of Obededom, porter of the temple (1 Paral. xxvi. 5).

AM'MON, grandson of Lot (Gen. xix. 34, 38).

AM'MONITES, descendants of Ammon. They destroyed the gigantic Zomzommim and occupied their country (Deut. ii. 20). God forbade Moses to attack them (Deut. ii. 19, 20). After the death of Othoniel, the Ammonites and Amalecites joined Eglon, king of Moab, in subduing the Israelites (Judg. iii. 13); in the time of Jephte, they again declared war on the Israelites, claiming the land that Moses had wrested from the Amorrhites, but Jephte defeated them at Aroer (Judg. x. 7-18; xi. 12-33), B. C. 1187. In the reign of Saul, Naas, king of the Ammonites, besieged Jabes of Galaad, but Saul relieved it (1 Kings xi. 11), B. C. 1095. David maintained friendly relations with the king of Ammon in his time, and on his death sent ambassadors to condole, but Hanon, the new king, treated the ambassadors ignominiously. David then conquered their country (2 Kings viii. 12; x. 1-14; xii. 26-31). They remained subject to the kings of Israel to the death of Achab, 897 B. C. (4 Kings i. 1). They invaded Juda, but were defeated by Josaphat (2 Paral xx. 1, 2); but after the fall of the kingdom of Israel, they occupied some of the territory of Ruben, Gad and Manasse (Jerem. xlix. 1). There are prophecies against them in Ps. lxxxii. 8; Jer. xlix. 1; Ezech. xxi. 20; xxv. 2-10; Amos i. 13; Soph. ii. 8). They were still cruel enemies of the Jews in the days of the Machabees (1 Mach. v. 6-43).

AM'NON, eldest son of David and Achinoam, dishonors his half-sister Thamar, and is assassinated in retaliation by her brother Absalom (2 Kings xiii. 1-28).

AMOC', one of the priestly families who returned from Babylon (2 Esdr. xii. 20).

A'MON, governor of Samaria under Achab, holds Micheas in prison (3 Kings xxii. 26).

A'MON, fourteenth king of Juda, son of Manasses and Messalemeth. He reigned twenty-two years, but only two in Jerusalem, 641-639 B. C.; he imitated his father's idolatry, and was killed by his own servants, and was buried in the garden of Oza (4 Kings xxi. 18-26; 2 Paral. xxxiii. 21-25).

AMORRHITES, a people descended from the fourth son of Chanaan, whose name was apparently Amor (Gen. x. 16). They first occupied the heights west of the Dead Sea (Gen. xiv. 7). They gradually drove the Moabites beyond the Arnon (Gen. xiv. 13; Num. xxi. 13, 26) and extended to Hermon (Deut. iii. 8; iv. 48). Moses conquered Sehon, king of the Amorrhites, whose capital was Hesebon, and occupied his territory on his refusing to permit the Israelites to pass through (Num. xxi. 21-31).

A'MOS, the third of the lesser prophets, was a herdsman. He lived in the time of Jeroboam II., 789 B. C., and for reproving the idolatry of Jeroboam II., and foretelling his death, was denounced by Amasias, priest of the golden calves at Bethel. He then retired to Thecue, in the tribe of Juda. His prophecies begin in the reign of Ozias, and announce God's judgments against the people of Israel and the neighboring nations. His prophecies comprise nine chapters (Amos i.-ix.) He is quoted by St. Stephen and St. James (Acts vii. 42; xv. 16).

A'MOS, one of the ancestors of our Lord (Luke iii. 25).

AMPHIP'OLIS, a city in Macedon, near Thrace. St. Paul and Silas passed by it after being delivered from prison at Philippi (Acts xvii. 1).

AMPLIA'TUS, a disciple mentioned by St. Paul (Rom. xvi. 8).

AM'RAM, eldest son of Caath, of the tribe of Levi; he married Jochabed, by whom he had Aaron,

Mary, and Moses. He died in Egypt, aged 137 (Ex. vi. 20; Num. iii. 19; 1 Paral. vi. 2, 18; xxiii. 12).

AM'RAPHEL, king of Sennaar, with three others, made war on the kings of the Pentapolis, and carried off Lot and his possessions; but was forced by Abraham to give them up, 1912 B. C. (Gen. xiv. 1).

AM'RI was general of the armies under Ela, king of Israel. While besieging Gebbethon, he heard that Zambri had murdered Ela and usurped the throne. He attacked Zambri in Thersa, and forced him to burn himself up in his palace with all his family, after a reign of seven days. Part of the nation recognized Thebni, who reigned four years. Amri reigned six years at Thersa, and six at Samaria, which he built after purchasing the mountain of Someron (3 Kings xvi. 9, 10, 24). There he ended his wicked reign (xvi. 28; Mich. vi. 16), 918 B. C.

A'NA, son of Sebeon, mentioned as having discovered in the desert hot springs, which the King James Bible erroneously renders *mules*.

A'NA, a town apparently on the Euphrates, above Babylon, where the name remains (4 Kings xviii. 34; 4 Kings xix. 13; Isaias xxxvii. 13; Gen. xxxvi. 24).

AN'AMELECH, a heathen god whose cruel worship in which children were burnt was carried from the Euphrates to Samaria (4 Kings xvii. 31).

ANANI'A, a city of Benjamin, occupied by the Jews after the captivity (2 Esd. xi. 32).

ANANI'AS, one of the three princely companions of Daniel brought up at the court of Nabuchodonosor. He there received the name of Sidrach (Dan. i. 6, 7). They refused to eat forbidden food (8-16), and to adore the statue of Nabuchodonosor (iii. 12), for which the three were cast into a fiery furnace (iii. 21); but God sent an angel (iii. 92, 95) and saved them from the action of the fire (iii. 24, 91, 92). Amid the flames they chanted the Benedicite, a canticle used to this day in the services of the church (iii. 52-90). It is rejected by Protestants. Nabuchodonosor bade them come forth, and they did so, unharmed, and not even singed by the fire (iii. 93, 94). They were promoted and honored by the king (97).

ANANI'AS, son of the perfumer, rebuilt part of the wall of Jerusalem after the return from Babylon (2 Esd. iii. 8).

ANANI'AS, high-priest, before whom St. Paul was arraigned, A. D. 58, and who ordered him to be struck in the mouth. St. Paul, not recognizing the high-priest, answered indignantly, but apologized on learning his dignity (Acts xxiii. 1-5); when St. Paul was sent to Cæsarea, Ananias followed and accused him before Felix, the governor (xxiv.)

ANANI'AS, one of the first Christians of Jerusalem, with his wife, Saphira. The faithful at that time had all things in common, and those who had houses and lands sold them, and laid the price at the feet of the apostles to be distributed to every one as he had need. Ananias and his wife had a piece of land which they sold, but laid only part of the price at the feet of the apostles. St. Peter called him to account, telling him that he had lied not to men but to God. And Ananias fell dead on the spot. When Saphira came in, she, too, falsely misrepresented the price they had received, when she, too, fell dead (Acts iv. 32-37; v. 1-11).

ANANI'AS, a disciple living in Damascus, who was directed by our Lord in a vision to go to Straight Street to Saul, who had just been converted and had arrived in Damascus. Ananias, in astonishment, replied that he had heard of him as a great persecutor, but our Lord said: Go thy way, for this man

is to me a vessel of election to carry my name before the Gentiles, and kings, and the children of Israel. For I will shew him how great things he must suffer for my name's sake. Ananias went to the house and laid his hands on Saul, who recovered his sight and received baptism (Acts ix. 10-18). There was no further mention of him in the Acts.

ANATH'EMA, a Greek word meaning set apart, separated, devoted. It is used especially to mark the absolute cutting off and separation of a man from the communion of the faithful, the number of the living or the privileges of society, or the devoting a person or thing to be destroyed by fire or otherwise. All were forbidden to have any idol in the house lest they should become an anathema like it (Deut. vii. 26); everything in idolatrous cities was to be destroyed. There shall nothing of that anathema stick to thy hand (Deut. xiii. 17). Jericho and all in it was to be an anathema (Jos. vi. 17; vii. 1, 11, 13; 1 Paral. ii. 7); God threatens to strike the earth with anathema, that is, with total destruction (Mal. iv. 6); St. Paul wishes to become an anathema for his brethren (Rom. ix. 3); anathema may be pronounced (Gal. i. 8; 1 Cor. xvi. 22); anathema incurred by nonfulfilment of a vow (Levit. xxvii. 29); place of Anathema (Judg. i. 17).

AN'ATHOTH, the city of Abiathar (3 Kings ii. 26); of the prophet Jeremias (Jer. i. 1; xi. 21; xxix. 27; xxxii. 7).

AN'CIENT OF DAYS, an expression used to designate God, in Dan. vii. 9, 13, 22.

AN'CIENTS OF ISRAEL, the heads of the twelve tribes and of the great families of Israel (Exod. iii. 16; iv. 29). Subsequently, Moses, by command of God, gathered unto him seventy men of the ancients of Israel, to whom God imparted some of the spirit he had conferred on Moses (Num. xi. 16, 17). The ancients continued under Josue (ix. 15; xxiii. 2; xxiv. 1; xxiv. 31).

AN'DREW, one of the twelve apostles of Jesus Christ, a native of Bethsaida, son of Jona, and brother of Simon Peter. He was a disciple of St. John, the Baptist, but followed our Lord when he was pointed out by the Precursor, and became the first disciple (John i. 39); then he took his brother, Simon, to him. They were with him at Cana, but then returned to their occupation as fishermen. While so engaged our Lord called them to become fishers of men, and they left everything and became his constant attendants (Matt. iv. 19). It was St. Andrew who gave him the five loaves and two fishes (John vi. 9). He appears also as introducing some Gentiles brought by St. Philip, and as asking when the destruction of the temple was to take place (John xii. 22). Eusebius, the earliest historian of the church, says he preached in Scythia. Others say that he preached also in Greece and was crucified at Patras, in Achaia.

ANDRONI'CUS, a nobleman left by Antiochus Epiphanes as his deputy at Antioch during his expedition to Cilicia. Manelaus, a false high-priest, bribed him with vessels stolen from the temple to put Onias, the real high-priest, to death, and Andronicus did so by treachery. Antiochus shed tears, remembering the modesty and sobriety of Onias, and caused Andronicus to be put to death where the sacrilegious wretch had committed the impiety against Onias (2 Mach. iv. 31-38).

ANER and ESCHOL, two Chanaanites who aided Abraham to retake Lot and his substance (Gen xiv. 13, 24).

ANGE, mountains of, on the left of Cilicia (Judith ii. 12).

AN'GELS, pure spirits created by God before man, and as it would seem from Job (xxxviii. 7) before the material world. Angel is from the Greek *angelos*, a messenger, the synonym of the Hebrew word *maleac*. God sends them to announce his will, to correct, punish, teach, rebuke, console (Ps. cii. 20; ciii. 4; Matt. iv. 1; xiii. 49; xxvi. 53). The mission and apparition of angels is constantly mentioned in Scripture. Different grades or choirs are named Seraphim (Isaias vi. 2, 6); Cherubim (Gen. iii.24); Thrones (Col. i. 16); Dominations (Col. i. 16); Virtues (Rom. viii. 38; 1 Pet. iii. 22); Powers (1 Pet. iii. 22; Col. i. 16); Principalities (Col. i.16); Archangels (Jude i. 9); and Angels; some of the angels rebelled against God and fell (Job iv. 18; Isaias xiv. 9; Ezech. xxviii. 3, 14, 17; John viii. 44); and were cast out of heaven (Isai. xiv. 12; Luke x. 18); and condemned to hell (Apoc. xx. 7); (See DEVIL; SATAN); the angels see God (Isai. vi. 2; Matt. xviii. 10); they are called sons of God (Job i. 6; xxxviii. 7); they are the ministers of God's will (Ps. cii. 20; ciii. 4; Matt. iv. 1; xiii. 49; xxvi. 53); they aid those who fear God (Ps. xxxiii. 8; xc. 11; Bar. vi. 6); are guardians of countries (Dan. iv. 10, 20; x. 10, 13, 20, 21; Acts xvi. 9); and of individuals (Matt. xviii. 10); angels sent by God to assist Agar (Gen. xvi. 7; xxi. 17); Abraham (xviii.; iii. 49); Daniel (vi. 22); Tobias (Tob. v. 6–12); St. Peter (Acts x. 19; xii. 7–11); Cornelius (Acts Abraham's bosom (Luke xvi. 22); an angel appears to Moses in the burning bush (Ex. iii. 2); the law given through angels (Heb. ii. 2); an angel guides the people of Israel (xii. 22; Num. xx. 16); God promises to send an angel to his people (Ex. xxiii. 20; xxxiii. 2); sends an angel to prevent Balaam cursing his people (Num. xxii. 22); to Josue (Jos. v. 13); an angel rebukes the people (Judg. ii. 1–4); an angel directs Gedeon (vi. 11–40; vii. 1–7); an angel appears to Samson's mother (xiii. 3–21); to Zacharias (Zach. ii., iii., iv., v., vi.); an angel punishes David (2 Kings xxiv. 16; 1 Paral. xxi. 15); directs Elias (3 Kings xix. 5; 4 Kings i. 3, 15); defeats the Assyrians (xix. 35); angels explain visions (Dan. viii. 16; ix. 21; x. 5, 10, 16); an angel leads the army of the Machabees (2 Mach. xi. 6–11); angels punish Heliodorus (2 Mach. iii. 25–27); an angel appears to St. Joseph (Matt. i. 20; ii. 13, 19); to Zachary (Luke i. 11, 20); to the blessed Virgin Mary (i. 26–38); to the shepherds (ii. 9, 15); to our Lord in his agony (xxii. 43); to the disciples after the Resurrection (Matt. xxviii. 2); the disciples after the Ascension (Acts i. 10); to St. Paul (Acts xxvii. 23); reveal the Apocalypse to St. John (Apoc. i. 1; xix. 10; xxii. 8); angels revered by the patriarchs (Gen. xviii. 2; xix. 1; Num. xxii. 31); Gedeon (Judg. vi. 11); but superstitious honors not to be paid to (Col. ii. 18); woman to have her head covered because of the

ST. ANNE, THE BLESSED VIRGIN AND THE INFANT JESUS.

xxii. 11); Lot (xix); Jacob (xxviii. 12; xxxii.); Elias (3 Kings xix. 5); the three children (Dan. x. 3; xi. 13); the eunuch of Queen Candace (viii. 26); to aid the sick (John v. 4); bear the just to angels (1 Cor. xi. 10); angels desire to know the mystery of the gospel (1 Pet. i. 12); will summon men to judgment (Matt. xxiv. 31; 1 Thess. iv. 15; 1 Cor. xv. 52); know not the day (Mark xiii. 32); will come with Christ to judge mankind (Matt. xvi. 27; 2 Thes. i. 7). Doctors and preachers called angels (Mal. ii. 7; iii. 1; Gal. iv. 14; Apoc. i. 20). The Sadducees denied the existence of angels (Acts xxiii. 8).

ANGELS of the Devil (Matt. xxv. 41); of Satan (2 Cor. xii. 7); of the dragon (Apoc. xii. 7); wicked angels (Ps. lxxvii. 49; Prov. xvii. 11; 2 Pet. ii. 4; Apoc. ix. 11, 14, 15).

AN'GER, the evil effects of this deadly sin shown in Gen. iv. 5; Job v. 2; Prov. xii. 13; xiv. 3; xv. 18; xix. 19; xxvii. 3; xxix. 22; Eccles. vii. 10; Ecclus. xxv. 23; xxviii. 13; xxx. 26; Matt. v. 22; Luke iv. 28; Gal. v. 20.

AN'IMALS, created on the fifth day (Gen. i. 24, 25); receive their names from Adam (ii. 20); first

ANOINTING.

mention of their being offered in sacrifice to God (iv. 4); offered by Noe (viii. 20); by Abraham (xv. 9; xxii. 13); under the Mosaic law (Num. xv.; xviii. 9; xix. 3); animals distinguished as clean and unclean (Gen. vii. 2, 3; viii. 20; Deut. xiv.; xv. 22; xxi. 5; Lev. xi.); to be offered by women at their purification (xii. 6, 8); animals seen in a dream by Ezech. (i. 4); seen in a vision by St. Peter (Acts x. 12); cruelty to animals forbidden (Gen. xxiii.; Exod. xxiii. 12); Num. xxxii. 24; Deut. v. 14; Prov. xii. 10; Ecclus. vii. 24).

AN'ISE, an aromatic seed, of which the scrupulous Pharisees made it a point to pay tithes (Matt. xxiii. 23).

AN'NA, wife of Elcana of Ramathaimsophim, an Ephrathite, prayed at Silo to be delivered from barrenness (1 Kings i. 10), and made a vow to the Lord (11); bears a son Samuel, B. C. 1155 (20); offers a sacrifice of thanksgiving (24, 25); her canticle (ii. 1–10); she dedicates her son to the service of the Lord (11, 18, 19).

AN'NA, wife of the elder Tobias, of the tribe of Nephthali, a captive at Ninive (Tob. i. 1, 2, 9); supports her blind husband by weaving (ii. 19); reproaches him on occasion of a kid (22, 23); her grief on the departure of her son (v. 23–28); she watched by the way daily for his return (xi. 5); tells her husband of his approach (6); their joy (11); her death (xiv. 14).

AN'NA, wife of Raguel, cousin of Tobias, and mother of Sara, whom young Tobias married (Tob. vii. 2).

AN'NA, daughter of Phanuel, of the tribe of Aser, a prophetess. She was a widow, having lived seven years in the married state, and persevered in holy widowhood to the age of eighty-four, serving God in the temple by prayer and fasting. When the Blessed Virgin at her purification presented the Infant Jesus in the temple, she with Simeon praised God, and spoke of the Saviour to all who looked for the redemption of Israel (Luke ii. 36–39).

AN'NAS, high-priest, exercising the functions alternate years with his son-in-law, Caiphas. As he was to assume power after the Pasch, our Lord was first taken before him (Luke iii. 2; John xviii. 13); St. Peter and St. John were arraigned before him soon after (Acts iv. 6).

ANNUN'CIATION of the Blessed Virgin (Luke i. 26–38).

ANOINT'ING. Prophets were anointed for their mission (3 Kings xix. 16); priests (Ex. xxix. 29; xl. 13; Num. iii. 3; Levit. iv. 3; xvi. 32); kings (1 Kings ix. 16; x. 1; xvi. 13; 3 Kings i. 34, 39; xix. 16; 4 Kings xi. 12; 1 Paral. xvi. 22; Ps. civ. 15); things set apart for the divine worship were anointed: Jacob's pillar (Gen. xxxi. 13); the tabernacle and its furniture (Ex. xxx. 26–28). The apostles, by our Lord's mission, anointed the sick (Mark vi. 13); this sacramental anointing prescribed (James v. 14). Christ, in Greek, means the Anointed (see Ps. ii. 2; Dan. ix. 25, 26); his anointing is from the Father (Ps. xliv. 8; Dan. ix. 24; Luke iv. 18; Acts iv. 27; x. 38; Heb. i. 9); the faithful are anointed (2 Cor. i. 21; 1 John ii. 20, 27).

ANT, cited as an example of diligence (Prov. vi. 6); of wisdom (xxx. 25).

ANTIOCH.

ANT'ICHRIST, the man of sin who is to precede the second coming of Christ (1 John ii. 18, 19; 2 Thess. ii. 3, 5; Apoc. xvi.–xix.); his defeat foretold (Isai. xi. 4); his conspiracy and fall (Ezech. xxxviii., xxxix.); his birth, progress and the fall of his empire foretold (Dan. vii. 8–26; 1 John ii. 18;

THE ANNUNCIATION.

2 John i. 7; 2 Thess. ii. 3); his persecution (2 Thess. ii. 4; Apoc. xi. 2, 7).

ANT'IMONY, a preparation of the metal called in our translation stibic stone, was used for darken ing the eye (4 Kings ix. 30; Jerem. iv. 30; Ezech. xxiii. 40); one of Job's daughters, Cornu Stibii, has a name meaning a vase of antimony (Job xlii. 14).

AN'TIOCH, capital of Syria, identified by St. Jerome with Reblat (Num. xxxiv. 11). It was the chief city of the kingdom of Syria (1 Mach. iii. 37; iv. 35; x. 68); Antiochus Eupator recaptures it (vi. 63; 2 Mach. xiii. 23, 26); Ptolemee crowned there (1 Mach. xi. 13); Jonathan sends troops to Antioch to support Demetrius (xi. 44); captured by Tryphon (1 Mach. xi. 56); the high-priest Onias concealed at (2 Mach. iv. 32, 36); the first Gentile church founded at Antioch (Acts xi. 20, 21); the disciples here first called Christians (xi. 26). St. Paul set out from Antioch on his journeys (Acts xi. 30; xiii. 4; xviii. 23).

AN'TIOCH in Pisidia. St. Paul at (Acts xiii. 14; xiv. 20; 2 Tim. iii. 11). It was also called Cæsarea.

ANTI'OCHIS, concubine of Antiochus Epiphanes, to whom that king gave Tharsus and Mallos, an act that led to a sedition (2 Mach. iv. 30).

ANTI'OCHUS II., Theos. His marriage and death foretold by Daniel (xi. 6).

ANTI'OCHUS IV., Epiphanes, son of Antiochus the Great, sent an envoy to Egypt to secure the regency, B. C. 173 (2 Mach. iv. 21): he then invaded and reduced much of Egypt (v. 1); hearing of troubles at Jerusalem, he returned, took the city, killed 80,000, took prisoners and sold 40,000. He also, aided by Menelaus, false high-priest, plundered the temple and profaned the sacred vessels (11–21). After conquering Egypt he sent Apollonius with an army to Judea, who treacherously slew many thousand adults, selling the women and young as slaves (24–26); he issued an edict commanding all to embrace his state religion; he ordered the temple to be profaned, the sacrifices of the law to be stopped, forbade the Sabbaths and Mosaic rites to be observed. He erected idolatrous temples and altars, on which swine and other unclean animals were offered. The penalty for disobedience was death (1 Mach. i. 43–52); on the fifteenth of the month Casleu he set up the abominable idol of desolation (Jupiter Olympius) on the altar of God (57); many Jews perished sooner than obey: women were put to death with their infants hung about their necks for circumcising them (64, 65); Mathathias and his brethren retired to the mountains; the aged Eleazar and the seven Machabee brothers were martyred at Antioch (2 Mach. vi., vii.); Judas Machabeus took up arms and defeated several armies; Antiochus went to Persia, hoping to wrest great wealth from that country, but hearing of Judas's victories and his recovery of Jerusalem and dedication of the temple, while on his way to punish the Jews he was struck down by disease, and though he promised to become a Jew if his life was spared, he died in great torments, B. C. 164 (1 Mach. vi. 16; 2 Mach. ix. 28, 29).

BRONZE FIGURE OF APIS.

ANTI'OCHUS V., Eupator, son of Epiphanes, succeeded his father at the age of nine. Lysias commanding his armies besieged Jerusalem, and was about to take it when he found it necessary to march on Antioch, where Philip had obtained control. But Demetrius Soter, the real heir, returning from Rome raised an army, captured Lysias and Antiochus, and put both to death, B. C. 162 (1 Mach. vi., vii.; 2 Mach. xiii., xiv.)

ANTI'OCHUS VI., Theos, son of Alexander Balas, was set up 145 B. C. by Tryphon, who won the aid of Jonathan and Simon Machabeus by giving them great powers. Jonathan won several victories over the forces of Demetrius, but Tryphon resolving to usurp the throne enticed Jonathan into Ptolemais and kept him a prisoner. Simon with his army saved Jerusalem, but Tryphon put Jonathan to death, and soon after subjected Antiochus to an operation under which he died (1 Mach. xi. 39, 63, etc.; xiii. 21–31).

ANTI'OCHUS SIDETES, son of Demetrius Soter, induced Simon to espouse his cause against Tryphon (1 Mach. xv. 1–3) by declaring Jerusalem and the temple free, and permitting him to coin money in his own name; but as Tryphon's troops deserted him, Antiochus refused the army sent him by Simon,

recalled his promises, and demanded the surrender of some towns. John Hircanus and Judas defeated the armies of Antiochus, but on the murder of Simon, Antiochus besieged Jerusalem, which was bravely defended by John Hircanus, but finally surrendered on favorable terms (1 Mach. xv. 25; xvi. 1–24).

AN'TIPAS, a faithful witness or martyr (Apoc. ii. 13).

ANTIP'ATER, son of Jason, one of the envoys of Jonathan Machabeus to Lacedæmon and Rome (1 Mach. xii. 16; xiv. 17–22).

ANTIPA'TRIS, a town between Jerusalem and Cæsarea to which St. Paul was taken (Acts xxiii. 31).

APES, imported as curiosities by Solomon (3 Kings x. 22; 2 Paral. ix. 21).

APHERE'MA, a toparchy added to Judea by the Syrian kings (1 Mach. xi. 34).

APHARSI'TES, Apharsathachites (1 Esd. iv. 9); Arphasachites (v. 6), tribes who were sent by the Assyrians to colonize the cities of Samaria.

APH'EC, Apheca (Jos. xv. 53), a city in Chanaan, whose king was slain by Josue (xii. 18); the Philistines encamped here when the ark was brought from Silo (1 Kings iv. 1, 2, 3). 2. Aphec, in the valley of Jezrahel, where the Philistines encamped before the battle of Gelboe (1 Kings xxix. 1). 3. Aphec in Aser, near Sidon (Jos. xix. 30; xiii. 4).

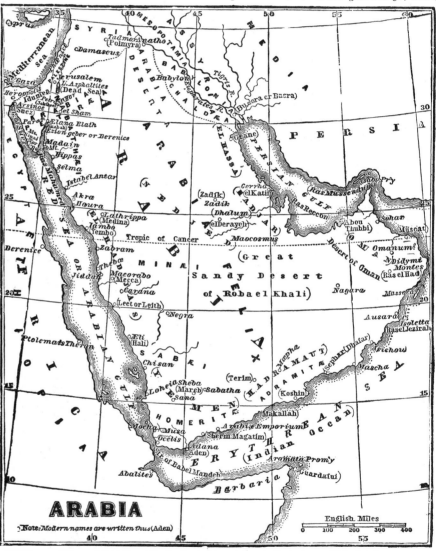

ARABIA

Note: Modern names are written thus (Aden)

English Miles

A'OD, son of Gera, of the tribe of Benjamin, and judge of Israel, succeeded Othoniel. Having been sent with tribute to Eglon, king of Moab, who had oppressed Israel for eighteen years, he slew the tyrant, and calling the people to arms seized the fords of the Jordan, and cut off all the Moabites to the number of ten thousand, 1245 B. C. (Judges iii. 15–30).

APAD'NO, a term of disputed meaning mentioned by Daniel (xi. 45) in speaking of the tabernacle of Antichrist.

APELL'ES, mentioned by St. Paul (Rom. xvi. 10). Tradition makes him bishop of Smyrna.

4. Aphec in Syria, near which Achab and Benadad fought (3 Kings xx. 26).

APOC'ALYPSE means Revelation, and is the title of the last of the Canonical books of the New Testament. It was written by St. John the Evangelist about the years 95–97 on the island of Patmos, to which he had been exiled by Domitian. It is not in the catalogue drawn up by the council of Laodicea, nor in that of St. Cyril of Jerusalem, but is cited as one of the inspired books by St. Justin, St. Irenæus, Origen, St. Cyprian, St. Clement of Alexandria, Tertullian, and all the Fathers from the fourth century. It contains twenty-two chapters; three addressed to seven bishops of cities in Asia Minor; fifteen on the persecutions of the church; four on the triumph of the church over its enemies, the marriage of the Lamb, and the happiness of the triumphant church.

APOC'RYPHA (concealed), a term applied to books not received in its canon by the church, namely, the prayer of Manasses, the third and fourth books of Esdras, the third and fourth books of Machabees, the Epistle of St. Barnabas, the book of Hermes and the 151st Psalm. Protestants apply the term Apocrypha to a large number of books received by the Latin and all Oriental Churches, and deny their inspiration.

APOL'LO, a Jew of Alexandria, came to Ephesus, and by his eloquence upheld the cause of Christianity, although he was only a catechumen and knew only the baptism of John. He was instructed by Aquila, and afterwards preached at Corinth. Some trouble arose, and he was with St. Paul at Ephesus, when he wrote his first Epistle to the Corinthians (Acts xviii. 24–26; 1 Cor. i.–iv.)

APOLLO'NIA, a city of Macedon (Acts xvii. 1).

APOLLO'NIUS, governor of Samaria, sent by Antiochus Epiphanes to Jerusalem, treacherously slaughtered many thousand people (1 Mach. i. 30, 31; 2 Mach. v. 24, 25); defeated and killed by Judas Machabeus, 147 B. C. (1 Mach. iii. 10–12).

APOLLO'NIUS, governor of Cœlo-Syria, general of Demetrius Nicanor, challenges Jonathan to meet him in the field (1 Mach. x. 69); on which Jonathan captured Joppe (74–76), and defeated Apollonius with great slaughter at Azotus, destroying that and other cities, with the temple of Dagon (77–85).

APOLLYON, the Greek name of Abadon, the destroying angel of the bottomless pit (Apoc. ix. 11).

APOS'TASY, abandonment of the true faith. The term apostate is used in Job xxxiv. 18; Prov. vi. 12; a general apostasy one of the signs of the coming of the last judgment (2 Thess. ii. 3).

APOS'TLE, one who is sent. It is applied distinctively to twelve disciples whom our Lord selected to found his church, and whom he sent, after his resurrection, throughout the world, to preach the gospel, teach all nations and baptize them in the

ARAB WOMAN WITH NOSE-RING. (Ayre.)

name of the Father, Son and Holy Ghost. He invested them with power to perform all kinds of miracles and supernatural cures. He gave them no written law: they were to teach men "to observe all things whatsoever he had commanded them," promising to abide with them (Matt. xxviii. 19), and to send them the Holy Ghost (Acts i. 5). The twelve apostles were Simon, to whom our Lord gave the name of Peter or Rock; Andrew his brother; Philip; John, the Evangelist, son of Zebedee, and James his brother; Bartholomew, Thomas, Matthew, Simon, Jude or Thaddeus, James, son of Alpheus, and Judas Iscariot. After the resurrection and

ascension of our Lord, Mathias was chosen instead of Judas. Paul is considered the apostle of the Gentiles. The vocation of the apostles (Luke vi. 13); they are sent into Judea (Matt. x. 5–42); excite the censure of the Jews by breaking off ears of wheat on the Sabbath day (Luke vi. 1); strive for pre-eminence (ix. 46); eat the Pasch with our Lord (Matt. xxvi. 20); sent into all the world (Matt. xxviii. 19; John xv. 16, 27; xx. 21; Acts i. 8; x. 42); they were guided by the Spirit of God (Mark xiii. 11; John xiv. 17; Acts i. 5; ii. 4; iv. 31; xix. 6; 1 Cor. ii. 12; 2 Cor. xiii. 3; 1 Pet. i. 11). The apostles hold a council at Jerusalem to decide questions as to Gentile converts (Acts xv. 4–22); their letter to the Gentiles (23–29); St. Paul commands the precepts of the apostles to be kept (41).

APPARIT'ION, of angels to Abraham (Gen. xviii. 2–22); of an angel to Jacob (Gen. xxxii. 24); of Samuel to Saul (1 Kings xxviii. 12); of a hand writing on the wall (Dan. v. 5); of an angel with the three children in the furnace (iii. 49); of an angel to Heliodorus (2 Mach. iii. 25); of angels at Jerusalem (v. 2); of many dead persons after the Crucifixion (Matt. xxvii. 53); of our Lord to Mary Magdalen (John xx. 16; Mark xvi. 9); to Peter (Luke xxiv. 34); to the disciples at Emmaus (Luke xxiv. 15); to the apostles (Mark xvi. 14; John xx. xxi; Acts i. 3, 4); to Thomas (John xx. 26); to the disciples (1 Cor. xv. 6); to Saul (1 Cor. xv. 8).

AP'PHUS, surname of Jonathan Machabeus (1 Mach. ii. 5).

AP'PII FO'RUM, a place near the port of Rome to which the Christians of Rome came to meet St. Paul (Acts xxviii. 15).

AP'PLE. The tree is mentioned in Cant. ii. 3; v. 1; viii. 5; Joel i. 12; the fruit in Prov. xxv. 11; Cant. ii. 5; vii. 8.

AQ'UEDUCT, or conduit of Ezechias, at Jerusalem (4 Kings xviii. 17; xx. 20; 2 Esdr. ii. 14; Isai. vii. 3; xxxvi. 2); the hill of the aqueduct is mentioned 2 Kings ii. 24. Aqueduct at Bethulia (Judith vii. 6).

AQ'UILA, a native of Pontus in Asia Minor, was converted with his wife Priscilla, by St. Paul (Acts xviii. 2); he was a tent-maker, and St. Paul lodged with him at Corinth (xviii. 3); he and his wife accompanied St. Paul to Ephesus, and risked their lives for him (Rom. xvi. 4); St. Paul in his second epistle to Timothy asks him to salute Aquila and Priscilla (iv. 19); mentions them (1 Cor. xvi. 19).

AR, a town in the land of Moab, destroyed by Moses (Num. xxi. 15, 28; Deut. ii. 18, 29); its desolation (Isai. xv. 1).

ARA'BIA, the country occupied by the Ismaelites, Edomites, people of Hor, Amalecites, etc. Mount Sina is mentioned as situated in Arabia (Gal.

MOUNTAINS OF ARMENIA.

iv. 25); the name occurs in 3 Kings x. 15; 2 Paral. ix. 14; Ps. lxxi. 15; Isai. xxi. 13; Jerem. xxv. 24; Ezech. xxvii. 21; 1 Mach. xi. 16; the gospel was preached there by St. Paul (Gal. i. 17); the people under the general name of Arabians are mentioned, 2 Paral. xvii. 11; xxi. 16; xxii. 1; xxvi. 7; 2 Esd. ii. 19; iv. 7; vi. 1; Ps. lxxi. 10; Isai. xiii. 20; 1 Mach. v. 39; xi. 17, 39; xii. 31; 2 Mach. v. 8; xii. 10, 11; Acts ii. 11).

A'RAD, king of Chanaan, attacks the Israelites, but is defeated (Num. xxi. 1–3).

ARA'DA, the twenty-first camp of the Israelites (Num. xxxiii. 24).

ARA'DIAN, a branch of the descendants of Chanaan (Gen. x. 18; 1 Paral. i. 16).

EGYPTIAN ARCHER AND QUIVER.
(From Wilkinson.)

A'RAM, fifth son of Sem (Gen. x. 22).

A'RAM, the residence of Balaam (Num. xxiii. 7), apparently Mesopotamia.

A'RAN, son of Thares, and brother of Abraham (Gen. xi. 26); father of Lot (27); died before his father (28).

ARA'PHA, a race of giants (2 Kings xxi. 18).

AR'ARAT, king of, to oppose Babylon (Jerem. li. 27); Sennacherib's sons flee to (Isai. xxxvii. 38).

AR'BATIS, a town in Galilee taken by Simon (1 Mach. v. 23).

AR'BEE, the city of, a name of Hebron (Gen. xxiii. 2; xxxv. 27).

ARBEL'LA, the district of Masaloth (1 Mach. ix. 2).

ARCH of triumph, erected by Saul, at Carmel (1 Kings xv. 12).

ARCH'ELAUS, son of Herod the Great, reigned in Judea (Matt. ii. 22).

ARCHIP'-PUS, mentioned by St. Paul (Coloss. iv. 17).

ARC'TU-RUS, a star in the constellation of the Great Bear (Job ix. 9).

AREOP'A-GUS, the place of assembly of the great Judges of Athens. St. Paul preaches there (Acts xvii. 19).

AR'ETAS, king of Arabia, to whom Damascus was subject when St. Paul escaped from the city (Acts ix. 23, 24; 2 Cor. xi. 32).

AREU'NA or Or'nan. While the pestilence was ravaging Jerusalem (1 Par. xxi. 18; 2 Kings xxiv. 18) an angel of the Lord commanded Gad to tell David to come and erect an altar to the Lord, on the threshing-floor of Areuna. The angel stays the plague there (16); David purchased it of Areuna, and built an altar on which he offered holocausts (24, 25; 1 Paral. xxi. 18-26).

AR'GOB, a country in Basan (Deut. iii. 4, 14; 3 Kings iv. 13).

AR'GOB, a place in Samaria where Phaceia, king of Israel, was killed (4 Kings xv. 25).

ARIARA'THES, king of Cappadocia, written to by the Romans in favor of the Jews (1 Mach. xv. 22).

A'RIE, a town in Samaria (4 Kings xv. 25).

A'RIEL, son of Gad, father of the Arielites (Num. xxvi. 17).

A'RIEL, a term meaning lion of God, applied to Jerusalem by Isaias (xxix. 1, 2), and to the altar by Ezechiel (xliii. 15).

A'RIELS of Moab, slain by Banaias (1 Paral. xi. 22).

ARIMATHE'A, the place of Joseph, who received the body of Christ, and buried it in his own monument (Luke xxiii. 51-56).

A'RIOCH, king of Pontus, makes war on Sodom and Gomorrha (Gen. xiv. 1).

NOE'S SACRIFICE ON LEAVING THE ARK.

ARISTAR'CHUS, a Macedonian of Thessalonica, companion of St. Paul at Ephesus (Acts xix. 29); on his return to Macedonia (xx. 4); when he sailed to Italy (xxvii. 2); St. Paul mentions him as a fellow-prisoner in his Epistle to the Colossians (iv. 10), and as a fellow-laborer in that to Philemon (24).

ARISTOBU'LUS, a Jew of a priestly family and preceptor of King Ptolemee, addressed by the Jews of Jerusalem (2 Mach. i. 10).

ARISTOBU'LUS; his household saluted by St. Paul (Rom. xvi. 11).

ARK, God commands Noe to build an ark 300 cubits long, fifty broad and thirty high (Gen. vi. 14-16); and to enter with his family and pairs of all living creatures (18-21; vii. 1, 2); Noe obeyed, and entered the ark (vi. 22; vii. 5-16) the seventeenth day of the second month (vii. 11); and on the twenty-seventh day of the seventh month it rested upon the mountains of Armenia. In the King James Bible, this is rendered mountains of Ararat, but the term Mount Ararat is not even in the Protestant Bible. The account of the Ark and Deluge are referred to in Wisd. x. 4; xiv. 6; by our Lord (Matt. xxiv. 37; Luke xvii. 26, 27); by St. Peter (1 Pet. iii. 20, 21; 2 Peter ii. 5).

ARK OF THE COVENANT. God's directions for its construction (Ex. xxv. 10-22); to be made by Besaleel and Ooliab (xxxi. 1-7); it was made accordingly of setim wood, two and a half cubits long, a cubit and a-half in breadth and height, covered within and without with gold. It had four gold rings, through which setim wood bars plated with gold were passed to carry it. There was a crown of gold on the ark, and a golden propitiatory of the entire length and breadth, with two cherubim of beaten gold at its ends, facing each other and covering the propitiatory with their wings (xxxvii. 1-9); Moses placed the testimony or tables of the law in it (xl. 18; Deut. x. 2; 3 Kings viii. 9); and set it in the tabernacle, drawing the veil before it (Ex. xl. 3-19); Aaron's rod was also placed in the ark (Num. xvii. 10); and the Book of the Law (Deut. xxxi. 26); and a gomor full of manna (Exod. xvi. 33, 34;

Heb. ix. 3, 4); all but the priests were forbidden to touch it (Num. iv. 5); or even approach it (Jos. iii. 4). It was carried by priests when the army moved. It was set down in the middle of the bed of the Jordan (Jos. iii. 17). The ark remained at Silo, but was brought in the time of Heli, the high-priest, to be borne against the Philistines at the battle of Aphec (1 Kings iv. 3, 4). The Israelites were defeated and the ark taken and placed by the Philistines in the temple of Dagon in Azotus (v. 1, 2); it overthrew and broke the idol of Dagon, and gave rise to a

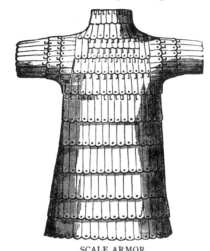

SCALE ARMOR.

plague (6–9); so that they sent it back in a cart drawn by kine which took it to Bethsames (vi. 1–15). For their irreverence many of the Bethsamites lost their lives; so that it was carried to Cariathiarim (vi. 19; vii. 2); it was removed by David to the house of Obededom (1 Paral. xiii. 5–13; 2 Kings vi. 2–11); and thence to Jerusalem (12); Oza being killed on the way for putting out his hand to hold it up (2 Kings vi. 7; 1 Paral xiii. 9, 10). When Solomon

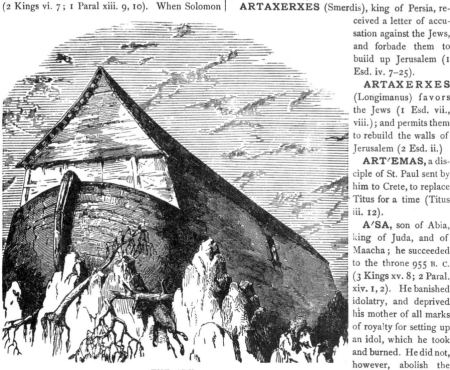

THE ARK.

erected the temple the ark was placed in the Holy of Holies within it (3 Kings viii. 3–6); there it

remained till the captivity, when it was hidden by Jeremias in a cave (2 Mach. ii. 5); seen by St. John in the temple of God in heaven (Apoc. xi. 19); it is spoken of as God's footstool (1 Paral. xxviii. 2; Ps. xcviii. 5; cxxxi. 7; Lam. ii. 1).

ARM, used as a symbol of power (Deut. v. 15; Ex. vi. 6; 1 Kings ii. 31; Ps. xvii. 35; Jerem. xvii. 5; Zach. xi. 17). It is also used for the shoulder of the victim (Ecclus. vii. 33; Lev. vii. 32; Exod. xxix. 22).

ARME'NIA. The ark rested on the mountains of Armenia (Gen. viii. 4).

AR'MONI, son of Saul, crucified by the Gabaonites (2 Kings xxi. 8).

ARNON, a torrent emptying into the Dead Sea on the east (Num. xxi., xxii.; Deut. ii., iii., iv.; Jos. xii., xiii.; Judges xi.)

AR'OER, a city of Gad, on the torrent of Arnon (Num. xxxii. 34; Deut. ii. 36; iii. 12; iv. 48; Jos. xii. 2).

ARPHAX'AD, son of Sem (Gen. xi. 10).

ARPHAX'AD, king of the Medes, built Ecbatana, defeated at Ragau (Judith i. 1–6).

AR'SA, governor of Thersa, in whose house Ela, king of Israel, was killed (3 Kings xvi. 10).

ARSA'CES, king of Persia, defeats and captures Demetrius Nicanor, 141 B. C. (1 Mach. xiv. 2, 3).

ARTAXERXES (Smerdis), king of Persia, received a letter of accusation against the Jews, and forbade them to build up Jerusalem (1 Esd. iv. 7–25).

ARTAXERXES (Longimanus) favors the Jews (1 Esd. vii., viii.); and permits them to rebuild the walls of Jerusalem (2 Esd. ii.)

ART'EMAS, a disciple of St. Paul sent by him to Crete, to replace Titus for a time (Titus iii. 12).

A'SA, son of Abia, king of Juda, and of Maacha; he succeeded to the throne 955 B. C. (3 Kings xv. 8; 2 Paral. xiv. 1, 2). He banished idolatry, and deprived his mother of all marks of royalty for setting up an idol, which he took and burned. He did not, however, abolish the high places (3 Kings xv. 10–14; 2 Paral. xv. 16); he fulfilled his father's vows by dedicating vessels in the temple (18); he

fortified several cities (2 Paral. xiv. 6); being menaced by Baasa, king of Israel, he sent treasures from

THE ARK OF THE COVENANT.

the temple to Benadad, king of Syria, to secure his alliance, for which he was censured by Hanani the prophet; for God had previously given him victory over the Ethiopians and Libyans. Asa threw the prophet into prison, and falling sick did not seek the Lord (2 Paral. xvi. 1–12).

AS'AEL, son of Sarvia, David's sister, and brother of Joab, was slain by Abner, whom he was

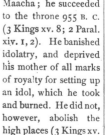

LEATHER CUIRASS.

pursuing after the battle of Gabaon (2 Kings ii. 18); for which Joab afterwards killed Abner (2 Kings iii. 26, 27). Asael was remarkably fleet of foot.

A'SAPH, son of Barachias, of the tribe of Levi, and of the family of Gerson, was a famous musician in the town of David (1 Paral. vi. 39). Several of the Psalms (xlix., lxxii., lxxxii.) bear his name. Many of his descendants returned from the captivity with Zorobabel (1 Esd. ii. 41; 2 Esd. vii. 45).

AS'CALON, a city of the Philistines, taken by the tribe of Juda after the death of Josue (Judges i. 18). David refers to the city in his lament over Saul (2 Kings i. 20).

ASSYRIAN CUIRASS.

ASCEN'SION of our Lord. After his resurrection, Jesus Christ for forty days shewed himself to his disciples, appearing to them and speaking to them of the kingdom of God. He enjoined them not to depart from Jerusalem until they received power from the Holy Ghost (Acts i. 3–8); then he led them out as far as Bethania (Luke xxiv. 50); to Mount Olivet, a sabbath day's journey from Jerusalem (Acts i. 12); and lifting up his hands he blessed them (Luke xxiv. 50). Then while they looked on he was raised up, and a cloud received him out of their sight (Acts i. 9). Two angels appearing, declared to them: This Jesus who is taken up from you into heaven, shall so come as you have seen him going into heaven (Acts i. 11; St. Mark xvi. 19). St. Helena erected a magnificent church of the Ascension on the spot.

ASEMO'NA or **HESMO'NA**, one of the stations of the Israelites in the desert (Num. xxxiii. 29, 30; xxxiv. 4, 5; Jos. xv. 4).

ASEN'APHAR, king of Assyria, who sent several nations to colonize Samaria. In their letter against the Jews, these people called him the great and glorious (1 Esd. iv. 10). He is supposed to be Salmanasar or Asor-Haddan.

AS'ENETH, daughter of Putiphare, and wife of the patriarch Joseph, to whom she bore Ephraim and Manasses (Gen. xli. 45, 50; xlvi. 20).

AS'ER, son of Jacob by Zelpha, hand-maid to Lia (Gen. xxx. 13); he had four sons, Jamne, Jesua, Jessui and Beria, and a daughter, Sara (Gen. xlvi. 17); Jacob's prophecy as to (xlix. 20).

AS'ER, one of the ten tribes descended from Aser, son of Jacob. They marched out of Egypt under Phegiel, son of Ochran, as their prince (Num. i. 13; ii. 27; vii. 72; x. 26); they numbered 41,500 (Num. i. 40, 41; ii. 28); they formed part of the camp of Dan on the north side (25–31); their offerings (vii. 72–77); they sent Sthur, son of Michael, to view the Promised Land (xiii. 14); Ahiud, son of Salomi, was appointed from Aser to divide the land (xxxiv. 27); in the census at Settim they numbered 53,400 (xxvi. 47); they stood on Mount Hebal to curse (Deut. xxvii. 13); Moses blesses the tribe (xxxiii. 24, 25); in the division they obtained the fifth lot—their territory (Jos. xix. 24–31); on the shore (Judg. v. 17; Ezech. xlviii. 2); failed to destroy the Chanaanites, and dwelt in their midst (i. 31, 32); keep the pasch (2 Par. xxx. 11).

ASH'ES. The ashes of a red cow, burnt entire, were used in a water of aspersion to cleanse the unclean (Num. xix. 1, 13); ashes were put on the head as a sign of mourning (2 Kings xiii. 19).

A'SIA, as used in the Bible, applies not to the continent, but to the western part of Asia Minor, of which Ephesus was the capital (1 Mach. viii. xi.–xiii.; 2 Mach. iii. 3; Acts ii., vi., xvi., xix.–xx., xxiii., xxiv., xxvii.; Rom. xvi.; 1 Cor. xvi.; 2 Cor. i.; 2 Tim. i.; 1 Pet. i.; Apoc. i.)

AS'IMA, an idol made and worshipped by the men of Emath in Samaria (4 Kings xvii. 30).

A'SIONGABER, a port on the Red Sea, one of the stations of the Israelites (Num. xxxiii. 35; Deut. ii. 8); Solomon had a fleet there (3 Kings ix. 26); Josaphat also (xxii. 49).

ASMO'DEUS, a demon who obsessed Sara, daughter of Raguel, and killed those married to her (Tob. vi. 14; iii. 8); expelled by the angel Raphael (viii. 2, 3).

SYMBOLIC GROUP OF ASIA. (From Group in Hyde Park.)

ASMO'NEAN, a name given to the dynasty of the Machabees.

AS'OR, capital of king Jabin, taken by Josue after the great battle of Merom (Jos. xi. 1, 7–11).

ASORHADDAN, son of Sennacherib, king of Assyria (1 Esd. iv. 2); took Jerusalem (2 Paral. xxxiii. 11).

AS'PHAR. The Dead Sea is called the Lake of Asphar (1 Mac. ix. 33).

AS'PHENEZ, master of the eunuchs of Nabuchodonosor (Dan. i. 3); gives new names to Daniel and his three companions (7).

ASP, a poisonous serpent. The wicked are said to have the venom of asps under their tongues (Ps. cxxxix. 4); and to close their ears to truth, as the asp does to the charmer (lvii. 5).

ASSID'EANS, a class of Jews distinguished for valor and zeal for the law of the Lord (1 Mach. ii. 42; vii. 13; 2 Mach. xiv. 6).

AS'SOS, a port in Troas to which St. Paul went after raising Eutychus to life at Troas (Acts xx. 13, 14).

ASSUE'RUS or Astyages, last king of Media (Dan. ix. 1; xiii. 65).

ASSUE'RUS or Artaxerxes, king of Persia, divorced his queen Vashti, and married Esther, a

REPRESENTATIONS OF A WINGED DEITY, SUPPOSED TO BE THE GOD ASSHUR, THE DEIFIED PATRIARCH OF ASSYRIA. (From Layard.)

Jewess. Haman, his prime minister, incensed at Mardochai, a Jew, for not rendering him sufficient honor, obtained of the king an edict for a general massacre of the Jews, and prepared a special gibbet for Mardochai. Esther interceded for herself and her people, and the Jews were delivered, Haman himself being put to death (Esther i.–xvi.)

ASSUE'RUS (Cambyses), king of Persia, before whom the Samaritans accused the Jews (1 Esd. iv. 6).

AS'SUR, son of Sem, founds the Assyrian empire (Gen. x. 22; 1 Paral. i. 17).

ASSYR'IA, ASSYR'IANS. The kingdom was on the Tigris (Gen. ii. 14); Balaam prophesies their overthrow by the Romans (Num. xxiv. 24); Phul, king of the Assyrians, invaded the kingdom of Israel, but Manahem by great tribute appeased him (4 Kings xv. 19); but Theglathphalasar, king of Assyria, took many cities of Israel, carrying off the people and the whole tribe of Nephthali to Assyria (29); B. C. 759; at the prayer of Achaz he laid waste Damascus (xvi. 9); Salmanasar, king of Assyria, overthrew the kingdom of Israel, and carried the rest of the ten tribes away as captives (xvii. 1–6); 730 B. C. Sennacherib, king of the Assyrians, invades Juda in the reign of Ezechias, but is defeated by an angel (4 Kings xviii. 13; xix. 35; 2 Paral. xxxii. 1–21); prophesies against the Assyrians (Isaias xiv. 25; xxx. 31; xxxi. 8).

AS'TAROTH or Astar'the, or Atergata, a goddess worshipped by the Sidonians (Judg. ii. 13; iii. 7; x. 6; 1 Kings vii. 3; xii. 10; xxxi. 10; 4 Kings xxiii. 13); Saul's armor hung up in the temple of Astaroth (1 Kings xxxi. 10); Solomon introduced her worship in Jerusalem (3 Kings xi. 5, 33); which Josias abolished (4 Kings xxiii. 13).

ATHA'LIA, daughter of Achab, or Amri, king of Israel (4 Kings viii. 18, 26), and wife of Joram, king of Juda. When Jehu put her son Ochozias to death, she killed all the princes of royal blood, in order to usurp the throne. Josaba, sister of Ochozias, saved Joas, son of that king, and he was brought up in the temple for seven years, when the high-priest Joiada proclaimed the young king. Athalia hearing the shouts of the people, rushed to the temple, but was seized, carried out and executed, 878 B. C. (4 Kings xi. 1–15).

ATH'ENS, a famous city of Greece. St. Paul preaches there (Acts xvii. 19–33).

AV'ARICE, to be avoided (Isai. xxxiii. 15; Matt. vi. 19; Mark viii. 36; Luke xii. 15; Eph. v. 3; Col. iii. 5; Titus i. 7, 11; Heb. xiii. 5; the wretchedness of the avaricious (Eccles. v. 9–19; vi. 2); their punishment (Prov. xv. 16, 27; xxviii. 22; Eccles. ii. 26; Isai. v. 8; lvi. 11; Ezech xxii. 13; Amos viii. 4; Mich. vi. 10; Hab. ii. 9; Ecclus. xxxi. 3; 1 Cor. vi. 10; 1 Tim. vi. 9); they slay themselves and the poor (Prov. i. 19; Eccles. iv. 8; Ecclus. xiv. 3).

ATHERSA'THA, a name or office of Zorobabel

ASSYRIAN BATTLE-SCENE.

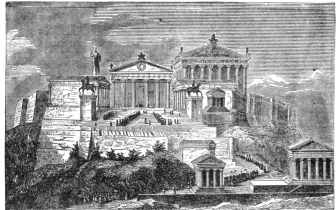

THE ACROPOLIS AT ATHENS.

(1 Esd. ii. 63; 2 Esd. vii. 65; 2 Esd. vii. 70); and of Nehemias (2 Esd. viii. 9).

ATONE'MENT, Day of, one of the most solemn and holy days of the Jewish year, observed on the tenth day of the seventh month. They were to afflict their souls, offer a holocaust, and refrain from all servile work (Lev. xxiii. 27–32).

ATTA'LIA, a port of Pamphylia, visited by St. Paul and St. Barnabas (Acts xiv. 25).

ATT'ALUS (Philadelphus), king of Pergamos. The Romans commend the Jews to him (1 Mach. xv. 22).

AUGUSTUS, Cæsar, first of the Roman emperors, orders the whole world to be enrolled (Luke ii. 1).

AVENGER OF BLOOD, the kinsman of a murdered man was to kill the murderer as soon as he apprehended him (Num. xxxv. 19; Deut. xix. 6). Three cities of refuge were provided, to which those who committed involuntary homicide could flee (Deut. xix. 2); but if he was found outside those cities, the avenger of blood could slay him (Num. xxxv. 26, 27).

AXA, or Achsa, daughter of Caleb, promised by her father to the man who took Cariath Sepher and marries Othoniel (Jos. xv. 16, 17; Judg. i. 12, 13; 1 Paral. ii. 49).

AZARIAS, or Ozias, king of Juda, came to the throne 810 B. C. at the age of sixteen. He was the son of king Amasias and Jechelia. He was struck with leprosy for attempting to offer incense in the temple, and lived apart from men, his son Joathan acting as regent. He reigned from 810–758 B. C (4 Kings xv. 1–7; 2 Paral. xxvi. 1–21; Matt. i. 9).

AZARI'AS, high-priest after Achimaas (1 Paral. vi. 9).

AZARI'AS, high-priest who opposed Ozias (2 Paral. xxvi. 17).

AZARI'AS, high-priest in the time of Ezechias (2 Paral. xxxi. 10).

AZARIAS, a prophet, son of Oded (2 Paral. xv. 1); sent by the Lord to Asa after his victory over Zara, king of Chus, to promise him prosperity, if he remained faithful (2 Paral. xv. 2).

AZARI'AS, name taken by the angel Raphael (Tob. v. 18).

AZARI'AS, son of Ozaias, accuses the prophet Jeremias with deceiving the people (Jerem. xliii. 2).

AZARI'AS, one of three thrown into the fiery furnace by Nabuchodonosor (Dan. iii. 49); see Ananias.

AZARI'AS, an officer left by Judas Machabeus in Jerusalem, who attacked Georgias near Jamnia, and lost two thousand men, 163 B. C. (1 Mach. v. 56).

AZO'TUS, a city of the Philistines; the Ark of the Covenant taken to it (1 Kings v. 1); burned by Jonathan Machabeus (1 Mach. x. 84); the apostle Philip borne to (Acts viii. 40).

AZO'TUS, Mount, Judas Machabeus killed near (1 Mach. ix. 15).

AZYMES or Unleavened Bread, Feast of (Lev. xxiii. 6; Matt. xxvi. 17). See PASCH.)

BA'AL or BEL, the god of the Phœnicians or Chanaanites, and apparently identical with the sun (4 Kings xxiii. 4, 11). The Jews frequently fell into the sin of worshipping Baal, and offered him human victims (Jerem. xxxii. 35; xix. 5; 4 Kings xvii. 16); erected altars to him in groves, on the high places, and on roofs of houses (3 Kings xvi. 31; 4 Kings xxiii. 4, 5, 12; 2 Paral. xxxiii. 3, 5; Jerem. xxxii. 29); they had priests for his worship (3 Kings xviii. 22; 4 Kings x. 19); this worship was attended with great impurity (3 Kings xiv. 24; xv. 12; xxii. 47; 4 King, xxiii. 7; Osee. iv. 14). Gedeon destroyed the altar of Baal (Judg. vi. 26, 30); Elias slew the priests of Baal (3 Kings xviii. 40); Jehu burned the idol (4 Kings xx. 20–28); Josias also (xxiii. 5).

BAA'LA, another name for Cariathiarim (Jos. xv. 9, 10).

BA'AL BER'IT, god of Sichemites, worshipped by the Jews after the death of Gedeon (Judg. ix. 4).

BA'ALIM, plural of Baal, but used generally for false gods (Judg. viii. 33).

BA'ALIS, king of the Ammonites, who sent Ismael to kill Godolias, governor of the Jews (Jerem. xl. 14).

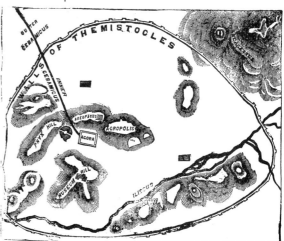

PLAN OF ATHENS, SHOWING THE POSITION OF THE AGORA OR "MARKET."

BA'AL PHAR'ASIM, scene of a battle where David defeated the Philistines (2 Kings v. 20).

BA'AL THAMAR, a place in the tribe of Benjamin, where the Israelites fought against that tribe (Judg. xx. 33).

CHART OF THE COUNTRY ROUND BABYLON, WITH LIMITS OF THE ANCIENT CITY. (According to Oppert.)

606 B. C. Nabuchodonosor marched on Jerusalem, and made king Joakim his servant (4 Kings xxiv. 1); but he revolted, and Nabuchodonosor, 599 B. C., carried off king Joachin with his nobles, soldiers and artificers as captives to Babylon. Sedecias, the next king, endeavored to revolt, but Nabuchodonosor returned 590 B. C., captured and destroyed Jerusalem with its temple, and overtaking Sedecias in his flight at Jericho, took him and put out his eyes (4 Kings xxiv., xxv.) Babylon was taken by surprise by the Medes and Persians under Cyrus, during a festival, as foretold (Jerem. li. 31–37; Isai. xxi. 1–9; Cyrus (536 B. C.) released the Jews from their captivity and permitted them to return to their country (1 Esd.; 2 Esd.) For prophecies against Babylon, see Ps. cxxxvi. 8; Isai. xiii., xiv.; xxi. 2; xlvii.; Jer. xxv. 12; l., li.; Baruch iv. 32; Mich. vii. 10; Hab. ii.) In the New Testament Babylon is applied to pagan Rome (1 Pet. v. 13; Apoc. xvii. 5; xviii. 2); as the capital of antichrist's kingdom (xiv. 8), and as a figure of the reprobate world (xvi. 19). In its prosperity Babylon was a city of fifteen miles square, lying on both sides of the Euphrates, connected by bridges, with a magnificent temple of Belus, palaces and hanging gardens, which were one of the wonders of the world.

BAC'CHIDES, general of Demetrius Soter, king of Syria, was sent against Judas Machabeus, and endeavored to entrap him. He killed sixty priests and Assideans and left the high-priest Alcimus with an army. He returned with new troops and pursued Judas to Laisa. Judas routed his right wing, but Bacchides enveloped him with the rest of his army, and Judas was slain, 157 B. C. (1 Mach. vii. 8–20; ix. 1–18); he subsequently attacked Jonathan, but lost a thousand men (ix. 49). Some time after he besieged Jonathan and Simon in Bethbessen, but was repulsed and made terms with the Machabees (1 Mach. ix. 60–73; 2 Mach. viii. 30).

BAC'CHUS, the god of wine, in whose festivi-

ties Antiochus forced the Jews to take part (2 Mach vi. 7; xiv. 33).

BAG'ATHAN, an officer of the guards of king Assuerus, conspires against his master (Esth. ii. 21).

AN ASSYRIAN KING.

BA'LA, Rachel's handmaid, who bore to Jacob Dan and Nephthali (Gen. xxix. 29; xxx. 3, 5).

BA'LA or Segor, one of the five cities (Gen. xiv. 2, 8).

BA'LAAM, son of Beor, a Mesopotamian prophet on the Euphrates, summoned by Balac, king of

ANCIENT BANQUET.

BA'ANA and Rechab, officers of Isboseth, who treacherously slew their master, but were punished by David (2 Kings iv. 2–12).

BA'ASA, son of Ahias, and general of Nadab's army. He treacherously slew his master during the siege of Gebbethon (953 B. C.), and usurped the throne. He exterminated the race of Jeroboam. For his idolatry he was rebuked by Jehu the prophet, but put the envoy of God to death. Baasa died at Thersa after a reign of twenty-four years (3 Kings xv. 27–xvi. 7; 2 Paral. xvi. 1–6).

BA'BEL (confusion), a tower which the descendants of Noe began to build in the plain of Sennaar, intending to make it reach heaven. God confounded their language, so that they could not understand each other. Then they ceased to build the city, and scattered into all lands (Gen. xi. 1–9).

BAB'YLON, the capital of Chaldea, built by Nemrod (Gen. x. 10); it was included in the Assyrian empire when the kingdom of the ten tribes was overthrown, and people were sent from Babylon to Samaria (4 Kings xvii. 24); but in the reign of Ezechias, Baladan, king of Babylon, sent presents to the king of Juda, who indiscreetly displayed his wealth (4 Kings xx.); for which the prophet Isaias rebuked him, foretelling the woes Babylon was to bring on his kingdom (xx. 14–18; Isaias xxxix. 1–6); the captivity of the Jews at Babylon was predicted (Lev. xxvi. 31–41; Deut. iv. 27; xxviii. 36, 49; 4 Kings xx. 17; Isai. vi. 12; xxvii. 10, 11; xxxix. 6; Jerem. i. 16; vi. 21–23; Ezech. ii.; Osee v. 5; vi. 11; x. 11; Joel i. 15; ii. 1; Amos ii. 5; Mich. iii. 12; iv. 10; Hab. i. 6; Soph. i.–iii.) In the year

Moab, to curse the Israelites. Warned by God he at first refused to go, but was at last permitted, yet was warned to act only by the divine command. An angel withstood him, and the ass he rode, beaten for not advancing, spoke. He was taken to the heights to curse the camp of Israel, but after offering sacrifice he blessed them. He foretold the greatness of Israel, the overthrow of many nations, the coming of the Messias, the captivity, the Roman conquest and the fall of that empire (Num. xxii., xxiii.) He gave wicked advice to Balac, and was killed among the

FIGURE OF ASTARTE FOUND IN ETRURIA.
(From Rawlinson's Herodotus, ii. 449.)

Madianites (Num. xxv. 1; xxxi. 8; 2 Pet. ii. 15; Apoc. ii. 14).

BA'LAC, son of Sephor, king of Moab, summoned Balaam to curse the children of Israel, but God did not permit them to attack him (Num. xxii. 5; Jos. xxiv. 9; Judg. xi. 25; Mich. vi. 5; Apoc. ii. 14).

BAL'ANAN, son of Achobor, seventh king of Edom (Gen. xxxvi. 38; 1 Paral. i. 49).

BALD, children of Bethel destroyed by bears for mocking the prophet Eliseus, and calling him bald head (4 Kings ii. 23, 24); baldness a disgrace (Isai. iii. 17, 24; xv. 2; Jerem. xlvii. 5; Ezech. vii. 18); Israelites forbidden to shave the head (Levit. xxi. 5).

BAL'DAD, a descendant of Abraham and Cetura, and a friend of Job (Job ii. 11; Gen. xxv. 2).

BALM, an aromatic (Gen. xxxvii. 25; xliii. 11; Ecclus. xxiv. 20, 21; Jerem. viii. 22; xlvi. 11; li. 8; Ezech. xxvii. 17.

BAL'TAS'AR, son of Evilmerodach, and grandson of Nabuchodonosor. At a great feast he used the sacred vessels of the temple of Jerusalem for himself and his guests to drink. Then a hand appeared writing on the wall. His magi could not interpret the words, but Daniel read, Mane, Thecel, Phares. Mane, God hath numbered thy kingdom and hath finished it; Thecel, thou art weighed in the balance and found wanting; Phares, thy kingdom is divided and given to the Medes and Persians. That very night Babylon was taken and Baltassar was slain, 538 B. C. (Dan. v. 1–31).

BANAI'AS, son of Joiada, captain of David's guards, the Cerethites and Phelethites (2 Kings xx. 23); he was David's counsellor (xxiii. 22; 1 Par. xi. 22); and famous for his exploits. He adhered to Solomon against Adonias, and was sent to execute

Joab, whom he succeeded as general (3 Kings ii. 35).

BA'NI, a family that returned from captivity (1 Esd. ii. 10); a Levite (2 Esd. viii. 7).

BAP'TISM of John. When St. John the Baptist began to preach penance, he instituted a baptism in the waters of Jordan. It did not remit sin, but disposed men to receive the real baptism to be instituted by Christ (Luke iii. 3; Matt. iii. 2, 11; xxi. 25; Mark i. 4–8). This baptism was continued by his disciples even after the death of our Lord (Acts xviii. 25; xix. 3).

BAP'TISM, a sacrament of the New Law instituted by Christ for the remission of sins (Matt. iii. 16; John iii. 5); and absolutely necessary for salvation (Mark xvi. 16; John iii. 5). Christ commanded his apostles to teach all nations, baptizing them in the name of the Father and of the Son and of the Holy Ghost (Matt. xxviii. 19); regenerating men in the sacrament (John iii. 5). Baptism was prefigured in the passage of the Red Sea (1 Cor. x. 2); in the pool of Bethsaida (John v. 2); in the Deluge (1 Pet. iii. 20). It was administered by the apostles (John iv. 2; Acts ii. 38; viii. 12, 36; xix. 4; xxii. 16); the eunuch of Queen Candace was baptized (Acts viii. 38); Saul (ix. 18); Cornelius and his family (x. 48); Lydia (xvi. 15); the jailor at Philippi (33); Crispus and others (1 Cor. i. 14); baptism saves through the resurrection of Christ (1 Pet. iii. 21; Titus iii. 5); takes away all sin (Ezech. xxxvi. 25; Zach. xiii. 1; Mark i. 4; Col. ii. 13; Heb. x. 22); there is but one baptism (Eph. iv. 5); it cannot be repeated (Heb. vi. 6); it can be conferred on infants (Gen. xvii. 14; Ex. iv. 25; John iii. 5; Acts ii. 39; xvi. 33; 1 Cor. xv. 22; 1 Tim. ii. 4); clothes us in Christ (Gal. iii. 27); applies to us the merits of his death (Rom. vi. 3); makes all believers one body (1 Cor. xii. 13).

BAP'TISM in the name of Jesus Christ (Acts ii. 38) is more generally interpreted to mean by the authority of Christ, and not as modifying Matt. xxviii. 10.

ASSYRIAN SPEARMAN. EGYPTIAN HEAVY-
(Fbn.) ARMED SOLDIER.

BAP'TISM with the Holy Ghost and with fire (Matt. iii. 11; Luke iii. 16).

BAP'TISM for the dead mentioned (1 Cor. xv. 29).

BA'RA, king of Sodom in the time of Abraham, who returned to him booty recaptured from Codorlahomor (Gen. xiv. 2, 17, 21).

BARAB'BAS, a noted robber, murderer, and rebel, whom the Jews preferred to our Lord when Pilate asked them which should be released (John xviii. 40).

ASSYRIAN BATTERING-RAM.

ROMAN BATTERING-RAM AND TOWER.

BAR'AC, son of Abinoem, chosen by God to deliver his people from bondage under Jabin, king of the Chanaanites, refused to obey the prophetess Debbora, but at last marched with her. He defeated Sisara near Mount Thabor. Sisara escaped, but was killed by Jahel, wife of Haber. Barac and Debbora, in a canticle, thanked God for the victory (Judges iv. v.); B. C. 1285.

BARJE'SU, or Elymas, a Jewish magician in the island of Crete, attached to the proconsul Sergius Paulus. He opposed Paul and Barnabas, but was reproached by St. Paul and struck with blindness (Acts xiii. 6).

BARJONA, son of Jona, St. Peter so called (Matt. xvi. 17).

BAR'NABAS, a disciple of Christ and companion of St. Paul in his apostolic labors. He was of the tribe of Levi, and born in Cyprus. He is also called Joseph. Barnabas introduced St. Paul to the apostles at Jerusalem (Acts ix. 26, 27). About the year 42 he was sent from Jerusalem to Antioch, and went to Tarsus to invite St. Paul to aid him (Acts xi. 22–26). The two saints visited Jerusalem with alms in the year 44 (Acts xi. 30). At Antioch they were directed by the Holy Ghost to be set apart for special work (xiii. 2). Their apostolic labors extended to Seleucia, Cyprus, Paphos, Perge, Antioch in Pisidia, Lystra, and Derbe. With St. Paul he opposed those who insisted on the circumcision of Gentile converts (xv. 2), and they were deputed to Jerusalem to have the point decided by the apostles

(xv. 22). From Antioch he proceeded to Cyprus again with his kinsman John Mark (xv. 39). He is said to have suffered martyrdom there. An epistle bearing his name is extant, and is very ancient, but has not been received as canonical.

BAR'SABAS, the surname of Joseph, one of the early disciples (Acts i. 23). He was apparently one of the seventy who had been witnesses of our Lord's ministry. He was proposed as successor of Judas Iscariot.

BAR'SABAS, surname of the apostle Jude (Acts xv. 22).

BAR'THOLOMEW, one of the apostles, was from Galilee (Matt. x. 3; Mark iii. 18; Luke vi. 14). He is said to have preached the gospel in India, Persia and Armenia. He is supposed by many to be identical with Nathaniel, Bartholomew being merely a patronymic. No evangelist speaks of both, and St. John (xxi. 2) seems to include Nathaniel among the apostles.

BAR'TIM'EUS, a blind man of Jericho, cured by our Lord while on his way to Jerusalem. When he heard that Jesus of Nazareth was passing, he began to invoke his aid, and could not be silenced (Mark x. 46–52; Matt. xx. 30).

BARUCH, the son of Nerias, was secretary and disciple of the prophet Jeremias. While that prophet was in prison, in the reign of Joakim, Baruch wrote down his prophecies and read them in the temple (Jerem. xxxvi. 4–10; 14–19); and he wrote them again after the king had destroyed the first roll (32). Jeremias consoled Baruch, who was afflicted at the sins of his countrymen (xlv). In the fourth year of Sedecias he went to Babylon with his brother Saraias, bearing a letter of Jeremias to the captive Jews (Jer. li. 59); he brought back a letter and alms (Baruch i.–v.) During the siege of Jerusalem he was imprisoned with Jeremias, till set free by Nabuzardan. He was accused of persuading Jeremias to oppose the emigration to Egypt (Jerem. xliii. 1–4), but went there with that prophet. His book is received as canonical by the church, but is rejected by Protestants.

BAS'AN, a kingdom east of the Jordan, extending to the desert between the river Jaboc and mount Hermon. Og was king when Moses defeated him near Edrai, and conquered the country (Deut. iii. 1–11.

BAS'EMATH. 1. Daughter of Elon, the Hethite, and wife of Esau (Gen. xxvi. 34). 2. Daughter of Ismael, third wife of Esau (Gen. xxvi. 2, 4, 10). 3. Daughter of Solomon, wife of Achimaas (3 Kings iv. 15).

BAS'ILISK, a kind of serpent (Ps. xc. 13).

BASK'ET for meal or bread (Gen. xl. 16; Exod. xxix. 3; Lev. viii. 2, 26; Num. vi. 15, 17, 19; Matt. xiv. 20; Mark vi. 43; Luke ix. 17; John vi. 13); for gathering grapes (Jer. vi. 9); for fruit (xxiv. 1,2; Deut. xxvi. 2, 4); other articles (Ps. lxxx. 7; 4 Kings x. 7).

THE BURIAL OF JESUS. (After Quintin Matsys.)

BAT, classed among the unclean animals (Lev. xi. 19; Deut. xiv. 18).

BATE or Epha, a Hebrew measure containing the tenth part of the chore or gomar. It held, according to Josephus, eight and two-third gallons, though Rabbinists make it about one-half (3 Kings vii. 26; 2 Paral. ii. 10; 1 Esdr. vii. 22; Ezec. xlv. 10).

BATH, bathing. The Hebrews bathed on their housetops and in their gardens (2 Kings xi. 2; Dan. xiii. 15).

BATH'UEL, son of Nachor and Melcha, was a nephew of Abraham, and father of Rebecca (Gen. xxii. 23)

BDELL'IUM, the gum of a tree found in Arabia, also in the land of Hevilath (Gen. ii. 12); manna the color of bdellium (Num. xi. 7).

BE'AN, the children of, malicious enemies of the Jews (1 Mach. v. 4).

BEANS, a vegetable (2 Kings xvii. 28; Ezech. iv. 9).

BEAR, an animal still found in the mountains of Palestine (1 Kings xvii. 34; 2 Kings xvii. 8). The constellation of the Great Bear (Job ix. 9).

BEARD, Israelites forbidden to shave the beard (Lev. xix. 27; xxi. 5); shaving it off as an insult (2 Kings x. 4); touched in salutation (xx. 9); anointed (Ps. cxxxii. 2); neglected or torn out in grief (2 Kings xix. 24; Isai. vii. 20; xv. 2; Jerem. xli. 5; Baruch vi. 30). The beard of a leper shaved (Lev. xiv. 9).

BEASTS, Daniel's vision of four beasts (Dan. vii. 3); another (viii. 3); mentioned in the Apocalypse (xvii. 3).

BEAT'ITUDES, the eight, pronounced by our Lord (Matt. v. 3; Luke vi. 20).

BED. The bed was originally very simple, the robe worn by day being the covering at night (Deut. xxiv. 13); even later the bedstead was so light as to be portable (1 Kings xix. 13, 15); subsequently they were highly adorned (Judith xiii. 8; Esth. i. 6); the furniture of an ordinary bedchamber (4 Kings iv. 10). Bed is used for the couch on which guests reclined (Esth. i. 6; vii. 8).

BEE, frequently mentioned in the Bible (Deut. i. 44; Judges xiv. 8; Ps. cxvii. 12; Isai. vii. 18).

BE'ELPHE'GOR, god of the Moabites. The Israelites initiated into his worship (Num. xxv. 3; xxxi. 16; Ps. cv. 28; Osee ix. 10).

BE'ELSEPHON, a station of the Israelites, where they crossed the sea (Exod. xiv. 2, 6).

BEEL'ZEBUB, a god adored at Accaron. Ochozias, when wounded, sent to consult him (4 Kings i. 2); in the New Testament used as a name for the devil (Matt. x. 25; xii. 24; Mark iii. 22; Luke xi. 15).

BE'HEMOTH, a monstrous animal supposed to be the hippopotamus (Job xl. 10).

BEL, first king of Babylon, worshipped as a god. The name is used sometimes to typify the kingdom (Isai. xlvi. 1; Jerem. li. **44**); Baruch reproaches them with asking a dumb idol to cure the dumb (vi. 40); Daniel detected the frauds of the priests of Bel (Dan. xiv. 2).

BE'LA, son of Beor, king of Denaba (Gen. xxxvi. 32).

BE'LA, son of Benjamin (Gen. xlvi. 21; Num. xxvi. 38; 1 Paral. viii. 1).

BEL'GA, chief of one of the courses of priests (1 Paral. xxiv. 14).

BE'LIAL (without yoke), used to mean a wicked, worthless, insubordinate man (Judg. xix. 22; 1 Kings ii. 12); used also to express Satan (2 Cor. vi. 15).

BEL'LY. Some make a god of their belly (Phil. iii. 19; Rom. xvi. 18).

BEN'ABIN'ADAB, governor of Nephath Dor, married Tapheth, daughter of Solomon (3 Kings iv. 11).

BENAD'AD, king of Syria, aided Asa, king of Juda, against Baasa, king of Israel, 938 B. C. (3 Kings xv. 18).

BENAD'AD II., king of Syria, attacked Achao, king of Israel, 901 B. C., but was defeated; he resumed the war the next year, but his army was destroyed at Aphec. He sought his life at the hands of Achab, who spared him (3 Kings xx. 3). Twelve years after he made war on Joram, son of Achab, but Eliseus defeated his plans (4 Kings vi. 8); some years after he besieged Samaria, and reduced the people to a fearful famine, but God sent a panic into his army, so that it fled from its camp (4 Kings vii., viii.)

BENAD'AD III., was thrice defeated by Joas, king of Israel, and lost all the conquests made by Hazael (4 Kings xiii. 3, 24, 25).

BEN'JAMIN, son of Jacob and Rachel, and the youngest of his children. Rachel, dying in giving him birth, called him Benoni (son of my pain); but Jacob called him Benjamin (son of the right hand) (Gen. xxxv. 18). When Jacob sent his sons into Egypt, he retained Benjamin (xlii. 4); Joseph, not trusting them, detained them till they brought Benjamin (xliii. 15, 20, 34; xliii. 7); Jacob reluctantly allowed him to go (8–15); Joseph concealed his joy, and by stratagem put his cup in Benjamin's sack (29, 34; xliv. 2, 12); Juda pleaded for him (18–34); then Joseph declared who he was, and wept and embraced Benjamin (xlv. 14); Jacob's prophecy (xlix. 27).

BEN'JAMIN. The tribe of Benjamin descended from the youngest son of Jacob. In the exodus from Egypt, Abidan, son of Gedeon, was prince of the tribe of Benjamin (Num. i. 11; ii. 22), and it numbered 35,400 (ii. 23), and at Settim 45,600 (xxvi. 41) men able to march on the west of the tabernacle (ii. 18); their offerings (vii. 60–65); their spy, Phalti (xiii. 10); Elidad chosen to divide the land (xxxiv. 21). Moses prophesies concerning the tribe (Deut. xxxiii. 12); the land allotted to the tribe was south of Ephraim, and between it and Juda, bounded by the Jordan, Cariathiarim, and from the valley of Hinnon to Bethel. They were skilful archers (1 Kings xx. 20, 36; 2 Kings i. 22; 1 Paral. viii. 40; xii. 2; 2 Paral. xvii. 17). The tribe for a fearful crime drew on it the other tribes, who slew all but 600, who escaped to the rock of Remmon (Judg. xix., xx.) The tribe gave the first king in the person of Saul (1 Kings ix. 1), and it adhered to Isboseth, his son (2 Kings ii.); on the revolt of Jero-

boam, it remained faithful to Roboam and his successors (3 Kings xii. 21) till the captivity. St. Paul belonged to this tribe.

BERE'A, a city in Macedonia, where St. Paul preached with great success (Acts xvii. 10, 13).

BER'ESCHIT (In the beginning), the Hebrew name for the book of Genesis.

BER'NICE, daughter of Agrippa the Great, and sister of the young Agrippa, with whom she listened to St. Paul's address to Festus (Acts xxv. 13–23).

BER'ODACHBAL'ADAN, king of Syria, condoles with Ezechias (4 Kings xx. 12).

BE'ROTH, a station of the children in the desert of Pharan (Deut. x. 6).

BER'SABEE, the Well of the Oath, where Abraham made a league with Abimelech (Gen. xxi. 31, 33). It was twenty miles south of Hebron, and one of the extreme points of the country, Dan being the other. Hence the expression, "from Dan to Bersabee" (2 Kings xvii. 11). It was in the tribe of Juda (Jos. xv. 28); and afterwards in Simeon (xix. 2).

BER'YL, a precious stone. The eighth jewel in the rational of the high priest was a beryl (Ex. xxviii. 20; xxxix. 13); an ornament of the king of Tyre (Ezech. xxviii. 13); in New Jerusalem (Apoc. xxi. 20).

BETHLEHEM.

BERZEL'LAI, of Rogel in the land of Galaad, an aged friend of David, who brought him provisions at Mahaim, at the time of Absalom's rebellion (2 Kings xvii. 27, 28). He returned to Jerusalem with David, but declined to remain at his court (xix. 33, 34); his sons are commended to Solomon (3 Kings ii. 7). (2) Priests after the captivity rejected from the priesthood (1 Esd. ii. 62; 2 Esd. vii. 64).

BES'ECATH or **BEZEC** (4 Kings xxii. 1), a city near Sichem, of which Adoni-Besec was apparently king. Saul reviewed his army here (1 Kings xi. 8).

BES'ELAM MITHRIDATES, an officer of the king of Persia, writes to him to prevent Jews rebuilding Jerusalem (1 Esd. iv. 7).

BES'ELEEL, son of Uri, and Mary the sister of Moses. He was gifted by God with wonderful skill in the working of metals and in invention. He was employed by Moses in constructing the tabernacle and all the articles used in divine worship (Exod. xxxi. 1–6).

BE'SOR, a brook in the southern part of Juda (1 Kings xxx. 9, 10, 21).

BETHA'NIA, at the foot of Mount Olivet, fifteen furlongs east of Jerusalem (John xi. 18; Mark xi. 1; Luke xix. 29). It was the residence of Lazarus, Mary and Martha, and here our Lord raised Lazarus to life (John xi. 1–45).

BETHA'NIA, a place beyond the Jordan where St. John baptized (John i 28).

BETHA'VEN, in the mountains of Benjamin, east of Bethel (Jos. vii 2; xviii. 12).

BETHBES'SEN. a city of Juda, where Simon and Jonathan Machabeus were besieged by Bacchides (1 Mach. ix. 62, 64).

BETH'EL, a city west of Hai (Gen. xii. 8). It was called Luza, but Jacob fleeing from Esau having seen in sleep the vision of angels, consecrated the stone on which he had slept, and named it Bethel, House of God (Gen. xxviii. 19); he afterwards built an altar there (xxxv. 7); in the days of the judges it was a holy place (Judg. xx. 31; xxi. 2); Debbora dwelt near it (Jud. iv. 4, 5); the Ark of the Covenant was near it (xx. 26; xxi. 4); Samuel the prophet visited it (1 Kings vii. 16); here Jeroboam set up the golden calves (3 Kings xii. 28, 29); it was acquired by the kingdom of Juda (2 Paral. xiii. 19); Elias and other prophets were there (4 Kings ii. 2);

there were priests there still later (4 Kings xvii. 28); Josias destroyed the heathen altars there (xxiii. 15–19). The prophets refer to it as a place of idolatry (Amos v. 5; Osee x. 15).

BETH'ER, a range of mountains (Cant. ii. 17).

BETH'IES'IMOTH, a town of Moab, assigned to Ruben (Jos. xiii. 20); its destruction foretold (Ezech. xxv. 9).

BETH'LEHEM (House of Bread), a city of Juda, ordinarily called Bethlehem of Juda, to distinguish it from Bethlehem in Zabulon (Jos. xix. 15). It is also called Ephrata (Gen. xlviii. 7; Mich. v. 2; Ruth i. 2; 1 Kings xvii. 12); Booz, one of the ancestors of David, was born there (Ruth i. 2, 19, 22; ii. 4; iv. 11); and David also (Luke ii. 4); the prophet Micheas (v. 2; Matt. ii. 6) foretold that the Messias was to be born there, and this prophecy was recognized by the priests. Our Lord Jesus Christ was born here in a stable (Matt. ii. 1; Luke ii. 4, 7); and here the shepherds and the wise men came to adore him. When Herod found that the wise men did not return, he ordered a massacre of all the children at Bethlehem of two years old and under that age (Matt. ii. 16, 18). Bethlehem is on a hillside, six miles south of Jerusalem. At the cave of the

BACTRIAN CAMEL.

Nativity there is a convent and a church dating back to the reign of Justinian.

BETHO'RON, a town in the tribe of Ephraim, ceded to the Levites (Jos. xxi. 22); it is frequently mentioned (Jos. x. 10, 11; 1 Kings xiii. 18; 2 Kings ii. 29; 1 Paral. vi. 68; 2 Paral. xxv. 13; 1 Mach. iii. 16, 24; iv. 29; vii. 39; ix. 50); Bethhoron, the upper, is named (Jos. xvi. 5; 2 Paral. viii. 5); and the lower (Jos. xvi. 3; xviii. 13; 3 Kings ix. 17; 2 Paral. viii. 7).

BETH'PHAGE', a little village at the foot of Mount Olivet, between Bethania and Jerusalem. From it our Lord sent his disciples to procure the ass on which he rode into Jerusalem before his passion (Matt. xxi. 2; Luke xix. 29; John xii. 14).

BETH'SABEE, daughter of Eliam, wife of Urias the Hethite. David seeing her bathing, was led by her beauty into the sin of adultery, and caused the death of Urias in order to marry her (2 Kings xi. 1-27); her child by this adulterous intercourse died, as the prophet Nathan foretold (xii. 18, 19); she subsequently bore him Solomon, Simmaa or Samua, Sobab, and Nathan (1 Par. iii. 5; 2 Kings v. 14); St. Matt. i. 6, 7, traces our Lord's descent from Solomon, and St. Luke (iii. 31) from Nathan. When Adonias, towards the close of David's reign, aspired to the succession, Bethsabee had Solomon crowned (3 Kings i. 34); after Solomon's accession, she asked him to give Abisag as wife to Adonias, which led to the death of the latter (3 Kings ii. 25). The thirty-first chapter of Proverbs is given as from Bethsabee.

BETHSA'IDA, the Hebrew name of a pool at Jerusalem, called also Probatica. It had five porches where the sick lay waiting for an angel to move the waters. The one who entered the water first after it moved was cured of his infirmity. Our Lord here cured a man helpless for thirty-eight years (John v. 1-9).

BETHSA'IDA, a city on the lake of Tiberias,

near the Jordan. It was the birthplace of the apostles St. Peter, St. Andrew, and St. Philip (John i. 44; xii. 21). Our Lord frequently visited it. He cured a blind man there (Mark viii. 22); on account of the incredulity of the people to his miracles he denounced woe to it (Luke x. 13; Matt. xi. 21).

BIBLE. The books of the Old Testament were first collected and revised by the Sanhedrim in the time of Esdras. The later books written or translated in Greek after the version by the seventy, known as the Septuagint, were added to it, and the whole of the Old Testament in this form passed into the hands of the Christian Church. After the establishment of the church, with greater power conferred upon her than the Sanhedrim had enjoyed, she accepted from time to time as inspired, works written by the apostles, St. Matthew, St. John, St. James, St. Jude, by St. Paul, and by disciples like St. Mark and St. Luke. From the council of Carthage (A. D. 397) to the council of Trent (A. D. 1576) she has fixed and adhered to a canon defining for the Christian world what books are to be held as inspired Scripture.

BIGAMY, the having two wives at the same time. The first example is among the family of Cain (Gen. iv. 19).

BIRDS created (Gen. i. 22; vii. 14); offered in holocaust (Lev. i. 14); laws as to nests of (Deut. xxii. 6).

BISH'OPS, election and duties (Luke xxii. 26; John x. 4-14; xxi. 15; Acts i. 24; vi. 3; xiv. 22; xx. 28; Rom. xv. 16-25; 1 Cor. iv. 1; 2 Cor. iii. 6; iv. 5; Eph. i. 16; iii. 2; 1 Tim. iii. 1; iv. 6; 2 Tim. ii. 15-24; 1 Pet. v. 2).

BITHYN'IA, a province in Asia Minor (Acts xvi. 7; 1 Pet. i. 1).

BIT'TERN, a bird (Lev. xi. 18; Sophonias

ii. 14); mistranslated cormorant in King James' Bible.

BIT'UMEN, the ark of Noe pitched with (Gen. vi. 14). The word is in the original Douay, but omitted in most editions of Challoner. Used for mortar in tower of Babel (xi. 3). Pits of, in the basin of the Dead Sea (Gen. xiv. 10). The mother of Moses smeared the basket with it (Ex. ii. 3). The Douay has *bitumen* in these places, but Challoner adopted from the King James Bible the indefinite expression *slime*.

BLAS'PHEMY, punished (Lev. xxiv. 11; 2 Esd. ix. 18; Tob. xiii. 16; Isai. i. 4; v. 24; xlviii. 11; lii. 5; Jerem. xxiii. 17; Ezech. xx. 27; 1 Mach. vii. 38; 2 Mach. viii. 4; xii. 14; xv. 24; Rom. ii. 24; 1 Tim. i. 20; Jude 8); against Jesus Christ (Matt. xxvii. 39; Luke xxiii. 39); against the Holy Ghost (Matt. xii. 31).

BLESSINGS, benedictions, Abraham is blessed by Melchisedec (Gen. xiv. 19); Jacob by Isaac (xxvii. 27; xxviii. 4); Jacob blesses his sons (Gen. xlviii., ix.); blesses Joseph's sons (xlviii. 15); the Israelites blessed by Aaron (Lev. ix. 22); by Balaam (Num. xxiii. 9); by Moses (Deut. xxxiii. 1); by Josue (Jos. viii. 33); by David (2 Kings vii. 8); by Solomon (3 Kings viii. 14); Josue blessed Ruben, Gad, and the half tribe of Manasses (Jos. xxii. 6); blesses Caleb (Jos. xiv. 13); Heli blesses Elcana (1 Kings ii. 20); Mathathias blesses the Machabees (1 Mach. ii. 69); David blesses spoils (1 Paral. xviii. 11); Simeon blesses the mother of our Lord (Luke ii. 34); Jesus Christ, our Lord, blesses the loaves and fishes before multiplying them (Matt. xiv. 19; Mark vi. 41; Luke ix. 16); he blesses the bread and wine at the moment when he institutes the Holy Eucharist (Matt. xxvi. 26; Mark xiv. 22); he blesses his disciples before ascending to heaven (Luke xxiv. 50, 51).

BLESS'ING of articles used in the divine worship—of Aaron's vestments (Ex. xxvii., xxviii.); of water for trial of jealousy (Num. v. 17); of an altar (Num. vii.; 2 Paral. vii.)

BLIND'NESS. The Sodomites blinded (Gen. xix. 11); Eliseus strikes the Syrians blind (4 Kings vi. 18); Tobias struck with blindness (ii. 11; xi. 15); the enemies of the Machabees (2 Mach. x. 30); Saul

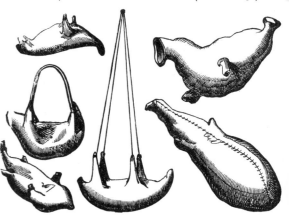

SKIN BOTTLES.

(Acts ix. 8, 18); Elymas (xiii. 11); blind men of Jericho (Matt. xx. 30); a man born blind (John ix. 1) and blind man of Bethsaida (Mark viii. 25) cured by our Lord. Spiritual blindness (Ps. lxviii. 24; cxlv. 8; Isai. xlii. 7-19; lix. 10; Wisd. ii. 21; Deut. xxviii. 28; Isai. vi. 10; John xii. 40; Rom. i. 21; xi. 10 Matt. xv. 14; Mark viii. 18; 2 Cor. iv. 4; Eph. iv. 18; 2 Pet. i. 9; 1 John i. 16; Apoc. iii. 17).

BLOOD. The effusion of blood was an essential part of sacrifice. "Without shedding of blood there is no remission" (Heb. ix. 22); the Old Testament dedicated with blood (18); the blood of the paschal lamb protects from death (Ex. xii. 7–23); the blood of a victim offered to God not to be poured upon leaven (Ex. xxiii. 18); blood of victims poured on the altar and sprinkled on the people (Ex. xxiv. 6, 8; xxix. 12, 20; Lev. i. 5, 11; iii. 2; iv. 7; v. 9, etc.; Heb. ix.) Blood being reserved especially to God, the Israelites were forbidden to eat it (Gen. ix. 4; Lev. iii. 17; vii. 27; xvii. 10, 12, 14; Deut. xii. 23; Acts xv. 20).

BLOOD OF CHRIST to be shed for the remission of sins (Matt. xxvi. 28; Mark xiv. 24; Luke xxii. 20; Acts xx. 28; Eph. i. 7; ii. 13; Coloss. i. 14, 20; Heb. ix. 7, 9, 12, 14–22; 1 Pet. i. 2, 19; 1 John i. 7; v. 6; Apoc. i. 5; vii. 14; xxii. 14); the bloody sweat in the garden (Luke xxii. 44); his blood actually shed on the cross (John xix. 34; 1 John v. 8); at the last supper he declares the chalice to be his blood (Matt. xxvi. 28; Mark xiv. 24; Luke xxii. 20; 1 Cor. xi. 25); he declares his blood to be drink indeed (John vi. 56); the drinking of it a condition of life everlasting (vi. 54–57); those who receive the Eucharist unworthily guilty of the Body and Blood of Christ (1 Cor. xi. 27); it pleads for us (Heb. xii. 24).

BLOOD, shedding of human. The first instance,

ANCIENT SARCOPHAGUS OR STONE COFFIN.

the murder of Abel (Gen. iv. 10); it cries to heaven for vengeance (iv. 10; Heb. xii. 24); man's blood not to be shed (Num. xxxv. 16–34; Ex. xx. 13; Matt. v. 21; Deut. v. 17; xix. 10); expiation of blood shed secretly (xxi. 1–9); the shedding of blood to be expiated by blood (Deut. xix. 13; Num. xxxv. 33); compensation for blood prohibited (31); cities of refuge provided for those who shed blood inadvertently (Num. xxxv. 6, 13, 15; Jos. xx. 2, 7, 9; Deut. xix. 4–7).

BLOOD, issue of, the menstrual discharge caused legal uncleanness (Lev. xv. 19–30; Matt. ix. 20; Mark v. 25; Luke viii. 43).

BLOOD, avenger of, the nearest relative of a murdered man, to kill the murderer (Num. xxxv. 19, 21); even an involuntary slayer, if found outside of city of refuge (27; Deut. xix. 6).

BOANER'GES, sons of thunder; the name given by our Lord to James and John, the sons of Zebedee (Mark iii. 17); as some think for the warmth of their zeal (Luke ix. 54).

BOC'CI, high-priest, son of Abisue (1 Paral. vi. 5).

BONDS AND CHAINS sent to various kings (Jer. xxvii. 2).

BONES, those of Joseph carried out of Egypt by Moses (Ex. xiii. 19); and buried in the land of promise (Jos. xxiv. 32); those of Saul and his sons

ANCIENT EGYPTIAN FUNERAL PROCESSION. (From Calliaud. Fbn.)

buried by the Jabesites (1 Kings xxxi. 13; 1 Paral. x. 12); transferred by David to the sepulchre of Cis, in the land of Benjamin (2 Kings xxi. 12–14); a man raised to life by the bones of Eliseus (4 Kings xiii. 21); bones burnt by Josias on the heathen altars to defile them (4 Kings xxiii. 16; 3 Kings xiii. 2); the bones of a holy man respected (4 Kings xxiii. 18); Ezechiel's vision of the dry bones (Ezech. xxxvii. 1–14); bones of the paschal lamb not to be broken (Ex. xii. 46); accomplishment of this figure in the person of Christ (John xix. 33, 36).

BOOK OF LIFE (Ex. xxxii. 32; Ps. lxviii. 29; Philip. iv. 3; Apoc. iii. 5; xiii. 8; xx. 12; xxi. 27); in Zachary's vision (Zach. v.); book of the seven seals (Apoc. v.)

BOOKS, of Moses, found in the temple (4 Kings xxii. 8); of Jeremias burned (Jer. xxxvi. 23); holy, burned by Antiochus (1 Mach. i. 59).

BOOT'Y, division of (Num. xxxi.); booty taken from king Agag to be destroyed (1 Kings xv.)

BO'OZ, son of Salmon and Rahab, marries Ruth (Ruth i.-iv.); one of the ancestors of our Lord (Matt. i. 5).

BO'OZ, one of the two columns of brass, which Solomon set up in the porch of the temple (3 Kings vii. 21); the other pillar was called Jachin. They were together thirty-five cubits high (2 Paral. iii. 15; 3 Kings vii. 15; Jerem. lii. 21); Booz was on the left (2 Par. iii. 7).

BO'RITH, a cleansing herb (Jerem. ii. 22).

BO'SES, a rock scaled by Jonathan when he attacked the Philistines (1 Kings xiv. 4).

BO'SOR or **BOS'RA,** a city beyond the Jordan assigned by Moses to the tribe of Ruben (Deut. iv. 43); a city of refuge (Jos. xx. 8; xxi. 27, 36); the prophets menaced Bosra with woe (Isai. xxxiv. 6; Jerem. xlviii. 24; xlix. 13, 22); Judas Machabeus captured and destroyed it (1 Mach. v. 26–28).

BOS'PHORUS, some of the Jews captive in (Abdias i. 20).

BOT'TLE, a leathern vessel for liquids (Ps. cxviii. 83; Matt. ix. 17); also earthen (Jerem. xix. 1).

BRACE'LETS (Num. xxxi. 50).

BRAM'BLE, Joatham's parable of the bramble chosen by the trees to be their king (Judges ix. 8–15).

BRASS, used for buckles of the tabernacle (Ex. xxv. 3; xxvi. 11; xxxvi. 18); for the altar, socket of pillars (xxvii. 1–18; xxxviii. 1–7, 9–19), the laver (8); Moses made a serpent of, which he set up (Num. xxi. 9);

castings of brass (3 Kings vii. 23; 2 Paral. iv.)

BRAZEN SERPENT, set up by Moses, at God's command, by looking at which those bitten by fiery serpents were cured (Num. xxi. 6–9); Jesus Christ refers to it as a figure of himself (John iii. 14); it did not heal by its own power (Wisd. xvi. 7); as the Jews paid it idolatrous honor, calling it Nohestan, king Ezechias destroyed it (4 Kings xviii. 4).

BREAD. Jesus the bread which came down from heaven (John vi. 41; 1 Cor. x. 16; xi. 27). See EUCHARIST. Unleavened bread to be eaten with the paschal lamb (Ex. xii. 18); bread brought to Elias miraculously (3 Kings xvii. 6); loaves of bread multiplied by Christ (Matt. xiv., xv.; Mark vi. 41; viii. 20; Luke ix. 13; John vi. 11).

BRETH'REN IN CHRIST (Matt. xii. 49; xxviii. 10; John xx. 17; Heb. ii. 12).

BRU'CHUS, a devouring insect, apparently a young locust (Lev. xi. 22; Ps. civ. 34; Joel i. 4; ii. 25; Nahum iii. 15, 16). See CATERPILLAR.

BUSH. The burning bush seen by Moses (Ex. iii. 2).

BUY'ING AND SELLING. How it should be done (Levit. xix. 35; xxv. 14; Deut. xxv. 13; Prov. xi. 1; Ecclus. xlii. 7; Jerem. xxxii. 6; 1 Cor. vii. 30; example set by Abraham (Gen. xxiii. 9–14); Esau sells his birthright (xxv. 33); Achab wishes to buy Naboth's vineyard (3 Kings xxi.)

BRICKS. The making of bricks is mentioned in regard to the tower of Babel (Gen. xi. 3); the Egyptians compelled the Jews to make brick (Ex. i. 14; v. 7); brick-kilns are mentioned in David's time (2 Kings xii. 31); Isaias reproaches the Jews with offering sacrifice on bricks, contrary to the law (lxv. 3).

BRIDE. The new Jerusalem coming down out of heaven compared to a bride adorned for her husband (Apoc. xxi. 2); the Bride is the church, the

EASTERN MODE OF BURIAL.

wife of the Lamb (9); her invitation to the nations (xxii. 17); for the adornment of a Hebrew bride, see Ruth iii. 3; Ezech. xxiii. 40; Eph. v. 26; her veil

(Gen. xxiv. 65; xxxviii. 14; 1 Cor. xi. 10); her white dress (Apoc. xix. 8); her stomacher or girdle (Jerem. ii. 32); her jewels (Cant. ix. 18; lxi. 10; Apoc. xxi. 2); perfumes (Ps. xliv. 9).

ANCIENT HARBOR OF CÆSAREA.

BRIDE′GROOM. His reception mentioned (John iii. 29; Isai. lxi. 10; Cant. iii. 11). See Marriage.

BUL′RUSHES, basket made of (Ex. ii. 3).

BUR′IAL. The first burial described in the Bible is that of Sara in the cave purchased by Abraham (Gen. xxiii. 4–19); the only instance of cremation is that of Saul and his sons (1 Kings xxxi. 12); aromatics were used to embalm the body (2 Paral. xvi. 14; Mark xvi. 1; Luke xxiii. 56; xxiv. 1; John xix. 39, 40), and the body was wrapped in linen cloths (John xi. 44; xix. 40). They had cemeteries without the cities (Ez. xxxix. 15).

BUT′TER is mentioned Gen. xviii. 8; Deut. xxxii. 14; Judg. v. 25; Job xx. 17; Isai. vii. 15, 22.

BURN′ING ALIVE, punishment of crime (Gen. xxxviii. 24; Levit. xx. 14).

BUF′FALO, used as food (3 Kings iv. 23).

CA′ATH, second son of Levi, and grandfather of Moses (Gen. xlvi. 11; Exod. vi. 18; Num. iii. 17). His family carried the ark of the covenant and the sacred vessels of the tabernacle (Num. iii. 17–31).

CABE, a measure, the sixth part of the seah, and the eighteenth part of the epha. During the siege of Samaria a cabe of the vegetable called pigeon's dung sold for five sicles (4 Kings vi. 25).

CAD′EMOTH, a wilderness from which Moses sent messengers to Sehon, king of Hesebon (Deut. ii. 26).

CA′DES, or **MISPHAT** (Gen. xiv. 7), a place in the desert of Sin, where Mary, the sister of Moses, died (Num. xx. 1), and where Moses struck the rock and made it yield water (11); this is "the water of contradiction" (13).

CA′DES, a town of which the king was killed by Josue (xii. 22); a town in the tribe of Juda (xv. 23); famous for its palm-trees (Ecclus. xiv. 18); a town in Galilee (1 Mach. xi. 63, 73).

CAD′UMIM, a torrent (Judges v. 21).

CÆSAR, or **CESAR,** the surname of Julius, applied generally to all the Roman emperors—to Tiberius (Matt. xxii. 21); to Nero (Acts xxv. 10).

CÆSARE′A, a port on the Mediterranean, built by Herod the Great. Herod Agrippa was struck here for his pride (Acts xii. 23); it was the residence of Cornelius, baptized by St. Peter (x. 1); St. Philip the deacon dwelt there (viii. 40); here Agabus predicted to St. Paul his bonds (xxi. 10, 11), and St. Paul was two years a prisoner here (xxiii.–xxv.)

CÆSAREA PHILIPPI, a city near Sidon and Damascus. Here Christ gave Simon the name of Peter, the rock on which he was to build his church, and promised him the keys of the kingdom of heaven (Matt. xvi. 13–19; Mark viii. 27); the woman cured of the issue of blood is said to have been of this place, and to have erected a statue of our Lord here.

CAGE, in the sense of a trap (Ecclus. xi. 32).

CAIN, the first-born of Adam and Eve (Gen. iv. 1); a husbandman (2); offered to the Lord fruits of the earth (3); but not acceptably (5); lures his brother Abel to the field and slays him (8); cursed by God (11); a mark set upon him (15); built a city called Henoch after his son (17); his descendants (17–24).

CAI′NAN, son of Enos (Gen. v. 9). Cai′nan, son of Arphaxad and father of Sale (Luke iii. 36).

CA′IPHAS, high-priest, son-in-law of Annas. When the council deliberated on the death of Christ, Caiphas said that it was expedient that one man should die, and that the whole nation should not perish. This he said not of himself, but because he was the high-priest of that year (John xi. 51, 52); when our Lord was arrested he was taken first to Annas, who came into office after the Pasch (Acts iv. 6), then to Caiphas (John xviii. 24); after hearing the witnesses, Caiphas adjured him to declare whether he was the Christ, the Son of God, and when Jesus declared that he was, the high-priest rent his garments, and declared him a blasphemer, and worthy of death. Caiphas again questioned him in the morning. He was with Annas in trying the apostles (Acts iv. 6).

CAI′US or **GAIUS,** a disciple of St. Paul; the host of that apostle at Corinth (Rom. xvi. 23), and accompanied him to Ephesus (Acts xix. 29); he is supposed to be the one to whom St. John addressed his third epistle (3 John i. 1).

CAL′AMUS, used in oil of unction (Ex. xxx. 23).

CA′LEB, son of Jephone of the tribe of Judas, one of the spies sent to examine the Promised Land (Num. xiii. 31); he and Josue reported favorably, and urged advancing into it, but the people, misled by the other spies, refused. God declared that none of them should enter it except Caleb and Josue (Num. xiii. 4–xiv. 30). When Josue entered the Promised Land, Caleb asked Hebron as his possession (Jos. xiv. 6–14); he conquered the sons of Enac, and gave Axa, his daughter, to Othoniel, for

THE CAMEL POST.

capturing Cariathsepher (xv. 13–19; xxi. 12; Judges i. 20).

CALF, the golden, worshipped as an idol by the Israelites at Mount Sinai (Ex. xxxii. 4; Deut. ix. 16);

by the Israelites when set up by Jeroboam (3 Kings xii. 28; 4 Kings x. 29; xvii. 16; Ps. cv. 19; Osee viii. 5, 6).

CALLIS'THENES, an officer of the king of Syria; sets fire to the doors of the temple; is himself burnt in his house (2 Mach. viii. 33).

CAL'VARY, or **GOLGOTHA** (the place of the skull), the spot near Jerusalem where our Lord was crucified (Matt. xxvii. 33; Mark xv. 22; Luke xxiii. 33; John xix. 17); and placed in the sepulchre. Here St. Helena erected the church of the Holy Sepulchre, which has always been a place of pilgrimage.

CAM'EL, a domestic animal, used as a beast of burthen in the East (Gen. xii. 16; xxiv. 10; xxxvii. 25; Judges vii. 12; 1 Kings xxvii. 9; xxx. 17; 4 Kings viii. 9; 3 Kings x. 2; 2 Paral. xiv. 14; Job i. 3; xlii. 12; Matt. iii. 4; Mark i. 6).

CAM'ELOPARDALUS, the giraffe, classed among clean animals (Deut. xiv. 5).

CAMP, used for the place called Mahanaim (Gen. xxxii. 21; 2 Kings ii. 9, 12, 29; xvii. 24; xix. 32).

CAM'UEL, father of the Syrians (Gen. xxii. 21).

CA'NA in Galilee, where our Lord wrought his first miracle by changing water into wine at the marriage feast (John ii. 1; Jos. xix. 28).

CANDA'CE, queen of Ethiopia, whose eunuch, after visiting Jerusalem to worship God, was converted and baptized by St. Philip (Acts viii. 27).

CAN'DLESTICK, seven-branched, in the tabernacle (Ex. xxv. 31); with seven lamps (Zach. iv. 2). The word is misleading, as there were no candles; it was a lamp-stand.

canonical and the New Testament; Protestants agreeing with neither, reject the deutero-canonical books, except a part of Esther.

CAN'OPY, a rich one used by Holofernes (Judith x. 19, etc.)

CANT'ICLE OF CANTI-CLES, a mysterious canonical book of the Old Testament, describing the union of Christ and his church.

CANT'ICLES. Besides the Psalms and the Canticle of Canticles, there are in the books of the Bible several canticles or poetical portions. The Canticle of Moses after passing the Red Sea (Exod. xv.); his Canticle on the wonderful works of God (Deut. xxxii.); Jethro's on learning of God's wonderful works (Ex. xviii.); Debbora's on her victory over Sisara (Judges v.); that of Anna, mother of Samuel (1 Kings ii.); David's (2 Kings xxii.); Tobias' (Tob. xiii.); Judith's in thanksgiving (Judith xvi.); that of the three children in the fiery furnace (Dan. iii. 52); the Magnificat of the Blessed Virgin (Luke i. 46); Simeon's (ii. 29); Zachary's (i. 68); Canticles of Sorrow, David's lament for Saul and Jonathan (2 Kings i. 18); on the ruin of Tyre (Ezech. xxvii. 2); on Egypt (xxxii. 18); that of Jeremias on the ruin of Jerusalem (Lam.)

CAPTIV'ITIES of the Jews. Phul, king of Assyria, and Theglathphalasar, king of Assur, carried away Ruben, Gad, and the half tribe of Manasses to Assyria, 750 B.C. (1 Paral. v. 26; 4 Kings xv. 19, 29); Salmanasar, after three years war, car-

THE SEVEN-BRANCHED CANDLESTICK, WITH ITS LAMPS.

ried the rest of the ten tribes away, 721 B.C. (4 Kings xvii. 3, 6); Sennacherib, 713 B.C., carried off many captives from cities of Juda (4 Kings xviii. 13); Nabuchodonosor took Jerusalem and carried away king Joachin and 10,000 soldiers, besides artificers, 598 B.C. (Dan. i. 2); 4 Kings xxiv. 14; Nabuzardan, his general, again took Jerusalem, with king Sedecias, and carried off the rest of the people (xxv. 11; 2 Paral. xxxvi. 20; Jerem. lii. 28–30). The Babylonian captivity lasted till the return under Zorobabel, 535 B.C. (1 Esd. ii. 1–70; 2 Esd. vii. 7–69); Esdras, 467 B.C. (1 Esd. viii. 1–14); and Nehemias, 454 B.C. Those who remained (Esth. viii. 9, 11) were known as the Dispersion (John vii. 35; 1 Peter i. 1; James i. 1).

CARBUN'CLE, a precious stone, the fourth in the rational (Exod. xxviii. 18; xxxix. 11; Ezech. xxviii. 13).

CAR'CAA, a town in Juda (Jos. xv. 3).

CAR'EHIM, birthplace of Jesbaam (1 Par. xii. 6.)

CAR'ETH, a town on the borders of Zabulon (Jos. xix. 15).

CA'RIA, a province of Asia Minor, in the extreme southeast (1 Mach. xv. 23).

CAR'IATH, a town in Benjamin (Jos. xviii. 28).

CAR'IATH or **CAR'IATHAIM**, occupied by the Emim (Gen. xiv. 5); assigned to Ruben (Num. xxxii. 37; Jos. xiii. 19); menaced (Jerem. xlviii. 1, 23; Ezech. xxv. 9).

CAR'IATHAIM, Levitical city in Nephthali (1 Paral. vi. 76).

CAR'IATH'ARBE (Hebron), (Jos. xiv. 15).

CAR'IATHIARIM or **CARIATHBAAL** (Jos. xv. 60), a city of Juda where the Ark of the Covenant remained for seven years (1 Kings vi.)

CAR'IATH SE'PHER (city of letters), taken by Caleb (Jos. xv. 15; Judg. i. 10–13).

CAR'ITH, a torrent beyond the Jordan, where Elias was miraculously fed (3 Kings xvii. 3, 5).

CAR'MEL, a city in the tribe of Juda (Jos. xv. 55); residence of Nabal (1 Kings xxv. 2–7).

CAR'MEL (vineyard of God), a mountain between the plains of Saron and Esdraelon, in the tribe

ARABIAN CAMEL.

CAN'ON, CANONICAL. The books of the Bible form three divisions, the proto-canonical, comprising the Pentateuch, Josue, Judges, Ruth, Kings, Paralipomenon, Esdras, Job, Psalms, Proverbs, Ecclesiastes, Canticles, Isaias, Jeremias, Ezechiel, Daniel, Osee, Joel, Amos, Abdias, Jonas, Micheas, Nahum, Habacuc, Sophonias, Aggeus, Zacharias, Malachias, forming the supposed canon of Esdras; the deutero-canonical books, Tobias, Judith, Esther, Wisdom, Ecclesiasticus, Baruch, parts of Daniel, Machabees, the books of the New Testament. The Catholic Church, from the Council of Carthage, A. D. 397, receives all; the Jews receive only the proto-canonical books, rejecting the deutero-

CAP, head covering (Dan. iii. 21).

CAPHAR'NAUM, a town on the lake of Genesareth (John vi. 17), and the chief residence of our Lord during the three years of his public life (Matt. iv. 13; Mark ii. 1); it is called his city (Matt. ix. 1); he called Matthew there (Matt. ix. 9); he preached here (Matt. iv. 17; Luke iv. 31); he reproached it with incredulity, and foretold its ruin (Matt. xi. 23).

CA'PER-TREE (Ecclesiastes xii. 5).

CAPH'TORIM, descendants of Mesraim, son of Cham (Gen. x. 14; 1 Paral. i. 12).

CAP'PADOCIA, the country between Mount Taurus and the upper Euphrates (Deut. ii. 23; Jerem. xlvii. 4; Amos ix. 7; Acts ii. 9; 1 Pet. i. 1).

of Aser (Jos. xix. 26). Elias, on Mount Carmel, defied the priests of Baal, and showed their impotence (3 Kings xviii. 19–45); while his sacrifice was consumed by fire from heaven. Eliseus also went to

MOUNT CARMEL AND ITS CONVENT.

Carmel (4 Kings ii. 25; iv. 25); its beauty is often referred to (4 Kings xix. 23, 24; Cant. vii. 5; Isai. xvi. 10; xxxv. 2; Jerem. xlvi. 18; Nahum i. 4).

CAR′PUS, disciple of St. Paul at Troas (2 Tim. iv. 13).

CARTHAGIN′IANS, inhabitants of the great city of Carthage, in the part of Africa now called Tunis (Ezech. xxvii. 12).

CAR′THA in Zabulon (Jos. xxi. 34), Carthan in Nephthali (32), Levitical cities.

CAS′LEU, a Jewish month, corresponding nearly to November (2 Esd. i. 1; Zach. vii. 1); on the 15th Antiochus Epiphanes profaned the temple (1 Mach. i. 57); Judas Machabeus purified and re-dedicated it on the 25th (2 Mach. i. 18); and established a festival observed by our Lord (John x. 22); and still kept by the Jews. The miraculous fire of Nehemias was also commemorated in this month (2 Mach. i. 18–22).

CAS′PHIN, a city taken with great slaughter by Judas Machabeus (2 Mach. xii. 13–16).

CAS′SIA, an aromatic used in the holy oil by Moses (Ex. xxx. 24); mentioned by David (Ps. xliv. 9).

CAS′SIA, Job's second daughter (xlii. 14).

CAST′ING OF METALS (2 Paral. iv. 17).

CAT, a domestic animal, mentioned only in Baruch (vi. 21).

CATERPILLAR (Bruchus), (2 Paral. vi. 28; Jer. li. 27).

CATHOLIC EPISTLES. That of St. James, the two of St. Peter, three of St. John, and one of St. Jude, are so called from being addressed to all the faithful. They refute the heresies of Simon, Nicolas, Cerinthus, and others.

CAVES, celebrated; that to which Lot retired (Gen. xix. 30); the double cave at Hebron, where Sara was buried (Gen. xxiii. 17); also Abraham (xxv. 9); the cave of Odollam, to which David fled (1 Kings xxii. 1; 2 Kings xxiii. 13; 1

Paral. xi. 15); the cave in the desert of Engaddi, where Saul was (1 Kings xxiv. 4).

CE′DAR, son of Ismael (Gen. xxv. 13; 1 Paral. i. 29); his descendants dwelt in tents (Cant. i. 4; Jerem. xlix. 28; Ps. cxix. 5; Isai. xlii. 11).

CE′DARS OF LI′BANUS (Judg. ix. 15; 4 Kings xiv. 9); employed in the temple of Jerusalem (3 Kings iv. 33; v., vii.–x.); used as symbols of beauty (Ps. xxxvi. 35; xci. 13; Cant. v. 15; Ecclus. xxiv. 17; Jerem. xxii. 7; Ezech. xxxi. 3, 8; Amos ii. 9).

CED′MONITES, inhabitants of Chanaan (Gen. xv. 19).

CED′RON, a torrent rising north of Jerusalem, and flowing between it and Mount Olivet into the Dead Sea (2 Kings xv. 23; 3 Kings xv. 13; 2 Paral. xv. 16; xxix. 16; xxx. 14; Jerem. xxxi. 40); crossed by our Lord (John xviii. 1).

CELESYRIA, the valley between Libanus and Anti-Libanus (1 Mach. x. 69; 2 Mach. iii. 5; iv. 4; viii. 8, 11).

CEL′IBACY, its excellence and advantages (1 Cor. vii. 7–9, 32, 34, 38).

CENCH′RA, the port of Corinth. St. Paul shaved his head here in fulfilment of a vow (Acts xviii. 18); he addresses the church there (Rom. xvi. 1).

CENDEBE′US, general of Antiochus Sidetes, who put him in command of the sea-coast, with orders to fortify Gedor and attack the Jews (1 Mach. xv. 38–41); Judas and John routed him near Modin (xvi. 1–10).

CEN′ERETH, a town in Nephthali (Jos. xix. 35; xi. 2; xii. 3; Deut. iii. 17); and a lake called also Genesar (1 Mach. xi. 67); also Genesareth, and Sea of Galilee (Matt. iv. 18).

CEN′EZITES, ancient inhabitants of Chanaan (Gen. xv. 19).

CENSERS.

CEN′SERS, vessels used for burning incense (Lev. x. 1; xvi. 12; Num. xvi. 37; 3 Kings vii. 50; Heb. ix. 4; Apoc. viii. 3).

CENTU′RION, a Roman officer commanding

AN EASTERN CARAVAN.

a hundred men. One obtains of our Lord the cure of his servant (Luke vii. 6); his faith praised (9); another confesses the divinity of Christ (Mark xv. 39; Luke xxiii. 47).

CE′PHAS, a Syriac word meaning rock, which our Lord gave to Simon as his name. The Greek word for rock, Petra, being feminine, the name became in that language Petros, in Latin Petrus, it being contrary to custom to give a feminine name to a man (John i. 42). St. Paul uses the name Cephas apparently for St. Peter (1 Cor. ix. 5; xv. 5); whether for him in Gal. ii. 9, 14, is disputed.

CE′PHAS, a disciple of St. Paul at Corinth (1 Cor. i. 12; iii. 22).

CERAS′TES, the horned adder. The word translated serpent, in Gen. xlix. 17, is in the Vulgate Cerastes, the name of a well-known and peculiar serpent, and the Hebrew word has the same meaning.

CER′EMONIES were connected with the divine worship, and at last prescribed in detail. Exterior worship (Gen. viii. 20) used by Melchisedec (xiv. 18); the ceremony of circumcision (xvii. 10); connected with the eating of the paschal lamb (Exod. xii., xiii.; Lev. xxiii. 5); used in the consecration of priests (Lev. ix.; xiv.; xxiii.; Num. i. 50; iv.–ix; xv.); prescribed for the singers in the temple (1 Paral. xxiii.); at the dedication of the first temple (3 Kings viii.); of the second (1 Esd. vi.); used at prayer (3 Kings viii. 22; xvii.; 1 Cor. xi. 4); ceremonies are signs of things to come (Exod. xiii. 9; Num. xv. 39; Ezech. xx. 12; 1 Cor. x. 11; 2 Cor. iii. 13; Heb. vii.; viii. 5; ix. 1; x. 1).

CER′ETHI, supposed to be a tribe of Philistines (1 Kings xxx. 14); some of whom were in David's bodyguard (2 Kings viii. 18; xv. 18; xx. 7; 3 Kings i.; 4 Kings xi. 19; 1 Paral. xviii. 17).

CETH′IM, son of Javan (Gen. x. 4; 1 Paral. vii. 1); the term is used for Macedonia (1 Mach. i. 1; Isai. xxiii. 1, 12; Jer. ii. 10); and Ceteans for Macedonians (viii. 5).

CETU′RA, second wife of Abraham, who bore him Zamran, Jecsan, Madan, Madian, Jesboc, and Sue (Gen. xxv. 1, 2; 1 Paral. i. 32).

CHAB′UL, land of, a term given by Hiram, king of Tyre, to twenty cities in Galilee ceded him by Solomon (3 Kings ix. 13).

CHAB′RI and **CHARMI**, priests in Bethulia (Judith viii. 9).

CHAINS. Samson was taken to Gaza in chains (Judg. xvi. 21); Sedecias to Babylon (4 Kings xxv. 7); Manasses (2 Paral. xxxiii. 11); God took the chains off the neck of Israel (Lev. xxvi. 13); we are to put our neck into the chains of wisdom (Ecclus. vi. 25); Jeremias ordered to put chains on his neck (xxvii. 2).

CHAIN of gold as an ornament for the neck (Gen. xli. 42; Prov. i. 9; Dan. v. 7; Ezech. xvi. 11; Isai. iii. 19).

CHALAN′NE, a city in Sennaar built by Nimrod (Gen. x. 10).

CHALCED′ONY, a precious stone (Apoc. xxi. 19).

CHAL′DE′A, the southern part of Babylonia (Jer. l.; li.; Ezech. xi.; xxiii.) Abraham was born at Ur, in the land of the Chaldees (Gen. xi. 28).

CHAL′DEES, the people of Chaldea (Gen. xi. xv.; 4 Kings xxiv., xxv.; 2 Paral. xxxvi.; 1 Esd. v.; 2 Esd. ix.; Isai. xiii.; xxiii.; xliii.; xlvii.–xlviii.; Jer. xxi.–xxii.; xxiv.–xxv.; xxxii.–xxxiii.; Ezech. i. 3, etc.; Dan. i. 4, etc.; Acts vii. 4).

CHAM, son of Noe (Gen. v. 31); his sin (ix. 22); Chanaan, his son, cursed (25); his posterity (x. 6–20); his sons were Chus, Mesraim, Phuth, and Chanaan (6); Egypt is called the land of Cham (Ps. lxxvii. 51; civ. 23; cv. 22).

CHA′MAAM, son of Berzellai, honored by David (2 Kings xix. 37–40).

CHAM′OIS, a clean animal, allowed to be eaten (Deut. xiv. 5).

xi. 17); Josias destroyed its temple (4 Kings xxiii. 13).

CHA′NAAN, grandson of Noe, cursed by him (Gen. ix. 25).

CHA′NAAN, land of, praised for its fertility (Deut. xi. 10; Exod. iii. 8); God promises it to Abraham and his seed (Gen. xii. 7; xvii. 8); renews the promise to Jacob (xxxv. 12); Moses leads the people out of Egypt to occupy it (Ex. xii.; Deut. xxxiv.); Josue and Caleb report in favor of it, but the people misled refuse to enter it, and die in the desert (Num. xiv. 6–38); Josue leads them into it (Jos. i.); divisions of (Gen. x. 19; Ex. xxiii. 31; Num. xxvi. 52; xxxiii. 54; xxxiv.; Josue xiii.–xix.; Ezech. xlvii. 13).

CHA′NAAN, woman of, obtains of our Lord the cure of her daughter (Matt. xv. 22).

CHANANE′AN, Simon, the apostle (Matt. x. 4).

THE VALLEY OF THE CEDRON.

CHARACA, inhabited by Jews called Tabianites (2 Mach. xii. 17).

CHARA′DRION, a bird forbidden as food (Lev. xi. 19; Deut. xiv. 18).

CHA′RAN or **HARAN**, a city in Mesopotamia where Abraham resided after leaving Ur (Gen. xi. 31–32; Acts vii. 2); Jacob fled to it (Gen. xxvii. 43; xxviii. 10; Judith v. 9).

CHAR′CAMIS, on the Euphrates, battles at (Isaias x. 9; 2 Paral. xxxv. 20; Jerem. xlvi. 2).

CHAR′IOTS used in war, Pharao's, overwhelmed in Red Sea (Ex. xiv. 7); used by Chanaanites at Merom (Jos. xi. 9); armed with scythes (2 Mach. xiii. 2; Judg. i. 19); of iron (Jos. xvii. 16); Sisara had nine hundred (Judg. iv. 3); captured by David (1 Paral. xviii. 4; 2 Kings viii. 4); Solomon's (3 Kings ix. 19, 22; x. 26); Josias mortally wounded in his chariot, removed to another (2 Paral. xxxv. 24); Elias the prophet carried off in a chariot of fire (4 Kings ii. 11); chariots seen in visions (Ezech. x.; Zach. vi. 1–8).

CHAR′ITY, a summary of the law (Matt. xxii. 37–39); Rom. xii. 9); superior to faith (1 Cor. xiii. 13); superior to sacrifices (Matt. xii. 7); is the bond of perfection (Col. iii. 14); charity covers sins (Prov. x. 12); is the end of the commandments (1 Tim. i. 5).

CHAS′LUIM, son of Mesraim (Gen. x. 14).

CHAS′TITY praised (Tob. vi. 16; Judith xv. 11; xvi. 26; Prov. xxii. 11; Wisd. iii. 13; iv. 1; vi 20; Ecclesiasticus vii. 28; xxvi. 20; Isai. i. 16; Zach. ix. 17).

CHEL′EAB, son of David by Abigail (2 Kings iii. 3); called Daniel (1 Paral. iii. 1).

CHEL′ION, son of Noemi (Ruth i. 1–9).

CHEL′MON, a city over against Esdraelon (Judith vii. 3).

CHER′OGRYLLUS, the rabbit or hedge-hog (Lev. xi. 5).

CHER′UBIM, an order of angels. They guard Paradise (Gen. iii. 24); represented on the ark of the covenant (Ex. xxv. 18; Ps. lxxix. 2; Ezech. xli. 18).

CHEST used for offerings for the reparation of the temple (4 Kings xii. 9, 10; Mark xii. 41).

CHILDREN of Hebrews drowned by Pharao (Ex. i. 22); the firstborn of the Egyptians struck dead (xi. 5); wicked children devoured by bears (4 Kings ii. 24); children of Bethlehem massacred by order of Herod (Matt. ii. 16); children blessed by our Lord (Mark x. 14; Luke xviii. 16); duty of children to parents (Gen. ix. 23; xxviii. 7; xxxvii. 14; Ex. xx. 12; xxi. 17; Levit. xix. 3; Deut. xxi. 18; xxvii. 16; Judges xiv. 1; 1 Kings ii. 22; xviii. 5; 3 Kings ii. 19; 4 Kings iii. 23; Ecclus. iii. 2; vi. 18; vii. 29; viii. 11; xxii. 3; xxiii. 18; xxv. 10; xxxii. 24; Tobias xiv. 5; Job viii. 4; Prov. i. 8; iv. 1; vi. 20; x. 1; xiii. 1; xv. 20; xix. 26; xxiii. 19; xxviii. 24; xxx. 17; Jer. xxxv. 16; Matt. x. 35; xix. 19; Mark x. 19; Luke ii. 51; Acts vii. 14; Col. iii. 20; 1 Peter v. 5).

CHIM′NEY (Ex. ix. 8) means rather the chafing dish used in warm countries; sinners shall pass like smoke out of a chimney (Osee xiii. 3).

CHLO′E, a Christian woman of Corinth, notifies St. Paul of the divisions there (1 Cor. i. 11).

CHO′BAR, a river of Assyria, on the banks of which Ezechiel received the message from God (Ez. i. 1).

CEDAR OF LEBANON.

CHA′MOS, a god of the Moabites (Num. xxi. 29); Solomon worshipped it in his old age (3 Kings xi. 7).

CHOD'CHOD, the Hebrew name for some precious stone (Ezech. xxvii. 16); perhaps jasper (Isai. liv. 12).

CHODOR'LAHOMOR, king of the Elamites,

WAR CHARIOTS.

one of the four kings who attacked the Pentapolis, and were pursued by Abraham (Gen. xiv.)

CHOIRS (2 Kings vi. 12; 2 Esd. xii. 31).

CHONE'NIAS, chief of the Levites, a skilful musician, directed the music when the ark of the covenant was brought to Jerusalem (1 Paral. xv. 22).

CHRIST'IAN, a disciple of Jesus Christ. The name was first given at Antioch (Acts xi. 26); they called each other brethren (Acts x. 23); the faithful (Ephes. i. 1); the saints (Acts xxvi. 10); believers (Acts iv. 32).

CHRIST, the anointed one (1 Kings ii. 10); David the Christ of the God of Jacob (2 Kings xxiii. 1; Ps. ii. 2; lxxxiii. 10; Lament. iv. 20; Hab. iii. 13).

CHRIST JESUS, the name of our Redeemer, Jesus being the Hebrew for Saviour, and Christ a Greek word meaning anointed. He is truly God, Creator of all things (John i. 3; Eph. iii. 9; Col. i. 16; Heb. i. 2); eternal (John xii. 34); one with the Father (John x. 30; xiv. 10; xvii. 21); truly the Son of God (Matt. xiv. 33; xvii. 5; Mark i. 11; v. 7; ix. 6; xv. 39; Luke i. 32, 35; iii. 22; John i. 1–34; vi. 70; ix. 35; xi. 27; xix. 7); the Word made flesh and truly man (John 1. 14; Col. ii. 9; 1 Tim. iii. 16; 1 John iv. 2; Matt. i. 23; Luke ii. 7); he is the mighty King of kings (Ps. ii. 6; xxi. 29; Ezech. xxxvii. 24; Col. ii. 10; 1 Tim. vi. 15; Apoc. i. 5; xvii. 14); all things have been subjected to him (Isaias ix. 6; Matt. xxviii. 18; Luke x. 22; John iii. 35; xvii. 2; Eph. i. 22). He is the Redeemer promised to Adam (Gen. iii. 15); to Abraham (Gen. xii. 3; xvii. 19; xxii. 18); to Isaac (xxvi. 4); to Jacob (xxviii. 14); to Juda (xlix. 10); foretold by Balaam (Num. xxiv. 17); by Moses (Deut. xviii. 18); by Anna (1 Kings ii. 10; by Nathan (2 Kings vii. 13); by David (Ps. ii., xxi., cix.); by Isaias (vii. 14; ix. 6; xi. 1; xxviii. 16; xl. 9; xlii. 1; xlv. 8; xlvi. 13; xlix. 1; lii. 10; liii.; lix. 20; ix. 1; lxii. 11; Jerem. xxiii. 5; xxx. 9; xxxi. 22;

xxxiii. 15; Bar. iii. 38; Ezech. xxxiv. 23; xxxvii. 24; Dan. ii. 44; vii. 13; ix. 25; Osee iii. 5; Joel ii. 23; Amos ix. 11; Abdias i. 21; Jonas ii. 1; Micheas v. 2; Nahum i. 15; Habacuc iii. 13; Sophonias iii. 15; Aggeus ii. 8; Zacharias ii. 10; iii. 8; vi. 12; Malachias iii. 1). He was foretold not only in general, but in detail. He was to be born of a virgin (Isaias vii. 14); of the house of David (Isaias xi. 1); in Bethlehem (Mich. v. 2); his passion prefigured in Isaac (Gen. xxii. 2); foretold (Ps. xxi.; Isai. liii.; Dan. ix. 26); his resurrection foretold (Ps. xv. 10); prefigured (Jonas ii. 1); his ascension foretold (Ps. xlvi. 6; lxvii. 19); he was announced by an angel (Luke i. 31); born at Bethlehem (Matt. ii. 1; John vii. 42; Mich. v. 2); of the Virgin Mary (Matt. i. 23; Luke ii. 7); announced by angels to the shepherds (Luke ii. 9); circumcised (Luke ii. 21); presented in the temple and recognized as the Messias by Simeon (Luke ii. 30); St. John bears testimony to him (Matt. iii. 11; John i. 29); baptizes him (Luke iii. 21); God the Father acknowledges him (Luke iii. 22; Matt. xvii. 5); he confirms his mission and doctrine by miracles (Matt. iv. 23; viii. 16; Acts x. 38); (see Miracles); he humbled himself to the form of a servant (Phil. ii. 7); bears the sins of all (Isaias liii. 4; 2 Cor. v. 21; Heb. iv. 15; vii. 27; 1 John iii. 5); suffered for us (Matt. xvi. 21; xvii. 12; xx. 18; xxvi. 37; xxvii.; Mark viii. 31; ix. 30; xv.; Luke xvii. 25; xviii. 31; xxiii.; John xviii.– xix.; Acts iii. 18; viii. 32; xvii. 3; Rom. viii. 32; Heb. ix. 28; xiii. 12; 1 Pet. ii. 21; iv. 1); he is betrayed by Judas (Matt. xxvi. 14; Mark xiv. 10; Luke xxii. 3; John xiii. 2); condemned by Caiphas (Matt. xxvi. 65, 66; Mark xiv. 64; Luke xxii. 71); by Pilate (Matt. xxvii. 26; Mark xv. 15; Luke xxiii. 24; John xix. 16); crucified and buried (Matt. xxvii. 35–49; Mark xv. 24–37; Luke xxiii. 32–46; John xix. 18–30; Acts ii. 23; iv. 10; xiii. 29; Rom. v. 6; vi. 10; viii. 34; xiv. 9; 1 Cor. ii. 2; xv. 3; 2 Cor. v. 15; xiii. 4; 1 Thess. v. 10); rose on the third day (Matt. xxviii. 6; Mark xvi. 6; Luke xxiv. 5; John xx. 9; Acts ii. 24; x. 40; xiii. 30; xvii. 31; Rom. iv. 25; viii. 34; xiv. 9; 1 Cor. xv. 4; 2 Tim. ii. 8); ascended into heaven (Mark xvi. 19; Luke xxii. 69; Acts i. 9; Rom. viii. 34; Eph. i. 20; Col. iii. 1; Heb. i. 13; x. 12; xii. 2; 1 Pet. iii. 22); he will come again to judge the living and the dead (Matt. xvi. 27; xxiv. 30; xxv. 31; Luke xvii. 24; xxi. 27; John v. 22; Acts i. 11; x. 42; Rom. ii. 16; 2 Cor. v. 10; 2 Tim. iv. 8; 1 Pet. iv. 5; Heb. ix. 28; Jude 1, 14; Apoc. i. 7; xxii. 12); he is the true light of the world (Isai. ii. 5; ix. 2;

xlix. 6; lx. 1; Matt. iv. 16; Luke ii. 32; John i. 4; iii. 19; viii. 12; ix. 5; xii. 35; 1 John ii. 8).

CHRYS'OLITE, a precious stone, the tenth in the rational (Exod. xxviii. 20; xxxix. 13; Apoc. xxi. 20; Ezech. x. 9; Dan. x. 6).

CHRYS'OPRASE, a precious stone of greenish color (Apoc. xxi. 20).

CHUB, a land near Egypt (Ezec. xxx. 5).

CHALDEAN SCULPTURE. (Layard ii. 348.)

CHURCH, called the kingdom of heaven (Matt. iii. 2; iv. 17; v. 3, 10, 19, 20; x. 7; xiii.; xvi. 19); kingdom of God (Mark i. 15; iv. 11; x. 14; Luke vi. 20; vii. 10; ix.; xi. 20; xxi. 31; xvii. 21; Acts xix. 8); of the Son of man (Matt. xvi. 28); of Christ and of God (Eph. v. 5); the church is a mystical body (1 Cor. xii. 12, 27; Eph i. 22; iii. 6; iv. 15; v. 23; Col. i.; ii.); the spouse of Christ (1 Cor. xi. 3; 2 Eph. v. 23; Gal. iv. 26; Apoc. xix. 7; xxi. 9); purchased by his blood (Acts xx. 28; 1 Cor. vii. 23; Eph. ii. 13; Col. i. 14; 1 John i. 7; Apoc. i. 5); built on a rock (Matt. xvi. 18); Christ the foundation and corner-stone (Ps. cxvii. 22; Isaias xxviii. 16; Matt. xxi. 42; Acts iv. 11; Rom. ix. 33; 1 Cor. iii. 11; Eph. ii. 20; 1 Pet. ii. 6;) the apostles are under him the foundation (Eph. ii. 20; Apoc. xxi.

CHRIST BEARING HIS CROSS.

14); especially St. Peter (Matt. xvi. 18); it is the house of God, the pillar and ground of truth (1 Tim. iii. 15); the gates of hell shall not prevail against it (Matt. xvi. 18); Christ will always be with it (Matt. xxviii. 20); the Holy Ghost will abide with it forever (John xiv. 26); God protects it (Ex. xiii. 21;

xxix. 45; Lev. xxvi. 12; Deut. vii. 21; xxiii. 14; xxvi. 3; 3 Kings vi. 13; Ps. xc. 1; cxxxi. 13; Isai. xli. 10; Jerem. xlvi. 28; Matt. xxviii. 20; Luke xxi. 15; John xiv. 23; 2 Cor. vi. 16). The church as the assembly of pastors (Matt. xvi. 19; xviii. 17; John xx. 23); the church as the assembly of the faithful (Num. xix. 20; xx. 4; Ps. xxi. 26; xxv. 12; xxxiv. 18; cvi. 32; cxlix. 1; Matt. xvi. 18; Acts v. 11; viii. 1; xvi. 5; Rom. xvi. 16, 23; 1 Cor. vi. 4; xi. 16; xii. 28; xiv. 5; 2 Cor. viii. 18, 23; xi. 8; xii. 13; Eph. v. 23; Philip. iv. 15; 1 Tim. iii. 5; James v. 14; Apoc. i. 11; xxii. 16).

CHURCH'ES of Asia designated by seven candlesticks shown to St. John (Apoc. i. 20); what is written to them (ii., iii.)

CHUS, son of Cham and father of Nemrod (Gen. x. 4–8; 1 Paral. i. 8–10).

CHU'SA, Herod's steward, whose wife Joanna ministered to our Lord (Luke viii. 3).

CHU-SA'I of Arach, a friend of David (2 Kings xv. 32).

CHU'-SAN RA-SATH'-AIM, king of Syria, overthrown by Othoniel (Judges iii. 10).

CIN'-ITES, nation dwelling west of the Dead Sea (Judges i. 16; 1 Paral. ii. 55; Num. xxiv. 21); in the time of Saul they were mingled with the Amalecites (1 Kings xv. 6); they were made captives by the Assyrians (Num. xxiv. 22).

CIN'NAMON, a spice used in the holy oil of unction (Ex. xxx. 23); mentioned Cant. iv. 14.

CIRCUMCIS'ION, a rite ordained by God as a sign of his covenant with Abraham (Gen. xvii. 10; Acts vii. 8); every male child was to be circumcised on the eighth day on pain of death (Lev. xii. 3; John vii. 22, 23); slaves also were circumcised (Gen. xvii. 12, 13; Ex. xii. 44); Moses neglecting to circumcise his son was menaced with death (Ex. iv. 24); Achior is circumcised after the defeat of Holofernes (Judith xiv. 6); Antiochus forbids it (1 Mach. i. 51); women put to death for performing it (64; 2 Mach. vi. 10); it was performed with stone knives (Ex. iv. 25; Jos. v. 2); St. John Baptist circumcised (Luke i. 59); it was a symbol of mortification of the heart (Deut. x. 16; xxx. 6); Jer. iv. 4; vi. 10; ix. 26; Rom. ii. 25–29; iii. 1; iv. 9; 1 Cor. vii. 18, 19; Eph. ii. 11); some Jews endeavored to undo it (1 Mach. i. 16);

our Lord submitted to be circumcised (Luke ii. 22), and the shedding of his blood is commemorated in a feast of the church; not necessary under the new law (Acts xv. 1–19; Gal. ii. 3; v. 2, 3; vi. 12; Phil. iii. 2, 3; Coloss. ii. 11); though St. Paul circumcised Timothy (xvi. 3).

CIRC'UMSPECTION recommended to Christians (Ephes. v. 15–21).

CIS, father of Saul (1 Kings ix. 1; Acts xiii. 21).

CIS'TERNS, for holding water (Gen. xxxvii. 20, 22, 24, 28, 29; Ex. xxi. 33); (in Challoner, *pit*), (Levit. xi. 36; Deut. vi. 11); a great one in Socho (1 Kings xix. 22); cistern of Sira (2 Kings iii. 26); of Bethlehem (xxiii. 15, 16, etc.); Jeremias compares false doctrines to broken cisterns that can hold no water (ii. 13).

CIT'IES, first built by Cain (Gen. iv. 17); Nemrod rules over many (x. 10; xi. 4, 8); cities first governed by kings (xiv. 1); four cities destroyed by fire from heaven (xix. 24); cities of refuge to which involuntary manslayers might fly, Sichem (1 Paral. vi. 67; Jos. xx. 7); Hebron (Jos. xx. 7; xxi. 13); Bosor, Ramoth, and Gaulon or Golan (Deut. iv. 43; Jos. xx. 8); Cedes (Jos. xx. 7); sacerdotal and Levitical cities (Jos. xxi. 2); cities cursed and given up to the Israelites to be destroyed (Deut. xx. 17); cities which refused passage to them (ii. 30); some preserved from destruction (ii. 19); cities divided by lot among the tribes (Jos. xiii.–xxii.)

CITTERNS, musical instruments (3 Kings x. 12).

CLAUD'IUS, Roman emperor, banishes the Jews from Rome (Acts xviii. 2); famine in his reign (xi. 28).

CLAUD'IUS LYSIAS, tribune at Jerusalem (Acts xxi. 31); rescues St. Paul (33); orders him to be scourged (xxii. 24); releases him on discovering him to be a Roman citizen (29); sends him to Felix at Cæsarea with a letter (xxiii. 23–30).

CLAU'DIA, a convert of St. Paul at Rome (2 Tim. iv. 21).

CLEAN of heart, blessed (Matt. v. 8).

CLEAN and unclean animals (Lev. xi. 2–31; Deut. xiv. 3–21; Acts x. 12); obligation not continued in the new law (Acts xv. 20).

CLEAN'NESS recommended (Matt. xxiii. 25; Luke xi. 39; 2 Cor. vii. 1).

CLEM'ENT, his name written in the Book of Life (Phil. iv. 3); generally regarded as the third successor of St. Peter.

CLEOPA'TRA, wife of Ptolomee Philometor (Esther xi. 1); (2) her daughter married Alexander Bales, king of Syria (1 Mach. x. 57, 58).

CLE'O-PHAS, or Alphæus, father of James, Simon and Jude, the apostles (Matt. x. 3; Mark iii. 18; Luke vi. 15; Acts i. 13); his wife was one of the holy women at the crucifixion (John ix. 25); our Lord appeared to him and another disciple on the way to Emmaus, the day of his resurrection (Luke xxiv. 18).

CLOUD. A pillar of cloud preceded the children of Israel in the desert (Ex. xiii. 21; xiv. 19; xl. 34; Num. ix. 17); it was a type of baptism, according to St. Paul (1 Cor. x. 2). Solomon's temple filled with a cloud, so that the priests could not stand (2 Par. v. 13, 14).

CO'A. Solomon imported horses from it (3 Kings x. 28; 2 Paral. i. 16).

COAT. Joseph's coat of divers colors (Gen. xxxvii. 3); his brethren dip it in blood and send it to Jacob (31, 32); if a man take away thy coat, let thy cloak go also (Matt. v. 40); the seamless coat of our Lord (John xix. 23).

COCK. A cock girded about the loins, cited as a thing that goes well (Prov. xxx. 31); Isaias foretells to Sobna that he shall be carried away as a cock is carried away (Isai. xxii. 17); Peter to deny his Lord before the cock crow (Matt. xxvi. 34; Mark xiv. 30); its crowing (xiii. 35).

COCKLE, a weed (Matt. xiii. 25).

COIN, of the tribute (Matt. xxii. 19).

ST. BERNARD WRITING COMMENTARIES ON THE HOLY SCRIPTURES.

COCY'TUS, a river, mentioned, Job xxi. 33.

COLOSSE', a city in Phrygia. St. Paul, while a prisoner in Rome, wrote an epistle to the church there (Col. i. 2).

COLOSS'IANS, St. Paul's epistle to the, one of the canonical books of the New Testament (Colos.)

COM'BAT between two bands of twelve, who are all slain (2 Kings ii. 16).

COMMAND'MENTS of God, twice written on stone on Mount Sinai (Ex. xx., xxxi. 18; xxxiv. 28); the first tables broken by Moses on witnessing the idolatry of the people (xxxii. 19); the second tables placed in the ark (xl. 18). The ten commandments (Exod. xx. 1–17; Deut. v. 6–21); to be loved (Ps. cxviii. 40, 127, 131, 159); to be kept if we wish to be saved (Matt. xix. 17); all the commandments reduced to two (Matt. xxii. 40).

COMMENTA'TORS. As the church treasured and preserved the Bible, most of the early fathers wrote in explanation of the Scriptures. St. Pantænus, a Sicilian, at Alexandria, was the first who devoted himself entirely to it. St. Clement, of Alexandria, a pupil of Pantænus (A. D. 190), wrote eight books of commentaries. Among his successors were Origen, St. Hilary, St. Ambrose, St. Jerome, St. Augustine, St. John Chrysostom, St. Cyril, of Alexandria, Theodoret, St. Isidore, Cassiodorus, and St. Gregory the Great, who all flourished before the close of the sixth century. Among later commentators of much of the Bible are St. Bede, Walafrid Strabo, Theophylact, St. Thomas Aquinas, St. Bernard, Hugo de Sancto Caro, Nicolas de Lyra, Maldonatus, Cornelius a Lapide, Menochius, Picquigny, and Calmet.

CON'CUBINE, used in the sense of inferior wife (2 Kings iii. 7; xx. 3; 3 Kings xi. 3; 2 Paral. xi. 21).

CONCU'PISCENCE forbidden and punished (Ex. xx. 17; Num. xi. 33; xxi. 5; Jos. vii.; Ecclus. xviii. 30; xix. 1; xlii. 11; Job xxxi. 1; Prov. vi. 25; Matt. v. 28; Mark iv. 19; Gal. v. 16; Col. iii. 5; 1 Thess. iv. 3; 1 Tim. v. 11; 2 Tim. ii. 22; 1 Cor. x. 6; 2 Pet. i. 4; 1 John ii. 16; James i. 14; iv. 1).

CONFESS'ION of sins (Gen. xli. 9; Lev. xvi.

21; xxvi. 40; Num. v. 7; Jos. vii. 19; 2 Kings xxiv. 17; 1 Esd. ix. 6; 2 Esd. ix. 2; Ps. xxxi. 5; xxxvii. 19; Prov. xvi. 3; xviii. 17; xxviii. 13; Ecclus. iv. 25, 31; v. 4; xxii. 27; Dan. ix. 5; Matt. iii. 6; xvi. 19; Luke xi. 4; xviii. 13; James v. 16; 1 John i. 8).

CON'FIRMATION, a sacrament, received by the Apostles at Pentecost (Acts ii.); conferred by them (viii. 17; Heb. vi. 2; Ephes. iv. 30). Its effects (1 Cor. xii., xiii.; Rom. xii. 6, 7; Eph. iv. 7).

CONFU'SION of tongues at Babel (Gen. xi. 9).

CON'SCIENCE, a good (Prov. xv. 15; Ecclus. xiii. 30; 2 Cor. i. 12; 1 John iii. 21); a guilty conscience (Wis. xvii. 10).

CO'OS, a port reached by St. Paul on his way to Jerusalem (Acts xxi. 1).

CONSUL'TING the Lord and his ministers (Gen. xxiv. 12; Ex. xi. 34; Lev. xxiv. 12; Num. ix. 8; xv. 34; xxvii. 4; Deut. v.; xvii. 8; Jos. ix. 14; Judg. i. 1; xviii. 5; xx. 18; xxi. 2; 1 Kings x. 22; xxiii. 4; xxx. 8; 2 Kings ii. 1; v. 19; xxi. 1; 3 Kings xiv. 2; xxii. 5; 4 Kings iii. 11; viii. 8; xxii. 13; 2 Paral. xviii. 4; xxxiii. 18; Ps. cxviii. 133; Isai. viii. 11; xxx.1; xlv. 11; Jerem. xxxvii. 16; xlii. 2; Ezech. xiv. 1; Zach. vii. 2; Job xii. 13; Ecclus. xxviii. 19; Luke xvi. 29).

CONTRADICT'ION, water of (Num. xx. 7).

CONTRIT'ION for sin, its necessity (Jer. vii. 3; Matt. iii. 2; iv. 17; Luke xiii. 3; xxiv. 47; Acts ii. 38; iii. 19; xxii. 17; xxvi. 20; xxvi. 20; pardon promised to true contrition (Deut. iv. 29; xxx. 2; 1 Kings vii. 3; 2 Paral. vii. 14; xxx. 6; xxxiv. 27; Job xiii. 23; Prov. xxviii. 13; Ecclus. xvii. 23; Isai. i. 16; xxx. 18; lv. 7; lix. 20; Jer. iii. 17; xviii. 8; xxix. 12; xxxi. 18; Ezech.

xviii. 21; Jon. iii. 9; Zach. i. 3; Acts iii. 19; xxvi. 18, 20).

CONVER'SION, of three thousand at Pentecost (Acts ii. 41); of five thousand (iv. 4); of the centurions after the crucifixion (Mark xv. 39; Luke xxiii. 47); of the thief crucified with our Lord (42); of Saul (Acts ix. 6); of king Manasses (2 Paral. xxxiii. 12).

CORBO'NA, Corban, gifts offered in the temple (Matt. xxvii. 6; Mark vii. 11).

CORE, a Hebrew measure equal to 75 gallons (Ezech. xlv. 14).

CORE, a Levite, revolts against the authority of Aaron: his punishment (Num. xvi.; xxvi. 10; Ps. cv. 18; Ecclus. xlv. 22).

CORIAN'DER, an aromatic seed, the manna resembled it (Exod. xvi. 31; Num. xi. 7).

COR'INTH, a city in Greece; visited by St. Paul, A. D. 52 (Acts xviii.); he lodged with Aquila and Priscilla, and preached to the Jews, but finding them obdurate, addressed the Gentiles. He remained here eighteen months, wrote two Epistles to the Thessalonians (Acts xviii. 18). After leaving them, he wrote two Epistles to them (1 Cor., 2 Cor.)

CORINTH'IANS, Epistles of St. Paul to the, canonical books of the New Testament.

COR'MORANT, a predatory bird (Lev. xi. 17; Deut. xiv. 17).

CORNE'LIUS, centurion of the Italian band stationed at Cæsarea, converted by a vision (Acts x. 1–3); instructed and baptized by St. Peter (34–48).

COR'NET, a musical instrument (1 Kings xviii. 6).

COR'NU STIB'II, a Latin translation of Kerenhappuch, the name of Job's third daughter (Job xlii. 14). It means Horn of Kohl, or stibic stone.

CORPSE, legal uncleanness incurred by touching (Num. xix. 16).

CORRECT'ION, fraternal, shown by example and precept (Gen. xxxvii. 21; Prov. ix. 8; x. 17; xii. 1; xiii. 1; xv. 31; xvii. 10; xxiv. 25; xxv. 12; xxvii. 5; xxviii. 23; Eccles. vii. 6; Ecclus. xx. 1; xxi. 7; Osee iv. 4; Matt. xviii. 15; Gal. ii. 11; 1 Tim. v. 20; 2 Tim. ii. 25; Heb. iii. 13; James v.

THE DISPUTE OF ST. THOMAS AQUINAS, ONE OF THE COMMENTATORS. (After Raphael.)

19); how it should be done (Matt. vii. 3; John viii. 7; Titus ii.)

COROZA'IM, a city in Galilee, on the west shore of the Lake of Tiberias. Jesus Christ wrought many miracles there, but reproaches it with incredulity (Matt. xi. 21; Luke x. 13).

CORRUP'TION. The body of Christ did not

CITY OF REFUGE.

undergo (Ps. xv. 10; Jon. ii. 7; Acts ii. 27, 31; xiii. 35, 37).

COUN'CIL OF JERUSALEM, held by the apostles to decide whether Gentile converts were required to observe the Mosaic law (Acts xv.)

COUN'CIL, Jewish court or Sanhedrim (Matt. v. 22; x. 17; Mark xiii. 9).

COUN'CIL of a Roman governor (Acts xxv. 12).

COUN'SEL of Tobias to his son (Tob. iv.); of the mother of the Machabees to her youngest son (2 Mach. vii. 27).

COURT, an open enclosure (Exod. xxvii. 9; xl. 31; Lev. vi. 16; 3 Kings vi. 36; vii. 12; 4 Kings xxiii. 12; 2 Paral. xxxiii. 5; Matt. xxvi. 58).

THE CREATION.

COV'ENANT of God with Noe (Gen. vi. 18; ix. 9); with Abraham (Gen. xv. 7; xvii. 2); with Isaac (Gen. xvii. 19; xxvi. 3); with Jacob (xxviii. 13); with the children of Israel (Ex. vi. 4; xix. 5; xxxiv. 27; Lev. xxvi. 1–42; Deut. v. 2; ix. 9; xxvi. 15).

COV'ETING forbidden (Ex. xx. 17; Deut. v. 21).

COV'ETOUSNESS. See AVARICE.

COW, sacrifice of a red cow for sin (Num. xix.; Heb. ix. 13).

COZ'BI, daughter of Sur, prince of the Madianites, killed with Zambri by Eleazar the priest (Num. xxv. 6–15).

CREA'TION of heaven and earth by God (Gen. i. 1; of man (26); of woman (ii. 21).

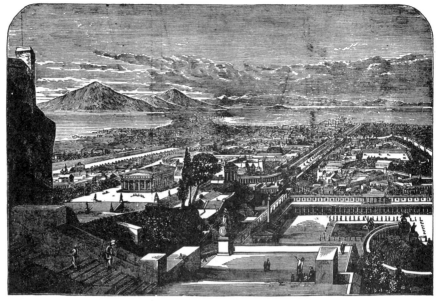

CORINTH.

CRES'CENS, a disciple of St. Paul, who mentions his going to Galatia (2 Tim. iv. 10).

CRETE, an island in the Mediterranean now called Candia (1 Mach. x. 67); St. Paul touched it off Gnidus (Acts xxvii. 7); and ran along to Phenice (12). St. Paul apparently preached there subsequently, and sent Titus as bishop to the island (Titus i. 5).

CRETES, Cretans, inhabitants of Crete (Acts ii. 11); their bad character (Titus i. 12).

CROSS. Our Lord bids his disciples to take up the cross and follow him (Matt. x. 8; xvi. 24; Mark viii. 34; Luke ix. 23; xiv. 27); he foretells his own death on the cross (John xii. 33; Mark viii. 31, 34); he carries his cross to Calvary (Luke xxiii. 26; John xix. 17; Mark xv. 21); the title affixed to the cross (Matt. xxvii. 37; Mark xv. 26; Luke xxiii. 38; John xix. 19); he dies on the cross (Matt. xxvii. 50; Mark xv. 37; Luke xxiii. 46; John xix. 30).

CROSS'ES and tribulations, the lot of all who wish to live piously (Ps. xxxiii. 20; Ecclus. ii. 1; Matt. xvi. 24; 1 Thess. iii. 3; 2 Tim. iii. 12); the folly of the cross (1 Cor. i. 18); crosses sent to us by God for our good (2 Cor. xi. 30; 1 Pet. iv. 17); crosses lead us to know God (Luke xxiv. 26, 46; John xii. 25; Acts xiv. 21; Rom. viii. 17; 2 Cor. iv. 8; v. 1; Phil. ii. 8; 2 Thess.

i. 5; Heb. xii. 2); they are to be borne patiently and joyfully (Matt. v. 12; x. 26; James i. 2).

CROWN. There was a golden crown surmounting the Ark of the Covenant (Ex. xxv. 11); the high priest wore a crown of gold on his mitre, inscribed

"Holiness" (Ecclus. xlv. 14; Wis. xviii. 24; Zach. vi. 11); David captured and wore a gold crown set with precious stones, weighing a talent, from Melchom, king of Ammon (2 Kings xii. 30; 1 Paral. xx. 2); Mardochai rides out wearing the crown of Assuerus (Esth. vi. 8; viii. 15); Ptolemee wore two

THE COUNCIL OR SANHEDRIM IN SESSION.

crowns (1 Mach. xi. 13); Alexander Bales sent a gold crown to Jonathan (1 Mach. x. 20); Alcimus gives a gold crown to Demetrius (2 Mach. xiv. 4); idols were crowned (Baruch vi. 9); crowns of gold were placed on the front of the temple at its dedication (1 Mach. iv. 57); the ancients cast their crowns before the throne of God (Apoc. iv. 10).

CROWN of thorns placed on the head of our Lord (John xix. 5).

CRU′CIFIXION, a punishment in Egypt (Gen. xl. 19); Saul's descendants suffer it (2 Kings xxi. 6–13); it was abolished by Constantine.

CRU′CIFIXION of our Lord, preceded by scourging (Matt. xx. 19; Mark xv. 15); he bore his own cross (Mark xv 21   Luke xxiii. 26; John xix.

SACRIFICE OF A RED COW FOR SIN.

17); was stripped of his garments on which the soldiers cast lots (Matt. xxvii. 35); nailed to the cross and set up between two thieves (Isai. liii. 12); watched by a centurion and a band of soldiers (Matt. xxvii. 54; Mark xv. 45; Luke xxiii. 47; John xix. 23); he dies on the cross (Matt. xxvii. 50; Mark xv. 37; Luke xxiii. 46; John xix. 30); his legs were not broken (33); but his side was opened with a spear

ANCIENT CROWNS.

(34); the apostles preached Christ crucified (Acts ii. 36; iv. 10; 1 Cor. i. 23; ii. 2); sinners crucify the Son of God again (Heb. vi. 6); Jerusalem called Sodom and Egypt, because our Lord was crucified there (Apoc. xi. 8).

CRYS′TAL (Job xxviii. 17; Ezech. i. 22; Apoc. iv. 6; xxi. 11).

CU′BIT, a measure, about nineteen or twenty inches (Gen. vi. 15; Deut. iii. 11, etc.)

CU′CUMBERS, a vegetable for which the Israelites in the desert longed (Num. xi. 5).

CUM′MIN, a plant like fennel (Isai. xxviii. 25, 27; Matt. xxiii. 23).

CUP. Pharao's cup (Gen. xl. 11); Joseph's found in Benjamin's sack (Gen. xliv. 5); David takes away Saul's cup (1 Kings xxvi. 12); Babylon compared to a golden cup (Jerem. li. 7); golden cup of abominations (Apoc. xvii. 4).

CUPBEARER, an officer of rank in Eastern courts (Gen. xl. 11; 3 Kings x. 5); Nehemiah was cupbearer to Artaxerxes (2 Esd. i. 11; ii. 1).

ANCIENT CUPS.

CUP of God's wrath poured out on guilty nations (Is. li. 17, 21; Jerem. xxv. 15, 27; Ezech. xxiii. 31–34; Apoc. xiv. 10–19).

CUTH′ITES, people of Cutha sent by the king of Assyria to Samaria (4 Kings xvii. 30).

CUT′TING or tattooing the flesh forbidden (Lev. xix. 28); it was done in mourning (xxi. 5; Deut. xiv. 1); in heathen worship (3 Kings xviii. 28).

CYM′BALS, musical instruments struck together (2 Kings vi. 5; 1 Paral. xiii. 8; xv.; xvi.; xxv.; 2 Paral. v.; Ps. cl. 5; 1 Cor. xiii. 1). Egypt is called the land of the flying cymbal (Isai. xviii. 1); alluding to the winged disk so frequent on Egyptian buildings.

CY′PRESS, a tree (Ecclus. xxiv. 17; l. 11; Cant. i. 16).

CY′PRUS, an herb (Cant. i. 13; iv. 13).

CY′PRUS, an island in the Mediterranean. Jews resided there in the days of the Machabees (1 Mac. xv. 23); native place of Barnabas (Acts iv. 36); the gospel preached in (Acts xi. 19); St. Paul visits it A. D. 42 (Acts xiii. 4–13; xv. 39; xxi. 3; xxvii. 4).

CYRE′NE, a city in Africa (Acts ii. 10); a place in Assyria (4 Kings xvi. 9).

CYRENIAN, a native of Cyrene. Simon bore the cross of our Lord (Matt. xxvii. 32; Mark xv. 21; Luke xxiii. 26); they had a synagogue at Jerusalem (Acts vi. 9); heard the apostles on Pentecost (ii. 10); helped to form the church at Antioch (xi. 20); Lucius, of Cyrene, one of the prophets and doctors there (xiii. 1); is venerated as the first bishop of Cyrene.

CYRI′NUS (Publius Sulpitius Quirinus) takes the census in Judea (Luke ii. 2).

CY′RUS, founder of the Persian monarchy, was announced by Isaias (xliv. 28; xlv. 1); he permits the Jews to return to Judea (2 Paral. xxxvi. 22; 1 Esd. i. 3; Dan. vi. 28; x. 1); he restores the sacred vessels of the temple (v. 7, 14).

DA′GON, the national god of the Philistines, represented as part man and part fish. His principal temples were at Gaza (Judges xvi. 21, 30); and Azotus (1 Kings v. 5, 6; 1 Paral. x. 10); the idol in the latter was overthrown when the Ark of the Covenant was placed in the temple (1 Kings v. 5); this temple was destroyed by Jonathan (1 Mach. x. 83; xi. 4).

DALAI′AS, counsellor of Joakim, tries to prevent the king from burning the prophecies of Jeremias (Jerem. xxxvi. 12, 25).

DAL′ETH, fourth letter of the Hebrew alphabet (Jerem. i. 4).

DALI′LA, a woman of the valley of Sorec, whom Samson loved, but who betrayed him to the Philistines (Judges xvi. 4–20).

DALMANU'THA, a place on the Sea of Galilee (Mark viii. 10).

DALMA'TIA, a province on the eastern shore of the Adriatic. St. Paul preached near it (Rom. xv. 19); and sent Titus there (2 Tim. iv. 10).

DAM'ARIS, an Athenian woman converted by St. Paul (Acts xvii. 34). St. Chrysostom records the tradition that she was the wife of Dionysius, the Areopagite.

DAMAS'CUS, one of the most ancient cities of Syria, watered by the Abana and Pharphar (Gen. xiv. 15; xv. 2); conquered by David (2 Kings viii. 5; 1 Paral. xviii. 5); in Solomon's time, Razon made himself king (3 Kings xi. 23, 24); it appears frequently in the wars of Israel and Juda (3 Kings xv. 18; 2 Paral. xvi. 2; 3 Kings xv. 20; 3 Kings xx. 26; 4 Kings vi. 24; vii. 6, 7; 4 Kings viii. 28; xiv. 28; xv. 37). Theglathphalasar slew Rasin, and laid Damascus waste, 742 B.C. (4 Kings xvi. 9; Isai. vii. 8; viii. 4; xvii.; Jerem. xlix. 23; Amos i. 5). In the time of the apostles, it was subject to king Aretas (2 Cor. xi. 32); Saul was proceeding to it to persecute the Christians, when he was arrested by our Lord. He was led blind to the Straight street in Damascus to the House of Judas, where Ananias cured and baptized him. The Jews sought his life for preaching Christ and he escaped from the wall in a basket (Acts ix. 1–25).

DAMNA'TION, eternal, prepared for the devil and the reprobate (Wis. v.; Job x. 22; Isai. xxiv. 22; xxx. 33; Dan. vii. 11; Matt. iii. 12; v. 29; xiii. 50; xxii. 13; Luke iii. 17; xvi. 23; Heb. x. 27; 2 Pet. ii. 4; Apoc. xix. 20; xx. 10; xxi. 8).

DAN, fifth son of Jacob (by Bala, Rachel's handmaid), (Gen. xxx. 6); he had but one son, Husim (xlvi. 23); Jacob's prophecies as to (Gen. xlix. 16.)

DAN, one of the twelve tribes. On leaving Egypt it numbered 62,700 fighting men, under their prince Ahiezer (Num. i. 12, 38, 39); they were on the north side (ii. 25); their offerings for the tabernacle (Num. vii. 66–71); they sent Ammiel to view the promised land (xiii. 13); Bocci was appointed from Dan to divide the land (xxxiv. 22); at Settim they numbered 64,400 (xxvi. 43); they stood on Hebal to curse (Deut. xxvii. 13); Moses' prophecy on (Deut. xxxiii. 22); their portion (Jos. xix. 40, 46, 47; Judg. xviii.); they capture the city of Lais and call it Dan (Judg. xviii. 28, 29); Samson was of Dan (Judges xiii.–xvi.); their territory was one extremity of the land, so that "from Dan to Bersebee" was used to express the whole country (Judg. xx. 1;

THE CRUCIFIXION. (After the painting by Van Dyke.)

2 Kings xxiv. 2, 15; 1 Paral. xxi. 2; 2 Paral. xxx. 5); Jeroboam set up a golden calf in Dan (3 Kings xii. 29); the city Dan taken by Benadad (xv. 20; 2 Paral. xvi. 4). The tribe disappears in Bible records; there is no genealogy in 1 Paral. ii.–viii.; and in the Apocalypse none of the tribe are mentioned among the elect (Apoc. vii. 4–8).

DANCE, used in religious ceremonies, after the passage of the Red Sea (Ex. xv. 20); after David's victory over Goliath (1 Kings xviii. 6); on Solomon's accession (3 Kings i. 40); on the evil effects of dancing see Ex. xxxii. 6; Judg. xi. 34; xvi. 21; Matt. xiv. 6.

DAN'IEL, a prophet who flourished at Babylon during the captivity, and author of one of the canonical books. He was carried away captive in the fourth year of Joakim, king of Juda, 606 B.C., and was one of the young nobles brought up at the court of Nabuchodonosor (Dan. i. 2, etc.); while a youth he, by his wisdom, delivered the chaste Susanna, falsely accused (Dan. xiii.;) he explained the vision of Nabuchodonosor of a statue of various metals, representing the great monarchies (ii. 1–48); he explained another vision of a tree cut down, foretelling the seven years' madness of the king (iv. 1–34; in the reign of Balthasar he had a vision of four animals coming out of the sea, representing the empires of the Chaldees, Persians, Greeks and Romans (Dan. vii.); also the persecution of the Jews under Antiochus (21, 25); the overthrow of the Persians by Alexander (viii.); when Balthasar profaned the sacred vessels of the temple, Daniel read the words written on the wall by the mysterious hand, and announced the death of the king and the fall of the monarchy that very night (Dan. v. 1–3; ix.); Darius the Mede made Daniel ruler of one of the provinces (vi. 1); he was again cast to the lions on the accusation of his enemies, and miraculously preserved (vi. 16–24); he foretold the coming and death of the Messias in seventy weeks (ix. 21–27); the angel Gabriel revealed to him the reign of Alexander, the division of his empire, the persecutions of Antiochus (x.; xi.) under Cyrus; he unmasked the priests of Bel, and destroyed the temple (xiv.), and a dragon worshipped by the people, for which he was again cast to the lions (xiv. 30, 31); but refreshed by Habacuc and delivered (32–41); his wisdom was proverbial (Ezech. xxviii. 3; xiv. 14, 20); his prophecies have come down to us partly in Hebrew, partly in Chaldee, and partly in Greek; the last portion is rejected by the modern Jews, who refuse to accept the New Testament and all other Greek Scriptures, and by

Protestants. Daniel died apparently during the captivity.

DAPH'CA, the ninth camp of the children of Israel in the desert (Num. xxxiii. 12).

TOMB OF CYRUS.

DAPH'NE, a place near Antioch where the high-priest Onias took refuge (2 Mach. iv. 33).

DAPH'NIS, a fountain (Num. xxxiv. 11).

DARI'US, the Mede, or Astyages (Dan. xiii. 65), uncle of Cyrus the Great, was the son of Assuerus (Dan. ix. 1); he overthrew his grandnephew Balthasar and began his reign at Babylon at the age of sixty-two, 538 B.C. (Dan. v. 31); he made Daniel governor of a province, and by an edict recognized the God of Daniel as "the living and eternal God" (vi. 2, 26).

DAGON, THE FISH GOD.

DARI'US (son of Hystaspes), renewed the order of Cyrus for the rebuilding of the temple (1 Esd. vi. 1).

DARI'US, the Persian (2 Esd. xii. 22), is supposed to be Dari'us Nothus, 425-404 B.C., or more probably Dari'us Codomanus, overthrown by Alexander (1 Mach. i. 1).

DARK CLOUD, God appears at Sinai in a (Ex. xx. 21).

DARK'NESS. Egypt struck with darkness for refusing to let the Israelites go (Ex. x. 21, 22); darkness over the whole earth at the crucifixion of our Lord (Matt. xxvii. 45); darkness is used for death (Job x. 21, 22); and for sin (John i. 5; iii. 19).

DA'THAN, son of Eliab of the tribe of Ruben, rebels with Core against Moses and Aaron, and is swallowed up by the earth (Num. xvi. 1-33; xxvi. 10; Deut. xi. 6; Ps. cv. 17; Ecclus. xlv. 22).

DATH'EMAN, a fortress besieged by Timotheus (1 Mach. v. 9).

DAUGH'TERS inherited in default of sons (Num. xxxvi. 6). The term daughter is used for any female descendant (Gen. xxiv. 3, 13; xxxi. 43); for women of a place or country (Gen. vi. 2; Num. xxv. 1; Deut. xxiii. 17; Luke xxiii. 28); for cities (Isai. x. 32; Jer. vi. 2; Zach. ix. 9).

DA'VID, son of Isai or Jesse, of the tribe of Juda, consecrated by Samuel as future king (1 Kings xvi. 13; 2 Kings ii. 4); he was renowned for valor, having slain a lion and a bear (1 Kings xvii. 34); he became Saul's armor-bearer and minstrel (1 Kings xvi. 21-23); when the giant Goliath defied the champions of Israel and no one dared accept the challenge, David met and slew him (49); Saul's son Jonathan and David became warm friends (xviii. 1, 3; xx. 8; xxiii. 18); Saul, jealous of David, attempted his life (xviii. 11); and sent him against the Philistines, promising his daughter Michol in marriage as a reward for victory; David's unexpected success embittered Saul, who showed such hostility to him that by Jonathan's advice he retired to Achis, king of Geth (xxi.); but there pretended insanity to avoid serving against his king and country (xxi. 13); he then retired to Maspha (xxii. 3); was delivered from Saul's pursuit (xxiii. 14); and spared the king when he was in his power (xxiv. 5; xxvi. 11); he married also Achinoam and Abigail, and resided at Siceleg; the Amelecites having captured the place and his family, he pursued and defeated them (xxx.); on the death of Saul at Mount Gelboe, he was anointed king at Hebron, and recognized by the tribe of Juda (2 Kings ii. 4, 10); the other tribes recognizing Isboseth, son of Saul (8-10); but David defeated him at Gabaon, and he was some time after assassinated by his own servants (2 Kings iv. 7); David was then, after seven years' reign at

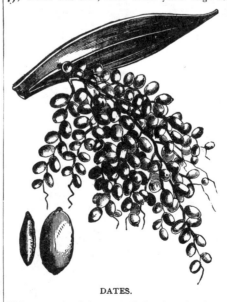

DATES.

Hebron, anointed king of all Israel, and reigned thirty-three years at Jerusalem (v. 5); he brought the

ark from Cariathiarim, and proposed to erect a temple (2 Kings vii. 2; 1 Paral. xvii.; xxiii.-xxvii.); but

THE THRONE OF CYRUS.

was told by the prophet Nathan that the work was for his son (2 Kings vii. 5-17); he freed Israel from paying tribute to the Philistines, defeated the Moabites, Adarezer, king of Soba, the Syrians, Edomites, and Ammonites (viii.; x.; xxi.); he fell into the sin of adultery, and to cover it contrived the death of Urias, for which he repented (xi.-xii. 13); his son Absalom rebels and forced David to flee from Jerusalem, but is defeated in battle and killed (xv.-xviii.); by numbering his people he draws down a pestilence (xxiv. 15); he caused Solomon his son by Bethsabee to be consecrated king (3 Kings i. 34); and died 1014 B.C. (3 Kings ii. 10); he composed Psalms, which form one of the canonical books, and have been used by the Jewish and Christian churches in divine worship; and in them he foretold of the Messias who was to be of his race; he is praised (Ecclus. xlvii. 2); our Lord is called the Son of David (Matt. i. 1; xv. 22; xxii. 45; Mark xii. 35; Luke xx. 41; Acts ii. 30); called a prophet (Acts ii. 30).

DEA′CONS, an order of clergy on the new law (Acts vi. 3); the qualities they should possess (1 Tim. iii. 8).

DEAD. How the dead are to be mourned (Lev. xix. 28; Deut. xiv. 1; xxxiv. 8; 2 Kings i. 11; iii. 32; x. 2; xii. 16; xiv. 2; xix. 1; xxi. 10, 13; Ecclus. xxii. 10; xxxviii. 16; 1 Mach. ix. 20; xii. 52; xiii. 26; Matt. ii. 18; Luke vii. 13; John xi. 33; Acts viii. 2; ix. 39; 1 Thess. iv. 12.)

DEAD SEA or Most Salt Sea (Lake Asphaltite), occupying the site of Sodom, Gomorrha, etc. (Num. xxxiv. 3, 12; Deut. iii. 17; Jos. xii. 3; xv. 5; xvi. 8).

DEAF MUTE cured by our Lord (Mark vii. 32).

DEATH is the penalty of sin (Gen. ii. 17; iii. 19; Rom. v. 12, 17; vi. 23; 1 Cor. xv. 21); sin causes a spiritual death (Eph. ii. 5; Coloss. ii. 13; 1 Tim. v. 6; James i. 15); all men are subject to death once (Jos. xxiii. 14; Job xiv. 5; Ps. lxxxviii. 49; Eccles. iii. 2; viii. 8; ix. 5; Ecclus. xvii. 3; xli. 1; John vii. 30; viii. 20; Heb. ix. 27); the hour of death is uncertain (Eccles. ix. 12; Matt. xxiv. 43; Luke xii. 40; 1 Thess. v. 2; 2 Thess. ii. 2; James i. 13); Christ overcame death (Isaias xxv. 8; Osee xiii. 14; Rom. vi. 9; 1 Cor. xv. 54; 2 Tim. i. 10; Heb. ii. 14; Apoc. i. 18; xxi. 4).

DE′MAS, of Thessalonica, a disciple of St. Paul (Coloss. iv. 14); ministered to him during his impris-

THE JEWISH CAPTIVES CONDUCTED BEFORE DARIUS.

onment in Rome, but loving the world, left him and went to Thessalonica (2 Tim. iv. 9).

DEME′TRIUS SOTER, king of Syria, son of Seleucus IV. He sent Bacchides against Judas Machabeus (1 Mach. vii.; 2 Mach. xiv.), and then Nicanor, who was defeated and slain (1 Mach. vii.; 2 Mach. xv.); but Bacchides sent again overwhelmed him. Demetrius was unable however to overthrow Jonathan, who sided with Alexander Balas against Demetrius (1 Mach. x. 1, 9), and Demetrius was killed, 150 B. C. (1 Mach. x. 49, 50).

DEME′TRIUS NICANOR, son of Soter, raised his standard in Cilicia (1 Mach. x. 67–69); won the favor of Ptolemy Philometor, who gave him his daughter Cleopatra in marriage and became king (x. 51–89; xi. 14–18); Jonathan Machabeus obtained his favor; Demetrius was finally driven out by Tryphon, was taken by the Parthians, but finally recovered his throne and was killed, 126 B. C. (1 Mach. xiii. 34–xiv. 38).

DEME′TRIUS, a silversmith of Ephesus, living by making little silver models of the temple of Diana, finding his trade injured by St. Paul, who converted the people to Christianity, raised a riot (Acts xix. 24).

DEME′TRIUS, a disciple praised by St. John (3 John 12).

DER′BE, a city in Lycaonia, to which St. Paul and St. Barnabas retired from Lystra (Acts xiv. 19); Gaius, a disciple, was a native of this place (xx. 4).

DES′ERT, or Wilderness of Sur, near the head of the Red Sea where Agar wandered (Gen. xvi. 7); —of Pharan, where Ismael took up his abode (Gen. xxi. 21); the Israelites wandered for a long time in this desert (Num. xiii. 1; Habac. iii. 3); of Sin, between Elim and Mount Sinai (Ex. xvi. 1; Num. xxxiii. 11, 12); another near Cadesbarné, also called of Cades (Ps. xxviii. 8; Num. xx. 1; xxxiii. 36); —of Sinai (Ex. xix. 2); of Cademoth (Deut. ii. 26); of Ziph, to which David fled (1 Kings xxiii. 15); of Maon (xxiii. 24); of Edom (4 Kings iii. 8); of Palmyra (2 Paral. viii. 4); of Egypt (Ezech. xx. 36); of Upper Egypt (Tobias viii. 3); of Deblatha (Ezech. vi. 14); where St. John preached (Matt. iii. 1); of Juda (Judges i. 16).

DESIR′ED of nations, the Messias (Agg. ii. 8).

DETRACT′ION, forbidden and punished (Ps. xiv. 3; c. 5; Prov. x. 18; xi. 13; xvi. 28; xx. 19;

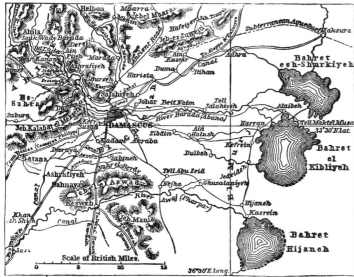

THE PLAIN AND LAKES OF MODERN DAMASCUS.
(This Map is from Fairbairn's Imperial Bible Dictionary.)

DEB′BORA, a prophetess, wife of Lapidoth, governed Israel in the days of the Judges, dwelling under a palm tree between Rama and Bethel (Judg. iv. 4, 5); she sent Barac to raise an army and attack Sisara, general of king Jabin's army, and composed a canticle on the victory (v.) 1285 B. C.

DEB′ORA, Rebecca's nurse, buried under an oak at Bethel (Gen. xxxv. 8).

DEC′ALOGUE, the Ten Commandments (Exod. xx. 2–17; Deut. v. 6–21).

DE′DAN, a country (Jerem. xxv. 23; xlix. 8; Ezech. xxv. 13; xxvii. 15; xxxviii. 13).

DED′ANIM, a Gentile nation (Isai. xxi. 3).

DED′ICATION of the temple by Solomon (3 Kings viii.; 2 Paral. v. 6–vii. 9); by Judas Machabeus (1 Mach. iv. 56; 2 Mach. ii. 9); dedication of the walls of Jerusalem (2 Esd. xii. 27).

DEL′UGE, an overflowing of the earth with water, announced (Gen. vi. 17–viii. 4); it lasts 150 days, beginning the 17th day of the second month, 2348 B. C.; it is never to occur again (ix. 11).

CONVENT OF MAR SABA, AND THE DEAD SEA.

xxvi. 20; Eccles. x. 20; Rom. i. 30; 2 Cor. xii. 20; 1 Pet. ii. 1; James iv. 11).

DEUTERO-CANONICAL books of the Old Testament are those books not included in the first canon ascribed to Esdras, but received by the Jewish church in the time of our Lord, and by the apostles and primitive church. They are rejected with the New Testament by the Jews. They are Tobias, Judith, Esther, Wisdom, Ecclesiasticus, Baruch, a part of Daniel, and the two books of the Machabees.

DEUTORON'OMY, or the Second Law, called in Hebrew Elle Haddebarim. It repeats and inculcates the ordinances given on Mount Sinai, and is the fifth and last of the Pentateuch, or five books of Moses. It was written on stones by Josue (Jos. viii. 32).

DEV'IL, the name given to the chief of the fallen angels. Sin entered the world through his

DEV'ILS or demons, evil spirits. All the gods of the Gentiles were devils (Ps. xcv. 5); men offered them sacrifices even of their own children (Ps. cv. 37; Baruch iv. 7; Levit. xvii. 7; 4 Kings i. 2, 3); this was specially forbidden (Lev. xvii. 7; Deut. xxxii. 17; 2 Paral. xi. 15; Ps. cv. 37); they are driven out of possessed persons by our Lord (Matt. viii. 16, 31; ix. 33; xvii. 17; Luke iv. 35; viii. 2, 28; ix. 43; xiii. 11); they are subject to the disciples (Luke x. 17; Acts v. 16; viii. 7; xvi. 18); they recognize Christ (Matt. viii. 29; Mark iii. 11; v. 7; Luke iv. 33, 41; viii. 28; Acts xix. 15; James ii. 19).

DIAN'A, goddess of hunting, worshipped especially at Ephesus. Her idol there was believed to have fallen from heaven (Acts xix. 35), and was revered in all Asia Minor (27). St. Paul's preaching drew so many from idolatry, that Demetrius, a silver-

Levi treacherously captured the city and slew the people (xxxiv. 1–31).

DI'NITES, one of the tribes sent to settle the country of the ten tribes (1 Esd. iv. 9); oppose the Jews (ib.)

DIONYS'IUS, the Areopagite, an illustrious Athenian converted by St. Paul (Acts xvii. 34).

DIOT'REPHES, a disciple mentioned 3 John i. 9.

DIP'SAS, a serpent whose bite caused a violent thirst (Deut. viii. 15).

DISCI'PLES, seventy were sent out by our Lord, two by two, to preach in the cities of Judea (Luke x. 1); their instructions (3); they return and give an account of their mission (17).

DISPER'SION, Jews of the, were those who remained in foreign countries after the captivity (James i. 1; 1 Pet. i. 1).

DAMASCUS, SYRIA.

jealousy (Wisd. ii. 24). He is always seeking to injure men (Gen. iii. 1; 2 Paral. xviii. 21; Job i. 11; Zach. iii. 1; Matt. viii. 28; Luke viii. 12; Acts xiii. 8; Eph. vi. 11; Apoc. ii. 10; xii. 9); he tempted our Lord (Matt. iv.); he transforms himself into an angel of light to deceive men (2 Cor. xi. 14); he goes about like a roaring lion (1 Pet. v. 8); he can act only as God permits (3 Kings xxii. 22; 2 Paral. xviii. 21; Job i. 12; ii. 6; Matt. viii. 31; Eph. ii. 2; 2 Tim. ii. 26; Apoc. xx. 7); he is the father and prince of the world and of all the wicked (John viii. 44; xii. 31; xiv. 30; xvi. 11; Acts xiii. 10; 2 Cor. iv. 4; Eph. ii. 2; 1 John iii. 10); his empire was destroyed by Christ (Matt. viii. 16; Luke x. 18; xi. 22; John xii. 31; Col. i. 13; 2 Tim. i. 10; Heb. ii. 14; 1 John v. 18; Apoc. xx. 9).

smith, who made silver temples as mementos, raised a riot (23–40).

DIDRACH'MA, a Greek piece of money (2 Mach. iv. 19; x. 20), and equivalent to the half-sicle which each Jew was obliged to pay annually to the temple (Matt. xvii. 23; Ex. xxx. 13).

DID'YMUS, the Greek name of Thomas (John xi. 16; xx. 24).

DI'ES (Jemima), the name of one of Job's daughters (Job xlii. 14).

DIE'VITES, one of the tribes sent to settle in the country of the ten tribes (1 Esd. iv. 9; 4 Kings xvii. 24).

DI'NA, daughter of Jacob and Lia (Gen. xxx. 21); ravished by Sichem, son of Hemor the Hevite, who then sought her in marriage: but Simeon and

DISOBE'DIENCE punished (Lev. xxvi. 14; Deut. xi. 28; xvii. 12; xviii. 19; 1 Kings xii. 15; 3 Kings xx. 36; 2 Paral. vii. 19; Jer. xi. 8); the disobedience of Adam and Eve (Gen. iii. 16); of Lot's wife (xix. 26); of the sons of Aaron (Lev. x. 1); of the Israelites (Num. xiv. 41; 1 Kings xiii. 11; xiv. 24; xv. 24; 2 Kings vi. 7; Jer. xxv. 3; xxvi. 4; Acts vii. 39).

DIVINATION by arrows (Ezech. xxi. 21, 22).

DIVINE, Jews forbidden to divine (Lev. xix. 26).

DIVI'NERS, soothsayers, interpreters unable to explain Pharao's dreams (Gen. xli. 8); Nebuchodonosor's (Dan. ii. 10); Balthasar's vision (Dan. v.).

DIVI'NING cup of Joseph (Gen. xliv. 5).

DIVIS'ION of the Promised Land among the

ten tribes (Jos. xiii.); share of the tribes of Ruben and Gad (Num. xxxii. 33; Jos. xiii. 8); of Juda (xv. 20); of Ephraim (xvi.); of Manasses (Num. xxxii. 33; Jos. xviii. 7; xvii. 1–11); of Benjamin (xviii.); of Simeon (xix.); of Zabulon (xix. 10); of Issachar (17); of Aser (24); of Nephthali (32); of Dan (40); of Levi (xxi. 4).

DIVORCE' forbidden (Matt. v. 32); permitted to the Jews (Deut. xxiv. 1); God punishes it (Mal. ii. 14).

DOC'TORS of the law taught by our Lord in childhood (Luke ii. 46); doctors come from all the cities of Judea and Galilee to hear him (v. 17); rebuked by our Lord (xi. 39); their hypocrisy unmasked (Matt. xvi. 1); condemned (Luke xi. 46); they are confounded (Matt. xxi. 24; xxii. 15; Mark xii. 13); they were to be heard, not to be imitated (Matt. xxiii. 3–6; Mark xii. 40); jealous of distinction (Matt. xxi. 15); they conspire the death of our Lord (John xii. 10; Matt. xxvi. 4); they seek means to put him to death (Luke xix. 47); they fear the people (48); resisted his miracles (John ix. 24); their blindness (39); they denied his mission (Luke xx. 2–4); compared to the rebellious vine growers (Luke xx. 9); seek to ensnare our Lord in his words (20); silenced (40); unable to answer the questions of our Lord (Matt. xxii. 46); corrupt Judas (xxvi. 15); they seize our Lord (John xviii. 3; Mark xiv. 43); they assemble to put him to death (Matt. xxvii. 1); deliver him to Pilate (2).

DOC'TRINE and TRUTH (Urim and Thummim), words on the Rational of Judgment (Ex. xxviii. 30).

SAMUEL ANOINTING DAVID.

watching and guarding (Job xxx. 1; Is. lvi. 10); devour corpses (3 Kings xiv. 11; xvi. 4; xxi. 19; xxii. 38; 4 Kings ix. 10; Jer. xv. 3; Ps. lxvii. 24); as a term of hatred or contempt (Ps. xxi. 17; 1 Kings xxiv. 15; 2 Kings iii. 8, etc.).

DOR'CAS or **TABITHA**, a Christian woman of Joppe, famous for her works of mercy (Acts ix. 36); restored to life by St. Peter (40, 41).

DOS'ITHEUS, a priest; took the book of Phurim or Esther to Egypt (Esth. xi. 1); an officer of Judas Machabeus (2 Mach. xii. 19, 35).

Ghost descends upon our Lord at his baptism in the form of a dove (Matt. iii. 16); we are to be as simple as doves (x. 16); a type of contemplation (Isai. xxxviii. 14; lix. 11); referred to (Ps. liv. 7; lxvii. 14; Jerem. xlviii. 28; Ezech. vii. 16; Osee vii. 11; Nah. ii. 7; Isai. lx. 8; Cant. i. 14; ii. 14).

DRACHM, a Greek coin (2 Esd. vii. 70–72; 2 Mach. xii. 43).

DRAG'ON, a creature of deserts like the ostrich (Job xxx. 29; Isai. xxxiv. 13; xliii. 20; **Jer. ix. 11**; x. 22; xiv. 6; xlix. 33; Micheas i. 8; Deut. xxxii. 33; Ps. xc. 13); a dragon worshipped at Babylon and killed by Daniel (Dan. xiv. 22); in the Apocalypse applied to the devil (Apoc. xii. 3); in Ezechiel to Pharao (Ezec. xxix. 3).

DRAG'ON, fountain at Jerusalem (2 Esd. ii. 13).

DRAUGHT of fishes, miraculous (Luke v. 6, 7).

DREAMS, God shows his will in (Gen. xlvi. 2; Num. xii. 6; 2 Kings vii. 4; Job iv. 13; vii. 14; xxxiii. 15; 1 Kings xxviii. 6; 2 Mach. xv. 11; Matt. i. 20; Acts xxiii. 11; xxvii. 23); they are not to be followed (Deut. xiii. 1; Eccles. v. 2; Ecclus. xxxiv. 1; Jerem. xxiii. 16; xxvii. 9; xxix. 8); impure dreams (Deut. xxiii. 10).

DRESS, vanity in dress reproved (Isai. iii. 18; Esth. xiv. 16; Matt. vi. 28; xi. 8; Mark xii. 38; Luke xvi. 19; 1 Tim. ii. 9; 1 Pet. iii. 3).

DROM'EDARY, an animal used as a beast of burden, swifter than the camel (Isai. lx. 6).

DROP'SY, our Lord cures a person afflicted with (Luke xiv. 2).

DROUGHT, in the kingdom of Juda, announced by Jeremias (Jerem. xiv. 3); in Israel by Elias (3 Kings xvii. 1–7; xviii. 2).

DRUNK'ENNESS and gluttony forbidden and punished (Prov. xxi. 17; xxiii. 1; Ecclus. xxiii. 6; **xxxi. 12, 17;** xxxvii. 32; Isai. xxii. 13; xxviii. 7; **xlvi. 12;** Ezech. xvi. 49; Joel i. 5; Mich. ii. 11; Hab. ii. 5; Wisd. ii. 7; Luke xii. 45; xxi. 34; Rom. xiii. 13; 1 Cor. v. 11)

SOUTHERN END OF THE DEAD SEA.

DO'DANIM, son or descendant of Javan (Gen. 4; 1 Paral. i. 7).

DOG, an unclean animal (Is. lxvi. 3); used for

DO'THAIN, DO'THAN, a town in Samaria (Gen. xxxvii. 17; 4 Kings vi. 13; Judith vii. 3).

DOVE sent out by Noe (Gen. viii. 8); the Holy

DRUSIL'LA, daughter of Herod Agrippa (Acts xxiv. 24).

THE PYRAMIDS OF EGYPT.

DUMB devil expelled (Luke xi. 14; Mark vii. 32).

EA'GLE, classed among unclean birds (Lev. xi. 13; Deut. xiv. 12); the bald eagle (Mich. i. 16); referred to by our Lord (Matt. xxiv. 28; Luke xvii. 37); the parable of the two eagles (Ezech. xvii. 3–10); its strong flight (2 Kings i. 23; Job ix. 26; Prov. xxx. 19; Jerem. iv. 13; Lam. iv. 19; Abd. 4); one of the four creatures in Ezekiel's vision had the head of an eagle (x. 14); hence applied symbolically to St. John the Evangelist. The eagle of the Apocalypse (iv. 7; viii. 13; xii. 14.)

EARS OF WHEAT. The disciples rebuked by the Pharisees for breaking on the Sabbath (Luke vi. 1; Matt. xii. 1).

EAR-RINGS, Earlets, early in use and apparently superstitions (Gen. xxxv. 4); sent as presents (Gen. xxiv. 22, 47; Job xlii. 11); given to make golden calf (Ex. xxxii. 2); for the sacred vessels (xxxv. 22); allusions to their use (Judg. viii. 24–26;

DEER.

Judith x. 3; Prov. xxv. 12; Isai. iii. 20; Ezech. xvi. 12; Osee ii. 13).

4 Kings xix. 15; Ps. cxiii. 15; cxx. 2; Prov. viii.; Esth. xiii. 10); suspended in space (Job xxvi. 7); covered with vegetation and animals (Gen. i. 10–12, 20–25); man created on earth (26, 27); cursed on account of Adam's sin (iii. 17, 18; iv. 2); overwhelmed with deluge on account of the sins of men (vii. 6, 10–12, 17); again peopled by Noe and his descendants (viii. 18); its final destruction (Apoc. xxi. 1).

EARTH'QUAKES, in the reign of Ozias (Zach. xiv. 5; Amos i. 1); at the crucifixion of our Lord (Matt. xxvii. 51); foretold (Apoc. vi. 12).

EB'ONY, imported into Tyre from Dedan (Ezech. xxvii. 15).

ECBAT'ANA, capital of the Medes (1 Esd. vi. 2; Tob. iii. 7; xv. 8; Jud. i. 1; 2 Mach. ix. 3).

ECCLE'SIASTES, one of the canonical sapiential books, written by Solomon, and called in Hebrew Coheleth or the Preacher (Eccles.)

ECCLE'SIAST'ICUS, one of the canonical sapiential books written by Jesus, the son of Sirach, and called in Hebrew Ben Sira. It was translated from the Hebrew by his grandson, and incorporated in the Septuagint.

ECH'O, rebounding from the mountains (Wisd. xvii. 18).

ECLIPSE' of the sun alluded to (Job xxxvi. 32; ix. 7; Ezech. xxxii. 7; Matt. xxvii. 45).

EDE'MA, a strong city in Nephthali (Jos. xix. 36).

E'DEN, sons of (Isaias xxxvi. 1).

E'DEN, Cain dwelt east of (Gen. iv. 16).

EDIS'SA, the name of Esther in captivity (Esth. ii. 7).

ED'NA, a priest (1 Esd. x. 30; 2 Esd. xii. 15).

ED'NAS, warriors who joined the party of David (1 Paral. xii. 20); a general of the army of Josaphat, king of Juda (xvii. 14).

E'DOM, another name of Esau (Gen. xxxvi. 1); used frequently for the country of his descendants. Edom opposes the Israelites (Num. xx. 14); not to be abhorred (Deut. xxiii. 7); subdued by David (2 Kings viii. 14); revolts (4 Kings viii. 20); defeated (xiv. 7; 2 Paral. xxi.; Isai. xxxiv. 6); prophecy against (Num. xxiv.; Ps. cxxxvi.; Isai. xxxiv.; lxiii.; Jerem. xlix.; Lam. iv.; Ezech. xxv.; xxxii.; xxxv.; xxxvi.; Amos, Abdias).

EG'LA, sixth wife of David and mother of Jethraam (2 Kings iii. 5).

EG'LON, king of the Moabites, oppressed the Israelites for eight years, but was slain by Aod, 1405 B. C. (Judg. iii. 12.)

E'GYPT, a country in the northeast of Africa, called the land of Cham (Ps. cv. 22); being settled by his son Mesraim (Gen. x. 6, 13); Abram went down to (Gen. xii. 10); Joseph sold to Ismaelite merchants going to Egypt (xxxvii. 25); Joseph's life in Egypt (xxxix–xli.); Jacob sends his other sons to Egypt for grain (xlii.–xliii.); goes down with all his family (xlvi.); his descendants oppressed and reduced to bondage (Ex. i. 8); as had been foretold (Gen.

WINGED CREATURE, WITH THE HEAD OF AN EAGLE.

xv. 13); Egypt smitten with plagues for refusing to let the Israelites depart (Ex. vii., viii., ix., x.); departure of the Israelites from (xii.; Deut. xvi.); Pharao pursuing is overwhelmed in the Red Sea (Ex. xiv.); the Israelites regret the food of Egypt (xiv. 11; xvi. 3; xvii. 3; Num. xi., xiv. xx.); Solomon marries the daughter of Pharao, king of Egypt (3 Kings iii. 1); Jeroboam fled to Sesac, king of Egypt (xi. 40); Osee applies to Sua, king of Egypt, for aid (4 Kings xvii. 4); Josias, king of Juda, defeated and slain by

EGYPTIAN BASKETS.   (From Wilkinson.)

Nechao, king of Egypt (4 Kings xxiii. 29; 2 Paral. xxxv. 20–24); Egypt overthrown by king of Babylon (4 Kings xxiv. 7; Jerem. xlvi. 2); Ptolemee, king of Egypt, overthrown by Antiochus (1 Mach. i. 17–21); Alexander Bales sends ambassadors to (x. 51); Ptolemee gives him his daughter in marriage (57); Ptolemee conquers Alexander and assumes the crowns of Egypt and Asia (xi. 13); prophecies against (Isai. xix., xx.; Jerem. xliii., xliv., xlvi.); called the Land with the winged Cymbal (Isai. xviii. 1); Joseph and Mary flee to with the infant Saviour (Matt. ii. 13).

E'LA, son of Baasa, king of Israel, reigned two years at Thersa, B. C. 930; and was assassinated by Zambri (3 Kings xvi. 6–10).

E'LAM, eldest son of Sem (Gen. x. 22; 1 Paral. i. 17); also the country settled by his descendants (Gen. xiv. 1, 9; Is. xi. 11; xxi. 2; Jer. xxv. 25; xlix. 34; Ezech. xxxii. 24); occupying part of Persia.

E'LAMITES, inhabitants of Elam (1 Esd. iv. 9); prophesied against (Jerem. xlix.)

ELCA'NA, general of Achas, king of Juda, killed by Zechri (2 Paral. xxviii. 7).

ELCHA'NAN, a brave warrior; son of David's uncle (1 Paral. xi. 26).

EL'DAD, one of the seventy ancients of Israel; Josue wished Moses to stop his prophesying, but Moses would not (Num. xi. 26–29).

ELE'AZAR, third son of Aaron, succeeds him in the high-priesthood (Num. xx. 26); he entered the promised land with Josue and divides it (Jos. xiv.

priest till the time of Heli, a descendant of Itha-mar.

THE FLIGHT INTO EGYPT.

ELE'AZAR, son of Saura, dies bravely in battle against Antiochus (1 Mach. vi. 43–46).

ELE'AZAR, son of Aminadab, appointed to guard the ark (1 Kings vii. 1).

ELE'AZAR, a venerable old man of Jerusalem, one of the chief scribes, put to death by Antiochus for refusing to eat the flesh of swine in violation of the law, or even pretend to do so (2 Mach. vi. 18–31).

ELE'AZAR, one of those who brought water to

ELE'AZAR, one of the ancestors of our Lord (Matt. i. 15).

ELECT', their small number (Matt. xx. 16); evil days shortened and postponed for the sake of (Matt. xxiv. 22; Mark xiii. 20).

ELECT' or ELECTA, a lady at Ephesus to

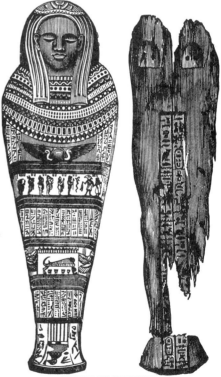

EGYPTIAN MUMMIES.

whom St. John addressed his second epistle. Some suppose it to be figurative for a church (2 John i. 1).

EL'EPHANT, used in war (1 Mach. i. 18; iii. 34; vi.; viii.; 2 Mach. xi., xiii., xiv.); elephants' teeth (ivory) (3 Kings x. 22).

E'LI, Eli, lama sabacthani, Hebrew words from

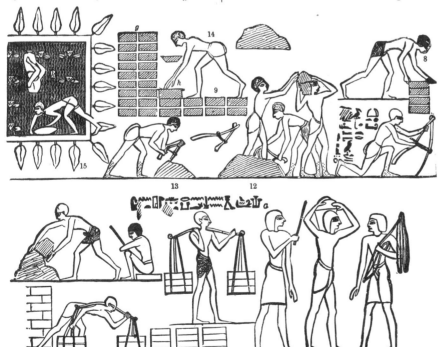

FOREIGN CAPTIVES EMPLOYED IN MAKING BRICKS AT THEBES. (Wilkinson.)

1); he dies at Gabaath, and is succeeded by Phinees (xxiv. 33); his family retained the office of high- | David from the cistern of Bethlehem (2 Kings xxiii. 9; 1 Paral. xi. 16).

Ps. xxi. 1, meaning "My God, my God, why hast thou forsaken me?" uttered by our Lord on the cross (Matt. xxvii. 46).

EGYPTIAN HEAD-DRESSES.

ELI′ACIM, son of Helcias, "over the house," high-priest, as some suppose, in the time of king Ezechias (4 Kings xviii. 18); his glory (Isai. xxii. 20–25); high-priest (Jud. iv. 5; 4 Kings xxii. 4; 2 Paral. xxxiv. 9; Baruch i. 7); called Joakim (Jud. xv. 9).

ELI′ACIM, king of Juda, surnamed Joakim. He was son of Josias, succeeded his brother Jechonias; he was placed on the throne by Pharao Nechao, 609 B.C.; he reigned wickedly (4 Kings xxiii. 34; xxiv. 5); called Eliakim (2 Paral. xxxvi. 4).

ELIA′DA, general under king Josaphat (2 Paral. xvii. 17).

ELI′AKIM, one of the ancestors of our Lord (Luke iii. 30).

ELI′AS, a famous prophet, a native of Thesbe, dwelling at Galaad, shuts up the heavens from raining (3 Kings xvii. 1); fed by ravens (6); multiplies the corn and oil of the widow of Sarephta (9–16); restores her son to life (17–24); Achab summons him (xviii. 1–20); Elias challenges the priests of Baal, shows his divine mission, and puts them to death (21–46); fleeing from Jezabel, he is fed by an angel in the desert (xix. 1–7); instructed by the Lord, he anoints Hazael king of Syria, and Jehu and Eliseus

EGYPTIAN MONARCH IN HIS CHARIOT.

(8–21); rebukes Achab for killing Naboth (xxi. 17–29); at the command of an angel he stops the messengers sent by king Ochozias to consult Beelzebub, and announces his death (4 Kings i. 3–8); two offi-

cers and their men destroyed by fire from heaven for intending evil to him (9–16); walks through the Jordan (ii. 8); goes up to heaven in a whirlwind and a fiery chariot (11); present at the transfiguration of our Lord (Matt. xvii. 3); he is to come again (Mal. iv. 5; Ecclus. xlviii. 10; Matt. xvii. 11; Mark ix. 11).

ELI′ASIB, a priest who went up with Zorobabel (2 Esd. iii. 1); high-priest (xiii. 28).

ELIC′IANS, the nation of king Erioch (Judith i. 6); supposed to be the Elamites.

ELIE′ZER DAMASCUS, Abraham's servant (Gen. xv. 2); goes to Mesopotamia to seek a wife for Isaac (Gen. xxiv. 10); brings Rebecca (61).

ELIE′ZER, son of Moses (Ex. ii. 22; xviii. 4); circumcised by his mother when the angel threatened the life of Moses for her neglect (iv. 24, 25); Jethro brings him to his father (xviii. 1–6).

ELIE′ZER, son of Dodau, a prophet who foretold to Josaphat that his fleet fitted out to co-operate with Ochozias should be wrecked in Asiongaber (2 Paral. xx. 37).

ELIE′ZER, a deputy sent by Esdras to the Jews at Chasphia (1 Esd. viii. 15–20).

E′LIM, sixth camp of the Israelites in the desert (Ex. xv. 27; Num. xxxiii. 9).

ELIM′ELECH, husband of Noemi, Ruth's mother-in-law, who went to the land of Moab (Ruth i. 2, etc.).

ELIO′DA, a son of David (2 Kings v. 16).

ELIPH′ALETH, or **ELIPHALET**, two sons of David (2 Kings v. 16; 1 Paral. xiv. 7; 1 Paral. iii. 6; iii. 8).

EL′IPHAZ, one of the friends of Job (Job ii. 11).

ELISE′US, son of Saphat, disciple and successor of the prophet Elias. He was of Abelmeula (3 Kings xix. 19; Ecclus. xlviii. 13); anointed by Elias (3 Kings xix. 16); he crossed the Jordan by striking it with the cloak of Elias (4 Kings ii. 14); sweetens water (20); multiplies oil (iv. 1–6); raised to life the child of the Sunamitess (iv. 32); heals the leprosy of Naaman, the Syrian (v. 14); blinds the Syrians (vi. 18); foretells plenty (vii. 1); his death (xiii. 14); his dead body restores a murdered man to life (21 Ecclus. xlviii. 15).

ELI′U, one of Job's friends; his address to Job (Job xxxii.)

ELIZ′ABETH, daughter of Aminadab, and wife of Aaron; she was mother of Nadab, Abiu, Eleazar and Ithamar (Ex. vi. 23).

ELIZ′ABETH, wife of Zachary (Luke i. 5); her maternity foretold (13); visited by the Blessed Virgin (39); her salutation recognizing her as mother of the Lord (41–45); gives birth to St. John the Baptist (57).

E′LUL, one of the months of the Jewish year,

nearly coinciding with August. The wall of Jerusalem was completed on the 25th (2 Esd. vi. 15; see 1 Mach. xiv. 27).

ELYMA′IS, a city in Persia, containing a temple of Nanea, which Antiochus endeavored to pillage (1 Mach. vi. 1–4; 2 Mach. i. 13).

EL′YMAS, or Barjesu, a magician who misled Sergius Paulus, governor of Cyprus, and was struck blind by St. Paul (Acts xiii. 7–9).

E′MATH, a city of Syria, assigned by Josue to the tribe of Nephthali (Jos. xix. 35); Thou, king of Emath, was on terms of amity with David (2 Kings viii. 9). It was taken by the kings of Juda and Israel (4 Kings xiv. 28); and by the Assyrians, who removed the people to Samaria (xvii. 24; xviii. 34).

EMBALM′ING, in use among the Jews (Gen. l. 2, 3; Luke xxiv. 1; John xix. 40).

EM′ERALD, a precious stone in the rational (Ex. xxviii. 17; xxxix. 10); alluded to (Tob. xiii. 21; Jud. x. 19; Ecclus. xxxii. 8; Ezech. xxviii. 13); in the wall of the New Jerusalem (Apoc. xxi. 19).

EM′ISSARY GOAT, chosen by lot (Lev. xvi. 8), to be offered by the high-priest, who was to pray that the sins of the people should light on him, and then turn him into the desert (20–22).

EMMAN′UEL, God with us, the name of the Messias (Isai. vii. 14; viii. 8; Matt. i. 23).

EM′MAUS, a hamlet near Jerusalem. Our Lord

DOOR INSCRIBED WITH PASSAGES FROM THE KORAN.

revealed himself after his resurrection to two disciples on their way to Emmaus (Luke xxiv. 13).

EM′PIRES, visions concerning the rise and fall of empires (Num. xxiv.; Dan. iv.–v.; viii.; xi.; Hab. ii.; Apoc. xvii., xviii.)

E′NAC, ENA′CIM, a race of giants (Num. xiii. 23, 29, 34; Jos. xv. 13, 14; Judg. i. 20; Deut. i. 28; ii. 10, 11, 21; ix. 2).

EN′DOR, the witch of, visited by Saul (1 Kings xxviii. 7–20); she evokes Samuel (14).

ENE′AS, a man of Lydda, paralyzed for eight years, cured by St. Peter (Acts ix. 33, 34).

EN′EMIES to be prayed for (Num. xvi. 22;

Luke vi. 28; xxiii. 34; Acts vii. 59); and loved (Prov. xxv. 21; Matt. v. 44).

ENGAD′DI or ASASONTHAMAR, a city near the Dead Sea; David dwelt in its strongholds (1 Kings xxiv. 1); Josaphat's enemies advance to (2 Paral. xx. 2); famous for vineyards (Cant. i. 13).

EN′GINES of war, what wood to be taken for (Deut. xx. 20); details as to (2 Paral. xxvi. 15; 1 Mach. v. 30; vi. 20, 31; 2 Mach. xii. 15, 27).

EN′NOM, En′non, the valley of the son of, east of Jerusalem (Jos. xv. 8; xviii. 16; 2 Esd. xi. 30); Topheth, where Moloch was worshipped, was here till defiled by Josias (4 Kings xxiii. 10; Jerem. vii. 31, 32).

EN′NON, near Salim, where St. John baptized (John iii. 23).

E′NOS, son of Seth (Gen. iv. 26; v. 11).

EN′VY, examples of (Gen. iv. 5; xxvi. 14; xxx., xxxi.; Exod. i.)

EPA′PHRAS instructs the Colossians (Coloss. i. 7); a fellow-prisoner with St. Paul in Rome (iv. 12; Philem. 23).

EPAPH′RODI′TUS, apostle of the Philippians (Phil. ii. 25); sent to Rome to minister to St. Paul (iv. 18).

EPENE′TUS, mentioned by St. Paul as the first-fruits of Asia in Christ (Rom. xvi. 5).

E′PHA or BATH, a Hebrew measure, holding, according to Josephus, a little more than eight gallons.

EPH′ESUS, a celebrated city in Ionia, Asia Minor. St. Paul visited it first A. D. 54 (Acts xviii. 19, 22); he soon returned and remained till 57, when Demetrius raised a riot which compelled him to retire; he was there again in 65; he wrote to the Christians of Ephesus from Rome (Eph.) Aquila,

bishop of Ephesus (1 Tim. iv. 14; 2 Tim. i. 6). The bishop praised (Apoc. ii. 1); but reproached with the cooling of his charity (4, 5).

DEFACED.

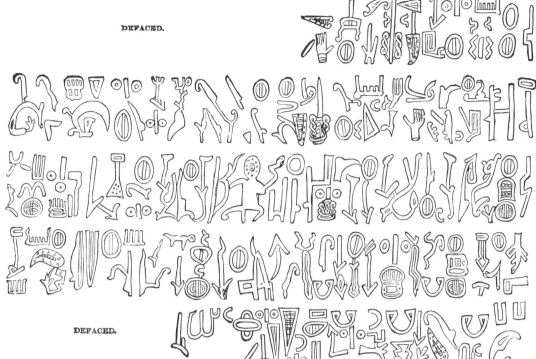

DEFACED.

INSCRIPTIONS AT EMATH.

EPH′PHETA, a Hebrew word meaning *Be thou opened* (Mark vii. 32–34).

E′PHOD, a priestly vestment. That of the high-priest was of gold and violet, and purple and scarlet, and fine linen, with two onyxes on the shoulders engraved with the names of the twelve tribes (Ex. xxviii. 6–9); over it was the rational of judgment (15); it was worn on approaching the tabernacle (43); it was carried away by the high-priest Abiathar when he fled to David (1 Kings xxiii. 6; xxx. 7); an ephod made of the gold taken by Gedeon from the Ismaelites proves destructive to his house (Judg. viii. 27).

EPH′RAIM, second son of the patriarch Joseph by Aseneth. Jacob, in blessing the sons, placed his right hand on Ephraim (Gen. xli. 52; xlvi. 20).

EPH′RAIM, tribe of. During the stay of the Israelites in Egypt, the sons of Ephraim attacked Geth and were slain (1 Paral. vii. 21); his descendants increased in Egypt so that they formed one of the twelve tribes; at the Exodus they numbered 40,500 men able to bear arms, under Elisama (Num. ii. 18, 19); their camp was on the west side (Num. ii. 18); their offerings (vii. 48–53); to view the land they sent Osee (Josue) son of Nun (xiii. 9); at Setim they numbered 32,500 (xxvi. 37); Camuel was

appointed to divide the land (xxxiv. 24); their territory (Jos. xvi.); Ammonites waste Ephraim (Judges x. 9); revolt against Jephte, defeated (Judges xii. 4); the fugitives detected at the ford of Jordan by the word Schibboleth (6); 42,000 of the tribe slain (6); formed part of the kingdom of Israel (3 Kings xii. 20; 2 Paral. x.); carried into captivity (4 Kings xvii. 5); Josue was of this tribe (1 Par. vii. 27).

EPHRA′TA, another name of Bethlehem (Gen. xxxv. 16, 19; xlviii. 7; Ruth iv. 11; Mich. v. 2).

EGYPTIAN ENSIGNS OR STANDARDS. (Fbn.)
From Champollion, 1, 2, 3, 4. From Wilkinson, 5, 7, 8. From Rossellini, 6, 9.

EPH′RATHITES, natives of Bethlehem (Ruth i. 2; 1 Kings xvii. 12).

EPHRA′TA, used in Ps. cxxxi. for the territory of Ephraim, and Ephrathite for a man of the tribe of Ephraim (3 Kings xi. 26).

EPH′REE, Pharao, king of Egypt, his fall foretold (Jerem. xliv. 30).

SPECIMEN OF ANCIENT EGYPTIAN ART.

Priscilla, and Apollo also labored here (Acts xviii. 2–18; xviii. 24). St. Paul consecrated St. Timothy

EPH'RON, son of Seor, sells the double cave to Abraham (Gen. xxiii. 16, 17; xxv. 9; xlix. 29).

RUINS OF EPHESUS.

EPH'RON, a mountain north of Juda (Jos. xv. 9).

EPH'RON, a city east of Jordan, taken by Judas Machabeas (1 Mach. v. 46; 2 Mach. xii. 27).

EPICURE'ANS, Greek philosophers, dispute with St. Paul (Acts xvii. 18).

EPIS'TLES, letters addressed by the apostles, and received as canonical books of the New Testa-

EUNICE, THE MOTHER OF TIMOTHY.

ment. They are the Epistles of St. Paul to the Romans, Corinthians (2), Galatians, Ephesians, Philippians, Colossians, Thessalonians (2), Timothy (2), Titus, Philemon, and Hebrews, the Epistle of St.

James, two Epistles of St. Peter, three of St. John, and one of St. Jude.

ERAS'TUS, treasurer of Corinth, a disciple of St. Paul (Rom. xvi. 23); follows him to Ephesus (Acts xix. 22); sent to Macedon; returns to Corinth (2 Tim. iv. 20).

ERIC'IUS, the hedgehog (Isai. xiv. 23; xxxiv. 11, 15; Soph. ii. 14); mistranslated bittern in the King James Bible.

ER'IOCH, king of the Elicians (Jud. i. 6).

E'SAU, son of Isaac and Rebecca (Gen. xxv. 25); sells his birthright to Jacob (xxv. 29–34); his wives (xxvi., xxviii., xxxvi.); sent out by Isaac to hunt for him (xxvii. 1–4); Jacob obtains his blessing by stratagem (5–30); he threatens Jacob's life (41); Jacob propitiates him (xxxii. 3–xxxiii. 3); their reconciliation (4).

ES'CHOL, an ally of Abraham at Mambre (Gen. xiv. 13, 24).

ES'COL, NEHELESCOL, a vale in Juda where the spies cut an enormous bunch of grapes (Num. xiii. 24, 25; xxxii. 9; Deut. i. 24).

ES'DRAS, a holy priest raised up to effect the return of the Jews from Babylon. He is supposed to have returned first with Zorobabel, 536 B. C., of which he wrote a description. When the enemies of the Jews raised obstacles to the rebuilding of the temple he returned to Babylon, and was sent to Jerusalem by Artaxerxes, 467 B. C. (1 Esd. vii. 1); he set out with a large body, and at the river Ahara was joined by others from Chasphia. He carried back the sacred vessels and published a fast; he deposed priests and Levites who had married heathen women and would not dismiss them (1 Esd. ix.–x.); he governed the Jews till the arrival of Nehemias (2 Esd. i. 1); after the restoration of the temple he read the law to the people (viii.); and solemnly renewed the covenant (ix., x.); he was of the race of Eleazar (1 Esd. vii. 5).

ES'DRAS, two canonical books of the Old Testament, called the first and second of Esdras; the second being also called the book of Nehemias. They relate the return of the Jews from Babylon, the rebuilding of Jerusalem, and the temple (1 Esd., 2 Esd.)

ES'DRAS, a priest who read the law to the people before a battle with the Syrians (2 Mach. viii. 23).

ES'DRELON, a plain in the tribe of Issachar (Jud. i. 8; iv. 5; vii. 3).

ES'THER, or EDISSA, daughter of Abihail, of the tribe of Benjamin (Esth. ii. 7, 15); when Assuerus deposed Queen Vashti, Esther was one of the beautiful maidens gathered for him to select a new queen, and was chosen (ii. 9); Aman, the king's minister, in his anger at Mardochai, Esther's uncle, obtained orders for a general massacre of the Jews (iii.–xiii.); Esther interceded with Assuerus, her people were delivered and Aman was put to death (xiv.–xvi.); a feast was established called Phurim (xi.); which is still kept by the Jews.

ES'THER, a canonical book written by Mardochai (Esth.)

E'THAM, third station of the Israelites in the desert (Ex. xiii. 20; Num. xxxiii. 6).

E'THAN, the Ezrahite, one of the wisest men of his time (3 Kings iv. 31; 1 Paral. ii. 6); but excelled by Solomon.

E'THAN, the rivers of (Ps. lxxiii. 15).

ETH'ANIM, one of the Jewish months, afterwards called Tisri (3 Kings viii. 2).

EGYPTIAN MUMMY CASES.

ETHBA'AL, king of Sidon and father of Jezabel (3 Kings xvi. 31).

ETHIO'PIA, a country in Africa, the modern Abyssinia (Gen. ii. 13; 4 Kings xix. 9; Jud. i. 9; Esth. i., viii., xiii., xvi.; Job xxviii. 19; Ps. lxvii. 32; Isai. xi., xviii., xx., xxxvii., xliii., xlv.; Jerem. xlvi. 9, etc.).

ETHIO'PIAN, Sephora so called (Num. xii. 1); Zara king of the Ethiopians (2 Par. xiv. 8); Candace queen (Acts viii. 27).

EUBU'LUS, a disciple of St. Paul (2 Tim. iv. 21).

EU'CHARIST, Holy, figured by the manna (Ex. xvi. 15; Ps. lxxvii. 24; John vi. 31); promised (52); instituted by our Lord (Matt. xxvi. 26; 1 Cor. xi. 23; Mark xiv. 22; Luke xxii. 19).

EUME'NES, king of Bithynia and Pergamos, joins the Romans against Antiochus the Great, and receives India, Media, and Lydia (1 Mach. viii. 8).

EU'NICE, a Jewess, mother of St. Timothy (Acts xvi. 1, 2).

EU'NUCH. Castration forbidden (Lev. xxii. 24; Deut. xxiii. 1); eunuchs appear, however, in the time of the kings (4 Kings viii. 6; ix. 32; xx. 18; xxiii. 11; xxv. 19; Isai. lvi. 3; Jer. xxix. 2; xxxiv. 19; xxxviii. 7; xli. 16; lii. 25; Acts viii. 27). Our Lord speaks of those who, by chastity, make themselves eunuchs for the kingdom of heaven (Matt. xix. 12).

EU'PATOR, surname of Antiochus, son of the Illustrious (1 Mach. vi. 17).

EUPHRATES, a river of Mesopotamia (Gen. ii. 14; Deut. xi. 24; 2 Kings viii. 3; Jer. xiii. 4; Apoc. ix. 14).

EUPOL'EMUS, one of Judas Machabeus' ambassadors to Rome (1 Mach. viii. 17; 2 Mach. iv. 11).

EU'ROAQUILO, the northeast wind (Acts xxvii. 14).

EU'TYCHUS, a young man of Troas, killed by falling from a gallery, but raised to life by St. Paul (Acts xx. 10).

EVAN'GELIST, a bearer of good tidings, the title given to Philip the deacon (Acts xxi. 8); St. Paul places evangelists as clergymen under the apostles and prophets (Eph. iv. 11); he bids Timothy do the duty of one (2 Tim. iv. 5). The title now applied to the authors of the four gospels, St. Matthew, St. Mark, St. Luke, and St. John.

EVE, the first woman, made out of a rib of Adam (Gen. ii. 21); induced by the serpent to eat the forbidden fruit (iii. 6); persuades Adam to eat thereof (6); her sentence (16); God makes her a garment of skins (21); mother of Cain (iv. 1); of Abel (2); of Seth (25); and of daughters (v. 4).

E'VILMER'ODACH, son and successor of Nabuchodonosor, takes king Joachin out of prison (4 Kings xxv. 27).

E'VIL, not to be returned for evil (Prov. xx. 22; xxiv. 29; Rom. xii. 14; 1 Cor. iv. 12; 1 Thess. v. 15; 1 Pet. iii. 9); we are to avoid evil (Prov. iii. 7; Isai. i. 16; Ezech. xviii. 21).

EVOCA'TION of the spirit of Samuel by the witch of Endor (1 Kings xxviii. 15; Ecclus. xlvi. 23).

EVO'DIA, a disciple mentioned by St. Paul (Phil. iv. 2).

EXCOMMU'NICA-TION (Matt. v. 29; xvi 19; 1 Cor. v. 3; 2 Thess. iii. 6; 1 Tim. i. 20; 2 Tim. iv. 15; Tit. iii. 10).

EX'ODUS, the second of the five books of Moses, and called in Hebrew Veelle Semoth. It describes the departure of the Israelites from Egypt (Ex.)

EX'ORCISTS, men appointed to expel evil spirits (Matt. xii. 27); some Jews assumed to do so in the name of Jesus Christ (Mark ix. 37; Luke ix. 40); the sons of Sceva attempting it, maltreated by the possessed (Acts xix. 16).

EX'PIA'TIONS, or expiatory sacrifices prescribed by God (Lev. v. 2–18; xxiii. 27, 28, 36).

EX'PIA'TION, feast of, one of the solemn feasts of the Jews on the tenth day of the seventh month (Lev. xvi. 29–34).

nations appointed to be destroyed (16, 17, 18).

THE TOMB OF ESTHER AND MORDECAI.

EXTERM'INANS, the Latin name of the angel of the bottomless pit (Apoc. ix. 11).

EXTREME' UNCTION, the use of the sacrament enjoined (James v. 14).

EYE, a good eye or intention (Ecclus xxxv. 12); the light of the body (Matt. vi. 22); an evil eye (Gen. vi. 2; Prov. vi. 13; Eccl. iv. 8; Ecclus. xiv. 8; xxxi 14; Matt. vi. 23; Mark vii. 22; 1 John ii. 16); the eye causes sin (Gen. iii. 6; xxxiv. 2; xxxviii. 15; xxxix. 7; 2 Kings xi. 2; xiii. 1; Prov. xxiii. 26; Ecclus. ix. 5; xxv. 28; xli. 25; xlii. 12; Judith x. 18; xii. 16; Dan. xiii. 8; Matt. v. 28; 2 Pet. ii. 14).

EZECHI'AS, king of Juda (4 Kings xvi. 20; xviii. 1; 2 Paral. xxix. 1); he destroyed all idols and heathen worship, and restored religion (4 Kings xviii. 4; 2 Paral. xxix.); threw off the Assyrian yoke (7); defeated the Philistines (8); Sennacherib attacking him is defeated by an angel (xix. 35); his health miraculously restored (xx. 7); consults Isaias (7–18; Isai. xxxvi.–xxxix.); shows his treasures to the Babylonian ambassador; is reproved (Isai. xxxix.); makes an aqueduct (4 Kings xx.); his death (21; 2 Paral. xxxii. 33).

EZE'CHIEL, son of Busi, a priest and prophet, taken to Babylon (Ezech. i. 3); where he prophesied (ii. 3); praised (Ecclus. xlix. 10).

POOL OF EZECHIAS AT JERUSALEM.

E'VI, king of Madian, killed by Phineas (Num. xxxi. 8).

EXTER'MINA'TION, God did not wish that of all the nations (Deut. xx. 10, 11);

EZE'CHIEL, the canonical book containing the prophecies of Ezechiel, one of the four great prophets (Ezech.)

FACE. God promises that his face shall go before the Israelites (Ex. xxxiii. 14); Jacob said: "I have seen God face to face" (Gen. xxxii. 30); "Make thy face to shine upon thy servant" (Ps. xxx. 17).

FAIRS OF TYRE (Ezech. xxvii. 12).

FAITH, a theological virtue (Hab. ii. 4; Matt. viii. 13; ix. 22; Mark v. 34; Rom. iii. 22; iv. 3; v. 1); its efficacy (Matt. ix. 2; xxi. 22; Mark xvi. 16; Luke xviii. 42; John i. 12; iii. 15; vi. 35; vii. 38; xi. 25; xiv. 12; xx. 29; Acts iii. 16; x. 43; xv. 9; xvi. 5; Rom. i. 16; iii. 22; Gal. iii. 8; Eph. ii. 8; Heb. xi. 1–39); faith without charity is lifeless (1 Cor. xiii. 2; Gal. v. 6; James ii. 24); faith is one (Eph. iv. 5).

FAITH'FUL, are delivered from the fate of sinners (Gen. vi., viii., xix.; Ex. viii.–xi.; xiv.; Num. xvi.; 1 Esd. viii. 22; Esth. vii.; 2 Pet. ii. 7).

FALSE PROPHETS, we are to beware of them (Deut. xiii. 1; xviii. 20; 3 Kings xxii. 6; Prov. xxviii. 10; Is. xxviii. 7; lvi. 10; Ezech. xiv. 9; xxii. 25; xxxiv.; Amos vii. 10; Mich. iii. 5; Zach. xiii. 2; Matt. vii. 15; Acts xx. 29; Col. ii. 8; 1 Tim. iv. 1; 2 Pet. ii. 1; 1 John iv. 1; Jude 4, 8).

FAM'INES (Gen. xii. 10; xxvi. 1; xli.; Ruth i. 1; 2 Kings xxi. 1; 3 Kings xvii.–xviii.; 4 Kings vi. 25; 2 Esd. v.; Acts xi. 28).

FARM, the term used (Luke xiv. 18; xv. 15).

FAR'THING, used for the Latin *quadrans* (Matt. v. 26; Mark xii. 42); for the *as* (Matt. x. 29); for the *dipondium* (Luke xii. 6).

FAST'ING recommended (Joel ii. 12; Matt. vi. 16; Mark ii. 20; Acts xiii. 2; xiv. 22; Rom. xiii. 13; 2 Cor. vi. 5; 1 Thess. v. 6; 1 Pet. i. 13; v. 8); fasting is meritorious (Judith iv. 8; viii. 6; Tob. xii. 8; Jer. xxxv. 14; Jonas iii. 7; Matt. xvii. 20); the Jews fasted when mourning for the dead (1 Kings xxxi. 13; 2 Kings i. 12; iii. 35; 1 Paral. x. 12; among the examples of fasting see Ex. xxxiv. 28; Judg. xx. 26; 1 Kings vii. 6; 2 Kings xii. 16; 3 Kings xix. 4; Ps. xxxiv. 13; Dan. x. 3; Joel i. 14; Matt. iv. 2; Acts x. 10; 1 Kings xiv. 24; 2 Paral. xx. 3; Jonas iii. 5; 1 Esd. viii. 21; Esth. iv. 16; Jerem. xxxvi. 9; fasting avails not without proper dispositions (Is. lviii. 3; Mark ii. 18; Luke xviii. 12).

FASTS. The appointed fasts of the Jews were in the fourth month for the breaking of the tables (Zach. viii. 19); in the fifth month for the destruction of Jerusalem (Zach. vii. 3); in the seventh month (viii. 19); also on the day of the atonement in that month (Levit. xxiii. 27); and in the tenth month (Zach. viii. 19).

FAT OF ANIMALS was prohibited as food (Lev. vii. 23, 25).

FEAR. We are to fear God and to keep him always before our eyes (Ex. xx. 20; Deut. iv. 10; vi. 2, 13; x. 12; xiii. 4; Jos. xxiv. 14; 4 Kings xvii. 36; 2 Paral. xix. 7; Ps. xxvi. 1; xxxii. 8; Prov. iii. 7; xiv. 2; xxiii. 21; Eccles. xii. 13; Ecclus. ii. 7; vii. 31; Jer. x. 7; xxxii. 39; Matt. x. 28; Luke xii. 5; 1 Pet. ii. 17; Apoc. xiv. 7).

FEAR OF GOD is the beginning of wisdom (Prov. ix. 10); is not opposed to faith (Eccles. viii. 12; Ecclus. v. 5; Rom. xi. 20; Heb. iv. 1); it is the beginning of the love of God (Ecclus. xxv. 16; Prov. xiv. 27); it is praised (Gen. xx. 11; Deut. vi. 24; Job xxviii. 28; Ps. cii. 17; cx. 5; cxi. 1; cxxvii.; Prov. x. 27; xvi. 6; xxxi. 30; Ecclus. ii. 18–23; x.

23; xv. 1; xxxiii. 1; xxxiv. 16, 19; Bar. iii. 7; Acts viii. 2; ix. 31); God fills the wicked with fear (Gen. xxxv. 5; Ex. xxiii. 27; Lev. xxvi. 36; Deut. ii. 25; xi. 25; xxviii. 10, 65; Jos. ii. 9; x. 10; Judg. iv. 15; vii. 21; 1 Kings vii. 10; 4 Kings vii. 6; 2 Paral. xiv. 14; xvii. 10; xx. 29; Judith xiv. 1; xv. 1; Ps. ix. 20; Jer. xlix. 37; 2 Mach. iii. 24). Abraham feared God (Gen. xxii. 12); the midwives (Ex. i. 17); the Israelites (xiv. 31); Abdias (3 Kings xviii. 3); Tobias (i., ii.); Sara (Tob. iii. 18; ix. 12; Judith viii. 8); Job (i. 8; xxxi. 23); Eleazar (2 Mach. vi. 30); Cornelius the centurion (Acts x. 2, 35).

FEASTS observed by the Jews; tne Pasch, or feast of the azymes or unleavened bread on the fifteenth day of the first month (Ex. xxiii. 15; Deut. xvi. 2; Matt. xxvi. 2; Mark xiv. 1; John xi. 55; Acts ii. 1; xx. 6); the feast of the First Fruits (Ex. xxiii. 16; Lev. xxiii. 15); the feast of Trumpets (Lev. xxiii. 24; 2 Paral. v. 3); feast of Atonement (Lev. xxiii. 27; Num. xxix. 7); feast of Tabernacles (Ex. xxiii. 16; Lev. xxiii. 34; Deut. xxxi. 10; 1 Esd. iii. 4; 2 Esd. viii. 15; 2 Mach. i. 9; x. 6); feast of Phurim (Esth. ix. 31); feast of the Dedication (1 Mach. iv. 56; John x. 22); on three great feasts of the year every male was required to appear before the Lord, by going up to the temple or tabernacle (Ex. xxiii. 17).

FE'LIX, governor of Judea, before whom St. Paul was brought at Cesarea, and who kept him two years in prison (Acts xxiii. 26, 27).

FES'TUS, governor of Judea, hears the cause of St. Paul (Acts xxiv. 27; xxv. 1–24).

FIGFAUNS, a desert creature (Jer. l. 39).

FIG—Ficus Carica. (Fbn.)

FIG-TREE, a common tree in Palestine (Deut. viii. 8; 3 Kings iv. 25; Micheas iv. 4; Zach. iii. 10); the barren fig-tree cursed by our Lord (Mark xi. 13–21); the parable of the fig-tree (Luke xiii. 6–9).

FIL'LET. The golden fillet (Eccles. xii. 6).

FIR-TREE (Isai. xiv. 8); fir-trees of Sanir (Ezech. xxvii. 5).

FIRE from heaven destroys Sodom and Gomorrah (Gen. xix. 24, 25, 28); kills Nadab and Abiu (Lev. x. 2; xvi. 1); destroys the rebellious Israelites (Num. xvi. 46, 49); descends on sacrifices (Judg. vi. 21; 3 Kings xviii. 38); destroys soldiers sent to seize Elias (4 Kings i. 10, 12); sacred fire found by

the Jews after their return from Babylon (2 Mach. i. 19; ii. 1).

FIRST-BORN of the Jews consecrated to God (Ex. xiii. 2; xxii. 29; Num. iii. 13; 1 Kings i. 24; Luke ii. 23); the first-born of the Egyptians slain (Ex. xii. 29).

FIRST-FRUITS to be offered to the Lord and his priests (Ex. xxii. 29; xxiii. 19; Lev. xxiii. 10, 39; Deut. xviii. 4; xxvi. 2; 2 Esd. x. 35; Num. xviii. 11)

FISH created on the fifth day (Gen. i. 20, 21); all without fins and scales declared unclean (Lev. xi. 9, 10); worship of forbidden (Deut. iv. 18); mode of taking (Hab. i. 15; Ezech. xxvi. 5; xlvii. 10; Isaias xix. 8); miraculous draught of fishes (Luke v. 6).

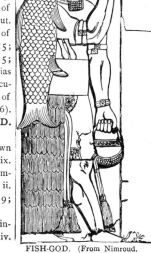

FISH-GOD. (From Nimroud. Layard.)

FISH'-GOD. See DAGON.

FLAX grown in Egypt (Ex. ix. 31); in the Promised Land (Jos. ii. 6; Osee ii. 5, 9; Isaias xix. 9).

FLEA, an insect (1 Kings xxiv. 15; xxvi. 20).

FLIGHT of the Holy Family into Egypt (Matt. ii. 13).

FLIGHT recommended in persecution (Matt. x. 23).

FLINT, a hard rock (Job xxviii. 9; Ezech. iii. 9).

FLOCK-TOW'ER (Gen. xxxv. 21).

FLUTE, a musical instrument (Dan. iii. 5–15).

FLUX. Bloody flux, dysentery, a disease (Acts xxviii. 8), of which St. Paul cured Publius.

FLY, an insect. All kinds of flies brought upon Egypt (Ex. viii. 21, 31; Ps. lxxvii. 45; civ. 31); dying flies spoil ointment (Eccles. x. 1); fly of Egypt (Isai. vii. 18).

FOR'EST of Bethel (4 Kings ii. 24); of Haret (1 Kings xxii. 5); near Bethaven (xiv. 25); castles in forests (2 Paral. xxvii. 4); forest of Libanus (3 Kings vii. 2); forest of Carmel, figurative (4 Kings xix. 24; Isai. xxxvii. 24).

FORGIVE'. We are to forgive one another (Matt. v. 24; vi. 14; xviii. 21; Mark xi. 25; Luke xi. 4; xvii. 4; Eph. iv. 32; Col. iii. 13).

FORGIVE SINS. The Son of man had power on earth to forgive sins (Matt. ix. 6; Mark ii. 10); he delegated the power to the apostles (Matt. xvi. 19; xviii. 18; John xx. 23); the thought of the scribes that God alone can forgive sins declared evil (Matt. ix. 4), and refuted by a miracle (Matt. ix. 6; Mark ii. 10; Luke v. 24).

FORGIVE'NESS of injuries. By Joseph (Gen. l. 21); taught by our Lord (Matt. v. 44; xviii. 35); practised (Luke xxiii. 34).

FORNICA'TION provokes God's anger (Deut. xxii. 21; Num. xxv. 6; Osee iv. 14; 1 Cor. vi. 9; Heb. xiii. 4); occasions of the sin to be avoided (Ecclus.

ix. 4; xlii. 12); forbidden in thought or desire (Ex. xx. 17; Matt. v. 28); idolatry often styled fornication (Judg. viii. 27), etc.

FORTUNA'TUS, disciple of St. Paul (1 Cor. xvi. 15, 17).

FOR'TUNE, a goddess, to whom apostate Jews offered libations (Isai. lxv. 11).

FOUN'TAIN. The dragon-fountain (Esdras ii. 13); fountain of Siloe (Isai. viii. 6; John ix. 7, 11); mysterious fountain (Zach. xiii.); fountain of Daphnis (Num. xxxiv. 11); fountain sealed up (Cant. iv. 12); the fountain of gardens (iv. 15); fountain in Jezrahel (1 Kings xxix. 1); fountain of Misphat (Gen. xiv. 7); fountain Rogel (Jos. xv. 7; xviii. 16; 2 Kings xvii. 17; 3 Kings i. 9); Samson's fountain (Judg. xv. 19); fountain of the sun (Jos. xv. 7); fountain of Taphua (Jos. xvii. 7).

FOWL, fatted fowl (3 Kings iv. 23).

FOX'ES, sent by Samson among the corn of the Philistines (Judg. xv. 4).

FRANK'INCENSE, a resin burned in divine worship (Ex. xxx. 34–36; Isai. lx. 6; Jerem. vi. 20); offered to our Saviour by the wise men (Matt. ii. 11).

FRAUD condemned (Jerem. ix. 6; Ecclus. xxxiv. 25; Prov. xii. 17; Mark vii. 22; Acts v. 2; Rom. i. 29).

FRIEND, not to be listened to against God (Deut. xiii. 6; xxxiii. 9); a pretended friend (John xiii. 18); Joab's friendship (2 Kings iii. 27; xx. 9); Ethai's friendship for David (2 Kings xv. 19); the friendship of David and Jonathan (1 Kings xix. 1; xx. 2, 30); the rich have many friends (Prov. xiv. 20); a true friend loves one at all times (xvii. 17); tells the truth (xxiv. 26); better than a brother (xviii. 24; xxvii. 10); some persons not to be taken as friends (xx. 19; xxii. 24); he who gives has many friends (xix. 6); marks of a true friend (xvii. 17; xxiv. 26; Eccles. iv. 9; Ecclus. vi. 11).

FRINGES. God commanded the Jews to have fringes, with ribbands of blue (Num. xv. 38; Deut. xxii. 12) on the garment, translated cloak, but evidently the taleth or vestment of prayer still worn by the Jews; skirt (Zach. viii. 23). The Pharisees accused of wearing them very large out of ostentation (Matt. xxiii. 5); it was apparently the fringe of our Lord's taleth that the women touched (Matt. ix. 20; Luke viii. 44); and others (Matt. xiv. 36; Mark vi. 56). The word fimbria, kraspedon, translated *hem*, being that used for the *fringes*.

FROGS, one of the plagues of Egypt (Ex. viii. 2, 7).

FRUITS of the promised land, their extraordinary beauty (Num. xiii. 25, 27; Deut. i. 24, 25); laws and ordinances concerning their gathering, and the offering of the first-fruits (Lev. xix. 23, 25).

FRU'MENTY or **FUR'METY,** polenta (Lev. xxiii. 14; Jos. v. 11; Ruth ii. 14; 1 Kings xvii. 17).

FUR'NACE, the three children cast into the fiery furnace (Dan. iii. 19); delivered (93).

GA'AL, son of Obed, rebels against Abimelech (Judg. ix. 26).

GAB'AA, or **GAB'AATH,** a town in Benjamin (Jos. xviii. 28); a crime against the wife of a Levite here drew on the tribe of Benjamin a war in which it was nearly annihilated (Judg. xix.; xx.); the birth-place of Saul (1 Kings x. 26; xxvi. 1); called Gabaath of Saul (Isai. x. 29); taken by Jonathan (1 Kings xiii. 3).

GAB'AON, a city in Chanaan, whose people obtained a pledge of safety from Josue by stratagem (Jos. ix. 3); Josue aided it against the Chanaanite kings (x. 3); and during this battle caused the sun to stand still (12, 13); the Gabaonites were made hewers of wood and drawers of water to the Israelites (ix. 23); Saul slew many of them (2 Kings xxi. 1); the country was punished by famine till David gave the Gabaonites seven sons and grandsons of Saul, whom the Gabaonites crucified (2 Kings xxi. 1–14).

GAB'AON, pool of (2 Kings ii. 13); combat at (14, 15).

GAB'BATHA, in Greek lithostrotos, a court in Pilate's palace paved probably with marble (John xix. 13).

GABE'LUS, of the tribe of Nephthali, living at Rages. Young Tobias was sent to obtain payment from him of ten talents of silver lent by his father (Tob. i.–ix.)

GA'BRIEL (power of God), one of the arch-angels, appears to the prophet Daniel (Dan. viii. 16; ix. 21); to Zachary, father of St. John the Baptist (Luke i. 11, 19); to the Blessed Virgin (26).

GAD, son of Jacob by Zelpha, Lia's handmaid (Gen. xxx. 9–11); he had seven sons (xlvi. 16); Jacob, in blessing him, announced that he was to lead the army (xlix. 19).

GAD, one of the twelve tribes, marched out of Egypt under Eliasaph, their prince (Num. i. 14; ii. 14); they numbered 45,650 (ii. 15); they were in the camp of Ruben on the south side (10–16); their offerings (vii. 42–47); their spy Guel (xiii. 16); numbered at Settim 40,500 (xxvi. 18); stood on Mount Hebal to curse (Deut. xxvii. 13); receives its share from Moses beyond the Jordan (Num. xxxii. 1–29; Deut. xxxiii. 20; Jos. xiii. 24); erect an altar which alarms the other tribes (Jos. xxii. 10); revolt under Jeroboam and form part of the kingdom of Israel; carried away captive by Theglathphalasar, king of Assyria (4 Kings xviii. 11).

TIBERIAS AND SEA OF GALILEE.

GAD, a prophet and friend of David (2 Kings xxiv. 11; 1 Kings xxii. 5); he gave David his choice of the three punishments for his sin (2 Kings xxiv. 12, 13); and directs him to raise an altar on the threshing-floor of Areuna (17).

GAD'DI, son of Susi, of the tribe of Manasses, one of the twelve spies (Num. xiii. 12).

GAD'DIS, surname of John, the eldest son of Mathathias (1 Mach. ii. 2).

GAD'ER, a city of the Chanaanites. Its king taken and put to death (Jos. xii. 13).

GAD'EROTH, a city south of Juda (2 Par. xxviii. 18).

GAD'GAD, a mountain in the desert of Pharan, the 29th station of the Israelites (Num. xxxiii. 32).

GAI'US or **CAIUS,** a disciple of St. Paul (Acts xix. 29; xx. 4; 1 Cor. i. 14; 3 John i.)

GAL'AAD, son of Machir, and grandson of Manasses (Num. xxvi. 29–31).

GAL'AAD, a part of Palestine, east of the Jordan (1 Kings xiii. 7). The mountains of Galaad were the commencement of Libanus (Jerem. xxii. 6); Jacob passed by the mountains of Galaad (Gen. xxxi. 21); Galaad was famous for its balm (Jerem. viii. 22; Gen. xxxvii. 25); Jephte was of Maspha in Galaad, and was apparently buried there (Judg. xi. 34; xii. 7).

GALA'TIA, a province of Asia Minor, south of the Black Sea (Acts xvi. 6).

GALA'TIANS, the Celtic people of Galatia. St. Paul preached to them A. D. 51, 54 (Acts xvi. 6; xviii. 23); and St. Peter also, as he addresses his epistle to them (1 Pet. i. 1); an army of Galatians attacking Babylonia were routed by Jews (2 Mach. viii. 20).

GALA'TIANS, Epistle of St. Paul to the, one of the canonical books of the New Testament written from Ephesus, A. D. 56 (Gal.)

GALGAL, a district and place west of the Jordan. Josue conquered the king of the nations of Galgal (xii. 23); the Israelites encamped in Galgal after passing the river, and set up the stones from the river bed (Jos. iv. 19, 20); here the people were circumcised (v. 2), and kept the Pasch (10); Saul made king at Galgal (1 Kings x. 8); Saul offered a holocaust in Galgal sinfully (xiii. 4-15); as the ark had rested there, it was a place of pilgrimage (Osee iv. 15; Amos iv. 4); idols also there (Judges iii. 19).

GAL'ILEE, under the Romans a large province. It included the cities given by Solomon to Hiram (Jos. xx. 7; 3 Kings ix. 11); so many strangers settled there that it was called Galilee of the Gentiles (Isai. ix. 1; Matt. iv. 15); in the time of our

SEA OF GALILEE, FROM THE NORTHWEST COAST.

Lord it was one of the three Roman provinces, Judea and Samaria being the others (Luke xvii. 11; Acts ix. 31). Nazareth, Cana, Tiberias, Capharnaum were all in Galilee (Luke i. 26; John ii. 1; vi. 1; Matt. iv. 13; ix. 1). Our Lord frequently preached and wrought miracles here (Matt. iv. 12; Acts x. 37); the apostles were all Galileans (Acts i. 11; Matt. xxvi. 73). Our Lord called a Galilean (69).

GAL'ILEE, Sea of (Mark i. 16); called also, of Genesareth and Tiberias.

GALL, as an emblem of bitterness (Job xx. 14; Jerem. viii. 14); gall of a fish used by Tobias in a miraculous way (Tob. vi. 9; xi. 4, 8, 13); gall and vinegar offered to our Lord on the cross (Matt. xxvii. 34).

GAL'LEYS, Balaam foretells the coming of the Romans in galleys to overthrow Assyrian and Hebrew (Num. xxiv. 24).

GALL'IO, brother of Seneca, the philosopher, and proconsul of Achaia. He refused at Corinth to hear the complaints of the Jews against St. Paul (Acts xviii. 12, 13).

GAMA'LIEL, doctor of the law, a Pharisee, master of St. Paul (Acts xxii. 3); he advised the Pharisees not to molest the apostles (v. 34-38).

GAMA'RIAS, son of Helcias, sent to Babylon by king Sedecias (Jer. xxix. 3, 4); one of the counsellors of king Joakim (xxxvi. 12).

GAR'DEN is used also in the sense of orchard. Gardens of pleasure (Ezech. xxxvi. 35; Joel ii. 3); paradise of pleasure (Gen. ii. 8); the king's garden (4 Kings xxv. 4; 2 Esd. iii. 15; Jer. xxxix. 4; lii. 7); contained the tombs of the kings (4 Kings xxi. 18, 26); gardens were places of devotion (Matt. xxvi. 36; John xviii. 1); the Jews made them scenes of idolatry (Isai. i. 29; lxv. 3; lxvi. 17); the garden of Solomon is referred to in Cant. iv. 12, 15; v. 1; vi. 1, 10; viii. 13).

GAR'AZIM, a mountain near Sichem, in Samaria. God commanded six tribes to stand on Garazim to bless those who kept the law, and six on Hebal to curse those who violated it (Deut. xi. 29; xxvii. 12; Jos. viii. 33); a temple was erected here by the Samaritans, Manasses, grandson of the high-priest Eliasib (2 Esd. xiii. 28), being, according to Josephus, the first schismatical high-priest; it became a temple of Jupiter, and was destroyed, but rebuilt as a temple to the true God. The Samaritan woman asked our Lord which public worship was right, that on Garazim or at Jerusalem, and he told her that salvation was with the Jews (John iv. 20-22).

GAR'LIC, a vegetable (Num. xi. 5).

GAR'MENT, woman healed by touching the hem of our Lord's garment (Matt. ix. 20); the soldiers cast lots for his garments (John xix. 23, 24); parable of the wedding garment (Matt. xxii. 11).

GAR'MENTS given by God to Adam and Eve after the fall (Gen. iii. 21); the Jews were accustomed to rend their garments in affliction (Gen. xliv. 13; Jos. vii. 6; Judg. xi. 35; 1 Kings iv. 12; 2 Kings xiii. 31; 3 Kings xxi. 27; 4 Kings v. 7; vi. 30; xi. 14; xviii. 37; xix. 1; xxii. 11, 19; Esth. iv. 1; Jer. xxxvi. 24; Joel ii. 13; 1 Mach. ii. 14; iii. 47; iv. 39; xi. 71; Matt. xxvi. 65; Acts xiv. 13; xvi. 22).

GAR'TERS (Num. xxxi. 50); slops (Douay); ornaments for the legs (Chall.), (Isai. iii. 20); were apparently gold anklets or bangles, still worn in the East.

GATES, used to represent a city or power (Gen. xxii. 17; xxiv. 60; Judg. v. 8; Ruth iv. 11; Ps. lxxxvi. 2; Matt. xvi. 18). Gates were then used for judgment, reception of ambassadors, etc. (Deut. xvi. 18; xxi. 19; xxv. 7; Jos. xx. 4; Judg. ix. 35; Ruth iv. 1, 11; Ps. cxxvi. 5). Gates of Jerusalem (2 Esd. iii. 1-31; xii. 38); at the gate of the temple called Beautiful St. Peter and St. John cured a lame man (Acts iii. 2).

GATH'ERER, the son of Vomiter. Chapter xxx. of Proverbs is given as his words. In Hebrew, it is Agur, the son of Jakeh.

GA'ZA, one of the cities of the Philistines (Gen. x. 19); within the territory of Juda (Jos. xv. 47; Judg. i. 18; 1 Kings vi. 17); Samson carried off its gates (Judg. xvi. 3); taken by Solomon (3 Kings iv. 24); it fell into the hands of the Philistines, but seem to have been taken by Ezechias (4 Kings xviii. 8).

GEB'BETHON, or Gabathon (Jos. xxi. 23), a city in the tribe of Dan, where Baasa killed Nabad, son of Jeroboam (3 Kings xv. 27).

GED'EON, son of Joas, of the tribe of Manasses, judge of Israel. He was raised up by God to deliver his people from the Madianites (Judg. vi. 11-24); he destroys the altar of Baal, from which he derives the surname of Jerobaal (25-32); God attests his mission by the miracle of the fleece (37-40); with only three hundred men he defeats the Madianites (vii.); he defeats and captures Zebee and Salmana, kings of Madian (viii. 4-12); destroys Succoth and Phanuel, which refused him aid (15-17); made

a golden ephod, which was worshipped at Ephra (27); died and was buried at Ephra (32).

GEHEN'NA, GEHENNON, the valley of Ennom, near Jerusalem, where Moloch was worshipped (Jerem. vii. 31); Josias defiled it to prevent the idolatry (4 Kings xxiii. 10; 2 Paral. xxxiv. 4); in the New Testament the word is used to mean *hell*, and is so translated (Matt. v. 22, 29, 30; x. 28; xviii. 9; xxiii. 15, 33; Mark ix. 42-46; Luke xii. 5; James iii. 6).

GE'HON, one of the rivers of Paradise, compassing all the land of Ethiopia (Gen. ii. 13); its overflow in the time of the vintage (Ecclus. xxiv. 37).

GEL'BOE, a mountain east of the plain of Esdraelon, where Saul was defeated and perished (1 Kings xxxi. 1-6; 2 Kings i. 6; xxi. 12; 1 Paral. x. 1).

GENEAL'OGIES of the descendants of Adam and Noe (Gen. x. 1, 5; 1 Paral. i. 4); of the descendants of Japheth (Gen. x. 1-5; 1 Paral. i. 5-7); of Cham (Gen. x. 6-20; 1 Paral. i. 8-16); of Sem down to Abraham (Gen. x. 21-29; xi. 10-32; 1 Paral. i. 17-27); of Esau (Gen. xxxvi. 10-43; 1 Paral. i. 35); of Abraham, Isaac, and Jacob (1 Paral. i. 34; ii. 1-55); of Juda and David (1 Paral. ii. 3-15); of other descendants of Juda (iv. 1-23); of the sons of Simeon (Gen. xlvi. 10; 1 Paral. iv. 24-37); of Ruben (Gen. xlvi. 9; 1 Paral. v. 1-8); of Gad (Gen. xlvi. 16; 1 Paral. v. 11-15); of Levi (Gen. xlvi. 11; 1 Paral. vi. 1-53); of Issachar (Gen. xlvi. 13; 1 Paral. vii. 1-5); of Nephthali (Gen. xlvi. 24; 1 Paral. vii. 13); of Manasses (Gen. xlvi. 20; 1 Paral. vii. 14-19); of Ephraim (Gen. xlvi. 20; 1 Paral. vii. 20-29); of Aser (Gen. xlvi. 17; 1 Paral. vii. 30-39); of Benjamin and Saul (1 Paral. viii. 1-40); of Jesus Christ (Matt. i. 1-17; Luke iii. 23-38).

GEN'ERATION used in the sense of creation (Gen. ii. 4); of genealogy (v. 1).

GENES'ARETH, lake of (Luke v. 1); or sea of Galilee (Matt. iv. 18; Mark vii. 31; John v. 1); or Sea of Tiberias (John vi. 1). It is called Sea of Cenereth (Num. xxxiv. 11); or Ceneroth (Jos. xii. 3). It is of oval shape, thirteen miles long, formed by the river Jordan. Much of our Saviour's public life was spent near it.

GEN'ESIS, the first book of the Pentateuch or Five Books of Moses. One of the canonical books of the Old Testament, and called in Hebrew Beresith. It contains the history from the Creation to the death of Joseph (Gen.)

GEN'TILES, a term used to express all other nations than the Jews (Ps. ii. 1, 8; ix. 6, 12, 21; Ezech. xxxvi. 6, 7, 23; Acts xvii. 4; 1 Cor. x. 32); conversion of the Gentiles (Gen. xlix. 10; Num. xxiv. 17; Deut. xxxii. 43; Ps. ii. 8; xxi. 28; lxvii. 32; lxxix. 1, 8; lxxxvi. 4; Is. ii. 2; xi. 10; Jer. ix. 26; Osee ii. 1; Mich. iv. 2; Soph. iii. 9; Zach. ii. 11; Matt. viii. 11; John x. 16; Acts viii. 26; 1 Cor. xii. 2).

GERA'RA, a city of the Philistines (Gen. x. 19); between Cades and Sur; Abraham abode at it (xx. 1); Isaac also (xxvi. 1, 6, 17); Asa king of Juda defeated the Ethiopians at Gerara (2 Paral. xiv. 13, 14).

GER'ASENS. The country of the Gerasens was on the Sea of Galilee. Our Lord here cured two men possessed by devils (Matt. viii. 28-34).

GER'GESITES, one of the seven nations of the land of Chanaan (Gen. xv. 21; Deut. vii. 1; Jos. iii. 10; xxiv. 11).

GER'SON, son of Levi and head of one of the great Levitical families (Gen. xlvi. 11; Ex. vi. 16; Num. iii. 21).

GESS'EN, a district of Egypt which Joseph assigned to his father and brothers (Gen. xlvi. 28; xlvii. 6); called also Ramesses (xlvii. 11); and Gosen (Jos. x., xi., xv.)

GES'SURI, a district near the Philistines (1 Kings xxvii. 8).

GESSU'RI, a district beyond the Jordan (Deut. iii. 14; Jos. xii. 5; xiii. 13); the people recognized Isboseth a king (2 Kings ii. 9).

GES'SUR of Syria, whose king's daughter David married, and who bore him Absalom (2 Kings xiii. 37; xv. 8; 1 Paral. ii. 23).

GETH, a city of the Philistines (1 Kings vi. 17); birth-place of Goliath (xvii. 4); it was taken by David (1 Paral. xviii. 1); rebuilt and fortified by Roboam (2 Paral. xi. 8); it was reconquered by Ozias (2 Paral. xxvi. 6); and by Ezechias; it was the most southerly town of the Philistines, as Accaron was the northern (1 Kings vii. 14; xvii. 52).

GETH'EPHER, or Geth in Opher (Jos. xix. 13); was the birth-place of the prophet Jonas (4 Kings xiv. 25).

GETH'SEM'ANI, a village on the Mount of Olives beyond the Cedron (John xviii. 1); to which our Lord retired to pray, and where he had the bloody sweat in the garden (Matt. xxvi. 36; Mark xiv. 32; Luke xxii. 39). A few olive trees still mark the spot near the tomb of the Blessed Virgin.

GI'ANTS; among the descendants of Cain (Gen. vi. 4); in Chanaan the Raphaim or Arapha (Gen. xiv. 5; Jos. xiii. 12; 2 Kings xxi. 18; 1 Paral. xx. 4); Enac, Enacim (Deut. i. 28).

GIB'BET, the king of Hai hung upon (Jos. viii. 29); Aman hanged on the gibbet he had prepared for Mardochai (Esth. vii. 10).

GIB'LIANS, people of Giblos prepared timber and stone for the temple (3 Kings v. 18).

GI'EZI, the servant of Eliseus (4 Kings v. 25); struck with leprosy for seeking a reward from Naaman (v. 26, 27).

GI'HON, a fountain west of Jerusalem, where Solomon was anointed king (3 Kings i. 33); Ezechias

GARDEN OF GETHSEMANI.

led its waters into Jerusalem to supply water in case of siege (2 Paral. xxxii. 30).

GIR'DLE of the prophet Jeremias, its signifi-

cation (Jer. xiii.); in the hands of the prophet Agabus (Acts xxi. 11).

THE EMISSARY GOAT SENT INTO THE DESERT.

GITH, a small grain raised in Palestine (Isai. xxviii. 25, 27).

GIVE. We are to give without accepting of persons, but especially to the faithful (Ecclus. iv. 36; vii. 36; Matt. v. 42; Luke vi. 30, 38; Rom. xii. 13; Gal. vi. 10); it is more blessed to give than to receive (Acts xx. 35).

GLASS. A sea of glass before the throne (Apoc. iv. 6; xv. 2); the golden walls of the New Jerusalem compared to (xxi. 18).

GLO'RY of God to be sought in all things (Jos. vii. 19; Ps. cxiii. (2) 1; Matt. vi. 9; John xvii. 4; Acts iii. 13; xii. 23; 1 Cor. vi. 20; x. 31; Philip. i. 20; Col. iii. 17; Tit. ii. 10).

GOATS. Ceremony of the emissary goat (Lev. xvi. 10); goats offered in sacrifice (ix. 3; xxiii. 19; Num. xv. 27; xxviii. 15, 22, 29; xxix. 16); wild goats (1 Kings xxiv. 3; Job xxxix. 1); goats as type of the wicked (Matt. xxv. 32, 33).

GOB, a place where two battles were fought with the Philistines (2 Kings xxi. 18); called Gazer in 1 Paral. xx. 4.

GOD, he is one in essence (Deut. iv. 35; vi. 4; xxxii. 39; 1 Tim. ii. 5; 1 Kings ii. 2; 2 Kings vii. 22; Wisd. xii. 13; Isai. xlv. 21; Mark xii. 29; John xvii. 3; 1 Cor. viii. 4, 6); in three divine persons (1 John v. 7; Matt. xxviii. 19; Mark i. 10, 11; ix. 6; Matt. iii. 16, 17; Luke iii. 22; ix. 35; John xiv. 26; xv. 26; 2 Cor. xiii. 13); eternal (Gen. xxi. 33; Ex. xv. 18; Job xxxvi. 26; Isai. xli. 4; lvii. 15; Dan. vii. 9; 2 Mach. i. 24; Rom. xvi. 26; Heb. i. 8; Apoc. xxi. 6); almighty (Gen. xvii. 1; xxxv. 11; xlviii. 3; 1 Kings xiv. 6; 2 Paral. xiv. 11; Wisd. xi. 23;

Job xlii. 2; Isai. xl. 10; xlvi. 9; lix. 1; Jer. xxxii. 17, 27; Zach. viii. 6; 2 Mach. i. 24; Mark

ix. 22; xiv. 36; Luke i. 37; xviii. 27; Eph. iii. 20; Apoc. xix. 6); omniscient and all seeing (Ex. iii. 19; Num. xii. 2; Deut. xxxi. 21; 1 Kings ii. 3; 2 Paral. xvi. 9; Job xiv. 16; xxviii. 24; xlii. 2; Ps. xxxii. 13; xxxvii. 10; Prov. xv. 3, 11; xxiv. 12; Isai. xxix. 15; xl. 27; xlviii. 4; Jer. i. 5; vii. 11; xvii. 10; xxiii. 24; xxxii. 19; Ezech. ii. 4; Wisd. i. 9; Ecclus. xvi. 16; xvii. 13; xxiii. 27; xxxix. 24, 29; 2 Mach. ix. 5; xii. 22; Matt. vi. 4; xxi. 2; Mark ii. 8; xiv. 13; John i. 48; xiii. 21; xvi. 30; xxi. 17; Acts ii. 23; xv. 8; Rom. viii. 27; 1 Thess. ii. 4; Heb. iv. 13; 1 John iii. 20); perfect (Matt. v. 48); infinitely good (2 Mach. i. 24; Matt. xix. 17; Luke xviii. 19); holy (1 Kings ii. 2; Apoc. xv. 4;); just (2 Mach. i. 25); immortal (1 Tim. vi. 16); immense and not to be confined (3 Kings viii. 27; 2 Paral. ii. 6; vi. 18; Job xi. 8; Ps. cxxxviii. 8; Isai. lxvi. 1; Matt. v. 35); Creator and Lord of heaven and earth (Gen. i. 1; xiv. 19; 1 Paral. xxix. 11; Ps. lxxxviii. 12; cxiii. (2) 16; Isai. xxviii. 16; xl. 28; li. 13; Jer. x. 12; xxxii. 17; Bar. iii. 32; Jonas i. 9; Ecclus. xxiv. 12; 2 Mach. i. 24; Matt. xi. 25; John i. 3; Acts iv. 24; xvii. 24; 1 Cor. viii. 6; Eph. iii. 9; Col. i. 16; Heb. i. 2, 10; iii. 4; xi. 3; Apoc. iv. 11; x. 6; xiv. 7); it is his right to be honored and glorified (Ps. cxiii. (2) 1; Isai. xlii. 8; 1 Tim. i. 17); to be served (Deut. vi. 13; x. 20; 1 Kings vii. 3; Matt. iv. 10; Luke iv. 8); it is his incommunicable right to be adored as God (Ex. xx. 5; Lev. xxvi. 1; Deut. v. 9; Matt. iv. 10); God governs all (Job xii. 10; Ps. cxiii. 3; cxxvi 1; Prov. xvi. 4, 9; Isai. xlviii. 7; Jer. xxvii. 5; Dan. ii. 21; Matt. xxv. 32; John v. 17; 2 Cor. iii. 5; Apoc. iv. 11); directs the ways of man (Prov. xx. 24; Jer. x. 23; Job xxxiv. 21); the heart of kings is in his hand (Prov. xxi. 1, 30); he gives power and glory (Dan. v. 18); he shows mercy to whom he pleases (Rom. ix. 15); works in us to will and to do (Phil. ii. 13; Heb. xiii. 21); God is the Father of all who obey him (Deut. xxxii. 6; Ps. cii. 13; Isai. lxiii. 16; Jer. iii. 4, 19; Mal. i. 6; ii. 10; Ecclus. xxiii. 1; Matt. xxiii,

9; Luke xi. 2; Rom. i. 7; viii. 15; 1 Cor. viii. 6; 2 Cor. vi. 18; Eph. iv. 6; 1 Thess. i. 3; 2 Thess. ii. 15); he is the Father of mercy and God of all comfort (2 Cor. i. 3); true, faithful and merciful (Ex. xxxiv. 6; Deut. vii. 9; xxxii. 4; Isaias xlix. 7; John iii. 33; Rom. iii. 4; 1 Cor. i. 9; 2 Thess. iii. 3; Tit. i. 2; Heb. x. 23; 1 John i. 9; Apoc. iii. 7, 14); no man can see God (Ex. xxxiii. 20; Deut. iv. 12; John i. 18; vi. 46; 1 Tim. vi. 16; 1 John iv. 12); neither God nor the things of God can be perfectly known or comprehended by the mind of man (Job xxxii. 8; Ps. xciii. 8; cxviii.; Isai. liv. 13; Matt. xiii. 11; xvi. 17; Luke viii. 10; x. 21; John i. 10; iii. 3; vi. 44, 64; xiv. 17; xvii. 6; Acts xvi. 14; Rom. i. 19; xi. 33; 1 Cor. ii.; Gal. i. 11; 1 Tim. vi. 16; Apoc. iii. 7); God is the protector of all who serve him (Gen. xvii. 1, 7; Ex. vi. 2; xx. 2; xxix. 45; Lev. xxvi. 11; Ps. xvii. 3; xlix. 6; Isai. xxx. 19; Jer. xxx. 22; xxxii. 38; Ezech. xxxvii. 23; John x. 28); God is the judge of all (Gen. xviii. 25; Deut. x. 17; Job xxxiv. 11; Ps. lxi. 13; xciii. 2; xcv. 10, 13; Ecclus. xxxv. 22; Isai. xi. 4; Jerem. xvii. 10; xxv. 14; Matt. xvi. 27; xxv. 31; 2 Tim. iv. 8; Heb. xii. 23); God is not the author of sin (Ex. xxiii. 7; 2 Paral. xix. 7; Judith v. 21; Job xxxiv. 10; Ps. xliv. 8; Prov. xv. 8; Ecclus. xv. 21; Rom. ix. 14; 2 Cor. vi 15); does not permit us to be tempted beyond what we are able (1 Cor. x. 13; James i. 13); punishes sin in this world (Deut. xxxii. 23; 3 Kings ix. 9; xxi. 29; Isai. xlv. 7; Jer. xi. 11; xxxii. 42; Baruch ii. 2; Amos iii. 6; Jonas iii. 10; Mich. i. 12; ii. 3); and eternally in hell (Ps. ix. 18; xxx. 18; Wisd. v. 14; Bar. ii. 17; Luke xvi. 22; 2 Pet. ii. 4; Matt. v. 29, 30; xviii. 9; xxiii. 33; Luke xii. 5; Apoc. xx. 9, 10).

GODO′LIAS, son of Ahican, left as governor in Jerusalem by Nabuchodonosor after the destruction of the city and temple (Jerem. xl.–xli.; 4 Kings xxv. 25). Killed by Ismahel, an emissary of Baalis, king of Ammon (Jerem. xli. 2).

GOG, prince of Mosoch and Thubal, in the land of Magog, announced by Ezechiel as a persecutor of the church (xxxviii.–xxxix.); also by St. John (Apoc. xx. 7).

GOLD, a precious metal, the first mentioned in the Bible as found in the land of Hevilath (Gen. ii. 11, 12); Solomon obtained gold from Ophir (3 Kings ix. 28) and Saba (x. 10); Jeremias mentions gold from Ophaz (x. 9); it was used for personal ornaments, and for the most sacred objects used in the public worship of God (Ecclus. xxxii. 7; Ex. xxv., xxviii., xxxvii.).

GOL′GOTHA, the Hebrew name of Calvary (Matt. xxvii. 33; Mark xv. 22; John xix. 17).

GOLI′ATH of Geth, a giant champion of the Philistines, who defied the armies of Saul (1 Kings xvii. 1–11); his height was six cubits and a span (10½ feet); David met him in the valley of Terebinth, armed only with a sling, and slew him (40–51).

GO′MER, son of Japheth (Gen. x. 2).

GO′MER, daughter of Debelaim, an unchaste or idolatrous woman, whom Osee was commanded to marry (Osee i. 2, 3).

GO′MOR, a Hebrew measure, the tenth part of the epha (Ex. xvi. 16–36).

GOMOR′RHA, one of the Pentapolis or five cities of the plain (Gen. x. 19); Bersa, its king, revolts against Chodorlahomor (xiv. 3, 4); but is defeated with his allies in the Woodland Vale (10); its wickedness provokes the divine vengeance (xviii. 20); destroyed by fire from heaven (xix. 24). The punishment of these guilty cities is frequently referred

to (Deut. xxix., xxxii.; Isai. i., xiii.; Jer. xxiii., xlix., l.; Amos iv.; Sophon. ii.; Matt. x. 15; Rom. ix. 29; Jude i. 7; 2 Pet. ii. 6).

GOOD HAVENS, a port in Crete, near the city of Thalassa, reached by St. Paul on his way to Rome (Acts xxvii. 8).

GOOD′NESS of God (Ex. xxxiv. 6, 7; 2 Kings xxiv. 14; Wis. xi. 24; Ps. xxxv. 6; lxxxv. 5; cii.; cxxxv.; cxliv. 8; Luke vi. 36; John iii. 16; 1 Cor. i. 3; Eph. ii. 4; 1 Tim. ii. 4; Titus ii. 11; iii. 4).

GOR′GIAS, general of Antiochus Epiphanes, sent by Lysias against the Machabees (1 Mach. iii. 38); defeated by Judas, near Emmaus (iv. 13–22; 2 Mach. viii.); he defeats Joseph and Azarias near Jamnia (1 Mach. v. 59, 60); nearly captured by Dositheus (2 Mach. xii. 35).

GORTY′NA, a city of Crete (1 Mach. xv. 23).

GREEK SOLDIER.

GOS′PEL, applied to the books of the four evangelists, St. Matthew, St. Mark, St. Luke, and St. John; four canonical books of the New Testament, Matt., Mark., Luke, John; used in the Bible to mean the doctrine of Jesus Christ, the Messias (Matt. iv. 23; ix. 35; xxiv. 14; xxvi. 13; Mark i. 14, 15; viii., x., xiii., xiv., xvi.; Acts xv. 7; xx. 24; 1 Cor. iv., ix., xv.; 2 Cor. ii., iv., viii.–xi; Gal. i., ii.; Eph. i., iii., vi.; Phil. i., ii., iv.; Coloss. i.; 1 Thess. i., ii., iii.; 2 Thess. i., ii.; 1 Tim. i.; 2 Tim. i., ii.; Philem.; 1 Pet. iv. 17; Apoc. xiv. 6). The preaching of the gospel foretold (Gen. xxviii. 14; Is. lv. 5; lxi.); we must not be ashamed of the gospel (Mark viii. 38; Rom. i. 16; 2 Tim. i. 8); obligation of supporting the priests, ministers of the gospel (Deut. xii. 19; 1 Thess. v. 12).

GO′ZAN, a river or district to which the ten tribes were carried (4 Kings xvii.–xix.; 1 Paral. v. 26; Isai. xxxvii. 11).

GRACE, a gratuitous gift of God (1 Cor. xii.; Eph. iv. 7; 1 Pet. iv. 10); it is supernatural, and makes the soul pleasing to God (Luke i. 28; ii. 40; John i. 16; Rom. i. 7; 1 Cor. xvi. 23; 2 Cor. i. 12; Gal. v. 4; Heb. xiii. 9; James vi. 6).

"GRACE to you and peace from God, our Father, and from the Lord Jesus Christ," a salutation used by St. Paul and St. Peter (Rom. i. 7; 1 Cor. i. 3; 2 Cor. i. 2; Gal. i. 3; Eph. i. 2; Phil. i. 2; Coloss. i. 3; 1 Thess. i. 2; 2 Thess. i. 2; Titus i. 4; Phil. 3; 1 Pet. i. 2; 2 Pet. i. 2); "Grace, mercy, and peace" (1 Tim. i. 2; 2 Tim. i. 2; see 2 John 3; Apoc. i. 4).

GRAPES, planted by Noe (Gen. ix. 20); in Egypt (xl. 10); not to be gathered in the year of

jubilee (Lev. xxv. 5); could be eaten in another's vineyard but not carried away (Deut. xxiii. 24); Nazarites forbidden to eat (Num. vi. 3); immense clusters of grapes found in the Promised Land (xiii. 25); treading out grapes (Job xxiv. 11; Jer. xlviii. 33; Amos ix. 13). "Do men gather grapes of thorns?" (Matt. vii. 16).

GRAT′ITUDE recommended (Num. xv. 18; Deut. iv. 9; 2 Paral. xv. 11; Wisdom xviii. 2; Acts xxiv. 21; Eph. v. 20; Phil. iv. 6; Col. ii. 7; iii. 15).

GRASS, a type of man's short life (Ps. xxxvi. 2; lxxxix. 6; Isai. xl. 6; Matt. vi. 30; Luke xii. 28; James i. 10).

GREEKS, used for Hellenist Jews, that is, those who spoke Greek (Acts vi. 1; ix. 29).

GRIF′FON, a bird of prey, and therefore unclean (Deut. xiv. 12).

GROAT, an English coin, now obsolete, but used for the drachma, a coin worth about fifteen cents.

GROATS, our Lord's parable of the (Luke xv. 8, 9).

HAB′ACUC, a native of Bezocher, a prophet, carried by an angel to relieve Daniel in the lion's den (Dan. xiv. 32); he is one of the twelve lesser prophets, and foretold in Juda the invasion of the Chaldeans (Hab.)

HAB′ACUC, one of the canonical books of the Old Testament (Hab.)

HA′BER, the Cinite, husband of Jahel, who killed Sisara (Judg. iv. 11–22).

HA′BOR, a city of the Medes, on the river Gozan (4 Kings xvii.–xviii.; 1 Paral. v. 26), to which the ten tribes were carried.

HACEL′DAMA, the field of blood, the potter's field, bought as a burial-place for strangers by the chief priests, with the money Judas brought back (Matt. xxvii. 8; Acts i. 19).

HAG′GITH, wife of David, and mother of Adonias (2 Kings iii. 4; 3 Kings i., ii.)

HA′I, a city east of Bethel (Gen. xii. 8); besieged in vain (Jos. vii. 5); finally taken and destroyed with all its people (viii. 19–26; x. 1, 2; xii. 9); the king hanged on a gibbet (viii. 29).

HAIR, the Israelites not to cut the hair roundwise (Lev. xix. 27); Samson's strength lay in his hair (Judg. xvi. 19); Absalom noted for his beautiful hair (2 Kings xiv. 26); the hair was cut in time of sorrow (Isaias iii. 17, 24; xv. 2; Jerem. vii. 29); or torn (1 Esd. ix. 3); the hair was anointed in time of joy (Ruth iii. 3; 2 Kings xiv. 2; Ps. xxii. 5; xliv. 8; Eccles. ix. 8; Matt. vi. 17; xxvi. 7; Luke vii. 46). The women curled their hair (Isai. iii. 24), and plaited it (Judith x. 3).

HA′LA, a city of the Medes, to which the ten tribes were carried (4 Kings xvii. 6; xviii. 11).

HALL, used for court of the high-priest (Luke xxii. 55), and for Pilate's judgment-hall in Matt. xxvii. 27; John xviii. 28; court of the palace (Mark xv. 16).

HAN′ANEEL, the tower of, part of the wall of Jerusalem (2 Esd. iii. 1; xii. 38; Jerem. xxxi. 38; Zach. xiv. 10). It was near the Fish-Gate.

HANANI′AS, son of Azur, of Gabaon, a false prophet in the reign of Sedecias, king of Juda, who opposed Jeremias (Jerem. xxviii.) Jeremias foretold his death that year, which took place (16, 17).

HAND, ordered to be cut off (Deut. xxv. 12); hands of idol Dagon cut off (1 Kings v. 5); a mysterious handwriting on the wall (Dan. v. 5); the cure of the withered hand (Luke vi. 10).

HA'RAN, a town perhaps in Mesopotamia, to which Thare proceeded with Abram and Lot, and where he died (Gen. xi. 31, 32); Abram set out from it at the age of seventy-five, after being called by God (xii. 1-4); Jacob fled from Esau to his uncle Laban in Haran (xxvii. 43; xxviii. 10; xxix. 4).

HARD'ENING of the heart comes from the sinner alone, not from God (Ex. iv. 21; Deut. xv. 7; Ps. xciv. 8; Heb. iii. 8, 15; iv. 7).

HARD'NESS of heart punished (Job xx. 19; Prov. xxi. 10; Matt. xviii. 30, 34; xxv. 42; James ii. 16); examples (Ex. i. 13; Deut. xxiii. 4; Judges viii. 6; 1 Kings xxv. 10; Amos i. 6; Luke xvi. 21).

HARE, classed among unclean animals (Lev. xi. 6; Deut. xiv. 7).

HA'RIM, the third of the twenty-four priestly families (1 Par. xxiv. 8; 1 Esd. ii. 39; x. 21).

HAR'LOT, a warning against (Prov. v. 3; vi. 24-26; vii. 13-27); the law against (Deut. xxiii. 17).

HAR'MA or **HORMA,** a city in the tribe of Juda and afterwards of Simeon (Jos. xv. 30; xix. 4); it was captured by the Israelites (Num. xxi. 3); it was originally called Sephaath (Judg. i. 17); the Israelites bound themselves by vow to destroy all belonging to the king of Arad; and called it Horma, or the Anathema; Josue took the king of Herma (Jos. xii. 14).

HARP, invented by Jubal, son of Lamech (Gen. iv. 21); David played on the harp to free Saul from the evil spirit (1 Kings xvi. 23); used in weddings (Gen. xxxi. 27); in divine worship (1 Paral. xiii. 8; xv. 16, 21; xxv. 1; 2 Par. v. 12; Ps. xxxii. 2; xlii.; lvi., etc.; Amos v. 23); in the vision of St. John (Apoc. v. 8; xiv. 2; xv. 2).

HART, a kind of deer, reckoned among the clean animals (Deut. xii. 15; xiv. 5; xv. 22; 3 Kings iv. 23); used as a figure of fleetness (Gen. xlix. 21; 2 Kings xxii. 34; Ps. xvii. 34; xli. 1; Cant. ii. 7, 9; iii. 5; Hab. iii. 19).

HAR'VEST, the Mosaic law as to (Lev. xxiii. 22); mysterious harvest (Apoc. xiv. 15).

HOUSE WITH A PARAPET.

HAS'EROTH, one of the stations of the Israelites in the desert (Num. xi. 34; xiii. 1; xxxiii. 17, 18; Deut. i. 1).

HA'TRED forbidden (Lev. xix. 17); hatred of God's enemies (Ps. cxxxviii. 21); reconciliation with our enemies commanded (Matt. v. 23); the world's hatred of the disciples of Christ (Mark xiii. 13); hatred of evil (Ps. xcvi. 10; Amos vi. 8).

HAV'OTHJAIR, towns or hamlets beyond the Jordan conquered by Jair (Num. xxxii. 41; Deut. iii. 14; Judg. x. 4).

HAWK, a bird of prey, forbidden as food (Lev. xi. 16; Deut. xiv. 15; Job xxxix. 13, 26).

HAZ'AEL, king of Syria; Elias was directed to anoint him (3 Kings xix. 15, 16); Eliseus predicted his elevation to the throne (4 Kings viii. 13); he put Benadad to death, 884 B.C., and as king ravaged Israel during the absence of Jehu (4 Kings x. 32, 33); in the reign of Joas he attacked Juda, took Geth, and marched on Jerusalem; Joas purchased peace with the treasures of the temple, 839 B.C. (4 Kings xii. 17); his army the next year took Jerusalem, and put many of the princes to death (2 Paral. xxiv. 23); he also desolated Israel (4 Kings xiii. 3); he died about 839 B.C.

HEAD, directions as to covering the head in prayer (1 Cor. xi. 4-6).

HEART, the heart is purified and sanctified by God (Ps. l. 12; John xiii. 10; xv. 3; xvii. 19; Acts xv. 9; 1 Cor. vi. 11; Eph. v. 26; Heb. i. 3; ix. 14; x. 14; xiii. 12); God accepts a man's heart or good-will for the deed (Gen. iv. 4; xxii. 12; Ex. xxv. 2; xxxv. 5; Deut. xix. 5; Matt. xv. 8; Mark xii. 43; Luke xxi. 3; 2 Cor. viii. 12).

HEARTH, cakes baked on the hearth (Gen. xviii. 6); it is used in Jerem. xxxvi. 22 for brazier or chafing-dish.

HEBRON.

HEATH'ENS, used in the New Testament in the sense of Gentiles (Matt. v. 47; vi. 7; xviii. 17).

HEAVEN, the firmament, created by God (Gen. i. 7, 8; Ps. xxxii. 6; cxxiii.; cxxxiii.; cxlv.); it proclaims his glory (Ps. xviii. 2; cxlviii. 4); heaven and earth shall pass away (Matt. xxiv. 35); a new heaven and new earth (Isai. lxv. 17; 2 Pet. iii. 13; Apoc. xxi. 1); heaven the abode of God and his angels and saints (Deut. iv. 39; Jos. ii. 11; 3 Kings viii. 23-49; 2 Paral. vi.; 2 Esd. ix. 6; Ps. x. 5; xiii. 2; xxxii. 23; lii. 3; cii. 19; cxxii. 1; Lament. iii. 50; Matt. v. 16, 45; vi. 9; vii. 10, 21; x. 32, 33; xxii. 30; Mark xii. 25; xiii. 32; Luke xxii. 43); manna styled bread from heaven (Ps. lxxvii. 24; civ. 40; John vi. 31, 32); the Holy Eucharist the true bread from heaven (32–52); the kingdom of heaven the church (Matt. iii. 2; iv. 17; v. 18; xiii. 11-47; etc.)

HE'BER, son of Sale (Gen. x. 24; xi. 14).

HE'BREW, the language of the Israelites. It is one of the Semitic languages, allied to the Phœnician and Arabic. It was written at first with the letters now called Old Hebrew or Samaritan, but during the captivity the square characters now used were adopted. The vowels generally were omitted. In the revival of Hebrew learning after the establishment of Christianity, a school at Masora introduced vowel points to fix the reading then in use. This differed from that previously in vogue, even as late as the time of the Septuagint; but as the Hebrew was a living tongue when the seventy translated into Greek, their rendering of names must be of higher authority than that of the Masoretic rabbis when the language was a dead one.

HE'BREWS, Epistle of St. Paul to the, one of the canonical books of the New Testament (Heb.)

HE'BREWS, the descendants of Abraham, and especially of Jacob (Gen. xiv. 13); chosen by God and separated from the other nations in Abraham (xii. 2, 7; xiii. 15; xv. 13; xvii. 8); the sons of Jacob go down to Egypt and dwell there (xlvi. 6); their rapid increase (Ex. i. 7); they are persecuted by Pharao (i.);

they are led out of Egypt by Moses (xii. 37); they wander in the desert (xiii. 18); they walk through the Red Sea (xiv. 22); cross the Jordan dry foot

COURT-YARD OF AN EASTERN HOUSE.

(Jos. iii.); occupy the promised land (iv. 12); each tribe receives the portion assigned to it (xiii.; xxii.); governed by Moses, and then by Josue (Ex.; Deut.; Jos.); then by judges (Judg.); they ask a king (1 Kings viii. 5); consequences (2 Kings v. 2); on the death of Solomon the kingdom divided into Juda and Israel (3 Kings xii. 16–19); the kingdom of Israel overthrown, 730 B. C., by Salmanasar, king of the Assyrians, and never restored (4 Kings xvii. 1–6); the kingdom of Juda overthrown, 590 B. C.; Jerusalem and the temple destroyed, the king taken and the people carried to Babylon (xxv.); Cyrus permits them to return and rebuild their city (1 Esd. i. 1); they are persecuted under the tyrant Antiochus (1 Mach. i.–iv.); revolt under the Machabees (v.)

HE'BRON, one of the oldest cities in the world (Num. xiii. 23); called also Cariatharbe (Jos. xiv. 15); Abraham dwells there (Gen. xiii. 18); he, with Sara and Isaac, interred there (xxxv. 27–29); assigned to Juda (Jos. xiv. 13); Josue takes it and kills king Oham (x. 3, 23, 37); taken by Othoniel (Judg. i. 10); a city of refuge (Jos. xx. 7; xxi. 11, 13); David reigns there (2 Kings ii. 3); Absalom revolts at (xv. 7–10); called also Mambre (Gen. xxiii. 19).

HE'BRON or HEBRONI, third son of Caath, head of one of the priestly families (Ex. vi. 18; Num. iii. 19–27; 1 Paral. vi. 2, 18; xxiii. 12, 19).

HEBRO'NA, one of the stations of the Israelites in the desert (Num. xxxiii. 34).

HE'LAM, a place where David defeated the Syrians and captured their chariots and horses (2 Kings x. 17; 1 Paral. xix. 18).

HEL'CIAS, grandson of Sellum, high-priest during the reign of Josias. In his time the law was found in the temple, 624 B. C.; (4 Kings xxii.–xxiii.; 2 Paral. xxxiv.)

HEL'CIAS, father of preceding; he flourished in the time of Ezechias (Baruch i. 7; 4 Kings xviii. 18).

HE'LI, of the race of Ithamar, high-priest, judged Israel forty years, 1156–1116 B. C. He succeeded Abdon (1 Kings i. 3); threatened by God for permitting the misconduct of his sons (ii. 27; iii. 12); falls back and dies on hearing of the capture of the ark and the death of his sons (iv. 18).

HELIODO'RUS, prime minister of Seleucus Philopator, king of Syria (2 Mach. iii. 7); sent to carry off the treasures of the temple, but was chastised by angels and carried off insensible (v. 18); cured by the prayers of Onias the high-priest (iii. 33).

HELIOP'OLIS, a city of Egypt. Joseph marries Aseneth, daughter of Putiphare, priest of Heliopolis (Gen. xli. 45; xlvi. 20); Ezechiel foretells that its sons shall fall by the sword (xxx. 17).

HELL, the pains of hell (Deut. xxxii. 22; Job xxiv. 19; Ps. xx. 10; cxi. 10; Ecclus. xxi. 10; Isai. v. 14; xxxiv. 9, 10; Jer. xv. 14; Mal. iv. 1; Matt. viii. 12; Luke xiii. 28; Apoc. xiv. 10); the punishment proportioned to guilt (Wisd. xi. 17; Luke xvi. 25; Apoc. xix. 20); it is endless (Isai. lxvi. 24; Matt. xxv. 41; 2 Thess. i. 9).

HE'LON, a Levitical city of the tribe of Dan (1 Paral. vi. 69).

HEM. See FRINGES.

HE'MOR, prince of Sichem, sells land to Jacob (Gen. xxxiii. 19); his city taken and he is slain for the sin of his son (xxxiv.)

HE'NOCH, a son of Cain (Gen. iv. 17); and a city built by Cain and named after his son (17).

HE'NOCH, son of Jared, of the race of Seth (Gen. v. 18); father of Mathusala (21); he lived 365 years (23); "and he walked with God and was seen no more, because God took him" (24).

HER, eldest son of Juda, cut off prematurely on account of his wickedness (Gen. xxxviii. 7).

HER'CULES. Jason, a usurper of the high-priesthood, sends money for sacrifices to this demi-god (2 Mach. iv. 19).

HER'ESY, used by St. Luke for sect; heresy of the Sadducees (Acts v. 17); of the Pharisees (Ch. sect),

(xv. 5; xxvi. 5); used for false doctrine by St. Paul (xxiv. 14; Acts xxiv. 5, Ch. sect; 1 Cor. xi. 19); foretold (1 Tim. iv.)

HER'ETICS, those who adhere to false doctrines. God permits them in order to try the faithful (1 Cor. xi. 19); there were heretics in the time of the apostles (1 Tim. i. 20; 2 Tim. ii. 18; 1 John ii. 18; 2 John 7; Apoc. ii. 15); it was foretold that there would be heresies (1 Tim. iv. 1; 2 Tim. iii.; 2 Peter ii.; iii.; Jude 18); they and their favorers to be avoided (Matt. vii. 15; Rom. xvi. 18; 2 Thess. iii. 14; 2 Tim. ii. 16; iii. 5; Tit. iii. 10; 2 John 10).

HER'MA, or Horma, a city of Chanaan (Jos. xii. 14).

HER'MAS and HER'MES, disciples mentioned by St. Paul (Rom. xvi. 14). A work called the Shepherd is ascribed to Hermas.

HERMOG'ENES, a disciple who deserted St. Paul (2 Tim. i. 15).

HER'MON, a mountain in the northeast of Palestine (Deut. iii. 8; iv. 48; Jos. xi. 17; xii. 1; Ps. cxxxii. 3); called Sarion by the people of Sidon, and Sanir by the Amorrhites.

HER'MON, or HERMO'NIIM, a mountain in the tribe of Issachar (Ps. xli. 7).

HER'OD THE GREAT, son of Antipater, appointed tetrarch of Judæa by Antony, B. C. 41; but was expelled by Antigonus, and fled to Rome. Appointed king of Judæa he took Jerusalem, B. C. 37; our Lord was born during his reign (Matt. ii. 1); when baffled by the wise men he ordered the massacre of the children of Bethlehem (16); his death (19).

HER'OD ANTIPAS, son of Herod the Great, made by his father tetrarch of Galilee (Matt. xiv. 1; Luke iii. 19; ix. 7; Acts xiii. 1); unlawfully takes Herodias, his brother's wife (Mark vi. 17), and casts St. John the Baptist into prison for rebuking him (Matt. xiv. 3; Mark vi. 18; Luke iii. 19, 20), and put him to death at the request of her daughter (Matt. xiv. 4; Mark vi. 19–27); Pilate sent our Lord to him (Luke xxiii. 7); he died in exile at Lyons, A. D. 39.

HER'OD PHILIP, son of Herod the Great and Mariamne, married Herodias, who left him for Herod Antipas (Mark vi. 17). Herod Philip II., son of Herod the Great and Cleopatra. He was tetrarch of Iturea and Trachonitis (Luke iii. 1); he built Cesarea Philippi, called after him (Matt. xvi. 13; Mark viii. 27).

HER'OD AGRIPPA, son of Aristobulus, and grandson of Herod the Great. Caligula made him king. He killed James, the brother of John, with the sword (Acts xii. 2); and imprisoned St. Peter (3); but the apostle was delivered by an angel (4–18); Herod then put the keepers to death (19), and went to Cesarea. He was incensed at Tyre and Sidon, but they appeased him (20). The people hailed him as a god, but he was struck by an angel, and died eaten up by worms (20–23).

HER'OD AGRIPPA II., called king Agrippa, went to Cesarea to salute Festus (Acts xxv. 13); hearing of St. Paul he wished to see him, and the apostle was brought before him (23); St. Paul addressed him eloquently (xxvi. 2–23); the sequel (24–32).

HERO'DIANS, a sect or party among the Jews. With the Pharisees they sought to ensnare our Lord (Matt. xxii. 16; Mark iii. 6; xii. 13).

HERO'DIAS, daughter of Aristobulus. She married Herod Philip I., but left him for Herod Antipas, who, to gratify her, put St. John the Baptist to death (Matt. xiv. 8).

HERO'DION, a kinsman of St. Paul (Rom. xvi. 11).

HER'ON, a wading bird, classed among the unclean (Lev. xi. 19; Deut. xiv. 16).

HETH, second son of Chanaan (Gen. x. 15; 1 Paral. i. 13).

HETH'ITES, descendants of Heth. They were friendly to Abraham (Gen. xxiii. 3); they opposed the Israelites (Jos. ix. 1; xi. 3); their kings are referred to (3 Kings x. 29; 4 Kings vii. 6); tributary (2 Paral. viii. 7).

HET'THIM, a land in which Luza was built by the house of Joseph (Judges i. 26).

HEV'ILATH, a land watered by the river Phison (Gen. ii. 14).

HE'VITES, a nation of Chanaan (Gen. x. 17; Ex. iii. 8, etc.)

HI'EL, of Bethel, rebuilt Jericho in the days of Achab. His son Abiram died when he laid the foundation, and his son Segub when he set up the gates, as Josue had foretold (3 Kings xvi. 34).

HIERA'POLIS, a city near Colosse and Laodicea (Coloss. iv. 13).

HIGH'-PLACES, in Hebrew Bamoth. Idolatrous rites and sacrifices were offered on summits of hills and other elevated spots, and these high-places were constantly condemned, as well as those who tolerated them (3 Kings iii. 2, 4; xii. 32; xiii. 2; xiv. 23). They were suppressed by Ezechias (4 Kings xviii. 4, 22; 2 Paral. xxxi. 1); and by Josias (4 Kings xxiii.; 2 Paral. xxxiv. 3).

HIGH'-PRIEST. Aaron appointed high-priest by divine authority (Ex. xxviii.), and consecrated with especial ceremonies (xxix.); the dignity to descend in his family (xxviii.; Num. xx. 25); it descended first in the line of Eleazar to his son Phineas (Judges xx. 28); then to Heli, of the family

THE HIGH-PRIEST IN HIS SACERDOTAL VESTMENTS.

of Ithamar (1 Kings iv. 18), in which it remained till the reign of Solomon, when it passed from Abiathar to Sadoc, of the house of Eleazar (3 Kings ii. 26). It descended in his family to the time of Sara-

ias, who was put to death at Reblatha by the king of Babylon (4 Kings xxv. 18–21). His successor, Josedec, died in captivity, but Jesus, his son, with Zorobabel, restored the temple and worship of God

THE HOLY.

(1 Esd. iv. 3; Agg. i. 1, 2; Zach. iii. 1; Ecclus. xlix. 14); in the persecutions of Antiochus, first to control, then to crush the Jewish church, the high-priesthood was degraded by Menelaus and Alcimus. The dignity was restored by the Machabees, priests of the course of Joiarib, and apparently of the house of Eleazar, and remained with them till Aristobulus was put to death by Herod. It was then sought by ambitious men, and in our Lord's time seems to have been held annually in turn by Annas and Caiphas (Matt. xxvi. 57; Luke iii. 2; John xviii. 13), who were succeeded by Theophilus (Acts ix. 1). The high-priesthood could not be instituted by man, but needed a divine vocation and installation (Heb. v. 4). God prescribed the vestments to be worn by the high-priest (Ex. xxviii., xxxix.) The high-priest alone could enter the Holy of Holies (Lev. xvi. 2). Jesus Christ the high-priest according to the order of Mechisedec (Heb. iv. 14; v.)

HILL OF THE FORESKINS (Jos. v. 3).

HIL'LOCK of Testimony (Gen. xxxi. 47).

HIN, a Hebrew measure, the sixth part of the bath (Ex. xxix. 40; Ezech. xlvi. 14).

HIND, the female of the stag, used as a figure of gentleness and affection (Prov. v. 19; Jer. xiv. 5).

HI'RAM, king of Tyre, a friend and ally of David (2 Kings v., vii.; 3 Kings v. 1); sent materials and workmen to erect David's palace (2 Kings v. 11; 1 Paral. xiv. 1); and also to erect the temple under Solomon (3 Kings v. 10; vii. 13; 2 Paral. ii. 13, 16); Solomon ceded twenty cities to him (3 Kings ix. 11); he aided in developing the commerce of the Jews (3 Kings ix. 27).

HO'BAB, son of Jethro, and brother-in-law of Moses, who persuaded him to accompany him (Num. x. 29).

HOLM TREE (Dan. xiii. 58).

HOLDA, a prophetess, wife of Sellum, consulted by king Josias and the high-priest Helcias, in regard to the book of the law (4 Kings xxii. 14).

HOLOCAUST, a sacrifice in which the whole animal was burnt on the altar, and no part eaten by the priest and offerer. Prescriptions in regard to them (Lev. vi. 9; vii. 8); the holocaust of a contrite heart (Ps. l. 21).

HOLOFER'NES, a Ninivite general, besieges Bethulia (Judith ii.–vii.); is visited and slain by Judith (xiii. 10).

HO'LY. God is essentially holy (Osee xi. 9; Apoc. iv. 8); men should be holy (Lev. xi. 44; xix. 2; Deut. xxvi. 19; Eph. iv. 24).

HO'LY! holy! holy! the perpetual praise in heaven (Apoc. iv. 8; Isai. vi. 3).

HO'LY, THE. The part of the tabernacle before the Oracle or Holy of Holies. In it stood the Altar of Incense, the Seven Branched Candlestick, and the Table of the Loaves of Proposition. (See TEMPLE.)

HO'LY OF HOLIES, the sanctuary or inmost part of the tabernacle and temple, where the Ark of the Covenant was kept behind the veil (Ex. xxv. 8; xxvi. 33; 3 Kings vi. 16); a sacrifice was to be offered by the high-priest annually before entering it (Lev. xvi. 2); a guard was kept constantly before it (Num. iii. 38).

HO'LY GHOST, the third person of the Blessed Trinity (Matt. xxviii. 19; 1 John v. 7; Ps. l. 13; Heb. ix. 14); proceeds from the Father (John xv. 26); and from the Son (xvi. 7, 14); he is the Paraclete (John xiv. 26); his mission (John xvi. 7); Mary, the Blessed Virgin, conceives by the Holy Ghost (Matt. i. 18, 20; Luke i. 35); he descends on Jesus at his baptism under the form of a dove (Matt. iii. 16; Mark i. 10; Luke iii. 22; John i. 32); our Lord commands baptism to be given in the name of the Father, and of the Son, and of the Holy Ghost (Matt. xxviii. 19); the Holy Ghost promised to the apostles and to the church (Ezech. xi. 19; xxxix. 29; Joel ii. 28; Matt. iii. 11; John vii. 39; xvi. 7); given to the apostles (John xx. 22); descends on the apostles (Acts ii.); on Cornelius (x. 44); on the faithful at Antioch (xi. 15); of Corinth (xix. 6); presides in the Council of Jerusalem (xv. 28); forbids St. Paul to preach in Asia (xvi. 6); foretells his imprisonment in Jerusalem (xxi. 11); teaches and enlightens the faithful (Ex. iv. 12; Ps. xxxi. 8; Isai. liv. 13; Mark xiii.

11; John vi. 45; xiv. 16, 26; xvi. 3; 2 Cor. i. 22; Eph. i. 13; ii. 18; 1 John ii. 27); prays for us (Rom. viii. 26); quickeneth (John vi. 64); the Holy Scrip-

HIGH-PRIEST OFFERING SACRIFICES.

tures inspired by (Mark xii. 36; Luke xii. 12; Heb. iii. 7; 2 Pet. i. 21; 2 Esd. ix. 30); fruits of the Holy Ghost (Gal. v. 22); gifts of the Holy Ghost (Isai. xi. 2); Elizabeth filled with the Holy Ghost (Luke i. 41); St. Peter (Acts iv. 8); Barnabas (xi. 24); blasphemy against the Holy Ghost (Mark iii. 29).

HO′LY WATER, its use prescribed (Num. v. 17).

HON′EY, the food laid up by the bee; sent by Jacob to Joseph (Gen. xliii. 11); abounded in Pal-

HUSKS OR PODS OF THE CAROB TREE.

estine (Ex. iii. 8, etc.; 1 Kings xiv. 25); sold to the Tyrian (Ezech. xxvii. 17); food of St. John the Baptist (Matt. iii. 4)); eaten by our Lord (Luke xxiv. 42).

HOOPOE, a bird classed as unclean (Lev. xi. 19; Deut. xiv. 18).

HOR, the mountain on which Aaron died (Num. xx. 29); it was in the uttermost borders of the land of Edom (xxxiii. 37).

HO′RAM, king of Gazer, defeated by Josue, 1450 B.C. (Jos. x. 33).

HO′REB, a mountain in Arabia Petræa, west of Sinai. Here God appeared to Moses in a burning bush (Ex. iii.); and here Moses made water issue from a rock (xvii. 6); Elias fled to Horeb from Jezabel (3 Kings xix. 8); it is sometimes mentioned as the same as Sinai (Ecclus. xlviii. 7; Malachi iv. 4).

HOR′MA or **HERMA,** the place of the anathema (Num. xxi. 3).

HORN, used to signify strength and power (Deut. xxxiii. 17; 1 Kings ii. 1; Ps. xxi. 22; lxxiv. 5, 6, 11; lxxxviii. 18, 25; cxi. 9; Ecclus. xlvii. 13); the horns of the altar, projections at the four corners (Ex. xxvii. 2; xxix. 12; Lev. iv. 7; Judith ix. 11; Ps. cxvii. 27); Moses coming from Sinai appeared as with horns of light (Ex. xxxiv. 35); horn used as vessel for liquids (1 Kings xvi. 1).

HOR′NETS sent before the Israelites (Ex. xxiii. 28; Deut. vii. 20; Jos. xxiv. 12).

HORSE, mentioned as domestic animal in Egypt (Gen. xlvii. 17); Job describes the war horse (Job xxxix. 19); frequently alluded to as used in war and with chariots (Ex. xv. 1; Deut. xi. 4, etc.); no mention made of its use in agriculture.

HORSE-LEECH, used as a type of the insatiable (Prov. xxx. 15).

HOSAN′NA, the cry of the people to our Lord when he entered Jerusalem (Matt. xxi. 9, 15; Mark xi. 9, 10; John xii. 13); it was from Ps. cxvii. 25, 26).

HOS′PITALITY commended (Isai. lviii. 7; Luke xiv. 13; Rom. xii. 13; 1 Tim. iii. 2; 3 John 5); examples of (Gen. xviii.; xix.; xxiv.; Judg. xiii. 15; 3

Kings xvii. 10); want of hospitality punished (Judg. viii. 5; xix. 18; 1 Kings xxv.; Wisd. xix. 13).

HOUSE built on the rock shall stand (Luke vi. 48; Matt. vii. 24; xvi. 18. See 2 Cor. v. 1; 2 Pet. i. 14).

HUMIL′ITY commended, Ecclus. iii. 20; vii. 19; Matt. v. 3; xviii. 4; xxiii. 7; Mark ix. 36; Rom. xi. 20; xii. 16; Philip. ii. 3; Col. iii. 12; James i. 9; iv. 10); God exalts the humble (1 Kings ii. 8; 2 Kings vi. 22; 2 Paral. xxxii. 26; xxxiii. 13; xxxiv. 27; Judith ix. 16; Ps. xxxiii. 19; Prov. xvi. 19; xviii. 12; xxix. 23; Isai. lxvi. 2; Matt. xi. 29; 1 Pet. v. 5); taught by our Lord's example (John xiii. 5).

HUR, king of Madian, killed by Phinees (Num. xxxi. 8).

HUSKS, mentioned in Luke xv. 16, are perhaps the pods of the carob (*ceratonia siliqua*), used to feed animals, and in times of scarcity for human food.

HY′ACINTH, a precious stone, one of the foundations of the New Jerusalem (Apoc. xxi. 20).

HY′ADES, a constellation (Job ix. 9).

HYMENE′US, condemned by St. Paul for false doctrines, declaring the resurrection past already (1 Tim. i. 20; 2 Tim. ii. 17, 18).

HYMN, sung by our Lord at the Last Supper (Matt. xxvi. 30; Mark xiv. 26); commended (Eph. v. 19; Col. iii. 16).

HYPOC′RISY condemned and punished (Job viii. 13; xiii. 16; xv. 34; xx.; xxvii.; xxxiv.; Prov. xxx. 12; Ecclus. i. 37; xix. 25; Isai. xxix. 13; Jer. ix. 8; Ezech. xxxiii. 31; Mal. iii. 14; 2 Mach. vi.

HYSSOP PLANT.

24; Matt. vi. 2; vii. 5; xxii. 18; xxiv. 51; 1 Thess. v. 22; 1 Tim. iv. 2; 2 Tim. iii. 5; 1 Pet. ii. 1).

HYS′SOP, a plant growing on walls (3 Kings iv. 33); it was used in various religious ceremonies, sprinkling the door-posts with the blood of the paschal lamb (Ex. xii. 22); in purifying lepers (Lev. xiv. 4, 51); in the sacrifice of the red cow (Num. xix. 6); hence David says, "Thou shalt sprinkle me with hyssop" (Ps. l. 9).

I'BEX, a mountain animal, mentioned in the Vulgate (1 Kings xxiv. 3; Job xxxix. 1); but translated wild goat.

I'BIS, a wading bird, common in Egypt. It is classed as unclean (Lev. xi. 17; Isai. xxxiv. 11). In Deut. xiv. 16 translated stork.

xvi. 38–42; xxv. 3; 2 Paral. v. 12; Ps. xxxviii.; lxi.; lxxvi.)

IDOL, an object set up to receive divine honors, either shapeless or the figure of an animal or false god; their making and adoration and service forbidden (Ex. xx. 4, 5; Deut. iv. 16); various idols are mentioned; Laban's (Gen. xxxi. 19); Moloch (Lev.xx. 2); the molten calf (Ex. xxxii. 4); Phogor (Num. xxv. 18); Baalim (Judg. x. 6); Dagon (1 Kings v. 4); Chamos (3 Kings xi. 7); two golden calves (3 Kings xii. 28); Astaroth (4 Kings xxiii. 13); idols set up by order of Antiochus (1 Mach. i. 57).

ILLYR'ICUM, a province on the Adriatic. St. Paul (Rom. xv. 19) says he preached from Jerusalem to Illyricum.

IMAGES forbidden to be made for worship (Ex. xx. 4; Levit. xxvi. 1; Deut. iv. 15); commanded to be made (Ex. xxv. 18–20; Num. xxi. 8); in Solomon's temple (3 Kings vi. 35; vii. 25; 2 Paral. iii. 10; iv. 3; v. 7); for Solomon's throne (ix. 18, 19).

IMPA'TIENCE punished (Ex. xiv. 11; xv. 24; xvi. 7; xvii. 2; Num. xi. 10; xiv. 1; xxi. 5; Job iii. 1; Prov. xii. 16; Ecclus. ii. 16).

IMPOSIT'ION of hands. Instances of (Gen.

IDOLS AND GODS OF EGYPT.

ICH'ABOD, son of Phinees, son of the high-priest Heli, born when the ark was taken (1 Kings iv. 19–22).

ICO'NIUM, capital of Lycaonia; St. Paul and Barnabas visit it after being driven from Antioch of Pisidia (Acts xiii. 51); converts made there forced to leave (xiv. 6; 2 Tim. iii. 11); revisited (Acts xiv. 20); the Christians there commend Timothy (Acts xvi. 1, 2).

IDITHUN, a Levite of the race of Merari, one of the four great leaders of the temple music (1 Paral.

IDOL'ATRY, the paying divine honors to idols or false gods a crime (1 Kings xv. 23); forbidden (Ex. xx. 4, 5; Deut. iv. 15); sin and folly of (Wisd. xiii.–xv.; Jer. x. 1–16; Isai. xlvi. 1); the Jews frequently fell into idolatry (Ex. xxxii. 4; Judges ii. 12; vi. 28; viii. 27; xiii. 1; xvii.; 3 Kings xi. 4–8; xii. 28; xiv. 9; xv. 13; xvi. 32; xviii.; xxi. 26; 4 Kings x. 18–28; xviii. 4; xxi. 2–7, 22; xxiii. 4–20; 1 Mach. i. 57).

IDUMEANS, Edomites, so called (Judith iii. 14; 2 Mach. x. 16).

xlviii. 14; Ex. xxix. 10; Lev. i. 4; Num. xxvii. 23; Dan. xiii. 34; Mark x. 16); used in the sacrament of confirmation (Acts viii. 17; xix. 6); in holy orders (vi. 6; xiii. 3; 1 Tim. iv. 14; v. 22; 2 Tim. i. 6).

INCENSE, used in divine worship (Ex. xxx. 8; xxxvii. 29); the altar of incense (Ex. xxx. 1; xxxvii. 25); Nadab and Abiu slain for offering incense when not commanded (Lev. x. 1); Zachary offers (Luke i. 9); offered by angels in heaven, the prayers of the saints (Apoc. viii. 3); the incense offered to God was prepared by his command (Lev. xvi. 12). The

Jews offered incense in the high places sinfully, and to false gods (3 Kings xxii. 44 ; 4 Kings xii. 3 ; xv. 35 ; xviii. 3, 4) ; and to the brazen serpent (4 Kings xviii. 4).

IN'CEST, carnal union between those related within the prohibited degrees. Its enormity (Lev. xviii. 6 ; xx. 12 ; Deut. xxii. 30 ; 1 Cor. v. 1) ; punished by St. Paul with excommunication (1 Cor. v. 1).

IN'DIA, mentioned as part of the kingdom of Assuerus (Esth. i. 1) ; mentioned (Job xxviii. 16 ; 1 Mach. viii. 8).

INDUL'GENCE granted by St. Paul to the incestuous man on his penance (2 Cor. ii. 10).

INFIDEL'ITY and incredulity punished (Num. xi. 33 ; xiv. 12 ; xx. 12 ; Judg. ii. 2 ; vi. 8 ; 2 Paral. xxiv. 22 ; Ecclus. ii. 15 ; Matt. xvii. 19 ; Mark xvi. 16 ; Luke i. 20 ; John iii. 18 ; viii. 24 ; Rom. xi. 20 ; Heb. iii. 18 ; iv. 2 ; xi. 6 ; Apoc. xxi. 8).

INGRAT'ITUDE punished (Rom. i. 21 ; 2 Tim. iii. 2).

JACOB'S WELL.

INHER'ITANCE, Jewish law as to (Num. xxvii. 6 ; Lev. xxv. 30).

INN, term used for the caravanserai of the East (Gen. xlii. 27 ; xliii. 21 ; Ex. iv. 24 ; 3 Kings xviii. 27 ; Luke ii. 7 ; x. 34).

IN'NOCENT, innocence, frequently associated with *hands* (Gen. xxxvii. 22 ; Ps. xxv. 6 ; lxxii. 13 ; Jerem. xlix. 12).

IN'NOCENTS, Holy, name given by the church to the children slain at Bethlehem by Herod (Matt. ii. 16–18). Their feast is celebrated (Dec. 28).

IN'STRUC'TION to be received with joy (Prov. i. 2).

IO'TA, the letter I in the Greek alphabet, which being the smallest letter, is used in the form of "jot" (Matt. v. 18) to express the least possible.

I'RA, priest of David (2 Kings xx. 26).

I'RON, Tubalcain, the first worker in (Gen. iv. 22) ; its hardness alluded to (Lev. xxvi. 19) ; its weight (Ecclus. xxii. 18) ; iron miraculously floats

on the water at the word of Eliseus (4 Kings vi. 6).

I'SAAC, son of Abraham and Sara. His birth foretold (Gen. xvii. 19 ; xviii. 10) ; born (xxi. 3) ; Abraham commanded to offer him in sacrifice (xxii. 2) ; laid on the altar (9) ; saved (12) ; Abraham sends to Mesopotamia to obtain a wife for him (xxiv.) ; he obtains Rebecca (51) ; marries her (67) ; she bears to him Esau and Jacob (xxv. 21–25) ; God promises that in his seed all nations shall be blessed (xxvi. 4) ; abode in Gerara (6) ; makes peace with Abimelech (31) ; blesses his sons, giving the blessing of the first-born to Jacob (xxvii.) ; sends Jacob to Mesopotamia (xxviii.) ; his death (xxxv. 28), 1716 B. C.

I'SAI, or Jesse, father of David (Ruth iv. 17, 22 ; 1 Paral. ii. 13 ; Matt. i. 5).

ISAI'AS, son of Amos, and the first of the four great prophets. He began to prophesy after the death of Ozias, 758 B. C., and prophesied during the reigns of Joatham, Achaz and Ezechias. He denounced the disorders of the Jews, and foretold the ruin of Judea, as well as Assyria, Babylon, Egypt, Moab, Tyre, etc. He announced the birth of the Messias under the name of Emmanuel (vii., viii.) ; he foretold the sufferings of the Messias, the call of the Gentiles, the rejection of the Jews, and the establishment of the church (xlix.–lvi. 8). He predicted the siege by Sennacherib and his defeat, the reign of Ezechias, and the reign of Cyrus. Isaias was consulted by Ezechias (xxxvii., xxxviii.) ; is praised by the son of Sirach (Ecclus. xlviii. 25) ; and is more frequently cited in the New Testament than any other prophet (Matt. iii., iv., viii., xii., xiii., xv. ; Mark i., vii. ; Luke iii., iv. ; John i., xii. ; Acts viii., xxviii. ; Rom. ix., x., xv.) According to tradition he was sawn in two by king Manasses. He wrote also the acts of Ozias (2 Par. xxvi. 22).

ISAI'AS, one of the canonical books of the Old Testament (Isai.) From 4 Kings xviii. 13 to xx. 19 are nearly identical with Isai. xxxvi. to xxxix. 8.

ISBOSETH or ISBAAL, son of Saul, was recognized as king on his father's death by all but the tribe of Juda (2 Kings ii. 10) ; after Abner's desertion (iii. 12) his power declined, and he was murdered by two of his officers, who took his head to David (iv. 6, 7).

IS'MAEL, son of Abraham by Agar, an Egyptian (Gen. xvi. 15) ; expelled with his mother on account of Sara (xxi. 14) ; they are miraculously relieved in the desert (15–20) ; dwells in Pharan and marries an Egyptian (21) ; he had twelve sons (xxv. 13–16) ; and a daughter Basemath who married Esau (xxxvi. 3, 10) ; he and Isaac buried their father in the double cave (xxv. 9).

IS'MAEL, son of Nathanias, kills Godolias, whom Nabuchodonosor had left as governor of Judea (Jer. xli. 2).

IS'RAEL, the name given to Jacob by the angel with whom he wrestled (Gen. xxxii. 28) ; it is also used for the people and inheritance of the Lord (Ex. iii. 1 ; vi. 6 ; xix. 2 ; Lev. xx. 2 ; Deut. vi. 9 ; ix. 3 ; x. 12 ; xxxii. 8 ; 1 Kings x. 18 ; xii. 1 ; 2 Kings vii. 23 ; 3 Kings viii. 53 ; Isai. xix. 25 ; xliii. 1 ; Jer. xiii. 11) ; the kingdom of Israel is that founded by Jeroboam, and including the ten tribes (3 Kings xii. 3) ; as foretold by the prophet Ahias (xi. 29 ; 2 Paral. x. 15) ; its history is given in the third and fourth books of Kings, and incidentally in 2 Paralipomenon. In the reign of Phacee, king of Israel, the tribe of Nephthali and many of other tribes were carried captives into Assyria by Theglathphalasar (4 Kings xv. 29) ; in the reign of Osee, last king of Israel, Salmanasar, king of Assyria, took Samaria and carried all the people away captives and placed them in Hala and Habor (xvii. 6) ; the sins which brought this judgment on them (7–18). Their captivity had been foretold (Deut. iv. 27) ; the Levites and many who clung to the true faith went to Jerusalem (2 Par. xi. 13) ; some in captivity remained faithful (Tobias).

IS'SACHAR, fifth son of Jacob, by Lia (Gen. xxx. 18) ; he had four sons, Thola, Phua, Job and Semron (xlvi. 13) ; in Jacob's blessing he is said to occupy fertile land, and to become tributary (xlix. 14).

IS'SACHAR, tribe of. In the Exodus they numbered 54,400 fighting men, under Nathanael, son of Suar, and camped next to Juda (Num. i. 28, 29 ; ii. 5, 6) ; their offerings (vii. 18–23) ; their spy, Igal, son of Joseph (xiii. 8) ; their prince to divide the land, Phaltiel (xxxiv. 26) ; they numbered at Settim 64,300 (xxvi. 25) ; Zabulon and Issachar blessed jointly (Deut. xxxiii. 18, 19) ; his allotment of the Promised Land was in the valley of Jezrael, between the Mediterranean and the Jordan (Jos. xix. 17–23) ; the captains of Issachar with Debbora and Barac (Judges v. 15) ; Thola, son of Phua, of the tribe of Issachar, judged Israel twenty-three years (x. 1, 2) ; after the revolt of Jeroboam, Baasa, of the tribe of Issachar, made himself king of Israel (3 Kings xv. 27 ; xvi. 6) ; succeeded by his son Ela (6–9) ; many of the tribe ate the Pasch of Ezechias, but unduly (2 Paral. xxx. 18) ; carried captives by Salmanasar (4 Kings xvii. 6).

IS'SUE OF BLOOD, a woman long afflicted with an issue of blood, cured by touching the fringes or hem of our Lord's garment (Matt. ix. 22).

IT'ALY, Balaam foretells the coming of conquerors from Italy to overthrow the kingdoms of Asia (Num. xxiv. 24) ; Isaias foretells the sign of salvation set up in (lxvi. 19) ; mentioned (Ezech. xxvii. 6 ; Acts xviii. ; xxvii. ; Heb. xiii. 24).

ITAL'IAN BAND, Cornelius was centurion of it (Acts x. 1).

ITHA'MAR, fourth son of Aaron. The high-priesthood came into his family in the person of Heli, and continued to the deposition of Abiathar (Ex. vi. 23; xxviii. 1; xxxviii. 21; Num. iii. 2; 1 Paral. vi. 3).

ITURE'A, a small province lying along Mount Hermon. It was settled by Jethur, son of Ismael (Gen. xxv. 15; 1 Paral. i. 31); the Itureans aided Ruben and Gad against the Agarites (1 Paral. v. 19); Philip was tetrarch of Iturea in the time of St. John the Baptist (Luke iii. 1).

I'VORY, material of the tusks of elephants, imported by Solomon from Tharsis (2 Paral. ix. 21); he made a throne of it (3 Kings x. 18; 2 Paral. ix. 17); used in house adornings (3 Kings xxii. 39; Ps. xliv. 9; Amos iii. 15; vi. 4; Esth. i. 6; Ezech. xxvii. 6); Achaz used it so that his palace is called an ivory house (3 Kings xxii. 39).

(Gen. xxv. 25); he bought Esau's birthright for a pottage of lentils (31); by his mother's aid he obtained his father's blessing as first-born by a stratagem (xxvii. 28); he fled to escape Esau's anger (42); and

JA'HEL, wife of Heber the Cinite, who slew Sisara, general of Jabin's armies, by driving a nail into his head while asleep in her tent (Judg. iv. 17).

JAHA'ZIEL, son of Zacharias, moved by the

JACOB RETURNING TO THE PROMISED LAND.

JA'BEL, son of Lamech and Ada, father of those who lodge in tents, and shepherds (Gen. iv. 20).

JA'BES, praised for his piety (1 Paral. iv. 9, 10); he is mentioned among the descendants of Juda, but nothing is known of him.

JA'BES GALAAD, a city in the tribe of Manasses, sacked by the Israelites for not joining in the war against Benjamin (Judges xxi. 8); besieged by Naas, king of Ammon, but relieved by Saul (1 Kings xi. 1); in gratitude they buried Saul and his sons honorably (1 Kings xxxi. 11, 12).

JA'BIN, king of Asor, alarmed at the conquests of Josue, united the various Chanaanite kings and met Josue at the waters of Merom with a host like the sands of the sea (Jos. xi. 4); but Josue routed them completely, pursuing them to Sidon. Then he took Asor and slew Jabin (6–10).

JA'BIN, another king of Asor (Jud. iv. 2); oppressed the Israelites for twenty years, but after the defeat of his army under Sisara, they overpowered and destroyed him (4–24).

JA'BOC, a ford where Jacob wrestled with an angel (Gen. xxxii. 22).

JA'CHANAN of Carmel, a city whose king was defeated by Josue (Jos. xii. 22). It became a Levitical city in the tribe of Zabulon.

JA'CHIN, one of the two bronze pillars on the porch of Solomon's temple. It means firmly established, and was on the right (3 Kings vii. 21).

JA'COB, son of Isaac and Rebecca, born 1836 **B. C.**; he was younger than his twin-brother Esau

went to his uncle Laban (xxviii. 10); at Bethel he had a vision of angels, and God promised that in his seed all nations of the earth should be blessed (Gen. xxviii. 11–22); served Laban for seven years for Rachel, but is deceived with Lia (xxix. 1–24); he served seven years more for Rachel (28); obtains the better share of the flocks (xxx.); returns home (xxxi. 17); fears Esau (xxxii. 7); wrestles with an angel at the ford of Jaboc (xxxii. 24); receives the name of Israel (xxxii. 28; xxxv. 10; 3 Kings xviii. 31); meets Esau and is reconciled to him (Gen. xxxiii. 1); has Ruben, Simeon, Levi, Juda, Issachar, Zabulon, and a daughter Dina by Lia; Joseph and Benjamin by Rachel; Dan and Nephthali by Bala, Rachel's handmaid; Gad and Aser by Zelpha, Lia's handmaid. He loved Joseph, and this excited the jealousy of his other sons, who proposed to kill him, but finally sold him to some merchants of Madian (Gen. xxxvii. 1–28); Jacob believes him dead (33); he sends his sons to Egypt in time of famine (xliii. 1); reluctantly allows Benjamin to go (13); his joy on learning that Joseph was alive and high in power in Egypt (xlv. 26–28); he goes down to Egypt with all his family (xlvi.; Deut. x. 22); adopts Joseph's two sons, Ephraim and Manasses (Gen. xlviii. 5); blesses his sons and dies (xlix.); he is buried with Abraham and Isaac (l. 7–13), as he had requested (xlix. 29); his praise (Ecclus. xliv. 25).

JA'COB'S WELL, near Sichar, where our Lord met the Samaritan woman (John iv. 5, 6).

JADA'SON, a river near which Nabuchodonosor vanquished Arphaxad (Judith i. 6).

spirit of the Lord, promises king Josaphat victory (2 Paral. xx. 14–17).

JAIL'OR, or keeper of the prison at Philippi, converted and baptized by St. Paul and Silas (Acts xvi. 23–34).

JA'IR, son of Manasses, took the cities in the land of Argob, and called it Havoth Jair (Num. xxxii. 41; Deut. iii. 14); he is supposed to be merely a descendant of Manasses through his mother, and to be

JA'IR, son of Segub, of the tribe of Juda; he had twenty-three cities in the land of Galaad (1 Paral. ii. 22, 23).

JA'IR, the Galaadite, judge of Israel after Thola; he governed twenty-two years, and had thirty sons, princes of as many cities in the land of Galaad, called Havoth Jair. He was buried at Camon, A. M. 2817 (Judges x. 3–5).

JAIR'US, ruler of the synagogue at Capharnaum, besought our Lord to save his dying daughter; on the way our Lord cured the woman with an issue of blood, and word came that the girl was dead. Jesus said to Jairus, "Fear not, believe only and she shall be safe," and going to the house he raised her to life (Luke viii. 41–56).

JAMES the Greater, son of Zebedee and Salome, and brother of St. John the Evangelist (Matt. iv. 21); he was of Bethsaida in Galilee, and a fisherman (Mark i. 19); he and his brothers were partners with St. Peter (Luke v. 10); chosen one of the apostles (Matt. x. 3; Mark iii. 17); their mother asked the preeminence for them in our Lord's kingdom (Matt. xx. 21); he witnessed the transfiguration of our

Saviour (Matt. xvii. 2); and wished him to draw down fire from heaven on a Samaritan city (Luke ix. 54); he and his brother called Boanerges or sons of thunder (Mark iii. 17); he saw Jesus Christ at the sea of Galilee after his resurrection (John xxi. 2, etc.), and at his ascension (Acts i.); he was put to death by the sword by Herod, A. D. 42 or 44 (Acts xii. 1).

JAMES the LESS, son of Alpheus (Matt. x. 3; Mark iii. 18; Luke vi. 15; Acts i. 13); or Cleophas, and Mary, sister of the Blessed Virgin (John xix. 25), and hence called the Brother of the Lord (Gal. i. 19); our Lord appeared to him a week after his resurrection (1 Cor. xv. 7); he is considered the first bishop of Jerusalem; St. Paul went to him (Gal. I. 19); and at the Council of Jerusalem he made the final discourse (Acts xv. 13); he was regarded with great veneration by the Jews, but was killed in the temple

Madai, Javan, Tubal, Mosoc, and Thiras (x. 2); by these were divided the islands of the Gentiles in their lands (5); he honors his father (ix. 23); is blessed by Noe (27).

JAR'AMOTH, a Levitical city of refuge (Jos. xxi. 29).

JA'RED, son of Malaleel and father of Henoch (Gen. v. 15).

JA'SA or **JAS'SA**, a city beyond the Jordan near which Moses defeated Sehon (Num. xxi. 23; Deut. ii. 32); it was assigned to the tribe of Ruben (Jos. xiii. 18); a Levitical city (1 Paral. vi. 78).

JA'SON, son of Eleazar, sent to Rome by Judas Machabeus to renew the alliance, 162 B. C. (1 Mach. viii. 17).

JA'SON, a Jew of Cyrene, who wrote the history of the persecutions under Antiochus Epiphanes and

JAS'PER, a precious stone. It was the sixth in the rational (Ex. xxviii. 18; xxxix. 11); the wall of the New Jerusalem was of jasper stone (Apoc. xxi. 18); and the first foundation was jasper (19); its brilliancy was such that the appearance of Him who sat on the throne is compared to it (iv. 3).

JA'VAN, fourth son of Japheth (Gen. x. 2).

JEAB'ARIM, one of the encampments of the Israelites in the land of Moab (Num. xxi. 11).

JEAL'OUSY, Trial of. The form of the trial before the priest (Num. v. 12-31).

JE'BUS, son of Chanaan and father of the Jebusites (Gen. x. 16; Jos. xv. 63).

JE'BUS, afterwards called Jerusalem, founded by Jebus (Jos. xv. 8; Judges xix. 10; 1 Paral. xi. 4).

JE'BUSITES, descendants of Jebus; they were warlike, and Israel could not destroy them (Judg.

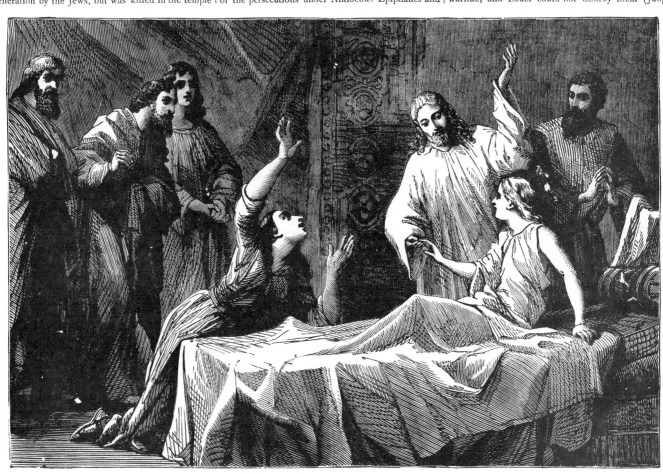

JAIRUS' DAUGHTER RAISED TO LIFE.

at the instigation of the high-priest Ananus; he was thrown down from a gallery and beaten to death; one epistle by him is in the New Testament.

JAMES, EPISTLE OF, one of the Catholic Epistles written by St. James the Less; a canonical book of the New Testament, enforcing the necessity of good works (James).

JAM'BRI. The children of Jambri sally out from Madaba, and kill John, brother of Simon and Jonathan Machabeus; his brothers avenge him (1 Mach. ix. 36-42).

JAN'NES and **MAMBRES**, two magicians who resisted Moses in Egypt (2 Tim. iii. 8).

JA'PHETH, son of Noe, born when his father was five hundred years old (Gen. v. 31); he was older than Cham (ix. 24), and some suppose him older than Sem; his sons were Gomer, Magog,

Eupator in five books (2 Mach. ii. 24). The second book of Machabees is abridged from it.

JA'SON, high-priest, bribed Antiochus Epiphanes to depose his brother Onias III. (2 Mach. iv. 8); he did all he could to abolish the worship of God, and introduce Greek idolatry (10-20); Menelaus, by similar bribery, then obtained the office (24); and Jason fled to the Ammonites (26); he subsequently attacked Jerusalem (v. 5-7); but failing to take it fled, and was imprisoned by Aretas; then escaped to Egypt and finally to Lacedæmon, where he died (8-10).

JA'SON, St. Paul's host at Thessalonica, risking his life to save the apostle during a sedition (Acts xvii. 7). If he is the same mentioned by St. Paul (Rom. xvi. 21) he was his kinsman. The Greeks honor him as bishop of Tharsis in Cilicia.

i. 21); they refused admission to David, who took the city (2 Kings v. 8); Solomon made them pay tribute (3 Kings ix. 20, 21; 2 Paral. viii. 7, 8).

JECHE'LIA, wife of Amasias, king of Juda, and mother of Azarias (4 Kings xv. 2).

JECHONI'AS, son of Josias (Matt. i. 11; Esther ii. 6); called Eliacim (4 Kings xxiii. 34, 35). Nechao made him king in place of his brother Joachaz, and called him Joakim (1 Paral. iii. 15; Jer. xxxvi. 1). He reigned eleven years under the domination of Nabuchodonosor, who carried him in chains to Babylon, but restored him (4 Kings xxiii. 36; xxiv. 1; 2 Paral. xxxvi. 5-8); he was a wicked prince; he threw the prophecies of Jeremias in the fire (Jer. xxxvi. 23); he revolted, and Nabuchodonosor besieged Jerusalem; Joakim was slain and buried like a dead ass, out of the city (Jer. xxii. 19).

JECHONI'AS, son of Joakim, is the name given by Jeremias (xxii. 24); to Joachin (4 Kings xxiv. 6; 2 Paral. xxxvi. 8).

JEC'SAN, son of Abraham and Cetura (Gen. xxv. 2).

JEC'TAN, son of Heber; his descendants occupied from Messa to Sephar (Gen. x. 26, 30).

JEC'TEHEL, a rock taken by Amasias, and over which he threw ten thousand Idumean prisoners (4 Kings xiv. 7; 2 Paral. xxv. 12).

JE'HU, son of Hanani, a prophet, sent by God to Baasa, king of Israel (3 Kings xvi. 1); put to death by Baasa (7); and the prophet Jehu, son of Hanani, reproached Josaphat, king of Juda, for aiding a wicked prince (2 Paral. xix. 2).

JE'HU, son of Josaphat, king of Israel, consecrated by Eliseus (3 Kings xix. 16); by the hand of one of his disciples (4 Kings ix. 1); on which he slew Joram (24); put to death Jezabel (33); and the house of Achab (x. 7–11); he abolished the worship of Baal, but not the golden calves (18–29.) He died after a reign of 28 years, 850 B. C. (4 Kings x. 35, 36); the prophet Osee foretold that the blood shed by Jehu should be avenged (Osee i. 4, 5).

JEM'INI, another name for Benjamin (Judg. iii. 15; 1 Kings ix. 1).

JEPH'TE, son of Galaad by a harlot, judge of Israel. Cast out of his father's house, he fled to Tob, and became the head of a predatory band (Judg. xi. 1–3). The people of Galaad promised to make him prince if he delivered them from the Ammonites (9, 10); he defeated them at Aroer (33); but he promised to offer as a holocaust the first that came out of the doors of his house when he returned (31), and the first was his only daughter; after she had mourned her virginity in the mountains with her companions for two months, Jephte "did to her as he had vowed" (39); the Hebrew maidens used annually to mourn her for four days (40); he defeated Ephraim at the fords of Jordan, killing

A STREET IN JERUSALEM.

42,000 (xii. 6); he judged Israel six years, and was buried in Galaad, 1181 B. C. (xii. 7).

JEREMI'AS, son of Helcias, of a priestly family, was born at Anathoth, in the tribe of Benjamin; he was sanctified by God as a prophet in his mother's womb (Jer. i., xxix. 27); he prophesied from 629 to 586 B. C.; he is forbidden to pray for the people (vii. 16); asks why the wicked prosper (xii. 1); commanded to buy a linen girdle (xiii. 1); forbidden to marry (xvi. 2); persecuted (xviii. 19; xxvi. 8); imprisoned by Phassur, the priest (xx. 2); complains that he is a laughing-stock for announcing the words of God (7); has a vision of two baskets of figs (xxiv.); Ahicam saves him from being put to death under Joakim (xxvi. 24); Jeremias makes chains and sends them to several kings, as tokens of their coming bondage (xxvii.); he exhorts men to pray for Babylon (xxix. 7); he predicts the birth of the Messias of a virgin mother (xxxi. 22); imprisoned by king Sedecias for announcing the coming ruin of the city (xxxii. 3); tries the Rechabites to show the Israelites how they neglected their duty (xxxv.); dictates his prophecies to Baruch (xxxvi. 4); God conceals him with Baruch (19); dictates his prophecies a second time after their destruction by Joakim (32); again imprisoned by Sedecias at the instigation of the nobles (xxxvii. 15; xxxviii. 6); he is saved by Abdelmelech, the Ethiopian (xxxviii. 12); finds favor with Nabuchodonosor (xxxix. 11); treated as a liar (xliii. 2); carries off the tabernacle, the ark, and the altar of incense, and hides them in the mountain where Moses saw the inheritance of God (2 Mach. ii. 5); advises Jews to remain at Jerusalem (Jer. xlii. 10); goes to Egypt (xliii. 6, 7); reproves the Jews there (xliv. 1); prophesies against the city of Hai (xlix. 3).

JEREMI'AS, one of the canonical books of the Old Testament (Jerem.); Lamentations of Jeremias (Lament.) and the prophecy of Baruch (Bar.) are considered as one book with the prophecies of Jeremias.

JER'ICHO, a city in the tribe of Benjamin; the stream watering the valley was bitter (4 Kings ii. 19), till made sweet by Eliseus; Jericho was miraculously taken by Josue, who, after sending in spies, marched

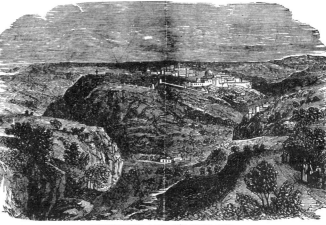

JERUSALEM AND ITS VALLEYS.

seven successive days around it, with the ark, blowing the trumpets, the walls fell, the city was taken and burnt (Jos. vi. 1–20); Josue cursed it (26); Hiel rebuilds it and incurs the curse (3 Kings xvi. 34); the scene of the good Samaritan is laid on the way to Jericho (Luke x. 33); called the city of the palm trees (Deut. xxxiv. 3; 2 Paral. xxviii. 15).

JEROBO'AM, son of Nabat, was an Ephrathite of Sareda; Solomon made him chief over the tributes of the house of Joseph (3 Kings xi. 28); Ahias the prophet foretold that he should rule over ten tribes (29–39); Solomon sought his life, but he fled to Egypt, where he remained till Solomon's death (40), and evidently fell into idolatry; returning, he put himself at the head of the discontented people (xii. 12); a revolt ensued, and ten tribes made Jeroboam king (20); to prevent the people from going up to Jerusalem, he set up a golden calf in Bethel, and another in Dan, for the people to worship, and instituted rites according to his own heart (27–33); he is reproved by a man of God (xiii.), and his hand withers when he tried to injure the prophet (xiii. 4), but is healed (6); Ahias prophesied the destruction of his family (xiv. 10); his death (20); his house destroyed (xv. 29); his idols continued, and constant reference is made to the sin of Jeroboam, son of Nabat, who caused Israel to sin (3 Kings xv.; xvi.;

PLAIN OF JERICHO.

xxii. 53; 4 Kings iii.; ix.; x.; xiii.–xv.; xvii.; xxiii.)

JEROBO'AM II., son of Joas, made king of Israel (4 Kings xiii. 13; xiv. 16); Osee prophesies in the reign of (Osee i. 1); prophesies against him (Amos vii. 9); his death (4 Kings xiv. 29).

JER'UEL, Josaphat defeated the Ammonites, Moabites, etc., in the desert of Jeruel (1 Paral. xx. 16).

JERU'SALEM, called Salem (Gen. xiv. 18); called Jebus (Jos. xviii. 28); besieged and taken by the tribe of Juda (Judg. i. 8); David takes the castle of Sion from the Jebusites (2 Kings v. 7); God chooses it as his abode (2 Paral. vi. 6; vii. 16); the capital of David and Solomon (2 Kings), and of the kings of Juda; David flees from (2 Kings xv. 14); taken by Joas, king of Israel, who dismantles it, 827 B.C. (4 Kings xiv. 13); besieged by Rasin, king of Syria, and Phacee, king of Israel, A.M. 3263 (4 Kings xvi. 5); by Nabuchodonosor, 599 B.C. (xxiv. 10; xxv. 1); burnt and destroyed (9); rebuilt (2 Esd. iii.; vi. 15); prophesies against Jerusalem and its people (4 Kings xxi. 12; xxiii. 27; Isaias i. 8; iii. 1; xxii. 10, 18; xxix. 1, 7; lxiv. 10; Jer. iv. 3, 9; vii.; xiii.; xvii. 19; xix. 3; xxi. 3; xxiii. 39; xxv. 9; xxxii. 3, 28; xxxiv. 1; xxxviii. 3; xxxix. 8; Ezech. iii.-v.; x.); its destruction by the Romans foretold (Dan. ix. 26; Zach. xiv. 2; Luke xix. 43; xx. 16; xxi. 6; John xi. 48); described by Esdras (2 Esd. iii.); captured by Judas Machabeus (1 Mach. iv. 37); Jerusalem in an allegorical sense as Holy Church (Ps. cxxi. 3; Isai. xxxiii. 20; liv. 11; lx.; lxii.; lxv.; Tob. xi.i. 19; Bar. v. 1, 5; Gal. iv. 26; Heb. xi. 10; xii. 22; Apoc. iii. 12); our Lord presented in the temple of Jerusalem (Luke ii. 22-38); found in the temple (46); our Lord's address to (Luke xiii. 34); he heals a man at the Probatica in Jerusalem (John v. 1); there at the Feast of Tabernacles (vii. 14); at the Feast of the Dedication (John x. 22); goes up to in triumph (Matt. xxi.; Mark xi.; Luke xix. 37; John xii. 12); weeps over it (Luke xix. 41); announces its destruction (Matt. xxiv. 15; Mark xiii.)

JESBIB'ENOB, a gigantic Philistine, slain by Abisai (2 Kings xxi. 16, 17).

JES'BOC, son of Abraham and Cetura (Gen. xxv. 2).

JESSE' or **ISAI**, father of David (Ruth iv. 29; Matt. i. 5; Luke iii. 32); Isaias announces a miraculous rod from the root of Jesse (Isai. xi. 1, 10; Rom. xv. 12).

JESUS CHRIST, the Messias. See CHRIST.

JE'SUS, or **JOS'UE**, son of Josedec, high-priest of the Jews after the Babylonian captivity; regulated the order and offices of the priests and Levites (1 Esd. iii. 3, 8); the prophet Aggeus urged him to hasten the rebuilding of the temple (Agg. i. 2); foretelling that the desired of nations should come (Zach. iii. 1-9); saw him in spirit crowned with a tiara, and also in iv. 2; vi. 11; associated with promises of the coming of the Orient or Messias. The son of Sirach praises him (Ecclus. xlix. 14).

JE'SUS, son of Sirach, author of the book of Ecclesiasticus (Ecclus., Prolog.)

JETH'RO, priest of Madian, father of Sephora,

wife of Moses (Ex. iii. 1); called also Raguel (ii. 18); unless we are to consider him son of Raguel and identical with Hobab (Num. x. 29); Moses remained forty years with Jethro before he returned to Egypt, and after reaching that country he sent back his wife and children to Jethro. After the Israelites reached Mount Sinai he came to the camp with them (Ex. xviii. 1); he offered sacrifice (12); advises Moses to appoint judges (21, 22); Moses seems to have invited him to accompany the Israelites (Num. x. 29-31.)

JE'SUS, called Justus, praised by St. Paul as a helper in the kingdom of God (Coloss. iv. 11).

JEW'ELS (Isai. iii. 21; lxi. 10; Apoc. xxi. 2).

JEWS, the name given first to the people of the kingdom of Juda, which consisted mainly of the tribe

JESUS CROWNED WITH THORNS.

of that name; but after the captivity it was applied to all Israelites. Their history before the time of our Lord is given in Esdras and Machabees. Jews persecute the apostles (Acts v. 18); three thousand converted (ii. 41); five thousand (iv. 4); the Greek Jews murmur as to the alms (vi. 1); the Jews rise against St. Stephen (vii.); the gospel preached to (xi. 19); they resist St. Paul (xiii. 45); abandoned for the Gentiles (46); persecute St. Paul (50); they had received many privileges over the Gentiles (Rom. iii. 1); their incredulity opposed (21); the cross a scandal to the Jews (1 Cor. i. 23); their hearts veiled and their mind hardened (2 Cor. iii. 14); they were in tutelage under the law (Gal. iv. 2); their reproba-

tion announced (Rom. x.); terrible judgment on that people (1 Thess. ii. 16); some saved (Rom. xi. 5); Christ promised to them (xv. 8); their future zeal (xi. 26).

JEZ'ABEL, daughter of Ethbaal, king of Sidon, and wife of Achab, king of Israel, a most impious woman (3 Kings xvi. 31); she and her husband maintained hundreds of idolatrous priests (xviii. 19); she kills many of the prophets of the Lord (4, 13); she menaced the prophet Elias with death (xix. 2); she employed false witnesses against Naboth in order to seize his vineyard, and compass his death (xxi. 7, 13); Jehu orders her to be cast down from a window, when the dogs devoured her (4 Kings ix. 33-36), as Elias had foretold (3 Kings xxi. 23). Her name has become proverbial for cruelty and wickedness. It is applied, in Apoc. ii. 20, to a false prophetess at Thyatira, who was leading the people to idolatry.

JO'AB, son of Sarvia, David's sister, and brother of Abisai and Azael, general of David's armies (2 Kings ii. 13); kills Abner treacherously after he had submitted to David (iii. 27); first to mount the walls of Sion when David took it (1 Par. xi. 6); reconciles Absalom and his father (2 Kings xiv.); kills Absalom contrary to David's orders (xviii. 14); his haughty bearing to David (xix. 5); assassinates his cousin Amasa (xx. 10); put to death by Solomon (3 Kings ii. 28, 34), pursuant to orders left by David (3 Kings ii. 6).

JO'ACHAZ, king of Juda. (See OCHOZIAS.)

JO'ACHAZ, son of Jehu, king of Israel (4 Kings x. 35; xiii. 1); his death (2).

JO'ACHAZ, son of Josias, king of Juda, called also Johanan (1 Paral. iii. 15; 2 Paral. xxxvi. 1; 4 Kings xxiii. 30); stripped of his kingdom by Nechao, and led prisoner to Egypt, where he dies (34; 2 Paral. xxxvi. 1, 4); his captivity foretold by Ezechiel (Ezech. xix. 4); succeeded by his brother Eliacim, or Joakim (4 Kings xxiii. 34; 2 Paral. xxxvi. 4).

JO'ACHIN, son of Joakim, by Nohesta, daughter of Elnathan (4 Kings xxiv. 8); reigns over Juda (2 Paral. xxxvi. 3); carried to Babylon by Nabuchodonosor (4 Kings xxiv. 12, 15; 2 Paral. xxxvi. 10); taken out of prison and restored to honor (xxv. 27); called Jechonias (Matt. i. 12; Jerem. xxiv. 1); succeeded by his uncle Mathanias, or Sedecias (4 Kings xxiv. 17).

JO'AKIM, son of Josias, brother of Joachaz, made king of Juda by Nechao, king of Egypt (4 Kings xxiii. 34; 2 Paral. xxxvi. 4); burns the books of Jeremias (Jerem. xxxvi. 23); his cruelty to the prophet Urias (xxvi. 20-23); conquered by Nabuchodonosor (4 Kings xxiv. 1); carried in chains to Babylon (2 Paral. xxxvi. 8); restored and rebels (4 Kings xxiv. 1); punished (2); his death (5); Jeremias prophesies that his body should be thrown out of Jerusalem unburied like an ass (Jer. xxii. 19); called also Eliacim.

JOAN'NA, wife of Chusa, Herod's steward, one

of the holy women, who ministered to our Lord of their substance (Luke viii. 3).

JOA'RIB, head of the first of the twenty-four priestly families established by David (1 Paral. xxiv. 7); the Machabees were descended from him (1 Mach. ii. 1).

JO'AS, son of Amalech, detained the prophet Micheas in prison by order of king Achab (3 Kings xxii. 26).

JO'AS, son of Ochozias; saved by his aunt Josaba when his grandmother Athalia slew all the children of Ochozias (4 Kings xi. 2); crowned king of Juda by Joiada, the high-priest; he repairs the temple (4 Kings xi. 12; xii. 4; 2 Paral. xxiii.; xxiv. 10); took all the treasures and precious vessels of the temple to purchase peace from Hazael, king of Syria (4 Kings xii. 18); kills Zacharias, the son of Joiada (2 Paral. xxiv. 22); slain by Josachar and Jozabad in the house of Mello (4 Kings xii. 20; 2 Paral. xxiv. 25); succeeded by Amasias (27; 4 Kings xii. 21).

JO'AS, son of Joachaz, king of Israel (4 Kings xiii. 10, 13).

JO'ATHAM or **JO'ATHAN,** king of Juda (4 Kings xv. 5, 32; 2 Paral. xxvi. 21; xxvii. 1); his death (xxvii. 9); succeeded by his son Achaz (4 Kings xv. 38); the prophets Isaias, Osee and Micheas prophesied in his reign (Isaias i. 1; Osee i. 1; Mich. i. 1).

JO'ATHAM, youngest son of Gedeon. He escaped when his brethren were massacred by Abimelech. At the coronation of the latter, he stood on Mount Garizim, reproached the people, and foretold woe to Sichem and Abimelech (Judg. ix. 5–20).

JOB, an upright man in the land of Hus (Job i. 1); a model of patience; his prosperity (i. 1–5); God permits Satan to afflict him (6–19); ii. 1–8); his wife mocks his faith (9); visited by his friends Eliphaz, Baldad and Sophar (11); Eliphaz accuses him of impatience (iv., v., xv., xxii.); Job maintains his innocence (vi.); Baldad accuses Job (viii.; xviii.; xxv.); Sophar reproves Job (xi.; xx.). Job maintains his innocence. Eliu also blames him (xxxii.–xxxvii.); God interposes (xxxviii.–xli.); Job submits and prays for his friends, and is restored to wealth and prosperity (xlii.)

JOB, one of the canonical books of the Old Testament, describing the trials and patience of the holy patriarch Job (Job).

JO'EL, eldest son of the prophet Samuel, made

ANCIENT JEWELRY. AN ENGRAVED CAMEO.

judge by his father, but he rendered unjust judgments (1 Kings viii. 1, 2; 1 Paral. vi. 33).

JO'EL, son of Phatuel, the second of the minor prophets. He prophesied in the kingdom of Juda, as Calmet thinks, in the reign of Josias. He exhorts the people to penance and foretells the coming miseries, and promises a teacher of justice (Joel).

JO'EL, a canonical book of the Old Testament, containing the prophecies of Joel.

JOHAN'AN, son of Caree, warned Godolias that Ismahel was sent to slay him (Jer. xl. 13); and offers to cut him off (15); after the death of Godolias, he marched against Ismahel, who fled (xli. 11–15); Johanan then led the people to Egypt by way of Bethlehem (16–18; 4 Kings xxv. 23–26).

JOHAN'AN or **JONATHAN** (2 Esd. xii. 11, 22); son of Joiada, and high-priest.

JOHN THE BAPTIST, precursor of our Lord, son of Zachary and Elizabeth, born (Luke i. 13, 57); circumcised (59); Zachary's speech restored (64); John's preaching (Matt. iii.); his food locusts and wild honey (Mark i. 6); he baptizes our Lord (Matt. iii. 16); points him out as the Messias (John i. 29); his humility (i. 19; iii. 28); sends his disciples to Jesus (Matt. xi. 2, 3); reproves Herod's sin (Mark vi. 18); Herodias lays snares for him (19); Herod casts him into prison (17); Herodias bids her daughter ask his head (24); Herod orders him to be beheaded (27); his martyrdom (Matt. xiv. 9; Mark vi. 27–29); called Elias (Matt. xi. 14; xvii. 12; Luke i. 17).

JOHN THE EVANGELIST AND APOSTLE, son of Zebedee, his vocation (Matt. iv. 21); chosen to be one of the twelve (x. 3; Mark iii. 17; Luke vi. 14); the disciple whom Jesus loved (John xiii. 23; xix. 26; xx. 2; xxi. 7, 20); wrote what he saw (xix. 35; xxi. 24; 1 John i. 1; Apoc. i. 2); witnesses the transfiguration (Matt. xvii. 1); at the Last Supper (John xiii. 23); at the crucifixion (xix. 26); wrote one of the Gospels, three Epistles, and during his exile at Patmos the Apocalypse or Revelation.

JOHN, GOSPEL OF ST. One of the canonical books of the New Testament, written by the Apostle St. John (John).

JOHN, EPISTLES OF ST. Three epistles of St. John the Apostle, canonical books of the New Testament (1 John, 2 John, 3 John).

JOHN, APOCALYPSE OF ST. One of the canonical books of the New Testament, containing revelations made to St. John the Apostle, in the island of Patmos (Apoc.)

JOHN MARK, a disciple, cousin of St. Barnabas, son of a Christian woman named Mary, at whose house the faithful assembled. St. Peter went to it after his miraculous deliverance from prison (Acts xii. 12); John Mark accompanied St. Paul and Barnabas to Antioch (Acts xii. 25; xiii. 13); St. Paul did not wish him as companion in Asia (Acts

xv. 37); he then went to Cyprus with St. Barnabas (39); with St. Paul in Rome (Coloss. iv. 10; Philemon 24); then with St. Timothy in Asia (2

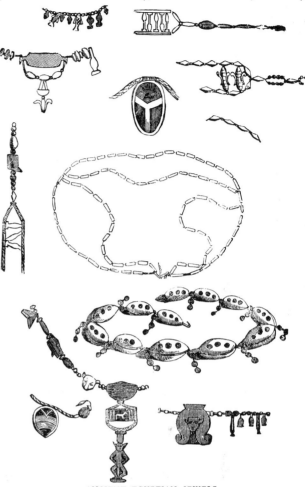

ANCIENT EGYPTIAN JEWELS.

Tim. iv. 11). He is believed to have died at Ephesus.

JOHN, kinsman of the high-priest (Acts iv. 6).

JOIA'DA, son of Eliasib, high-priest (2 Esd. xii. 20). His wife Josaba or Josabeth, sister of Ochozias, saved young Joas in a bedchamber. Joiada preserved him in the temple, and after seven years proclaimed him king, and put Athalia to death (4 Kings xi.; xii.; 2 Paral. xxiii.; xxiv.); he overthrew the worship of Baal, and restored the temple of God; he died 844 B. C., aged one hundred and thirty (2 Paral. xxiv. 15).

JO'NADAB, son of Semmaa, and nephew of David, wickedly advised Amnon, and brought misery on the house of David (2 Kings xii. 3, etc.)

JO'NADAB, son of Rechab, chief of the Rechabites. Jehu takes him to witness his destruction of the house of Achab and of the priests of Baal (4 Kings x. 15, 16); forbids his followers to drink wine, plant fields or vineyards, or build houses (Jerem. xxxv. 6–10).

JO'NAS, son of Amathi, fifth of the minor prophets, was a Galilean, a native of Geth in opher (4 Kings xiv. 25); many have believed him to be the son of the widow of Sarepta raised to life by Elias (3 Kings xvii. 17); he lived in the reigns of Joas and Jeroboam II., kings of Israel. God ordered him to go and announce to Ninive its destruction (Jonas i. 1): he sought to avoid the mission by flight, and embarked at Joppe for Tharsis. A storm arising, the sailors cast lots to find who caused their peril. The lot fell on Jonas, who confessed who he was, and

sought to save him from his father's anger (xix.; xx.); he met David secretly in the desert of Ziph when Saul was pursuing him (xxiii.); he was killed with

Bacchides besieged him, 158 B. C. (ix. 64), but failed to capture the place and subsequently made peace. He then governed the people at Machmas. Alexander Bales and Demetrius Soter both sought his friendship. He declared for Alexander, and in 152 B. C. assumed the high-priesthood (1 Mach. x.); Alexander treated him with great honor, but in 148 B. C. Demetrius Nicator sent Apollonius against him. Jonathan took Joppe and defeated Apollonius at Jamnia (1 Mach. x.); he besieged the citadel of Jerusalem, then held by Demetrius, but finally obtained it by aiding the king to reduce Antioch (1 Mach. xi.); Demetrius soon became hostile, when Jonathan espoused the cause of young Antiochus and renewed alliance with Sparta and Rome (1 Mach. xii.); he overawed the armies of Demetrius, and punished the Zabadean Arabs. Tryphon allured Jonathan to Ptolemais, threw him into prison and massacred his attendants (1 Mach. xiii.); Simon, his brother, sent a large ransom which Tryphon demanded, but the treacherous general put Jonathan and his sons to death at Bascama, 143 B. C. Simon buried him at Modin and erected a magnificent tomb (1 Mach. xiii. 27).

JON'ATHAN, son of Absalomi, one of the generals of Jonathan Machabeus, took Joppe (1 Mach. xiii. 11).

ANCIENT EASTERN JEWELS AND ORNAMENTS.

bade them cast him into the sea, and the sea would grow calm. A great fish swallowed Jonas, who was three days and nights in its belly. He cried to the Lord, who caused the fish to cast him on the shore. Then the Lord repeated his command to Jonas. He entered Ninive crying, "In forty days Ninive shall be destroyed." The king and his people were converted, and did penance in sackcloth and ashes, and God revoked the sentence against them. Jonas was grieved that his prophecy did not come to pass, and God made an ivy, which he had caused to grow up and shade the prophet, to wither away (Jonas i.–iv.); Jonas also foretold that Jeroboam II. would restore the ancient limits of the kingdom of Israel (4 Kings xiv. 25); our Lord refers to the preaching of Jonas (Matt. xii. 41; Luke xi. 32), and makes Jonas' three days' burial in the belly of the fish a type of his own burial and resurrection (Matt. xii. 39, 40; xvi. 4; Luke xi. 29–31); he was frequently painted in the catacombs as a type.

JON'ATHAN, a Levite, son of Gersam and grandson of Moses, became an idolatrous priest in the house of Michas, and then at Dan or Lais (Josue xvii. 7–xviii. 31).

JON'ATHAN, son of Saul and devoted friend of David. With no one but his shield-bearer, he attacked the Philistines at Machnas and caused a panic, in which they slew each other (1 Kings xiii.; xiv.); Saul, pursuing the enemy, cursed any one who ate before evening; Jonathan, ignorant of this, ate a little wild honey, and when it was disclosed by lot, Saul would have slain him, but the people interposed. Jonathan became attached to David from the time of his victory over Goliath (1 Kings xviii.), and

his father in the battle at Mount Gelboe (1 Kings xxxi. 1, 2); David composed a touching lamentation for him (2 Kings i. 18–27), and befriended his son Miphiboseth (2 Kings ix. 7; xxi. 7).

JON'ATHAN, son of the high-priest Abiathar, informs Adonias that David had proclaimed Solomon his successor (3 Kings i. 42, 43).

JON'ATHAN, high-priest, son of Joiada (2 Esd. xii. 11).

JON'ATHAN, scribe of king Sedecias, and persecutor of the prophet Jeremias (Jerem. xxxvii 14–19).

JON'ATHAN, surnamed Apphus, son of Mathathias and brother of Judas Machabeus (1 Mach. ii. 5), succeeds his brother as commander of the army of Israel (ix. 28, 29); defeats Bacchides near the Jordan, and crosses the river in safety, 161 B. C. (ix. 44); when Bacchides returned with a fresh army Jonathan retired to Bethbessen in the desert, where

Mach. xiii. 11).

JOP'PE, a city and port of Palestine, on the Mediterranean, now called Jaffa. Hiram sends rafts of timber for Solomon to Joppe (2 Paral. ii. 16);

THE JORDAN ON THE ROAD FROM NABULUS (ancient Sichem) TO ES-SALT
(ancient Ramoth-galaad?).

Jonas embarked at (Jonas i. 3); St. Peter restores Dorcas to life at (Acts ix. 40); Cornelius by order of an angel sends messengers to St. Peter at Joppe (x. 5, 32)

JO'RAM, son of Thou, king of Emath in Syria, sent to congratulate David on his victory over Aderezer, king of Syria, 1004 B. C. (2 Kings viii. 10).

JO'RAM, son and successor of Josaphat, king of Juda (3 Kings xxii. 51; 4 Kings viii. 16); he married Athalia, daughter of Amri (2 Paral. xxii. 2), or Achab (4 Kings viii. 18; 2 Paral. xxi. 6); he puts his six brothers to death (2 Paral. xxi. 4); the Edomites revolt, and though he defeated he could not subdue them (4 Kings viii. 20–22; 2 Paral. xxi. 8–10); Lobna also revolted (10), and his kingdom was ravaged by the Philistines and Arabs (16); he built high places, and encouraged idolatry (11); Elias wrote to rebuke him and announce his chastisement (12–15); he died miserably, and was not buried in the sepulchre of the kings (18–20); all his sons were killed by the Arabs except Ochozias, who succeeded him (xxii. 1).

JO'RAM, son of Achab, king of Israel (4 Kings i. 17; iii. 1); defeats Mesa, king of Moab (iii. 4–27); is saved by Eliseus, but tries to kill the prophet (4 Kings iii., vii.); makes war on Hazael, king of Syria, and is wounded at Ramoth-Galaad (4 Kings viii. 28, 29; ix. 14, 15); his wickedness (iii. 2, 3); he goes to meet Jehu at Jezrahel, who shoots him through the heart with an arrow (ix. 24); his body flung into Naboth's vineyard (25).

JOR'DAN, a river of Palestine, running from Anti-Libanus to the Dead Sea. There were fords opposite Jericho (Jos. ii. 7; Judg. iii. 28; xii. 5); at Bethbera or Bethabara (Gen. xxxii. 10; Judg. vii. 24; xii. 6); all the country beyond the Jordan selected by Lot (Gen. xiii. 10); villages beyond given to the Israelites (Num. xxxii.); Josue passes it miraculously with the children of Israel (Jos. iii. 15–17; iv. 1); sets up a monument in the bed (iv. 8); the waters of the Jordan divided by the prophet Elias (4 Kings ii. 8); by Eliseus, with the mantle of Elias (14); St. John the Baptist at (Matt. iii. 5); he baptizes our Lord in the Jordan (Luke iii. 21).

JOS'ABA, daughter of Joram, and wife of the high-priest Joiada, saves Joas, the son of her brother Ochozias, when Athalia sought to murder all her grandsons (4 Kings xi. 2, 3).

JO'SACHAR, son of Semaath, and Jozabad, son of Somer, kill Joas, king of Juda (4 Kings xii. 21).

JOS'APHAT, king of Juda, son of Asa, by his queen Azuba (3 Kings xv. 24; xxii. 41); he kept in check the king of Israel, fortified the cities of Juda, and those conquered by Asa from Israel; he abolished the idolatry in the high-places and groves. He sent Levites through his kingdom to instruct the people (2 Paral. xvii. 7); he made the Philistines and Arabs tributary. He made an alliance with the wicked king Achab to attack Ramoth, against the words of the prophet Micheas, and was nearly slain in battle (3 Kings xxii.; 2 Paral. xviii.) The prophet Jehu rebuked him (2 Paral. xix. 1, 2); the Moabites, Ammonites, and Meonians made war on him, but he

JOSEPH SOLD BY HIS BRETHREN.

was delivered by prayer (2 Paral. xx. 1–3); he agreed with Ochozias, king of Israel, to fit out a fleet at Asiongaber, but God defeated his design (2 Paral. xx. 35, 36); he died in Jerusalem, and was buried in the royal sepulchre 889 B. C., after a reign of twenty-five years (2 Paral. xxi. 1; 3 Kings xxii. 51).

JOS'APHAT, valley of. The Lord will assemble all nations there to judge them (Joel iii. 2, 12); some suppose it the Valley of Blessing, near the Dead Sea (2 Par. xx. 26), where Josaphat's enemies from Moab, Ammon and Mt. Seir slew each other (22); others think it the valley between Jerusalem and Mount Olivet.

JOS'EDECH, high-priest, succeeds his father Saraias (1 Paral. vi. 14, 15; 1 Esd. iii. 2); he apparently died in Babylon, and his son Jesus restored the temple.

JO'SEPH, son of Jacob and Rachel, born 1745 B. C. (Gen. xxx. 24); God favored him with prophetic dreams (xxxvii. 5); he denounced the wickedness of his brothers (Gen. xxxvii. 2, 4); out of jealousy and revenge they resolved to put him to death, but sold him to the Ismaelites (xxxvii. 28; Ps. civ. 17), who took him to Egypt and sold him to Putiphar; his mistress, failing to lead him to sin, accused him and had him imprisoned (xxxix. 17, 20); having shown his ability in interpreting dreams, he was sent for to explain a dream of king Pharao (xli. 24, 25); the king, admiring his wisdom, set him over all Egypt, and he married the daughter of Putiphar (45); his brethren sent down by their father in the time of famine to obtain food in Egypt, where Joseph had accumulated grain, bow down reverently to him without recognizing him (xlii. 6; xliii. 26); he detains Simeon, and compels them to bring his own brother Benjamin, and then discovers himself to them (xlv. 1); his two sons Ephraim and Manasses blessed and adopted by Jacob (xlviii. 5); Jacob's words as to Joseph (xlix. 22); his death (l. 24), 1635 B. C.; his bones carried out of Egypt as he had directed (Ex. xiii. 19); buried at Sichem (Jos. xxiv. 32); words of Moses as to Joseph (Deut. xxxiii. 13). There was no tribe of Joseph, but his sons Ephraim and Manasses, having been adopted by Jacob, the descendants of each formed a tribe.

JO'SEPH, son of Jacob (Matt. i. 16); or Heli (Luke iii. 23); spouse of the Blessed Virgin Mary (Matt. i. 16); called a just man (19); his anxiety relieved by an angel (20); his obedience (24); warned by an angel to fly into Egypt (ii. 13, 14); and subsequently to return (19, 20); dwells at Nazareth (23); working as a carpenter (xiii. 55).

JO'SEPH or **JOSE,** son of Mary of Cleophas (Mark xv. 40; Matt. xiii. 55; xxvii. 56). He was brother of St. James the Less.

JO'SEPH BARSABAS, surnamed the Just, must have been one of the first disciples of our Lord, being one of those who companied with the apostles, beginning with the baptism of John until the Ascension (Acts i. 21, 22); he and St. Mathias were proposed for the apostleship left vacant by the fall of Judas (23). According to Eusebius, he was one of the seventy disciples, and once having drunk poison was miraculously preserved.

JO'SEPH OF ARIMATHEA or **RAMA-THA,** was a senator among the Jews and a secret disciple of Christ (John xix. 38). He took no part in the councils against our Lord (Luke xxiii. 51); and after his crucifixion went boldly to Pilate and asked for the body to inter it (Mark xv. 43; John xix. 38); he laid it in a new tomb which he had made for himself on Calvary, and closed it with a heavy slab prepared for the purpose (Matt. xxvii. 60; John xix. 40, 41).

JOSI'AS, son of Amon, king of Juda, and of Idida, daughter of Hadaiah, of Besecath (4 Kings xxii. 1, 2); he began to reign at the age of eight, 641 B. C. (4 Kings xxi. 24; xxii. 1); his birth foretold by a prophet (3 Kings xiii. 2); in his twentieth year he purified Juda and Jerusalem from high-places, groves, idols and superstitious figures (2 Paral. xxxiv. 1, 2, 3, etc.); he did so even in Ephraim, Manasses, Simeon, and Nephthali (6); he repaired the temple, and when the high-priest Helcias found the book of the law in the temple, he consulted the prophetess Holda, read the book to the people, made a covenant with the Lord, banished idolatry (4 Kings xxii., xxiii.; 2 Paral. xxxiii., xxxiv.); he celebrated the Pasch with solemnity (2 Paral. xxxv. 1; 4 Kings xxiii. 21); in 610 B. C., Pharao Nechao, king of Egypt, marching to attack Carchemis, on the Euphrates, wished to march across Juda, but Josias opposed him and was mortally wounded at Mageddo, near Mount Carmel. He died in Jerusalem of his wounds, 610 B. C. (4 Kings xxiii. 30; 2 Paral. xxxv. 23); Jeremias wrote a lamentation on his death (2 Paral. xxxv. 25); and the son of Sirach extols him (Ecclus. xlix.); the prophets Jeremias, Baruch, Joel, and Sophonias flourished in his reign.

JOS'UE, the son of Nun, or Nave (Osee, Num. xiii. 9, 17; Jesus, Ecclus. xlvi. 1), was of the tribe of Ephraim born 1544 B. C.; he is at first called the minister of Moses (Ex. xxiv. 13; Deut. i. 38); his servant (Ex. xxxiii. 11); defeated the Amalecites, 1491 B. C. (Ex. xvii. 9, 10); he remained on Mt. Sinai while Moses received the divine communications (xxiv. 13); he was constantly at the tabernacle (xxxiii. 11); in his zeal for Moses he wished to prevent others from prophesying (Num. xi. 28, 29); he was sent from Cadesbarne with other spies to examine the Promised Land (xiii. 17); but only he and Caleb recommended it (xiv. 6). When Moses was near his end, by command of God he imposed hands on Josue before Eleazar the priest (xxvii. 18-23); and Moses then announced to the people that he was to be their leader (Deut. xxxi. 3); and gave instructions to Josue (7); and God gave him a charge in the tabernacle of the testimony (14, 23); and repeated it

after the death of Moses (Jos. i. 1-9); he sent spies to Jericho (ii.); crossed the Jordan (iii.); raised a monument to commemorate the miracle (iv.); is visited by an angel (v. 13); captures Jericho by the sound of his trumpets (vi.); takes the city of Hai (viii.); blesses the people (33); is deluded by the Gabaonites (ix.); aids them (x.); the sun and moon stop at his command during his battle with the five kings of the Amorrhites at Gabaon (x. 13); he defeats thirty-one kings (xii.); receives his share in the distribution of the land (xix. 49); assembles the princes of each tribe, gives them his last advice, and recalls God's benefits to them (xxiv. 1-24); dies at the age of one hundred and ten (29); and was buried

JOSEPH INTERPRETING PHARAO'S DREAM.

at Thamnathsare, on Mount Ephraim (30; Judges ii. 8); his praise (Ecclus. xlvi. 1-10).

JOUR'NEY. The Sabbath day's journey was limited by the Jewish law to 2,000 paces from the walls of the place (Ex. xvi. 29; Acts i. 12).

JU'BAL, son of Lamech and Ada, "he was the father of them that play on the harp and the organ" (Gen. iv. 21).

JU'BILEE. The year of jubilee was the fiftieth, that after seven weeks of years (Lev. xxv. 8); during this year no ground was sown, or reaped, only what grew spontaneously was gathered; lands returned to their original owners; Hebrew slaves were

liberated, with their wives and children (xxv. 9-34).

JU'DA, fourth son of Jacob and Lia, born in Mesopotamia, 1755 B. C. (Gen. xxix. 35); advised his brothers to sell Joseph, not kill him (xxxvii. 26); married Sue, a Chanaanite woman, who bore him Her, Onan and Sela. His two elder sons were punished by God. Juda had also by Thamar, widow of Her, Phares and Zara (xxxviii.); made himself responsible for the safety of Benjamin (xliii. 8, 9); his humble address to Joseph on Benjamin's arrest (xliv. 16-34); Jacob in his blessing foretold the royal power in the line of Juda, and that the sceptre should not be taken away from Juda till the Expectation of nations came (xlix. 8-12).

JU'DA. The tribe of Juda, descended from Juda, son of Jacob, marched out of Egypt with 74,600 fighting men under Nahasson, their prince (Num. i. 7, 27); they camped on the east (ii. 3, 4); first in rank among the tribes (Num. ii. 3; vii. 12; Judges i. 2); their offering (Num. vii. 12-17); Caleb was sent from Juda to view the Promised Land (xiii. 7); and to divide it (xxxiv. 19); at Settim they numbered 76,500 (xxvi. 19-22); Moses' blessing on Juda (Deut. xxxiii. 7); their share in the Promised Land (Jos. xv.); Achan, of the tribe of Juda, by his disobedience causes Israel to be defeated at Hai (Jos. vii.); the tribe could not destroy the Jebusites (xv. 63); with the tribe of Simeon it defeats the Chanaanite and Pherezite (Judg. i. 2-20); the Ammonites waste Juda (x. 9); deliver Samson to the Philistines (xv.); God appoints Juda the leader in the war against Benjamin (Judg. xx. 18); Booz, husband of Ruth, of the tribe of Juda (Ruth); David, his descendant, selected by God to succeed Saul (1 Kings xvi.); anointed king over Juda (2 Kings ii. 4); only the house of Juda followed David (10); becomes king of Israel and Juda (v. 5); all but Juda and Benjamin revolt from Roboam (3 Kings xii. 20, 23); the royalty remains in the house of David (2 Kings vii. 12; 1 Paral. xvii. 11; 2 Paral. vi. 6).

JU'DA. The kingdom of Juda is that governed by Roboam and his descendants, embracing the tribes of Juda and Benjamin, with the Levites. It lasted from 970 B. C. to 588 B. C.

JU'DAS MACHABE'US, son of Mathathias, a priest of the sons of Joarib (1 Mach. ii. 4); succeeded his father as leader of the faithful in their war against Antiochus Epiphanes (ii. 49, 70), B. C. 166; he defeated Apollonius (1 Mach. iii. 11); and Seron (13-23); Antiochus sent Gorgias against Judas, who defeated him at Emmaus (iv.); he then routed Lysias at Bethhoron (iv. 28, 29), 160 B. C.; he then went up to Jerusalem, purified the temple, restored the altar and sacred vessels, and on the 25th of Casleu, the ninth month, renewed the worship of God after the dedication of the temple (iv. 37-52); soon after he defeated Timotheus and Bacchides, and returned laden with booty (2 Mach. viii. 30; x. 24).

He fortified Bethsura to protect Jerusalem from the Idumeans (1 Mach. iv. 61); he took Bosor, and marched to the relief of Datheman, defeated Timotheus and laid Astaroth Carnaim in ashes (1 Mach. v.); he defeated Lysias at Bethsura (2 Mach. xi. 1–28); he chastised Joppe and Jamnia, and took the strong city of Ephron. At Odollam he found idols on the persons of some of his fallen soldiers, and sent to Jerusalem to have sacrifices offered for them, a testimony to the Jewish practice of prayer for the dead (2 Mach. xii. 40). Antiochus Eupator came in person with a large army and besieged Bethsura, and then Jerusalem, till domestic troubles compelled him to make peace (1 Mach. vi.; 2 Mach. xiii.) Demetrius, the next king, sent Bacchides against Judas. Bacchides entered Jerusalem, set up Alcimus as high-priest (1 Mach. vii.; 2 Mach. xiv.) Judas soon drove him out and made terms with Nicanor, the next general sent against him, till Demetrius ordered Nicanor to seize Judas. The war was renewed; Nicanor, repulsed at Caphar Salama, threatened to destroy the temple unless Judas was delivered up, but the valiant priest defeated and slew him at Bethoron, 161 B. C. Demetrius then sent Bacchides against him. Judas was at Bethel with 3,000 men, but alarmed at the force approaching, most of these deserted him. Judas, with only 800 men, attacked Bacchides and routed his right wing, but was surrounded by the main body, and after a desperate action slain. He was buried by his brothers in the sepulchre of the family at Modin (1 Mach. ix. 19).

JU′DAS ISCAR′IOT (probably of Iscarioth in the tribe of Ephraim), called to be an apostle (Matt. x. 4; Mark iii. 19; Luke vi. 16); entrusted with the money contributed (John xii. 6); yields to avarice and becomes a thief (6); betrays our Lord for thirty pieces of silver (Luke xxii. 4; Matt. xxvi. 21, 46, 49); a prey to remorse, he brought back the money to the chief-priests, hung himself with a halter, and burst asunder (Matt. xxvii. 4; Acts i. 18).

JU′DAS the Galilean, raises an insurrection, but his adherents are scattered (Acts v. 37).

JUDEA AS DEPICTED ON COINS STRUCK BY THE EMPEROR VESPASIAN.

JU′DAS, surnamed Barsabas, sent from Jerusalem to Antioch with St. Paul and Barnabas to convey the decision of the council (Acts xv. 22–33).

JUDE, surnamed Thaddeus, or Lebbeus (Matt. x. 3; Mark iii. 18), and Z e l o t e s, sometimes called the brother of the Lord (Matt. xiii. 55; Mark vi. 3); brother of St. James the Less (Acts i. 13); one of the apostles (Matt. x. 3; Mark iii. 18; Luke vi. 16). At the last supper he asked our Lord why he did not manifest himself to the world (John xiv. 22).

JUDE, Epistle of St., one of the canonical books of the New Testament, a Catholic epistle, written by the apostle St. Jude (Jude).

JU′DAS writes in the name of the senate and people of Jerusalem to Aristobulus, preceptor of king Ptolemee (2 Mach. i. 10).

JU′DAS, host of St. Paul at Damascus (Acts ix. 11).

JUDE′A, the name given after the Babylonian captivity to the part occupied by the Jews.

JUD′GES. These were leaders raised up by God to govern or deliver his people after the death of Josue (Judg. ii. 16); their rule continued till Saul was made king (1 Kings viii.) They were Othoniel, Aod, Debora and Barac, Gedeon (Abimelech), Thola, Jair, Jephte, Abesan, Ahialon, Abdon, Heli the high-priest, Samson, Samuel, 1434–1095 B. C.

JUD′GES, one of the canonical books of the Old Testament, written it is believed by the prophet Samuel, containing the history of the Israelites from death of Josue to the time of Heli (Judg.)

JUD′GES, instituted by Moses on the advice of Jethro (Ex. xviii. 25); their duties and functions (Ex. xxi.; xxii.; xxiii.; Lev. xxiv. 11; Deut. i. 13, 16; xvii.; xxv. 1.; xxvii. 19; 1 Kings viii. 3; xii. 5; 2 Paral. xix. 6; Ps. lxxxi. 2–8; Prov. xxviii. 21; Ecclus. iv. 5; x.; Isai. v. 16; x. 1–3; Jer. v. 1; Luke xviii. 2; xxiii. 13; John viii. 15; James ii. 4).

JUDG′MENT. We should examine before judging after the example of God himself (Gen. iii.

11; xi. 5; xviii. 21; Ex. iii. 8; xxiii. 2; Deut. xiii. 14; xvii. 9; xix. 18; Jos. vii. 19; xx. 1–5; Judg. xx 3, 12; Prov. xviii. 13; 1 Mach. vii. 7); we must not judge others without authority (Ecclus. xi. 9; Luke vi. 37); nor judge according to appearance only (John vii. 24; Deut. i. 16); we must not judge rashly (Matt. vii. 1; xii. 7; Luke vii. 33; John ix. 16; Acts xxviii. 4; Rom. xiv. 4, 13; 1 Cor. iv. 5; 1 Tim. v. 21).

JUDG′MENT. The last judgment, foretold by our Lord, and reserved to him alone (John v. 22); described (Matt. xxv. 31–46; Apoc. vi. 17; vii.; xiv. 7).

JU′DITH, of the tribe of Ruben, daughter of Merari, and widow of Manasses. She lived in Bethulia, and passed her widowhood in holy seclusion (Judith viii. 4, etc.); when the city was besieged by Holofernes, and Ozias the ruler of the city promised to surrender if God did not send relief within five days (viii.), she rebuked them for tempting the Lord (viii. 11), and resolved to endeavor to save the city. She bade them pray for her (33); and putting on hair-cloth and ashes, implored the assistance of God (ix.); she then went with her handmaid to the camp of the Assyrians; Holofernes, taken by her beauty, gave her liberty to go forth each night to pray; and having invited her to a banquet, was overcome with wine. Then Judith, praying to God for strength, beheaded him with his own sword, and went forth, bearing his head to Bethulia (x.–xiii.); the Israelites attacked the Assyrians, who, finding their general slain, fled before the Hebrews (xiv., xv.); she praised God for his mercy in a canticle (xvi. 2–21); she died at the age of 105, and was buried in Bethulia (28).

JU′DITH, one of the canonical books of the Old

Testament, describing the deliverance of Bethulia by Judith (Judith).

JU'LIA, a Christian woman of Rome saluted by St. Paul (Rom. xvi. 15).

ANCIENT LAMPS.

JU'NIAS, kinsman and fellow-prisoner of St. Paul, "of note among the apostles" (Rom. xvi. 7).

JU'NIPER TREE. Elias rests under one near Bersabee when fleeing from Jezabel (3 Kings xix. 4).

JU'PITER, the chief deity honored by the Romans, and by the Greeks under the name of Zeus. Antiochus made the temple of Jerusalem a temple of Jupiter Olympius, and that in Garizim of Jupiter Hospitalis (2 Mach. vi. 2); when St. Paul and Barnabas cured the cripple at Lystra, the people took them to be gods, and wished to sacrifice to Barnabas as Jupiter (Acts xiv. 11, 12).

JUST, JUST'ICE. The perfection of justice cannot be attained in this life (Gen. vi. 5; Ex. xxxiv. 7; Num. xiv. 18; 3 Kings viii. 46; 2 Paral. vi. 36; Job iv. 17; ix. 2, 15, 20; xxv. 4; Ps. xiii. 1; l. 7; cxxix. 3; cxlii. 2; Prov. xx. 9; Eccles. vii. 21; Wis. xii. 10; Jer. xxx. 11; Mich. vii. 2; Nah. i. 3; Matt. vi. 12; Luke xvii. 10, 14; Rom. iii. 9, 23; vii.; Gal. iii. 22; Eph. ii. 3; 1 John i. 8). Increase in justice the fruit of good works (Ecclus. xviii. 22; Rom. ii. 13; James ii. 22, 24; Apoc. xxii. 11); who are truly just (Luke i. 6; John viii. 36; xvii. 17, 19; 1 Cor. vi. 11; Heb. xi.)

JUST, book of the, referred to (2 Kings i. 18; Jos. x. 13).

JUST'ICE, regulations for administering (Ex. xviii. 21–26; xxiii. 1; Deut. xix.; xxi.)

JUST'IFICATION attributed to faith and other virtues (Ex. xx. 6; Prov. x. 12; Wis. xi. 24; Ecclus. i. 27; Ezech. xviii. 21, 22; Matt. x. 28; Luke vii., xv., xviii., xix.; Rom. viii. 23; 1 Cor. viii. 4; Gal. v. 6; 1 Pet. iv. 8; 1 John iv. 7); our merit comes from Jesus Christ, and there is no merit before the first justification and remission of sins (Gen. xv. 6; Isai. xlv. 26; liii. 8, 12; Jerem. xxiii. 6; xxxiii. 16; Dan. vi. 22; Hab. ii. 4; Zach. ix. 9; Acts x. 43; xiii. 39; Rom. vi. 16; x. 4, 10; 1 Cor. i. 30; Gal. ii. 16; v. 5; Phil. iii. 9; Tit. iii. 7; 1 Pet. iii. 18).

JUS'TUS, surname of Joseph, called Barsabas, (Acts i. 23); also of Titus, a Christian at Corinth, with whom St. Paul lodged (Acts xviii. 7); also of Jesus, a disciple of St. Paul (Col. iv. 11).

KEY, first mentioned (Judges iii. 25). The key of the house of David (Isai. xxii. 22; Apoc. iii. 7); our Lord gives St. Peter the keys of the kingdom of heaven (Matt. xvi. 19); the keys of death and hell (Apoc. i. 18; ix. 1; xx. 1).

KINE, fat and lean, seen in Pharao's dream (Gen. xli. 2).

KING'DOM OF HEAVEN (Matt. iii. 2); iv. 17; v. 3, 10, 19, 20; vii. 21; viii. 11; x. 7; xi. 11, 12; xiii. 11, 24, 31, 33, 44, 45, 47, 52; xvi. 19; xviii. 3, 4, 23; xix. 12, 14, 23, 24; xx. 1; xxii. 2; xxiii. 13; xxv. 1).

KING'DOM OF GOD (Matt. vi. 33; xii. 28; xiii. 38; xxi. 31, 43; Mark i. 14, 15; iii. 24; iv. 11, 26, 30; viii. 39; ix. 46; x. 14, 15, 23–25; xii. 34; xiv. 25; xv. 43; Luke i. 43; vi. 20; vii. 28; viii. 1, 10; ix.; x. 9, 11; xi.; xii. 13, 32; xiii.; xiv. 15; xvi. 16; xvii. 20, 21; xviii., xix., xxi., xxii., xxiii. 51; John iii. 3, 5; xviii. 36; Acts i. 3; viii. 12; xiv. 21; xix. 8).

KING'DOM (Matt. vi. 10; viii. 12; ix. 35; xiii. 19; xxiv. 14); "kingdom of my Father" (Matt. xxvi. 29; Mark xi. 10).

KING'DOM OF GOD, spiritual, interior and eternal (Gen. xlix. 10; Num. xxiv. 17; 1 Kings ii. 10; viii. 7; 1 Paral. xvii. 14; xxviii. 7; Ps. ii. 6; ix. 8; xxi. 28; xliv. 7; lxxix. 2; cix.; cxliv. 11; Isaias ix. 6; xi.; xxxii. 1; xl. 9; xlii. 1; Jerem. xxiii. 5, 6; xxxiii.; Ezech. xxxiv. 23; xxxvii. 24; Dan. ii. 44; iv. 23; vii. 14, 27; ix. 24, 25; Osee iii. 5; Mich. iv. 1, 3; v. 1; Zach. ix. 9; Matt. xiii.; Luke i. 32; xxi. 31; xxii. 29; xxiii. 2; John vi. 15; xii. 14–34; xviii. 33–36; 1 Tim. i. 17; Heb. i. 8; ii. 9).

KING'DOM OF ISRAEL, comprising ten tribes, founded by Jeroboam (3 Kings xii. 3, 9, 16).

KING'DOM OF JUDA, comprising the tribes of Juda and Benjamin with the Levites.

KINGS AND PRINCES: their duty and authority (Deut. xvii. 19; 1 Kings viii.; 3 Kings ii. 2; x. 9; 2 Par. ix. 1; xix. 5; Job xxxiv. 30; Ps. ii. 10; Ps. c.; Prov. xiv. 28; xix. 12; xx. 8, 26; xxviii. 15; xxix. 4, 14; xxxi. 4; Wisd. vi. 10; Jer. xxii. 2). The heart of kings is in the hand of God (Prov. xxi. 1); kings first mentioned (Gen. xiv. 1, 2, 5, 6, 10, 18; xx.; xxvi. 1); the Israelites first have a king (1 Kings xi. 15).

KINGS, four canonical books of the Old Testament, called First and Second Kings or Samuel, the first written it is generally believed by the prophet Samuel and concluded by the prophets Nathan and Gad, who wrote the second also. The Third and Fourth of Kings called in Hebrew First and Second. These books contain the history of the Israelites from the time of Samuel to the commencement of the Babylonian captivity (1 Kings, 2 Kings, 3 Kings, 4 Kings).

KISS, a symbol of peace and charity (Gen. xxix. 13; xlv. 15; xlviii. 10; Ex. iv. 27; Luke xv. 20; Acts xx. 37; Rom. xvi. 15; 1 Cor. xvi. 20; 2 Cor. xiii. 12; 1 Thess. v. 26; 1 Peter v. 14); Joab's perfidious kiss (2 Kings xx. 9); Judas' (Matt. xxvi. 49).

KITE, a bird of prey, forbidden as unclean (Lev. xi. 14; Deut. xiv. 13).

KNEEL'ING IN PRAYER (3 Kings xix. 18; 2 Paral. vi. 13; xxix. 30; 1 Esd. ix. 5; Dan. vi. 10; Mich. vi. 6; Luke xxii. 41; Rom. xiv. 11; Philip. ii. 10).

KNOWL'EDGE of good and evil (Gen. ii. 9); knowledge of the holy (Prov. ix. 9, 10); knowledge puffed up (1 Cor. viii. 1); knowledge falsely so called (1 Tim. vi. 20).

LA'ABIM, third son of Mesraim, son of Cham (Gen. x. 13).

LA'BAN, son of Bathuel and grandson of Nachor. He receives Abraham's servant, who comes to ask Rebecca as a wife for Isaac (Gen. xxiv. 29); Jacob takes refuge with him in Mesopotamia (xxviii.); agrees to serve him seven years for his daughter Rachel (xxix.); is deluded with Lia (24, 25); serves him seven years more for Rachel (27); their agreement for the division of the flocks (xxx. 25–43); he pursues Jacob and charges him with stealing away his gods (xxxi. 30); he makes a covenant with Jacob (45–55).

LA'BOR as well as sorrow, common to all men (Gen. iii. 17; Ex. xx. 9; xxxiv. 21; Deut. v. 13; Tob. ii. 19; Ps. cxxvii. 2; Prov. vi. 6; x. 4; xiv. 4; xx. 4; Eccles. v. 11; Ecclus. xxix. 29; John xxi. 3; Acts xviii. 3; xx. 34; Eph. iv. 28; 1 Thess. ii. 9; iv. 11); labor does not enrich unless blessed by God (Gen. iii. 17; xxvi. 3, 12; xxx. 27; Deut. viii. 17, 18; Job xlii. 12; Prov. x. 22; Ecclus. xi. 6); the laborer is worthy of his wages (Lev. xix. 13; Deut. xxv. 4; Ecclus. vii. 22; xi. 18; Jerem. xxii. 13; Mal. iii. 5; Matt. x. 10; 1 Cor. ix. 9, 14; James v. 4); labor praised (Prov. xii. 11; xiii. 4; xiv. 23; xxiv. 27; xxviii. 19); labor forbidden at certain times (Ex. xvi. 23; xx. 10; xxxv. 2; Lev. xix. 3; xxiii. 3; xxvi. 2; Num. xv. 32; Deut. v. 12; 2 Esd. ix. 14; x. 31; xiii. 19; Matt. xii. 2).

LACEDEMO'NIANS, ancient allies of the Jews (1 Mach. xii. 5; see 2 Mach. v. 9).

LA'CHIS, a city of the Amorrhites, the king of Lachis, with others besieged Gabaon (Jos. x. 5, etc.);

THE LAVER.

but was taken and hanged (26); Josue then took the city and destroyed it (31–34); Roboam rebuilt and fortified it (2 Paral. xi. 9); Amasias fled to Lachis and was slain there (4 Kings xiv. 19; 2 Paral. xxv.

27); taken by Sennacherib in the reign of Ezechias (4 Kings xviii. 17); reoccupied after the captivity (2 Esd. xi. 30).

LAD'DER, Jacob's mysterious ladder (Gen. xxviii. 12).

LAKE AS'AN (1 Kings xxx. 30); probably near Asan, a town in the tribe of Juda (Jos. xv. 42); and later of Simeon (xix. 7).

LAKE AS'PHAR, the same as Lake Asphaltites or the Dead Sea. It was originally the Woodland Vale (Gen. xiv. 3)); the site of the Pentapolis, or the five Cities of the Plain, Sodom, Gomorrah, Adama, Seboim and Segor, which were almost entirely destroyed by fire from heaven (Gen. xix. 24, 25); and became the "Salt Sea" (Gen. xiv. 3); Jonathan and Simon encamped near it after the death of Judas (1 Mach. ix. 33).

LAKE OF TIBERIAS (see SEA OF GALILEE, or TIBERIAS).

LAHE'LA, a province beyond the Euphrates to which Theglathphalasar carried away the tribes of Ruben and Gad and the half tribe of Manasses (1 Paral. v. 26; 4 Kings xv. 19, 29).

LA'IS, a city in the land of Rohab, taken by the tribe of Dan and rebuilt under the name of Dan (Judg. xviii.)

LAI'SA, a place near Berea, where Judas Machabeus was defeated and killed by Bacchides and the apostate high-priest Alcimus (1 Mach. ix. 5).

LAMB, the young of the sheep offered in sacrifice by Abel, "firstlings of the flock" (Gen. iv. 4); given as a testimony (xxi. 28); used by Jacob in purchasing land at Sichem for an altar (xxxiii. 19); under the Mosaic law a lamb to be offered morning and evening (Ex. xxix. 38; Num. xxviii. 3); the rite of

THE BRAZEN LAVER.

the paschal lamb instituted to commemorate their deliverance from Egypt (Ex. xii. 5-46; Lev. ix. 3; xxiii. 12); it was a type and figure of our Lord (John

xix. 36; 1 Pet. i. 19); our Lord called the Lamb of God (John i. 29, 36; Apoc. v. 6; xiii. 8; xiv. 1); he is followed by virgins (xiv. 4).

LAME, any descendant of Aaron who was lame was not to act as priest (Lev. xxi. 18); firstlings, when lame, not to be sacrificed (Deut. xv. 21); lame persons cured by our Lord (Matt. xi. 5; xv. 30; xxi. 14; Luke vii. 22; xiv.); a lame man cured by St. Peter at the beautiful gate (Acts iii. 3–8); the lame cured by St. Philip (viii. 8); by St. Paul (xiv. 7).

LAM'ECH, son of Mathusael, of the race of Cain, father of Jabel, and Jubal and Tubalcain (Gen. iv. 18–22).

LAM'ECH, son of Mathusala, and father of Noe; he lived to the age of 777 years (Gen. v. 25–31.)

LAMENTA'TIONS OF JEREMIAS, a canonical book of the Old Testament, being the canticles of that prophet over the destruction of the holy city of Jerusalem and the temple of God (Lam.) His lamentations for king Josias were long preserved (2 Paral. xxxv. 25).

LAM'IA (Isai. xxxiv. 14); translated sea-monster (Lam. iv. 3).

LAMPS, vessels of pottery or metal in which oil was burnt to give light. Lamps were placed on the article improperly translated candlestick, placed before the veil of the tabernacle (Lev. xxiv. 2, 4); lamps in pitchers used by Gedeon in defeating the Madianites (Judg. vii. 16–20); Zacharias has a vision of a golden candlestick with seven lamps (Zach. iv. 2); seven lamps before the throne of God (Apoc. iv. 5); lamps borne in a wedding ceremony by virgins (Matt. xxv. 1). The word lamp is also used in the sense of flame (Gen. xv. 17; Job xli. 10; 1 Mach. vi. 39).

LAMP'SACUS, a city of Mysia. The consul Lucius writes to it in favor of Simon (1 Mach.xv.16,23).

LAM'UEL, king, author of ch. xxxi. Prov.; supposed to be a name for Solomon.

LAN'GUAGE of the whole earth confounded at Babel, giving rise to a diversity (Gen. xi. 9). The language in which most of the Old Testament was written was the Hebrew; part of Daniel in Chaldaic; Wisdom, Machabees, and the New Testament in Greek, except the gospel of St. Matthew, which some believe to have been written in Syriac.

LAODICE'A, a city in Phrygia, on the river Lycus. The angel or bishop of the church of Laodicea blamed for lukewarmness (Apoc. iii. 15, 16);

RUINS OF LAODICEA.

his presumption (17); he may rise again by penance (19). The apostle St. Paul wrote an epistle to the church there (Col. iv. 16).

LAP'IDOTH, husband of the prophetess Debora (Judg. iv. 4).

LA'RUS, bird classed among the unclean (Lev. xi. 16; Deut. xiv. 15).

LAT'CHET, the strap of the shoe or sandal (Gen. xiv. 23; Luke iii. 16).

LAT'IN, the language of the Romans (Luke xxiii. 38; John xix. 20).

LAT'TICE, a screen to window or balcony (4 Kings i. 2; Prov. vii. 6; Cant. ii. 9).

LAUGH'TER, avoided (Eccles. ii. 2); turned into sorrow (James iv. 9).

LAVER, a vessel of brass in the tabernacle for the priests to wash their hands (Ex. xxx. 18); made of the metal mirrors of the women (xxxviii. 8); consecrated (Lev. viii. 10); in Solomon's temple (3 Kings vii. 26), (see SEA); Christ cleansed the church by the laver of water in the word of life (Eph. v. 26). He has saved us by the laver of regeneration (Tit. iii. 5).

LAW. The term is used to mean all that God commanded under the patriarchs and the Mosaic dispensation as contrasted with the gospel. First precepts imposed by God on Adam (Gen. ii. 16); violated (iii. 4, 6); the decalogue given to Moses (Ex. xx.; Deut. v.); the tables of the law given (Ex. xxxi. 18; Deut. v. 22); broken (Ex. xxxii. 19; Deut. ix. 17); second tables (Deut. x. 1); the law read to the people (xxxi. 9, 11; Jos. viii. 33; 4 Kings xxiii. 2; 2 Esd. viii. 8; ix. 4; 2 Mach. viii. 19, 23); the law gives only knowledge of sin (Rom. iii. 20; vii. 1, 7; Gal. iii. 19); produces wrath (Rom. iv. 15); makes sin abound (v. 20); good in itself (1 Tim. i. 8); ceremonial law abolished as impotent (Heb. vii. 18); the law of God cannot be fulfilled without the aid of his Spirit (Deut. v. 29; Ps. cxviii. 34; Luke xviii. 22; Acts xv. 10; Rom. viii. 2); Christ came to fulfil it (Matt. v. 17); he abolishes the ceremonies (Matt. xv. 20; Mark vii. 2; Acts x. 15; xv. 10; Rom. vi. 14; vii. 17; viii. 1, 3; Gal. iii. 13; iv. 5; Eph. ii. 13; 1 Pet. i. 11); the new law consists in charity (Matt. v. 44; vii. 12; John xiii. 34; Rom. xiii. 10; Gal. v. 14; vi. 2; I Tim. i. 5).

LAW, doctor of the (Matt. xxii. 35).

LAWYER, used for one of the scribes (Mark xii. 28; Luke x. 25; xi. 45; Titus iii. 13).

THE LILY OF SYRIA.

LAY'MEN not to intrude into sacred things contrary to their duty (Lev. x. 1; Num. i. 51; iii. 10); nor rashly touch the sacred vessels (Num. i. 51; iv. 15, 19, 20; xviii. 7; 2 Kings vi. 6; I Paral. xiii. 10; 2 Paral. xxvi. 19).

LAZ'ARUS, the poor but just man at the door of the rich man (Luke xvi. 20).

LAZ'ARUS, brother of Martha and Mary (John xi. 1); they seem to have been children of Simon the leper of Bethania (Matt. xxvi. 7); he fell sick when our Lord was beyond the Jordan, and his sisters sent word to our Lord; but Lazarus died before he arrived and was buried. Jesus going to the tomb, called him, and he came forth alive (John xi. 1–45); our Lord entertained by them, and Mary anoints his head and feet (Matt. xxvi. 7; Luke vii. 37–50; John xi. 2; xii. 3); the chief priests think to kill Lazarus also (John xii. 10).

LEAGUE. God forbade the Israelites to form any league with the people of Chanaan (Ex. xxiii. 32); they are punished for disobeying (Judg. i. 24, 27; 2 Paral. xix. 2).

LEAV'EN (Lev. vii. 12; Deut. xvi. 3); used as a figure of corrupt doctrine (Matt. xvi. 6; I Cor. v. 6).

LEB'BEUS. See JUDE.

LEB'NA, a camp of the Israelites in the desert (Num. xxxiii. 21).

LEB'NA, a city besieged and taken by Josue (Jos. x. 29), and its king put to death (31).

LEEKS, a well-known vegetable (Num. xi. 5).

LE'GION, used to mean a large number (Matt. xxvi. 53; Mark v. 9; Luke viii. 30).

LEGS of persons crucified broken to hasten death (John xix. 31); our Saviour's were not broken on the cross, fulfilling a prophecy (Ex. xii. 46; Num. ix. 12).

LEND'ING commended (Deut. xxiii. 20; Ps. cxi. 5); usury forbidden (Ezech. xviii. 8).

LENT prefigured by the fast of Moses (Ex. xxiv. 18; xxxiv. 28); of Elias (3 Kings xix. 8); of our Lord (Matt. iv.)

LEN'TILS. Esau sells his birthright for a pottage of lentils (Gen. xxv. 33, 34).

LEOP'ARD, referred to for its fierceness (Isai. xi. 6; Jerem. v. 6; Osee xiii. 7); its spots (Jerem. xiii. 23); its swiftness (Hab. i. 8).

LEP'ERS excluded and kept in uninhabited places (Levit. xiii. 46; 4 Kings vii. 3; Luke xvii. 12); healed (4 Kings v. 14; Matt. viii. 2; Mark i. 40; Luke xvii. 14).

LEP'ROSY of men (Levit. xiii.); in houses (xiv. 34–48); of garments (xiii. 47–59); God strikes sinners with leprosy (Num. xii.; Deut. xxiv. 9; 4 Kings xv. 5); their dress prescribed (Lev. xiii. 45); sacrifices and rites for the cleansing of a leper (xiv. 2–32); for the purification of a house (48–53).

LE'SA, a town on the southern limit of Chanaan near the Dead Sea (Gen. x. 19).

LET'TER of the law killeth (2 Cor. iii. 6).

LET'TERS of the alphabet in Hebrew were twenty-two. See ALPHABET.

LET'TERS of Sennacherib to the king of Jerusalem laid before the tabernacle (4 Kings xix. 14); of the Samaritans to Artaxerxes accusing the Jews (I Esd. iv. 11–16); reply (18); letter of the Jews to Darius (v. 6, 17); in form of edict, given by Artaxerxes to Esdras (vii. 11); of Jeremias to the captives (Baruch vi.); of the Machabees to the Lacedemonians (I Mach. xii. 5); of the Jews in Jerusalem to those in Alexandria (2 Mach. i. 1–9); of the senate of Jerusalem and Judas to Aristobulus (i. 10–19); others (xi. 16, 22).

LE'VI, third son of Jacob and Lia, born in Mesopotamia, 1756 B.C. (Gen. xxix. 34); with his brother Simeon he massacres the Sichemites in revenge for the outrage on Dina (xxxiv. 25); Jacob's dying reproach (xlix. 5, 6); he went down into Egypt with his three sons, Gerson, Caath and Merari (Gen. xlvi. 11); he died aged 137; genealogy of the sons of (Ex. vi. 16).

LE'VI, tribe of, to be scattered among the other tribes (Gen. xlix. 7); Moses and Aaron of this tribe (Ex. ii.; iv. 14); selected by God for his special service (Num. viii. 6); they numbered 23,000 on leaving Egypt, but were not reckoned with the rest and received no possession (Num. xxvi. 62); Josue assigned them none (Jos. xiii. 33); Moses blesses the tribe (Deut. xxxiii. 8–11).

LEVI'ATHAN, a marine monster of great size (Job iii.; xl.) Leviathan the bar serpent, and leviathan, the crooked serpent (Isai. xxvii. 1).

LE'VITES. Their zeal against the worshippers of the golden calf (Ex. xxxii. 26); God makes the Levites his ministers instead of the first-born of Israel (Num. iii. 12, 41; viii. 16); their abode, right, subsistence (Lev. x. 12; xxv. 32; Num. xviii. 21, 24; xxxv. 2–7; Deut. x. 8; xii. 12, 19; xiv. 27; xviii. 1; xxvi. 11; Jos. xiii. 14, 33; xviii. 7; xxi.; 2 Esd. x. 33, 37; xiii. 10; Ecclus. vii. 32; Ezech. xlviii. 13); their ministry (Num. i. 49; iii.; iv. 1; viii.; xviii. 2, 23; Deut. x. 8; Jos. iii. 6; I Paral. vi. 31; ix. 14; 2 Paral. xix. 8; Ezech. xliv. 10); cities assigned to the Levites in the various tribes (Jos. xxi.); Jeroboam expels them from their cities in the ten tribes (2 Paral. xi. 14); outrage committed against a Levite of Ephraim by the men of Gabaa (Judg. xix. 22); consequent destruction of the tribe of Benjamin (xx. 40–48).

LEVIT'ICUS, a canonical book of the Old Testament, one of the five books of Moses; it relates to the public worship of God, and is the ritual of the Mosaic law (Lev.)

LI'A, oldest daughter of Laban, imposed on Jacob as a wife by deceit (Gen. xxix. 23); she bore him six sons, Ruben, Simeon, Levi, Juda, Issachar, Zabulon, and a daughter Dina: she gave her handmaid Zelpha to Jacob as a wife. She died in the land of Chanaan, and was interred in the double cave (Gen. xlix. 31).

LIB'ANUS, a celebrated mountain, that separates Syria from Palestine (Deut. iii. 25; Jos. ix. 1; xi. 17; Judg. iii. 3; ix. 15); famous for its cedars (3 Kings iv. 33; 4 Kings xiv. 9; 2 Paral. ii. 8, 16; I Esd. iii. 7; Ps. xxxvi. 35; xci. 13; Cant. iii. 9; Ecclus. xxiv. 17; Isai. ii. 13).

LIBA'TION, or drink offering, a mode of sacrifice in which wine was poured out (Gen. xxxv. 14; Ex. xxix. 40; Num. xxviii. 7); not to be offered on the altar of incense (xxx. 9); David made a libation of the water of Bethlehem (2 Kings xxiii. 16); Achaz offered libations on the altar of Damascus (4 Kings xvi. 13; Jerem. i., vii., xi., xviii., xix., xxxii., xliv.; Ezech. xx. 28).

LIB'ERTY, evangelical (John viii. 32; Rom. vi. 18; viii. 2, 21; I Cor. vii. 22; Gal. v. 13; James i. 25; ii. 12; 2 Pet. ii. 19); evil and condemned liberty (Job xi. 12; Jer. xxxiv. 17; I Peter ii. 16).

LIB'ERTINES, a term meaning freedmen. There was at Jerusalem a synagogue of libertines, who procured the death of St. Stephen (Acts vi. 9).

LI'BRARY at Babylon (I Esd. v. 17; vi. 1); of Nehemias at Jerusalem (I Mach. ii. 13).

LIB'YA, an African province (Acts ii. 10).

LIGHT. Jesus Christ is the light of the world (Isai. ix. 2; xlix. 6; lx. 1, 19; John i. 5; viii. 12; ix. 5; xii. 36, 46; I John i. 5; ii. 8); how Christians are the light of the world (Prov. iv. 18; Isai. lxii. 1; Matt. v. 15; Rom. ii. 19; Phil. ii. 15).

LION.

LIL'Y. Parable of the lily (Matt. vi. 28; Luke xii. 27).

LI'NUS, a disciple mentioned by St. Paul (2 Tim. iv. 21); St. Irenæus, Eusebius, and other early writers attest that he succeeded St. Peter as bishop of Rome. He is commemorated Sept. 23; and by the Greek church Nov. 5.

LI'ON, a wild animal of tropical countries, famous for its majesty and strength. Samson kills a lion (Judg. xiv.); David (1 Kings xvii.); a lion kills a prophet (3 Kings xiii.); lions destroy the colonists sent to the kingdom of Israel (4 Kings xvii. 25); Daniel cast into the lion's den (Dan. vi., xiv.); the devil compared to a roaring lion (1 Pet. 5, 8); Juda to a lion's whelp (Gen. xlix. 9); Israel to a lion and a lioness (Num. xxiii. 24); Dan to a lion's whelp (Deut. xxxiii. 22); its strength (2 Kings i. 23); its boldness (Wis. xi. 18); its ravages (Ezech. xxii. 25); its terrible roar (Amos iii. 8; Soph. iii. 3). The lion of the tribe of Juda (Jesus Christ) (Apoc. v. 5).

LITHOSTRO'TOS, a place paved with stones or mosaic; the place was Pilate's judgment-seat; was called in Hebrew Gabbatha (John xix. 13).

LITT'LE CHILDREN blessed by our Lord (Matt. xix. 14; Mark x. 14).

LIZ'ARD, forbidden as unclean food (Lev. xi. 30).

LOAVES OF PROPOSITION placed on the golden table every Saturday (Ex. xxv. 30; Lev. xxiv. 5–8); to be eaten only by the priests (9).

LOAVES, miraculously multiplied by our Lord (Matt. xiv. 19–21; xv. 32–38; Mark vi. 35–44; viii. 1–9; Luke ix. 13; John vi. 11).

LOB'NA, or **LABANA,** a city of Juda (Jos. xv. 42); given to the children of Aaron (Jos. xxi. 13); revolts from Juda (4 Kings viii. 22); besieged by Assyrians (xix. 8).

LO'CUSTS, a devouring species of grasshopper,

LOAVES OF PROPOSITION.

sent as a plague upon Egypt (Ex. x.); not forbidden to be used as food (Lev. xi. 22); their coming threatened as a punishment (Deut. xxviii. 38; Joel i.

4); the food of St. John the Baptist (Matt. iii. 4; Mark i. 6).

LO'IS, grandmother of Timothy (2 Tim. i. 5).

PLAGUE OF LOCUSTS BROUGHT UPON EGYPT.

LOST BOOKS of the Bible. Book of the patriarch Enoch (Jude 14); Book of the Covenant (Ex. xxiv. 7); Book of the Wars of the Lord (Num. xxi. 14); Book of the Just (Jos. x. 13; 2 Kings i. 18); Book of the Law of the Kingdom, by Samuel (1 Kings x. 25); Book of the Words of the Days of Solomon (3 Kings xi. 41); Book of the Words of the Days of the Kings of Juda (3 Kings xiv. 29; xv. 7, 23, etc.); Book of the Words of the Days of the Kings of Israel (3 Kings xiv. 19; xv. 31); Book of Samuel the seer; Book of Nathan the prophet; Book of Gad the seer (1 Paral. xxix. 29); Books of Ahias the Silonite (2 Par. ix. 29); Book of the Prophet Semeias (2 Par. xii. 15); Book of the Prophet Jehu (2 Par. xx. 34); Book of Mardochai (Esth. ix. 20); Words of Hozai (2 Par. xxxiii. 19); Parables of Solomon (3 Kings iv. 32); Poems of Solomon; Natural History (3 Kings iv. 33); the Predictions of the Prophet Addo (2 Paral. ix. 29; xii. 15); Acts of Ozias, by Isaias (2 Paral. xxvi. 22); Book of the Days of the Priesthood of John Hircanus (1 Mach. xvi. 24); Descriptions of Jeremias (2 Mach. ii. 1); History of the Jews by Jason of Cyrene (2 Mach. ii. 24); Epistle of St. Paul to the Laodiceans (Col. iv. 16).

LOST COIN, parable of the (Luke xv. 8).

LOT, son of Aran, and nephew of Abraham (Gen. xi. 27); leaves Chaldea with Abraham (31); they separate to avoid the collisions between their herdsmen (xiii. 11); taken prisoner, but rescued by Abraham (xiv.); escapes from the destruction of Sodom (xix. 17; 2 Pet. ii. 7); his wife changed into a pillar of salt for looking back (Gen. xix. 26; Wis. x. 7; Luke xvii. 32); dwells in a cave with his

daughters (30); Moab and Ammon, his sons by them (37, 38).

LOTS, sometimes permitted to be cast (Lev. xvi. 8; 2 Esd. xi. 1; Prov. xvi. 33; xviii. 18; Ezech. xxi. 19; Jon. i. 7); the promised land divided by lot among the tribes (Num. xxvi. 55; xxxiii. 54; Jos. xviii. 10; xix.); Josue casts lots to discover Achan's crime (Jos. vii. 14); Samuel casts lots to discover whom God has chosen as king of his people (1 Kings x. 20); Saul casts lots to discover who had transgressed his command (xiv. 41); the apostles cast lots to select a successor to Judas (Acts i. 26); the soldiers cast lots on our Saviour's garments (John xix. 24).

LOVE. We are to love God above all things (Ex. xx. 6; Deut. v. 10; vii. 9; x. 12; xxx. 6; Jos. xxii. 5; Ecclus. vii. 32; Matt. x. 37; 1 Cor. ii. 9); love is the fulfilling of the law (Wisd. vi. 19).

LUC'IFER, the king of Babylon, symbolically the devil (Isai. xiv. 12).

LU'CIUS of Cyrene, one of the prophets of the church at Antioch (Acts xiii. 1).

LU'CIUS, a relative of St. Paul (Rom. xvi. 22).

LU'DIM, son of Misraim (Gen. x. 13).

LUKE, evangelist, physician, a disciple of St. Paul (Col. iv. 14); his companion on his journeys (Acts xx. 6; 2 Tim. iv. 11); writes one of the gospels and the Acts of the Apostles.

LUKE, ST., Gospel of, one of the canonical books of the New Testament, embracing the history of our Lord, with many details evidently from the Blessed Virgin, her canticle, Zachary's, etc. (Luke).

LU'NATIC cured by our Lord after his apostles had tried in vain (Matt. xvii. 14).

LUTE, a musical instrument (2 Kings vi. 5).

LU′ZA, the ancient name of Bethel (Gen. xxviii.)

LU′ZA, a town in Arabia Petræa, built by a man of Bethel (Judg. i. 25, 26).

LYC′AONIA, a province of Asia Minor, part of Cappadocia; St. Paul preached in Iconium and Lystra, cities of Lycaonia, A. D. 45 (Acts xiv.)

LYC′IA, a maritime province in Asia Minor. St. Paul landed at Lystra in Lycia on his way to Rome to appear before Nero, 60 A. D. (Acts xxvii. 5).

LY′DA (1 Mach. xi. 34); or Lydda, east of Joppe, founded by Samad (1 Par. viii. 12); St. Peter visited it (Acts ix. 32); and cured Eneas of the palsy (33, 34).

LYD′IA, a woman of Thyatira, a dealer in purple, residing at Philippi, in Macedonia; she was converted and baptized by St. Paul, with her whole family. The apostle, at her instance, took up his abode with them (Acts xvi. 14–40).

LYD′IA, a province of Asia Minor, settled by the descendants of Lud (Gen. x. 22; Isaias lxvi. 19).

LY′DIA, a province of Egypt, settled by Ludim, son of Misraim (Gen. x. 13; Jer. xlvi. 9; Ezech. xxvii. 10; xxx. 5).

LYRE, a musical instrument (Isai. v. 12).

LYSA′NIAS, tetrarch of Abilene, at the time when St. John the Baptist began to preach (Luke iii. 1).

LYS′IAS, general of the army of Antiochus Epiphanes, left by him as regent (1 Mach. iii. 32); he sent a powerful army under Ptolemee, Nicanor and Gorgias against the Machabees, but Judas defeated them. The next year Lysias took the field in person, but was routed (1 Mach. iv. 28, 29). After the death of Antiochus, he seized the regency and continued the war, and advanced to Bethsura and was defeated (2 Mach. xi.) He returned with Eu-

pator and laid siege to Jerusalem, but as Philip was at Antioch to claim the regency, Lysias made terms with Judas, but treacherously broke down the wall (1 Mach. vi. 62; 2 Mach. xiii. 2); then he took Antioch and killed Philip, but was the next year defeated and killed by Demetrius, 162 B. C. (1 Mach. vii. 4; 2 Mach. xiv. 2).

LYSIM′ACHUS, son of Ptolemee, translated Esther into Greek (Esth. xi. 1).

LYSIM′ACHUS, brother of Menelaus, the high-priest, killed by the people while he was endeavoring to plunder the treasury of the temple (2 Mach. iv. 39).

THE ADORATION OF THE THREE KINGS.

LYS′TRA, a city in Lycaonia, where St. Timothy was born. St. Paul and St. Barnabas having preached here and cured a cripple, the people wished to offer them sacrifice as gods, but they soon after stoned them (Acts xiv.)

LYS′TRA in Lycia (Acts xxvii. 5); is in Greek called Myra.

MAA′CHA, or **MACHATI,** a province which Josue spared (Jos. xiii. 13); the king of Maacha aided the Ammonites against David (2 Kings x. 8, 9); Seba took refuge there (2 Kings xx. 15); the

tribe of Manasse extended to (Deut. iii. 14; Jos. xii. 5).

MAA′CHA, son of Nachor (Gen. xxii. 24).

MAA′CHA, daughter of Tholmai, king of Gessur, and wife of David, to whom she bore Absalom and Thamar (2 Kings iii. 3; 1 Paral. iii. 2).

MAA′CHA, daughter of Abessalom (3 Kings xv. 2); wife of Roboam, king of Juda (Michaia, 2 Paral. xiii. 2); mother of Abia, and (grand) mother of Asa (3 Kings xv. 10, 13, 14).

MAA′RA OF THE SIDONIANS (Jos. xiii. 4).

MAASI′AS, son of Ananias, contributed to rebuild Jerusalem (2 Esd. iii. 23).

MAA′SIA, one of the priests who assisted Esdras in reading the law (2 Esd. viii. 4).

MACE-DO′NIA, a Grecian kingdom; alms sent thence to the poor of Jerusalem (Rom. xv. 26; 2 Cor. viii. 1); St. Paul called to Macedonia (Acts xvi. 9).

MACH′-ABEES, seven brothers of this name and their mother put to death at Jerusalem in presence of Antiochus Epiphanes; their heroic fortitude (2 Mach. vii.)

MACH′-ABEES, two canonical books of the Old Testament, describing the attempt of Antiochus to force a state religion on the Jews, and the heroic resistance and triumph of the faithful under the brave priests of the house of Mathathias (1 Mach.; 2 Mach.)

MACHABE′US, surname of Judas, one of the sons of Mathathias (1 Mach. ii. 4).

MAC′ELOTH, one of the stations of the Israelites in the desert (Num. xxxiii. 25).

MACH′MAS, a place east of Bethaven (1 Kings xiii. 2).

MADA′BA, or **MEDA′BA,** a city beyond the Jordan in the tribe of Ruben (Jos. xiii. 16); the Moabites seized it (Isai. xv. 2); the people of

Madaba treacherously slew John Gaddes, brother of Judas Machabeus, and were punished (1 Mach. ix. 36.)

MAD′AI, third son of Japheth (Gen. x. 2).

MAD′AN, third son of Abraham and Cetura (Gen. xxv. 2; 1 Paral. i. 32).

MAD′IAN, fourth son of Abraham and Cetura (Gen. xxv. 2; 1 Par. i. 32).

MAD′IANITES, a people lying east of the Red Sea (Ex. ii. 15; Hab. iii. 7); and east of the Dead Sea, south of Moab. They were defeated by Adad, king of Edom (Gen. xxxvi. 35); Moses took refuge among them and married Sephora, daughter of Jethro (Ex. ii. 15–22); the Madianites led the Israelites into debauchery and the worship of their idol Phogor (Num. xxii. 4; xxv. 6, 15); God's sentence on them (17); an army under Phinees, son of the high-priest Eleazar, attacked them and destroyed all their cities. He killed five of their kings, Evi, Recem, Sur, Hur, and Rebe (xxxi. 2–8); the Madianites oppressed the Israelites in the days of the Judges and were defeated by Gedeon (Judges vi., vii.)

MAD′ON, a city of Chanaan; Jobab, its king, joined Jabin, king of Asor, against Josue, but he was taken and put to death and his city destroyed (Jos. xi. 1; xii. 19).

MA′ELETH, a term in the title of Ps. lii.; and meaning a musical instrument, or the dance.

MAG′ALA, the place where the Israelites were encamped when David slew Goliath (1 Kings xvii. 20).

MAG′DAL, a place in Egypt near the Red Sea where the Israelites encamped (Ex. xiv. 2). Jews dwelt there in the time of Jeremias (Jerem. xliv. 1).

MAG′EDAN, a district in the Sea of Galilee (Matt. xv. 39).

MAG′DALEN, MARY, was delivered from seven devils by our Lord, and afterwards ministered to him of her means (Luke viii. 2; Mark xv. 40); she did

MANDRAKES.

not desert him during his passion, but stood under the cross (John xix. 25); when the disciples discovered that the body was no longer in the sepulchre (Matt. xxviii. 5; Mark xvi. 5; John xx. 1) Mary

remained there weeping (John xx. 11); our Lord appeared to her, though she did not at first recognize him (Mark xvi. 9; John xx. 15); he directed her to announce his resurrection to the other disciples (17). Some suppose her to be the sinful woman who anointed our Lord's feet at the house of Simon the Pharisee (Luke vii. 37); and others suppose her to be the sister of Lazarus.

MAG′ETH, a city beyond the Jordan taken by Judas Machabeus (1 Mach. v. 36).

MAGIC′IANS, God threatens those who resort to them (Lev. xx. 6). Saul put them out of the land (1 Kings xxviii. 3).

MAG′ISTRATES, obedience to (1 Pet. ii. 14).

MAGNIF′ICAT, or Canticle of the Blessed Virgin (Luke i. 46).

MA′GOG, son of Japheth (Gen. x. 2); the land of Magog (Ezech. xxxviii. 2; xxxix. 6); the nation (Apoc. xx. 7).

MAHANA′IM, or **MANAIM**, scene of Jacob's vision, called also "The camp" (Gen. xxxii. 2); Levitical city arose there in the tribe of Gad on the torrent Jaboc (Jos. xxi. 37; 1 Paral. vi. 89); it was Isboseth's capital (2 Kings ii. 8, 12); David took refuge there during Absalom's rebellion (2 Kings xvii. 24; xix. 32).

MA′HATH, son of Amasai, assists king Ezechias in purifying the temple (2 Par. xxix. 12).

MAH′ATH, an ancestor of our Lord (Luke iii. 26).

MA′HELETH, also called Basemath, daughter of Ismael, and wife of Esau (Gen. xxviii. 9).

MA′HELETH, a word in the title of Ps. lxxxvii.; the same as Maeleth.

MAIDEN. The ravishing of a maiden caused the destruction of Sichem (Gen. xxxiv.); the violation of a maiden punished by the law of Moses (Deut. xxii. 23); a maiden sacrificed by her father (Judges xi. 39); a maiden restored to life by our Lord (Luke viii. 54).

MALACHI′AS, the last of the twelve minor prophets. The name means Angel of the Lord. Nothing is known of him.

MALACHI′AS, one of the canonical books of the Old Testament containing the prophecies of Malachias. He foretells the coming of St. John the Baptist, the two advents of the Messias (Mal. iii. 1); the abolition of the ancient sacrifice, and the perpetual offering of a clean oblation (Mal. i. 11); it is cited (Mark i. 2; ix. 11; Luke i. 17; Rom. ix. 13).

MAL′ALEEL, son of Chanaan (Gen. v. 12). He lived 895 years.

LOT'S WIFE—A PILLAR OF SALT.

MAL′ASAR, the officer appointed over Daniel, Ananias, and their companions (Dan. i. 11).

MAL′CHUS, servant of Caiphas, the high-priest; he was one of the party sent to seize our Lord. St. Peter cut off his ear, but our Saviour cured the wound (John xviii. 10).

MAL′EDICT′ION, ceremonies of (Deut. xxvii. 15; xxviii. 16–68).

MAL′TA or **MELI′TA**, an island in the Mediterranean. St. Paul was shipwrecked there, A. D. 60. While taking up a bundle of sticks to make a fire, a serpent stung him. The people expected to see him die, but when he shook it into the fire, they regarded him as a divinity. The apostle cured Publius, the governor, of a fever, and remained there three months (Acts xxviii.)

MAM′BRE, an Amorrhite, an ally of Abraham, who aided him to pursue the victorious kings (Gen. xiv. 13).

MAM′BRE, Vale of, a valley near Hebron (Gen. xiii. 18; xiv. 13), where Abraham long dwelt, and where the three angels appeared to him (xviii. 1); he purchased a double cave that looked towards Mambre for a burial-place for Sara (xxiii. 19); Isaac and Esau bury Abraham there (xxv. 9); Isaac continued to dwell there (xxxvii. 27); Jacob returned to it (27).

MAM′BRE. The torrent of Mambre (Judith ii. 14).

MAM′BRES, one of the two magicians who opposed Moses in Egypt (2 Tim. iii. 8).

MAM′MON, a Syriac word meaning riches. Our Saviour says we cannot serve God and mammon

(Matt. vi. 24; Luke xvi. 13); and again he bids us make to ourselves friends of the mammon of iniquity, that is, make for ourselves friends in eternity by the riches which lead so many to sin (9).

MAM'UCHAN, one of the seven counsellors of king Assuerus (Esth. i. 14, 16).

MAM'ZER, a Hebrew term for bastard. They were not to be admitted to the church to the tenth generation (Deut. xxiii. 2).

MAN created to the image of God (Gen. i. 26; ii. 7; Ecclus. xvii. 1; Job x. 8; Ps. cxviii. 73; James iii. 9); created just and upright (Eccles. vii. 30); created immortal (Wis. ii. 23); cursed after his sin (Gen. iii. 17); blessed in Christ (xii. 3); he is dust and ashes, and will return to the earth; compared to grass (Gen. ii. 7; iii. 19; Job xxxiii. 6; Eccles. xii. 7; Ecclus. xxxiii. 10; xli. 13; Ps. lxxxi. 7; cii. 15; cxxviii. 6; cxliii. 4; Isai. xl. 6; xlv. 9); to a tent (Isai. xxxviii. 12; 2 Pet. i. 13); he is in the hands of God like clay in the hands of a potter (Ecclus. xxxiii. 13); his nothingness appears in his birth (Wis. vii. 1–3); wherein he is like unto the beasts (Eccles. iii. 19); his thoughts are timid (Wis. ix. 14); he is subject to error (Lev. x. 1; Num. xv. 39; Deut. xii. 8; 1 Kings xv. 9; 2 Kings vi. 6; Prov. xii. 15; xiv. 12; xxi. 2; Isai. v. 21; xiv. 13; lv. 8; Matt. iii. 14; xvi. 22; John xii. 5; xiii. 8); known by his words and actions (Ecclus. xix. 27; xxvii. 7; Matt. vii. 16; Luke xi. 33); the duty and authority of man towards his wife (Gen. ii. 23; iii. 16; Num. v. 12–18; xxx. 7–13; Deut. xx. 7; xxiv. 1, 5; Prov. v. 18; xviii. 22; xxxi. 10; Eccles. ix. 9; Ecclus. vii. 26; ix. 1; xv. 2; xxvi. 3; Mal. ih. 14, 16; 1 Cor. vii.; Eph. v. 22; Col. iii. 18; Tit. ii. 4; 1 Tim. ii. 11; 1 Pet. iii. 1); man must be born again in order to enter the kingdom of heaven (Matt. xviii. 3; John iii. 3; 1 Cor. iv. 15; Gal. iv. 19; Eph. iv. 22; Col. iii. 9; Tit. iii. 5; James i. 18; 1 Pet. i. 23; ii. 2).

MAN OF GOD. One who prophesied against Jeroboam (3 Kings xiii. 1–10); deceived by an old prophet, he ate and drank when God had forbidden him (18), and is killed by a lion (24); the prophet buries him (30); Josias spares his sepulchre (4 Kings xxiii. 18).

MAN'AHEM, son of Gadi, sixteenth king of Israel. He attacked and killed Sellum, who had slain Zacharias and usurped the throne, 771 B. C. He destroyed all the towns from Thapsa to Thersa, because they would not acknowledge him. He taxed his people very heavily in order to pay the tribute exacted by Phul, king of Assyria. He reigned ten years wickedly at Samaria (4 Kings xv. 14–22; 1 Paral. v. 26; Osee v. 13).

MAN'AHEN, foster-brother of Herod (Antipas) the tetrarch. He was one of the prophets at Antioch to whom the Holy Ghost revealed the mission of Saul and Barnabas (Acts xiii. 1, 2).

MANAS'SES, eldest son of Joseph (Gen. xli. 51; xlvi. 20); adopted by Jacob (xlviii. 5); Joseph tried to place Jacob's hand on the head of Manasses (17–19); Jacob's prophecy as to Manasses (19, 20).

MANAS'SES, tribe of, one of the twelve tribes of Israel. On going out of Egypt, its prince was Gamaliel, son of Phadassur (Num. i. 10); his fighting men numbered 32,200 (ii. 20); at Settim 52,700 (xxvi. 34); they marched on the west side. They made their offerings the eighth day (vii. 54); Moses assigned to Gad, Ruben, and the half-tribe of Manasses the kingdoms of the Amorrhites, or Galaad, and Basan, east of the Jordan (xxxii. 33), and they took

MARY, MOTHER OF GOD.

possession (39–42; Jos. xiii. 29); Josue allots lands to the other half-tribe, west of the Jordan (Jos. xvii. 1–18); Gedeon, of the tribe of Manasses, delivers Israel from the Madianites (Judg. vi.); carried into captivity (4 Kings xv. 29; xvii. 6); some remained, who ate the Pasch proclaimed by king Ezechias, but not according to the law (2 Paral. xxx. 18); carried away captive with the rest of Israel (4 Kings xvii. 6).

MANAS'SES, son of Ezechias and of Haphsiba, and king of Juda, began to reign 698 B. C. (4 Kings xx. 21; xxi. 1; 2 Paral. xxxiii.) He plunged into every form of idolatry, restoring the old Chanaanite worship, setting up altars to Baal, groves and high-places, and in the very temple he set up altars to the host of heaven and an idol of the grove (Astarthe). He had his son passed through fire in honor of Moloch, and had recourse to all kinds of magic and superstition. He was cruel, and shed innocent blood (4 Kings xxi. 16); God by his prophets foretold the judgments to come on Juda and Jerusalem (10–15); Isaias is generally believed to have been one of these prophets, and to have been sawed in two by order of Manasses. In 676 B. C. the king of Assyria sent an army which carried Manasses a prisoner to Babylon (2 Paral. xxxiii. 11, 12). There he repented and prayed, and did penance. He was restored to his kingdom and abolished idolatry, doing much to restore the worship of the true God (12–17); his penitent prayer and the acts of his reign were written down by Hozai (19); a prayer bearing his name is extant, but has never been received as canonical. He restored the walls of Jerusalem, and died after a reign of fifty-five years (4 Kings xxi. 18; 2 Paral. xxxiii. 20).

MANAS'SES, husband of Judith, died of a sunstroke at Bethulia (Judith viii. 2, 3).

MAN'DRAKE, a plant to which important powers were ascribed. Ruben finds some, and obtains a favor for his mother (Gen. xxx. 14).

MA'NE, one of the three Chaldean words that appeared on the wall at Baltassar's feast (Dan. v. 25).

MAN'GER. Our Lord laid in a manger at Bethlehem (Luke ii. 7, 12).

MAN HU, Hebrew words meaning "What is this?" used by the Israelites on seeing manna, whence the name (Ex. xvi. 15).

MANIL'IUS, TITUS, Roman ambassador to the Jews 163 B. C. (2 Mach. xi. 34–38).

MAN'NA, or MAN, the food with which God nourished the children of Israel in the deserts of Arabia for forty years after the eighth encampment. The manna began to fall on Friday, the sixteenth day of the second month, 1491 B. C., and continued to fall every day except the Sabbath till they crossed the Jordan, 1451 B. C. It was small, like coriander seed, of the color of bdellium (Num. xi. 7); and as it were beaten with a pestle (Ex. xvi. 14); it had to be gathered before the sun rose (Ex. xvi. 21), a gomor for each person, and if more were gathered it measured no more (18); it was beaten or ground, then boiled and made into cakes (Num. xi. 8); if kept over for any day but the Sabbath, it swarmed with worms (Ex. xvi. 20); the book of Wisdom calls it "the food of angels, bread from heaven, prepared without labor, having in it all that is delicious, and the sweetness of every taste" (Wisd. xvi. 20); it ceased after they ate the corn of the Promised Land (Jos. v. 12). Our Lord cites it as a figure of the Holy Eucharist (John vi. 31–35, 48–59); and St. John calls the Eucharist "a hidden manna" (Apoc. ii. 17).

MANU'E, of Saraa, in the tribe of Dan, father

of Samson. An angel appeared to his wife, and promised her a son, who was to be a Nazarite (Judg. xiii. 2–7); at Manue's prayer the angel reappeared, Manue offered a kid in sacrifice, and the angel ascended in the flame of the altar (8–20).

MA'ON, a city in the southern part of the tribe of Juda (Jos. xv. 55). Nabal dwelt near it, and David spent a long time in those parts.

MA'OZIM, a god whom Daniel foretold Antiochus was to worship (Dan. xi. 38, 39); together with a strange god whom his fathers knew not.

MA'RA, or bitterness. The first camp of the Israelites in the desert of Etham; Moses sweetened the waters with wood (Ex. xv. 23; Num. xxxiii. 8).

MA'RA, a name adopted by Noemi (Ruth 20).

MARAI'OTH, son of Achitob, and high-priest (1 Par. ix. 11; 1 Esd. vii 3).

MARANA'-THA (The Lord cometh), an anathema or menace among the Jews (1 Cor. xvi. 22).

MARDO'-CHAI, son of Jair, of the race of Saul and tribe of Benjamin. He was taken to Babylon with king Jechonias by Nabuchodonosor, 599 B. C. (Esth. ii. 5, 6), and is identified by some with the one in 1 Esd. ii. 2. On the deposition of Vashti, Mardochai's niece Esther was selected by Assuerus as his queen. While at the palace door Mardochai heard a plot formed by two eunuchs against the king's life. He gave information, and the conspirators were put to death (Esth. ii. 21); but he received no reward. Aman became the king's favorite and received the highest honors, but all was as nothing because Mardochai did not do him reverence. In revenge he obtained of the king an edict for a general massacre of the Jews. Mardochai urged Esther to ask the king to recall it. Meanwhile, the king, while sleepless, had the chronicle of his reign read to him. When they came to Mardochai's service, he asked what reward had been bestowed on him. Finding that none had, he summoned Aman and asked what should be done to the man whom the king wished to

honor. Aman thinking it to be himself, said that he should be clothed in the royal robes and be led through the city splendidly mounted, his horse held by the highest noble. The king bade him do all this for Mardochai. Esther inviting the king to a banquet, confessed her origin and her relationship to Mardochai. She pleaded for her people, the edict was revoked, and Aman hung on the gibbet he had prepared for Mardochai (Esth. vii.–xii.) The book of Esther is usually ascribed to Mardochai.

MARE'SA, a city of the tribe of Juda (Jos. xv.

MARY AND HER DIVINE SON, IN CHRISTIAN ART.

44); scene of Asa's victory over Zara (2 Par. xiv. 9); birthplace of Micheas (Mich. i. 15).

MARK, ST., one of the four evangelists. He was a disciple of St. Peter (1 Pet. v. 13); he is believed to have accompanied the apostle to Rome, and to have written his gospel there. According to tradition, he was put to death at Alexandria, in Egypt, in the year 68.

MARK, ST., Gospel of, one of the canonical books of the New Testament (Mark).

MAR'RIAGE, instituted by God (Gen. i. 27; ii. 21–24); it is indissoluble (Gen. ii. 21; Matt. v. 32; xix. 7; 1 Cor. vii. 10); Mosaic law regarding marriage (Lev. xviii. 6); the brother in certain cases to marry the widow of his deceased brother (Deut. xxv. 5, 10); or the nearest kinsman if no brother survived (Ruth iii. 12; iv. 4–10); law for marriage of daughters inheriting on failure of sons (Num. xxxvi. 3, 4); form of marrying a captive woman (Deut. xxi. 13, 14); question of the Sadducees as to marriage (Mark xii. 18); marriage with unbelievers forbidden (Ex. xxxiv. 16; 2 Cor. vi. 14); holy virginity superior to marriage (1 Cor. vii. 27–40); but marriage not sinful (vii. 28, 36); those who forbade marriage condemned as heretics (1 Tim. iv. 3); marriage a figure of the union between Christ and his church (Cant. Eph. v. 32; Apoc. xix. 7).

MAR'RIAGE FEAST AT CANA honored by the presence of Jesus Christ and his first miracle (John ii.); the marriage feast of the Lamb (Apoc. xix. 7, 9); parable of the marriage feast (Matt. xxii. 2–14; Luke xiv. 7); parable of the wise and foolish virgins at the marriage feast (Matt. xxv.)

MAR'THA, sister of Lazarus and Mary, resided at Bethania. She complained to our Lord that Mary sat at his feet listening, while she had all the work to do, but he declared that Mary had chosen the better part (Luke x. 38–42); when Lazarus fell sick, both sisters sent to Jesus (John xi. 3); on his arrival, Martha went forth to meet him (20). She professed her belief in the resurrection (24); and in our Lord as the Christ the Son of God who had come into the world (22, 27). She told Mary of his arrival (28). Martha served at table to our Lord in the house of Simon, the leper (John xii. 2).

MA'RY, sister of Moses, watches him when exposed (Ex. ii. 4); her canticle (xv. 20); murmurs, and is struck with leprosy (Num. xii. 1–10; Deut.

xxiv. 9); Moses prays for her and she is cured after seven days (Num. xii. 13-15); a prophetess (Ex. xv.

THE THREE MARYS AT THE SEPULCHRE.

20; Mich. vi. 4). She died at Cades in the desert of Sin, and was buried there (Num. xx. 1).

MA'RY, mother of God, foretold and prefigured (Gen. iii. 15; Ps. xliv. 11; xlv. 5; lxxiv. 2; lxxxvi. 3; cxxxi. 8; Prov. xxxi. 10, 29; Cant.; Ecclus. xxiv.; Isai. vii. 14; xi. 1; xix. 1; xlv. 8; Jer. xxxi. 22); called the mother of our Lord (Luke i. 43); the mother of Jesus (Matt. ii. 13; John ii. 3); the angel Gabriel sent to her to announce that she is to be the mother of the Messias by the action of the Holy Ghost (Luke i. 26); her love of holy virginity (34); her humility and obedience to the will of God (38); she learns of Elizabeth's miraculous pregnancy (36, 37), and proceeds to visit her (39, 40); at her coming, John the Baptist leaps in his mother's womb, and Elizabeth is filled with the Holy Ghost, and recognizes her as mother of her Lord, her wonder that she should visit her (41-45); Mary's canticle, the Magnificat (46-55); she remained three months with Elizabeth and returned to her own home in Nazareth (i. 26-56); Joseph relieved by an angel from his anxiety as to Mary (Matt. i. 18-25); she sets out with him for Bethlehem to be enrolled according to the decree of Cesar Augustus (Luke ii. 4, 5); she gives birth to our Lord in a stable at Bethlehem (Matt. i. 16; Luke ii. 7); she kept in her heart all that the shepherds told her (Luke ii. 19); the wise men find Jesus with Mary, his mother (Matt. ii. 11); she presents him in the temple (Luke ii. 22); Simeon foretells her sufferings (34); by the warning of an angel she flees to Egypt with Joseph and the infant Saviour (Matt. ii. 20); returns to Nazareth after the death of Herod (23); she loses her divine Son and finds him in the temple with the doctors of the law (Luke ii. 42-51); at the marriage feast of Cana in Galilee (John ii. 1); followed him in his ministry (Mark iii. 31; Luke viii. 19); at the foot of the cross (John xix. 25) St. John given to her as a son (xxvi. 26); she remains with that apostle (27); receives the Holy Ghost with the apostles (Acts

i. 14); declared to be blessed by the angel Gabriel (Luke i. 28); by St. Elizabeth (42, 45); by a pious woman (Luke xi. 27); she declares that all generations shall call her blessed (i. 48); as seen by St. John in the Apocalypse (xii. 1).

MA'RY, the sister of Lazarus, and Martha, at Bethania. She sat at the feet of Jesus (Luke x. 39); commended (42); sends for our Lord when Lazarus was sick (John xi. 3); beloved by our Lord (5); falls at the feet of Jesus (32); anoints his head and feet and wipes them with her hair (xii. 3; Matt. xxvi. 7); her memory to be preserved (Matt. xxvi. 13).

MA'RY, wife of Zebedee and mother of James and John (Matt. xxvii. 56); called also Salome (Mark xv. 40).

MA'RY, mother of John Mark. Her house was a place where the apostles and the faithful assembled (Acts xii. 12).

MA'RY of Cleophas (John xix. 25), supposed to be the mother of James the Less, Joseph, Simon and Jude (Matt. xiii. 55; xxvii. 56; Mark vi. 3); she followed our Lord to Calvary (John xix. 25), and prepared spices to embalm his body (Luke xxiii. 56); visits the sepulchre and learns that he is risen (Luke xxiv. 1); our Lord appears to her and the other women (Matt. xxviii. 9).

MA'RY, a convert who labored for the faith at Rome (Rom. xvi. 6).

MA'RY MAG'DALEN. See MAGDALEN.

MAS'AL, a city in the tribe of Aser, assigned to the Levites of the family of Gerson (Jos. xxi. 30; 1 Paral. vi. 74).

MASER'EPH-OTH, the waters of, near Sidon. Josue pursued the Chananaite kings to them (Jos. xi. 8; xiii. 6).

MAS'EPHA, a city in the tribe of Juda (Jos. xv. 38).

MAS'PHA, in the mountains of Galaad, in the tribe of Gad. Laban and Jacob make a covenant there (Gen. xxxi. 49); Jephte resided there (Judg. xi. 11, 29, 34); the Moabites were in possession of a place called Maspha (1 Kings xxii. 3).

MAS'PHA, a district at the foot of Mount Hermon, inhabited by the Hevites (Jos. xi. 3, 8).

MAS'SA, seventh son of Ismael (Gen. xxv. 14).

MASS. The holy sacrifice of the mass foretold in the Old Testament (Lev. xxvi. 9-12; Ps. xxii. 5; cix. 4; Isai. ii. 3; xix. 19; lvi. 7; lxi. 6; lxvi. 20; Jerem. xxxi. 31; xxxiii. 18; Dan. xii. 11; Am. ix. 11; Mal. i. 11); it is shown under various figures (Gen. xiv. 18; xv. 9; xxii. 13; Ex. xii. 5, 24; xxv. 30; xxix. 2, 15; Lev. ii. 11; 1 Kings xxi. 4; 3 Kings xix. 6; 4 Kings iv. 41; Dan. viii. 12); it is called the continual sacrifice (Dan. xi. 31; xii. 11); there shall always be priests to offer it (Jerem. xxxiii. 18, 21); it is instituted by Jesus Christ (Matt. xxvi. 26-30; Mark xiv. 22-26; Luke xxii. 17-20; 1 Cor. xi. 24); the place of offering is an altar (Heb. xiii. 10; 1 Cor. ix. 13).

THE MOABITE STONE.

MASSO'RA, a Hebrew word meaning *tradition*. It is applied to the traditional reading of the Hebrew, and to the vowel points, accents, and punctuation introduced by Massoretic scholars.

MAS'TER and **MIS'TRESS.** Their authority and duty in regard to servants (Ex. xx. 10; xxi. 2, 20, 26; Lev. xxv. 48; Deut. v. 14, 21; Job xxxi. 13; Prov. xxix. 19; Jerem. xxxiv. 9, 14; Ecclus. vii. 22; xxxiii. 31; Eph. vi. 9; Col. iv. 1); masters, though wicked, to be obeyed (Matt. xxiii. 3; 1 Pet. ii. 18).

MAS'TIC TREE (Dan. xiii. 54).

MA'THAN, priest of Baal, slain at his altar by order of the high-priest Joiada (4 Kings xi. 18).

MA'THAN, son of Eleazar and father of Jacob (Matt. i. 15).

MATH'AT, son of Levi and father of Heli, one of the ancestors of our Lord (Luke iii. 23).

MATHA'TA, son of Nathan (Luke iii. 31).

MATHATHI'AS, sixth son of Idithun of the race of Core, head of the fourteenth family of Levites (1 Paral. xxv. 3).

MATHATHI'AS, son of John of the family of Joiarib. When Apollonius came to Jerusalem with the impious orders of Antiochus, he retired to Modin (1 Mach. ii. 1); the envoys of the king having reached Modin to establish idolatry, Mathathias protested, and slew a Jew who went to offer incense to an idol, and with him the king's officer (1 Mach. ii. 23–25). He overturned the altar and called on the faithful to follow him. He retired to the mountains with his five sons, John, Simon, Judas Machabeus, Eleazar, and Jonathan. Attacked by the idolaters on the sabbath day, they were massacred, not wishing to fight on that day (ii. 38); Mathathias then gathered the Assideans, punished idolaters, destroyed altars, and circumcised the people (45, 46); after beginning the war of liberation, he blessed his sons, exhorted them to observe the law (1 Mach. ii. 49–68), and died at Modin, 161 B. C. (1 Mach. ii. 69).

MATHU'SALA, son of Henoch (Gen. v. 22); he dies at the age of 969 years (27).

MAT'RIMONY, a sacrament (Eph. v. 22).

MATTHEW, ST., apostle and evangelist, called also Levi; was son of Alpheus (Mark ii. 14; Luke vii. 27); and a publican or tax-gatherer (Mark ii. 14). He was at his duties when our Lord called him (Matt. ix. 9; Mark ii. 14; Luke v. 27). He invited our Lord to his house, where Christ rebuked the Pharisees (Matt. ix. 10, etc.) The prevailing opinion is that he preached among the Parthians and died by martyrdom.

MATTHEW, Gospel of St., one of the canonical books of the New Testament, written by St. Matthew, and containing the earliest life of our Lord. It is by some said to have been written in Syriac, and by others in Greek (Matt.)

MATTHIAS, ST., apostle. He was one of those who had followed our Lord from his baptism by St. John (Acts i. 21, 22); after the ascension he was chosen to take the place of Judas Iscariot (23–26). He is supposed to have preached and died in Colchis.

MEAL, multiplied by the prophet Elias (3 Kings xvii. 16).

MEAS'URE (Metreta), (2 Par. ii. 10; iv. 5; John ii. 6).

MEAS'URE. With the same measure that men shall mete withal, it shall be measured to them again (Ex. xxi. 23; Judg. i. 7; 1 Kings xv. 33; 2 Kings xxii. 25; Prov. xxii. 23; Isai. xxxiii. 1; lxv. 6; lxvi. 4; Jer. l. 15, 29; li. 49; Ezech. xvi. 59; Joel iii. 7; Luke vi. 38); measures and weights must be just

(Lev. xix. 35; Deut. xxv. 13; Prov. xvi. 11; xx. 10; Ezech. xlv. 10; Mich. vi. 11; Am. viii. 5).

ME'DAD and **EL'DAD,** two men whom God filled with his Spirit to aid Moses in governing his people (Num. xi. 26–30).

MEDES. The ten tribes of Israel removed as captives to the country of the Medes (4 Kings xvii. 6; xviii. 11; Tob. i. 16; v. 14); the Medes conquer Babylon (Dan. v. 31; Isai. xiii. 17, 18).

ME'DIA, the country of the Medes (Jerem. li. 28; 1 Mach. vi. 56; xiv. 1); Arsaces, king of Media and Persia (1 Mach. xiv. 2).

MEEK'NESS commended (Ecclus. i. 35; Matt. v. 4; Gal. vi. 1; Eph. iv. 2; Col. iii. 12; Tit. iii. 2); especially to ministers of the Lord (2 Tim. ii. 25); mildness is one of the fruits of the Holy Ghost (Gal. v. 23); we are taught meekness by the example of Josue (Jos. vii. 19); of David (1 Kings xxv. 32; 2 Kings xvi. 10); of our Lord (Matt. xi. 29).

MEGIL'LOTH, a name applied by the Jews to Ecclesiastes, Canticle of Canticles, Lamentations, Ruth, and Esther.

MEL'CHA, daughter of Aram, and sister of Lot. She married Nachor; her children were Hus, Buz, Camuel, Cased, Azau, Pheldas, Jedlaph, and Bathuel (Gen. xxii. 20; xxiv. 15).

MEL'CHI, son of Addi, one of the ancestors of our Lord (Luke iii. 28).

MEL'CHIAS, head of the fifth of the twenty-four priestly families (1 Paral. xxiv. 9).

MEL'CHIAS, son of Herem, aided in building the walls of Jerusalem (2 Esd. iii. 11).

MEL'CHIAS, son of Rechab, built the Gate of the Dunghill at Jerusalem (2 Esd. iii. 14).

MEL'CHIAS, son of a goldsmith, built part of the wall of Jerusalem (2 Esd. iii. 30, 31).

MEL'CHIAS, son of Amelech. Jeremias is cast into the dungeon of Melchias (Jerem. xxxviii. 6).

MELCHIS'EDECH, king of Salem, and priest of the Most High God (Gen. xiv. 18); his genealogy is not given (Heb. vii. 1); when Abraham pursued and defeated the kings who had carried off Lot and his goods (Gen. xiv. 17–19) Melchisedech met him in the vale of Save, bringing forth bread and wine, for he was the priest of God; he blessed Abraham and gave him tithes (18–20), a figure of Christ (Ps. cix. 4; Heb. vii. 1).

MELCHISU'A, third son of Saul, slain with his father at Gelboe (1 Kings xxxi. 2).

MEL'CHOM, god of the Ammonites (4 Kings xxiii. 13; Sophon. i. 5).

MEL'ITA, same as Malta (Acts xxviii. 1).

MEL'LO, a city near Sichem; the people of these two places made Abimelech, son of Gedeon, king (Judg. ix. 6, 20).

MEM'MIUS, QUINTUS, one of the Roman ambassadors to king Antiochus Eupator, wrote to the Jews, ratifying all the acts of Lysias (2 Mach. xi. 34–36).

MEMPHIS, a city of Egypt. The princes of Memphis deceive Egypt (Isai. xix. 13); Jews resided there in the time of Jeremias (xliv. 1; xlvi. 14; Osee ix. 6); its destruction foretold (Jerem. xlvi. 19; Ezech. xxx. 16); God will destroy its idols (Ezech. xxx. 13).

MEN'ELAUS, son of Simon, of the tribe of Benjamin, succeeded Jason as high-priest, 172 B. C., by usurpation and bribery. He betrayed his country and religion (2 Mach. iv. 24); and was put to death by Antiochus, 162 B. C. (xiii. 4–8).

MEN'NA, son of Mathatha, one of the ancestors of our Lord (Luke iii. 31).

MEN'NI, a kingdom invited to war on Babylon (Jer. li. 27).

MEPH'AATH, a city in the tribe of Ruben, given to the Levites of the house of Merari (Jos. xiii. 18; xxi. 36).

MERAI'OTH, son of Zaraias, one of the high-priests (1 Paral. vi. 6).

MER'CURY, a god worshipped by the Greeks and Romans as the god of commerce. Paul was taken for this deity by the men of Lystra (Acts xiv. 11).

MER'CY. We must show mercy to our neighbor (1 Kings xv. 6; 2 Paral. xxviii. 9, 15; Ps. cxi. 5, 8; Prov. xiv. 21, 22, 31; Osee vi. 11; Mich. vi. 8; Zach. vii. 9; Matt. v. 7; ix. 13; xii. 7; xxiii. 23; xxv. 42; Luke vi. 36; Rom. xii. 13; Gal. vi. 16; Col. iii. 12; 1 Tim. v. 10).

MER'IBBAAL, son of Jonathan, more generally called Miphiboseth (1 Paral. viii. 34; ix. 40; 2 Kings iv. 4).

MER'OB or **MICHOL,** eldest daughter of Saul, promised to David but given to Hadriel, son of Bezellai of Molathi (1 Kings xiv. 49; xviii. 17, 19); her six sons were crucified by the Gabaonites (2 Kings xxi. 8).

MER'ODACH, an ancient king of Babylon, worshipped as a god (Jer. l. 2).

MER'ODACH BALADAN, king of Babylon, hearing of the recovery of king Ezechias, sent to congratulate him (Isai. xxxix. 1).

MER'OM, waters of, Jabin and the other kings of Chanaan assembled here to resist Josue (Jos. xi. 5).

MER'OME, a district where the children of Zabulon and Nephthali exposed their lives (Judg. v. 18).

MER'OZ, a place near the torrent of Cison. The people of this place would not aid their brethren in the battle against Sisara, and were cursed (Judg. v. 23).

MER'RHA, a mercantile town or country (Bar. iii. 23).

MES or **MOS'OCH,** fourth son of Aram (Gen. x. 23; 1 Paral. i. 17).

ME'SA, king of the Moabites, rich in flocks. He paid a tribute of one thousand lambs and as many rams (4 Kings iii. 4). He revolted against Joram, king of Israel. Joram, with Josaphat, king of Juda, and the king of Edom, besieged him in his capital. Mesa offered his son in sacrifice on the wall, when they retired (iii. 5–27; 1 Paral. ii. 42).

MESOPOTA'MIA, a province between the Euphrates and Tigrus. It is famous in Scripture. Phaleg, Heber, Thare, Abraham, Nachor, Sara, Rebecca, Lia, Rachel, and the sons of Jacob were born there (Gen. xi.–xxx.)

MES'RAIM, son of Cham (Gen. x. 6); his descendants settled in Egypt.

MESSI'AS. He is promised to Adam (Gen. iii. 15;) to Abraham (xii. 3; xxi. 12; xxii. 18); he is to have a precursor (Mal. iii. 1); his birth of a virgin announced (Isai. vii. 14; Jerem. xxxi. 22); the time of his coming revealed to Daniel (Dan. ix. 24); the place of his birth designated (Mich. v. 2; Matt. ii. 6); his reign described (Jer. xxiii. 5); he is to enter the second temple (Agg. ii. 8; Mal. iii. 1); he is to abide among men (Isai. xii. 6); he is to be rejected by his people (xlix. 7, 9); he is called Jesus or Saviour (Matt. i. 21, 25); Christ, or the Anointed (Matt. xxvi. 68; John i. 41; iv. 25; vii. 41; xi. 27; Acts xvii. 3; xviii. 28); he is the Lamb of God (John i. 29, 36).

METH'CA, encampment of the Israelites in the desert (Num. xxxiii. 28, 29).

MEZ'UZOTH; name given by the Jews to Deut. vi. 4–9, written on parchment, and hung on the doors or worn.

MI'CHAEL, an archangel, fights against Satan for the people of God (Dan. x. 13; xii. 1; Jude 9; Apoc. xii. 7).

MI'CHAS, son of a widow of Ephraim, made a silver ephod, and set it up in his house, making his son priest, and afterwards a Levite. The tribe of Dan carried off idol and priest, and the worship was established at Lais or Dan. Jonathan, grandson of Moses, became priest. This idolatry continued till the fall of the kingdom of Israel (Judg. xvii., xviii.)

MICH'EAS, son of Jemla, a prophet, summoned before Achab and Josaphat (3 Kings xxii. 10; 2 Paral. xviii. 12); he announces their defeat (3 Kings xxii. 17; 2 Paral. xviii. 16); struck on the cheek by Sedecias (3 Kings xxii. 24; 2 Paral. xviii. 23); Achab orders him to be imprisoned; his prophecy fulfilled (2 Kings xxii. 26–38; 2 Paral. xviii. 25–34).

MICH'EAS of Morasthi, one of the twelve minor prophets. He prophesied in the days of Joathan, Achaz, and Ezechias, kings of Juda, and was a cotemporary of Isaias, using similar language (Isai. ii. 2; Mich. iv.; Isai. xxvi. 21; Mich. i. 3).

MILETUS.

MICH'EAS, one of the canonical books of the Old Testament, containing the prophecies of Micheas of Morasthi. He foretold the destruction of the ten tribes, and the destruction of Jerusalem. He foretold the coming of the Messias, his birth at Bethlehem, and the establishment of the church (Mich.)

MI'CHOL, daughter of Saul, promised to David (1 Kings xviii. 21); given to him in marriage (xviii. 27); saves him from Saul's anger by letting him down from a window and placing a figure in his bed (xix. 12); Saul afterward gave her as a wife to Phalti or Phaltiel (xxv. 44); David demands her from Isboseth, and she was restored to him (2 Kings iii. 13–16); she ridiculed David dancing before the ark of the covenant, and remains childless (vi. 16–23).

MID'WIVES, their courage saves the children of the Hebrews (Ex. i. 17).

MILE'TUS, a city of Ionia, St. Paul at (Acts xx. 15, 17); Trophimus left sick at (2 Tim. iv. 20).

MIL'ITARY MUSTERINGS among the Jews (Judg. vii. 1, 24; xii. 1; xix. 29; 1 Kings xi. 7, 9).

MIN'ISTERS OF THE GOSPEL, what is due them (1 Cor. iv.)

MIPHIB'OSETH, son of Jonathan and grandson of Saul (2 Kings iv. 4); David favors him on account of his father (ix. 7); a cripple (3, 13); his servant Siba calumniates him to David (xvi. 3); he alone of Saul's family escaped a violent death; he is called also Meribbaal (1 Paral. ix. 40); he justifies himself before David (2 Kings xix. 24–30).

MIR'ACLES, signs, prodigies, wonders decreed by God from all eternity, coeval with the laws of nature, and executed in time, to show his power, authority, or goodness. Moses works miracles to prove his mission (Ex. iv. 3, 9); he afflicts Egypt by a miracle with a series of plagues (vii.–ix., xiv.); he leads the Israelites through the Red Sea (xiv. 21); causes water to issue from a rock (xvii. 6).

MIR'ACLES OF ELIAS. He raises to life the son of the widow of Sarephta (3 Kings xvii. 17–24); draws down fire from heaven on his holocaust which he had soaked with water (xviii. 34–38); obtains rain (41–45); draws down fire from heaven on officers sent to arrest him (4 Kings i. 10); divides the water of Jordan and passes over on dry ground (ii. 8).

MIR'ACLES OF ELISE'US. He sweetens the waters of Jericho (4 Kings ii. 19–22); draws vengeance on disrespectful children (23, 24); multiplies the widow's oil (iv. 2–7); raises to life the child of the Sunamitess (iv. 18–37); cures Naaman's leprosy (v. 1–14); punishes Giezi's avarice and falsehood by leprosy (27); blinds the Syrians (vi. 18); his relics raise a dead man to life (xiii. 21).

MIR'ACLES OF JESUS CHRIST. He changes water into wine at the marriage feast of Cana in Galilee (John ii. 1–10); cures the sick and crippled (Matt. iv. 24; viii. 16; ix. 35; xi. 2; xiv. 14; xv. 30; Mark i. 34; vi. 5; Luke iv. 40; v. 15; vi. 18; ix. 11); cures the possessed (Matt. iv. 24; viii. 16; Mark i. 26–39; iii. 23; Luke iv. 41; vi. 18; xi. 15); the deaf, dumb, and blind (Matt. xi. 5; xv. 30); cleansed lepers (Matt. xi. 5; viii. 2; Mark i. 40; Luke v. 12). He heals the centurion's servant (Matt. viii. 5; Luke vii. 2); the mother-in-law of Peter (Matt. viii. 14); he stills the tempest on the Sea of Galilee (Matt. viii. 26; Mark iv. 39; Luke viii. 24); cures a possessed man and allows the devils to enter swine (Matt. viii. 28; Mark v. 1; Luke viii. 27); he heals a paralytic (Matt. ix. 1; Mark ii. 3; Luke v. 18); cures the woman suffering from an issue of blood (Matt. ix. 20; Mark v. 25; Luke viii. 43); raises to life the ruler's daughter (Matt. ix. 22; Mark v. 22; Luke viii. 41); heals two blind men (Matt. ix. 27); a dumb man possessed (Matt. ix. 32; Luke xi. 14); feeds five thousand people with five loaves and two fishes (Matt. xiv. 17; Mark vi. 35; Luke ix. 12; John vi. 5); he walks on the water (Matt. xiv. 26; Mark vi. 48); he heals the daughter of the woman of Chanaan (Matt. xv. 22; Mark vii. 24); he cures a deaf mute (Matt. ix. 32; Mark vii. 32; Luke xi. 14); feeds four thousand persons with seven loaves and a few fishes (Matt. xv. 34; Mark viii. 5); cures a blind man (Mark viii. 22); a deaf and dumb man possessed (Matt. xvii. 14; Mark ix. 16; Luke ix. 37);

St. Peter by his direction obtains money from a fish (Matt. xvii. 26); he cures Bartimeus of blindness (Matt. xx. 30; Mark x. 46; Luke xviii. 35); he curses the barren fig tree and causes it to wither (Matt. xxi. 19; Mark xi. 13); he raises to life the son of the widow of Naim (Luke vii. 11); he heals a woman bent by infirmity for eighteen years (Luke xiii. 11); he cures a person of dropsy (Luke xiv. 2); he cleanses ten lepers (Luke xvii. 12); he restores the ear of Malchus which St. Peter had cut off (Luke xxii. 51); he gives sight to a man blind from birth (John ix. 6); he raises Lazarus to life (John xi. 44); he gives Peter and John a miraculous draught of fishes (xxi. 6); he strikes Saul with blindness (Acts ix. 8).

MIR'ACLES OF THE APOSTLES and Disciples of our Lord. Jesus Christ confers on them the power to work miracles (Matt. x. 1; Mark iii. 15; xvi. 17; Luke ix. 1); St. Peter and St. John cure a lame man at the Beautiful Gate (Acts iii. 1); St. Peter cures Eneas (ix. 33); he raises Tabitha to life (ix. 36); he cures many (Acts v. 12); he cures the sick by his shadow (15); St. Paul raises a young man to life (Acts xx. 9, 10); he heals a cripple (xiv. 9); works more than common miracles (xix. 11); cures the sick and possessed by handkerchiefs and aprons from his body (xix. 12); unharmed by the sting of a poisonous serpent; he cures Publius and all the sick of Melita (Acts xxviii. 5–9); strikes Elymas blind (Acts xiii. 6–11).

MIR'ACLES asked and refused (Mark viii. 11; Luke xxiii. 8).

MIR'ROR. The women of Israel give their mirrors (King James has absurdly looking-glasses) to make the laver of brass (Ex. xxxviii. 8). Wisdom is the unspotted mirror of God's majesty (Wisd. vii. 26). Looking-glass (Isai. iii. 23) and glass (1 Cor. xiii. 12; James i. 23) should also be mirror.

MI'SACH (Dan. iii. 12), or Misael (i. 7), one of the three companions of Daniel, the former being the Chaldean name given him. He was one of the three cast into the fiery furnace. See ANANIAS.

MIS'ERIES of human life (Job vii.; xiv.); they are the consequences of sin (Gen. iii. 16–19); described (Wisd. vii. 3; Eccles. iii. 19; ix. 3; Prov. xiii. 21; Ecclus. iii. 29).

MI'SOR, a city in the tribe of Ruben, given to the Levites of the family of Merari (Jos. xxi. 36); supposed to be Mephaath (1 Paral. vi. 78, 79).

MIS'PHAT, the fountain of Misphat, "the same as that of Cades" (Gen. xiv. 7). It is the same as the Water of Contradiction (Num. xx. 13).

MITE (Latin *minutum*), a coin, value 1½ cents. The widow throws her mites into the treasury (Luke xxi. 2).

MI'TRE, worn by Aaron (Ex. xxix. 6; Ecclus. xlv. 14), and his sons (Ex. xxix. 9; xxxix. 26, 30; Lev. viii. 13).

MITHRIDA'TES, the son of Gazabar. Cyrus delivered the vessels of the temple to prince Sassabasar, by the hand of Mithridates (1 Esd. i. 8).

MITHRIDA'TES. Beselam Mithridates writes against the Jews (1 Esd. iv. 7).

MIT'YLENE, capital of the island of Lesbos, visited by St. Paul on his way from Corinth to Jerusalem, A. D. 58 (Acts xx. 14).

MNA, fifteen sicles make a mna (Ezech. xlv. 12); the word is translated pound (3 Kings x. 17, etc.).

MO'AB, son of Lot and his eldest daughter (Gen. xix. 31–37).

MO'AB, the country of the Moabites, beyond the

Jordan and the Dead Sea, on the banks of the river Arnon; prophecies against it (Num. xxi. 29; xxiv. 17; Ps. lix. 10; cvii. 10; Isai. xv. 1–9; Jerem. xlviii. 1; Ezech. xxv. 8; Amos ii. 1; Soph. ii. 8).

MO'ABITES, a people descended from Moab, son of Lot. The Amorrhites conquer part of their country (Judg. xi. 13), which Moses conquered and gave to the tribe of Ruben. Moses spared the Moabites, and the Israelites were forbidden to attack them (Deut. ii. 9); Balac bribes Balaam to curse the Israelites (Num. xxii. 5; xxiii.); excluded from the temple (Deut. xxiii. 3); under Eglon they oppress the Israelites (Judg. iii. 12); David makes them tributary (2 Kings viii. 2); under Mesa they shake off the yoke of the kings of Israel (4 Kings i. 1; iii. 5); delivered into the hands of Israel (4 Kings iii. 24); make incursion into the land of Israel (xiii. 20); excluded from dignities (Deut. xxiii. 3; 2 Esd. xiii. 1); Ruth, a Moabitess (Ruth).

MO'DIN, a city in the tribe of Dan, on a mountain of the same name. It was the residence of Mathathias (1 Mach. ii. 1); near the sea (xiii. 29); Judas wins a victory near Modin (2 Mach. xiii. 9–14); the tombs of the Machabees at (1 Mach. ii. 70; ix. 19; xiii. 25, 30; xiv. 4).

MO'LOCH, god of the Ammonites (Lev. xviii. 21; xx. 2); called also in some places Melchom (4 Kings xxiii. 13; 1 Paral. xx. 2; Jer. xlix. 1; Amos i. 15; Soph. i. 5); the Israelites forbidden to consecrate their children to Moloch (Lev. xviii. 21; xx. 2–5); children were sacrificed to it (4 Kings xvii. 31; Ps. cv. 37; Isai. lvii. 5; Ezech. xvi. 21; xxiii. 39); David captured a rich crown used on the idol (1 Paral. xx. 2).

MON'EY struck in Judea (1 Mach. xv. 6); silver weighed passed as money (Gen. xxiii. 15, 16; xxxvii. 28; xliii. 21; xxiv. 22).

MOLOCH.

MONTHS of the Jewish year: Nizan or Abib (Ex. xiii. 4; 2 Esd. ii. 1), corresponding nearly to March; Zio (April), (3 Kings vi. 1); Sivan (May), (Bar. i. 8); Thammuz (June); Ab (July); Elul

MOSES' ROD CHANGED TO A SERPENT.

(August), (1 Mach. xiv. 27); Ethanim (September), (3 Kings viii. 2); Bul (October), 3 Kings vi. 38); Casleu (November), (2 Esd. i. 1; 2 Mach. i. 9); Thebat (December); Sebat (January); Adar (February), (Esther iii. 7; 1 Mach. vii. 43).

MORI'A, a mountain on which Solomon's temple was built (2 Paral. iii. 1).

MORT'IFICA'TION of the flesh inculcated (Rom. vi. 12; viii. 12; Gal. v. 16; Eph. iv. 22; Col. iii. 5; Tit. ii. 12; 1 Pet. ii. 1; iv. 6; Heb. xii. 1; 1 Cor. ix. 27).

MO'SA, son of Caleb (1 Paral. ii. 46).

MO'SA, son of Zamri, descendant of Jonathan (1 Paral. viii. 37; ix. 42, 43).

MO'SEL, a city mentioned by Ezechiel (xxvii. 19).

MOS'ERA, an encampment of the Israelites near Mount Hor, where Aaron died (Deut. x. 6).

MOS'EROTH, an encampment of the Israelites (Num. xxxiii. 30).

MO'SOCH, sixth son of Japheth (Gen. x. 2).

MO'SES, son of Amram and Jochabed, of the tribe of Levi, was born in Egypt, 1571 B. C. His sister Mary and his brother Aaron were older than he. Some time before his birth Pharao, king of Egypt, ordered all male Hebrew children to be killed at their birth (Ex. i. 16); his mother concealed him for three months (ii. 2); and then placed him in a basket of bulrushes and laid it in the river Nile. The daughter of Pharao going to bathe saw the child, and compassionately resolved to adopt it. A Hebrew woman was called to nurse it, and was really Jochabed herself (9); the princess after three months took him and gave him the name Moses, and he was brought up at court and instructed in all the wisdom of the Egyptians (Acts vii. 20–22); when he was forty years old he slew an Egyptian who was oppressing an Israelite (Ex. ii. 11, 12; Acts vii. 23, 24);

afterwards when endeavoring to prevent two of his countrymen from quarreling, he was reproached with the death of the Egyptian (Ex. ii. 13, 14; Acts vii. 26–28); Moses then fled to Madian, and after defending the daughters of Raguel or Jethro, a priest, remained with him and married his daughter Sephora, who bore him two sons, Gersam and Eliezer (Ex. ii. 22); God appeared to him in a burning bush on Mount Horeb, and commanded him to assemble the ancients of Israel, and go with them to the king of Egypt and demand the release of his people (Ex. iii.); God gave him miraculous powers, and associated Aaron with him (Ex. iv.); Pharao refused to let the Israelites go, and oppressed them more grievously (Ex. v.); on which Moses smote Egypt with nine plagues, and finally with the death of their first-born (Ex. vii.–xii.); the Israelites escaped by observing the rite of the paschal lamb then instituted (Ex. xii.); he then led the Israelites out of Egypt after they had been there 430 years (xii. 40), to return to the land of Chanaan which God promised them (Ex. iii. 8; xiii. 5); he led them by the way of the desert, God showing the way by day in a pillar of cloud and by night in a pillar of fire (xiii. 18, 21); Pharao pursued them and overtook them at the Red Sea, which divided when Moses stretched forth his hand, allowing the children of Israel to pass through, but overwhelmed the Egyptian army when it followed (Ex. xiv.); Moses composed and sang a canticle to praise God (xv.); the people murmured for food, and God sent quails, also manna, a food which lasted for forty years (xvi.); when they murmured for water at Raphidim, Moses struck the rock and water came forth, but as he showed doubt, God declared that he should not enter the promised land (Ex. xvii.; Num. xx.); the Amalecites attacked them here but were defeated by the prayer of Moses (xvii. 8–14); Jethro here brought to Moses Sephora and her children (xviii. 5); Moses appointed judges over the people (25); he went up Mount Sinai, and received from God the ten commandments on two tables of stone and directions for the government of the people, the worship of God and the ministry (Ex. xix.–xxxi.; Levit.

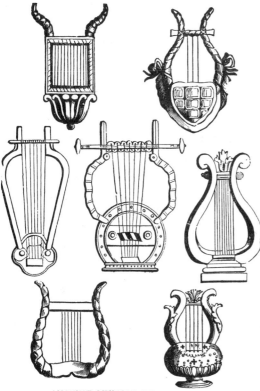

ANCIENT MUSICAL INSTRUMENTS.

i.–xxvii.; Deut. i.–xxxii.); during his stay on the mountain the people induced Aaron to make a golden calf, which they worshipped. Moses descending threw down the tables of the law and broke them. Then, at the head of the Levites, he cut his way through the idolaters, killing 23,000 men (Ex. xxxii. 1–28); Moses then hewed two tables, on which God inscribed the commandments (Ex. xxxiv.; Deut. x.);

THE MYRTLE.

when he came down his face was radiant with light so that he had to cover it (Ex. xxxiv. 30); he caused the tabernacle, with the Ark of the Covenant, and

the altars, lavers, and table, as well as the vestments for Aaron and his sons, to be made as God had directed (Ex. xxxvi.–xxxix.; Num. viii.–x.); when the tabernacle was set up God filled it with his majesty (xl.); the people frequently murmured against Moses, and even Aaron and Mary joined, but God justified his servant (Num. xi.–xii.); when they approached the Promised Land, Moses sent spies from each tribe to reconnoitre the land, but they all except Josue and Caleb spoke so strongly against it that the people refused to advance; in consequence the people were condemned to wander in the desert for forty years, and of all who came out of Egypt only Josue and Caleb lived to enter the Promised Land (Num. xiii.; xiv.); Moses condemned Core, Dathan, and Abiron, who rebelled against Aaron, and they were swallowed up alive (Num. xvi.); he defeated Arad, king of Chanaan, at Horma (Num. xxi. 3); Sehon, king of the Amorrhites, at Jasa (23); Og, king of Basan, at Edrai (33–35); the king of Moab, and the kings of the Madianites (xxii.; xxxi. 8); when the people were bitten by fiery serpents, he set up a brazen serpent, and all who looked on it were cured (Num. xxi. 9); Moses allotted lands to the tribes of Ruben, Gad, and half of Manasses, on the east side of Jordan (Num. xxxii.); he blessed the people, and having seen the Promised Land from Phasga, on Mount Nebo, and died there at the age of 120 (Deut. xxxiii.–xxxiv.); he was buried in the valley of Moab over against Phogor (xxxiv. 6); and his burial-place is unknown to man. The archangel Michael disputed with the devil for his body (Jude 9); Moses prayed constantly for his people (Ex. xiv. 15; xvii. 4, 11; xxxii. 11, 13, 31; Num. xi. 2; xiv. 13, 17; xxi. 7; Deut. ix. 18, 26); he is praised (Deut. xxxiv. 7, 8, 10; Ecclus. xlv. 1); he appears with Elias at the Transfiguration of our Lord (Matt. xvii. 3); he is the first of the inspired writers, having prepared the Pentateuch, that is, Genesis, Exodus, Leviticus, Numbers, Deuteronomy.

MOUNT AB'ARIM, one of a chain of mountains connected with Phasga and Nebo, extending from the mountains of Galaad to the plains of Moab (Num. xxvii. 12–14; Deut. xxxii. 49–52).

MOUNT of AM'ALECH, in the tribe of Ephraim (Judg. xii. 15).

MOUNT CAL'VARY, the place of our Lord's crucifixion (Matt. xxvii. 33; Mark xv. 22; Luke xxiii. 33; John xix. 17).

MOUNT CAR'MEL, on the Mediterranean, between Dora and Ptolemais, in the tribe of Aser (Jos. xix. 26); Elias confounds the priests of Baal at Mount Carmel by drawing down

fire from heaven (3 Kings xviii.); Eliseus goes to Mount Carmel (4 Kings ii. 25); its beauty a type (Amos i. 2; ix. 3).

MOUNT EPHRAIM (Jos. xxiv. 30; Judges ii. 9; 2 Paral. xix. 4).

MOUNT ENGAD'DI, near the Dead Sea (Jos. xv. 62).

MOUNT GA'AS, in the tribe of Ephraim (Jos. xxiv. 30; Judg. ii. 9).

MOUNT GAR'AZIM, where the Samaritans had their temple.

MOUNT GEL'BOE, in the plain of Jezrael, where Saul and his sons perished in battle (1 Kings xxxi. 1; 1 Paral. x. 1; 2 Kings i. 6).

MOUNT HE'BAL, near Garizim, curses invoked at (Deut. xi. 29; xxvii. 13); Josue built an altar there (Jos. viii. 30).

MOUNT HER'MON, beyond the Jordan, near Libanus (Deut. iii. 8; Jos. xi. 3; xii. 4; xiii. 5; Judg. iii. 3; 1 Paral. v. 23; Ps. lxxxviii.; cxxxii. 3; Cant. iv. 8).

MOUNT HOR, in Edom or Idumea (Num. xx. 22); the Israelites at (xx.; xxi.); Aaron dies there (xxxiii. 38; Deut. xxxii. 50).

MOUNT HO'REB, near Sinai, in Arabia Petræa. God appears to Moses in a burning bush on (Ex. iii. 1; Deut. i. 2); the Israelites at (Ex. xxxiii.; Deut. i., iv., xviii.; 3 Kings viii., xix.); Moses draws water from the rock (Ex. xvii. 6); God makes a covenant with the Jews at (Deut. v. 2); Elias reaches it by miraculous food (3 Kings xix. 8).

MOUNT'AINS OF JUDA, the mountains in the south of their territory tending to Idumea (Luke i. 39, 65).

THE MUSTARD OF PALESTINE.

MOUNT LIB'ANUS (Deut. i. 7; Jos. i. 4; Judg. iii. 3; 3 Kings iv. 33; 4 Kings xiv. 9; 2 Paral. ii. 8; 1 Esd. iii. 7, etc.) See LIBANUS.

MOUNT MORI′A, on which the temple was built (2 Paral. iii. 1).

MOUNT NE′BO, part of the mountains of Abarim. Moses died there (Num. xxxii. 3; Deut. xxxiv. 1).

MOUNT OF OL′IVES or **OLIVET,** near Jerusalem (Zach. xiv. 4); our Lord arrives at (Matt. xxi. 1; Mark xi. 1; Luke xix. 29; John viii. 1); while sitting on he foretells the destruction of Jerusalem (Matt. xxiv. 3; Mark xiii. 3); he passes the night on (Luke xxi. 37); received with hosannas and palms on descending from it (Luke xix. 37); he went to it after the Last Supper (Matt. xxvi. 30; Mark xiv. 26; Luke xxii. 39); ascends to heaven from (Acts i. 12).

MOUNT PHA′RAN, in Arabia Petræa (Gen. xiv. 6; Deut. i. 1).

MOUNT PHAS′GA, beyond the Jordan (Num. xxi. 20); Deut. xxxiv. 1).

MOUNT SEIR or **EDOM** (Gen. xiv. 6).

MOUNT SEMERON, on which Samaria was built (2 Paral. xiii. 4).

MOUNT SI′NAI, in Arabia Petræa (Deut. xxxiii. 2), where Moses received instructions and the tables of the law from God. Spiritual meaning of (Gal. iv. 24).

MOUNT SI′ON, on which the city of David was built (Deut. iv. 48).

MOUNT THA′BOR, in upper Galilee, north of the Great Plain (Judg. iv. 6); it is generally regarded as the scene of the transfiguration of our Lord; it was in the tribe of Zabulon (Jos. xix. 22; 1 Parai. vi. 77); Barac defeats Sisara there (Judg. iv. 14); referred to (Ps. lxxxviii. 13; Jerem. xlvi. 18; Osee v. 1).

MOUNT′AIN, our Lord's sermon on the (Matt. v.–vii.); our Lord is tempted by Satan on a mountain (Matt. iv. 8); he is transfigured on a mountain (Matt. xvii. 1; Mark ix. 1); he retires on a mountain to pray (Matt. xiv. 23; Mark vi. 46; Luke vi. 12); he enters Jerusalem in triumph from Mount Olivet (Luke xix 37); he is crucified on the mountain (Matt. xxvii. 33; Mark xv. 22; Luke xxiii. 33; John xix. 17); ascends to heaven from a mountain (Acts i. 12).

MOURN′ING OF EGYPT, a place so called (Gen. l. 11).

MOUSE, MICE, rodent animals, classed as unclean (Lev. xi. 29); Azotus overrun with mice (1 Kings v. 6); the Philistines send to the Israelites golden mice according to the number of their cities in order to be delivered (vi. 18); Israelites compared to mice (Judith xiv. 12); those who ate them to be consumed (Isai. lxvi. 17).

MUR′DER, forbidden, committed, punished (Gen. iv.; ix. 5, 6; xxxvii. 18; Ex. xx. 13; Lev. xxiv. 17; Deut. xix. 11; xxvii. 24; 2 Kings iv. 7, 12; 3 Kings ii. 5; 4 Kings xxi. 16; Prov. vi. 17; xxviii. 17; Ecclus. xxxiv. 27; Lam. iv. 13; Ezech. xi. 6; xxii. 2; xxiv. 6; Osee iv. 2; Matt. xix. 18; xxiii. 35; John viii. 44; Rom. xiii. 9; Gal. v. 21); the law permits killing a night robber (Ex. xxii. 2); law as to involuntary killing (Deut. xix. 4; Jos. xx. 3); concealed murders (Deut. xxi. 1).

MUR′MURERS, their guilt and punishment (Ex. xiv. 11; xv. 24; xvi. 2–8; xvii. 3; Num. xi. 1; xii. 1, 9, 10; xiv. 2, 20; xvi. 3; xvii. 13; xxi. 5; Deut. i. 27; Jos. ix. 18; Wisd. i. 11; Matt. xx. 11; Luke xv. 2; xix. 7; John vi. 41; Acts vi. 1; 1 Cor. x. 10; Jude 16).

SACRED MUSIC AND ITS PATRONESS—SAINT CECILIA.

MU′SICAL INSTRUMENTS, the harp and organ invented (Gen. iv. 21); trumpets used in divine worship (1 Paral. xvi. 42); psalteries, harps, cymbals (xv. 16–21; 2 Paral. xxix. 25; Ps. xxxii. 2; xci. 4; cvii. 3; cl. 3–5); timbrel (Ex. xv. 20; Ps. lxxx. 3); flute, sackbut and symphony (Dan. iii. 5).

MUS′TARD SEED, parable of the (Matt. xiii. 31; Luke xvii. 19; Mark iv. 31); faith as of a mustard seed (Matt. xvii. 19; Luke xvii. 6).

MYRRH, used in sacred oils (Ex. xxx. 23); as a perfume (Esth. ii. 12; Ps. xliv. 9; Cant. i. 12;) one of the gifts offered to our Lord by the wise men (Matt. ii. 12); offered to our Lord on the cross (Mark xv. 23); used in embalming him (John xix. 39).

MYRTLE TREES, vision of the (Zach. i. 8).

MYS′IA, a province in Asia Minor. St. Paul preached there (Acts xvi. 7, 8).

MYS′TERY of the kingdom of God confided to the apostles only (Matt. xiii. 11; Mark xiv. 11; Luke viii. 10); the apostles made the dispensers of the mysteries of God (1 Cor. iv. 1); the mystery of faith (1 Tim. iii. 9); the mystery of God complete (Apoc. x. 7).

NA′AMA, an Ammonitess, wife of Solomon, and mother of Roboam (3 Kings xiv. 21; 2 Paral. xii. 13).

NA′AMAN, general of the armies of Benadad, king of Syria, highly esteemed, but a leper (4 Kings v.); one of his slaves, a Jewish girl, induces him to go to the prophet Eliseus, who bade him bathe seven times in the Jordan. He did it reluctantly, but was cured. He became a worshipper of the one true God. His leprosy passed to Giezi, the prophet's servant, in punishment of his avarice and falsehood (4 Kings v.; Luke iv. 27).

NA′AMATHITE, Sophar, one of Job's friends, is called "the Naamathite," but whether from the name of a tribe or town is unknown (Job ii. 11; xi. 1; xx. 1; xlii. 9).

NA′ARATHA, a city in the tribe of Ephraim (Jos. xvi. 7).

NAA′RIA, fifth son of Sechenias (1 Paral. iii. 22); he was one of the leaders of the 500 Simeonites who extirpated the Amelecites of Mount Seir (iv. 41).

NA′AS, king of the Ammonites, besieged Jabes, of Galaad (1 Kings xi. 1), and demanded that every man should put out one eye. They sent for aid to Saul, who by threat of extirpation to all who did not rally to him, raised an army and cut the Ammonite army to pieces (1 Kings xi. 1–11); Naas subsequently showed kindness to David (2 Kings x. 2), so that on his death David sent ambassadors to his son Hanon to condole with him (x. 1, 2).

MOUNT NEBO

NA'AS, father of David, Abigail and Sarvia (2 Kings xvii. 25); the same as Isai or Jesse (2 Kings xvii. 25; 1 Par. ii. 13).

NAAS'SON, a place in the tribe of Nephthali (Tob. i. 1).

NAB'AJOTH, oldest son of Ismael (Gen. xxv. 13; xxviii. 9; xxxvi. 3; 1 Par. i. 29; Isai. lx. 7).

NA'BAL, a rich man of the tribe of Juda, and house of Caleb, living in the wilderness of Maon. He refused provisions to David, and escaped David's vengeance by the intercession of Abigail. He died soon after apparently of fright at the danger he had incurred (1 Kings xxv. 2–38).

NA'BO, an idol of the Babylonians (Isai. xlvi. 1; Jerem. xlviii. 1).

NABO.—Assyrian Statue in British Museum.

NA'BOTH, an Israelite of Jezrahel. He refused to sell his vineyard to king Achab. Jezabel had Naboth falsely accused of blasphemy and treason, unjustly condemned and put to death. Achab then seized the vineyard, but Elias denounced the judgments of God on Achab and Jezabel (3 Kings xxi. 1–24).

NAB'UCHODO-NOSOR (Saosduchin), king of Ninive, defeats Arphaxad, king of the Medes (Judith i. 5); sends Holofernes to reduce the nations to him (ii. 1); his army defeated before Bethulia (xv. 1).

NAB'UCHODO-NOSOR, king of Babylon. He reconquered Charcamis from Nechao, king of Egypt, and took Jerusalem, carrying away captive Joakim, whom Nechao had put on the throne (2 Paral.

xxxv.; xxxvi. 4–6); he left him, however, as tributary, and on his rebellion three years after, sent roving tribes against him, 603 B. C. (4 Kings xxiv. 2); in the second year of his reign he had a mysterious dream, which Daniel, a captive, interpreted (Dan. i. 1–44); Joachim, king of Juda, having revolted, Nabuchodonosor besieged and took Jerusalem, and carried off the king, and all but the poorest of the people, and all the treasures and vessels of the temple, 599 B. C. He left Sedecias as king, but he too revolted, and Nabuchodonosor again besieged the city, and after suspending the siege to meet and defeat Pharao Ephree, took Jerusalem, and destroyed the city and temple, 588 B. C. (4 Kings xxv. 11; Jerem. xxxix. 10). He reduced Sidon, Moab, Ammon, Edom and Tyre (Jerem. xlviii., xlix.; Ezech. xxvi.; Isai. xiv. 2, 8); he conquered Egypt, 571 B. C. (Ezech. xxix. 17–20); Daniel explained another mysterious dream (Dan. iv. 1); in 569 B. C. he was stricken with insanity, and ate grass like a beast, and was not restored for seven years (Dan. iv. 26–30); on his recovery he erected a golden statue, and cast the three Hebrew children into a fiery furnace for refusing to worship it (Dan. iii.) He died 562 B. C.

NAB'UTHEANS, a tribe in the desert, friendly to the Machabees (1 Mach. v. 25; ix. 35).

NAB'UZARDAN, general of Nabuchodonosor, destroyed the temple and walls of Jerusalem, and carried off the remnant of the people (4 Kings xxv. 8; Jerem. xxxix. 9, 11); on the death of Godolias, he ravaged Judea, and reduced the Ammonites (Jer. lii. 30).

NA'CHON. Oza was struck for his rashness at the floor of Nachon (2 Kings vi. 6).

NA'CHOR, son of Sarug, and father of Thare (Gen. xi. 22).

NA'CHOR, son of Thare (Gen. xi. 27).

NA'DAB, eldest son of Aaron, struck dead for offering fire not taken from the altar, 1490 B. C. (Lev. x. 1–3; Num. iii. 4).

NA'DAB, son of Jeroboam, king of Israel. He reigned two years, B. C. 954–2, and was assassinated by Baasa, at the siege of Gebbethon (3 Kings xiv. 20; xv. 25–28).

NAHA'LIEL, one of the encampments of the Israelites in the desert (Num. xxi. 19).

NAHAS'SON, son of Aminadab (Ruth iv. 20); prince of the tribe of Juda on leaving Egypt (Num. i. 7; ii. 3; vii. 12).

NA'HUM, the Elcesite, the seventh of the twelve minor prophets. He was a native of Elcese or Elcesai, supposed to be a town in Galilee. He prophesied after the captivity of the ten tribes, and foretold the destruction of Ninive.

NA'HUM. One of the canonical books of the Old Testament, containing the prophecies of Nahum (Nah.)

NA'IM, a village in Galilee, near Hermon, where our Lord raised to life the widow's son, whom they were carrying to the grave (Luke vii. 11–18).

NA'JOTH, a place near Ramatha. David fled to it from Saul (1 Kings xix. 19); Samuel dwelt there with the sons of the prophets (23).

NA'KED. It is an obligatory work of mercy to clothe them (Isai. lviii. 7; Ezech. xviii. 7; Tob. i. 20; Matt. xxv. 36, 38).

NAME. The name of God to be reverenced, and not taken in vain (Ex. xx. 7; Deut. v. 11; xxviii. 58; Ps. cx. 9; Mich. iv. 5; 1 Tim. vi. 1).

NAME of Jesus announced by an angel (Matt. i. 21; Luke i. 31); given to him at his circumcision (Matt. i. 25; Luke ii. 21); the power of the name of Jesus (Phil. ii. 9, 10); miracles wrought in the name of Jesus (Acts iii. 6; iv. 10; xix. 13); all our works to be done in the name of (Col. iii. 17); baptism in the name of (Acts viii. 12, 16).

NANE'A, a Persian goddess. Antiochus Epiphanes endeavored to plunder her temple at Elymais, but his emissaries with their leader were entrapped and slain (2 Mach. i. 13–16; 1 Mach. vi. 1–4).

NARCIS'SUS, St. Paul mentions his household as converts (Rom. xvi. 11).

NA'THAN, a prophet; sent to David to prevent his building the temple (2 Kings vii. 4; 1 Paral. xvii. 1); reproves him for his adultery and murder (2 Kings xii. 4;); induces David to anoint Solomon as king (3 Kings i.); wrote an account of the reigns of David and Solomon (1 Paral. xxix. 29; 2 Paral. ix. 29; xxix. 25).

NA'THAN, son of David and Bethsabee (2 Kings v. 14); and father of Mathatha (Luke iii. 31).

NA'THAN, brother of Joel, one of David's bravest warriors (2 Kings xxiii. 36; 1 Paral. xi. 38).

NA'THAN, one of the leading Jews who returned with Esdras from Babylon, and was sent by him to Eddo (1 Esd. viii. 16).

NATHAN'AEL, prince of the tribe of Issachar in the exodus (Num. i. 8; vii. 18).

NATHAN'AEL, fourth son of Jesse, and brother of David (1 Par. ii. 14; 1 Kings xvi. 6, 8, 9).

NATHAN'AEL, a doctor of the law, sent by Josaphat through his kingdom to instruct the people (2 Paral. xvii. 7).

NATHAN'AEL, a disciple of our Lord. Philip told him that they had found the Messias, and our Lord showed his knowledge of him (John i. 45–49); our Lord appeared to him after his resurrection (xxi. 2). Many think him to be the same as Bartholomew, which is only a patronymic name.

NATHANMELECH, eunuch of king Manasses, having charge of the chariots consecrated to the sun (4 Kings xxiii. 11).

NATHIN'ITES, men given by David and the princes for the service of the Levites (1 Esd. viii. 20; ii. 58).

NAZ'ARETH, in Galilee, in the tribe of Zabulon, on the side of Thabor. Here our Lord resided most of his life, from his return from Egypt to the commencement of his public ministry (Luke ii. 51; iv. 16); he preached in the synagogue (iv. 16); the people would not hear him, but attempt to kill him (30). In the inscription placed by Pilate on the cross, he is called of Nazareth (John xix. 19).

NAZ′ARITES, persons bound to God by vows (Gen. xlix. 26; Num. vi. 18–21; Judg. xiii. 5, 7; xvi. 17; Matt. ii. 23; Acts xviii. 18); abstinence practised by them (Judg. xiii. 7; Amos ii. 12; Num. vi. 3).

NEAP′OLIS, a city in Macedonia, visited by St. Paul (Acts xvi. 11).

NEB′AHAZ, god of the Hivites (4 Kings xvii. 31).

NE′BO, a mountain in Moab where Moses died (Deut. xxxiv. 1).

NECHA′O, king of Egypt, conquered Carchamis, and killed Josias, king of Juda, in battle at Mageddo 610, B. C. (4 Kings xxiii. 29, 30; 2 Paral. xxxv. 20); he deposed Joachaz at Rebla, and made Eliacim king, calling his name Joakim (4 Kings xxiii. 33–35; 2 Paral. xxxvi. 3, 4); he is defeated by Nabuchodonosor (4 Kings xxiv. 7).

NE′HELES′COL, the torrent of the cluster of grapes, the point reached by the spies, and called so from the immense cluster they found (Num. xiii. 25).

NEHEMI′AS, son of Helchias, born at Babylon during the captivity. He was of a priestly family (2 Mach. i. 18, 21; 2 Esd. i. 1; x. 1); he is called Athersatha (1 Esd. ii. 63; 2 Esd. vii. 65); he fasted, prayed, and humbled himself before the Lord to obtain from the king permission to rebuild Jerusalem. King Artaxerxes noticing his sadness, asked the reason, and granted his request. He went to Jerusalem, and finding the people well disposed, showed his authority, and they began to rebuild the walls. Sanaballat, and other enemies of the Jews, endeavored to thwart the plan and kill him; but the work was completed (2 Esd. i.–vi.); the walls and gates were then dedicated, and the Feast of Tabernacles celebrated (viii., xii.); as much of the city within the walls was unoccupied, he drew many into the city, and corrected many abuses (xi.); he compelled those who had married heathen women to dismiss them, provided for the maintenance of the priests, and the observance of the Sabbath, and all the people publicly renewed the covenant with the Lord (ix., x., xiii.); the fire of temple had been hidden in a well; water poured from this by Nehemias on the altar restored the sacred fire (2 Mach. i. 18); he also collected the sacred books (ii. 13, 14); he returned to Babylon to obey the king's orders (2 Esd. v. 14; xiii. 6), but is said to have died at Jerusalem, 424 B. C. The second book of Esdras bears the name of Nehemias, and seems drawn from the commentaries of Nehemias mentioned in 2 Mach. ii. 13.)

NEIGH′BOR. Who is our neighbor? (Luke x. 29); we are to love our neighbor as ourself (Matt. v. 43; xxii. 39; Mark xii. 31; Rom. xiii. 9); he that loveth his neighbor fulfilleth the law (Rom. xiii. 8); we are not to judge our neighbor (James iv. 13).

NEM′ROD, son of Chus, a stout hunter before the Lord (Gen. x. 8, 9); he founded the kingdom of Babylon (x.); it included Arach, Achad, and Chalanne in the land of Sennaar.

NE′OPHYTE, one newly converted, not to be made a bishop (1 Tim. iii. 6.)

NE′PHI, or **NEPHTHAR,** the place where the fire from the altar had been hidden, and whence the

water rekindled the fire at the prayer of Nehemias (2 Mach. i. 36).

NEPH′THALI, sixth son of Jacob, born of Bala, Rachel's handmaid (Gen. xxx. 8); his sons were Jasiel, Guni, Jeser, and Sallem (Gen. xlvi. 24); Jacob, in blessing him, says: Nephthali, a hart let loose and giving words of beauty (Gen. xlix. 21).

NEPH′THALI, the tribe of. On leaving Egypt it numbered 53,400, and at Settim 45,400, men able to bear arms (Num. i. 42, 43; xxvi. 50). Their prince was Ahira, the son of Enan (Num. ii. 29); the Promised Land was viewed by Nahabi, son of

NAZARETH.

Vapsi (xiii. 15); Moses promised it abundance, and the possession of the sea and the south (Deut. xxxiii. 23); its share in the Promised Land was the sixth lot, on the Jordan, bounded by Zabulon on the south, Aser on the west, and Juda on the east (Jos. xix. 32); they failed to exterminate the Chanaanites (Judg. i. 33); with Zabulon they defeat Jabin's army under Sisara (Judg. iv. 6); they were the first to be carried captives to Assyria (4 Kings xv. 29); Isaias predicted that they should see the light of the Messias (Isai. ix. 1); and our Lord preached frequently in the territory of Nephthali (Matt. iv. 13, 15). See TOBIAS.

NE′REUS, a disciple of St. Paul (Rom. xvi. 15).

NER′GEL, a god of the Cuthites, worshipped at Samaria (4 Kings xvii. 30).

NER′EGEL and **SERESER,** mentioned among the princes of Babylon (Jer. xxxix. 3, 13).

NE′RO, Roman emperor, some of his household received the faith (Phil. iv. 22). St. Paul appealed to him when arrested in the temple of Jerusalem (Acts xxv. 10–12); and appeared before him (2 Tim. iv. 16, 17). According to tradition, Nero put St. Peter and St. Paul to death.

NES′ROCH, a god of the Assyrians, in whose temple Sennacherib was slain by his own sons (4 Kings xix. 37; Isai. xxxvii. 38).

NET. The parable of the net (Matt. xiii. 47); the net is mentioned in Exodus xxvii. 4; the apostles leave their nets (Matt. iv. 18, 20; Mark i. 18); their nets breaking at the miraculous draught of fish (Luke v. 6).

NETTLES, a stinging plant (Prov. xxiv. 31; Isai. xxxiv. 13; Osee ix. 6).

NEW MOON. The Hebrew months were lunar

and began with a new moon. Sacrifices were appointed for this time (Num. xxviii. 11–15; x. 10; 1 Paral. xxiii. 31; 4 Kings iv. 23; Ezech. xlv. 17; that of the month Tizri was most solemn (Lev. xxiii. 24; Num. xxix. 1); God rejected the new moons on account of their sins (Isai. i. 14); Judith did not fast on the new moons, being holidays (Judith viii. 6).

NEW TEST′AMENT, the new covenant in the blood of our Lord, foretold (Jer. xxiii. 3); Christ the intermediator by his blood (Matt. xxvi. 28; Heb. ix. 15; xii. 24; xiii. 20). The term is used to comprise the collected canonical books since the birth of Christ, namely, the four gospels, the Acts of the Apostles, Epistles of St. Paul, St. James, St. Peter, St. John, St. Jude, and the Apocalypse.

NICA′NOR, son of Patroclus (2 Mach. viii. 9); commander of the elephants under Antiochus Epiphanes, made governor of Judea (xiv. 12); sent into Judea by Lysias (1 Mach. iii. 38, 39; 2 Mach. viii. 9, 10); but was defeated by Judas with the loss of 9,000 men (2 Mach. viii. 24); Nicanor was sent again about four years later, and endeavored to entrap Judas, but was again routed at Capharsalama (1 Mach. vii. 26–32); he threatened to destroy the temple if Judas was not given up (33–35); being reinforced, he again met Judas at Adarsa, where he was defeated and slain (39–43) 161 B. C.

NICA′NOR, one of the seven deacons appointed at Jerusalem soon after the descent of the Holy Ghost (Acts vi. 5, 6).

NICODE′MUS, a Pharisee and disciple of Christ. He is called by St. John "a ruler of the Jews" (John iii. 1); and by our Lord "a master in Israel" (iii. 10); he came to our Lord by night and was instructed by him (iii. 1–21); when the Pharisees sent ministers to arrest our Lord, Nicodemus protested against judging any one unheard (vii. 50); they asked him whether he was a Galilean (52); after our Lord's crucifixion, he took a mixture of myrrh and aloes and went with Joseph of Arimathea, took down his body, bound it with spices, and laid it in the sepulchre (xix. 39–42).

NICOLA′ITES, early heretics mentioned by St. John (Apoc. ii. 6, 15).

NIC′OLAS, a proselyte (that is, a Gentile converted to Judaism) of Antioch. He was one of the seven deacons chosen at Jerusalem after the descent of the Holy Ghost (Acts vi. 5).

NICOP'OLIS, a city of Epirus, where St. Paul passed the winter of A. D. 64, and to which city he summoned Titus (Tit. iii. 12).

NI'GER, surname of Simon, one of the prophets and doctors at Antioch (Acts xiii. 1).

NILE, the famous river of Egypt (Gen. xv. 18; 3 Kings viii. 65; 4 Kings xxiv. 7; Amos ix. 5); Isaias alludes to its fertilizing the country (xxiii. 3); Josue calls it the troubled river that watereth Egypt

THE NILE AT LUXOR.

(xiii. 3); Jeremias speaks of the troubled water of Egypt (ii. 18). The name Nile is in Isaias xxiii. 23.

NIN'IVE, a great city of Assyria, built by Assur (Gen. x. 11); it does penance at the preaching of Jonas (Jon. iii. 5); Sennacherib slain in (4 Kings xix. 36; Isai. xxxvii. 37); Nabuchodonosor reigns in (Judith i. 5); the Israelites were taken to as captives (Tob. i.); its destruction or desolation foretold (Tob. xiv. 5; Nah. i.; Soph. ii. 13); on the day of judgment it will condemn the Jews (Matt. xii. 41).

NI'SAN, one of the months of the Jewish year, called in the earlier books Abib; but Nisan in 2 Esd. ii. 1; Esther iii. 7, 12; xi. 2.

NI'TRE, an alkali mentioned (Prov. xxv. 20; Jerem. ii. 22).

NOADI'AS, a false prophet, who endeavored to thwart Nehemias (2 Esd. vi. 14).

NOBE, a priestly city. David here received from Achimelech loaves of proposition and the sword of Goliath (1 Kings xxii. 9; xxi. 1).

NO'DAB aided Ruben, Gad and Manasses against the Agarites (1 Paral. v. 19).

NO'E, son of Lamech, born 2948 B. C. (Gen. v. 28, 29); he begat Sem, Cham, and Japheth (v. 31; vi. 10); in the general wickedness, Noe found grace before the Lord (vi. 8); he was a just and perfect man, and walked with God (9); by God's command he built an ark, and entered it with his wife, his sons and their wives, and a certain number of all animals and birds (vi. 13–22; vii. 1–16); and they were preserved from the deluge which covered the whole earth (vii. 17–24); when the ark rested on the mountains of Armenia, he sent out a raven, and then a dove, but waited for God's direction to leave the ark. His first act was to build an altar, and offer a sacrifice to God (viii. 16–22); God blessed Noe, gave him certain precepts, and established a covenant with him (ix. 1–17); Noe cursed Chanaan, son of Cham, for disrespect to him when unwittingly

overcome with wine (ix. 25); he lived 350 years after the flood, and died at the age of 950 (28, 29); St. Peter calls him a preacher of divine justice (2 Pet. ii. 5); and the son of Sirach praises him (Ecclus. xliv. 17).

NOE'MA, sister of Tubalcain; is one of the four antediluvian women mentioned by name (Gen. iv. 22).

NOE'MI, a Moabitess, widow of Elimelech, and mother-in-law of Ruth (Ruth i. 2–iv. 17).

NOHEST'A, daughter of Elnathan, wife of king Joachim, and mother of king Joachin (4 Kings xxiv. 8).

NOHEST'AN, the name given in the days of king Ezechias to the brasen serpent made by Moses (Num. xxi. 8), and which he destroyed, as it was worshipped (4 Kings xviii. 4).

NO'PHE, a city of the Moabites (Num. xxi. 30).

NO'PHETH, a province (Jos. xvii. 11).

NORTH, a Jewish priest making offerings was required to face the north (Lev. i. 11).

NOV'ELTY. We are to fly novelty, and adhere to the doctrine of the elders (Prov. xxii. 28; Ecclus. viii. 11; Jer. vi. 16; Rom. xvi. 17; Gal. i. 6–8; 1 Tim. vi. 20; 2 Tim. iv. 3; 2 Pet. iii. 17; 1 John ii. 24; 2 John 7; Jude 17–20).

NUM'BERING AND GENEALOGY of the descendants of Adam (Gen. v. 1); of the descendants of Sem, Cham and Japheth (x. 1); of Nachor (xxii. 20); of Abraham by Cetura (xxv. 1); of Ismael (xxv. 12–17); of Jacob and his sons when he went to Egypt (xlvi. 8); of the Israelites in Egypt (Ex. i. 1); of the princes of Israel (vi. 14); of the articles intended for the worship of God (xxxix.); of men able to bear arms (Num. i. 1–46); of the tribe of Levi (iii. 1; iv. 2; xxvi. 57); of the heads of families at Mount Sinai (x. 13); of men twenty years old and over (xxvi. 4); of booty taken (xxxi. 26); of kings conquered by the people of God (Jos. xii. 1); of cities captured (xv.); the numbering of the people by David is punished by God (2 Kings xxiv.; 1 Paral. xxi. 5); of Asa's officers and troops (2 Paral. xiv. 8); of the people of the kingdom of Juda carried captive to Babylon (4 Kings xxiv. 14–16; xxv. 11; 2 Paral. xxxvi. 20); of those who returned from Babylon to Jerusalem under Cyrus (1 Esd. ii. 1–62); of those with Esdras under Artaxerxes (viii. 1–16); of those who married heathen women (x. 17, 44); of those who rebuilt the walls of Jerusalem (2 Esd. iii. 1); of those who returned with Zorobabel (vii. 6); of those who renewed the covenant (ix. 1); of those who settled in Jerusalem (xi. 3); a census of all nations under the Roman sway ordered by Augustus (Luke ii. 2); mysterious numbering of the elect (Apoc. vii. 4–8).

NUM'BERS, canonical book of the Old Testament, one of the five books of Moses (Num.)

NUNC DIMITTIS, the canticle of the holy old man Simeon in the temple at the Presentation of our Lord (Luke ii. 29).

OAK OF WEEPING. Debora, nurse of Rebecca, buried under it (Gen. xxxv. 8); Josue renews the covenant of the people with God under the oak of Sichem (Jos. xxiv. 26); the oak of Basan (Ezech. xxvii. 6).

OATH. Covenant between Isaac and Abimelech bound by oath (Gen. xxvi. 31); the force of an oath (Ex. xxii. 11; Lev. v. 4; vi. 3; Num. xxx. 3; Deut. i. 35; vii. 8; Jos. ii. 17; vi. 22). The oath of the children of Israel at Maspha (Judg. xxi. 1, 18); the breaking of an oath punished (3 Kings viii. 31).

O'BED, son of Booz and Ruth, and grandfather of David (Ruth iv. 21, 22); one of the ancestors of our Lord (Matt. i. 5).

OBED'EDOM, son of Idithun, a Levite (1 Paral. xvi. 38); after the death of Oza, David placed the Ark of the Covenant in the house of Obededom (2 Kings vi. 10–12; 1 Paral. xiii. 13); God blessed him with a numerous family (1 Paral. xxvi. 4); Obededom and his sons were appointed doorkeepers of the temple (1 Paral. xv. 18, 21).

OBE'DIENCE to God rewarded (Gen. xii. 4; xvii. 9; xxvi. 5; Ex. i. 17; xix. 5; xx. 6; xxiii. 22, 25; Lev. xx. 22; xxvi. 3; Deut. iv. 40; vii.; xi.; xiii. 4; xvii. 19; xviii. 15; xxiv. 8; xxvii. 10; xxviii. 1, 12; Jos. xxi. 43; 1 Kings xii. 14; 4 Kings x. 30; 2 Paral. vii. 17; Prov. i. 8, 33; xv. 31; Ecclus. xxxv. 7; Isai. i. 19; xlviii. 18; lv. 2; Jer. vii. 23; xi. 4; xvii. 24; xxxv.; Dan. iii.; 2 Mach. viii. 30; Matt. iv. 19; vii. 24; viii. 21; xv. 3; Luke v. 4; x. 16; John ii. 7; Acts iv. 19; v. 29; Rom. xvi. 19; Phil. ii. 8, 12; 1 Thess. iv. 1; 1 Pet. i. 14; Jam. i. 22).

OBE'DIENCE to superiors (Prov. xxi. 28; xxv. 12; Ecclus. iii. 7; Rom. i. 30; Eph. vi. 1, 5; Coloss. iii. 20, 22; 2 Tim. iii. 2; Heb. xiii. 17). Our Lord's example (Luke ii. 51; Phil. ii. 8).

O'BOL, the twentieth part of the sicle (Ex. xxx. 13).

O'BOTH, one of the encampments of the Israelites in the desert (Num. xxi. 10; xxxiii. 43).

OCHO'ZATH, friend of Abimelech, who accompanied him to Isaac (Gen. xxvi. 26).

OCHOZI'AS, king of Juda, son of Joram and Athalia, began to reign 885 B. C., at the age of twenty-two (4 Kings viii. 24) or forty-two (2 Paral. xxii. 2); he was a wicked prince; he joined Joram, king of Israel, in a war against Syria. Joram was wounded in battle, and Ochozias visited him at Jezrahel, when Jehu approached. They went to meet him, and Jehu shot Joram with an arrow. Ochozias fled, but was struck by Jehu's servants and died at Mageddo (4 Kings ix. 21–27; 2 Paral. xxii. 9); Athalia, his mother, killed all his sons but one, and Jehu slew all his brothers' sons (8, 10).

OCHOZI'AS, son of Achab, king of Israel (3 Kings xxii. 40); he served Baal (54); he and Josaphat, king of Juda, built ships in Asiongaber to go to Tharsis (2 Paral. xx. 36); he fell through the lattices of his upper chamber, and sent to consult Beelzebub, the god of Accaron, whether he should recover (4 Kings i. 2); Elias met the messengers and told them that he should die (4); then Ochozias twice sent officers and soldiers, but they were destroyed by fire (9–12); a third officer begged the prophet to spare his life and go with him. Elias went to Ochozias and told him he was to die, and he did, 896 B. C. (13–16).

O'DED, a prophet of the Lord. When Phacee, king of Israel, had slain 120,000 of the people of Juda, and carried away 200,000 as captives to Samaria, Oded reproached him with his cruelty, urged them to release the captives. Some of the chief men of Israel seconded him, and the captives were released and clothed and taken back to Jericho, 741 B. C. (2 Paral. xxviii. 6–15).

ODOL'LAM, ODULLAM, the king of Odullam was slain by Josue (Jos. xii. 15); and David fled to the cave of Odollam (1 Kings xxii. 1).

OF'FERINGS of Cain and Abel (Gen. iv. 3, 4); of Noe (viii. 20); of Melchisedech (xiv. 18); sin offerings (Ex. xxix. 36); the evening and morning offerings (39, 41; xxx. 7, 8, 20; Num. xxviii. 3–8); offerings made by the people to construct the tabernacle, the Ark of the Covenant, etc. (Ex. xxv. 2, 3; xxx. 12, 16; xxxv. 5–9; Lev. i. 2–15; ii. 1–13; iii. 3–8; iv. 3–28; v. 6–18; vi. 6–26; vii. 3–38; viii. 14, 22; ix. 7–18; xii.; xv.; Num. vii.; xviii.; Deut. xii.; Jos. viii. 31; xii.)

OG, king of Basan; he was the last of the race of giants, his iron bed long preserved in Rabbath measuring nine cubits long and four broad (Deut. iii. 11). When the Israelites had conquered the Amorrhites, Og marched with all his people to Edrai, but Moses defeated him, slaying him, his sons, and his people (Num. xxi. 33–35; Deut. xxix. 7; xxxi. 4; Ps. cxxxv. 20).

O'HAM, king of Hebron, one of the five who besieged Gabaon; he was defeated, taken, and hanged by Josue (Jos. x. 3–26).

OIL, the purest and clearest oil of olives was to be burned in the sanctuary (Ex. xxvii. 20; Lev. xxiv. 2); oil was used in anointing and consecrating (Ex. xxx. 24; Ex. xl. 11; Lev. viii. 2, 10; xiv. 26); the prophet Elias by a miracle causes the cruse of oil of the widow of Sarephta not to be diminished (3 Kings xvii. 14); Eliseus multiplies the oil of the widow of the prophet (4 Kings iv. 4); in the sacrament of extreme unction, the sick are anointed with oil in the name of the Lord (James v. 14).

OIL OF UNCTION, divine injunctions as to its importance, and the manner of making it (Ex. xxix. 7, 21; xxx. 25, 31; xxxi. 11; xxxv. 15; xl. 9, 11; Lev. viii. 2, 10; x. 7; xxi. 10, 12; Num. iv. 16).

OLIVE FRUIT.

OINT'MENT, use of among the Jews (Ex. xxv., xxx., xxxv., xxxvii., xxxix.; 4 Kings xx. 13; 1 Paral. ix. 30; Judith xvi. 10; Esth. xiv. 2; Ps. cxxxii. 2; Eccles. vii. 2; Ezech. xxiii. 41; Cant. i. 2; Dan. x. 3; Amos vi. 6; Matt. xxvi. 7, 12; Mark xiv. 3; Luke vii. 37; John xi. 2; xii. 3).

OLD MAN. The old man—meaning our sinful life—to be put away (Eph. iv. 22; Col. iii. 9); to be crucified with Christ (Rom. vi. 6).

OL'IVE. The dove let out by Noe brings him a branch of olive (Gen. viii. 11); our Lord on the Mount of Olives (John xviii. 1); the church compared to an olive tree (Rom. xi. 17, 24). See OIL.

OL'IVET. Mount Olivet, or of Olives, the scene of the agony of our Lord, and his betrayal, and his seizure by his enemies (Zach. xiv. 4; Matt. xxi. 1; xxiv. 3; xxvi. 30; Mark xi. 1; xiii. 3; Luke xxii. 39; John viii. 1).

OLYM'PIAS, one of the early Christians saluted by St. Paul (Rom. xvi. 15).

OLYM'PIAN JOVE, a deity of Greece and Rome. His statue set up in the temple of Jerusalem by Antiochus Epiphanes (2 Mach. vi. 2; 1 Mach. i. 62), where it remained three years, till Judas Machabeus restored the worship of God, 161 B. C. This idol was the abomination of desolation spoken of by Daniel (ix. 27).

O'MAR, second son of Eliphas, and grandson of Esau (Gen. xxxvi. 11, 15).

ONES'IMUS, a Phrygian, slave to Philemon, and subsequently a disciple of St. Paul, who converted him, and sent him back to his master (Philem. 10); he was sent to Colosse (Col. iv. 9).

ONESIPH'ORUS, served the church greatly in Asia, and came to Rome in the year 65, where he found St. Paul in prison and almost forsaken, and relieved him to the best of his power (2 Tim. i. 16–18).

ONI'AS, high-priest of the Jews to whom Arius, king of the Spartans, wrote a letter (1 Mach. xii. 20).

ONI'AS, high-priest of the Jews when Heliodorus was sent by Seleucus to plunder the temple, but was chastised by an angel. He recovered by the prayers of Onias (2 Mach. iii. 1–40); Simon, of the tribe of Benjamin, accused him as a traitor (iv. 2), but Onias went to Antioch and justified himself (4, 5); his brother Jason induced Antiochus, the Illustrious, by money to confer the high-priesthood on him, and did all in his power to introduce idolatry (7–22), till he was set aside for Menelaus, the brother of Simon. That wicked man sold the sacred vessels of the temple, and Onias who was at Antioch rebuked him. Andronicus, at the instigation of Menelaus, lured Onias from his sanctuary by a false oath and slew him (23–34). Antiochus mourned his death and punished his murderer (37, 38); his eulogy (2 Mach. iii. 1, 2.)

ON'YCHA, an aromatic (Ex. xxx. 34); said to be a sea-shell.

ON'YX, a precious stone. There was one in the fourth row on the rational of judgment (Ex. xxviii. 20).

OXEN TREADING OUT CORN.

OO'LIAB, son of Achisamech, of the tribe of Dan, appointed with Beseleel to manufacture the tabernacle and its contents (Ex. xxxv. 34).

OOL'IBA and **OOLLA,** names employed in Ezechiel to represent the kingdoms of Jerusalem or Juda, and Samaria or Israel (Ezech. xxiii. 4).

OOLIBA'MA, wife of Esau, and daughter of Ana, a Horrite (Gen. xxxvi. 18); she is called Judith (xxvi. 34); she bore three sons, Jehus, Ihelon, and Core (xxxvi. 18). Two of her descendants (xxxvi. 25), one of them a duke of Edom, bore the same name (41; 1 Paral. i. 52).

O'PHEL. The wall of Ophel was part of the walls of Jerusalem. Joathan built much on it (2 Paral. xxvii. 3); Manasses built a wall from the Fishgate to Ophel (xxxiii. 14); after the return from Babylon, the Nathinites dwelt there (2 Esd. iii. 26; xi. 21).

O'PHER, second son of Madian, and grandson of Abraham and Cetura (Gen. xxv. 4).

O'PHER, a city, whose king was slain by Josue (Jos. xii. 17).

OPHIO'MACHUS, a kind of edible locust (Lev. xi. 22).

O'PHIR, one of the sons of Jectan (Gen. x. 29; 1 Paral. i. 23).

O'PHIR, a port or region from which the Jews in the days of Solomon received gold and thyine wood (3 Kings ix. 28; x. 11; xxii. 49; 1 Paral. xxix. 4; 2 Paral. viii. 18; ix. 10).

OPH'NI and **PHINEES,** sons of Heli, the high-priest, called children of Belial, that is, wicked men (1 Kings ii. 12); they robbed the sacrifices (13–17), and committed sins of impurity in the very temple (22); Heli rebuked, but feebly (23–25); their death foretold (34); both killed in battle by the Philistines (iv. 4, 11, 17).

OR'ACLE, the propitiatory on the Ark of the Covenant (Ex. xxv. 18, 20; xxxvii. 6; xl. 18; Lev.

xvi. 2, 13, 15); in Solomon's temple the term is applied to the inner temple, or holy of holies (3 Kings vi. 5–31; vii. 49; viii. 6, 8; 2 Paral. iii. 6; iv. 20; v. 7, 9). Moses consulted the oracle and God answered him from the propitiatory (Num. vii. 89); David consulted the oracle (2 Kings xxi. 1).

OR'DERS, a sacrament (Luke xxii. 19; John xx. 22; 1 Tim. iv. 14; v. 22; 2 Tim. i. 6; Tit. i. 5).

OR'DINA'TION of priests in the primitive church one of the cares of the apostles (Acts xiv. 22).

O'REB and **ZEB**, princes of the Madianites. They were taken by the tribe of Ephraim at the fords of the Jordan, while fleeing from Gedeon, and put to death, 1245 B. C. (Judg. vii. 24, 25).

O'RIENT, one of the names of the Messias (Zach. vi. 12; Luke i. 78).

ORIG'INAL SIN, the sin of Adam and Eve

xxii. 9; xxxi. 17; Prov. xxiii. 10; Isai. i. 17, 23; James i. 27). They are under the protection of God (Ps. ix. 14, 18; lxvii. 6; cxlv. 9; Prov. xxiii. 10).

ORTHO'SIAS, a sea-port in Phœnicia to which Tryphon fled (1 Mach. xv. 37).

OR'YX, an animal mentioned (Deut. xiv. 5; Isai. li. 20); correctly translated in the Douay, but Challoner introduced "wild goat" and "wild ox" from the King James.

O'SEE, the original name of Josue (Num. xiii. 9, 17).

O'SEE, son of Beeri, the first of the twelve minor prophets. He prophesied in the kingdom of Israel, in the reign of Jeroboam II., while Ozias, Joathan, Achaz and Ezechias reigned in Juda. He denounced the idolatry and vice of the ten tribes, and foretold their captivity.

Caleb promised his daughter Axa to the man who took Cariathsepher. Othoniel undertook it and succeeded, 1445 B. C. (Jos. xv. 15–17). After Josue's death, the Israelites fell for eight years under the sway of Chusan Rasathaim, king of Mesopotamia, but Othoniel defeated him, and delivered Israel, which enjoyed peace for forty years (Judg. iii. 8–11).

OVERREACHING or **CIRCUMVENTING** in business forbidden (1 Thes. iv. 6).

OWL, a nocturnal bird, classed as unclean (Lev. xi. 16, 17; Deut. xiv. 15).

OX, OXEN (Gen. xii. 16; xx. 14; xxi. 27, etc.); ox treading out the corn not to be muzzled (Deut. xxv. 4); an ox goring a man to be put to death (Ex. xxi. 28–31); the theft of an ox (xxii. 1); to rest on the Sabbath (xxiii. 12); cut in pieces by Samuel and sent to the tribes (1 Kings xi. 7); sacrifices of (Levit. i. 2; iii. 1; xxii. 19; Num. vii. 23; 2 Kings vi. 13; 3 Kings viii. 63; xviii. 23).

O'ZA, son of Abinadab, drives the cart containing the Ark of the Covenant (2 Kings vi. 3); takes hold of it at the floor of Nachon (6); struck dead (7); the place called the "Striking of Oza" (8).

O'ZI, son of Bocci, high-priest (1 Paral. vi. 5; 1 Esd. vii. 4).

OZI'AS, king of Juda, called also Azarias (4 Kings xv. 1); son of Amasias and Jechelia (2 Paral. xxvi. 1, 3; Matt. i. 9); ascended the throne at the age of sixteen, 900 B. C., and reigned fifty-two years (1 Paral. xxvi. 3); he built Ailath (2), and towers in Jerusalem and the wilderness (9, 10); and towns in the Philistine country (6); he defeated the Philistines, Arabians and Ammonites (7); encouraged agriculture (10); sought the Lord in the days of Zacharias (5); but, under Azarias, attempted to offer incense in the temple

THE ORACLE OR PROPITIATORY ON THE ARK OF THE COVENANT.

in eating the forbidden fruit (Gen. iii. 6); by reason of it all men are conceived in sin (Job xiv. 4; Ps. l. 7; Rom. v. 12; 1 Cor. xv. 21; Eph. ii. 3); Jeremias sanctified in his mother's womb (Jer. i. 5); St. John the Baptist (Luke i. 41, 44); Mary, mother of God, alone being conceived without sin (Gen. iii. 15).

ORI'ON, a constellation mentioned by Job (Job ix. 9); and by Amos (v. 8).

OR'NAN, the Jebusite, owned the threshing-floor over which the angel appeared threatening Jerusalem for David's sin in numbering the people (1 Paral. xxi. 15–26); David bought the spot, and as directed by God, erected an altar there, and offered a sacrifice (2 Kings xxiv. 24). Ornan is also called Areuna. The site was afterwards taken for Solomon's temple.

ORONA'IM, a place in Moab (Isai. xv. 5).

OR'PHA, a Moabitess, wife of Chelion, son of Elimelech and Noemi (Ruth i. 4); she remained in the land of Moab (14).

OR'PHANS, to be cared for as a work of mercy (Ex. xxii. 22; Deut. x. 18; xxiv. 17; xxvii. 19; Job

O'SEE, one of the canonical books of the Old Testament, containing the prophecies of Osee (Os.)

O'SEE, son of Ela. He conspired against Phacee, son of Romelia, killed him, and made himself king of Israel, 739 B. C. (4 Kings xv. 30); he was wicked, but not one of the worst (4 Kings xvii.); he sought the aid of Sua, king of Egypt, to throw off the Assyrian yoke, but Salmanasar, after three years' siege, took Samaria, slaughtered the people, and destroyed the city (Osee xiv. 1; Mich. i. 6); the ten tribes were then carried captive to Assyria.

OS'PREY, a bird of prey, forbidden as unclean (Lev. xi. 13; Deut. xiv. 12).

OS'TRICH, a tall bird of the desert, forbidden as unclean (Lev. xi. 16; Deut. xiv. 15). The King James erroneously translates it owl. It is referred to as dwelling in deserts (Job xxx. 29; Isai. xxxiv. 13; xliii. 20); her mode of laying her eggs in the sand and her speed are mentioned (Job xxxix. 13–18); (King James has peacock) (Lam. iv. 3).

OTHO'NIEL, son of Cenez, of the tribe of Juda.

and was struck with leprosy and remained so till death, dwelling apart, his son Joatham being regent (4 Kings xv. 5; 2 Paral. xxvi. 4, 16–22); he was buried in the field of the royal sepulchres (23); he is reproached also with not abolishing the high-places (4 Kings xv. 4).

OZI'AS, son of Micha, prince of Juda (Judith viii. 34), and one of the ancients of Bethulia, receives Achior (Judith vi. 19); is rebuked by Judith for setting a time as a limit to God's mercy (viii. 10–27); he approves her plan (28–34); he praises her for her courageous act in killing Holofernes (xiii. 23–25).

O'ZIEL, son of Caath and grandson of Levi (Ex. vi. 18); he was brother to Amram, father of Moses and Aaron (20); his sons were Misael, Elisaphan and Sethri (22); his descendants (Num. iii. 27; 1 Paral. vi. 2).

PAINT'ING the eyes with stibic stone (kohl), a practice among Oriental women (4 Kings ix. 30; Jer. iv. 30; Ezech. xxiii. 40). Some editions of

Challoner have incorrectly "paint the *face*," instead of "the *eyes*," an error adopted from King James.

PAINT'INGS on the walls among the Chaldeans (Ezech. xxiii. 14).

PAL'ACE OF KING SOLOMON, built in thirteen years (3 Kings vii. 1; ix. 10; x. 4); with a second or inner palace called "the house of the forest of Libanus" (vii. 2–12).

PAL'ESTINE, the country of the Palestines or Philistines (Jerem. xlvii. 1).

PAL'ESTINES, people of Palestine or Philistines (Gen. xxi. 33, 34; xxvi.; Ex. xxiii. 31; Amos ix. 7); the Sea of the Palestines (Ex. xxiii. 31).

PALM-TREE OF DEBBORA, where that prophetess judged Israel, between Rama and Bethel, in the mountains of Ephraim (Judg. iv. 5); the just man compared to a palm-tree (Ps. xci. 13); wisdom compared to (Ecclus. xxiv. 18).

PALM-TREES. The children of Israel encamped at Elim, where there were seventy palm-trees (Ex. xv. 27; Num. xxxiii. 9); Jericho called the city of the Palms (Deut. xxxiv. 3; Judg. i. 16; iii. 13; 2 Paral. xxviii. 15); in the decorations of Solomon's temple (3 Kings vi., vii.); in Ezechiel's (Ezech. xl., xli.); branches of palms borne as a sign of joy, and used in the Feast of Tabernacles (2 Esd. viii. 15; 1 Mach. xiii. 51; 2 Mach. x. 7; xiv. 4); the people of Jerusalem receive our Lord with branches of palms (John xii. 13); the elect seen by St. John with palms in their hands (Apoc. vii. 9).

PALM'ER-WORM (Joel i. 4; ii. 25; Amos iv. 9).

PALMI'RA, or **PALMYRA,** a city in the wilderness built by Solomon (3 Kings ix. 18; 2 Paral. viii. 4). It was in a desert on the confines of Arabia Deserta. It was called Tadmor in Hebrew.

PAL'SY, a disease. Our Lord cured several afflicted with it (Matt. iv. 24; viii. 6; ix. 2; Mark ii. 3; Luke v. 18); the apostle cures several in Samaria (Acts viii. 8); St. Peter cures Eneas (ix. 33).

PAMPHYL'IA, a province in Asia Minor, west of Cilicia and bordering on the Mediterranean (1 Mach. xv. 23); St. Paul and St. Barnabas preached in Pamphylia (Acts xiii. 13; xiv. 23); John Mark left them in Pamphylia (xv. 38); the sea of Pamphylia (xxvii. 5).

PA'PER. The term is used in Tob. vii. 16, 2 John 12, and was writing material made of papyrus or some similar substance.

PA'PHOS, in Cyprus. St. Paul there struck Elymas blind and converted Sergius Paulus (Acts xiii. 7–12).

PAR'ABLES. Apologues used to convey instruction. In the Old Testament: Balaam's (Num. xxiii. 18; xxiv. 5); Joatham's parable of the trees electing a king (Judg. ix. 7–15); Nathan's parable of the one ewe lamb (2 Kings xii. 1–4); that of the woman of Thecua (2 Kings xiv. 5–7); that of the prophet to Achab (3 Kings xx. 39); that of the thistle and the cedar (4 Kings xiv. 9); Isaias' parable of the vineyard (Isai. v. 1–6); Solomon composed three thousand (3 Kings iv. 32).

PAR'ABLES OF OUR LORD. That of the house built on the rock and the house built on sand (Matt. vii. 24; Luke vi. 48); that of the unclean spirit (Matt. xii. 43); the parable of the sower (Matt. xiii. 3; Mark iv. 1; Luke viii. 5); the parable of the good seed and the cockle (Matt. xiii. 24); the kingdom of heaven likened to a mustard-seed (Matt. xiii. 31; Mark iv. 31); to leaven (Matt. xiii. 33); to a hidden treasure (44); to a pearl of great price (45);

to a net (47); the parable of the blind leading the blind (Matt. xv. 14; Luke vi. 39); the parable of the lost sheep (Matt. xviii. 12; Luke xv. 4); the parable of the unforgiving servant (Matt. xviii. 23); the parable of the laborers in the vineyard (Matt. xx. 1–16); the parable of the two sons (Matt. xxi. 28–30); the parable of the husbandmen (xxi. 33–41); the parable of the King's marriage-feast for his son (Matt. xxii. 2–14; Luke xiv. 16); the parable of the evil servant (Matt. xxiv. 43–51; Luke xii. 37); parable of the wise and the foolish virgins (Matt. xxv. 1–12); the parable of the talents (Matt. xxv. 14–30; Luke xix. 12–27); the parable of the vineyard and the husbandmen (Mark xii. 1–10; Luke xx. 9–16); the parable of the Good Samaritan (Luke x. 30–37); the parable of the importunate friend (Luke xi. 5–9); the parable of the rich man taken suddenly away (Luke xii. 16–21); the parable of the great supper (Luke xiv. 16–24); parable of the lost groat (Luke xv. 8, 9); the parable of the prodigal son (Luke xv. 11–32); the parable of the unjust steward (Luke xvi. 1–9); parable of the rich man and Lazarus (Luke xvi. 19–31); parable of the unprofitable servants (Luke xvii. 7–10); parable of the unjust judge (Luke xviii. 2–7); the parable of the Pharisee and the publican (Luke xviii. 10–14).

PAR'ACLETE', a Greek word meaning comforter, applied by our Lord to the Holy Ghost (John xiv. 16, 26; xv. 26; xvi. 7).

PAR'ADISE OF PLEASURE, God places man in (Gen. ii. 8); casts Adam and Eve from it (iii. 23, 24); a heavenly paradise promised (Luke xxiii. 43); called by St. Paul the third heaven (2 Cor. xii. 2, 4).

PARALIPOM'ENON or **CHRONICLES,** two canonical books of the Old Testament, being a supplement to the books of Kings (1 Paral., 2 Paral.)

PAR'ASCEVE', a Greek word meaning preparation, and applied by the Jews to Friday as the day when preparation was made for the Sabbath. Our Lord was crucified on the parasceve of the Pasch (John xix. 11, 31, 41); and St. Matthew calls the next day the day that followed the day of preparation or Parasceve (Matt. xxvii. 62).

PARCH'MENT. Skin dressed for writing material. St. Paul refers to his parchments (2 Tim. iv. 13).

PAR'DON. We are to pardon those who sin against us (Ecclus. xxviii. 8; Matt. v. 23; xviii. 22, 35; Luke xvii. 3; Eph. iv. 32).

PA'RENTS. The duties of parents to their children declared (Gen. xviii. 19; xxi. 19; xxiv. 2; xxv. 6; xxxiv. 4, 30; xlix. 2; Ex. x. 2; xii. 26; xiii. 14; xxi. 9; Lev. xix. 29; Num. xxx. 6; Deut. iv. 9; vi. 7, 20; xi. 19; xxi. 18; xxii. 15, 19; xxxii. 46; Jos. iv. 21; 1 Kings ii. 23; iii. 13; 3 Kings ii. 1; Tob. i. 10; iv.; x. 13; xiv. 5, 12; Job i. 5; Ps. lxxvii. 5; Prov. i. 8; iv. 1; v. 7; xiii. 1, 24; xix. 18; xx.

7; xxii. 6, 15; xxiii. 13; xxix. 17; Ecclus. iv. 23; vii. 25; viii. 11; xvi. 1; xxv. 10; xxvi. 13; xxx. 1, 11; xxxiii. 22; xlii. 5; Dan. xiii. 3; 1 Mach. ii. 49, 64; 2 Mach. vi. 24, 28; vii. 1–41; Matt. x. 37; Eph. vi. 4; Col. iii. 21; 2 Tim. iii. 15; Tit. ii. 4).

PAR'MENAS, one of the first deacons appointed by the apostles (Acts vi. 5).

PAR'OS. David prepared a great quantity of marble of Paros for the building of the temple (1 Paral. xxix. 2).

PARTH'IANS, people of ancient Persia, mentioned in Acts ii. 9.

PAR'TRIDGE, hatches eggs she does not lay (Jerem. xvii. 11); hunted in the mountains (1 Kings xxvi. 20); caged (Ecclus. xi. 32).

PASCH, a Hebrew word meaning passage, and applied to the greatest holiday of the Jews, instituted to commemorate their deliverance from Egypt when the angel of death passed over their houses sparing their first-born. Its institution, and the eating of the paschal lamb (Ex. xii. 43; xxiii. 15; Lev. xxiii. 5;

THE PALMER-WORM.

Ezech. xlv. 21); it was kept on the tenth day of the first month of the Jewish year (Ex. xii. 18); it was celebrated in the desert (Num. ix. 2–5); regulation as to those unable to eat it from uncleanness (10–12); penalty on those who wilfully neglect it (13); the Pasch kept at Galgal (Jos. v. 10); in the time of Josias, king of Juda (4 Kings xxiii. 21); in the time of king Ezechias (2 Paral. xxx. 1–27); in the time of Esdras (1 Esd. vi. 19); the Pasch celebrated by our Lord, the first time (John ii. 13); the second (v. 1); the third (vi. 4); the last (Matt. xxvi. 17).

PAS'CHAL LAMB, directions as to the mode of eating (Ex. xii. 7–11); it was a figure of our Lord (John i. 36; Apoc. v. 6; xxi. 9, 14, 22, 27; xxii. 3, 14).

PAS'SION, a term applied to the sufferings of our Lord. His passion was foretold by Isaias (Isai. lii. 14; liii.; lxiii. 1–6); foretold by himself (Matt. xx. 18, 19; Mark xiv. 18, 21, 27; Luke ix. 22; xxii. 15, 21, 22; John xiii. 21); passion according to St.

Matthew (Matt. xxvi., xxvii.); according to St. Mark (Mark xiv., xv.); according to St. Luke (Luke xxii., xxiii.); according to St. John (John xviii., xix.)

PAS'TORS. Duties of pastors, teachers, and other superiors, their authority (Ex. xviii. 13; Lev. xxiv. 22; Num. xi. 16, 24; xxv. 4; Deut. i. 13, 17; x. 1; xiii. 1; xvii. 9; xviii. 8; xix. 11; Acts xx. 28, 31; Rom. ix. 3; xii. 8; xiii. 1; 1 Cor. iv. 14; 2 Cor. xi. 28, 29; Tit. ii. 1; iii. 1; Heb. xiii. 17; 1 Pet. ii. 13).

PA'TIENCE OF GOD towards men (Gen. vi. 3; Ex. xxxiv. 6; Num. xiv. 18; Ps. lxxxv. 15; cii. 8;

THE COUNTRIES Embraced within the **TRAVELS OF ST. PAUL**

Jos. i. 10; 1 Kings viii. 11; 3 Kings iii. 9; 2 Paral. xix. 6; Ps. lxxxi.; Prov. xx. 8; xxvii. 24; xxix. 4; 14; xxxi. 4; Wisd. i. 1; vi.; Ecclus. vii. 6; x. 1, 24; Isai. i. 23, 26; x. 1; xxxii. 1; Jerem. xxii. 2; xxvii.; Ezech. xxii. 6, 12; xxxiv. 4; xlv. 9; Osee xiii. 10; Mich. iii. 9; Matt. xviii. 12; xxii. 21; xxiv. 45; John

cxliv. 8; Eccles. viii. 12; Wisd. xi. 24; xv. 1; Isai. xxx. 18; Joel ii. 13; Jon. iv. 2; Nah. i. 3; Matt. xviii. 27; Rom. ii. 4; 1 Tim. i. 16; 2 Pet. iii. 9).

PA'TIENCE IN AFFLICTIONS (Gen. xl., xli.; Job ii. 9; vii. 2; Prov. xv. 18; xvi. 32; xxv. 15; Ecclus. i. 29; Tob. ii. 12; Matt. v. 39; Rom. v.

3; xii. 12; xv. 4; 2 Cor. vi. 4; Gal. v. 22; Eph. iv. 2; 1 Thess. v. 14; 1 Tim. vi. 11; 1 Peter ii. 20; 2 Pet. i. 6; Heb. xi. 25; James v. 7).

PA'TRIARCHS. This name is applied to the heads of families before the time of Moses, who worshipped the true God: Adam, Lamech, Noe, Sem, Phaleg, Heber, Abraham, Isaac, Jacob and his twelve sons. (See 1 Paral. viii. 28; Tob. vi. 20; Acts ii. 29; vii. 8, 9; Heb. vii. 4).

PATRO'BAS, a Christian of Rome, saluted by St. Paul (Rom. xvi. 14).

PAUL, ST., apostle of the Gentiles. His original name was Saul (Acts vii. 59; ix. 1; xiii. 1); he was of the tribe of Benjamin (Rom. xi. 1; Phil. iii. 5), born at Tarsus in Cilicia, and a Roman citizen by birth (Acts xxii. 3, 28); he was a Pharisee, brought up at the feet of Gamaliel (Acts xxii. 3); at first a fierce persecutor of the church at Jerusalem, dragging away men and women to prison (Acts viii. 3; xxii. 4); he obtained of the high-priest letters to Damascus to do the same there (ix. 2; xxii. 5); near Damascus he was surrounded by a bright light, and fell to the ground, when our Lord asked him, "Why persecutest thou me?" He asked, "Who art thou, Lord?" and was answered, "I am Jesus, whom thou persecutest." He at once yielded to grace, and was led blind to Damascus (ix. 4–9); Ananias, warned supernaturally, went to him, restored his sight, and baptized him (10–18; xxii. 6–16); he preached at Damascus, visiting Arabia for a time (Gal. i. 17), till the Jews sought his life, when he was let down from the wall in a basket, and he returned to Jerusalem (Acts ix. 20–26; 2 Cor. xi. 33); he labored there among Jews and Gentiles, till he received while in a trance in the temple a special call to the Gentiles (Acts xxii. 21; Rom. xi. 13; xv. 16; Gal. ii. 2, 8; 2 Tim. i. 11); he was then sent to Tarsus, by way of Cesarea (Acts ix. 30); St. Barnabas took him from Tarsus to Antioch, where they converted so many that the disciples were first called Christians (Acts xi. 25, 26); they took the alms of the faithful to Jerusalem in the time of famine (30); the Holy Ghost renews his vocation to the Gentiles (xiii. 2, 4), and he with Barnabas went to Seleucia, and then to Cyprus (4); there he struck blind Elymas, or Barjesu, a magician, who diverted people at Paphos, from the faith (6–11); converted the proconsul Sergius Paulus (7–12); from this time he is called Paul (xiii. 9, 13); he then preached in Perge, in Pamphylia (13), at Antioch, in Pisidia (14–50), at Iconium (xiii. 51–xiv. 5), at Lystra, where he cured a cripple, and where Sts. Barnabas and Paul were taken for Jupiter and Mercury, but where St. Paul was soon after stoned (6–18); at Derbe (19); thence they returned to Perge, and by way of Attalia to Antioch (20–25); they go to Jerusalem to consult the apostles on questions that had arisen (xv. 2); return with the decision of the council of Jerusalem (22, 30); St. Paul and St. Barnabas then separated, St. Paul visiting the churches in Syria and Cilicia to enforce the decree of the council (xv. 41; xvi. 4); at Derbe took Timothy as his associate (xvi. 1–3), and preached in Phrygia, Galatia, and Mysia (xvi. 6, 7); at Troas he was called in a vision to Macedonia (9), and sailed to Samothracia, Neapolis, Philippi (11, 12); converts Lydia (14); delivers a girl from an evil spirit (16–18); he and Silas condemned to be beaten and cast into prison; an earthquake followed, and the keeper was converted; set free by the magistrates (22–40); preaches at Thessalonica, Berea, and at Athens, in the midst of the Areopagus, converting Dionysius and Damaris (xvii.); preaches at Corinth, residing with Aquila and Priscilla a year and a half (xviii. 1–11); brought before the proconsul Gallio (12–16); Paul then sailed to Syria, went to Ephesus, Ceserea, and Jerusalem to fulfil a vow (18–22); then to Antioch, Galatia, and Phrygia (23); miracles wrought by him in Ephesus (xix. 11, 12); sends Timothy and Erastus to Macedonia (xix. 22); paganism declines so that Demetrius raises a riot against him (23–40); preaches at Troas, and restores Eutychus to life (xx. 6–12); returns to Jerusalem by way of Assos, Mitylene, Samos, and Miletus, whence he sent for the ancients of the church of Ephesus (13–17); his address to them (18–35); then by way of Coos, Tyre, Ptolemais (xxi. 1–7); stays with St. Philip, the evangelist, one of the seven deacons at Ceserea (8), and is warned by Agabus, the prophet, of his coming imprisonment (10–14); reports to St. James the result of his missions (18); goes to the temple with four men who had a vow on them (26); seized and dragged out of the temple and beaten, but is rescued by the tribune (xxi. 29–37); he addresses the people (xxii. 1–22); the tribune orders him to be scourged, but he claims to be tried as a Roman citizen (24–29); brought before Ananias, the high-priest, and the council (xxii. 30; xxiii. 1, 2); his address (xxiii. 3–6); a plot formed to kill him (12–15); sent by the tribune to the governor Felix, at Ceserea (22–35); accused by Ananias; his defence (xxiv. 1–21); Portius Festus, his successor, asks St. Paul to go to Jerusalem to be tried (xxv. 9); he appeals to Cesar (11); appears before king Agrippa (xxv. 22–xxvi. 32); sent to Rome under Julius, the centurion, sails to Lystra, thence in an Alexandrian ship; at Good Havens, in Crete (xxvii. 1–8); keeping on against St. Paul's advice, they are wrecked on Melita; he is unharmed by the sting of a serpent, cures Publius, and all the sick on the island; after three months' stay, continue the voyage to Syracusa, Rhegium, Puteoli (xxviii. 1–13); reaches Rome. where he is allowed to dwell by himself with a soldier as guard (16); his address to the Jews (17–28); remains two years there (29–31); he wrote from Rome the Epistles to Philemon, to the Colossians, Ephesians, and Philippians (Philem.,Col., Eph.,Phil.), and also, as is most probable, the Epistle to the Hebrews (Heb. xiii. 24), after the release of Timothy, who joined him in the Epistle to the Philippians (Heb. xiii. 23); he may have carried out his promise to visit the Jewish converts in Palestine (Heb. xiii. 23); but he went to Ephesus, and left St. Timothy there (1 Tim. i. 3); preached in Crete, and made St. Titus bishop (Tit. i. 5), and visited Macedonia, as he had promised (Phil. ii. 24; i. 25, 26); the first Epistle to St. Timothy is supposed to have been written at this time from Macedon; he wrote an Epistle to Titus, apparently from Nicopolis; he preached at Troas, and left some books and clothes with Carpus (2 Tim. iv. 13); then visited St. Timothy at Ephesus (2 Tim. i. 4), and went to Miletus, where he left Trophimus sick (2 Tim. iv. 20); his various sufferings (2 Cor. xi. 23–27); after this he returned to Rome, where he converted some of Nero's household, and was thrown into prison. Onesiphorus with difficulty found him (2 Tim. i. 16); when he wrote, St. Luke alone was with him (iv. 11); he appeared before Nero (iv. 16, 17); he urged St. Timothy to come to him quickly (8, 21), as he expected to be put to death (6, 7); according to the constant tradition of the church, he was beheaded June 29, A. D. 66, at Rome, and buried on the Ostian

way. St. Paul labored with his hands so as to be a burthen to none (Acts xx. 33; 2 Cor. xi. 9, 11; xii. 13; 1 Thess. ii. 9; 2 Thess. iii. 8).

PAUL. Epistles of St. Paul. Fourteen epistles of St. Paul are held by the church as canonical Scriptures of the New Testament—one to the Romans (Rom.); two to the Corinthians (1 Cor.; 2 Cor.); one to the Galatians (Gal.); one to the Ephesians (Eph.); one to the Philippians (Phil.); one to the Colossians (Col.); two to the Thessalonians (1 Thess.; 2 Thess.); two to Timothy (1 Tim.; 2 Tim.); one to Titus (Tit.); one to Philemon (Phil.), and one to the Hebrews, or Jewish Christians in Palestine (Heb.)

PAULUS, SERGIUS, converted by St. Paul at Paphos. He was Roman pro-consul of Cyprus, and styled a prudent man (Acts xiii. 7–12).

PEACE offered to the cities of Chanaan before attacking them (Deut. xx. 10).

PEACE, temporal and spiritual (Gen. xiii. 6, 8; xxvi. 22; xlv. 24; Lev. xxvi. 6; Num. vi. 27; Ecclus. xxv. 2; xxviii. 15; Jer. xxix. 7; Matt. v. 9; Mark ix. 49; Luke xiv. 32; Acts ix. 31; Rom. xii. 18; 1 Cor. xiv. 33; Eph. iv. 3; 2 Tim. ii. 22; 1 Pet. iii. 11; Heb. xii. 14; James iii. 18; Apoc. vi. 4); interior peace between God and those who love him (Isai. ii. 4; ix. 7; xi. 7; lxvi. 12; Osee ii. 14, 20; Mich. iv. 3; Zach. ix. 10; Luke ii. 14; xxiv. 36; John xiv. 17; xvi. 33; xx. 19; Acts x. 36; Rom. v. 1; Eph. ii. 14; Phil. iv. 7); false teachers and worldlings promise peace when there is no peace (Jer. vi. 14; viii. 8–11; xiv. 13; xxiii. 17; Ezech. xiii. 10, 16; Mich. iii. 5; John xiv. 27; 1 Thess. v. 3).

PEACE be to this house, a salutation prescribed by our Lord (Matt. x. 12; Luke x. 5); Peace be to you, a salutation used by our Lord (Luke xxiv. 36; John xx. 21, 26).

PEACE'MAKERS blessed (Matt. v. 9; James iii. 18).

PEACE-OFFERINGS, directions in regard to (Lev. iii. 1; vii. 11); the portion of the priest (28).

PEACOCKS brought by Solomon's ships every three years from Tharsis (3 Kings x. 22; 2 Paral. ix. 21).

PEARL, used in comparison (Prov. xxv. 12); cast not pearls before swine (Matt. vii. 6); the pearl of great price (xiii. 45, 46); worn by women (1 Tim. ii. 9); in the gates of the New Jerusalem (Apoc. xxi. 21).

PEL'ICAN, a bird used in a simile in Ps. ci. 7.

PELU'SIUM, a city called the strength of Egypt, Ezechiel's prophecy against (Ezech. xxx. 15, 16). It is the modern Damietta.

PEN. David compares his tongue to the pen (calamus) of a scrivener (Ps. xliv. 2); Job wishes his words written with an iron pen (stylus) (Job xix. 24); a man's pen (stylus) (Isai. viii. 1); the lying pen of scribes hath wrought falsehood (Jer. viii. 8); the pen of iron with the point of a diamond (xvii. 1).

PEN'ANCE. The penance of Adam (Gen. iii. 17, 23); the Ninevites do penance at the preaching of Jonas (Jon. iii.; Matt. xii. 41); the penance of the Jews under Esdras (1 Esd. iii. 12, 13); penance preached by St. John the Baptist (Matt. iii. 2, 11; Mark i. 4; Luke iii. 3); by our Lord (Luke xiii. 3); baptism of penance (Mark i. 4).

PEN'ANCE and satisfaction for sin (Ps. vi. 7; 2 Cor. vii. 10).

PEN'CIL, a style for writing (4 Kings xxi. 13).

PEN'NY, used in English translations for the

Roman silver coin denarius (value fifteen cents) (Matt. xx. 2; Mark vi. 37; xii. 15; Luke xx. 24; John vi. 7; Apoc. vi. 6).

PENTAP'OLIS, the five cities of the Plain, Sodom, Gomorrha, Adama, Seboim and Segor (Wisd. x. 6).

PENTATEUCH, the Greek name (meaning five books) commonly applied to the five books written by Moses, Genesis, Exodus, Leviticus, Numbers, Deuteronomy. Called "The Book of the Law of Moses" (2 Paral. xxv. 4; 2 Esd. viii. 1); "the book of Moses" (2 Paral. xxxv. 12; 1 Esd. vi. 18; 2 Esd. xiii. 1); "the law of Moses" (1 Esd. vii. 6); "the book of the law of the Lord by the hand of Moses" (2 Paral. xxxiv. 14).

PENTE'COST, a great Jewish feast kept on the fiftieth day after the Pasch, hence its Greek name. It is called the feast of the first-fruits (Ex. xxiii. 16; Lev. xxiii. 15–21); feast of weeks (Ex. xxxiv. 22); Pentecost (2 Mach. xii. 32; Acts ii. 1).

PER'FUMES (Ps. xliv. 9; Cant. iv. 11; Prov. xxvii. 9; vii. 17; Isai. iii. 24).

PER'GE, a city of Pamphylia, where St. Paul and St. Barnabas preached (Acts xiii. 14; xiv. 24).

PER'GAMUS, a city of Mysia. Antipas, a faithful witness of Christ, martyred there (Apoc. ii. 13); the Nicolaites there (15); some who advised eating things offered to idols (14); called a place where Satan dwelleth (13); the angel or bishop urged to do penance (16).

PER'JURY, law relating to (Lev. v. 4; xix. 12); committed and punished (3 Kings viii. 31; Jer. vii. 9; Zach. v. 3; Mal. iii. 5; 1 Tim. i. 10); the perjury of Pharao (Ex. viii. 8, 15, 28); of Saul (1 Kings xix. 6); of Eupator (1 Mach. vi. 62); of Alcimus (vii. 15, 18); of Demetrius (xi. 53); of Trypho (xiii. 15, 19); of Andronicus (2 Mach. iv. 34); of the people of Joppe (xii. 3).

PERSECUTION. The persecution of Antiochus (2 Mach. vi., vii.); Saul's persecution at Jerusalem (Acts ix. 1; 1 Tim. i. 13); Herod's (Acts xii.); persecutions foretold by our Lord (Luke xxi. 12; Mark xiii. 9).

PERSEP'OLIS, a city of Persia; Antiochus Epiphanes defeated in an attempt to rob the temple (2 Mach. ix. 2).

PERSEVERANCE. The necessity of (1 Paral. xxviii. 7; Job ii. 3; Prov. iv. 13; xxiii. 17; Ezech. xviii. 24; Ecclus. ii. 3; xi. 21; xxv. 5; Matt. x. 22; xv. 22; xxiv. 13; Luke ix. 60; John vi. 65; Acts i. 14; ii. 42; xi. 23; xiii. 43; Heb. iii.; 2 Pet. ii. 20; 1 John ii. 24; Apoc. ii. 16).

PERSIA, a powerful kingdom in Asia. Daniel predicts three kings in Persia, and then a mighty one who shall make war on Greece (Xerxes), (Dan. xi. 2); Antiochus goes to levy tribute in Persia (1 Mach. iii. 31); Antiochus attempts to plunder the temple of Nanea, at Elymais, in Persia (1 Mach. vi. 1, 5, 56; 2 Mach. i. 12–16; ix. 1, 21); Jews led to Persia (i. 19); Nehemias sent by king of Persia (20); Arsaces, king of Persia and Media (1 Mach. xiv. 2). See ELAM.

PER'SIANS, people of Persia (Ezech. xxvii. 10; xxxviii. 5; Judith xvi. 12). See ELAMITES, PARTHIANS.

PER'SIS, a Christian woman of Rome saluted by St. Paul as "the dearly beloved who hath much labored in the Lord" (Rom. xvi. 12).

PERSONS. Respect of persons condemned (Jas. ii. 1; Rom. ii. 11; Col. iii. 25; Eph. vi. 9; 2 Paral. xix. 7).

PESTILENCE sent to punish the sin of David (2 Kings xxiv. 15).

PETER, ST., called originally Simon (Matt. iv. 18; x. 2); Barjona (Matt. xvi. 17), son of John or

struction of Jerusalem (Mark xiii. 3, 4); at the Last Supper refuses to let Christ wash his feet (John xiii. 6–10); declares that he will not be scandalized (Matt. xxvi. 33); his denial of Christ foretold (34, 35;

(x. 1–48); justifies it (xi. 5–17); arrested by Herod (xii. 3); miraculously delivered (4–19); presides in the council at Jerusalem (xv. 7–29); St. Paul tarried with him fifteen days at Jerusalem (Gal. i. 18); the gospel of the circumcision committed to Peter (ii. 8); addresses an epistle to the faithful in Pontus, Galatia, Cappadocia, Asia, and Bithynia (1 Pet. i. 1); and also a second (2 Pet. iii. 1). According to the uninterrupted tradition of the church, he was put to death at Rome, at the same time as St. Paul, to whom he alludes in his second epistle, and he there (2 Pet. i. 14) says that our Lord had signified his approaching death to him. For his primacy, see Matt. x. 2; xvi. 18; Mark iii. 16; Luke vi. 14; his commission to confirm the faith as infallible guide (Luke xxii. 32); as pastor of pastors (John xxi. 17).

ST. PETER SET FREE BY AN ANGEL.

Jona (John i. 42; xxi. 15–17); our Lord bestows on him the surname Cephas (Rock), (John i. 42); a Syriac term, rendered into Greek and made masculine by the word Petros, Peter (Mark iii. 16); whence he is constantly styled Simon Peter (Matt. xvi. 16; Luke vi. 14; ix. 20; John vi. 8, 69; xx. 2, 6); and so styles himself (2 Pet. i. 1); he was a native of Bethsaida, and brother of Andrew (John i. 44); Andrew, a disciple of St. John the Baptist, on the testimony of St. John that Jesus was the Lamb of God, told his brother Simon, "We have found the Messias," and brought him to Jesus (John i. 29–42); he afterwards called them while casting their nets into the sea (Matt. iv. 18; Mark i. 16); he cured Peter's wife's mother of a fever (Matt. viii. 14, 15; Luke iv. 38, 39); our Lord teaches from his ship (Luke v. 3); after the miraculous draught of fishes, Peter left all and followed him (Luke v. 2–11); the reward promised him (Mark x. 28–30); he names Peter the first of his twelve apostles (Matt. x. 2; Mark iii. 16; Luke vi. 14); walks on the water at the command of Jesus (Matt. xiv. 23–31); asks an explanation of a parable (xv. 15; Mark vii. 17); acknowledges Jesus as the Christ, the Son of the living God, by revelation from the father (Matt. xvi. 16, 17); our Lord blessed him, declared him to be the rock on which he should build his church, and that he would give him the keys of the kingdom of heaven with power to bind and loose (18, 19); rebuked for urging our Lord not to undergo his passion and death (23; Mark viii. 32, 33); his answer at Capharnaum (John vi. 69); witnesses the Transfiguration (Matt. xvii. 1–9; Mark ix. 1–8; Luke ix. 28–36); obtains the tribute-money from a fish (Matt. xvii. 23–26); asks about forgiving injuries (xviii. 21; Luke xvii. 4); asks about the de-

Mark xiv. 29, 30); he takes a sword (Luke xxii. 38); with our Lord in the garden of olives (Matt. 36–40); cuts off the ear of Malchus (51; John xviii. 10); denies Christ, is converted, and weeps bitterly (Matt. xxvi. 69–75; Luke xxii. 55–62; John xiii. 37, 38; xviii. 15–27); after the resurrection the holy women directed by the angel to tell St. Peter of it (Mark xvi. 7); Magdalen tells him (John xx. 2); he goes to the sepulchre (Luke xxiv. 12; John xx. 6); our Lord appears to him (Luke xxiv. 34; 1 Cor. xv. 5); at the Sea of Galilee, St. Peter casts himself into the water in order to reach our Lord quickly (John xxi. 7); draws in the net (11); our Lord questions him, and commissions him to feed his sheep and his lambs, and foretells the manner of his death (15–19); Peter inquires in regard to John (21); after the ascension he perseveres with the rest in prayer (Acts i. 13, 14); says that one must be made a witness in the place of Judas (16–22); after the descent of the Holy Ghost preaches (ii. 14–40); three thousand are baptized that received his word (41); Peter and John cure the lame man at the Beautiful Gate (iii. 1–8); addresses the people (12–26); they are apprehended (iv. 1); Peter's address to the high-priest and ancients (8–12); forbidden to speak or teach in the name of Jesus (18); their reply (19, 20); Peter condemns the sin of Ananias and Saphira (v. 1–10); his shadow cures the sick (15); the answer of Peter and the apostles to the high-priest after the angel delivered them from prison (29); Peter and John go to Samaria (viii. 14); Peter's answer to Simon Magus (20–23); Peter healeth Eneas at Lydda (ix. 32–35); raises Tabitha to life at Joppe (36–43); receives Cornelius, the centurion, into the church in consequence of a vision

PHA′CEE, son of Romelia, king of Israel, kills Phaceia, and usurps his throne, 759 B. C. (4 Kings xv. 25, 27); made war on Jerusalem (Isai. vii. 1; 2 Paral. xxviii. 6); in one day he slew 120,000 men of Juda, and carried away 200,000 women, boys and girls, and immense booty (6–8), but releases his prisoners at the prayer of the prophet Oded (9–15); Theglathphalasar carried off the tribe of Nephthali and many others, and Phacee was slain by Osee, who formed a plot against him, 739 B. C. (4 Kings xv. 29, 30).

CRUCIFIXION OF ST. PETER.

PHACE′IA, king of Israel, succeeds his father Manahem, 761 B. C. (4 Kings xv. 23); after a wicked reign of two years, he was killed by his captain Phacee, in Samaria, in the tower of the king's house near Argob (24, 25).

PHAL'TI, son of Raphu, one of the twelve spies sent to view the promised land (Num. xiii. 10).

PHAL'TI or **PHALTIEL**, son of Lais. Saul gave Michol, David's wife, to him, but David demanded her from Isboseth, and Phalti gave her up with grief (1 Kings xxv. 44; 2 Kings iii. 15).

PHAN'UEL, the name given by Jacob to the place where he wrestled with the angel (Gen. xxxii. 30); a city of the same name was afterwards built there, but Gedeon, after the defeat of the Madianites, destroyed the tower and the people, for refusing to join him (Judges viii. 8, 17); Jeroboam, son of Nabat, rebuilt it (3 Kings xii. 25).

PHA'RAM, king of Jerimoth, ally of Adonibesec, put to death and hanged by Josue (Jos. x. 3, 24–26).

PHA'RAN, a desert in Arabia Petræa. Codorlahomor ravaged the country up to it (Gen. xiv. 6); Agar fled to it with Ismael (xxi. 21); the Israelites marched to it from Sinai (Num. x. 12); spies sent from it (xiii. 3, 27); Sinai called the mountain of Pharan (Deut. xxxiii. 2; Hab. iii. 3); David retires to it (1 Kings xxv. 1, 2); Adad taken there (3 Kings xi. 18).

PHA'RAO, a name common to several kings of Egypt. The first mentioned in the Bible lived in the days of Abraham; struck with ulcers for carrying off Sara (Gen. xii. 17). The second in the time of Jacob (Gen. xxxix. 1); his dreams interpreted by Joseph (xli. 16, 25); appoints Joseph minister (40); sends the people to Joseph for bread (55); receives Jacob and his sons, and gives them the care of his flocks (xlvii. 6, 7), and the land of Ramesses (11); acquires all the land of Egypt (20, 21); permits Joseph to go to Chanaan to bury his father (l. 6). The third oppresses the children of Israel (Ex. i. 8, 11); orders the male children to be destroyed (22); his daughter saves Moses (ii. 5–10); he seeks to kill Moses (15); refuses to allow the Israelites to depart (v. 2); his hardened conduct punished by a series of plagues (vi.–x.); the death of his firstborn (xii. 29); he allows the Israelites to depart (xii. 31; xiii. 17); and then pursues them (xiv. 5, 6); enters the Red Sea, which closes on him and his army (23–28). The fourth mentioned is the one whose daughter Solomon married (3 Kings iii. 1). The fifth, Pharao Nechao, conquered Carchemis, killed Josias, king of Juda, and deposed Joachaz, but was defeated by Nabuchodonosor (4 Kings xxiii.–xxiv.; 2 Paral. xxxv.–xxxvi.) Against the sixth, Ephree, Jeremias prophesied (Jer. xliv. 30).

PHAR'ATHON, a place in the mountain of Amalec, in the tribe of Ephraim; birthplace of Abdon, judge of Israel, who was buried there (Judg. xii. 15); called Phara (1 Mach. ix. 50).

PHA'RES, son of Juda and Thamar (Gen. xxxviii. 29); his sons were Hesron and Hamul (Num. xxvi. 21).

PHA'RES, one of the words written on the wall during the sacrilegious banquet of Balthasar, and explained by Daniel (Dan. v. 28).

PHAR'ISEE and **PUBLICAN**, the parable of (Luke xviii. 10); a Pharisee invites Jesus to dine (Luke vii. 36); scandalized that he allows a sinful woman to approach him (39); our Lord proposes a parable to him.

PHAR'ISEES, a strict sect of the Jews, censured by our Lord (Matt. iii. 7; vii. 29; xvi. 6, 11, 12; xxiii.; Luke xi. 42, 43; xii. 1; Mark ii. 18; viii. 15; John viii. 15); conspire against him (Matt. xxvi. 4; Luke xxii. 2; John xi. 47); St. Paul appeals to their doctrinal pride (Acts xxiii. 6).

PHAR'PHAR, one of the rivers of Damascus, referred to by Naaman (4 Kings v. 12).

PHARU'RIM, a locality near the entrance of the temple (4 Kings xxiii. 11).

PHASE (passage), another name for the Pasch (Ex. xii. 11; Lev. xxiii. 5; Num. ix. 2).

PHAS'ERON. The children of Phaseron struck in their tents by Jonathan (1 Mach. ix. 66).

PHAS'GA, a mountain beyond the Jordan in the land of Moab, whence Moses saw the promised land (Deut. iii. 27; xxxiv. 1); Moses dies there (5); Balaam builds seven altars on it (Num. xxiii. 14).

PHAS'SUR, son of Emmer, a priest, prince of the house of the Lord, struck Jeremias and put him in prison (Jerem. xx. 1–3); the prophet announced that he would die a captive in Babylon (xxi. 1); Sedecias sent him to Jeremias (xxxviii. 1).

PHATU'RES, a city and district of Egypt (Jer. xliv. 1, 15; Ezech. xxix. 14; xxx. 14).

PHAU, a city in Idumea, of which Adar was king (Gen. xxxvi. 39; 1 Paral. i. 50).

PHE'BE. St. Paul mentions her as in the ministry of the church that is in Cenchre (the port of Corinth) (Rom. xvi. 1); asks the Romans to receive her, as she had assisted many and him also (2).

PHEG'IEL, son of Ochran, prince of the tribe of Aser (Num. vii. 72).

PHEL'ETHI, guards of David (2 Kings viii. 18; xx. 23; 3 Kings i. 38; 1 Paral. xviii. 17).

PHEL'TIAS, son of Banaias, prince of the people; Ezechiel sees him in a vision, as an announcement of his death (Ezech. xi. 1–4).

PHENENNA, second wife of Elcana (1 Kings i.)

PHENICE', a port in the island of Crete. St. Paul advised wintering there (Acts xxvii. 12).

PHER'EZITES, people of the land of Chanaan (Gen. xiii. 7); Josue told the tribe of Ephraim to attack them (Jos. xvii. 15); Solomon subjugated them (3 Kings ix. 20); in the time of Esdras some Jews had married among them (1 Esd. ix. 1).

PHERMES'TA, son of Aman, put to death with his father (Esther ix. 9).

PHESDOM'IM, a place in the tribe of Juda. The Philistines defeated at (1 Paral. xi. 13, 14); the borders of Dommim are mentioned (1 Kings xvii. 1).

PHETE'IA, the nineteenth course of priests (1 Paral. xxiv. 16).

PHET'RUSIM, son of Mizraim (Gen. x. 14).

PHI'COL, general of the army of Abimelech, king of Gerara, in the time of Abraham (Gen. xxi. 22); also in the time of Isaac (xxvi. 26).

PHIGEL'LUS, a disciple who abandoned St. Paul at Rome (2 Tim. i. 15).

PHIHI'HAROTH. The children of Israel ordered to encamp over against it (Ex. xiv. 2).

PHILADEL'PHIA, a city of Mysia in Asia Minor. The bishop is praised for his zeal (Apoc. iii. 7, 9).

PHILAR'CHES, a wicked associate of Timotheus, slain in battle by Judas Machabeus (2 Mach. viii. 32).

PHIL'EMON, a rich man of Colosse, converted with his wife Appia by Epaphras, a disciple of St. Paul (Coloss. iv. 12; i. 7, 8). Onesimus, one of his slaves, robbed him and fled to Rome, where he was converted by St. Paul. The apostle sent him back to his master with an epistle (Philem.)

PHIL'EMON, St. Paul's Epistle to, one of the canonical books of the New Testament (Philem.)

PHILE'TUS, an early heretic condemned by St. Paul. He taught that the resurrection was already past, and subverted the faith of some (2 Tim. ii. 17, 18).

PHIL'IP, foster-brother of Antiochus Epiphanes, was a Phrygian (1 Mach. vi. 15, 55; 2 Mach. ix. 29); he was made governor of Jerusalem (2 Mach. viii. 8; v. 22); he used every means to force the Jews to renounce their faith (2 Mach. vi. 11). Antiochus at his death made him regent, but Lysias seized the government, and Philip went to Egypt for aid (2 Mach. ix. 29); he seized Antioch, but Lysias retook it and put Philip to death (1 Mach. vi. 55–63).

PHIL'IP, son of Herod the Great, and brother of Herod, tetrarch of Galilee. He was tetrarch of Iturea and the country of Trachonitis (Luke iii. 1); his wife Salome was the daughter of Herodias, who asked the head of John the Baptist (Matt. xiv. 6–11).

PHIL'IP, otherwise Herod Philip, son of Herod the Great and Mariamne II., daughter of Simon the high-priest. He married Herodias, who bore him Salome (see last article) (Mark vi. 17; Matt. xiv. 3).

PHIL'IP, ST., one of the twelve apostles, a native of Bethsaida in Galilee. Our Saviour called him by saying "Follow me" (John i. 43); Philip told Nathanael that he had found the Messias, and took him to Jesus (45–51); the next year he was made one of the apostles (Luke vi. 14; Matt. x. 3); at the feeding of the five thousand our Lord asked Philip, "Whence shall we buy bread that these may eat?" (John vi. 5–7); he introduced some Gentiles to our Lord (John xii. 20, 22); at the Last Supper he asked to see the Father, and our Lord declared that he and the Father were one (John xiv. 8, 10). He is said to have preached in Phrygia.

PHIL'IP, ST., the deacon. He was the second of the seven deacons chosen by the apostles (Acts vi. 5); he resided at Cesarea in Palestine, where his four daughters, virgins, were endowed with prophecy (xxi. 8, 9); he preached in Samaria (Acts viii. 5); expelled unclean spirits, cured the palsied and lame (7, 8); baptized many (12); among other Simon Magus (13); at the bidding of an angel he went to the road from Jerusalem to Gaza (viii. 26); met and converted the eunuch of Candace, queen of the Ethiopians (27–39); Philip was then taken to Azotus, and preached as he returned to Cesarea (40); in the year A. D. 58 St. Paul tarried for some days with St. Philip at Cesarea (Acts xxi. 10).

PHILIP'PI, a city of Macedonia. St. Paul preached there, A. D. 52 (Acts xvi. 12, 13); converted Lydia, and delivered the pythonical girl (14–18); was scourged and imprisoned, but the jailer is converted by a heavenly light (22–33); the magistrates alarmed (35–39); the faithful there relieved St. Paul on several occasions (Philip. iv. 16); they sent money to him in Achaia, and sent Epaphroditus to him in Rome (Philip. iv. 16, 18).

PHILIP'PIANS, Epistle to, written by St. Paul. One of the canonical books of the New Testament (Philip.)

PHIL'ISTIA, PHIL'ISTHIIM, the country of the Philistines, Palestine (Ex. xv. 14; Isai. xiv. 31).

PHIL'ISTINES, a people from the island of Cappadocia (Amos ix. 7; Jerem. xlvii. 4); they expelled the Hevites (Deut. ii. 23); they persecute the Israelites (Judg. iii. 3; x. 7; 1 Kings iv.; v.; xiii. 5; xvii. xxiii. 1; xxix. 1; xxxi. 1; 2 Kings v. 17, 22; xxi.

15, 18); they are defeated (Judg. iii. 31; xv. 9; 1 Kings vii. 11; xiv.; xviii. 27; xix. 5; xxiii. 5; 2 Kings viii. 1: 4 Kings xviii. 8); prophecies against

PLOUGHS AND YOKES OF ASIA MINOR.

the Philistines (Isai. xiv. 29; Jerem. xlvii. 1, 4; Ezech. xxv. 15; Amos i. 8; Soph. ii. 5; Zach. ix. 6; Joel iii. 4); their country assigned to the tribe by Josue (Jos. xiii. 2, 3); oppress the Israelites in the times of Samgar (Judg. iii. 31); Samson (Judg. xv., xvi.); Samuel (1 Kings vi.); and Saul (1 Kings xiii.); and disarm them (1 Kings xiii. 19); reduced by David (2 Kings v. 17; viii. 1); revolt against Joram (2 Paral. xxi. 16; xxvi. 6, 7); ravaged Juda in the days of Achaz (2 Paral. xxviii. 18); reduced by Ezechias (4 Kings xviii. 8).

PHILOL'OGUS, saluted by St. Paul (Rom. xvi. 15).

PHILOS'OPHERS, their false wisdom shown by their crimes (Rom. i. 21, 24; iii.)

PHIN'EES, son of Eleazar, and grandson of Aaron, third high-priest of the Jews, B. C. 1433–1414 (Ex. vi. 25; Judges xx. 28); by his zeal against the idolatry of the Madianites, he appeases the wrath of God (Num. xxv. 7; Ps. cv. 30); the priesthood promised to him (Num. xxv. 12); is sent to the tribes of Ruben and Gad, and half-tribe of Manasses (Jos. xxii. 13); his address to them (16–20); their reply (21–28); declares them not guilty of revolt (31); he is praised (Ecclus. xlv. 28–31); his family retained the high-priesthood till the time of Heli.

PHIN'EES, son of the high-priest Heli, united with his brother Ophni in wickedness (1 Kings i. 3); slain with him in punishment of his sins (iv. 11).

PHI'SON, one of the four great rivers that watered Paradise; it compassed all the land of Hevilath, where gold groweth (Gen. ii. 11).

PHI'THOM, a city in Egypt, built for Pharao by the Israelites (Ex. i. 11).

PHLEG'ON, a convert mentioned by St. Paul (Rom. xvi. 14).

PHO'GOR, a mountain beyond the Jordan, near Nebo and Phasga (Num. xxiii. 28; Deut. xxxiv. 6).

PHO'GOR, an idol of the Madianites (Num. xxv. 18; xxxi. 16); the Israelites encamped in the valley opposite the temple of Phogor (Deut. iii. 29; iv. 46).

PHRYG'IA, one of the provinces of Asia Minor; people from it at Jerusalem on Pentecost (Acts ii. 10); St. Paul passes through (xvi. 7); confirming the disciples (xviii. 23).

PHU'A and **SEPH'ORA**, midwives of the Israelites in Egypt (Ex. i. 15, 16), disobey the king's cruel order, and are rewarded by God (18–21).

PHUL, king of Assyria (4 Kings xv. 19), came into the land of the kingdom of Israel, at the prayer of king Manahem (Osee v. 13; 4 Kings xv. 19; 1 Paral. v. 26).

PHU'NON, one of the stations of the Israelites in the wilderness (Num. xxxiii. 42, 43).

PHU'RIM, meaning lots, the name of a solemn feast among the Jews, in honor of their delivery from Aman (Esth. ix. 26, 28, 31).

PHUTH, third son of Cham (Gen. x. 6).

PHYLAC'TERY, rolls of parchment, containing words of the law, worn on the forehead and left wrist, based on Ex. xiii. 9; our Lord reproached the Pharisees with making them wide out of ostentation (Matt. xxiii. 5).

PI'ETY. True piety to God recommended (Ex. xii. 24; xx.; xxiii. 25; Deut. v. 11; x. 12; Jos. xxii. 5; Ps. ii. 11; xlix. 14; Zach. viii. 16; Rom. xii.–xiv.); includes obedience (1 Kings xv. 22; Ps. xxxix. 7; Prov. iii. 1; John xii. 26); serves God in spirit (Philip. iii. 3); flies evil (Isai. i. 16; lviii. 6; Jer. xxii. 3; Ezech. xviii. 6; Zach. vii. 9); does mercy (Mich. vi. 8); leads to reconciliation with our brother (Matt. v. 24); removes causes of scandal (29); causes us to offer the other cheek to the smiter (39); to give what we have (Luke iii. 11); to feed the hungry (Matt. xxv. 35; 1 Kings xxi. 6; 2 Kings xvi. 1); God punishes those who have no piety (Deut. xxiii. 4; Judg. viii.; 1 Kings xxv.)

PIG'EONS offered in sacrifice (Gen. xv. 9; Lev. i. 14; xii. 6; xiv. 22; xv. 14, 29; Num. vi. 10; Luke ii. 24).

PI'LATE. Pontius Pilate, governor of Judea for the Roman emperor. Christ was brought before his tribunal (Luke xxiii. 1; Mark xv. 1; Matt. xxvii. 2); does not answer (14); warned by his wife not to condemn the just man (Matt. xxvii. 19); asks whether he is king of the Jews (Mark xv. 2; Luke xxiii. 3; John xviii. 33); finds no cause in him (Luke xxiii. 4); sends him to Herod (7); seeks to release him

(John xix. 12); asks what is truth, but does not wait to hear (John xviii. 38); washes his hands, but condemns our Lord for fear of the Jews (Matt. xxvii. 24; Luke xxiii. 24); causes him to be scourged and delivered to them (Matt. xxvii. 26; Mark xv. 15; John xix. 1); his soldiers crown Jesus with thorns (Matt. xxvii. 29; John xix. 2); writes the inscription (John xix. 19); his answer to the Jews (22); Joseph of Arimathea asks him for our Lord's body (Matt. xxvii. 58; John xix. 38); the Pharisees ask him for a guard for the sepulchre (Matt. xxvii. 62–65).

PIL'GRIMAGES, their utility, when made with devotion (3 Kings viii. 41; 4 Kings v. 5; Acts viii. 27).

PIL'GRIMS or strangers to be received kindly (Ex. xii. 4, 49; xxii. 21; xxiii. 9; Lev. xix. 33; xxiii. 22; Num. xxxv. 15; Deut. i. 16; x. 18; xxiv. 14, 17; xxvi. 11; Ezech. xlvii. 22; Zach. vii. 10; Heb. xiii. 2); we are all pilgrims and strangers in this world (Gen. xv. 13; xxiii. 4; xlvii. 9; 1 Paral. xxix. 15; Ps. cxviii. 19; Phil. iii. 20; Heb. xiii. 14; 1 Pet. ii. 11).

PIL'LAR OF CLOUD AND FIRE guiding the Israelites in the desert (Ex. xiii. 21).

PINE TREE, mentioned by Isaias xliv. 14.

PIN'NACLE OF THE TEMPLE. The devil places our Lord on (Matt. iv. 5).

PISID'IA, a province of Asia Minor, north of Pamphylia. St. Paul preached at Antioch, in Pisidia (Acts xiii. 14; xiv. 23).

PITS OF SLIME (Gen. xiv. 10) were pits of bitumen, and the word is so in the Douay and in correct Bibles.

PLAGUES. Egypt is struck with a series of plagues for the obstinacy of Pharao (Ex. vii.–ix.; xiv.); plague brought on the people of Israel by the vain glory of David (2 Kings xxiv. 15).

PLAIN OF ESDRELON (Judith i. 8); of Jordan (Deut. iii. 10); of the wilderness (Deut. iii. 17).

PLEDGE, certain things not to be taken in (Deut. xxiv. 6).

PLEI'ADES, a constellation named in the book of Job (Job xxxviii. 31).

PLOUGH'SHARE. Samgar slays six hundred men with a ploughshare (Judg. iii. 31); the Israelites sharpen them for weapons (1 Kings xiii. 20). The King James has goad, but incorrectly.

POME'GRANATES, a fruit. The Israelites complain in the desert of Sin that they had none (Num. xx. 5); ornaments like the fruit were on the hem of the high-priest's ephod (Ex. xxviii. 33, 34); on

PILLAR OF FIRE.

the tops of the pillars in Solomon's temple (3 Kings vii. 18, 20); a paradise of pomegranates (Cant. iv. 13; vi. 10; vii. 12).

PONT'US. Arioch, king of Pontus, an ally of Codorlahomor, against the kings of the Pentapolis (Gen. xiv.) This Pontus, in Hebrew Ellasar, is supposed by some to have been in Arabia.

PONT'US, a province of Asia Minor, mentioned in the account of Pentecost (Acts ii. 9); St. Peter addresses his first epistle to the Christians there (1 Pet. i. 1); Aquila was of Pontus (Acts xviii. 2).

POOL OF BETHSAIDA or PROBATICA, at Jerusalem (John v. 2); miraculous cures when an angel stirred the water (4); Christ heals a man there who had been thirty-eight years infirm (8).

POOL OF EZECHIAS, at Jerusalem (2 Esd. iii. 16).

POOL OF FIRE (Apoc. xix. 20; xx. 9; xxi. 8).

POOL OF SILOE (Sent: John ix. 7), (2 Esd. iii. 15); flows silently (Isai. viii. 6); our Lord cures a blind man by sending him to wash in it (John ix. 7, 11).

POOR. God's commandments as to the poor (Ex. xxii. 22–26; xxiii. 3–11; Lev. xiv. 21; xix. 10; xxiii. 22; Deut. xv. 8–11); the Lord is a refuge for the poor (Ps. ix. 10); he hears the poor (lxviii. 34); he lifts up the poor man (cxii. 7); the poor man better than a vain-glorious man (Prov. xii. 9); better than a perverse rich man (xix. 1; xxviii. 6); better a poor, wise child than a foolish old king (Eccles. iv. 13); he who giveth to the poor shall not want (Prov. xxviii. 27); we are to give alms to the poor (Ecclus. iv. 1); blessed are the poor in spirit (Matt. v. 3; Luke vi. 20); the poor have the gospel preached to them (Matt. xi. 5; Luke iv. 18; vii. 22); our Lord tells us that we have the poor always with us to relieve (Mark xiv. 7; John xii. 8; Matt. xxvi. 11); no distinction between rich and poor is to be made in the church (James ii. 2–6).

POPE, or CHIEF BISHOP. St. Peter, by Christ's ordinance, was raised to this dignity (Matt. xvi. 18, 19; Luke xxii. 31, 32; John xxi. 15; Matt. x. 2; Acts v. 29; Gal. ii. 7, 8).

PORCH, before Solomon's temple (3 Kings vi. 3; 1 Paral. xxviii. 11; 2 Paral. iii. 4; viii. 12; xv. 8; xxix. 17; John x. 23; Acts iii. 11; v. 12); in Ezechiel's (Ezech. xlii., xlvi.); in Solomon's palace (3 Kings vii. 6); at the Probatica (John v. 2).

PORPHIR'ION, a river bird, apparently the purple gallinule, classed among the unclean birds (Lev. xi. 18; Deut. xiv. 17).

POS'IDO'NIUS, an officer sent by Nicanor to Judas Machabeus (2 Mach. xiv. 19).

POST (messenger) (Esth. iii. 13); couriers (15); runners (Prov. xxiv. 34); posts sent with letters (2 Paral. xxx. 6, 10); my days have been swifter than a post (Job ix. 25).

POT, full of flesh and bones, a figure used by the prophet Ezechiel (Ezech. xxiv. 3).

POTT'AGE (4 Kings iv. 39).

POTTER, referred to (Jerem. xviii. 3; Ecclus. xxxviii. 32, 33); man is in the hand of God as clay in the hand of a potter (Ecclus. xxxiii. 13); the clay cannot dictate to the potter (Rom. ix. 21); Judas' money used to buy a potter's field (Matt. xxvii. 7, 10).

POUND, the word used in English translations for the Greek mna, a coin worth $15 (1 Esd. ii. 69; 2 Esd. vii. 72; Luke xix. 13, 25); also a weight (3 Kings x. 17; 1 Mach. xiv. 24; xv. 18).

POW'ER, in the sense of veil (1 Cor. xi. 10).

POW'ERS, every soul to be subject to the high powers (Rom. xiii. 1, 3; 1 Pet. ii. 13–16).

POW'ERS, an order of angels (Col. i. 16).

PRAISE. We are under obligation to chant the praises of God (Ps. xlvi. 2; cxlvi. 7; cxlix. 1; Isai. xii. 4; Eph. v. 19; Col. iii. 17; Heb. xiii. 15; James v. 13); we cannot do it worthily (Ps. xci. 2; cv. 2; cxviii. 164; cxliv. 3; Ecclus. xliii. 2); to be chanted from the heart (Ps. lxxxiii. 3; Ecclus. xliii. 32; Col. iii. 16).

PRAY'ER. Conditions of a good prayer (Num. xi. 16, 24; Deut. iv. 7; Judg. x. 10, 15; 1 Kings i. 11; 2 Kings xxii. 2, 7; 3 Kings iii. 7; Tob. iii. 11; Judith iv. 12; Ecclus. xxxv. 26; Isai. lxv. 24; Amos vii. 2; Matt. vi. 5, 9; vii. 7; xviii. 19; xx. 20; xxvi. 39; Mark xiii. 33; Luke xviii. 1; xxii. 40; John iv. 23; xv. 7; xvi. 23; Acts i. 14; ii. 42; iv. 24, 31; Rom. viii. 26; xii. 12; 1 Cor. xiv. 13; Eph. vi. 18; Col. iv. 2; 1 Thess. v. 17; 1 Tim. ii. 1; Heb. xiii. 18; 1 Peter iii. 12; 1 John vi. 4; James iv. 3; v. 13; Apoc. xix. 5; xxii. 9); prayers duly made are heard (Gen. xvi. 11; xxi. 17; Ex. ii. 24; iii. 7; vi. 5; xxii. 23, 27; Deut. iv. 7; xv. 9; 1 Kings iii. 9, 10; ix. 16; xii. 18; 3 Kings xiii. 6; xvii. 22; xviii. 36; 4 Kings xiii. 23; xx. 5; 2 Paral. xxxii. 24; xxxiii. 13; Tob. iii. 24; Ps. iii. 5; iv. 4; ix. 13; xvii. 7; xxi. 25; xxxiii. 7; xlix. 15; liv. 17; cxvii. 5; cxix. 1; cxliv. 19; Prov. xv. 29; Ecclus. iv. 6; xxi. 6; xxxv. 16–21; xlviii. 22; Isai. xxx. 19; xxxvii. 15, 21; lv. 6; Jer. xxix. 12; Lam. iii. 56; Dan. xiii. 44; Jon. ii. 3; Zach. xiii. 9; 2 Mach. iii. 22; John ix. 31; Acts x. 4); why some prayers are not heard by God (Deut. i. 45; xxxi. 18; Judg. x. 10; 1 Kings viii. 18; Ps. xvii. 42; Prov. i. 28; xxi. 13; xxviii. 9; Ecclus. xxxiv. 29, 31; Isai. i. 15; Jer. vii. 16; xi. 11; xiv. 12; xv. 1; Ezech. viii. 18; xiv. 16, 20; Mich. iii. 4; Zach. vii. 13; 2 Mach. ix. 13; Heb. xii. 17); examples of the prayers of saints (Gen. xxxii. 9; Ex. xxxii. 11, 13; Num. xiv. 19; Deut. ix. 26; 3 Kings viii. 15; 2 Paral. vi. 16; xiv. 11; xx. 6, 12; 1 Esd. ix. 6; 2 Esd. i.; Tob. viii. 7; xiii. 1; Judith ix. 2; xvi.; Esth. xiv. 3; Wisd. ix.; Ecclus. xxiii. 1; xxxvi. 1–11; li.; Isai. xxxiii. 2; lxiv.; Jer. x. 24; xvii. 13, 14; xviii. 19; xxxii. 16; Lam. v.; Bar. i. 17, 21; ii. 6; iii. 1, 9; Dan. ix. 4; xiii. 42; Jon. ii.; Hab. iii.; 1 Mach. vii. 37; 2 Mach. vi. 30; Acts iv. 24); praying in the name of Jesus (John xiv. 13; xv. 16; xvi. 23, 26; 1 John v. 14); of ourselves we cannot pray as we ought (Matt. xx. 20; Mark x. 35; Rom. viii. 26; James iv. 3); we must pray without ceasing (Ps. cxviii. 62; Matt. vii. 7; Luke xi. 9; xviii. 1; Acts x. 2; Col. iv. 2; 1 Thess. iii. 10; v. 17; 1 Tim. v. 5; 2 Tim. i. 3); we are bound to pray for those who preach (Eph. vi. 19); we are bound to pray for one another (Jer. xlii. 2, 20; Bar. i. 13; 2 Mach. i. 6; 1 Thess. v. 25; 1 Tim. ii. 1; James v. 16); prayers for the dead holy and wholesome (2 Mach. xii. 43).

PRAY'ER. A Jewish house of prayer (Acts xvi. 13).

PREACH THE GOSPEL. The apostles are commanded by our Lord to preach the gospel to all nations (Matt. xxviii. 19; Mark xvi. 15; Luke ix. 60; xxiv. 47; Acts ii. 14; iii. 12; iv. 8; x. 42; xiii. 16).

PREACH'ER (1 Tim. ii. 7; 2 Tim. i. 11).

PREDES'TINATED. Those whom God foreknew, he also predestinated (Rom. viii. 29); whom he predestinated, them he also called (30); God hath predestinated us unto the adoption of children (Eph. i. 5, 11).

PRES'ENCE OF GOD (1 Paral. xvi. 27; Ps. xv. 11; xvii. 7; lxvii. 9; Isai. lxiv. 1; Jer. v. 22; Ezech. i.; Dan. vii. 9; Nah. i.; Hab. iii.; Apoc. i.)

PRESENTA'TION, applied especially to the offering of the first-born son to God in the temple (Ex. xiii. 2; xxii. 29; Num. iii. 13); our Lord was presented in the temple by the Blessed Virgin (Luke ii. 22).

PRES'ENTS, bribes. God is not to be gained by bribes (Deut. x. 17); judges are forbidden to receive bribes (Ex. xviii. 21; xxiii. 8; Num. xxxv. 31; Deut. xvi. 19; xxvii. 25; Job xxxvi. 18; Ecclus. iv. 36); those who receive bribes shall be punished (Job xv. 34; Ps. xxv. 10; Isai. i. 23; v. 23; Ezech. xiii. 19; xxii. 12; Mich. iii. 11); he who hates bribes shall live (Prov. xv. 27; Isai. xxxiii. 15); they pervert the order of justice (Prov. xvii. 23; xxviii. 21); they blind the judges (Ecclus. xxix. 31); they make room for a man before princes (Prov. xviii. 16); many are the friends of him that giveth gifts (xix. 6); a secret present quencheth anger (xxi. 14); he that maketh presents shall purchase victory, but carrieth away souls (xxii. 9); Abraham refuses presents from the king of Sodom (Gen. xiv. 22); Jacob sends presents to Esau (Gen. xxxii. 13–21); Balaam refuses the presents of Balac (Num. xxii. 18); Samuel's sons, Ophni and Phinees, corrupted by presents (1 Kings viii. 3); Samuel never took a bribe (1 Kings xii. 3); a prophet refuses the presents of Jeroboam (3 Kings xiii. 8); Eliseus refuses the presents of Naaman (4 Kings v. 16); Daniel refuses the gifts of Balthasar (Dan. v. 17); those are happy who receive no bribes (Ps. xiv. 5; Isai. xxxiii. 15; xlv. 13; Acts xx. 35); the high-priesthood obtained by Jason through bribery (2 Mach. iv. 8); by Menelaus (24); Judas bribed to betray our Lord (Matt. xxvi. 15; Mark xiv. 10).

PRI'APUS, an obscene idol. Maacha, mother of king, was priestess of Priapus (3 Kings xv. 13); Asa abolished the worship, broke the idol in pieces, and burnt it (13; 2 Paral. xv. 16).

PRIDE forbidden and punished (Gen. iii. 17; xi. 5, 7; Ex. v. 2; xiv. 26; 1 Kings xvii.; 4 Kings xviii. 19; xix. 35; Tob. iv. 14; Judith ix. 16; xiii.; Prov. vi. 17; xi. 2; xiii. 10; xv. 25; xvi. 5, 18; xviii. 12; xxv. 6; xxix. 23; Ecclus. x. 9–16; xxv. 4; Isai. iii. 15–17; ix. 9; x. 9; xiv. 9; xxxvi.–xxxvii.; xlvii. 8; Jer. xlviii. 29; xlix. 16; Ezech. xvi. 49; xxviii. 2; xxxi. 10; Dan. iv. 19, 27; v. 22; Abd. i. 3; Mal. i. 4; 2 Mach. ix. 4, 6; Luke i. 51; x. 15; xiv. 7, 11; xviii. 11; xxii. 24; Acts xii. 21; Rom. i. 30; xi. 20; 2 Tim. iii. 2; 1 Pet. v. 5; 2 Pet. ii. 10; Jude 16; Apoc. xviii. 1–24).

PRIESTS under the patriarchal law, Melchisedec (Gen. xiv. 18); Raguel or Jethro (Ex. ii. 16; xviii. 12); under the Mosaic law, confined to the family of Aaron; their duty and office (Ex. xxix. 44; xxx. 7; Lev. x. 1, 6; xxi.–xxii.; xxiv. 3; Num. iii. 10; iv. 5, 11; x. 8; xviii. 1, 7; Deut. xxi. 5; 1 Kings ii. 28, 35; 1 Paral. vi. 49; 2 Paral. xxvi. 17; Ezech. xliv. 15, 20; Heb. v. 7; x. 11); entitled to tithes (Num. xviii. 26–28); special tithes every third year (Deut. xxvi. 28; xxvi. 12); the redemption money for the firstborn of man or beast (Num. xviii. 15, 16); to a portion of the spoil taken in war (Num. xxxi. 28); to the loaves of proposition, and parts of animals offered in sacrifice (Num. xviii.; Lev. vi., vii., x.); to the first fruits (Ex. xxiii. 19; Lev. ii., x., xxii.; Deut. xxvi.); after entering the promised land, thirteen cities were assigned to the priests, viz.: Hebron, Lobna, Jether, Estemo, Holon, Dabir, Ain, Jera, Bethsames, Gabaon, Gabae, Anathoth, Almon (Jos. xxi. 13–18); in the time of David the priests numbered 38,000 (1 Paral. xxiii. 3), and were divided by him into twenty-four courses (1 Paral. xxiv. 1–19; 2

Paral. xxiii. 8), each of which served in turn for a week, the duties being assigned by lot (Luke i. 9); after the captivity only four courses could be found (I Esd. ii. 36–39); punishment of wicked priests (Num. xvi.; 1 Kings ii. 22; iii. 17; 3 Kings ii. 26; Isai. i. 11; Jer. ii. 8; viii. 10; Osee iv. 6, 9; v.; Mal. i., ii.; 1 Mach. vii. 5, 9, 21); the priest was the judge of difficult questions (Deut. xvii. 9, 12; Mal. ii. 7); of leprosy (Levit. xiii.)

PRIESTS under the new law. Jesus Christ, priest forever, according to the order of Melchisedech (Ps. cix. 4); our high-priest (Heb. v. 6; x.

THE RETURN OF THE PRODIGAL SON.

21); there are priests of God and of Christ (Apoc. xx. 6); we have an altar, and priests who serve at it (Heb. xiii. 10; 1 Cor. ix. 13); priests ordained by the apostles (Acts xiv. 22), and by Titus, under the authority of St. Paul (Tit. i. 5); St. Paul consults the priests at Jerusalem (Acts xv. 2); priests are to rule well (1 Tim. v. 17); accusations against a priest to be under two or three witnesses (19); priests to be called in in time of sickness (James v. 14).

PRIEST'HOOD in the old law. Laws relating to it (Lev. viii., xvi., xxi., xxii.); its insufficiency (Heb. ix., x.); the priesthood of Melchisedech (Heb. vii. 1–14); the excellence of the priesthood of Christ (Heb. vii. 19); the priesthood of the new law (1 Tim. iv. 14).

PRINCE OF DEVILS (Matt. ix. 34; xii. 24); Beelzebub (Luke xi. 15), prince of this world (John xii. 31; xiv. 30; xvi. 11; 1 Cor. ii. 6, 8).

PRINCE of the kings of the earth, Jesus Christ (Apoc. i. 5).

PRIN'CES of the twelve tribes (Ex. vi.; Num. i., vii.; John vii. 48; Acts iv. 8; xiv. 5).

PRINCIPAL'ITIES, an order of angels (Col. i. 16).

PRIS'CA or PRIS'CILLA, wife of Aquila, early converts. They were compelled to leave Rome when Claudius expelled all Jews (Acts xviii. 2), and settled in Corinth (1); St. Paul remained with them, as they were tent-makers (2); they went with St. Paul to Ephesus (18); they returned to Rome, where St. Paul salutes the church in their house (Rom. xvi. 5); calls them his helpers in Christ (3), and says that they laid down their own necks for his life; and that not only he but all the churches of the Gentiles thank them (4).

PRIS'ONERS, Abraham delivers Lot when a prisoner (Gen. xiv. 16); David rescues the prisoners taken at Siceleg (I Kings xxx. 18); Abdemelech delivers Jeremias when a prisoner (Jer. xxxviii. 10); an angel delivers St. Peter (Acts xii. 7); we should visit the prisoners (Tob. i. 15; Matt. xxv. 36; 2 Tim. i. 16; Heb. xiii. 3); God does not forsake (Gen. xxxix. 21; Wis. x. 13; Isai. xlii. 7; Acts v. 19; xii. 7; xvi. 26).

PROBAT'ICA, a pool at Jerusalem, called also Bethsaida, with five porches (John v. 8). See POOL OF BETHSAIDA.

PROCHO'RUS, one of the seven deacons first appointed by the apostles at Jerusalem (Acts vi. 5).

PROCON'SUL, a governor of a province, appointed by the Roman senate. Sergius Paulus, proconsul of Cyprus (Acts xiii. 7–12); Gallio, proconsul of Achaia (xviii. 12); at Ephesus (xix. 38).

PROD'IGAL SON, the parable of the (Luke xv. 11).

PROFANE'. Esau called profane for selling his birthright (Heb. xii. 16); the Jews considered it profane to eat with Gentiles (Gen. xliii. 32); one who did not eat of the peace-offering in season deemed profane (Lev. xix. 7); forbidden food styled profane (Isai. lxv. 4).

PROM'ISED LAND, God's promises in re-

gard to it (Gen. xii. 7; xiii. 15; xv. 7, 8; xxii. 17); renewed to the Hebrew people (Ex. xiii. 5; xxxiii. 2); shown to Moses (Deut. xxxiv.); though he is not allowed to enter; its remarkable fruits (Lev. xxvi. 4, 5; Deut. i. 21, 25; iii. 25; xi. 10, 14); its limits (Num. xxxiv. 2); described (Jos. xiii.–xix.; Ex. iii.); portioned beyond the Jordan among the tribes of Ruben, Dan, and the half-tribe of Manasse (Num. xxxii. 1); among the other tribes (Jos. xiii.–xxi.)

PROM'ISES. God makes promises subject to conditions (Deut. xviii. 8, 9; xxviii.; Lev. xxvi.; 1 Kings ii. 30; Ezech. xviii.; xxxiii. 15, 19; Mark xvi. 16; John iii. 16, 36; vi. 47; viii. 31; xiii. 17; xv. 7, 14; Rom. viii. 17; Col. i. 23; Heb. iii. 14; 2 Pet. i. 4; Apoc. ii.–iii.; xxi. 7).

PROPH'ECIES. The use to be made of prophecies (2 Pet. i. 19; 1 Cor. xii. 10; 1 Thess. v. 20); of the Apocalypse (Apoc. i. 3; xxii.)

PROPH'ET, from a Greek word, means one who foretells. The Jews called them first Seers (1 Kings ix. 9); also men of God (4 Kings vi. 6); their disciples were called Sons of the Prophets (4 Kings ii. 3); Aaron is called the prophet, that is, the spokesman of Moses (Ex. vii. 1); Abraham is called a prophet (Gen. xx. 7); a prophet is promised by Moses (Deut. xviii. 15); alluded to afterwards (John i. 25; vii. 40); really our Lord Jesus Christ (Matt. xxi. 11; Mark i. 15; John iv. 19); no prophet arose like unto Moses (Deut. xxxiv. 10); a prophet sent to the Jews in the days of Gedeon (Judg. vi. 8); Samuel a prophet (1 Kings iii. 20); the prophet Gad (1 Kings xxii. 5; 2 Kings xxiv. 11); the prophet Nathan (2 Kings vii. 2; xii. 25; 3 Kings i. 8–45; 1 Paral. xvii. 1); the prophet Ahias, the Silonite (3 Kings xi., xiv.); an old prophet slain for disobedience (xiii.); the prophet Jehu (3 Kings xvi.); Elias, the prophet (3 Kings xviii., etc.; Ecclus. xlviii. 1); Eliseus (3 Kings xix. 16); the prophet Jonas (4 Kings xiv. 25; Jonas; Matt. xvi. 4); the prophet Isaias (4 Kings xix. 2; 2 Paral. xxvi. 22; Ecclus. xlviii. 23; Isaias; Matt. viii. 17; Mark ii. 2; vii. 6; John xii. 38; Acts viii. 28, 30); the prophet Semeias (2 Paral. xii. 15); the prophet Addo (2 Paral. xiii. 22); the prophet Azarias (2 Paral. xv. 8); the prophet Hanani (2 Paral. xvi. 7); the prophets Asaph, and Heman, and Idithum (2 Paral. xxxv. 15); the prophet Jeremias (2 Paral. xxxvi. 12; Jer.; Lam.; Bar.; 2 Mach. ii.; xv.; Matt. xvi. 14); the prophet Aggeus (1 Esd. v. 1; Agg.); Zacharias (1 Esd. v. 1; Zach.); Noadias (2 Esd. vi. 14); the prophet Amos (Tob. ii. 6; Amos); Baruch (Bar.); Ezechiel (Ezech.); Daniel (Dan.; Matt. xxiv. 15); Habacuc (Dan. xiv. 32; Hab.); Osee (Os.); Micheas (Mich.); Sophonias (Soph.); Zacharias (Zach.); Malachias (Mal.); Joel (Acts ii. 16; Joel); St. John the Baptist, a prophet and more than a prophet (Matt. xi. 9); a prophet of the Most High (Luke i. 76); he himself humbly says he is not the prophet (John i. 21); the prophet Agabus (Acts xi. 28; xxi. 10); prophets from Jerusalem (Acts xi. 27); at Antioch (xiii. 1); all the prophets and the law bear testimony to Christ (Matt. xi. 13); many prophets wished to see him (Luke x. 24); the city of Jerusalem reproached with slaying the prophets and then building them honorable tombs (Matt. xxiii. 37; Luke xiii. 34).

PROPH'ETS, false; our Lord warns us against them (Matt. vii. 15); it is foretold that there will be many (Matt. xxiv. 11, 24; Mark xiii. 22; Luke vi. 26; 2 Peter ii. 16; 1 John iv. 1); Hananias (Jerem. xxviii.); Barjesu (Acts xiii. 6).

PROPH'ETESSES, Mary, sister of Moses (Ex. xv. 20); Debbora (Judg. iv. 4); Holda (4 Kings

xxii. 14; 2 Paral. xxxiv. 22); Anna (Luke ii. 36).

PROPIT′IATORY, otherwise called the Oracle. It was the cover of the Ark of the Covenant; it was of gold, with two cherubim at each end, facing, and their wings touching. From this God gave his oracles when consulted by Moses or the high-priest (Ex. xxv. 22; Num. vii. 89).

PROP′OSIT′ION, LOAVES OF. They were the twelve loaves which the priest of the week placed every Sabbath, that is Saturday, on the golden table in the Holy before the Lord. They represented the twelve tribes. When the fresh loaves were placed, those of the previous week were removed and could be eaten by the priests only. The offering was accompanied with incense and salt (Lev. xxiv. 5–9; Num. iv. 7; Heb. ix. 2); David, when pressed by hunger, ate the loaves of proposition (1 Kings xxi. 4; Matt. xii. 4).

PROS′ELYTE, a Gentile who was received into the Jewish church (1 Paral. xxii. 2; 2 Paral. ii. 17; xxx. 25; Tob. i. 7; Ezech. xiv. 7; Matt. xxiii. 15; Acts ii. 11).

PROV′ERBS, one of the canonical books of the Old Testament written by Solomon (Prov.) Chapter xxx. is given as the words of Gatherer, the son of Vomiter, in Hebrew of Agur, the son of Jakeh. Chapter xxxi., the words of king Lamuel, Prov. i. 16, is cited, Rom. iii. 15; iii. 7; Rom. xvi. 16; iii. 11, 12; Heb. xii. 5, 6; Apoc. iii. 19; iii. 34; James iv. 6; x. 12; 1 Pet. iv. 8; xi. 31; 1 Pet. iv. 18; xvii. 13; Rom. xii. 17; 1 Thess. v. 15; 1 Pet. iii. 9; xvii. 27; James i. 19; xx. 9; 1 John i. 8; xx. 20; Matt. xv. 4; Mark vii. 10; xxv. 21, 22; Rom. xii. 20; xxvi. 12; 2 Pet. ii. 22; xxvii. 1; James iv. 13, 14.

PSALMS, one of the canonical books of the Old Testament, called in Hebrew Tehillim, that is, hymns of praise. The author of a great part of them was king David, while some are supposed to have been composed by those whose names they bear. They are one hundred and fifty in number, and are divided by the Hebrews into five books. In numbering the Psalms, the Hebrew makes two of what is Ps. ix. and Ps. cxiii. in the Vulgate, and in our English Catholic Bibles; and of what is Ps. cxiv. and cxv., and Ps. cxlvi., cxlvii., they make one. The Psalms are greatly used in the Jewish forms of prayer, whole psalms and verses said responsively, and the usage passed to the Catholic church, which uses them in the same way in her mass and office.

A WOMAN'S PURIFICATION AFTER CHILDBIRTH.

PSALMS, GRADUAL. The Gradual Psalms are cxix. to cxxxiii. They are so called either from the fifteen steps by which the people ascended to the

temple, or that the voice in singing was raised by certain steps.

PSALMS, PENITENTIAL (Ps. vi., xxxi., xxxvii., l., ci., cxxix., and cxlii.) are so called as they all express sorrow and contrition.

PTOLEMA′IS, a city of Phœnicia, on the Mediterranean (Accho, Judg. i. 31), (1 Mach. v. 15); Simon pursued the enemy to the gates of Ptolemais (22, 55); taken by Alexander Bales (x. 1); Demetrius allots it to the Jews (x. 39); Ptolemee and Alexander meet there, and Jonathan also (56–60); Demetrius at (xi. 22, 24); Jonathan entrapped into Ptolemais by Tryphon, and slain there (xii. 45, 48); Antiochus made Machabeus governor from Ptolemais to the Gerrenians (2 Mach. xiii. 24, 25); St. Paul stopped there on his way to Jerusalem (Acts xxi. 7).

PTOL′EMEE, a name born by the kings of Egypt, from Ptolemee, son of Lagus, to the conquest of the country by the Romans.

PTOL′EMEE, PHILOMETOR, son of Ptolemee Epiphanes. He was attacked by Antiochus Epiphanes, king of Syria (1 Mach. i. 19); forms an alliance with Alexander Bales (x. 51); makes war on him, takes Antioch, and assumes the crown of Syria (xi. 13); defeats Alexander in battle (15); dies (18).

PTOL′EMEE MACER, governor of Cyprus for king Ptolemee Philometor, went over to Antiochus, the Illustrious (2 Mach. x. 13); bribed by Menelaus to obtain the favor of Antiochus (2 Mach. iv. 45, 46); Philip seeks his aid, but Judas defeated his troops (viii. 8; 1 Mach. iii. 38, 39); just to the Jews (2 Mach. x. 12); accused to Eupator, poisons himself (13).

PUB′LICANS, farmers or gatherers of taxes. They were despised among the Jews (Matt. v. 46; ix. 11; xi. 19; xviii. 17; xxi. 32; Luke iii. 12); St. Matthew, the apostle, was one when our Lord called him (Luke v. 27); several converted by our Lord (Matt. xxi. 32; Luke v. 27; vii. 29; xv. 1); Zacheus, the chief of the publicans at Jericho, converted (xix. 1–10); our Lord's parable of the publican and the Pharisee (Luke xviii. 10).

PUB′LIUS, chief man of the island of Malta, received St. Paul into his house after his shipwreck (Acts xxviii. 7); St. Paul cures his father of a fever and dysentery (8).

PU′DENS, a disciple mentioned by St. Paul in his second Epistle from Rome to Timothy (2 Tim. iv. 21). He is supposed to have been a Roman senator, converted by St. Peter.

PU′PIL OF THE EYE, often referred to as a symbol of something to be carefully guarded (Deut. xxxii. 10; Ps. xvi. 8; Prov. vii. 2; Ecclus. xvii. 18; Lam. ii. 18; Zach. xii. 8).

PURG′ATORY. Passages proving its existence (2 Mach. xii. 43, 46; Matt. v. 25; xii. 32; 1 Cor. iii. 15; Phil. ii. 10; 2 Tim. i. 18;

RACHEL'S TOMB.

1 Pet. iii. 19; 1 John v. 16; Apoc. v. 3, 13; xxi. 27).

PURIF′ICATION. Purification a legal ceremony, to be performed by a woman after the birth of her child (Lev. xii. 6); the Blessed Virgin obeys the law (Luke ii. 22); purification part of the ceremonial of one who made a vow (Acts xxi. 25).

PURIF′ICATIONS, law relative to (Lev. xii. 4, 5; xiv. 23, 49; xv. 28; 1 Paral. xxiii. 28); purification of the temple after the heathen rites (1 Mach. i. 18, 36; ii. 20; x. 5; 2 Mach. x. 3, 6); water-pots for purifying according to the manner of the Jews (John ii. 6); dispute between John's disciples and the Jews concerning purifications (iii. 25).

PU′RITY, cleanness of heart and body recommended (Matt. xxiii. 25; Luke xi. 39; 2 Cor. vii. 1).

PUTE′OLI, a city of Italy, reached by St. Paul on his way to Rome, A. D. 61 (Acts xxviii. 13); finding brethren there, he remained several days (14).

PUT′IPHAR, a eunuch, chief captain of the army of Pharao (Gen. xxxvii. 36); he purchased Joseph, and made him steward of his house (xxxix. 4); his wife tempts Joseph (7), and being repulsed falsely accused him (8–18); Putiphar believing his wife cast Joseph into prison (20).

PUTIPHA′RE, priest of Heliopolis. His daughter Aseneth was given to Joseph as his wife by Pharao (Gen. xli. 45).

PYGARG′, an animal with a white rump, a species of antelope, allowed to be eaten (Deut. xiv. 5).

PYG′MEANS, are said to have hung their quivers on the walls of Tyre, and perfected its beauty (Ezech. xxvii. 11).

PYR′AMIDS, Simon set up seven pyramids at Modin, for his father, mother and four brethren (1 Mach. xiii. 28).

PYTHON′ICAL SPIRIT. A girl with a pythonical spirit at Philippi, whose divinings were a great gain to her master, was delivered from the spirit by St. Paul (Acts xvi. 16).

QUAILS, a well-known bird. God sent flocks of them to feed the Israelites in the desert (Ex. xvi. 13; Ps. civ. 40; Wis. xvi. 2); they gathered and dried them (Num. xi. 32), but were punished by a plague (33).

QUARTUS, a Christian at Corinth (Rom. xvi. 23).

QUAR'RELS, to be avoided (Ecclus. viii. 2, 4, 19; Phil. ii. 15; iii. 6; 1 Thess. ii. 10; iii. 13; v. 23).

QUARTERS OF JERUSALEM, after the return from Babylon, named in 2 Esd. iii. 3.

QUEEN OF SABA, comes to visit Solomon (3 Kings x. 13; 2 Paral. ix. 1, 9, 12); the queen of the south will rise in judgment against the Jews (Luke xi. 31). Queen, used to mean the mother of the reigning king, who in the East exercised greater influence than the wife (4 Kings x. 13; 2 Paral. xv. 16; xxii. 10).

QUEEN OF HEAVEN, the goddess Astarte, or the moon. Hebrew women offered cakes to her (Jer. vii. 18; xliv. 17-19, 25).

QUESTIONS. Useless questions to be avoided (Gen. iii. 1, 6; Prov. xxv. 27; Eccles. vii. 11; Ecclus. iii. 22; Matt. xxiv. 3; John xxi. 21; Acts i. 6; 1 Tim. i. 4; vi. 3; 2 Tim. ii. 16; Tit. iii. 9).

RABBA, Rabbath of the children of Ammon, a strong place east of the Jordan, the chief town of the Ammonites. The iron bed of Og was preserved there (Deut. iii. 11); David sent Joab to besiege it (2 Kings xi. 1); they made frequent sallies (17); finally taken by David (xii. 26-31); Moloch was worshipped there in the days of Amos (Amos i. 14); still important in the days of Nabuchodonosor (Jerem. xlix. 2, 3; Ezech. xxi. 20).

RABBI', Rabboni, a term signifying master, applied to our Lord (Matt. xxiii. 7, 8; xxvi. 25, 49; Mark ix. 5; xi. 21; xiv. 45; John i. 38, 49; iii. 2, 26; iv. 31; vi. 25; ix. 2; xi. 8; Mark x. 51; John xx. 16).

RAB'SACES, general of the army of Sennacherib, king of the Assyrians; his horrible blasphemies (4 Kings xviii. 17; Isai. xxxvi., xxxvii.)

RAB'SARES, a prince of the court of Nabuchodonosor, at Babylon (Jerem. xxxix. 3).

RA'CA, a term of contempt (Matt. v. 22).

RA'CHEL, youngest daughter of Laban, feeds her father's flocks (Gen. xxix. 9); Jacob meets her and kisses her (10, 11); she announces his arrival (13); Jacob being in love with her offers to serve seven years for her (18); is deceived with Lia, but serves seven years more for Rachel, and marries her (28); Laban gives her Bala for her servant (29); she remained barren (31); her grief (xxx. 1); gives Bala to Jacob as a wife (3); Rachel bears Joseph (22-24); she steals her father's idols (xxxi. 19); and hides them (34); bears Benjamin near Ephrata or Bethlehem (xxxv. 16-18); dies and is buried there (19); Jacob erects a pillar over her sepulchre (20).

RAGAU (1 Paral. i. 25; Luke iii. 35), or Reu (Gen. xi. 18, 19); son of Phaleg.

RAGAU, a place where Nabuchodonosor, king of Ninive, defeated Arphaxad, king of the Elamites (Judith i. 5, 6).

RAGES, a city of Media, situated in the mountains of Ecbatana. Gabelus, to whom the elder Tobias had lent money, resided here, and he sent his son to obtain it (Tob.)

RAG'UEL, or Jethro, father-in-law of Moses. See JETHRO.

RAG'UEL, father of Sara, who married the younger Tobias. He lived at Rages, a city of the Medes (Tob. iii. 7); he had one daughter Sara (vi. 11); he receives Tobias and the angel (vii. 1); as instructed by the angel (vi. 13). Tobias asks Sara

as his wife (vii. 10); Raguel gives her (15, 16); digs a grave for Tobias (viii. 11); blesses the Lord for his safety (16); gives Tobias half his possessions (24); sends Tobias and Sara home (x. 10-13).

RA'HAB, a woman of Jericho, entertains Josue's spies (Jos. ii. 1; Heb. xi. 31; James ii. 25); conceals them from the officers of the king (Jos. ii. 3-5); she recognized the true God (11); makes the spies swear to show mercy to her father's house, and give her a token (13); lets them down from a window (15); a scarlet cord a made a sign of safety to her (18); Josue orders her and her family to be spared (vi. 17); she is saved with her kindred and goods (23); she married Salmon, prince of Juda (Matt. i. 5); to whom she bore Booz, great-grandfather of David (Ruth iv. 21, 22; 1 Paral. ii. 11).

RA'HAB, a city or country, by some supposed to be Egypt (Ps. lxxxvi. 4).

RA'HUEL, son of Esau and Basemath, daughter of Ismael (Gen. xxxvi. 4, 17).

RAIN'BOW, God set a rainbow in the sky as a sign of his covenant with Noe (Gen. ix. 12; Ezech. i. 28).

RAISINS, dried grapes (1 Kings xxv. 18; xxx. 12; 2 Kings xvi. 1).

RAM. Eliu is said to have been of the kindred of Ram (Job xxxii. 2); apparently the same as Aram.

RAM, the male of the sheep, offered in sacrifice by Abram, as directed by God (Gen. xv. 9); one given as a substitute for Isaac (xxii. 13); ram skins used in the tabernacle (Ex. xxv., xxvi., xxix., xxxv., xxxvi., xxxix.); offered in sacrifice under the law (Levit. v., vi., viii., ix., xvi., xix., xxiii.; Num. vi., vii., xv., xxiii., etc.); seen in a vision by the prophet Daniel (Dan. viii. 3).

RA'MA, a city of Benjamin (Jos. xviii. 25); between Gabaa and Bethel (Judg. iv. 5; xix. 13); Jeremias restored to liberty at Rama (Jerem. xl. 1-3); Rachel mourning for her children at Rama (Jerem. xxxi. 15); applied to the massacre of the innocents (Matt. ii. 8).

RA'MA, a wooded height near Gabaa (1 Kings xxii. 6; 1 Esd. ii. 26; 2 Esd. vii. 30; Isai. x. 29; Osee v. 8).

RAMATH (Jos. xix. 21); Beer-Ramath (xix. 8); Ramoth to the south (1 Kings xxx. 27); a city in the tribe of Simeon.

RAMA'THA, a town in Samaria, given by Demetrius to Jonathan (1 Mach. xi. 34).

RAMATHAIMSOPHIM, in Mount Ephraim, the home of Elcana, father of Samuel (1 Kings i. 1).

RAM'ATHLE'CHI (The lifting up of the jawbone, the place where Samson slew a thousand Philistines with the jawbone of an ass (Judg. xv. 14 -17).

RAMES'SES, a city built by the Hebrews during their bondage in Egypt (Ex. i. 11).

RAMES'SES, a district of Egypt assigned to Jacob and his family when they went to Egypt (Gen. xlvii. 11). The Israelites set out from it under Moses (Ex. xii. 37; Num. xxxiii. 3).

RAM'ETH (Jos. xix. 21), Ram'oth (1 Paral. vi. 73), a Levitical city in the tribe of Issachar.

RAMOTH GALAAD, a city in the tribe of Gad (Jos. xiii. 26); a city of refuge (Deut. iv. 43; Jos. xx. 8); given to the Levites (Jos. xxi. 37; 1 Par. vi. 80); it became a source of contest between the kings of Israel and Syria (3 Kings xxii.); Joram, king of Juda, grievously wounded while besieging (4 Kings viii. 28, 29; 2 Paral. xxii. 5); Jehu conse-

crated king there (4 Kings ix.); Achab killed in battle with the Syrians before Ramoth (2 Paral. xviii.)

RAN'SOM OF LANDS AND HOUSES regulated by express law (Lev. xxv. 23-31).

RAPE, the law against (Deut. xxii. 28, 29).

RAPH'AEL, son of Semeias, a valiant man (1 Paral. xxvi. 7); a Levite and porter of the temple.

RAPH'AEL, one of the seven angels constantly before the throne of God (Tob. xii. 15); he appeared in human form (v. 5), and guided young Tobias to Ecbatana, expelled the devils who beset Sara, obtained her in marriage for Tobias (vi.-viii.), received the money from Gabelus (ix.), guided him safely home, and cured the blindness of the elder Tobias (Tob. xi.)

RAPH'AIM, a race of gigantic men in Chanaan. Chodorlahomor and his allies smite them in Astarothcarnaim. Their territory promised to the descendants of Abraham (xv. 20); in Moses' time, Og, king of Basan, ruled over the remnant of the race (Jos. xii. 3); they were overthrown and destroyed by Moses (xiii. 12). The valley of Raphaim kept the name to the time of Isaias (Jos. xv. 8; 2 Kings v. 18; 1 Paral. xiv. 9; Isai. xvii. 5); Saphai, of the race of the Raphaim, was a Philistine champion, and was slain by Sobochai (1 Paral. xx. 4), as were Goliath and his brother (5, 6).

RAPH'IDIM, the encampment of the Israelites after leaving the desert of Sin (Ex. xvii. 1); there was no water there, and Moses obtained water by striking the rock (1-6; Num. xxxiii. 14, 15); they set out from it for Sinai (Ex. xix. 2).

RAPH'ON, a city beyond the Jordan, near Carnaim. Judas Machabeus defeated Timotheus there (1 Mach. v. 37).

RAPT TO THE THIRD HEAVEN, St. Paul was (2 Cor. xii.)

RAS'IN, king of Syria, with Phacee, king of Israel, invades Juda, and besieges Achaz in Jerusalem (4 Kings xv. 37, 38; xvi. 5, 6); Rasin also took Aila (4 Kings xvi. 6), and carried away great booty to Damascus (2 Paral. xxviii. 5); Theglathphalasar, king of the Assyrians, to protect Achaz, took Damascus, and slew Rasin (4 Kings xvi. 9).

RAT'IONAL OF JUDGMENT, a precious, embroidered vestment, worn on the breast of the high-priest, with four rows of precious stones, on each of which was graven the name of one of the twelve tribes (Ex. xxviii. 15-28).

RAZI'AS, one of the ancients of Jerusalem, called the "Father of the Jews," accused to Nicanor of observing the law (2 Mach. xiv. 37); 500 soldiers sent to seize him (39); strikes himself with his own sword (41-46).

RAZON, son of Eliada, fled from his master Aderezer, king of Soba (3 Kings xi. 23); became captain of a band of robbers, and finally king of Damascus (24); hostile to king Solomon (25).

REAP'ING, directions as to (Lev. xxiii. 22).

RE'BE, one of the five princes of the Madianites, slain by Phinees, son of Eleazer (Num. xxxi. 8; Jos. xiii. 21).

REBEC'CA, daughter of Bathuel, and wife of Isaac. Abraham sent Damascus Eliezer to Haran to obtain a wife for Isaac of his kindred (Gen. xxiv. 1-14); Rebecca met him at the well, and gave him to drink, and watered his camels (15-20); receives presents and reports his coming (22-28); Rebecca asked as wife to Isaac (49); Laban and Bathuel give her (51); she goes with her maids (58-62);

meets Isaac at the Well of the Living and Seeing, and becomes his wife (62–67; xxv. 20); she bears Esau and Jacob (25); with Isaac at the court of Abimelech in Gerara (xxvi. 8); aids Jacob to deceive Isaac and supplant Esau (xxvii. 1–41); advises him to flee to Laban (42, 43); complains of the daughters

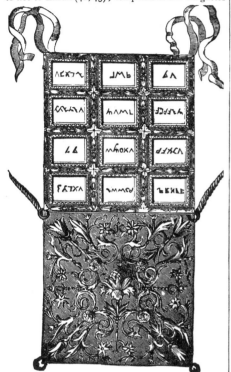

THE RATIONAL OF JUDGMENT.

of Heth, whom Esau married (46); buried in the double cave (xlix. 31).

REBLA′THA, a city in the land of Emath in Syria; Rebla was on the boundary of the promised land, over against the fountain of Daphnis (Num. xxxiv. 11); Pharao Nechao fined and bound Joachaz in Rebla (4 Kings xxiii. 33); Sedecias was brought before the king of Babylon and blinded in Reblatha (xxv. 6; Jerem. xxxix. 5, 6; lii. 9, 10); Saraias, the high-priest, and others, put to death there (lii. 24–27).

RE′CEM, one of the princes of Madian, put to death by Phinees, after the abomination of Beelphegor (Num. xxxi. 8).

RE′CHAB and **BAANA**, assassins of Isboseth, son of Saul (2 Kings iv. 2); put to death by David (12).

RECH′AB, father of Jonadab, founder of the Rechabites (4 Kings x. 15, 23); Calor (Chamath) is given as the father of the house of Rechab (1 Paral. ii. 55).

RECH′ABITES, were Cinites, descendants of Jethro (1 Paral. ii. 55); they were employed in the service of the temple; they dwelt in tents (Jer. xxxv. 6, 7); they were to drink no wine, build house, sow seed, or plant vineyard, or have any (6, 7); their head in the time of Jeremias was Jezonias (3); he tempted them to drink wine (5); they refused to disobey the commands of Jonadab (6–10); and their fidelity was cited to the Jews to their confusion (11–18); and the promise made that there shall not be wanting a man of the race of Jonadab standing before the Lord forever (19). Melchias, apparently a Rechabite, aided in building the wall of Jerusalem after the captivity (2 Esd. iii. 14).

REC′OMPENSE due to works (Gen. iv. 7; xv.

1; Ps. cxviii. 112; Prov. xi. 18; Wis. v. 16; Ecclus. ii. 8; xi. 24; xviii. 22; xxxvi. 18; li. 30, 38; Isai. iii. 10; Jerem. xxxi. 16; Matt. v. 12; xx. 8; John iv. 36; Rom. iv. 4; 1 Tim. v. 18).

REC′REATION, when becoming, permitted (1 Paral. xxix. 9; 2 Esd. xii. 42; Ps. lxvii. 4; Luke i. 14; 1 Thess. v. 16); not to be indulged in after the manner of the heathen (Eccles. ii. 2; vii. 3; Osee ix. 1; Amos vi.; Prov. ii. 14; James iv. 9).

REDEEM′, REDEMP′TION. Land among the Jews could not be sold forever. The owner who was forced to sell could always redeem, and in the year of jubilee, when all that was sold returned to the owner, except houses in cities. The houses of Levites in cities could always be redeemed (Lev. xxv. 23–32). Nothing consecrated to the Lord could be redeemed, except unclean beasts (xxvii. 28–33).

REDEEM′ER, a name applied especially to Jesus Christ, who has redeemed us from the bondage of Satan. Job declares his faith in a Redeemer to come (Job xix. 25); David (xviii. 15; lxxvii. 35); Isaias xli. 14; xliii. 14; xliv. 6, 24; xlvii. 4; xlviii. 17; xlix. 7, 26; liv. 5, 8; lix. 20; lx. 16; lxiii. 16; Jerem. l. 34; Lam. iii. 58.

REDEMP′TION, Christ came to give his own blood as a redemption for many (Matt. xx. 28; Mark

ROMAN SOLDIER.

x. 45); we have redemption through him (Col. i. 14); he gave himself for our redemption (1 Tim. ii. 6).

RED SEA, between Egypt and Arabia. Moses leads the Israelites to it (Ex. xiii. 18); the Israelites

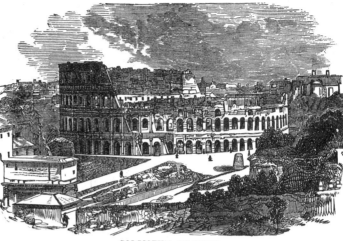

COLOSSEUM AT ROME.

traverse it on foot through the bed miraculously (xiv. 20); Pharao and his host are overwhelmed in it (Ex. xv. 4; Ps. cv. 7, 9; cxxxv. 15; 1 Mach. iv. 9; Acts vii. 36; Heb. xi. 27); the Israelites march from the banks of the Red Sea (Ex. xv. 22); designated as a boundary (xxiii. 31). Solomon had ports on the Red Sea (3 Kings ix. 26).

REED, placed in the hands of our Lord in mockery instead of a sceptre (Matt. xxvii. 29).

REEDS, valley of (Josue xvi. 8).

REE′MA, or **REGMA**, son of Chus (Gen. x. 7). His descendants sent spices, gold, and precious stones to Tyre (Ezech. xxvii. 22).

REF′UGE, cities and places of, assigned for cases of involuntary shedding of human blood (Ex. xxi. 13; Deut. iv. 41; xix. 2, 7; Jos. xx.; 3 Kings i. 50; ii. 28).

REGEN′ERATION, necessary for salvation (John iii. 5); it changes earthly to spiritual affections (Rom. viii. 5, 13); it makes men pass from infidelity to faith (John i. 12; Gal. iii. 16; 1 John v. 1); it is a renewal of the heart by the Holy Ghost (Titus iii. 5; Gal. iv. 6); it is a participation in the Divine nature (2 Pet. i. 4; Col. ii. 11); it is the justification of the sinner (1 Cor. vi. 11; Eph. v. 8); the regenerate must lead an entirely new life (Rom. vi.; vii. 6; xii. 1; Eph. iv. 22; Col. iii. 9; 1 Cor. v. 7; 2 Cor. v. 15; 1 Pet. iv. 1).

RE′I, one of David's counsellors who did not join the party of Adonias (3 Kings i. 8).

REINS, kidneys. The Hebrews regarded them as the seat of joy, grief, pleasure. God is called searcher of the heart and reins (Ps. vii. 10; Wis. i. 6; Apoc. ii. 23; Jerem. xvii. 10; xx. 12; xi. 20); Try me, burn my reins and my heart (Ps. xxv. 2).

REL′ICS. Virtue possessed by the relics and garments of the saints, and miracles wrought by their means exemplified in the mantle of Elias, dividing the waters of Jordan so that Eliseus passed over on foot (4 Kings ii. 14); in the bones of the prophet Eliseus which raised to life a man slain by robbers (xiii. 21); in the hem (fringe) of our Lord's garment (Matt. ix. 20; xiv. 36); in the handkerchiefs and linen of St. Paul (Acts xix. 12); in the shadow of St. Peter (v. 15).

REM′MON, a town in the tribe of Simeon (Jos. xix. 7; xv. 32; 2 Esd. xi. 29; Zach. xiv. 10).

REM′MON, a rock to which the remnant of the tribe of Benjamin escaped (Judg. xx. 45; xxi. 13).

REM′MON, AMTAR, a city or cities in the tribe of Zabulon (Jos. xix. 13).

REM'MON PHARES, an encampment of the Israelites in the desert (Num. xxiii. 19).

REM'MON, an idol worshipped at Damascus.

ROME—THE OSTIAN GATE.

Naaman obliged to visit a temple of Remmon, with the king of Damascus, his master (4 Kings v. 18).

REM'PHAN. St. Stephen citing (Amos v. 25–27); speaks of "the star of your god Remphan," but the name is not now in Amos (Acts vii. 43).

REND'ING of garments a sign of grief (Gen. xxxvii. 30; 2 Paral. xxxiv. 27; 1 Esd. ix. 3; Job i. 20; ii. 12); we are to rend our hearts and not our garments (Joel ii. 13).

REPENT'ANCE, see PENANCE.

REPROBA'TION of the Jews, leads to the salvation of the world (Rom. xi. 1).

REPU'DIATION of a wife permitted among the Jews; the manner in which it was performed (Deut. xxiv. 1, 3; Jer. iii. 8; Matt. v. 31; xix. 7).

REP'UTATION preferable to riches (Prov. xxii. 1; Ecclus. xli. 15, 16); it is lawful to defend our reputation and innocence against accusations (Jos. xxii. 22; 1 Kings i. 15; 3 Kings xviii. 18; Jerem. xxxvii. 13; John xviii. 23; Acts ii. 15; vi. 14; vii. 2; xxviii. 17).

REPU'TED unto justice (Rom. iv. 3–6; Gen. xv. 6).

RE'SA, son of Zorababel, one of the ancestors of our Lord (Luke iii. 27).

RE'SEN, a city of Assyria, built by Assur, between Ninive and Chale (Gen. x. 12).

RE'SEPH, a city of Syria (4 Kings xix. 12; Isai. xxxvii. 12).

RESPECT' of persons forbidden. There is none with God (Lev. xix. 15; Deut. i. 17; x. 17; 1 Kings xvi. 7; Prov. xviii. 5; xxviii. 21; Isai. xi. 3; Mal. ii. 9; Matt. xxii. 16; Gal. ii. 6; Eph. vi. 9; James ii. 9; 1 Pet. i. 17).

RES'PHA, daughter of Aia, concubine or inferior wife of Saul. She is abused by Abner (2 Kings iii. 8). Saul had on some occasion put to death a number of Gabaonites (1 Kings xxi.); God punished the crime by a three years' famine. David summoned the Gabaonites to know what they demanded. They asked seven sons or grandsons of Saul. David gave up Respha's two sons, and five sons of a daughter of Saul (xxi. 8); the Gabaonites crucified them (9); Respha watched the bodies, protecting them against the birds and beasts of prey, from the beginning of the harvest till the water dropped out of heaven (10).

RES'SA, a station of the Israelites in the desert (Num. xxxiii. 22).

REST of God promised to his people (Heb. iv. 9); the just have assured rest and peace (Wis. iii. 3; iv. 1; Isai. lvii. 2; Luke xvi. 22; Apoc. xiv. 13); to find rest for the soul (Jer. vi. 16; Matt. xi. 29); the day of the rest of the Lord (Ex. xxiii.); sabbath rest consecrated by law (Lev. xxiii. 3).

RES'URRECTION. The resurrection of Jesus Christ foretold by the prophets (Ps. iii. 6; ix. 15; xv. 10; xxi. 31; xl. 11; Osee vi. 3; Isai. liii. 10–12; Zach. vi. 12, 13); foretold by himself (Matt. xxvi. 61; Mark xv. 58; John ii. 19); it is the foundation of our faith (1 Cor. xv. 14, 17, 20; 2 Cor. v. 15; 1 Thess. iv. 13; 2 Tim. ii. 8).

RES'URRECTION of the dead (Ex. iii. 6; Job xiv. 12; xix. 25, 26; xxi. 30; Isai. xxvi. 19; lxvi. 14; Ezech. xxxvii. 1–10; Daniel xii. 2; Jonas ii. 11; Soph. iii. 8; 2 Mach. vii. 9; xii. 44; Matt. xxii. 23, 31; Luke xx. 35; John v. 21, 28; vi. 39; xi. 24; Acts xxiv. 15; 1 Cor. xv.; 2 Cor. iv. 14; v.; Coloss. iii. 4; Phil. iii. 21; iv. 3; 1 Thess. iv. 13, 16; 2 Tim. ii. 11; Apoc. xx. 12).

RETH'MA, an encampment of the Israelites in the desert (Num. xxxiii. 18).

REU or RAGAU, son of Phaleg. He died 1974 B. C., aged 239 (Gen. xi. 18, 20; 1 Paral. i. 25; Luke iii. 35).

REUM BELTEEM writes to the king to oppose the rebuilding of Jerusalem (1 Esd. iv. 8–23).

REV'ELATIONS and visions (Jos. v. 13; 1 Kings xxviii. 14; 2 Mach. iii. 24; v. 2; x. 29; xi. 8; Apoc.)

REVIEW' of the army of Israel by Saul (1 Kings xi. 8).

RHEG'IUM, a port in southern Italy. St. Paul arrives there on his way to Rome (Acts xxviii. 13).

RHINOCEROS. Strength of Egypt compared to (Num. xxiv. 8).

RHODE, a damsel at the house of John Mark (Acts xii. 13); in her amazement at the appearance of St. Peter she omits to open the gate (14).

RHODES, St. Paul reaches on his way to Rome (Acts xxi. 1).

RHOD'OCUS, a traitor in the army of Judas Machabeus; he is discovered and imprisoned (2 Mach. xiii. 21).

RICH. How the rich should treat the poor (Lev. xxv. 35; Deut. xv. 7, 10; Job xxxi. 16; Ps. lxi. 11; Prov. xiv. 31; xix. 17; xxi. 13; xxii. 7; xxviii. 27; Eccles. xi. 1; Ecclus. iv. 4; vii. 36; xxix. 12; xxxi. 8; Matt. vi. 19; xix. 21; Luke xiv. 13; xvi. 9; xvi. 25; xviii. 22; Acts ii. 45; iv. 34). The vanity of riches, and contempt for them; we are not to put our trust in them (Ps. xxxviii. 7; xlviii.; li. 9; Prov. x. 2; xv. 16; xviii. 11; xxii. 16; xxiii. 4; xxviii. 11; xxx. 8; Eccles. v. 9, 12; vi. 2; Ecclus. x. 10; xiv. 3; xxxi. 3; Isai. ii. 7; Jerem. xvii. 3, 11; xxii. 13; Ezech. vii. 19; Luke viii. 14; 1 Tim. vi. 9; James

i. 11); riches called unjust (Ecclus. v. 10); the wicked rich are cursed (1 Kings xxv. 2; Job xx. 19; xxvii. 19; Jer. xv. 13; Am. vi. 1; viii. 4; Hab. ii. 6; Luke vi. 24; xvi. 19; James v. 1).

RICH MAN AND LAZARUS, a parable of our Lord (Luke xvi. 19–31).

RIN'NA, son of Simeon (1 Paral. iv. 20); compare Gen. xlvi. 10.

RIPH'ATH, second son of Gomer, and grandson of Japheth (Gen. x. 3; 1 Paral. i. 6).

RIV'ERS. Four rivers, Phison, Gehon, Tigris and Euphrates, water Paradise (Gen. ii. 11–14); rivers represented as exulting, clapping their hands at the coming of Christ to judge the earth (Ps. xcvii. 8); the waters of the Nile turned into blood (Ex. vii.); the Euphrates mentioned (Gen. ii. 14; Deut. i. 7; 2 Kings viii. 3; 4 Kings xxiii.; 1 Paral. v. 9); the Abana and Pharphar, rivers of Damascus (4 Kings v. 12); the Tigris (Gen. ii. 14; Tob. vi. 1); Ezechiel at the river Chobar (Ezech. i. 3; iii. 15); our Lord baptized in the river Jordan. See JORDAN.

ROBO'AM, son of Solomon, by Naama, an Ammonite woman (3 Kings xiv. 21), began to reign 1014 B. C., at the age of 41; after Solomon's death he went to Sichem to be installed king (xii. 1); the people demanded a diminution of the taxes, but influenced by bad advisers, he answered roughly (xii. 11, 13); all the tribes except Juda and Benjamin revolt, and follow Jeroboam, and make him king (19, 20); God forbids Roboam to make war on Israel (2 Paral. xi. 3); Sesac, king of Egypt, made war on Roboam; took Jerusalem, and plundered the temple and palace (xii. 2–9); Roboam replaced the golden shields of Solomon with shields of brass (10); his death—he is succeeded by his son Abiam (16); Roboam's wife was Maacha, the daughter of Abessalom (3 Kings xv. 2).

ROCK, struck by Moses, gives water in abundance (Ex. xvii. 6); and the rock was Christ (1 Cor. x. 4); the remnant of the tribe of Benjamin flee to the rock of Remmon (Judg. xx. 47); Samson held the rock of Etam (xv. 8); David pursued by Saul, took refuge in caves in the rocks at Maon (1 Kings xxiii. 25, 28); at Odollam (1 Kings xxii. 1) Engaddi, there were caves to hold all his men, and where Saul abode for a time (1 Kings xxiv. 2, 5); Josue shut up the five captured kings in the cave of Maceda

ROME—THE PANTHEON.

(Jos. x. 16); during the Madianite oppression, the Jews took refuge in caves in the rocks (Judg. vi. 2); the Cinites dwelt in the hollows of the rocks (Num. xxiv. 21); Oreb slain at the rock Oreb (Judg. vii. 25);

xvii. 32; xxxi. 3); the rock of salvation (Deut. xxxii. 13); the apostle Simon is called Cephas, Peter, that is, the rock: "Thou art Peter, and on this rock I will build my church" (Matt. xvi. 18); a rock of offence (Rom. ix. 33); the sepulchre in which our Lord was laid was hewn out of a rock by Joseph of Arimathea (Mark xv. 46); at the crucifixion, the rocks were rent by an earthquake (Matt. xxvii. 51).

ROD. The rod of Moses was changed into a serpent near the burning bush (Ex. iv. 3); it was again changed before Pharao (vii. 10); Aaron's devours rods which the magicians had changed into serpents (12); it changes water into blood (20); Moses directed to lift up his rod, and stretch his hand over the Red Sea to divide it (xiv. 16); strikes the rock Horeb, and obtains water for the Israelites (xvii. 5, 6); the rod of Aaron blossoms, to prove the divine institution of his priesthood (Num. xvii. 8); God orders it to be kept in the tabernacle of the testimony (10).

ROD, as an instrument of correction (Prov. x. 13; xiii. 24; xxii. 8; xxvii. 15; Acts xvii. 22; 2 Cor. xi. 25).

ROE, used (Deut. xii., xiv., xv.; 2 Kings ii. 18; 3 Kings iv. 23; 1 Par. xii. 8; Cant. ii., iv.; vii., viii.; Ecclus. xi., xxvii.), evidently for an antelope, and probably the gazelle. The original Douay has *doa* in Deut.

RO'MA, concubine or inferior wife of Nachor (Gen. xxii. 24).

ROMANS, their fame (1 Mach. viii. 1); form an alliance with the Jews (1 Mach. viii. 17, 27, 29); their republican form of government praised (1 Mach. viii. 2, 14, 16); Roman Christians (Rom. i. 8); predictions that the Romans were to destroy Jerusalem and the temple of the Lord (Num. xxiv. 24; Isai. v. 26; vi. 11; Dan. ix. 16; Luke xix. 41; xxi. 20; John xi. 48); Judea subject to the Romans in the time of our Lord (Luke iii. 1).

ROMANS, Epistle to the, written by St. Paul, one of the canonical books of the New Testament (Rom.).

ROME. Judas Machabeus sends Eupolemus and Jason as ambassadors to Rome (1 Mach. viii. 17); the treaty (23–28); a second embassy (xii.); Jonathan's death heard in Rome (xiv. 16); strangers from Rome at Jerusalem on the day of Pentecost (Acts ii. 10); Jews expelled from Rome by the em-

ROME—THE MAUSOLEUM OF HADRIAN.

peror Claudius (xviii. 2); St. Paul at Rome (xxviii. 16, 30, 31).

ROS, son of Benjamin (Gen. xlvi. 21).

ROSE, wisdom compared to a rose-plant in Jericho (Ecclus. xxiv. 18; xxxix. 17; l. 8); used for crowns (Wisd. ii. 8).

RU'BEN, eldest son of Jacob and Lia, born (Gen. xxix. 32); commits incest with Bala, his father's concubine (xxxv. 22), therefore not accounted the first-born (1 Par. v. 1); endeavored to deliver Joseph out of the hands of his brethren (xxxvii. 21, 22); rends his garments on not finding him in the cistern (29, 30); makes himself responsible for the safe return of Benjamin (xlii. 37); not blessed on account of his sin (xlix. 3, 4); his sons, Henoch, Phallu, Hesron, and Charmi (xlvi. 9).

RU'BEN, tribe of, numbered 46,500 fighting men when they came out of Egypt (Num. ii. 10, 11), and 43,730 at Settim (xxvi. 7); they were under their prince Elisur, son of Sedear (i. 5; ii. 10); his gifts to the tabernacle (vii. 30–35). They ask lands beyond the Jordan (Num. xxxii. 1–5); the reply of Moses (6–15); their promise (16–19); Moses gives Ruben, Dan, and the half-tribe of Manasses Galaad, the kingdoms of Sehon and Og (29, 33; Deut. iii. 12; xxix. 8; Jos. iv. 12; xiii. 23); the children of Ruben built Hesebon, Eleale, Cariathaim, Nabo, Baalmeon, and Sabama (Num. xxxii. 37); last words of Moses as to Ruben (Deut. xxxiii. 6); the tribe erect an altar, and are called to account (Jos. xxii. 10); they fight against the Agarites (1 Paral. v. 19), and took great booty (21), and occupied their land (22); join David (xii. 37); Adina, son of Siza, their prince (xi. 42), and afterwards Eliezer, son of Zechri (xxvii. 16); Theglathphalasar, king of Assyria, carries them away into captivity, when Beera was prince (v. 6, 26; 4 Kings xv. 29); Judith was of the tribe of Ruben (Judith viii. 1).

RUE, a bitter herb. The Pharisees were so exact as to pay their tithe of it (Luke xi. 42).

RU'FUS, son of Simon, the Cyrenian (Mark xv. 21); supposed to be the one saluted by St. Paul (Rom. xvi. 13).

RU'IN. Temporal chastisements often foretold in the Scriptures (Ex. xxxiv. 12; Lev. xxvi. 30; Judg. viii. 27; 2 Kings xv. 14; Ps. cv. 29; cix. 6; Prov. xii. 13; xxix. 16; Ecclus. xxxi. 38); they are often announced by the prophets (Isai. iii. 6; viii. 14; xxiii. 13; lxiv. 11; Jer. vi. 21; Bar. iv. 31; Ezech. xxvi. 15; xxxi. 16; Os. ix. 8); the ruin of Jerusalem foretold (Luke xix. 41; xx. 16; xxi. 6; John xi. 48); the ruin of Jerusalem visited by Nehemias (2 Esd. ii. 13, 15).

RUTH, a Moabitess, marries Chelion, son of Elimelech and Noemi (Ruth i. 2–4); when Noemi, after the death of her husband and sons, resolved to return to the land of Israel, Ruth would not leave her (5–17); gleans in the fields of Booz (ii. 1–8); she is favored by him (8–18); claims him as a husband by the law of affinity (iii.); on refusal of a nearer kinsman to marry her and take the field of Elimelech, Booz marries her (iv.); Isai, father of David, was their grandson (iv. 22).

RUTH, a canonical book of the Old Testament, giving the history of Ruth, and placed between Judges and Kings (Ruth).

ROME—THE MODERN CAPITOL.

SAA'NANIM, a city of the tribe of Nephthali (Jos. xix. 33).

SAA'RIM (1 Paral. iv. 31); or **SARAIM** (Jos. xv. 36), a city of the tribe of Juda, and then of Siméon.

SA'BA, son of Chus (Gen. x. 7); a son of Rhegma (x. 7); a son of Jectan (x. 28); a son of Jecsan (xxv. 3).

SA'BA, the queen of (3 Kings x.); the queen of the south (Matt. xii. 42; Luke xi. 13); having heard the fame of Solomon, she came to Jerusalem with a rich retinue and presents (3 Kings x. 1–3) she tried him with hard questions, but he answered all (1–3); she acknowledged his greatness and his wisdom: "the half hath not been told me; thy wisdom and thy works exceed the fame which I heard" (7); she blessed God who had raised him to the throne (8), and made him rich presents of gold, spices and precious stones (10; 2 Paral. ix. 1–9); the kings of Saba shall bring gifts to the Lord (Ps. lxxi. 10; Jerem. vi. 20; Isai. lx. 6); Saba sold gold, precious stones and spices to Tyre (Ezech. xxvii. 22, 23).

SABACTHA'NI, a Hebrew word that occurs in Ps. xxii. 2; cited by our Lord on the cross, and meaning "thou hast abandoned me" (Matt. xxvii. 46; Mark xv. 34).

SAB'AIM (Isai. xlv. 14), apparently Sabeans.

SABA'MA, a city of the tribe of Ruben (Num. xxxii. 38; Jos. xiii. 19); taken by the Moabites after the tribe of Ruben was carried off (Isai. xvi. 8; Jerem. xlviii. 32); Saban (Num. xxxii. 3) is probably the same place; famous for its vineyard (Isai. xvii. 8, 9).

SAB'AOTH, a Hebrew word meaning hosts, armies, and retained in the expression Lord God of Sabaoth, or Lord God of Hosts (Jerem. xi. 20; Rom. ix. 29; James v. 4).

SAB'ARIM, a place near Hai and Bethel, to which Josue pursued the enemy after his miraculous victory (Jos. vii. 5); a frontier town (Ezech. xlvii. 16).

SABA'THA, third son of Chus (Gen. x. 7).

SABATHA'CA, fifth son of Chus (Gen. x. 7).

SAB'BATH, a Hebrew word meaning rest; God created the world in six days, and rested on the seventh, which is the Sabbath or rest. Hence, the seventh day of the week or Sabbath, our Saturday, was commanded to be kept holy by rest from all work (Gen. ii. 2, 3). Its sanctification commanded

(Ex. xvi. 23; xx. 8-10; xxiii. 12; xxxi. 14-17; xxxiv. 21; xxxv. 2; Lev. xix. 3; xxiii. 3, 15; xxv. 4; Num. xv. 32; xxviii. 9; Deut. v. 12-14: 2 Esd. xiii. 16-

THE ROE (properly, Gazelle).

22; Isai. lvi. 2, 4; lviii. 13; lxvi. 23; Jer. xvii. 21-27; Ezech. xx. 12; xxii. 8; 1 Mach. i. 48; ii. 32, 41; 2 Mach. xv. 1; Matt. xii. 1, 10; Mark ii. 23; iii. 2; vi. 2; Luke iv. 16, 31; vi. 1; xiii. 10, 14; xiv. 1; John v. 10; vii. 22; ix. 14; Acts xiii. 14-27, 44; xv. 21; xviii. 4; Heb. iv. 10); violation of the commandment by doing work on the Sabbath day to be punished by death (Ex. xxxi. 14; xxxv. 2); a man detected gathering sticks on that day put to death by order of God (Num. xv. 32-36); journey which it was lawful to make on the Sabbath (Acts i. 12); our Lord accused of violating the Sabbath, and allowing his disciples to do so (Matt. xii. 1, 11; Mark ii. 23, 27; Luke xiii. 15; John vii. 23); he is Lord of the Sabbath (Matt. xii. 8).

SABE'ANS, carry off the flocks of Job (Job i. 15); children of Tyre to be sold by the Jews to the Sabeans (Joel iii. 8).

SACHA'CHA, a city of Juda (Jos. xv. 61).

SACKBUT, a musical instrument (Dan. iii. 5, 7, 11).

SACKCLOTH, worn by the orientals in time of mourning and penance (Gen. xxxvii. 34; Job xvi. 16; 2 Kings iii. 31; 3 Kings xx. 31; Esth. iv. 1-3; Ps. xxix. 12; Jonas iii. 5; Isai. xx. 2; Zach. xiii. 4; Matt. xi. 21).

SAC'RIFICE to be offered to God alone (Ex. xxii. 20; Lev. xvii. 3, 5, 8); victims offered to God to be without blemish (Lev. i. 3; iii. 1; xxii. 19; Num. xxviii. 3, 31; Deut. xv. 21; Ezech. xliii. 23; Mal. i. 8, 14); God shows by fire from heaven and otherwise what sacrifices please him (Gen. iv. 4; viii. 20; xv. 17; Lev. ix. 24; Judg. vi. 21; xiii. 19; 3 Kings xviii. 38; 1 Paral. xxi. 26; 2 Paral. vii. 1; 2 Mach. i. 22; ii. 10); the daily sacrifice under the Mosaic law (Ex. xxix. 38; Num. xxviii. 3; 1 Esd. iii. 2); the various sacrifices of the Mosaic law: 1. Holocaust, in which the whole animal was consumed on the altar (Gen. viii. 20; xxii. 2; Ex. x. 25; xviii. 12); there was a special altar of holocaust (Ex. xxxviii. 1); how and when offered (Lev. i. 1-17). 2. Peace offerings (Lev. iii.), in which certain parts, the fat,

kidneys, etc., were burnt on the altar (iii. 9, 16), the rest eaten by the priests and offerer. 3. Sin offering, in which the same parts were burned on the altar, and the rest on a pile of wood without the camp (iv.); God forbids the sacrifices of children (Lev. xviii. 21; Deut. xii. 31; xviii. 10; Judg. xi. 38; 4 Kings iii. 27; xvi. 3; xvii. 17; xxi. 6; 2 Paral. xxviii. 3; Ps. cv. 37; Ez. xxiii. 37); the sacrifices of the wicked rejected by God (Gen. iv. 5; 1 Kings xv. 21; Ps. xxxix. 7; xlix. 8; l. 18; Prov. xv. 8; xxi. 27; Ecclus. xxxv. 15; Isai. i. 11; xliii. 23; lxi. 8; lxvi. 3; Jer. vi. 20; vii. 21; xiv. 12; Osee v. 6; viii. 13; ix. 4; Amos v. 22; Mich. vi. 7; Mal. i. 7, 13; Matt. x. 13; Mark xii. 33; Heb. x. 5); the sacrifices and feasts, in which the victims were eaten, were to be celebrated with joy (Gen. xxxi. 46; Ex. xviii. 12; xxxii. 6; Num. xxv. 2; Deut. xii.; xxvii. 7; 1 Kings i. 4; ix. 12; xvi. 5; 2 Kings xv. 12; 3 Kings i. 9; iii. 15; 1 Paral. xxx. 21).

SAC'RIFICE of the new law announced by Malachias (Mal. i. 11); called the continual sacrifice (10); to be offered till our Lord comes to judge the world (1 Cor. xi. 6); sacrifice offered for the dead (2 Mach. xii. 43).

SACRILEGE committed in the temple by Lysimachus at the advice of Menelaus (2 Mach. iv. 39); St. Paul accuses the Jews of (Rom. ii. 22).

SADDUCEES, a sect among the Jews, so called from Sadoc, their founder. They denied the existence of angels, and the resurrection of the body (Matt. xxii. 23; Mark xii. 18; Luke xx. 27; Acts xxiii. 8; iv. 1); they persecute the apostles (Acts iv. 1-3; v. 17); divided against the Pharisees (xxiii. 6, 8).

SADNESS. The sad countenance of the just corrects the sinner (Prov. xxv. 23; Eccles. vii. 4); the heart of the wise is saddened at the sight of evil (5); the sadness of Jesus Christ in the garden of olives (Matt. xxvi. 38).

SADOC, high-priest of the race of Eleazar, made high-priest after Saul put Achimelech to death (1 Kings xxii. 17, 18); he followed David with the ark on the revolt of Absalom (2 Kings xv. 24); sent to by David (xix. 11, 12); did not join the adherents of Adonias (3 Kings i. 8); anoints Solomon king (39).

SAINTS. They are to pray for us (Jerem. xv. 1; 2 Mach. xv. 14; Apoc. v. 8; viii. 3); God confers grace on us, in view of their prayers and merits (Gen. xxvi. 5, 24; Exod. xxxii. 13, 14; 3 Kings xi. 12, 13, 32-34; xv. 4, 5; 4 Kings xix. 34; xx. 6; Isa. xxxvii. 35; Ecclus. xliv. 24); prayer to the saints does not dishonor the Mediator (Rom. xv. 30; Col. iv. 3; Eph. vi. 19; 1 Thess. v. 25; 2 Thess. iii. 1; Heb. xiii. 18); they offer our prayers to God (Tob. xii. 12; Apoc. v. 8; viii. 3); they reign with Christ in heaven (2 Cor. v. 8; Philip. i. 23; Apoc. iv. 4); it is praiseworthy to call them to mind (Ecclus. xliv.; John xii. 26; Ps. cxxxviii. 17); God is praised in his saints (Ps. cxlix. 5); they perform miracles in life and after death; they shall judge the world (Wis. iii. 8; v. 1; Matt. xix. 28; Jude 14); they shall be like angels of God (Matt. xxii. 30).

SALAM'IEL, son of Surisaddai, prince of the tribe of Simeon (Num. i. 6); his offerings (vii. 36 37; x. 19).

SALAMI'NA, a city of Cyprus, visited by St Paul and St. Barnabas (Acts xiii. 5).

SALA'THIEL, son of Jechonias or of Neri (1

Paral. iii. 17); he died at Babylon during the captivity; he descended from Solomon through Roboam.

SA'LA, son of Cainan and grandson of Arphaxad (Gen. xi. 12-15; Luke iii. 35). He died at the age of 433.

SALE and purchase of land. The earliest recorded is that of the double cave bought by Abraham for a burial-place (Gen. xxiii. 16). Sale of his birthright by Esau (Gen. xxv. 29-34); sale of inheritance could not be perpetual among the Jews (Lev. xxv. 28).

SAL'EBIM, a city in the tribe of Dan (Jos. xix. 42; 3 Kings iv. 9; Judg. i. 35). It is mentioned in connection with Bethsames and Ajalon.

SALE'CHA, a city in Basan, in the half tribe of Manasses, beyond the Jordan (Deut. iii. 10; Jos. xii. 4; xiii. 11).

SA'LEM, one of the names of Jerusalem. It means peace, and is so translated in Ps. lxxv. 3; Melchisedech was king of Salem (Gen. xiv. 18; Heb. vii. 1, 2).

SA'LEM, a city of the Sicheonites, at which Jacob arrived on his return from Mesopotamia (Gen. xxxiii. 18).

SA'LEPH, second son of Jectan (Gen. x. 26).

SA'LIM, the district in which Saul sought the lost asses (1 Kings ix. 4).

SA'LIM, a place on the Jordan where St. John the Baptist baptized (John iii. 23).

SALI'SA, the land of Salisa was near Mount Ephraim (1 Kings ix. 4).

SAL'LEM, fourth son of Nephthali (Gen. xlvi. 24).

SAL'MA or **SAL'MON,** son of Naasson (1 Paral. ii. 11; Ruth iv. 20; Matt. i. 4.); called the father, that is, founder of Bethlehem (1 Paral. ii. 51, 54). His son Booz married Ruth (Ruth iv. 10).

SALMA'NA, one of the princes of the Madianites defeated by Gedeon (Judg. viii. 5).

SALMANAS'AR, king of Assyria (Salmana, Osee x. 14); he invades the kingdom of Israel (Tob. i. 2); subdued it and compelled Osee, son of Ela, to pay him tribute (4 Kings xvii. 3); when Osee sought the aid of Sua, king of Egypt, Salmanasar besieged Osee, bound him, and cast him into prison (4); he besieged Samaria three years, and carried Israel or the Ten Tribes away, and placed them in Hala and Habor, cities of the Medes (6; xviii. 9-11); Tobias enjoyed the favor of Salmanasar (Tob. i. 14).

SAL'MON, the same as Salma.

SALMO'NA, one of the encampments of the Israelites in the desert (Num. xxxiii. 41).

SALMO'NE, a port in the island of Crete, reached by St. Paul on his way to Rome, A. D. 60 (Acts xxvii. 7).

SALO'ME, is the name of the daughter of Herodias, who danced before Herod, and asked the head of St. John the Baptist (Mark vi. 17-24; Luke iii. 19).

SALO'ME, wife of Zebedee,

SACKCLOTH.

and mother of St. James the greater, and St. John, the evangelist (Matt. xxvii. 56; Mark. xv. 40); she was one of the pious women who followed our Lord to minister to him (Matt. xxvii. 56); on one occasion she asked that her sons might sit at his right and left hand in his kingdom (Matt. xx. 20–22); she remained with the Blessed Virgin under the cross (Mark xv. 40; Matt. xxvii. 55, 56); she was one of those who bought spices to anoint Jesus, and went early on Sunday morning to the sepulchre (Mark xvi. 1, 2); and were met by Jesus as they returned to Jerusalem (Matt. xxviii. 9, 10).

SAL'PHAAD, son of Hepher, of the tribe of Manasses. He died without male issue, leaving five daughters, but they received their share in the promised land, with the rest of the tribe (Num. xxvi. 33; xxvii. 1, 2; Jos. xvii. 3).

SALT. Lot's wife is changed into a pillar of salt (Gen. xix. 26); salt was required to be offered with all oblations (Lev. ii. 13; Mark ix. 48); it was the symbol of a covenant with God (Num. xviii. 19); the city of salt (Jos. xv. 62); Abimelech sowed salt on the site of Sichem, after destroying it (Judg. ix. 45); the prophet Eliseus sweetens the waters of Jericho by putting salt in them (4 Kings ii. 20–22); its use as a seasoning (Job vi. 6); its weight referred to (Ecclus. ii. 18); frost compared to it (xliii. 21); new-born children washed with salt (Ezech. xvi. 4); the apostles called by our Lord the salt of the earth (Matt. v. 13); salt worthless if it lose its savor (Matt. v. 13; Mark ix. 49; Luke xiv. 34); used in the sense of discretion and wisdom (Col. iv. 6).

SALT SEA. The Dead Sea called the most Salt Sea (Num. xxxiv. 3, 12; Deut. iii. 17; Jos. xii. 3; xv. 2, 5; xvi. 8; xviii. 19).

SALT WATER cannot yield sweet (James iii. 12).

SAL'UMITH, daughter of Dabri, of the tribe of Dan. Her son, by an Egyptian, blasphemed the name of God, and was stoned by order of God (Levit. xxiv. 10–23).

SALMANASAR PUTTING OUT THE EYES OF CAPTIVES.

SALUTA'TION. The angelical salutation, that of the angel Gabriel to the Blessed Virgin (Luke i. 29).

SALUTA'TIONS of St. Paul to various Chris-

tians (Rom. xv. 33; xvi. 3–16; Coloss. iv. 15; 2 Tim. iv. 19); general salutations (1 Cor. xvi. 19, 20; Phil. iv. 21; Coloss. iv. 15; 1 Thess. v. 26).

SAMARIA.

SALVA'TION is the one thing necessary (Luke x. 42); to be worked out with fear (Phil. ii. 12); was with the Jews and not with the Samaritans; comes from the Jews (John iv. 22); the salvation of the world is the work of Jesus Christ alone (Matt. i. 21; Luke iii. 6; John iv. 42; Acts iv. 9–12; xi. 14, 17; Rom. xi. 14, 26; 1 Cor. i. 18, 21; iii. 15; ix. 21, 22; x. 33; 1 Tim. i. 15; ii. 4; Tit. iii. 5).

SA'MA, a city of the tribe of Juda (Jos. xv. 26).

SAMA'A, brother of David, and father of Jonathan, one of his heroes (2 Kings xxi. 21; 1 Paral. xx. 7).

SAMA'A and **SAMAIAS** join David when he was persecuted by Saul (1 Paral. xii. 3, 4).

SAMA'OTH OF JEZER, commander of an army under David and Solomon (1 Paral. xxvii. 8).

SAM'ARITE. The Samarite is given as the tenth son of Chanaan (Gen. x. 18).

SAMA'RIA, a city built by Amri, king of Israel, on Mount Someron, which he bought for two talents of silver (3 Kings xvi. 24); it became the capital of the Ten Tribes, which Sichem and Thersa had been. Besieged by Benadad, king of the Syrians (3 Kings xx. 1); again by Benadad, king of Syria (4 Kings vi. 24); besieged for three years by Salmanasar, who took it after three years, and carried off all the people (xvii. 6); the prophets frequently foretold its ruin (Isai. vii. 30; Ezech. xxiii.; Osee viii.; xiv.; Amos iii. 12; Mich. i. 5); the king of the Assyrians sends colonies to occupy cities of Samaria (4 Kings xvii. 24); a priest carried captive came to teach them to worship the Lord (28); they worshipped him as well as their various false gods (29–34); these Samaritans opposed the rebuilding of Jerusalem by the Jews (1 Esd. iv.; 2 Esd. iv.); a city of the Samaritans refused to receive our Lord, because he was going to Jerusalem (Luke ix. 52, 53); our Lord passed through Samaria, and stopped at Sichar (John iv. 5); Philip preached Christ in the city of Samaria (Acts viii. 5); performs great miracles (6–8, 13); converts many, among others Simon Magus (9–13); the apostles

send St. Peter and St. John to Samaria to confirm the converts (14–25).

SAMAR'ITANS, heathen nations sent by the king of Assyria to occupy Samaria (4 Kings xvii. 24); adopt the worship of the true God (29–34); had a temple on Mount Garizim (John iv. 20); oppose the rebuilding of Jerusalem (1 Esd. iv.; 2 Esd. iv.); one of their cities refuses to receive our Lord (Luke ix. 52, 53); our Lord converts a Samaritan woman at Jacob's well near Sichar (John iv. 5–38); abides there two days, and converts many (39–42); Philip preaches to the Samaritans (Acts viii. 5–13); St. Peter and St. John confirm them (14–25); they preach the gospel to many countries of the Samaritans (25); the parable of the good Samaritan (Luke x. 33).

SAM'GAR, son of Anath, third judge of Israel. He slew six hundred Philistines with a ploughshare, and defended Israel (Judg. iii. 31).

SA'MIR, a city in the tribe of Ephraim, residence of Thola, judge of Israel (Judg. x. 1).

SA'MOS. The Romans wrote to the governor of Samos in favor of the Jews in the time of Simon Machabeus (1 Mach. xv. 23); St. Paul lands there on his way to Jerusalem (Acts xx. 15).

SAMOTHRA'CIA, an island in the Egean Sea. St. Paul touched there on his way from Troas to Macedonia (Acts xvi. 11).

SAM'SAI, one of those who wrote to king Artaxerxes against the Jews (1 Esd. iv. 8, 9, 17, 23).

SAM'SON, judge of Israel, son of Manue, of the tribe of Dan (Judges xiii. 2–4); his birth foretold to his mother by an angel (3); he was to be a Nazarite (5); Manue himself sees the angel (11–14); Manue offers a kid to the Lord, and the angel went up in the smoke of the sacrifice (20). Samson is born A. M. 2849 (24); the spirit of the Lord comes upon him (25); tears a lion to pieces (xiv. 5); eats a honeycomb from the mouth of the dead lion (9); his riddle to the Philistines (14); his wife seeks the solution and reveals it (17); slays thirty men (19); his wife given to another (20); destroys the corn, vineyards, and oliveyards of the Philistines with fire (xv. 1–6); the Philistines kill his wife and her father (7); he makes a great slaughter of them (8); dwells in a cavern of rock Ectam (8); the Philistine army against Juda encamps at Lechi (9); he is bound and delivered to the Philistines, but bursts his bonds and

witch of Endor (xxviii. 15; Ecclus. xlvi. 23); his praise (xlvi. 16; Jerem. xv. 1; Acts iii. 24; xiii. 20).

SANABALL'AT, governor of the Samaritans,

SAPHATHI'A, son of David and Abbital (2 Kings iii. 4; 1 Paral. iii. 3). He is mentioned as the fifth son, but no more is recorded of him or his mother.

SAPHATI'A, one of the sons of king Josaphat (2 Paral. xxi. 2).

SAPHATI'A, son of Mathan, accuses the prophet Jeremias of discouraging the people by his predictions (Jerem. xxxviii. 1).

SAP'PHIRE, a precious stone. It was in the second row of gems in the rational (Ex. xxviii. 18); Job mentions it (Job xxviii. 6, 16; Cant. v. 14; Ezechiel i., x., xxviii.); it is referred to as the first foundation of the new Jerusalem (Tob. xiii. 21; Isai. liv. 11; Apoc. xxi. 19).

SAPHI'RA, wife of Ananias, falls dead on hearing of the death of her husband (Acts v.)

SA'RAI, daughter of Thare, and wife of Abraham (Gen. xi. 29; xx. 12); she married him in the land of Ur (xi. 31); passes as his sister (xii.); Pharao takes her, but is punished (xii. 15-17); gives her handmaid Agar to Abraham (xvi. 3), but afflicts her so that she runs away (6); overhears the angel promise Abraham a son by her and laughs (xviii. 10); she denies it (15); her name changed to Sara (xvii. 15); Abimelech, king of Ge-

SAMSON'S RIDDLE.

kills one thousand men with the jaw-bone of an ass (13-17); refreshed by a spring from a tooth in the jaw-bone (19); carries off the gates of Gaza (xvi. 1-3); his love for Dalila (4); she seeks to learn the secret of his strength, and discovers it (5-17); she betrays him, cuts his hair, and gives him up to the Philistines (18-20); they blind him, and put him in a prison to grind (21); after his hair had grown they took him into a temple of Dagon, to make sport for them (22-25); he pulls away the pillars, and the temple fell on the multitude, killing more in death than he had done in life (26-30); his burial (31). He judged Israel twenty years (xv. 20; xvi. 31).

SAMUEL, judge of Israel, son of Elcana and Anna; his mother's grief at her barrenness, and her prayers (1 Kings i. 1-19); birth of Samuel (20); she dedicates him to God at Silo (24-28); he ministers before the Lord, and becomes great (ii. 18, 21); he slept in the temple (iii. 3); receives a message from God for the high-priest Heli (4-18); Samuel recognized as a faithful prophet (20, 21); after the death of Heli, he addresses the people, and becomes judge (vii. 3-6); abolishes idolatry (3, 4); the Philistine army overthrown by thunder at Masphath (10, 11); recovers the cities from Accaron to Geth (14); dwells at Ramatha (17); appoints his sons Joel and Abia judges (viii. 2); the people ask a king (5); Samuel's reply by direction of God (6-18); the people insist (19); God reveals to him the coming of the man he had chosen (ix. 15, 16); Samuel anoints Saul (x. 1); he calls the people together in Maspha (17), and announces that God had chosen Saul (24); he writes the law of the kingdom (25); Samuel's address to the people (xii.); he rebukes Saul for offering sacrifice (xiii. 13); he rebukes him for keeping booty of the Amalecites, and slays Agag (xv. 12-35); consecrates David as king (xvi. 13); dies, and is buried in Ramatha (xxv. 1; xxviii. 3); he appears to Saul, evoked by the

and an enemy of the Jews. He was a native of Horon, in the land of Moab (2 Esd. ii. 10); he taunts Nehemias (19); his anger at the rebuilding of the walls of Jerusalem (iv. 1, 7); forms a league against the Jews (vi. 2); writes to Nehemias (5-7); he gains a false prophet, Semeias (12-14); during the absence of Nehemias, he induced Manasses, grandson of the high-priest Eliasib, to marry his daughter, but Nehemias expelled him (xiii. 28).

SANC'TUARY. The Holy, or part of the tabernacle or temple before the veil (Ex. xxvi. 33; 3 Kings viii. 8). See HOLY.

SAND, used as a type of great number. God promises Abraham a posterity as numerous as the sand of the sea, which cannot be numbered (Gen. xxxii. 12); the harvest of Egypt compared to it (Gen. xli. 49); the armies of the Chanaanites (Jos. xi. 4); the camels of Madian (Judg. vii. 12); the Philistine armies (1 Kings xiii. 5); as a symbol of weight (Prov. xxvii. 3; Ecclus. xxii. 18); a grain of sand the most insignificant thing, "As a pebble of the sand, so are a few years compared to eternity" (Ecclus. xviii. 8); instability, the house built on the sand (Matt. vii. 26).

SAN'DALS, a usual protection for the feet in warm countries (Judith x. 3; xvi. 11; Mark vi. 9).

SAPH or SAPHAI, of the race of giants, killed by Sabochai (2 Kings xxi. 18; 1 Paral. xx. 4).

SA'PHAN, the scribe, informs king Josias of the finding of the law of the Lord in the temple (4 Kings xxii. 10; 2 Paral. xxxiv. 20).

rara, takes her (xx. 2); bears Isaac (xxi. 2, 3); asks to have Agar and Ismael cast out (10); she died in Hebron at the age of 127 (xxiii. 1, 2); Abraham buys the double cave, and inters her in it (3-20).

SA'RA, daughter of Raguel. She had been given to seven husbands, who were killed by a devil named Asmodeus (Tob. iii. 8); taunted by her maidservant (7, 9, 10); her prayer (11-23); the angel Raphael tells Tobias to ask her hand (vi. 13); he does so (vii. 10); she marries him (15, 16); the devil is exorcised (viii.); she sets out with Tobias (x. 10);

RUINS OF SARDIS.

she bore him seven sons in Ninive (xiv. 5); they return to her father from Ninive after the death of the parents of Tobias (xiv. 14).

SARA'A, a city of Juda, fortified by Roboam (2 Paral. xi. 10).

SARA'A, in the tribe of Dan, birthplace of Samson (Judg. xiii. 2).

SARAI'A, the last high-priest of the Jews before the captivity. He was taken by Nabuzardan, and taken to Reblatha, where Nabuchodonosor put him to death, 588 B. C. (Jerem. lii. 24–27; 4 Kings xxv. 18–21).

SARAI'A, son of Helcias, high-priest (2 Esd. xi. 11).

SARA'IAS, brother of Baruch, went to Babylon with king Sedecias (Jerem. li. 59); he bore a letter from Jeremias.

SAR'ASAR, second son of Sennacherib, assassinates his father in the temple of Mesroch (4 Kings xix. 37; 2 Paral. xxxii. 21; Tob. i. 24; Isai. xxxvii. 38).

SAR'DIS, a city in Asia Minor. The angel or bishop of Sardis is blamed for his works (Apoc. iii. 1, 2); the faithful of the church of Sardis who persevere in good are praised (4).

SAR'DIUS STONE, a precious stone, in the first row on the rational (Ex. xxviii. 17); mentioned by Ezechiel (xxviii. 13; Apoc. xxi. 20).

SAR'DONYX, a precious stone (Job xxviii. 16).

SARE'A, a city in the tribe of Juda (Jos. xv. 53).

SARE'DA, a city in the tribe of Ephraim, birthplace of Jeroboam, son of Nabat (3 Kings xi. 26).

SAREDA'THA, a city in the tribe of Ephraim (2 Paral. iv. 17).

SAREPH'TA, or **SAREPTA** (Luke iv. 26), a city of the Sidonians. Elias is sent there (3 Kings xvii. 9); he is received by a widow woman, whose meal and oil he makes inexhaustible till rain fell (10–16); he raises her son to life (17–24); Sarepta mentioned (Abd. xx.)

SA'RID, a city of Zabulon (Jos. xix. 10).

SARO'HEN, a city of the tribe of Simeon (Jos. xix. 6).

SA'RON, a district beyond the Jordan in the tribe of Gad (1 Paral. v. 16; xxvii. 29); its fertility was proverbial (Isai. xxxiii. 9; xxxv. 2).

SA'RON, a city whose king was taken and slain by Josue (Jos. xii. 18).

SA'RON, a place near Lydda (Acts ix. 35).

SARSA'CHIM, one of the Babylonian generals (Jer. xxxix. 3).

SAR'THAN, a city on the Jordan, to which the waters rolled back when Josue crossed it (Jos. iii. 16); Solomon cast vessels for the temple near Sarthan (3 Kings vii. 46).

SA'RUG, son of Reu or Ragau (Gen. xi. 20–22); he died at the age of two hundred and thirty, 1955 B. C.

SAR'VIA, sister of David and mother of Joab, Abisai and Asael (2 Kings ii. 18; 1 Paral. ii. 16).

SAS'SABAS'AR, prince of Juda. Cyrus delivered to him the vessels of the temple of Jerusalem (1 Esd. i. 8); the name is probably the Babylonian term for Zorobabel; the foundation of the temple is ascribed to both (Zach. iv. 9; 1 Esd. v. 16).

SA'TAN, the devil, tempts Job (Job i. 6; ii. 1; xii. 7); tempts David to number his people (1 Paral. xxi. 1); opposes Jesus the high-priest (Zach. iii. 1); tempts our Lord (Matt. iv. 10; Mark i. 13); seeks to tempt the apostles (Luke xxii. 31); enters into Juda (Luke xxii. 3; John xiii. 27); taketh the good seed out of hearts (Matt. iv. 15); tempts Ananias (Acts v. 3); sinners will be delivered to (1 Cor. v. 5; 1 Tim.

i. 20); transfigures himself into an angel of light (2 Cor. xi. 14); the devil (Apoc. xii. 9; xx. 2); loosed from prison (xx. 7).

SAUL, son of Cis, of the tribe of Benjamin, first king of the Israelites. He goes to seek his father's asses (1 Kings ix. 3); resolves to consult Samuel (9); God reveals to Samuel that he was to be the king (15); anointed king by Samuel (x. 1); he prophesies (11); Samuel presents him to the people (24); some of the army join him (26); others deride him (27); he sets out from Gabaa to relieve Jabes of Galaad besieged by Naas (xi. 1–6); summons the people and raises an army of 330,000 men (8); slaughters the Ammonites (11); he is made king in Galgal (15); he waits in Galgal for Samuel, and as he delayed he offers sacrifice (xiii. 9, 10); is rebuked (13, 14); Jonathan attacks the Philistines and throws them into confusion, so that they slay each other (xiv. 14); the rash curse of Saul (24); he defeats Moab, Ammon, Edom, the king of Soba, and the Philistines (47); and Amalec (48); he had three sons, Jonathan, Jessui and Melchisua, and two daughters, Merob and Michol. His wife was Achinoam (49, 50); he is sent to destroy Amalec, but spares Agag the king and saves much booty; he is rebuked by Samuel, who hewed Agag to pieces (xv.); Saul is troubled by an evil spirit (xvi. 14, 15); David, by the music of his harp, relieves him from it (23); Goliath, the champion of the Philistines, defies the army of Saul, but is slain by David (xvii. 1–51); the Philistines are defeated (51, 52); the praise of David excites the anger and jealousy of Saul (xviii. 5–9); but he gives him his daughter Michol to wife on his slaying two hundred Philistines (17–27); he attempts to pierce David with his spear (xviii. 10; xix. 10); he pursues him (xx.–xxiii.); Doeg the Edomite, by his orders, slays the high-priest Achimelech and eighty-five priests, and destroyed Nobe, their city (xxii. 18, 19); the Ziphites tell him of David's abode (xxiii. 19); pursues him to the desert of Maon (25); recalled to meet the Philistines (28); accidentally places himself in the power of David, who cut off the hem of his robe (xxiv. 5); David then addressed him (9–16); he is reconciled to David, who promised not to destroy his seed (22); he again pursues David (xxvi. 1–3); David enters his tent at night, and carried off his spear and cup of water, but would not let Abisai hurt him (3–13); he is again reconciled to David (17–25); he puts away all the magicians and soothsayers out of the land (xxviii. 3); when the Philistines invade the land, he camped at Gelboe (4); saw that his army was discouraged (5); consults the Lord in vain (6); goes to a woman with a divin-

ing spirit at Endor (7); she evokes Samuel, who tells him that he and his sons are to die the next day (15–19); defeated by the Philistines (xxxi. 1); his sons, Jonathan, Abinadab and Melchisua, slain (2); Saul himself wounded by arrows (3); falls on his sword (4); his head cut off (9); his armor put in the temple of Astaroth (10); his body hung on the wall of Bethsan (10); the men of Jabes Galaad recover the bodies of Saul and his sons and bury them (12, 13); his children by Respha crucified (2 Kings xxi. 9).

SAVE, a vale where Abraham defeated Chodorlahomor and his allies and rescued Lot (Gen. xiv. 17).

SA'VIOUR, our Lord Jesus Christ. See CHRIST.

SA'VIOUR OF THE WORLD, Pharao gives Joseph an Egyptian name with this meaning (Gen. xli. 45).

SA'VIOUR, Othoniel called a Saviour (Judg. iii. 9); Aod (15; 2 Esd. ix. 27).

SA'VIOUR, Almighty God, Saviour of Israel (1 Kings xiv. 39; 4 Kings xiii. 5); David invokes

THE MOLTEN SEA.

God as his Saviour (2 Kings xxii. 2, 3; Ps. xvii.; 1 Paral. xvi. 35); Esther (Esth. xv. 5).

SCAN'DAL. We are not to scandalize our neighbor by our life or words (Lev. iv. 3; Num. xxxi. 16; 2 Kings xi. 14; 1 Esd. viii. 22; Prov. xxviii. 12; 2 Mach. vi. 24; Matt. xvii. 26; xviii. 6; Mark ix. 41; Luke xvii. 2; Rom. xiv. 13, 21; 1 Cor. viii.; x. 32; 2 Cor. vi. 3; 1 Thess. v. 22); we are obliged to flee from all that may prove a scandal to us (Ex. xxxiv. 12; Deut. vii. 2, 16; xiii.; Matt. v. 29; xvi. 22; Mark ix. 42; Rom. xvi. 17).

SCENOPEG'IA, the Greek term for the Jewish feast of tabernacles (1 Mach. x. 21; 2 Mach. i. 9, 18; John vii. 2).

SCEP'TRE, not to pass from Juda till the coming of the Messias (Gen. xlix. 10).

SCE'VA, a Jewish priest. His sons attempt to exorcise an evil spirit in the name of Christ, but are put to flight by the demons (Acts xix. 11–16).

SCHIB'BOLETH, an ear of corn. The Ephraimites after their defeat by Jephte detected at the ford of Jordan by this word (Judg. xii. 6).

SCIN'IPHS. Insects sent as a plague on Egypt (Ex. viii. 16–18).

SCOR'PION, a venomous insect (Deut. viii. 15; Ezech. ii. 6; Ecclus. xxvi. 10; Apoc. ix. 3, 5).

SCOR'PION, the ascent of the (Num. xxxiv. 4; Jos. xv. 3).

SCOR'PIONS, scourges with sharp metal points, Roboam threatens his people with (3 Kings xii. 11, 14; 2 Paral. x. 11, 14).

SCOURG'ING. This punishment inflicted on our Lord (Matt. xix. 19; Mark xv. 15); on the apostles (Acts v. 40; xvi. 22; 2 Cor. xi. 25).

SCREECH OWL, forbidden as unclean (Lev. xi. 17).

SCRIBES, doctors of the law among the Jews (2 Kings viii. 17; xx. 25; 4 Kings xii. 10; 1 Paral. xxiv. 6; 2 Paral. xxxiv. 13; 2 Esd. viii. 1; Jer. xx. 36; 1 Mach. v. 42; vii. 12; 2 Mach. vi. 18); they and the Pharisees oppose and persecute our Lord (Matt. v. 20; vii. 29; xvi. 21; xvii. 10; xx. 18; xxiii. 2, 13, 14; xxvi. 57; xxvii. 41; Mark i. 22; ii. 6, 16; iii. 22; vii. 1, 6; viii. 31; ix. 10, 13; x. 33; xi. 18, 27; xii. 28, 32, 35, 38; xiv. 1, 43, 53; xv. 1, 31; Luke v. 21, 30; vi. 7; ix. 12; xv. 2; xx. 1, 19, 39, 46; xxii. 2, 66; xxiii. 10; John viii. 3; Acts iv. 5; vi. 12).

SCRIP, David puts stones in a shepherd's scrip to fight Goliath (1 Kings xvii. 40); the apostles forbidden by our Lord to carry a scrip for a journey (Matt. x. 10; Mark vi. 8; Luke ix. 3).

SCRIP'TURES. The origin of the Holy Scriptures, and how they are to be used (Ex. xvii. 14; xxxiv. 27; Deut. xvii. 18; xxxi. 9; Jos. i. 8; 2 Esd. viii. 3; Isai. xxx. 8; xxxiv. 16; Jer. xxx. 2; xxxvi. 2, 10; Bar. i. 14; Dan. x. 21; Matt. iv. 4; Luke xvi. 29; John v. 39; Acts xv. 21; xvii. 11; Rom. iv. 23; xv. 4; 1 Cor. ix. 9; x. 11); God gives the true understanding of them (2 Pet. i. 20); some abuse the difficult things therein (iii. 16); the apostles have not written all things (John xxi. 25; 1 Cor. xi. 34; 2 Thess. ii. 14; 2 John 12; 3 John 13); the priests are the depositaries and interpreters of the Scriptures (Deut. xxiv. 8; Ezech. xliv. 24; Mal. ii. 7).

SCULP'TURE, or graven image to the likeness of anything, expressly forbidden to the Jews, and why (Ex. xx. 4; Lev. xxvi. 1; Deut. iv. 16; Jos. xxiv. 14; Ps. xcvi. 7); sculptured figures in the tabernacle (Ex. xxxvii. 7, 8, 9); precious stones cut and engraved (xxxix. 6).

SCYTH'IANS mentioned as types of barbarity, scalping men (2 Mach. iv. 47); mentioned Col. iii. 11.

SEA, created (Gen. i. 10, 22); Job's description of the sea (Job vi. 3; vii. 12; ix. 8; xi. 9; xiv. 11; xxvi. 12; xxviii. 14; xxxvi. 30; xxxviii. 8–16; xli. 22); David's (Ps. viii. 9; xxiii. 2; xxxii. 7; lxiv. 6, 8; lxviii. 3; ciii. 25; cxxxiv. 6); Solomon's (Prov. viii. 29); the sea receives all the waters (Eccles. i. 7; Lam. ii. 13; Ezech. i. 16; xxvi. 3); Jesus stills the sea (Matt. viii. 26); he walks on the sea (Matt. xiv. 24; Mark vi. 48).

SEA, THE MOLTEN, set up in Solomon's temple instead of the laver, five cubits high and thirty in circumference, made of brass captured from Aderezer (1 Paral. xviii. 8). It stood on twelve oxen, resting on bases; and the whole had wheels to move it (3 Kings vii. 33–37); Achaz took the sea down and placed it on a stone pavement (4 Kings xvi. 17); it was finally broken up by the Chaldeans (xxv. 13).

SEA OF THE DESERT, the Dead Sea, so called (Deut. iii. 17; Jos. xii. 3).

SEA OF GALILEE (which is that of Tiberias) (John vi. 1; xxi. 1); Jesus walking by the Sea of Galilee calls Peter, Andrew, James, and John (Matt.

iv. 18–22; Mark i. 16); he stills the tempest on the sea (Matt. viii. 24–27; Mark iv. 1–40; Luke viii. 25); the swine rush into the sea in the country of the Gerasens (Matt. viii. 28–34; Mark v. 13); teaches by the sea (Matt. xiii. 1; Mark v. 1–12); walks on the sea (Matt. xiv. 26–28; Mark vi. 47–49; John vi. 1–25); multiplies loaves on a mountain by the sea, and crosses to Magedan (Matt. xv. 29–39; Mark vii. 31); Peter obtains money from a fish in the Sea of Galilee (Matt. xvii. 36); Jesus teaches the multitudes near the sea, and calls Levi (Mark ii. 13, 14); appears to his disciples after his resurrection at the Sea of Galilee (John xxi.)

SEAL, Aman seals the orders of Assuerus with the king's ring (Esth. iii. 12); the priests of Bel ask king Nabuchodonosor to seal the temple door with his ring (Dan. xiv. 10); put me as a seal upon thy heart, and a seal upon thy arm (Cant. viii. 6); a sealed fountain (iv. 12); God's sealed treasures (Deut. xxxii. 34); Job says God has sealed up his offences (Job xiv. 17); Jeremias seals a deed for land (Jer. xxxii. 10); St. John sees in the Apocalypse a book with seven seals (Apoc. v.)

SEAT OF MAJESTY, the Son of Man sitting upon as judge (Matt. xix. 28; xxv. 31; Heb. viii. 1; xii. 2; Apoc. xxii. 3).

SE'BA, son of Bochri, of the tribe of Benjamin, revolts against David after the overthrow of Absalom (2 Kings xx. 1, 2); Joab besieges him in Abela beth Maacha (xx. 15); the people cut off his head and throw it over the wall (22).

SE'BAT, one of the months of the Jewish year.

SEBE'NIAS, a priest in the time of David who sounded the trumpet before the ark (1 Paral. xv. 24).

SEB'EON, the Hevite. Esau marries his granddaughter (Gen. xxxvi. 2); his sons (24).

SEB'IA, of Bersabee, wife of Ochozias, king of Juda, and mother of king Joas (4 Kings xii. 1; 2 Paral. xxiv. 1).

SEB'OIM, one of the cities of the Pentapolis, destroyed by fire from heaven (Gen. x. 19; xiv. 2, 8; Deut. xxix. 23; Osee xi. 8); the valley of Seboim (1 Kings xiii. 18); a city in the tribe of Benjamin (2 Esd. xi. 34).

SE'CHEM, of the tribe of Manasses, son of Galaad, and father of the Sechemites (Num. xxvi. 31; Jos. xvii. 2; 1 Paral. vii. 19).

SECHE'NIAS, son of Obdia, of the race of David (1 Paral. iii. 21–24).

SECHE'NIAS, head of the tenth family of priests (1 Paral. xxiv. 11; 1 Esd. viii. 3, 5).

SECHE'NIAS, son of Jehiel, advises the sending away of Gentile wives (1 Esd. x. 1–4).

SECHRO'NA, a city in the tribe of Juda (Jos. xv. 11).

SE'CRET OF A KING. It is good to hide (Tob. xii. 7).

SECTS, numbered among the works of the flesh (Gal. v. 20); originated by lying teachers, who bring upon themselves swift destruction (2 Pet. ii. 1); authors of described (10).

SECUN'DUS, a disciple of St. Paul. He was of Thessalonica, and followed St. Paul from Greece to Asia (Acts xx. 4).

SECURE' (JOAS), one of the descendants of Juda (1 Paral. iv. 22).

SEDA'DA, a city of Syria, on the frontier of the promised land (Num. xxxiv. 8; Ezech. xlvii. 15).

SEDECI'AS, called also Matthanias. He was uncle of Joachim, king of Juda, whom Nabuchodo-

nosor deposed and carried away to Babylon (2 Paral. xxxvi. 11; Jer. xxxvii. 1; 4 Kings xxiv. 15); setting Matthanias on the throne, and calling him Sedecias (17); he was then twenty-one (18); his reign was wicked (19); he revolted against the king of Babylon, who besieged Jerusalem, and reduced it to terrible distress (xxiv. 20; xxv. 4); when the walls were breached Sedecias fled, but was overtaken, defeated, and taken in the plains of Jericho (5); he was carried to Reblatha, where Nabuchodonosor slew his sons, put out his eyes, and then took him in chains to Babylon (6, 7; 2 Paral. xxxvi. 11–20); all this had been foretold by the prophets Jeremias and Ezechiel (Jer. xxvii. 22; xxxvii. 16; Ezec. xiii. 3; xvii. 16; xx.) He reigned eleven years, and the kingdom of Juda ended with him.

SEDECI'AS, son of Chanana, a false prophet in Samaria (3 Kings xxii. 11; 2 Paral. xviii. 10); another false prophet burned alive by the king of Babylon (Jer. xxix. 22).

SEDIT'ION punished (Num. xvi. 31).

SEDUCE'. We are warned not to allow evil teachers to seduce us (Matt. xxiv. 4–11; Mark xiii. 5–12; Luke xxi. 8; Rom. xvi. 18; 1 Cor. iii. 18; xv. 33; Eph. v. 6; 2 Thess. ii. 3); Satan seduceth the whole world (Apoc. xii. 9).

SEED. Parable of the seed (Matt. xiii. 24–30; Mark iv. 3–9).

SE'GOR, one of the cities of the Pentapolis, situated at the south end of the Dead Sea, preserved for the sake of Lot (Gen. xix. 22); called also Bala (Gen. xiv. 2).

SE'GUB, son of Hial, of Bethel, died when his father hung the gates of Jericho, having rebuilt it in defiance of Josue's prophetic curse (3 Kings xvi. 34; Jos. vi. 26).

SE'HON, king of Hesebon, defeated the king of Moab, and took much territory (Num. xxi. 26); commanded the Amorrhites beyond the Jordan; Moses sent to him to ask permission to pass through his territory (Num. xxi. 21; Deut. ii. 26); he refused (Num. xxi. 21; Deut. ii. 30); raised an army to oppose them, and marched into the desert; gave them battle at Jasa (Num. xxi. 23; Deut. ii. 32); was defeated and slain (Num. xxi. 24; Deut. i. 4).

SE'HON, the city of Hesebon (Num. xxi. 27, 28; Jer. xlviii. 45).

SE'IR, the Horrite; his descendants (Gen. xxxvi. 20–30; 1 Paral. i. 38, 39).

SEIR, MOUNT, a range east and south of the Dead Sea (Deut. i. 2); mentioned (Gen. xiv. 6; Jos. xxiv. 4; Deut. ii. 5; 2 Paral. xx. 10; Ezech. xxxv. 2).

SE'IR, a mountain on the frontiers of the tribes of Juda and Dan (Jos. xv. 10).

SE'IRA, the mount or country of Seir, inhabited by the Edomites (4 Kings viii. 21).

SEI'RATH, a place to which Aod went after killing Eglon, king of Moab (Judg. iii. 26).

SE'LA, son of Juda by Sue (Gen. xxxviii. 5); his posterity (1 Paral. iv. 21).

SE'LA, a place in the tribe of Benjamin (Jos. xviii. 28).

SEL'CHA, a city in the kingdom of Og, beyond the Jordan (Deut. iii. 10; 1 Paral. v. 11).

SEL'EBIN, a city in the tribe of Dan (Jos. xix. 42).

SE'LEC, an Ammonite; one of the heroes of David's army (2 Kings xxiii. 37; 1 Paral. xi. 39).

SELE'MIAS, a priest appointed to receive the tithes and first-fruits (2 Esd. xiii. 13).

SELE'MIAS, son of Abdeel, sent by king Joakin to arrest Jeremias (Jer. xxxvi. 26).

SELE'MIAS, Juchal, son of, sent by king Sedecias to ask the prayers of Jeremias (Jer. xxxviii. 1, 3).

SELE'MITH, son of Zechri, a descendant of Moses, guardian of the treasures of the temple (1 Paral. xxvi. 26).

SELEU'CIA, a city of Syria, situated on the Mediterranean at the mouth of the Orontes. Ptolemee Philometor extends conquests to it (1 Mach. xi. 8); St. Paul and St. Barnabas embarked there to go to Cyprus (Acts xiii. 4).

SELEU'CUS (surnamed Philopator, son of Antiochus the Great), king of Asia, allowed out of his revenues the cost of the sacrifices in the temple of Jerusalem (2 Mach. iii. 3); sends Heliodorus to plunder the temple (7–40); called by Daniel "one most vile and unworthy of kingly honor" (Dan. xi. 20); the prophet foretold his death: "in a few days he shall be destroyed, not in rage nor in battle" (20); he was assassinated by Heliodorus.

SE'LIM, a city in the tribe of Juda (Jos. xv. 32.)

SEL'LA, wife of Lamech, and mother of Tubalcain and Noema (Gen. iv. 21, 22).

SEL'LA, the descent of. Joas, king of Juda, assassinated by his servants in the house of Mello, in the descent of Sella (4 Kings xii. 20).

SEL'LAI, one of the chief priests who returned from the captivity with Zorobabel (2 Esd. xii. 6, 20).

SEL'LEM, son of Nephthali (Num. xxvi. 49).

SELLERS and **BUYERS** driven out of the temple by our Lord (John ii. 14–16).

SEL'LUM, son or native of Jabes, conspired against Zacharias, king of Israel, and slew him publicly (4 Kings xv. 10); he usurped the throne, but reigned only one month in Samaria, 771 B. C. (4 Kings xv. 13).

SEL'LUM, son or native of Thecua, husband of the prophetess Holda, in the days of Josias, king of Juda (4 Kings xxii. 14).

SEL'LUM, fourth son of Josias, king of Juda (1 Paral. iii. 15; Jer. xxii. 11); he is the same as Joachaz, who was carried into Egypt (4 Kings xxiii. 30–34).

SEL'LUM, son of Nephthali (1 Paral. vii. 13; Gen. xlvi. 24).

SEL'LUM, son of the high-priest Sadoc, and progenitor of the high-priest Helcias (1 Paral. vi. 12, 13); called also Mosollam (ix. 11).

SEL'LUM, son of Core (1 Paral. ix. 19, 31); apparently escaped when the rest were swallowed up (Num. xxvi. 11).

SEL'LUM, son of Cholhoza, restored the gate of the fountain, and the wall to the pool of Siloe (2 Esd. iii. 15).

SEL'LUM, Ezechias, son of, induces the Israelites to treat the people of Juda humanely (2 Paral. xxviii. 12).

SEL'LUM, son of Alohes, lord of half the street of Jerusalem, with his daughters built part of the wall (2 Esd. iii. 12).

SEL'MON, a mountain near Sichem. Abimelech's stratagem at (Judg. ix. 48); mentioned by David (Ps. lxvii. 15).

SEL'MON, an Ahohite, one of David's heroes (2 Kings xxiii. 28).

SEM, son of Noe, born 2646 B. C., apparently younger than Japheth, and older than Cham (Gen. vi. 10); entered the ark with his father; blessed by Noe for not treating him with disrespect, like Cham (ix. 26); his sons were Elam, Assur, Arphaxad,

Lud, and Aram (x. 22); he lived to the age of 600 (xi. 10, 11); Abraham descended from Sem through Arphaxad (11–27). He is the ancestor of the Semitic family of nations.

SEMAI'A, a false prophet gained by Tobias and Sanaballat, endeavors to alarm Nehemias (2 Esd. vi. 1–14).

SE'MATHITES, a tribe allied to Cariathiarim (1 Paral. ii. 53).

SEME'BER, king of Seboim, one of the allies of the kings of the Pentapolis (Gen. xiv. 2).

SEM'EGARNABU, general of Nabuchodonosor (Jerem. xxxix. 3).

SEM'EI, second son of Gerson and grandson of Levi (Ex. vi. 17; Num. iii. 18; 1 Paral. vi. 17; xxiii. 7); head of the family of Semeites (Num. iii. 21; 1 Paral. xxiii. 7, 10; Zach. xii. 13).

RABSACES BEFORE SENNACHERIB.

SEM'EI, son of Gera, a kinsman of Saul, cursed and stoned David, as he left Jerusalem, at the time of Absalom's rebellion (2 Kings xvi. 5, 13); after his return he seeks and obtains pardon (2 Kings xix. 16, 17); David charges Solomon not to let him go unpunished (3 Kings ii. 9); Solomon ordered him to build a house in Jerusalem, and not to go out of it, under pain of death, if he passed Cedron (37); three years after he went to Geth in pursuit of runaway servants (40); and he was put to death (46).

SEMEI'AS, a prophet sent to Roboam, king of Juda, to forbid him to make war on the Ten Tribes (3 Kings xii. 22; 2 Paral. xi. 2; xii. 5, 7).

SEME'IAS, a Levite sent by king Josaphat to instruct the people (2 Paral. xvii. 8).

SEME'IAS OF NEHELAM, a false prophet at Babylon, wrote to Jerusalem against Jeremias (Jerem. xxix. 24–32).

SE'MER, sold Mount Somer or Semeron, on which Amri, king of Israel, built Samaria (3 Kings xvi. 24).

SEM'ERON or **SOMER,** the mountain on which Samaria was built (2 Paral. xiii. 4); a battle had been fought there between Abia, king of Juda, and Jeroboam, in which Abia was victorious (2 Par. xiii.)

SEM'ERON, a city of the Chanaanites (Jos. xi. 1; xii. 20).

SEM'LA, king of Masreca, in Idumea (Gen. xxxvi. 36).

SEM'MA, of Arari, son of Age, one of David's champions (2 Kings xxiii. 11); he defeats the Philistines (12); brings to David water from the cistern of Bethlehem (16).

SEM'MAA, brother of David, and father of Jonadab (2 Kings xiii. 3).

SEM'RAN, son of Issachar (Num. xxvi. 24).

SEN. Samuel set up the Stone of Help between Masphath and Sen, to commemorate a victory over the Philistines (1 Kings vii. 12).

SEN'AA. The children of Senaa were a body of 3950, who returned from Babylon (2 Esd. vii. 38).

SENE', steep cliffs like teeth between Machmas and Gabaa; Jonathan and his armor-bearer crept by it to attack the Philistines (1 Kings xiv. 4).

SEN'NA, a city in the south of the promised land (Num. xxxiv. 4).

SEN'NAAB, king of Adama, one of the cities of the Pentapolis, defeated by Amraphel and his allies (Gen. xiv. 2).

SEN'NAAR, a country of Babylonia. Calanne was built here by Nemrod (Gen. x. 10); here the descendants of Noe began to build the tower of Babel (Gen. xi. 2); Amraphel, king of Sennaar, was powerful in the time of Abraham (xiv. 1); the name is given to the country of Babylon (Dan. i. 2; Zach. v. 11).

SENNACH'ERIB, king of Assyria, son and successor of Salmanasar, reigned 714–704 B. C. Ezechias, king of Juda, threw off the yoke of the Assyrians (4 Kings xviii. 7), which Theglathphalasar had imposed on Achaz (4 Kings xvi. 10; 2 Paral. xxviii. 20, 21); Sennacherib marched against him, and took all the strong cities of Juda (4 Kings xviii. 13; 2 Paral. xxxii. 1); while besieging Lachis, he received proposals of submission from Ezechias, but he demanded 300 talents of silver and thirty talents of gold (4 Kings xviii. 14); Ezechias paid it, stripping the very doors of the temple (16), but Sennacherib, instead of retiring, sent a part of his army under Tharthan, Rabsares, and Rabsaces, to demand

CHURCH OF THE HOLY SEPULCHRE AT JERUSALEM.

the surrender of the city (17); they met envoys of Ezechias, and not only insulted them, but blasphemed the God of Israel (19–35); Sennacherib then besieged Lobna (4 Kings xix. 8), and wrote a letter to Ezechias in the same strain of insult and blasphemy (10–13; Isai. xxxvi. 1); hearing of the advance of Tharaca, king of Ethiopia, he advanced to meet him, and never invested the city of Jerusalem (4 Kings xix. 32), an angel of the Lord having slain 185,000 men in his camp in one night (35; Isai. xxxvii. 36; 1 Mach. vii. 41; 2 Mach. viii. 19; Tob. i. 21; Ecclus. xlviii. 24); Sennacherib then returned to Ninive (4 Kings xix. 36), and was assassinated in the temple of Nesroch by his two sons Adramelech and Sarasar, as Isaias had foretold (Isai. x. 33; xxxi. 8; xxxiii. 1).

SENSEN'NA, a city in the tribe of Juda (Jos. xv. 3).

SE'ON, a city in the tribe of Issachar (Jos. xix. 19).

SEO'RIM, the fourth of the twenty-four courses of priestly families (1 Paral. xxiv. 8).

SEPH'A'ATH, a city in the tribe of Simeon (Judg. i. 17).

SEPHA'MA, a city of Syria, on the frontiers of the promised land (Num. xxxiv. 10, 11).

SEPH'AMOTH, David sent there the spoils he took from the Amalecites (1 Kings xxx. 28).

SEPH'AR, a mountain in the East, apparently in or near Armenia (Gen. x. 30).

SEPHARVA'IM, a tribe or people sent by Salmanazar to colonize the kingdom of Israel after the removal of the ten tribes (4 Kings xvii. 24, 31); they were perhaps from the Sephar mountains (Gen. x. 30); they were idolaters, and worshipped Ana and Ava as their gods or kings (4 Kings xviii. 34; Isai. xxxvii. 13; 4 Kings xix. 13); they offered their children in sacrifice to these gods (4 Kings xvii. 31); when they settled in Samaria many were destroyed by lions (xvii. 25, 26), and to propitiate the god of the country, a Jewish priest was sent to them (28), after which time they worshipped both the true God and their old divinities (33).

SEPHA'TA, a valley near Maresa (2 Paral. xiv. 10), where Asa defeated Zara.

SEPHE'LA, a district in which Simon built and fortified Adiada (1 Mach. xii. 28).

SE'PHER, one of the encampments of the Israelites in the desert (Num. xxxiii. 23).

SEPH'ET, a city in the tribe of Nephthali (Tob. i. 1).

SEPH'ORA, one of the seven daughters of Raguel, priest of Madian (Ex. ii. 16–21); driven away from the well by shepherds, but protected by Moses (16, 17); marries Moses (21); bears Gersam and Eliezer (22; xviii. 3, 4); went with him to Egypt, but on the way circumcised her son with a very sharp stone, when the Lord would have killed Moses for his negligence (iv. 25); sent back to Madian by Moses (xviii. 2); she and her two sons brought to Moses in Raphidim, by Jethro her kinsman (5); Aaron and Mary call her an Ethiopian (Num. xii.)

SEPH'ORA, one of the mid-wives of the Israelite women in Egypt, who saved the children (Ex. i. 15).

SEP'TUAGINT. The ancient Greek version of the Old Testament, made in Egypt, as is generally stated, in the reign of Ptolemy Philadelphus, by seventy-two learned Jews, and the translation took the name Septuagint, meaning seventy, from this fact. As Greek became the prevailing language through Asia Minor, Palestine, and Egypt, this version came into general circulation. It was used by our Lord and his apostles, as is evident from places where it is cited in the New Testament, and does not correspond with the modern Hebrew text. The Septuagint version of Deut. vii. is cited (Matt. iv. 4); of Deut. vi. 16 in Matt. vi. 7; of Osee vi. 6 in Matt. ix. 13; of Lev. xix. 18 in Matt. xix. 19; of Ps. viii. 2 in Matt. xxi. 16; of Ps. cxviii. 22, 23, in Matt. xxi. 42; of Ex. iii. 6 in Matt. xxii. 32; of Ps. cx. 1 in Matt. xxii. 44; of Zach. xiii. 7 in Matt. xxvi. 31.

SEP'ULCHRE, HOLY. The tomb in which our Lord was laid on Mount Calvary. It had been hewn in the rock by Joseph of Arimathea, for his own use (Matt. xxvii. 60); our Lord's body was laid there by Joseph and Nicodemus (Matt. xxvii. 57–60; Mark xv. 43–46; Luke xxiii. 50–53; John xix. 38–42); the sepulchre was sealed and guarded at the desire of the Jewish priests (Matt. xxvii. 60, 66); Mary Magdalen and the other Mary, mother of Joseph, sat over against it (Matt. xxvii. 61; Mark xv. 47; Luke xxiii. 55); the same with Salome, went to the sepulchre early on the first day of the week. The stone rolled back by an angel who sat on it, terrifying the guards (Matt. xxviii. 1–4; Mark xvi. 4; Luke xxiv. 2; John xx. 1); they entered (Mark xvi. 5); but found not the body of the Lord (Luke xxiv. 3); but saw angels who told them that the Lord had risen (Matt. xxviii. 5, 7; Mark xvi. 5–7; Luke xxiv. 4–8); they went out of the sepulchre, and ran to tell the disciples (Matt. xxviii. 8; Mark xvi. 8); going back they told them (Luke xxiv. 9); St. Peter and St. John went to the sepulchre and entered it (Luke xxiv. 12; John xx. 3–8); our Lord appears to Mary Magdalen at the sepulchre (Mark xvi. 9; John xx. 11–17);

Isaias predicts that his sepulchre shall be glorious (Isai. xi. 10).

SEP'ULCHRE of David (Acts ii. 29).

SEP'ULTURE. It is one of the works of mercy to bury the dead (Gen. xxiii. 19; xxv. 9; xxxv. 19, 29; Num. xx. 1; Deut. x. 6; xxi. 23; Jos. xxiv. 30; Judg. xii. 7; 1 Kings xxv.; 2 Kings ii. 32; 3 Kings ii. 10, 34; xi. 43; xiii. 30; xiv. 31; 4 Kings xiii. 20; 2 Paral. xvi. 14; xxiv. 16; xxxv. 24; Tob. i. 20; ii. 4, 7; iv. 3, 18; viii. 14; xii. 12; xiv. 12, 16; Ecclus. vii. 37; xxxviii. 16; Matt. xiv. 12; xxvii. 58; John xix. 39; Acts viii. 2; xiii. 29; 1 Cor. xv. 4).

SER, a city in the tribe of Nephthali (Jos. xix. 35).

SER'APHIM, an order of angels, seen by Isaias in a vision; they had six wings, covering their faces with two, their feet with two, and flying with two (Isai. vi. 2).

SERGIUS PAULUS, proconsul or governor of the island of Cyprus, converted by St. Paul (Acts xiii. 7). See PAUL.

SER'MON of our Lord on the Mount (Matt. v. 3, 12; Luke vi. 20); sermon or discourse to Nicodemus (John iii. 3); on his divinity (John v. 17–32); on St. John the Baptist (33, 35; Matt. xi. 2, 19; Luke vii. 24–35); on the incredulity of the Jews (Matt. xi. 20); on the bread from heaven (John vi. 26); on humility (Matt. xviii. 1, 5); on correction and fraternal charity (15–22); on purity of heart (xv. 8; Mark vii. 6); on the cross (Matt. xvi. 24); on the love of God (Luke x. 27); on prayer (i. 13); before and after the Last Supper (Matt. xxvi.; Mark xiv.; Luke xxii.; John xiii. 12–38; xiv.–xvi.); sermon of St. Peter on Pentecost (Acts i. 16; ii. 14); of St. Paul in the synagogue (xiii. 16); before the Areopagus (Acts xvii. 22); before Felix, the pro-consul (xxiv. 10).

THE BIRTH OF OUR SAVIOUR ANNOUNCED TO THE SHEPHERDS BY ANGELS.

SE'RON, general of the army of Antiochus Epiphanes (1 Mach. xiii. 13, 23); he undertook to overthrow Judas Machabeus, but was routed at

Bethoron, and his army fled to the territory of the Philistines.

SER′PENT. The devil, under the figure of a serpent, seduces Eve (Gen. iii. 1, 5); it is cursed (14); prediction that the woman shall crush his head (iii. 15); miraculous serpent produced by the rod of Moses (Ex. iv. 3, 4; vii. 10); imitated by Pharao's magicians, who make their rods turn into serpents (12); that of Aaron devours those of the magicians (12); Moses sets up the brazen serpent in the wilderness (Num. xxi. 8); did not heal by its own power (Wisd. xvi. 7); was a figure of Jesus Christ (John iii. 14); worshipped by the Jews under the name of

SHIELDS.
1. Assyrian. 2, 3. Persian. (From Layard, Ker Porter. Fbn.)

Nohestan, till destroyed by king Ezechias (4 Kings xviii. 4).

SERPENT WORSHIP (Wis. xi. 16; Dan. xiv. 22–26).

SE′RUG, son of Ragau, and father of Nachor (Gen. xi. 20; 1 Paral. i. 26).

SER′VANTS and HANDMAIDS. Their duty (Gen. xxiv.; xxxi. 39; Ex. xxii. 28; 4 Kings v. 20, 25; Prov. xiv. 35; xix. 10; xxix. 19; Ecclus. x. 28; Luke xii. 37, 45; 1 Cor. vii. 21; Col. iii. 22; 1 Tim. vi. 1; Heb. xiii. 17; 1 Pet. ii. 18); how they should be treated by their masters (Deut. v. 14; xii. 12).

SER′VITUDE or BONDAGE. Law limiting the time during which a Hebrew might remain in bondage (Lev. xxv. 39, 40); the Hebrews rebellious to God's commandments, are reduced to servitude by Theglathphalasar, king of Assyria (4 Kings xv. 29); by Salmanasar (xvii. 6; xviii. 11); those who violate the law of God are under the servitude of sin (John viii. 34; Rom. vi. 17, 20).

SE′SAC (SESONCHIS), king of Egypt, declared war on Roboam, king of Juda, in the fifth year of Roboam's reign, 971 B.C. He took the strong places, and advanced to Jerusalem (3 Kings xiv. 25; 2 Paral. xii. 2); his army consisted of 1,200 chariots, 60,000 horsemen, and footmen beyond number (2 Paral. xii. 3); he took the strongest cities of Juda (4); he captured Jerusalem and plundered the temple and the palace (3 Kings xiv. 26; 2 Paral. xii. 9).

SE′SAC, a term in Jer. xxv. 26; li. 41, used apparently for Babylon.

SE′SAI, one of the three brothers, giants of the race of Enac, whom Caleb drove out of Hebron (Jos. xv. 14).

SETH, son of Adam and Eve, born after Cain and Abel. He died at the age of 912, 2962 B.C. (Gen. v. 3–8); his descendants long have served the true religion, and are called the sons of God (vi. 2); father of Enos (iv. 26; v. 6).

SET′IM WOOD, supposed to be the acacia or locust. The Ark of the Covenant was made of it (Ex. xxv. 5, 10; Deut. x. 3).

SEX′TARY, a measure (Lev. xiv. 10).

SHEEP, parable of the lost sheep (Luke xv. 4; Matt. xviii. 12); seven sheep offered by Abraham (Gen. xxi. 29); Jacob's sheep (Gen. xxx. 38); sheep offered in sacrifice (Lev. iii. 6; iv. 32; xiv. 10; Num. vi. 14; xv. 4); our Lord compares the good to sheep (Matt. xxv. 32, 33); his sheep know him (John x. 27), and hear his voice (x. 3); he gives his life for his sheep (x. 11); he had other sheep, but would bring all into one sheepfold (x. 16); he commands Peter to feed his sheep and his lambs (xxi. 17).

SHEET, containing mysterious animals seen in a vision by St. Peter (Acts x. 11).

SHEP′HERD, THE GOOD. A figure of Christ (John x. 2); he lays down his life for his sheep (John x. 11); he seeks the lost sheep (Luke xv. 4; Matt. xviii. 12); leaving this world after his resurrection, he commissions Peter to feed his sheep

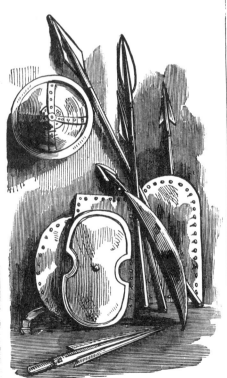

ANCIENT JEWISH SHIELDS AND SPEARS.

and his lambs (John xxi. 17); his birth first revealed to shepherds (Luke ii. 8).

SHEPHERD′S ROD, the prophet Zach-

arias has a vision of shepherds' crooks (Zach. xi. 7).

SHIPS. Men trust their lives even to a little

AN ANCIENT SHIP.

wood, and passing over the sea by ship are saved (Wis. xiv. 5); the course of a ship through the waves a type of earthly things (v. 10); the ark (Gen. vi.); Zabulon in the road of ships (Gen. xlix. 13); Dan applied himself to ships (Judg. v. 17); Solomon built a fleet of ships at Asiongaber, near Ailath, on the Red Sea (3 Kings ix. 26); Josaphat built ships at the same place, but as he did it in conjunction with the wicked king of Israel, they were destroyed (3 Kings xxii. 49; 2 Paral. xx. 36, 37); Jonas thrown into the sea from a ship (Jon. i. 5); ships on the Sea of Galilee (Matt. iv. 21; Mark i. 19); Jesus preaches from a ship (Mark iv. 1; Luke v. 3); Jesus in a ship during a storm on the Sea of Galilee (Mark iv. 37; vi. 47); St. Paul's voyages in ships from Philippi to Troas (Acts xx. 6); from Coos to Rhodes and Patara (xxi. 1); thence in another vessel to Tyre (3); on a ship of Adrumetum to Lystra in Lycia (xxvii. 5); then in a ship of Alexandria, which was wrecked off Melita (xxvii. 6; xxviii. 10); then in the Castors, an Alexandrian ship, to Puteoli (11–13).

SHOE, meaning of the custom of taking off a shoe and presenting it to another (Deut. xxv. 9; Ruth iv. 7, 8); St. John the Baptist declares himself unworthy to loose our Lord's shoe (Matt. iii. 11; Mark

SICLE, SHOWING THE CUP OF MANNA PRE-
SERVED IN THE ARK.

i. 7; John i. 27); the apostles directed not to carry shoes (Matt. x. 10; Luke x. 4); Moses commanded to take off his shoes, as the ground whereon he stood was holy (Ex. iii. 5); those eating the paschal lamb to have shoes on their feet (xii. 11); the shoes of the Israelites did not wear out in the desert (Deut. xxix. 5); the shoe of Aser to be iron and brass (Deut. xxxiii. 25).

SHOUL'DER OF VICTIMS OFFERED IN SACRIFICE. Directions as to (Ex. xxix. 22; Lev. vii. 34; x. 14; Num. vi. 19).

SI'BA, Saul's servant, appointed to take care of Miphiboseth (2 Kings ix. 9); he slanderously accuses his master of ingratitude and treachery to David, and obtains his property (xvi. 2); he goes to David, and proves his innocence (xix. 17); David restores half his property (29).

SIC'ELEG, a city in the tribe of Simeon (Jos. xix. 5), given to David by Achis, king of Geth (1 Kings xxvii. 6); in David's absence the Amalecites took and burned it, and carried off David's wives and children (xxx. 1, 2); he pursued them, and recovered what he lost (18, 19).

SI'CHEM, son of Hemor, ravishes Dina (Gen. xxxiv. 2); killed by Simeon and Levi (26).

SI'CHAR or **SI'CHEM,** a city near which Jacob bought a field (Gen. xxxiii. 19); Joseph's bones laid there (Jos. xxiv. 32; Acts vii. 16); our Lord converts the Samaritan woman there (John iv. 5).

the coast of (Matt. xv. 21; Mark vii. 24); reaches Sidon (31); the people of Sidon come to hear him (Luke vi. 17); St. Paul visits (Acts xxvii. 3).

SIDO'NIANS, people of Sidon. They called Mount Hermon Sarion (Deut. iii. 9); Maara, one of their cities (Jos. xiii. 4); left by the Lord that by them he might instruct Israel (Judg. iii. 1–3); oppressed the Israelites (x. 11, 12); their easy mode of living (xviii. 7); worshipped the goddess Astarthe, or Astaroth, as Solomon did also (3 Kings xi. 5; 4 Kings xxiii. 13); they were great workers in wood (3 Kings v. 6); Jezabel, daughter of Ethbaal, king of the Sidonians (xvi. 31).

SI'DRACH, the Chaldean name of Ananias (Dan. i. 7).

SIEGE of Bethulia by Holofernes (Judith vii.); of Bethsura (1 Mach. xi. 65); of Gabaa by the tribes of Israel (Judg. xx. 19, 43); of Gaza (i. 18; Amos i. 6, 7; 1 Mach. xiii. 43); of Hai (Jos. vii. 5; viii. 1–26); of Jebus by David (1 Paral. xi. 5); of Jericho by Josue (Jos. vi. 1–21); of Jerusalem by the chil-

Josue's covenant with Rahab (Jos. ii. 18); the death of Ophni and Phinees a sign that the priesthood was to pass from the house of Heli (1 Kings ii. 34); Samuel anointed and kissed Saul as a sign that God had anointed him to be prince over his inheritance (x. 1); the sound of one going on the tops of the pear trees a sign that God gave David victory over the Philistines (2 Kings v. 24); the destruction of Sennacherib's army a sign to Ezechias (4 Kings xix. 29); the shadow turning back on the dial of Achaz a sign that Ezechias would recover, and he and Jerusalem be delivered from the king of the Assyrians (Isai. xxxviii. 8); the swaddling clothes and manger a sign that the infant is the Saviour, Christ the Lord (Luke ii. 11, 12). Signs and monuments in memory of things past: the paschal lamb a memorial of the deliverance of the Israelites from Egypt (Ex. xii. 1–14); the fringes or hem worn by the Jews a memorial of the commandments of God (Num. xv. 38, 39); the censers of Core, Dathan, and Abiron beaten into plates and nailed on the altar as a sign that no stranger should offer incense (xvi. 38–40); Aaron's rod that blossomed kept as a token of the rebellious children of Israel (xvii. 10); twelve stones set up by Josue as a sign of the miraculous crossing of the Jordan (Jos. iv. 6); God sends signs to show his omnip-

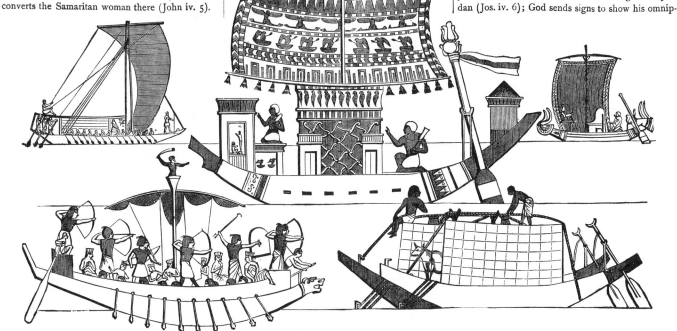

ANCIENT SHIPS.

SI'CLE, a Hebrew weight (10 dwts.), and also a coin, 46 cents (Gen. xxiii. 15; 1 Mach. x. 40).

SIC'YON, a city of Peloponnesus, to which the Romans wrote in favor of the Jews (1 Mach. xv. 23).

SIDE, a port in Pamphylia, to which the Romans wrote in favor of the Jews (1 Mach. xv. 23).

SI'DON, a famous city of Phœnicia, on the limits of the Promised Land (Gen. x. 19); and of Zabulon (xlix. 13); Josue pursued Jabin and his allies after the battle of Merom as far as great Sidon (Jos. xi. 8); the land of Aser extended to (xix. 28); but Aser could not take it (Judg. i. 31); the Jews worship the gods of Sidon (x. 6); Lais at a distance from Sidon (xviii. 7); the census takers of David go to Sidon (2 Kings xxiv. 6); its destruction foretold (Isai. xxiii.; Jer. xxvii. 3; xlvii. 4; Ezech. xxviii.; Joel iii. 4, 8); our Lord declares that if he had wrought his miracles in Tyre and Sidon they would have been converted (Matt. xi. 21, 22; Luke x. 13, 14); he visits

dren of Juda (Judg. i. 8); by those of Benjamin (21); by David (1 Paral. xi. 5); by the Philistines and Arabians, 886 B. C. (2 Paral. xxi. 16); by Joas, king of Israel, 839 B. C. (2 Paral. xxv. 23, 24); by the king of Egypt (2 Paral. xxxvi. 3); by Nabuchodonosor, 607 B. C. (2 Paral. xxxvi. 6); 597 B. C. (4 Kings xxv. 1); by Nabuzardan, B. C. 586 (4 Kings xxv. 8, 9); by Antiochus Epiphanes, 170 B. C. (1 Mach. iii. 45; vi. 62); by Judas Machabeus (2 Mach. x. 1; 1 Mach. iv. 37); that by Titus foretold by our Lord (Luke xix. 43); of Rabba by Joab (2 Kings xi. 1); of Samaria (3 Kings xx.; 4 Kings xviii. 9, 10); of Sichem and Thebes by Abimelech, 1235 B. C. (Judg. ix. 26–50); of Tyre (Ezech. xxvi. 4).

SIGNS of things to come. The rainbow a sign of God's covenant with Noe (Gen. ix. 12); circumcision a sign of God's covenant with Abraham (Gen. xvii. 11); the Sabbath a sign of God's covenant with the Israelites (Ex. xxxi. 13); a scarlet cord a sign of

otence, his truth, his justice, and his goodness: the changing of Moses' rod into a serpent (Ex. iv. 2–6); the turning of the waters of Egypt into blood (vii. 17); the sending of quails and manna to the Israelites (xvi.); the dividing of the waters of the Jordan (Jos. iii. 10–17); the rending of the altar, a sign that Josias would immolate heathen priests there (3 Kings xiii. 1–5); the widow's pot and cruse a sign (xvii. 14); the fire consuming the sacrifice of Elias (xviii. 38); Achab's miraculous victory over the Syrians (xx. 13–29); the cure of Naaman's leprosy (4 Kings v. 14); the going back of the shadow on the dial of Achaz (xx. 9); Christ stilling the sea (Matt. viii. 26); the cure of the palsy a sign of the forgiveness of sin (ix. 2); Peter's walking on the water a sign that the vision was really our Lord (xiv. 28); our Lord reproaches the people that unless they saw signs and wonders they did not believe (John iv. 48); the scribes and Pharisees ask a sign from him (Matt. xii.

38; Mark viii. 11; Luke xi. 16); no sign to be given that generation but the sign of Jonas, the prophet (Matt. xii. 39; Mark viii. 12; Luke xi. 29); the Pharisees and Sadducees ask a sign (Matt. xvi. 1); the sign of the prophet Jonas again said to be the only one to be given (4); the sign of his second coming (xxiv. 3–51; Mark xiii. 4–37; Luke xxi. 7–36); the sign of the Son of man in heaven (Matt. xxiv. 30); signs shall follow them that believe (Mark xvi. 17); the Lord confirmed the work of the apostles with signs that followed (20); our Lord a sign which shall be contradicted (Luke ii. 34); signs in the sun and moon (xxi. 25); Herod hoped to see some sign wrought by our Lord (Luke xxiii. 8); the Jews ask a sign, and he replied, "Destroy this temple, and in three days I will build it up," speaking of the temple of his body (John iii. 18–21); many believed, seeing the signs he did (23); the word sign used for miracle in John iii. 2; iv., vi., vii., ix.–xii., xx.; Acts ii. 22, 43; iv., v., vii., viii., xiv., xv.; 2 Cor. xii. 12; 2 Thess. ii. 9); the sign of the living God (Apoc. vii. 2; ix. 4); signs in heaven (xii. 1, 3; xv. 1).

SI'HOR, a place in the tribe of Aser (Jos. xix. 26).

SI'LAS or SYLVANUS, one of the chief men among the brethren (Acts xv. 22), sent by the apostles with Judas to Antioch, with the decrees of the council of Jerusalem (27); after Barnabas parted from him, St. Paul chose Silas, who accompanied him to Syria and Cilicia (40, 41), then to Lystra, Phrygia, and Galatia, and finally to Macedonia (xvi. 1–12); at Philippi they were beaten and imprisoned (22, 23); while praying and praising God at midnight, an earthquake shakes the prison (25, 26); the jailer falls at the feet of Paul and Silas (29), and is baptized (33); at Thessalonica (xvii. 1); sent away to Berea (10); remains there with Timothy (14); apparently the same as the Sylvanus in whose name as well as those of Paul and Timothy, the two epistles to the Thessalonians are written (1 Thess. i. 1; 2 Thess. i. 1); and the one mentioned in 2 Cor. i. 19.

SI'LENCE, usefulness of (Prov. xvii. 28; Eccles. iii. 7; Ecclus. xx. 6; xxxii. 12).

SILK, worn by Mardochai (Esth. viii. 15); merchants of silk mourn the destruction of Babylon (Apoc. xviii. 12).

SI'LO, a famous city in the tribe of Ephraim (Jos. xviii.), not far from Sichem. The tabernacle of the testimony was set up here, B. C. 1444 (Jos. xviii. 1); lots cast here to divide the land among the tribes (10; xix. 51); the ark remained there till it was taken by the Philistines (Judg. xviii. 1; 1 Kings iv. 17); Israel assembled at Silo to fight against the tribes beyond the Jordan, who had erected an altar (Jos. xxii. 12); they went to Silo to consult the Lord as to the war against Benjamin (Judg. xx. 18); they returned to Silo to mourn over the destruction of the tribe of Benjamin (xxi. 2–25); Elcana went up on the appointed days to adore and to offer sacrifice to the Lord of Hosts in Silo (1 Kings i. 3). Anna brings Samuel to the house of the Lord in Silo (24); the Lord appeared to Samuel in Silo (1 Kings iii. 21); the Ark of the Covenant taken from Silo to the camp of Israel (iv. 3, 5); Heli falls dead in Silo (18); Jeroboam's wife goes to the prophet Ahias in Silo (3 Kings xiv. 2–4); the Almighty bids the Jews see what he had done in Silo (Jerem. vii. 12, 14); and the destruction of the temple to be like that of Silo (xxvi. 6, 9); men came from Silo after the death of Godolias (xli. 5).

SILO'E (Sent), a fountain at the foot of the walls of Jerusalem, on the east side, between the city and the brook Cedron, supposed to be the same as Rogel (Jos. xv. 7; xviii. 16; 2 Kings xvii. 17; 3 Kings i. 9); the waters flowed silently (Isai. viii. 6); the Jews represented as rejecting them (6); after the captivity, Sellum, son of Cholhoza, built the walls of the pool of Siloe unto the king's garden (2 Esd. iii. 15); our Lord sent a blind man, telling him go, wash in the pool of Siloe, and when he did so he saw (John ix. 1–41).

SIL'OE, a tower which fell and crushed eighteen men (Luke xiii. 4).

SIM'EON, son of Jacob and Lia, born 1757 B. C. (Gen. xxix. 33; xxxv. 23); he, with Levi, avenges the violence done to Dina by the slaughter of the Sichemites (xxxiv. 25–31); taken and bound by Joseph in Egypt (xlii. 25, 36); Jacob, in his prophetical words, calls Simeon and Levi vessels of iniquity waging war (xlix. 5); and he cursed their fury and wrath (6, 7); his sons were Jamuel, Jamin, Ahod, Jachin, Soar, or Zare, and Saul (Ex. vi. 15; Num. xxvi. 12–14).

SIM'EON, one of the twelve tribes of Israel. When they left Egypt their prince was Salamiel, the son of Surisaddai (Num. i. 6; x. 19); and they numbered 59,300 fighting men, in the camp of Ruben, on the south side (ii. 13); and at Settim, 22,200 (xxvi. 14); the offerings of the tribe (vii. 36–41); Saphat, the son of Huri, was sent by Moses from this tribe to view the land (xiii. 6); Zambri, son of Salu, prince of the tribe of Simeon, slain by Phinees for sinning with Cozbi, a Madianite, when the people fell into idolatry and vice (xxv. 6–18); in the division of the land their representative was Samuel, son of Ammiud (xxxiv. 20); they were among the tribes on Garizim, to bless the people (Deut. xxvii. 12); the lands allotted to Simeon in the possession of Juda (Jos. xix. 1–9); Simeon and Juda attack the Chanaanites and Pherezites, and slew 10,000 in Bezee, capturing Adonibezec, cutting off his fingers and toes (Judges i. 3–7); Simeon, with Juda, defeated the Chanaanites of Sephaath, and captured Horma (17); 7,100 of the tribe of Simeon joined David in Hebron (1 Paral. xii. 25); Ozias, of the tribe of Simeon, one of the rulers in Bethulia (Judith vi. 11); twelve thousand of the tribe signed in the Apocalypse (Apoc. vii. 7).

SIM'EON, son of Ruben, one of the ancestors of Judith (Judith viii. 1; ix. 2).

SIM'EON, grandfather of Mathathias, of the house of Phinees, the high-priest (1 Mach. ii. 1).

SIM'EON, a just and devout man in Jerusalem, waiting for the consolation of Israel (Luke ii. 25); the Holy Ghost promised that he should not see death before he had seen the Christ of the Lord (26); at the time of the purification of Mary, and the presentation of the child Jesus, he came by the spirit into the temple (27); he took the child into his arms and uttered the canticle "Nunc Dimittis" (29–32); blessed Joseph and Mary, foretold that the child is for the fall and the resurrection of many (34), and told Mary that a sword should pierce her own heart (35).

SIM'EON, son of Juda, one of the ancestors of our Lord (Luke iii. 30).

SIM'ERON, fourth son of Issachar (1 Paral. vii. 1). See SEMRON.

SIM'MAA (SAMUA, 2 Kings v. 14; 1 Paral. xiv. 4), son of David and Bethsabee (1 Paral. iii. 5).

SI'MON, cousin of our Lord (Matt. xiii. 55; Mark vi. 3), son of Cleophas and Mary, one of the twelve apostles of our Lord. He was surnamed the Chananean (Matt. x. 4), or Cananean (Mark iii. 18), or Zelotes (Luke vi. 15; Acts i. 13); according to Eusebius, he was crucified by Atticus, governor of Palestine, in the reign of Trajan, A. D. 107.

SI'MON, son of Ozias, high-priest of the Jews; he founded the height of the temple, the double building, and the high walls (Ecclus. l. 2); he enlarged the entrance and the court (5); his eulogy (6–23).

SI'MON MACHABEUS, surnamed Thasi, son of Mathathias, prince and high-priest till 135 B. C. His father commended him as a man of counsel (1 Mach. ii. 65); he commanded 1,500 men in the successful battle against Nicanor, 166 B. C. (2 Mach. viii. 22); in 163 B. C., with 3,000 men, he fought many battles in Galilee, killed 3,000 of the enemy, delivered the Jews there, and returned with them and rich spoils (1 Mach. v. 17–23); he joined battle with Nicanor in 161 B. C., although surprised at the sudden coming of his superior forces (2 Mach. xiv. 17); in 148 B. C. he aided Jonathan to take Joppe (1 Mach. x. 74–76), and to defeat Apollonius at Azotus (82); young king Antiochus made him governor from Tyre to Egypt (xi. 59); he took Bethsura (65), and Joppe (xii. 33), and built Adiada in Sephela (38); on the arrest of Jonathan by Tryphon, he exhorted the people, and was hailed as leader (xiii. 8); he marched to Addus to meet Tryphon (13), and sent money and hostages to obtain the release of Jonathan (19); he followed Tryphon closely (20), buried Jonathan in Modin (25), and set up seven pyramids (27–30); fortifies and provisions the towns (33); sends to king Demetrius, who confirms him in his possessions (34–41), and people began to write: "The first year under Simon, the high-priest, the great captain and prince of the Jews" (42); he took Gaza (43–48), and made it his habitation, after cleansing it from idols (65); the castle of Jerusalem surrenders to him (49, 50); he enters it 142 B. C., with great solemnity (51); fortifies the mountain, and dwells there (53); rules in peace (xiv. 1–15); renews alliance with Rome and Sparta (16–49); Antiochus, son of Demetrius, confirms his authority (xv. 1–9); Simon aids him (26), but Antiochus refused aid, and demanded Joppe, Gazara, and Jerusalem (27–31); Simon offers him a hundred talents (35), but Antiochus sent Cendebeus against him (38, 39); Simon's sons defeat him (xvi. 8); Ptolemee his son-in-law slays Simon and his sons at Doch (11–16).

SI'MON, of the tribe of Benjamin, overseer of the temple, quarrels with Onias, the high-priest, tells Apollonius, governor of Celesyria, that there was great wealth in the temple, and induced king Seleucus to send Heliodorus to seize it (2 Mach. iii. 4–7); calls Onias a traitor (iv. 2).

SI'MON, THE CYRENIAN, forced by the Jews to carry the cross of our Lord (Matt. xxvii. 32), as he was coming out of the country (Mark xv. 21); he was apparently a disciple, for he is mentioned as father of Alexander and Rufus (21).

SI'MON, THE PHARISEE, desired our Lord to eat with him (Luke vii. 36); while our Lord was at meat, a sinful woman anointed his feet, washed them with her tears, and kissed them (37, 38); Simon's reflections (39); the lesson taught him by our Lord (40–50).

SI'MON, THE LEPER, resided at Bethania, near Jerusalem (Matt. xxvi. 6; Mark xiv. 3; John xi., xii.); he invites Jesus to his table; Lazarus, Mary and Martha are there, and a woman anoints our Lord's head (Matt. xxvi. 7; Mark xiv. 8); and

Mary anoints his feet, and wipes them with her hair (John xi. 2; xii. 1–3).

SI′MON BARJONA, or son of John. See PETER.

MOUNT SION

SI′MON NIGER, a prophet at Antioch (Acts xiii. 1); one of those who imposed hands on St. Paul and Barnabas (3).

SI′MON, a tanner at Joppe. St. Peter abode many days with him (Acts ix. 43) in his house by the sea (x. 6); here Peter had a vision, and is called to visit Cornelius the centurion (19–23).

SI′MON MAGUS, converted at Samaria by Philip, the deacon, after he had seduced the people and bewitched them with his magical practices (Acts viii. 9–13); when he saw the gifts of the Holy Ghost, after the imposition of hands by the apostle, he offered St. Peter money to obtain the power (18); St. Peter bid him keep his money to perish with him, for imagining that the gift of God could be purchased with money (20), and exhorted him to penance (22, 23); Simon asked the apostle to pray for him (24), but he fell away. From him any sale of ecclesiastical functions is called Simony.

SIM′ONY. It is forbidden to sell the gifts of God (4 Kings v. 22, 26; Dan. v. 17; Matt. x. 9; Acts xx. 35; 1 Cor. ix. 15; 2 Cor. xi. 9; xii. 13).

SIMPLE OF HEART. God reveals himself to them (Isai. xxix. 18, 24; xxxii. 4; Eccles. ix. 15; Matt. xi. 25; Luke ii. 9; v. 8; x. 21; Acts iv. 13; 1 Cor. i. 26; ii. 1); simplicity and uprightness of heart commended (Gen. xx. 6; Job i. 8; Matt. x. 16; Acts ii. 46; Rom. xvi. 18; Eph. vi. 5; Col. iii. 22.)

SIN. Its origin (Gen. ii. 17; iii. 6; Rom. v. 12; 1 Cor. xv. 21). Original sin, of our first parents, through which we are conceived and born in sin (Job xiv. 4; xv. 14; Ps. l. 7; Rom. iii. 9, 23); effects of sin (Gen. viii. 21;

ROMAN SLINGER. (From Column of Antoninus. Fbn.)

Ecclus. xvii. 30; Rom. vi. 23; vii. 8, 11, 13, 21; Gal. v. 17; Eph. ii. 3); sin is taken away by Jesus Christ (John i. 29; Rom. v. 9–19; vi. 3; vii. 24; viii. 1, 2; Gal. iii. 22); God alone remits sin by his own authority (Ex. xxxiv. 7; Ps. xviii. 13; xxxi. 5; cii. 12; Isai. xliii. 25; xliv. 22; Jer. xxxi. 34; xxxiii. 8; Mich. vii. 18; Matt. xviii. 18; John xx. 23); Christ had power to forgive sins (Matt. ix. 6; Mark ii. 10; Luke v. 24); he delegated the power to the apostles (Matt. xvi. 19; xviii. 18; John xx. 23); all sin is remitted through the merits of Christ (Isai. liii.; Dan. ix. 24; Matt. i. 21; ix. 2; xi. 27; xx. 28; xxvi. 28; Luke xxiv. 47; Acts ii. 38; x. 47; xiii. 38; Rom. iv. 25; 1 Cor. vi. 11; xv. 3; 2 Cor. v. 15; Gal. i. 4; Eph. i. 7; Col. i. 14; 1 Tim. i. 15; Tit. ii. 14; Heb. i. 3; ix. 12–14; 1 Pet. i. 19; iii. 18; 1 John i. 7; ii. 12; iii. 16; Apoc. i. 5).

SIN against the Holy Ghost (Mark iii. 29; Luke xii. 10; Heb. vi. 6); sin which cries to heaven for vengeance (Gen. iv. 10; xviii. 20; Ex. xxii. 23, 27; Ecclus. xxxv. 18; James v. 4); it frequently occurs that many are punished for the sin of one (Gen. iii.; Num. xvi. 21; Jos. vii.; Judg. xix. 25; 2 Kings xxiv.); sin against nature (Gen. xix.; Judg. xix. 22; Lev. xx.; Rom. i. 27; 1 Cor. vi. 10; 1 Tim. i. 10); sin of ignorance (Lev. iv. 2; v. 15; Num. xv. 27; Luke xxiii. 34; John ix. 41; xv. 24; Acts iii. 17; 1 Tim. i. 13); sin committed through malice (Num. xv. 30; Ecclus. x. 14; Matt. xxviii. 13; John xi. 53; Acts iv. 18; v. 3; Heb. vi. 5; x. 6); confession of sins (Gen. xli. 9; Lev. xvi. 21; xxvi. 43; Num. v. 7; Jos. vii. 19; 2 Kings xxiv. 17; 1 Esd. ix. 6; 2 Esd. ix. 2; Ps. xxxi. 5; xxxvii. 19; Prov. xvi. 3; xviii. 17; xxviii. 13; Ecclus. iv. 25, 31; vii. 34; xvii. 27; Dan. ix. 5; Matt. iii. 6; xvi. 19; Luke xi. 4; xviii. 13; James v. 16; 1 John i. 8); the penalty of sin is not always remitted although the sin is forgiven (Num. xiv. 20; 2 Kings xii. 14; xxiv. 12–25; 1 Paral. xxi. 10); the sinful woman at the feet of our Lord (Luke vii. 37).

SIN, a desert south of the Promised Land, in Arabia Petræa, near Edom (Num. xxxiv. 3); the Israelites reached it after crossing the Red Sea, between Elim and Sinai (Ex. xvi. 1; xvii. 1; Num. xxxiii. 11, 12); here the Israelites murmured (Ex. xvi. 2); and God sent manna (xvi. 4–35); they left it and advanced to Raphidim (xvii. 1); Moses obtains water for them by striking a rock in the desert of Sin (Deut. xxxii. 51; Num. xxvii. 14); the spies viewed the land from the desert of Sin to Rohob (Num. xiii. 22); it was one of the limits of the Promised Land (Num. xxxiv. 3).

SI′NA or **SI′NAI**, a mountain in Arabia (Gal. iv. 25; Heb. xi. 18); the Israelites reached it after leaving Raphidim (Num. xxxiii. 15; Ex. xix. 2); God commands Moses to sanctify the people, promising to come down on Mount Sinai on the third day (11); every one touching the mountain menaced with death (12); the Lord comes in a cloud with fire and smoke, and the sound of a trumpet (18, 19); he calls Moses into the mount (20); God gives the law to Moses (xx.–xxxi.); Moses, Aaron, Nadab, Abiu, and seventy ancients of Israel go and behold the God of Israel (xxiv. 9, 10); Moses was there forty days and forty nights (18); and received the two tables of stone engraved by the hand of God (xxiv. 12; xxxii. 15, 16); during his absence the people fall into idolatry (xxxii.); their punishment (xxxii. 28); the tables are renewed (xxxiv. 1); the tabernacle set up (xl.); the people are numbered at Sinai (Num. i. 1); they march from Mount Sinai (x. 33).

SINCER′ITY commended (1 Cor. v. 8; 2 Cor. i. 12; ii. 17; Phil. i. 10, 17; ii. 20; 2 Pet. iii. 1).

SIN′EW. Jews forbidden to eat the sinews of the legs of animals (Gen. xxxii. 32).

SIN′ITE, eighth son of Chanaan (Gen. x. 17).

SI′ON, the mountain in Jerusalem on which the temple was built. David's city was north of the ancient one (Ps. xlvii. 3; 2 Kings v. 7); David captures the castle of Sion (2 Kings v. 7; 1 Paral. xi. 5); the ark of the covenant carried to (2 Kings vi.); hence it is called the holy mountain (Ps. ii. 6); and God is said to dwell there (Ps. ix. 12; xix. 3; lxxiii. 2; lxxv. 3; cxlv. 10; Ecclus. xxiv. 15; Joel iii. 21); and to love it (Ps. lxxvii. 68; lxxxvi. 2; cxxxi. 13); Jerusalem called the Daughter of Sion (Ps. ix. 15; lxxii. 28; Cant. iii. 11; Isai. i. 8; iii. 16; x. 32; xvi. 1; Jer. iv. 31; vi. 23; Lam. i. 6; Mich. iv. 10; Soph. iii. 14; Zach. ii. 10; ix. 9); salvation to come from Sion (Ps. xiii. 7; lii. 7; Isai. xxxvii. 32).

SI′ON. Mount Hermon also so called (Deut. iv. 49; Ps. cxxxii. 3; Ecclus. xxxiv. 17).

SI′OR, a city in the tribe of Juda (Jos. xv. 54).

SI′RA. Abner was brought back from the cistern of Sira, before Joab slew him (2 Kings iii. 26).

SIRACH, father of Jesus, the author of Ecclesiasticus, who is often called merely the son of Sirach, Ben-Sira (Ecclus. l. 29; li. 1).

SMYRNA.

SI′RENS, to dwell in the ruined temples of pleasure in Babylon (Isai. xiii. 22).

SIS, an ascent near Jerusalem (2 Paral. xx. 16).

SI'SAI, a giant of the race of Enac (Num. xiii. 23; Jos. xv. 14).

SIS'ARA, general of the army of Jabin, king of Asor, sent against the army of Barac and Debbora, on Mount Thabor, composed of the men of Nephthali and Zabulon (Judg. iv. 1–6); he marched from Haroseth of the Gentiles, his abode (iv. 2), with 900 chariots (13); defeated by Barac, and leaping from his chariot, fled on foot (15); came to the tent of Jahel, wife of Haber, the Cinite (17), who drove a nail into the temple of his head, as he lay asleep (21); he had oppressed the Israelites for twenty years (3).

SI'VA, secretary of King David (2 Kings xx. 25).

SI'VAN, one of the months of the Jewish year (Bar. i. 8).

SLIME. Man formed out of the slime of the earth (Gen. ii. 7). In most editions of Challoner's Bible, slime, adopted from the King James Bible, is incorrectly used for bitumen, the correct word in the old Douay, in Gen. vi. 14; xi. 3; xiv. 10; Ex. ii. 3.

SLING, or **SLING'ER**, one of the earliest weapons used to throw stones. The tribe of Benjamin were so expert in its use that they could hit even a hair (Judges xx. 16). David used it in defeating Goliath (1 Kings xvii. 40–50); slingers in the war with Moab (4 Kings iii. 25).

SLOTH, SLOTH'FULNESS, causes David to fall into sin (2 Kings xi.); produces poverty (Prov. x. 4; xx. 13; xxviii. 19); casteth into a deep sleep (xix. 15); it led to the iniquity of the people of Sodom (Ezech. xvi. 49); teaches much evil (Ecclus. xxxiii. 29).

SLOTH'FUL, SLUG'GARD. The sluggard referred to the ant (Prov. vi. 6, 11); compared to vinegar and smoke (x. 26); a fool (xii. 11); always poor (xxi. 5); willeth and willeth not (xiii. 4); cast down by fear (xviii. 8); will not bring his hand to his mouth (xix. 24); toils not in spring; begs in summer (x. 5; xx. 4; xxvi. 15); hideth his hand under his armpit (xxvi. 15); saith "There is a lion in the way" (13); is wiser in his own conceit than seven men that speak sentences (16); his path a hedge of thorns (xv. 19); the sluggard is pelted with a dirty stone (Ecclus. xxii. 1); if any man will not work, neither let him eat (2 Thess. iii. 10).

SMYR'NA, a city of Asia Minor, on the Archipelago. The church in Smyrna is one of the seven to which our Lord sent messages (Apoc. i. 10); the message (ii. 8–11).

SO'BA, a kingdom in the land of Hemath, in Syria (1 Paral. xviii. 3); Saul defeated the king of Soba (1 Kings xiv. 47); David defeated Aderezer, son of Rohob, king of Soba (2 Kings viii. 3; 1 Paral. xviii. 3, 4); the Syrians of Damascus attempted to aid Aderezer, but were also defeated (1 Paral. xviii. 5; 2 Kings viii. 5); David took great spoil, especially brass, out of Bete and Beroth (8, 12); cities of Soba, Thebath, and Chun (1 Paral. xviii. 8); the Syrians of Soba aid the Ammonites against David (2 Kings x. 6–8; 1 Paral. xix. 6); but he defeats them at Helam (2 Kings x. 17, 18). Razon fled from Aderezer, king of Soba (3 Kings xi. 23); Solomon's brazen sea and pillars made of brass captured from Soba (1 Paral. xviii. 8).

SO'BAB, son of David and Bethsabee (2 Kings v. 14; 1 Paral. iii. 5; xiv. 4).

SO'BACH, general of Aderezer's army from beyond the Euphrates; defeated by David and mortally wounded at Helam, 1036 B. C. (2 Kings x. 16, 17).

SO'BAL, the same as Soba (Judith iii. 14).

SO'BI, son of Naas, of Rabbath, brings provisions to David during his flight from Absalom (2 Kings xvii. 27).

SOB'NA, scribe of king Ezechias (4 Kings xviii. 18); he was sent to Rabsaces, to hear Sennacherib's terms (19–27); he was a priest, and had charge over the temple (Isai. xxii. 15, 19); had prepared a magnificent sepulchre for himself (16); to be deposed from the ministry (19); carried off like a cock (17); die in exile (18).

SO'BOCHAI, of Hurathi, one of David's heroes, slew the giant Saph, at Gob (2 Kings xxi. 18; 1 Paral. xx. 4).

SOBRI'ETY and **TEMPERANCE** commended (Tob. vi. 17; Eccles. v. 11; Ecclus. xxxi. 9, 32–41; Dan. i. 8, 11; Rom. xiii. 13; xiv. 17; 1 Cor. vii.; Gal. v. 23; 1 Tim. iii. 2; 2 Tim. i. 7; Tit. i. 8; ii. 6, 12; 1 Pet. i. 13; 2 Pet. i. 6).

SOC'COTH, a city beyond the Jordan, between the torrent Jaboc and the river. Jacob returning from Mesopotamia pitched his tents there, and built a house, called it Socoth (Gen. xxxiii. 17); the people of Soccoth refuse provisions to Gedeon (Judg. viii. 5); he takes and destroys it (16, 17).

SOC'COTH, a station of the Israelites in the desert. They marched to it from Ramesse (Ex. xii. 37; Num. xxxiii. 5); the sacrifice of the paschal lamb, enjoined annually, and the consecration of the first-born to God (Ex. xiii.); they marched thence to Etham (xiii. 20; Num. xxxiii. 6); guided by the pillar of cloud and of fire.

SO'CHOTHBE'NOTH, a god worshipped by the Babylonian colonists sent to Samaria (4 Kings xvii. 30).

SO'DI, a river of Babylon (Bar. i. 4).

SOCI'ETY. We are to seek the company of the good and fly that of the wicked (Gen. xix. 15; Lev. xiv.; Num. xvi. 25; xxv. 2; Jos. xxiii. 7; 2 Paral. xix. 2; Tob. i. 5; Job xxxi. 1; Ps. xxv. 4, 8; xxxvi. 1; Prov. i. 10; iv. 14; vi. 25; xiii. 20; xx. 19; xxii. 10, 24; xxiii. 6, 17; xxiv. 1, 21; xxix. 27; Ecclus. vi. 35; viii. 1, 18; ix. 21; xii. 10; xiii. 1, 20; Jer. xvi. 8; 2 Tim. iii. 5; iv. 14; 1 John iii. 10; 2 John i. 11; Apoc. xviii. 4).

SOD'OM, the chief city of the Pentapolis, situated in a beautiful and fertile plain, like the paradise of the Lord (Gen. xiii. 10); Lot, Abraham's nephew, resided there (xiii. 12); the people exceedingly wicked (13); it is sacked by Chodorlahomor and his allies (xiv. 11); the king of Sodom went out to meet Abraham after his victory in the vale of Save (17); God threatens its destruction (xviii. 20–22); Abraham intercedes for it (23–33); angels received by Lot in Sodom (xix. 1); they bid Lot leave the city with his wife and daughters (15); God rains brimstone and fire on Sodom and Gomorrha (Gen. xix. 24; Deut. xxix. 23; **Wis. x. 6, 7**); pride, fulness of

bread, abundance, idleness, and cruelty to the poor led to her destruction (Ezech. xvi. 49).

SO'HAR, fifth son of the patriarch Simeon, son of Jacob (Gen. xlvi. 10; Ex. vi. 15); called Zara, Zare (Num. xxvi. 13; 1 Paral. iv. 24).

SOLEM'NITY, a great holiday (Ex. x. 9; xiii. 6; xxiii. 15; Lev. xxiii. 6; Num. xxviii. 17; Deut. xvi.; 2 Paral. vii., viii.; 1 Esd. iii. 4); the solemnities of the old law rejected (Mal. ii. 3).

SOLIC'ITOUS. We are not to be too solicitous for the goods of this world (Ex. xxxiv. 21; Lev. xxv. 20; Deut. viii. 3; Job v. 5; Ps. liv. 23; cxliv. 15, 16; Prov. x. 3; xiii. 25; Matt. vi. 25; x. 9, 29; xiii. 22; xvi. 7; Luke viii. 14; xii. 22; xiv. 18; xxi. 34; Philip. iv. 6; Heb. xiii. 5; 1 Pet. v. 7).

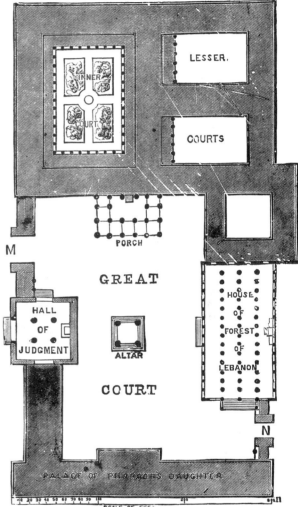

DIAGRAM PLAN OF SOLOMON'S PALACE. By J. Fergusson, Esq.

SOLID, a coin; the word in Hebrew seems to be the Persian daric. The princes of the people, in the time of David, offered 10,000 silver solids for the erection of the temple (1 Paral. xxix. 7); after the captivity the heads of families contributed 60,000 solids of gold (1 Esd. ii. 69; viii. 27); the borrower will pay only one-half solid (Ecclus. xxix. 7).

SOL'OMON, king of Israel, son of David and Bethsabee, born 1033 B. C.; his birth foretold (2 Kings vii. 12); his birth (xii. 24); David swears to Bethsabee that her son Solomon shall succeed him (3 Kings i. 17); Adonias seeks to be proclaimed king (i. 5); David renews his promise to Bethsabee (28); Solomon is anointed king in Gihon, by Sadoc, the high-priest (39); he receives the last charge of David (ii. 1–9); he succeeds to the throne (12); put his brother Adonias to death (25); deposed Abiathar

THE SOWER.

from the high-priesthood (27); makes Sadoc high-priest (35); puts Joab to death (34); his judgment on Semei (36–46); marries Pharao's daughter (iii. 1); offers sacrifice at Gabaon (2 Paral. i. 3); asks of the Lord wisdom; God's promise (3 Kings iii. 11–14; 1 Paral. 7–12); judgment as to the child claimed by two women (3 Kings iii. 16–28); his riches and wisdom (3 Kings iv.; x. 4, 24; 2 Paral. ix.; Luke xi. 31); Hiram, king of Tyre, agrees to furnish material and workmen for the temple (3 Kings v.; 2 Paral. ii.); Solomon builds the temple (3 Kings vi.; 2 Paral. iii., iv.); he erects palaces for himself and his queen (3 Kings vii.); he dedicates the temple (viii.; 2 Paral. v.–vii.); the Lord appears to him (3 Kings ix. 1–9); he gives Hiram, king of Tyre, twenty cities (12); he built Gazer, Bethhoron, Baalath, and Palmyra (3 Kings ix. 17, 18; 2 Paral. viii. 4, 5); the queen of Saba visits him; his commerce and riches (3 Kings x.; 2 Paral. ix.; Luke xi. 31); the Chanaanites made tributary (1 Paral. viii. 7); anointed king the second time (1 Paral. xxix. 22); married women of idolatrous nations (3 Kings xi. 1); had seven hundred wives, and three hundred concubines (3); led by his wives to idolatry, he worshipped Astarthe and Moloch (5); and built a temple for Chamos and Moloch (7, 33); God declares that in punishment he will take the kingdom out of his son's hand, and give ten tribes to Jeroboam (35); the peace of his kingdom troubled by Adad, Razon, and Jeroboam (14–40); Solomon seeks the life of Jere-

boam (40); Solomon died 975 B. C., after reigning forty years (3 Kings xi. 43; 2 Paral. ix. 30, 31).

SO′MER, sold to Amri, king of Israel, the village and mountain where Samaria was built (3 Kings xvi. 24).

SOMO′RIA, son of Roboam and Abihail (2 Paral. xi. 18, 19).

SON′ OF MAN. The Messias so called by the prophet Daniel (Dan. vii. 13); our Lord constantly so styled himself (Matt. viii. 20; ix. 6; xi. 19; xii. 32, 40); the term used by St. Luke and St. John (Acts vii. 55; Apoc. i. 13; xiv. 14).

SONS′ OF GOD, the descendants of Seth so called (Gen. vi. 2); they are corrupted by intermarriage with the descendants of Cain (Gen. vi. 2).

SOOTH′SAYERS. It is forbidden to ask anything of soothsayers, to be defiled by them (Lev. xix. 31); Saul put all the magicians and soothsayers out of the land (1 Kings xxviii. 3); the Jews reproached with resorting to soothsayers like the heathen (Isai. ii. 6); the soothsayers of Nabuchodonosor cannot explain his dream (Dan. ii. 27); the soothsayers of Baltassar cannot explain the mysterious hand-writing on the wall (v. 7, 11).

SO′PATER, son of Pyrrhus, of Berea, set out from Ephesus, and stayed for St. Paul at Troas (Acts xx. 4); he is supposed by some to be identical with Sosipater, spoken of by St. Paul as a kinsman (Rom. xvi. 21).

SO′PHACH, general of Aderezer's army (1 Paral. xix. 16).

SO′PHAR, the Naamathite, one of the friends of Job (Job ii. 11); reproves Job for justifying himself (xi.); Job's reply (xii.); Sophar declares the shortness of the prosperity of the wicked, and their sudden downfall (xx.); Job's answer (xxi.); Sophar is refuted by God himself (xxxviii.); he went and did as the Lord had spoken to him (xlii. 9).

SOPHONI′AS, son of Maasias, second priest next to Saraias, the high-priest (4 Kings xxv. 18); he is sent on several occasions to the prophet Jeremias, by king Sedecias (Jer. xxi.; xxix.; xxxvii.; lii.); after the capture of Jerusalem by the Chaldees, he was sent to Reblatha, where Nabuchodonosor put him to death (4 Kings xxv. 21).

SOPHONI′AS, son of Chusi, and grandson of Godolias, one of the twelve minor prophets. His name means watchman of the Lord, or The Hidden of the Lord. According to common opinion he was a native of Sarabatha, and of the tribe of Simeon.

He prophesied in the reign of Josias, king of Juda (Soph. i. 1); he announced the coming judgment on the kingdom of Juda for its sins; the captivity and return; the destruction of Ninive; and judgments on the Philistines, Moab and Ammon.

SOPHONI′AS, one of the canonical books of the Old Testament (Soph).

SO′REC, a torrent in the tribe of Dan. Dalila, the betrayer of Samson, dwelt there (Judg. xvi. 4).

SOR′ROWFUL. Men to be made sorrowful to lead them to penance (2 Cor. vii. 9).

SOS′IPATER and **DOSITHEUS**, two captains under Judas Machabeus, defeat ten thousand men of the army of Timotheus, left in a hold (2 Mach. xii. 19); they capture Timotheus himself, but release him on his promise to set free the Jews in his hands (24, 25).

SOS′IPATER. See SOPATER.

SOS′THENES, ruler of the synagogue at Corinth, beaten before Gallio's judgment seat (Acts xviii. 17).

SOS′THENES, a Christian whose name is joined with St. Paul's as addressing the Corinthians (1 Cor. i. 1).

SOS′TRATUS, governor of the castle built by the Greeks in the upper city at Jerusalem, demands of Menelaus the money he had promised Antiochus Epiphanes (2 Mach. iv. 27, 28); both summoned before the king (28); made governor of the Cyprians (29).

SOUL. God breathed into man's face the breath of life, and he became a living soul (Gen. ii. 7). The soul is immortal (Eccles. xii. 7); he that gaineth it is wise (Prov. xi. 30); the Lord loveth souls (Wis. xi. 27); God wishes our whole soul (Isai. xxviii. 20); what doth it profit a man if he gain the whole world, and suffer the loss of his own soul? Or what exchange shall a man give for his soul? (Matt. xvi. 26; Mark viii. 36, 37); we are to love the Lord with our

WOMEN WITH THE DISTAFF SPINNING.

whole soul (Deut. vi. 5); the souls of the just are in the hand of God (Wis. iii. 1); the souls of the just dwell with God after death (2 Cor. v. 8; Phil. i. 23; Apoc. xiv. 13).

SOW'ER, parable of the sower (Matt. xiii. 3; Mark iv. 3; Luke viii. 5).

SPAN, a measure (1 Kings xvii. 4; Ex. xxviii. 16).

SPARROW. Not a sparrow falls to the ground without God's will (Matt. x. 29); we are not to fear, as we are of more value than many sparrows (Luke xii. 6, 7); sparrows offered as a sacrifice (Lev. xiv. 4).

SPARTANS, Arius, king of the Spartans, forms an alliance with the high-priest Onias (1 Mach. xii. 20); claims to be of the stock of Abraham (21); Jonathan renews the alliance (6); his death lamented at Sparta (xiv. 16).

SPEAK. There is a time to speak (Prov. xv. 23; Eccles. viii. 5; Ecclus. xi. 8; xx. 6; xxxiii. 9; xxxiii.); how we are to speak (Job vi. 29; Prov. xv. 4; xvi. 20, 23; xxix. 11; Ecclus. iii. 24; v. 16; vi. 5; Col. iv. 6; James v. 12); we are not to speak rashly, but to examine what is said (Ps. cxi. 5; Prov. xx. 15; xxi. 23; Eccles. xii. 10; Ecclus. xxiii. 7; xxviii. 29; xxxii. 16; James i. 19; iii. 7).

SPICES', use of (Ex. xxv. 6; xxx. 23, 34; Cant. iv. 16; vi. 1; Luke xxiii. 56).

SPIDER'S WEB. The hypocrite's trust compared to (Job viii. 14; Isai. lix. 5).

SPIES. Twelve men, one from each tribe, sent by Moses to view the Promised Land; all but Caleb and Josue exaggerate the dangers of attempting to conquer it (Num. xiii.; xiv. 6; Deut. i. 22).

SPIK'ENARD, an aromatic (Cant. i. 11; iv. 13, 14; Mark xiv. 3).

SPIN'NING, mentioned (Ex. xxxv. 25; Prov. xxxi. 19; Matt. vi. 28).

SPIR'IT. God a spirit (John iv. 24; 2 Cor. iii.

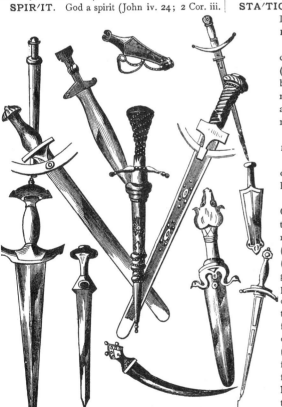

ANCIENT SWORDS.

17; Gen. i. 2; Job xxvi. 13; xxxiii. 4; Ps. cxxxviii. 7; Ecclus. i. 9).

SPIRIT in the sense of life (Job xii. 10; Ezech. xxxvii. 8).

SPIR'IT to be tried (1 Cor. xiv. 32; 1 Thess. v. 21; 1 John iv. 1).

SPONGE, a sponge full of vinegar was raised to our Lord on the cross (Matt. xxvii. 48; Mark xv. 36; John xix. 29).

SPRINK'LING of blood (Ex. xii. 22; Heb. ix. 19; Lev. xvi. 14); sprinkling with hyssop (Ps. l. 9); with water (Num. viii. 7; xix. 12); of the blood of Jesus Christ (1 Pet. i. 2).

STACH'YS, a disciple of St. Paul, saluted by him (Rom. xvi. 9).

STAC'TE, a precious gum used in compounding the holy incense (Ex. xxx. 34); mentioned (Gen. xxxvii. 25; xliii. 11; Ezech. xxvii. 19).

STARS, names of remarkable stars, Arcturus, Orion, the Hyades (Job ix. 9); Arcturus, Pleiades (xxxviii. 31); Joseph sees himself worshipped by eleven stars (Gen. xxxvii. 9); a star shall rise out of Jacob (Num. xxiv. 17); the morning stars praised God (Job xxxviii. 7); the wise men led by a star to Bethlehem (Matt. ii. 2); the woman in the Apocalypse crowned with stars (Apoc. xii. 1).

STATER, a coin (46 cents) (4 Kings vii. 1; xvi. 18; Jer. xxxii. 9; Ezech. iv. 10); found miraculously in the mouth of a fish caught by St. Peter at our Lord's direction (Matt. xvii. 26).

STA'TIONS or **ENCAMPMENTS** of the Israelites in the desert (Num. xxxiii. 1-49).

STAT'UE OF SALT. Lot's wife changed into a statue or pillar of salt (Gen. xix. 26); a mysterious statue seen by Nabuchodonosor (Dan. ii. 31-36); its meaning explained by Daniel (37-45); a golden statue erected by Nabuchodonosor for all to adore (iii. 1-15).

STEALING forbidden (Ex. xx. 15).

STELLIO, a kind of lizard, reckoned unclean (Lev. xi. 30); in kings' houses (Prov. xxx. 28).

STEPHEN, ST., protomartyr. One of the seven deacons first chosen by the apostles at Jerusalem (Acts vi. 5); a man full of faith and the Holy Ghost (5); ordained by imposition of hands (6); full of grace and fortitude, he did great wonders and signs among the people (8); Jews of various synagogues dispute with him, but are unable to resist the wisdom and spirit that spoke (9, 10); false witnesses suborned to accuse him of blasphemy against Moses and God (11); brought before the council (12); false witnesses (13, 14); his face like the face of an angel (15); his reply to the high-priest (vii. 2-53); the Jews gnash their teeth at him (54); looking up he saw the glory of God and Jesus standing at the right hand of God, and so declared (55); they rushed upon him, dragged him out of the city and stoned him, laying their garments at the feet of Saul (57); his last words: Lord Jesus, receive my spirit (58); Lord, lay not

this sin to their charge (59); Saul consented to his death (59).

STERIL'ITY in Egypt foretold by Joseph (Gen.

EMBLEMS ON THE STANDARDS OF THE TRIBES.

xli. 30); in Israel foretold by Eliseus (4 Kings vi. 25).

STERIL'ITY in a wife, a disgrace among the Jews, as in Sarai (Gen. xi. 30); Rebecca (xxv. 21); the wife of Manue (Judg. xiii. 2); Anna (1 Kings i. 2); Michol (2 Kings vi. 23); God promises his faithful freedom from it (Deut. vii. 14; Ps. cxii. 9; Cant. iv. 2); in view of the woes to befall Jerusalem our Lord pronounces the barren blessed (Luke xxiii. 29).

STEPHANAS, one of the first converts at Corinth, baptized with his whole family by St. Paul, A. D. 52 (1 Cor. i. 16); he went to Ephesus to meet St. Paul, A. D. 56 (xvi. 17); and apparently was one of the bearers of the first epistle to the Corinthians to the faithful there.

STHARBUZANAI, an officer of the Persian kings, demands of the Jews their authority for rebuilding the temple and walls of Jerusalem (1 Esd. v. 3); he writes a letter to king Darius (6); the letter (7-17).

STIB'IC STONE (kohl), a preparation of antimony used in the East by women to paint the eyes (4 Kings ix. 30; Jer. iv. 30; Ezech. xxiii. 40). The Douay has paint the *eyes;* many editions of Challoner, following King James', incorrectly altered it to face. Job's daughter, Cornu Stibii (Heb. Keren happuch), means a horn of Stibic stone (Job xlii. 14).

STING OF THE FLESH (2 Cor. xii. 7).

STOMACHER or **GIRDLE** worn by women (Jer. ii. 32).

STONE, set up as a title by Jacob (Gen. xxviii. 22; xxxi. 45, 46, 51, 52); Hebrews ordered to set up stones after passing the Jordan and to inscribe the commandments on them (Deut. xxvii. 2, 4); Josue renews the order (Jos. iv. 5); stones set up in Galgai (Jos. iv. 19); Josue sets up a great stone under the oak that was in the Sanctuary of the Lord (Jos. xxiv. 26, 27); Samuel sets up the Stone of Help (1 Kings

vii. 12); a mysterious stone, figure of the church, seen by Daniel in a vision (Dan. ii. 35); Chanaanites slain by stones from heaven (Jos. x. 11); altars built of untrimmed stones (Deut. xxvii. 5).

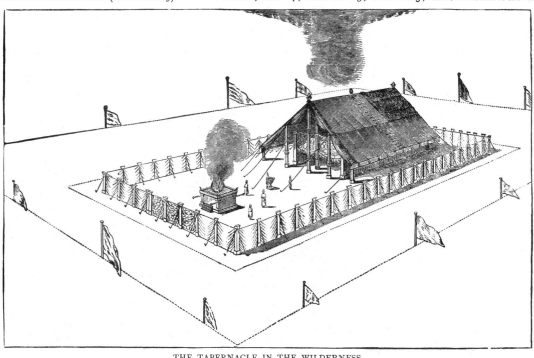

THE TABERNACLE IN THE WILDERNESS.

STONE OF BOSRA, son of Ruben, one of the bounds of Juda (Jos. xv. 6); the Stone of Help (1 Kings iv. 1; v. 1; vii. 12); Adonias gives a feast at the stone of Zoheleth (3 Kings i. 9); David and Jonathan at the stone Ezel (1 Kings xx. 19); Christ, the corner-stone (Eph. ii. 20); the stone rejected (Ps. cxvii. 22; Matt. xxi. 42; Mark xii. 10; Luke xx. 17).

STONE KNIVES, used in circumcision (Ex. iv. 25; Jos. v. 2).

STONES, PRECIOUS (3 Kings vii. 9, 11; 1 Paral. xxix. 2; 2 Paral. xxxii. 27); two onyxes engraved in the ephod (Ex. xxxix. 6); twelve stones in the rational of judgment, viz.: Sardius, topaz, emerald, carbuncle, sapphire, jasper, ligurius, agate, amethyst, chrysolite, onyx and beryl (10–13; xxviii. 17–20); amethyst (Apoc. xxi. 20); beryl (Ex. xxviii. 20; Ezech. xxviii. 13; Apoc. xxi. 20); carbuncle (Ex. xxviii. 18; Ecclus. xxxii. 7; Ezech. xxviii. 13); chrysolite (Ezech. x. 9; xxviii. 13; Dan. x. 6; Apoc. xxi. 20); chrysoprase (Apoc. xxi. 20); emerald (Tob. xiii. 21; Judith x. 19; Ecclus. xxxii. 8; Ezech. xxviii. 13; Apoc. xxi. 19); jasper (Isai. liv. 12; Ezech. xxviii. 13; Apoc. iv. 3; xxi. 11, 18, 19); onyx (Gen. ii. 12; Ex. xxv. 7; xxviii. 9, 20; xxx. 34; xxxv. 9, 27; xxxix. 6, 13; 1 Paral. xxix. 2; Ezech. xxviii. 13); sapphire (Tob. xiii. 21; Job xxviii. 6, 16; Cant. v. 14; Isai. liv. 11; Lam. iv. 7; Ezech. i. 26; x. 1; xxviii. 13; Apoc. xxi. 19); sardius (Ezech. xxviii. 13; Apoc. xxi. 20); topaz (Job xxviii. 19; Ps. cxviii. 127; Ez. xxviii. 13; Apoc. xxi. 20).

STO′NING, a punishment among the Jews (Lev. xx. 2, 7; xxiv. 14, 16, 23; Num. xv. 35; Deut. xiii. 10; xxii. 21, 24; 3 Kings xxi. 13; Acts vii. 58).

STORK, forbidden as food (Deut. xiv. 16).

STORM, stilled by our Lord on the Sea of Galilee (Matt. viii. 26; Mark vi. 51; Luke viii. 24); St. Paul wrecked by a storm on Melita (Acts xxvii. 41).

STO′RAX, Jacob sends some as a gift to Joseph (Gen. xliii. 11).

STRIFE forbidden (Prov. xxvi. 20; xvii. 14; xxv. 8; xxvi. 17; Rom. xiii. 13; 1 Cor. iii. 3; Gal. v. 20; Philip. ii. 3; 2 Tim. ii. 23; Tit. iii. 9; James iii. 14).

STRIPES, when inflicted (Deut. xxv. 2); stripes inflicted on St. Paul (2 Cor. xi. 24; Acts xvi. 23).

STUB′BORNNESS (2 Paral. xxx. 8; Ps. xciv. 8; Heb. iii. 13).

STUMB′LING-BLOCK, Christ a stumbling-block to the Jews (1 Cor. i. 23; Isai. viii. 14; Rom. ix. 32; 1 Pet. ii. 8).

SUB′URBS of the cities of refuge assigned to the Levites (Num. xxxv. 3–5).

SU′A, king of Egypt (Sevechos); his aid is sought by Osee, king of Israel (4 Kings xvii. 4), 717 B. C.

SU′AL. The Philistines made an irruption into the land of Sual (1 Kings xiii. 17).

SU′BA, a kingdom of Syria (2 Paral. viii. 3). See SOBA.

SUB′AEL, son of Amram, head of a family of Levites (1 Paral. xxiv. 20).

SUB′AEL, eldest son of Gersom, son of Moses (1 Paral. xvi. 24).

SUB′AEL, son of Heman, a Levite (1 Paral. xxv. 20).

SUB′UEL, son of Gersom, and grandson of Moses (1 Paral. xxiii. 16).

SUE, sixth son of Abraham and Cetura (Gen. xxv. 2).

SUE, daughter of a Chanaanite, and wife of Juda (Gen. xxxviii. 2); she bore Her, Onan and Sela.

SU′HITE. Baldad, one of the friends of Job, was a Suhite (Job ii. 11); supposed to mean a descendant of Sue, son of Abraham.

SULAMI′TESS, a name given to the spouse in the Canticles (vi. 12; vii. 1).

SUN, created (Gen. i. 16; Job ix. 7; xxxi. 26; xli. 21; Ps. ciii. 19); seen in a dream (Gen. xxxvii. 9); stopped in its course by Josue (Jos. x. 13); its motion (Eccles. i. 5, 6); worshipped by the heathens (Wis. xiii. 2; Job xxxi. 26; 4 Kings xxiii. 5–11); darkened at the death of Christ (Luke xxiii. 45); at the last judgment (Matt. xxiv. 29; Luke xxi. 25; Apoc. vi. 12; ix. 2); the Sun of Understanding (Wis. v. 6).

SU′NAM, a city in the tribe of Issachar (Jos. xix. 18); the Philistines encamped there (1 Kings xxviii. 4); Eliseus raised to life the child of his hostess at Sunam (4 Kings iv. 8).

SUNAMI′TESS, a woman of Sunam. Abisag, wife of David, is so called (3 Kings i. 3, 15; ii. 17–22); the hostess of Eliseus (4 Kings iv. 12–36).

SUN-DIAL of Achaz. The shadow moves back on it at the prayer of Isaias (4 Kings xx. 11).

SUPERSTIT′ION. Festus applies the term to the Jewish faith (Acts xxv. 19); St. Paul applies it to heretical ideas (Col. ii. 23); he calls the Athenians too superstitious (Acts xvii. 22).

SUPH, a Levite, ancestor of Elcana, and founder of the family of Suphim or Sophim (1 Kings i. 1; 1 Paral. vi. 35); the land of Suph was named from him (1 Kings ix. 5).

SU′PHAM, son of Benjamin (Num. xxvi. 39); called Mophim (Gen. xlvi. 21).

SUP′PER, the Paschal, or last celebrated by our Lord (Luke xxii. 14).

SUR, a city in Arabia Petræa, giving name to the desert of Sur (Gen. xvi. 7; Ex. xv. 22; 1 Kings xv. 7; xxvii. 8).

SUR, the gate of Sur was one of the gates of the temple (4 Kings xi. 6).

SURISAD′DAI, father of Salamiel, prince of the tribe of Simeon in the exodus (Num. i. 6).

SU′SA, scribe of David (1 Paral. xviii. 16).

SU′SA or **SU′SAN,** capital of Persia (Dan. viii.

PERSIAN SWORD, OR ACINACES.

2); its castle (2); here Daniel had the vision of the ram and the goat (viii.); it is the scene of the events recorded in the book of Esther (Esth.); Nehemias was at Susan when he obtained permission to rebuild the walls of Jerusalem (2 Esd. i. 1).

SUSAN'NA, daughter of Helcias, and wife of Joakim, of the tribe of Juda, during the captivity of Babylon. She was falsely accused of adultery by two impious and impure judges, but her innocence was shown by Daniel (Dan. viii.)

SUSAN'NA, one of the holy women who followed our Lord and ministered to him (Luke viii. 2, 3).

SWALLOW alluded to (Isai. xxxviii. 14; Jer. viii. 7; Bar. vi. 21; Tob. ii. 11).

SWEAR. When and under what conditions it is lawful to swear (Gen. xiv. 22; xxi. 24; xxii. 16; xxiv. 2; xxvi. 31; xxxi. 53; xlii. 15; xlvii. 31; Ex. xxii. 11; Lev. v. 4; Num. xiv. 21; xxx.; Deut. vi. 13; Jos. ii. 12; 1 Kings xix. 6; xxiv. 23; xxx. 15; 2 Kings iii. 35; xix. 7; 3 Kings i. 29; 2 Paral. xv. 14; 1 Esd. x. 5; Job xxvii. 2; Ps. xiv. 4; xxiii. 4; Ecclus. xxiii. 9, 12; Isai. xiv. 24; xlv. 24; Jer. iv. 2; xii. 16; li. 14; Heb. vi. 13, 17; Apoc. x. 6); unlawful oaths forbidden (Gen. xxv. 33; Ex. xx. 7; xxiii. 13; Jos. ix. 15; xxiii. 7; Judg. xxi. 1, 7, 18; 1 Kings xiv. 24; xxviii. 10; 3 Kings xix. 2; Jer. v. 2, 7; Soph. i. 5; Zach. viii. 17; Matt. xxiii. 16–22); we should not swear without due cause (Matt. v. 34; James v. 12).

SWEAT. Man condemned to eat his bread in the sweat of his face (Gen. iii. 19); our Lord's bloody sweat in the Garden of Olives (Luke xxii. 44).

SWORD, a flaming sword placed before the paradise of pleasure (Gen. iii. 24); Abraham carried one when going to sacrifice Isaac (xxii. 6); Esau to live by the sword (xxvii. 40). The ordinary swords had apparently only one sharp edge, as two-edged swords are specially alluded to (Heb. iv. 12; Apoc. i. 16); figuratively, the Sword of the Spirit, which is the Word of God (Eph. vi. 17).

SYCAMORE, a tree growing in the plains (3 Kings x. 27; 2 Paral. i. 15; ix. 27; Isai. ix. 10); Zacheus ascended a sycamore tree in order to see our Lord (Luke xix. 4).

Thess. i. 1); St. Peter sends his first Epistle by him (1 Pet. v. 12).

SYN'AGOGUE, or Assembly of the Ancients

THE ARK OF THE COVENANT, THE ALTARS, TABLE OF LOAVES OF PROPOSITION, AND OTHER FURNITURE OF THE TABERNACLE.

(Num. iv. 34; xxxi. 13; Luke viii. 41, 49); it persecutes Jesus Christ (John ix. 22); gives letters to Saul to persecute the church (Acts ix. 2); accursed (Apoc. ii. 9; iii. 9). The word is sometimes rendered Congregation.

SYNAGOGUE, place where Jews met on the Sabbath to read the law and pray. There were at Jerusalem, besides those of the ordinary residents, synagogues of the libertines or freedmen, Cyrenians, Alexandrians, Cilicians (Acts vi. 9); the presiding officer of a synagogue called a ruler (Luke viii. 41; John iv. 46; Acts xviii. 8, 17); our Lord habitually taught in the synagogues (John xviii. 20; Matt. iv. 23; ix. 35; xii. 9; xiii. 54; Mark i. 21–29, 39; iii.

whose servant our Lord healed, had built a synagogue for the Jews at Capharnaum (Luke vii. 5). The Pharisees sought the first seats in (Matt. xxiii. 6).

SYRACUSE', a city in Sicily, at which St. Paul touched on his way to Rome (Acts xxviii. 12).

SYRIA. Mesopotamia of Syria, between the Euphrates and Tigris (Gen. xxviii. 2, 5, 6; xxxiii. 18; xxxv. 9, 26; xlvi. 15); Syria of Damascus (2 Kings viii. 5); Syria of Soba or Celesyria (Judith iii. 1; 1 Mach. x. 69; 2 Mach. iii. 5, 8; iv. 4; viii. 8); Benadad, king of Syria (2 Kings xx.; 4 Kings vi.); Rasin, king of Syria (Isai. vii.)

SYRIANS, become tributary to David (2 Kings viii. 6); Syrians of Soba, Rohob, Istob and Maacha, join the Ammonites against David (x. 6, 8); defeated (13, 18); the Syrians, under Benadad, besiege Samaria, and are defeated (3 Kings xx.); again at Aphec (26–30); war against Israel (4 Kings vi. 8); blinded and led into Samaria (vi. 18); under Benadad besiege Samaria (vi. 24); panic-struck they raise the siege (vii. 6, 7); conquered and led away captive by the Assyrians (4 Kings xvi. 9); their desolation and ruin foretold (Isai. xvii. 1; Jer. xlix. 23; Amos i. 3).

SYROPHŒNICIAN WOMAN, her daughter cured by our Lord (Mark vii. 25).

TAB'EEL, one of those who opposed the rebuilding of the temple (1 Esd. iv. 7).

TAB'EEL, Rasin, king of Syria, and Phacee, king of Israel, conspire to make the son of Tabeel king of Israel (Isai. vii. 1, 6).

TAB'ERNACLE, the tent in which the worship of God was conducted before the erection of the temple. Its construction and adornment prescribed by God (Ex. xxvi. 1–35); it was rectangular, thirty cubits long, ten wide, and ten high, with curtains at the sides (1–6); the roof of goats' hair, and a second one of rams' skins (7, 14); it was upheld by boards

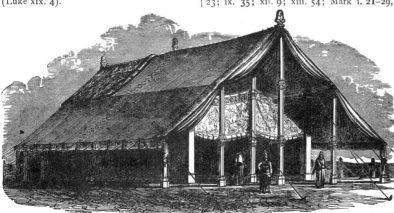

THE TABERNACLE.

SYLVANUS (see SILAS), a disciple of St. Paul, preaches to the Corinthians (2 Cor. i. 19); joins in the address of the Epistle to the Thessalonians (1

1; vi. 2; Luke iv. 15–44; vi. 6; xiii. 10; John vi. 60); St. Paul preaches in (Acts ix. 20; xiii. 5, 14; xvii. 1, 10, 17; xviii. 4, 19; xix. 8); the centurion

of setim wood, mortised and joined (15–29); it was divided into two parts (1), the holy, twenty cubits long and ten wide. In this stood the table of the loaves of proposition, the seven-branched candlestick, and the altar of gold, on which incense was burned (xxvi., xl.) Within was (2) the sanctuary or holy of holies, ten cubits square, containing the ark of the covenant. It was separated from the outer part by a precious veil hung on four columns of setim wood, plated with gold (xxvi. 36); and a similar curtain was at the entrance of the holy. Around the tabernacle was a court, one hundred cubits long, and fifty wide, enclosed by curtains hanging from silver-plated setim pillars, in brass sockets (xxvii. 9–18); the altar of holocaust stood in this court, opposite the entrance to the holy (xl. 6); it was made and set up as God

golden crown, and a smaller crown above. It had four gold wings at the corners under the crown, and was carried by gold-plated setim wood bars, passed through the rings (Ex. xxv. 23–28).

TABLES OF STONE. God gave to Moses two tables on Mount Sinai, of testimony written with the finger of God (Ex. xxiv. 12; xxxi. 18); as he came down from the mountain, seeing the idolatry of the people, being very angry, threw the tables out of his hand, and broke them at the foot of the mount (xxxii. 19); then God commanded him: Hew thee two tables of stone like unto the former, and I will write upon them the words which were in the tables which thou brokest (xxxiv. 1); Moses cut the tables, such as had been before (4); and God wrote upon the tables the ten words of the covenant (28); and

TAPH'ETH, daughter of Solomon, and wife of Ben Abinadab (3 Kings iv. 11).

TAPH'NES, queen of Egypt. Pharao gave her sister in marriage to Adad, son of the king of Edom (3 Kings xi. 19, 20).

TAPH'NIS, a city of Egypt (Jer. ii. 16; xliii. 7–9); xliv. 1; xlvi. 14); some of the Jews retire to it contrary to the voice of the Lord (xliii. 7); Jeremias hid stones in the vault under the brick wall at the gate of Pharao's house in Taphnis (9), and foretold that Nabuchodonosor would set his throne there (10); the sceptres of Egypt to be broken there (Ezech. xxxi. 18); Jeremias is said to have been buried there.

TAPH'SAR, a word used in Jer. li. 27, and supposed to mean Satraps.

TAPH'UA, a city on the border of Manasses (Jos. xvi. 8; xii. 17); also a city in the tribe of Juda (Jos. xv. 34).

TAPH'UA, a fountain, the land of that name (Jos. xvii. 7).

TAPH'UA, a district on the borders of the half tribe of Manasses, but belonging to the tribe of Ephraim (Jos. xvii. 8).

TAR'SUS, capital of Cilicia, spoken of by St. Paul as "no mean city" (Acts xxi. 39). He was born and long resided there (**Acts** ix. 11; xxi. 39;

REARING THE TABERNACLE.

had commanded, and he filled it with his majesty (xl. 32); it was carried by the Levites (Num. i. 50, 53); the various vessels and articles used there are described (Num. iv. 5–14); its ministers or servants (iv. 15–28; xviii. 2, 3, 5, 7).

TAB'ERNACLES, Feast of, or Scenopegia; a feast during which the Jews lived in tents or booths, made of bough, in memory of their wandering in the desert (Lev. xxiii. 34–42); our Lord observed the feast (John vii. 2).

TABITHA, a pious widow of Joppe, called in Greek, Dorcas. She was full of good works, clothing the widows (Acts ix. 36, 39); she fell sick and died (37); but the disciples sent for St. Peter, who was at Lydda (38); he went and saw the evidence of her good works (39); then kneeling down he prayed, and said: "Tabitha, arise," and she sat up (40).

TABLE FOR THE LOAVES OF PRO-POSITION. It was of setim wood, two cubits long, one broad, and one and a half high, overlaid with the purest gold, with a golden ledge, having a

when he came down he held the two tables of the testimony (29); these were deposited in the ark of the covenant (xl. 18); and remained there till the destruction of the temple and city of Jerusalem, when the ark was removed by the prophet Jeremias (2 Mach. ii. 5).

TAD'MOR, a city built by Solomon; called also Palmyra (3 Kings ix. 18; 2 Paral. viii. 4).

TAL'ENT, a weight used in computing money (Ex. xxv. 39; xxxviii. 24, 27; 2 Kings xii. 30; 3 Kings xvi. 24; xx. 39; Matt. xviii. 24; xxv. 15). The talent of silver was worth $1,663; the talent of gold $26,608.

TAM'ARICK, a plant in the desert (Jer. xvii. 6).

TALITHA CUMI, Syriac words, meaning "My daughter, arise," used by our Lord (Mark v. 41).

TAN'IS, an ancient city of Egypt, built seven years after Hebron (Num. xiii. 23); miracles wrought there by Moses (Ps. lxxvii. 12, 43); Isaias reproaches its princes with folly (Isai. xix. 11, 13); the Jews send for aid to Tanis (xxx. 4).

xxii. 3); St. Barnabas preaches in (xi. 25).

TEB'BATH, the Madianites, after their defeat by Gedeon, fled to Tebbath (Judges vii. 23).

TE'BETH, fourth month of the civil year of the Jews (Esth. ii. 16); the feast of the dedication of the temple (1 Mach. iv. 59; John x. 22) fell in this month.

TEHIN'NA, father of the city of Naas; one of the men of Recha (1 Paral. iv. 12).

TE'LEM, a city of the tribe of Juda (Jos. xv. 24).

TEMPEST on the sea of Galilee stilled by our Lord (Matt. vii. 26; Mark vi. 51; Luke viii. 24).

TEMPLE OF JERUSALEM. God forbids David to build it (2 Kings vii. 5–12); he foretells that Solomon shall build it (13); Solomon agrees with Hiram for materials and workmen (3 Kings v. 1–18); he began it in the month Zio, the 480th year after their departure from Egypt (vi. 1), 1003 B. C.; it was sixty cubits long, twenty cubits broad, and twenty cubits high, with a porch in front ten cubits deep (2, 3); the front of the porch was supported by two great pillars of brass called Jachin and Booz, with lily work at the top (3 Kings vii. 21). The door-posts were of olive wood, and the doors of fir, with cherubim and palm trees in high relief plated with gold (vi. 33, 34); the holy was forty cubits long by twenty broad (vi. 17); beyond that was the oracle or holy of holies, twenty cubits square (20); the walls of the temple were of stone cut and dressed before they were brought there (3 Kings vi. 7); the holy and holy of holies or oracle were wainscoted with cedar, wrought and carved (18); the ceiling of deal (2 Paral. iii. 5); the floors of precious marble (6), overlaid with gold (3 Kings vi. 30); the inner walls were covered with plates of gold (3 Kings vi. 21; 2 Paral. iii. 5); these gold plates were carved with divers figures and carvings, cherubim, and palm trees in relief (3 Kings vi. 29), and little chains interlaced one with another (2 Paral. iii. 5); at the entrance to the oracle were little doors of olive wood, with pentagonal posts, and doors of olive wood, with cherubim and palm trees in high relief, all overlaid with gold (3 Kings vi. 31, 32); before it hung a veil of silk, wrought with cherubim in colors (2 Paral. iii. 14). In the holy of holies were two cherubim of olive wood ten cubits high, their wings touching the opposite wall; these were overlaid with gold (3 Kings vi. 23–28); and the ark was placed so that they covered it with their wings (2 Paral. v. 7, 8). The temple was finished in Bul, the eighth month in the eleventh year, the work having lasted seven years (3 Kings vi. 38); it was dedicated in Ethanim, the seventh month, 1003 B. C., and the ark carried to its place (3 Kings vii. 1–9; 2 Paral. vii. 10); a cloud filled the house of the Lord, the glory of the Lord filled it (2 Paral. v. 14; 3 Kings viii. 11); Solomon addressed the assembly of Israel (12–21); his prayer (23–61; 2 Paral. vi.); after the prayer fire from heaven consumed the immense number of holocausts offered (vii.); the ceremonies lasted for seven days (3 Kings viii. 65; 2 Paral. vii. 8, 9); God appeared to Solomon and declared that he had chosen that as a place of sacrifice (12–22); Achaz profanes the temple, stripping it to give to the king of the Assyrians (xxviii. 21); he took away all the vessels and broke them and closed the temple (24); he removed the brazen altar and set up a heathen one (4 Kings xvi. 15); Ezechias reopened it and restored the service of God (2 Paral. xxix.); it is profaned by Manasses, who set up heathen altars and a molten statue in it and in the courts (xxxiii. 4, 5, 7); but, repenting, removed them (15); the ark removed by Jeremias (2 Mach. ii. 4); Solomon's temple burned down by Nabuchodonosor (4 Kings xxv. 9). SECOND TEMPLE: God chargeth Cyrus to build him a house in Jerusalem (1 Esd. i. 2); the Jews contribute means (5, 6); Cyrus restores the vessels of the temple (7–11); Josue, the son of Josedec, collects material and workmen (iii. 8); the foundations laid with hymns (10, 11); enemies oppose the work and it is suspended till the second year of the reign of Darius (iv. 1–25); it was then resumed by his order to be sixty cubits long and sixty high (vi. 3); it was completed the third day of the month of Adar, in the sixth year of Darius, 515 B. C., and was dedicated with great solemnity (15–22); it was plundered by

Antiochus, the Illustrious (1 Mach. i. 23, 24); profaned by heathen altars and idols, and immolation of unclean beasts (49, 50); Judas Machabeus, after defeating Lysias, restored the temple and altars, and adorned the front of the temple with crowns of gold and escutcheons, and celebrated the dedication with great pomp (1 Mach. iv. 38–58; 2 Mach. x. 1–8); and instituted the yearly feast of the dedication in the month Casleu (1 Mach. iv. 59; 2 Mach. x. 8); the temple was adorned with rich presents (2 Paral. i.–v.; 2 Mach. iii. 2); prophesies against the temple (Lev. xxvi. 31; 3 Kings ix. 7; 4 Kings xxi. 12; Ps. lxxiii. 7; Is. lxvi.; Jer. vii. 4, 30; xxvi. 6, 12; Dan. ix. 26; Am. ix. 1; Mich. iii. 12; Zach. xi. 1; Matt. xxiv. 2); profaners of the temple punished (Isai. lxvi. 3; 2 Mach. iii. 25, 26; Matt. xxi. 12; John ii. 15); the spiritual temple and house of God (2 Kings vii. 13; Prov. ix. 1; Agg. ii. 8; Matt. vii. 24; xvi. 18; John ii. 19; 1 Cor. iii. 16; vi. 19; 2 Cor. vi. 16; Eph. ii. 20; 1 Tim. iii. 15; Heb. iii. 6; 1 Pet. ii. 5); the

xiv. 9); temple of Babylon (Dan. i. 2); of Nanea in Persia (2 Mach. i. 13).

TEMPT. It is forbidden to tempt God (Ex. xiv. 11; xvii. 2; Deut. vi. 16; Judith viii. 11; Matt. iv. 7; 1 Cor. x. 9); how God tries and tempts his own (Gen. xxii. 1; Ex. xv. 25; xvi. 4; xx. 20; Deut. viii. 2; xiii. 3; Judg. ii. 22; iii. 1; 2 Paral. xxxii. 31; Tob. ii. 12; Job i. 12; Wisd. iii. 5; Ecclus. ii. 4; xxxii. 18; Zach. xiii. 9; Rom. v. 4; 1 Cor. x. 13; 2 Pet. ii. 9; Apoc. ii. 10).

TENT. Jabel the father of such as dwell in tents (Gen. iv. 20); the Lord appeared to Abraham as he was sitting in the door of his tent at Mambre (xviii. 1); he pitched his tent at Bersabee (xxvi. 25); the Israelites pitch their tents at Sinai (Ex. xix. 2).

TEPID'ITY in the service of God, terrible warning against (Apoc. iii. 15, 16; Luke ix. 62).

TER'EBINTH, valley of the (1 Kings xvii. 2; xxi. 9).

TER'PHALITES, one of the nations sent

TARSUS.

temple is the house of prayer, God hears those who pray there (Isai. lxvi. 7; Matt. xxi. 13; 3 Kings ix. 3; viii. 29; 2 Paral. vi. 19); Jesus and his disciples often went up to the temple to pray (Matt. xxiv. 1; Mark xi. 11; xii. 35; Luke ii. 27; Acts ii. 46; iii. 11; v. 20, 21, 25; xxii. 17); God needs no temple to serve as his abode; the prophet Ezechiel sees in a vision the temple rebuilt, and describes it in detail (Ezech. xl.–xlviii.)

TEM'PLE, schismatic, erected by the Samaritans on Mount Garizim (2 Mach. v. 23); under the reign of Antiochus, Jupiter Hospitalis worshipped there (vi. 2); although the worship of the true God was restored there, our Lord condemned it (John iv. 22).

TEM'PLES. Many heathen temples are mentioned; that of Dagon at Gaza (Judg. xvi. 23); at Azotus (1 Kings v. 2; 1 Mach. x. 84); of Astaroth (1 Kings xxxi. 10); of Baal at Samaria (3 Kings xvi. 32); of Remmon at Damascus (4 Kings v. 18); of Chamos and Moloch erected by Solomon on the hill over against Jerusalem (3 Kings xi. 7); of Nesroch at Ninive (Isai. xxxvii. 38); of Bel at Babylon (Dan.

to occupy the country of the ten tribes (1 Esd. iv. 9).

TER'TIUS, the secretary of St. Paul, who wrote the epistle to the Romans (Rom. xvi. 22).

TERTUL'LUS accuses St. Paul before Felix (Acts xxiv. 2–9).

TEST'AMENT, the Old and the New (Gal. iv. 24; Heb. ix. 15; xiii. 20).

TEST'AMENT, OLD, the collection of inspired books written before the coming of our Lord.

TEST'AMENT, NEW, the collection of inspired books written since the coming of our Lord.

TEST'IMONY, false testimony forbidden (Ex. xx. 16; xxiii. 1; Deut. v. 20; Ps. xxvi. 12; xxxiv. 11; Prov. xix. 5, 9; xxi. 28; xxiv. 28; xxv. 18; Matt. xix. 18; Rom. xiii. 9); false testimony given against Naboth (3 Kings xxi.); against Susanna (Dan. xiii. 34); against Jesus (Matt. xxvi. 59; xxviii. 13); against St. Stephen (Acts vi. 11); against St. Paul (Acts xxi. 28); a faithful witness (Apoc. ii. 13); no one is to be condemned on the testimony of a single witness (Num. xxxv. 30; Deut. xix. 15; John viii. 17; 1 Tim. v. 19; Heb. x. 28).

TET′RARCH, the ruler of the fourth part of a country. Herod called tetrarch of Galilee (Matt. xiv. 1; Luke iii. 1, 19; ix. 7; Acts xiii. 1); Philip, tetrarch of Iturea and Trachonitis (Luke iii. 1); Lysanias, tetrarch of Abilina (Luke iii. 1).

THA′BOR, a mountain of Galilee, on the borders of Issachar (Jos. xix. 22); Debbora and Barac assembled their army on Thabor (Judg. iv. 6); Osee reproaches the princes of Israel for spreading a net upon Thabor (Osee v. 1); it is by tradition regarded as the place of our Lord's transfiguration.

THA′BOR, the oak of, on the way to Bethel (1 Kings x. 3).

THA′DAL, king of the nations, one of the kings allied against the Pentapolis (Gen. xiv. 1).

THAD′DEUS, surname of the apostle St. Jude (Mark iii. 18).

THA′HATH, one of the encampments of the Israelites in the desert (Num. xxxiii. 26).

THALAS′SAR, a province of Asia; Rabsaces, officer of Sennacherib, alludes to it (Isai. xxxvii. 12); written Thelassar (4 Kings xix. 12).

THALAS′SA, a city in Crete (Acts xxvii. 8).

THA′MAR, wife of Her, and then of Onan, sons of Juda (Gen. xxxviii. 6); returns to her father's house (11); tempts Juda (13–18); bears him Phares and Zara (27; xlvi. 12).

THA′MAR, daughter of David, by Maacha, daughter of Tholmai, king of Gessur; she is violated by her brother Amnon (2 Kings xiii. 14).

THA′MAR, daughter of Absalom, remarkable for her beauty (2 Kings xiv. 27).

THA′MAR, a city of Judea (Ezech. xlvii. 19; xlviii. 27).

THAM′NA or **THAMNA′THA,** a city of the Philistines (Jos. xv. 10, 57); where Samson married a wife (Judg. xiv. 1, 2, 5; 1 Mach. ix. 50).

THAM′NA, concubine of Esau, and mother of Amalec (Gen. xxxvi. 12).

THAM′NA, duke of Edom, after Adad (1 Paral. i. 51; Gen. xxxvi. 40).

THAM′NAN, a city near Ajalon (2 Paral. xxviii. 18).

THAM′NATHSARA (Jos. xix. 50) or **THAM′-NATHSARE′,** a city in the tribe of Ephraim, where Josue was buried (Jos. xxiv. 30).

THA′NAC, a city in the half tribe of Manasse beyond the Jordan (Jos. xxi. 25).

THAN′ATHS′ELO, a city of Ephraim (Jos. xvi. 6).

THANKSGIV′ING, enjoined (2 Cor. ix. 12; Philip. iv. 6; Col. ii. 7; iv. 2; Apoc. vii. 12).

THAP′SA, a city in the tribe of Ephraim, taken by Manahem, king of Israel, who perpetrated horrible cruelties there (4 Kings xv. 16, 17).

THAP′SA, an important city near the Euphrates (3 Kings iv. 24).

THA′RA, a eunuch who conspired against Assuerus (Esth. xii. 1).

THARA′CA, king of Ethiopia, marches with a large army to support king Ezechias against Sennacherib (4 Kings xix. 9; Isai. xxxvii. 9).

THARE′, son of Nachor, and father of Nachor, Aran, and Abram. He went with Abram from Ur of the Chaldees, to Haran in Mesopotamia, and died there (Gen. xi. 31, 32); he fell into idolatry (Jos. xxiv. 2, 14).

THARE′, a camp of the Israelites in the desert (Num. xxxiii. 27).

THARE′LA, a city in the tribe of Benjamin (Jos. xviii. 27).

THA′RES (Esth. ii. 21; vi. 2). See THARA.

THAR′SIS, second son of Javan (Gen. x. 4).

THAR′SIS, one of the highest satraps in Persia (Esth. i. 14).

THAR′SIS, a country to which Solomon sent his fleets (3 Kings x. 22; 2 Paral. ix. 21); Holofernes pillaged the children of Tharsis (Judith ii. 13); silver in plates was imported from Tharsis (Jer. x. 9); the kings of Tharsis mentioned (Ps. lxxi. 10); Jonas fled to (Jon. i. 3).

THAR′THAC, a false god of the Hevites (4 Kings xvii. 31).

THAR′THAN, one of the officers sent by Sennacherib to Ezechias (4 Kings xviii. 17).

THA′SI, the surname of Simon Machabeus (1 Mach. ii. 3).

THATHAN′AI, governor of Samaria, opposes the rebuilding of Jerusalem (1 Esd. v. 6); writes against the Jews to king Darius (7); he is ordered to leave them in peace (vi. 6); obeys (13).

THAU, the last letter of the Hebrew alphabet; in the ancient character it had the form of a cross. It is the sign put on the forehead of God's elect (Ezech. ix. 4, 6).

THE′ATRE, a place of public amusement or assembly (Acts xix. 29).

THE′BATH, a town of Syria, taken by David (1 Paral. xviii. 8).

THEBES, a city in the tribe of Ephraim. Abimelech killed by a woman while besieging it (Judg. ix. 50; 2 Kings xi. 21).

THEB′ET, one of the months of the Jewish year.

THEB′NI, son of Gineth, contends with Amri for the crown of Israel (3 Kings xvi. 21); Thebni died (22).

THEC′EL, "weighed in the balance." One of the mysterious words written on the wall at Balthasar's feast and interpreted by Daniel (Dan. v. 25).

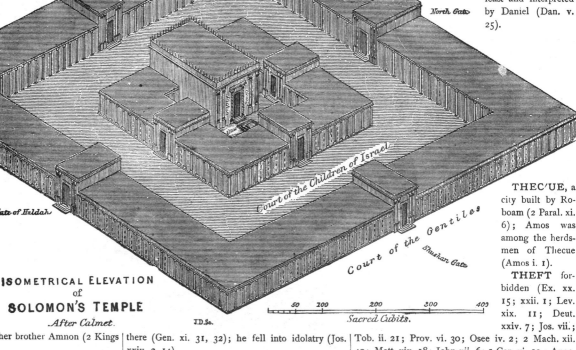

Gate of Tabor · North Gate · Gate of Huldah · Court of the Children of Israel · Court of the Gentiles · Shushan Gate

ISOMETRICAL ELEVATION
of
SOLOMON'S TEMPLE
After Calmet.
J.D.So.

50 100 200 300 400
Sacred Cubits.

THEC′UE, a city built by Roboam (2 Paral. xi. 6); Amos was among the herdsmen of Thecue (Amos i. 1).

THEFT forbidden (Ex. xx. 15; xxii. 1; Lev. xix. 11; Deut. xxiv. 7; Jos. vii.; Tob. ii. 21; Prov. vi. 30; Osee iv. 2; 2 Mach. xii. 40; Matt. xix. 18; John xii. 6; 1 Cor. vi. 10.; Apoc. ix. 21); laws relative to restoration (Ex. xxii. 4); relative to a stolen deposit (7); a night robber breaking into a house may be slain (32); cannot be killed by day without homicide.

THEG′LATHPHALASAR, king of the Assyrians, defeats the Assyrians, and carries off most of the ten tribes to Assyria (4 Kings xv. 29).

THELHAR′SA and **THEL′MALA,** Babylonian cities (1 Esd. ii. 59).

THE′MA, son of Ishmael (Gen. xxv. 15; Job vi. 19).

THE′MAN, son of Eliphaz and grandson of Esau (Gen. xxxvi. 11).

THE′MANITES, land of (Gen. xxxvi. 34).

THE′ODAS, a man who rose up according to Gamaliel, affirming himself to be somebody; but he was slain, and those who believed in him, some 400 were scattered (Acts v. 36).

THEODO'TIUS, a Syrian, one of the deputies sent by Nicanor to Judas Machabeus to treat of peace (2 Mach. xiv. 19).

THEOPH'ILUS, the person to whom St. Luke addressed his gospel, and the Acts of the Apostles.

THER'APHIM, "that is to say, idols" (Judg. xvii. 5; xviii. 14; Osee iii. 4).

THER'SA, a city whose king was slain by Josue (Jos. xii. 24); it became a city in the kingdom of Israel. Jeroboam made it his abode (3 Kings xiv. 17); it was also the capital under Baasa (xv. 21, 33); under Ela (xvi. 9); under Zambri (15); under Amri (23), till he built Samaria (24); Manahem went from Thersa to Samaria to slay Sellum and usurp his throne (4 Kings xv. 14).

THER'SA, youngest of the five daughters of Salphaad (Num. xxvi. 33; xxvii. 1; xxxvi. 2, 3; Jos. xvii. 3).

THES'BE, a city in Galaad beyond the Jordan, the native place of the prophet Elias, who is called Elias the Thesbite (3 Kings xvii. 1; 4 Kings i. 3, 8; ix. 36).

THESSALONI'CA, capital of Macedonia; St. Paul preached Christ in the synagogue there, A. D. 52; converting many Jews and Gentiles (Acts xvii.); the Jews raised a riot, and failing to seize St. Paul and Silas, dragged Jason and others to the rulers. The faithful sent St. Paul and Silas away by night (Acts xvii. 1–10); St. Paul thanks the Philippians for sending twice to Thessalonica means for his use (Phil. iv. 16); mentions Demas going there (2 Tim. iv. 9); with Sylvanus and Timothy wrote two epistles from Corinth to the faithful at Thessalonica (1 Thess.; 2 Thess.)

THESSALO'NIANS', two Epistles of St. Paul to the; canonical books of the New Testament (1 Thess., 2 Thess.)

THIEVES, those who corrupt the Word of God called thieves (Jer. xxiii. 30; John x. 1).

THIGH, touched in taking an oath (Gen. xxiv. 2, 9; xlvii. 29).

THI'RAS, seventh son of Japheth, son of Noe (Gen. x. 2).

THOBADO'NIAS and THOBIAS, Levites sent by king Josaphat through the cities of Juda to instruct the people in their religion (2 Paral. xvii. 8).

THO'CHEN, a city of Simeon (1 Paral. iv. 32).

THOGOR'MA, third son of Gomer (Gen. x. 3; 1 Paral. i. 9).

THOGOR'MA, a country that sent horses and mules to Tyre (Ezech. xxvii. 14); it lay in the north (xxxviii. 6).

THO'HU, grandfather of Samuel (1 Kings i. 1; 1 Paral. vi. 34).

THO'LA, eldest son of Issachar (Gen. xlvi. 13; Num. xxvi. 23; 1 Paral. vii. 1, 2).

THO'LA, tenth judge of Israel, son of Phua, the uncle of Abimelech (Judg. x. 1); he was of the tribe of Issachar, and dwelt at Samir, in Mount Ephraim

(1); he judged Israel twenty-three years, and was buried at Samir (2).

THO'LAD, a city in the tribe of Simeon (1 Paral. iv. 29).

THOL'MAI, son of Enach, of the race of giants; he was slain by the Israelites (Num. xiii. 23; Jos. xv. 14).

THOL'MAI (2 Kings iii. 3); or Tholomai (2 Kings xiii. 17). He was son of Ammiud, king of Gessur, and father of Maacha, wife of David (2 Kings iii. 3; 1 Paral. iii. 2); Absalom, after killing his brother Amnon, fled to his grandfather Tholmai in Gessur (2 Kings xiii. 37).

THOM'AS, SAINT, one of the twelve apostles, called also Didymus (John xx. 24), the name meaning twin; he was called to the apostleship (Luke vi. 13–15); on hearing of the death of Lazarus, he said, "Let us go and be with him" (John xi. 16); at the Last Supper he said to Jesus: "Lord, we know not whither thou goest, and how can we know the way?"

PRIEST.   HIGH PRIEST.   LEVITE.

TABLE OF LOAVES OF PROPOSITION.   THE ARK OF THE COVENANT.   GOLDEN CANDLESTICK.

ALTAR OF INCENSE.   ALTAR OF HOLOCAUSTS.   LAVER.

DRESS OF PRIESTS AND FURNITURE OF THE TEMPLE.

(John xiv. 5); after the resurrection, when told that our Lord had appeared to the other apostles, he refused to believe, unless he actually saw and touched him (John xx. 25); eight days after, our Lord appearing again, made him place his finger and hand in the wounds, and reproached him with his incredulity (27); St. Thomas exclaimed: "My Lord and my God" (28); our Lord replying, said: "Blessed are they that have not seen, and have believed" (29).

THO'PHEL, a place beyond the Jordan on the borders of the wilderness (Deut. i. 1).

THO'PO, a fortified city (1 Mach. ix. 50).

THORNS, part of man's punishment (Gen. iii. 18); a figure of the cares of life (Matt. xiii. 22; Mark iv. 19); our Lord crowned with thorns (Matt. xxvii. 29; Mark xv. 17; John xix. 2); earth bringing forth thorns and briars is reprobate (Heb. vi. 8).

THOU, king of Emath, in Syria, sent his son Joram to congratulate David on his victory over Aderezer, and to offer him vessels of gold, silver and brass (2 Kings viii. 8–11).

THOUGHTS, God abhors wicked thoughts (Matt. xv. 19; Mark vii. 21; Zach. viii. 17; Prov. vi. 18); God knows the thoughts of the heart (3 Kings viii. 39; 2 Paral. vi. 30; Job xlii. 2; Ecclus. xlii. 20; Isai. xxix. 15; Matt. ix. 4; John ii. 25; Heb. iv. 12); known to those to whom God reveals them (4 Kings v. 26; vi. 12; Dan. ii. 29).

THRAC'IANS, in the army of Gorgias, one saves him (2 Mach. xii. 35).

THREE TAV'ERNS, St. Paul arrives at a place so called near Rome (Acts xxviii. 15).

THRESHING-FLOOR of Areuna, or Ornan, the Jebusite; the angel of Lord sent to strike the people for David's sin stood by it (2 Kings xxiv. 16; 1 Paral. xxi. 15); the angel commanded Gad to tell David to build an altar there (18; 2 Kings xxiv. 18); David bought it of Areuna, and built an altar there (24, 25; 1 Paral. xxi. 25, 26); the temple of Solomon was erected there. Oza killed at the threshing-floor of Chidon (1 Paral. xiii. 9).

THRONE. Description of Solomon's throne (3 Kings x. 18); of the mysterious throne of the Lord (Apoc. iv. 2–10).

THRONES, an order of angels (Coloss. i. 16).

THU'BAL, fifth son of Japheth (Gen. x. 2; 1 Paral. i. 5; Ezech. xxvii., xxxii., xxxviii., xxxix.)

THUN'DER, in Egypt (Ex. ix. 23); at Mount Sinai (xix. 16); in Mardochai's dream (Esth. xi. 5); in Job (xxvi., xxxviii.); voice like thunder in testimony of our Lord (John xii. 29); in the Apocalypse (Apoc. iv., vi., viii., x., xiv. 2; xv., xix. 6).

THYATI'RA, a city on the borders of Mysia and Lycia. The church there was one of the seven in Asia, to whom bishops are sent in the Apocalypse

(Apoc. i. 11); the bishop praised for his faith, charity and patience (ii. 19); reproached with allowing a woman to spread false doctrines (20–24).

THEBES, IN EGYPT—THE RAMESSEION.

THY'INE TREES brought from Ophir (3 Kings x. 11); the rails of Solomon's temple and palace, citterns and harps made of it (12).

TIBE'RIAS, sea of, the sea of Galilee so called (John vi. 1; xxi. 1).

TIBE'RIAS, a city on the sea of Galilee (John vi. 23).

TIBE'RIUS, adopted son and successor of Augustus. St. John the Baptist began his preaching in the fifteenth year of his reign (Luke iii. 1).

TI'CHON. The prophet Ezechiel speaks of the house of Tichon, which is by the border of Aaran (Ezech. xlvii. 16).

TI'GRIS, one of the four great rivers of Paradise (Gen. ii. 14); Tobias reaches it (vi. 1); Nabuchodonosor defeated Arphaxad near it (Judith i. 5, 6); the son of Sirach alludes to its floods in the days of the new fruits (Ecclus. xxiv. 35); Daniel has a vision near the Tigris (Dan. x. 4).

TILL'AGE of the soil a penalty imposed on the human race (Gen. iii. 17).

TI'GER, a wild animal mentioned (Job iv. 11).

TIM'BREL, a musical instrument (Gen. xxxi. 27; 1 Kings xviii. 6; Isaias v. 12; 1 Mach. ix. 39).

TIME. Things should be done in their time (Eccles. iii. 2; viii. 5; Ecclus. xx. 6; xxxii. 29; Rom. xiii. 11); the seventh angel in the Apocalypse declares that Time shall be no longer (Apoc. x. 6). Time used in Daniel for year (Dan. iv. 13).

TIMON, one of the first seven appointed deacons (Acts vi. 5).

TIMOTHEUS, general of king Antiochus Epiphanes, defeated by Judas Machabeus, with the loss of 20,000 men (2 Mach. viii. 30); again beyond the Jordan (1 Mach. v. 6, 7); killed at Gazara (2 Mach. x. 37).

TIMOTHEUS, another general under the same king, and governor of the countries beyond the Jordan, defeated by Judas and Jonathan (1 Mach v. 11, 12; 2 Mach. xii. 20); flees to Carnion (21); falls into the hands of Dositheus and Sosipater, who spare his life (25).

TIMO'THY, SAINT, a disciple of St. Paul, son of Eunice, a Jewess, and a pagan father (Acts xvi. 1); he was born at Derbe or Lystra. St. Paul praises the piety of Eunice and her mother Lois (2 Tim. i.

5); St. Paul circumcised him before taking him to aid him in the ministry (Acts xvi. 3); he was ordained with imposition of the hands of the priesthood (1 Tim. iv. 14; 2 Tim. i. 6); he accompanied St. Paul to Macedonia (Acts xvi. 12); Philippi, Thessalonica and Berea (Acts xvii. 1–14); he remained at Berea till St. Paul summoned him to Athens (15); he was then in Corinth (xviii. 5); and from Ephesus St. Paul sent him again to Macedonia (xix. 22); St. Paul, in writing to the Thessalonians, joins St. Timothy and St. Silas with himself (1 Thess.; 2 Thess.); he labored at Corinth (1 Cor. iv. 17; 2 Cor. i. 19); he was with St. Paul in Macedonia when he wrote his second Epistle to Corinthians (2 Cor. i.); he salutes the Romans (Rom. xvi. 21); St. Timothy accompanied St. Paul on his way to Jerusalem (Acts xx. 4); and was with him, A. D. 60–62, when he wrote to the Philippians, the Colossians and to Philemon; the next year St. Paul mentions that St. Timothy was out of prison (Heb. xiii. 23); in A. D. 64, he left him at Ephesus (1 Tim. i. 3, 4); of which city he is always reckoned the first bishop. St. Paul addressed two epistles to him (1 Tim.; 2 Tim.) He is recorded to have suffered martyrdom at Ephesus while endeavoring to prevent heathen

rites. The bishop of Ephesus reproached in the Apocalypse (Apoc. ii. 1–3); is by some supposed not to be St. Timothy.

TIM'OTHY, St. Paul's two Epistles to; canonical books of the New Testament (1 Tim.; 2 Tim.)

TISRI', the first month of the civil year, and the seventh of the ecclesiastical year.

TITAN. Judith, in her canticle, says of Holofernes: "Neither did the sons of Titan strike him" (Judith xvi. 8).

TITHES, first paid by Abraham to Melchisedech (Gen. xiv. 20); Jacob promises to offer tithes to the Lord (xxviii. 22); prescribed by the law of Moses (Ex. xxii. 29; Lev. xxvii. 30–34).

TITLE, used in the sense of a monument (Gen. xxviii. 18; xxxi. 45; xxxiv. 14; xxxv. 20; Levit. xxvi. 1; 2 Kings xviii. 18).

TI'TUS, a disciple of St. Paul, a Gentile by birth (Gal. ii. 3); converted by St. Paul who calls him his son (Tit. i. 4); St. Paul took him to Jerusalem, A. D. 51 (Gal. ii. 1); he would not consent to be circumcised; he was sent to Corinth to still the troubles there, A. D. 56 (2 Cor. xii. 18); he joined St. Paul in Macedonia (2 Cor. vii. 6, 15); he set out for Corinth (2 Cor. viii. 5–17); carrying St. Paul's second Epistle to the Corinthians. He was made bishop of Crete, A. D. 63 (Tit. i. 5); and St. Paul summoned him to Nicopolis (Tit. iii. 12). He is said to have died and been buried in the island of Crete.

TI'TUS. St. Paul's Epistle to, one of the canonical books of the New Testament (Tit.)

TI'TUS JUSTUS, St. Paul abides with him at Corinth (Acts xviii. 7).

TOB, a country beyond the Jordan (Judg. xi. 3, 5); called Tubin (1 Mach. v. 13); suffering of Jews there (13); Judas among them (2 Mach. xii. 17).

TOBI'AS THE ELDER, of the tribe of Nephthali (Tob. i. 1); faithful to the Lord (6); marries Anna (9); his works of mercy, especially burying the dead (19, 20); fled during persecution of Sennacherib (23); buries a dead man (ii. 1–9); blinded by dung from a swallow's nest (11); his patience (12–

THESSALONICA.

23); his instructions to his son (iv.); sends his son to collect money of Gabelus at Rages (v.); the angel Raphael sent as a guide (v. 5, 6); cured of his blindness by Raphael's directions (xi. 8–15); seeks to reward the guide (xii.); praised by Raphael (xii. 12, 13); his canticle (xiii.); died at Ninive, aged 102 (xiv. 2).

TOBI'AS THE SON. Instructions given him by his father (Tob. iv.); sent to Rages to collect money of Gabelus (Tob. v.); the angel Raphael becomes his guide (22–28); takes a fish in the Tigris (2–4); keeps parts by command of the angel (4, 8, 9); is directed by him to marry Sara (12); entertained by Raguel (vii. 1–9); he asks Sara as his wife (10); their marriage (15, 16); exorcises the devil who had afflicted her by following the angel's directions (viii.); asks Azarias to go to Gabelus (ix. 1); sets out for his father's home (10, 11); his parents long for him (x. 1–7; xi. 5, 6); he reaches home and cures his father's blindness (9–17); buries his parents and leaves Ninive (xiv. 14); his death (16).

TOBI'AS, one of the canonical books of the Old Testament, containing the history of Tobias (Tob.)

TOBI'AS, one of the four from whom God orders the prophet Zachary to receive gold and silver for a crown for Jesus, the high-priest (Zach. vi. 10, 14).

TOMB, bought by Abraham in the land of Hebron (Gen. xxiii. 16); Sara buried there (19); Rachel's tomb erected near Bethlehem (xxxv. 20; xlviii. 7); Jacob's tomb in the land of Hebron (xlvii. 30); Joseph's tomb at Sichem, in land bought by Jacob (Jos. xxiv. 32); Aaron's tomb on Mount Hor (Num. xx. 29); tomb of Moses in the valley of Moab, unknown to men (Deut. xxxiv. 6); Josue's tomb at Thamnathsare (Jos. xxiv. 30); Samson's (Judg. xvi. 31); that of Absalom (2 Kings xviii.); that of Ochozias at Je-

rusalem (4 Kings ix. 28); Judith's at Bethulia (Judith xvi. 28); tombs of the Machabees at Modin (1 Mach. xiii. 25, 29); tomb of our Lord sealed and guarded (Matt. xxvii. 60, 66).

TONGUE. We are to beware of an evil tongue (Lev. xix. 16; Job v. 21; Ps. li. 4; cxxxix. 4, 12; cxl. 3; Prov. iv. 24; xv. 2; xvi. 28; xvii. 20; xviii.; xxi. 23; xxx. 11.; Eccles. v. 2; Wis. i. 11; Ecclus. v. 16; xxv. 11; xxviii.; 1 Cor. xv. 33; James i. 19; iii. 5, 8); the tongue is to be bridled (Prov. xii. 14; xiii. 2, 3; xvii. 27; xviii. 21; Ecclus. xiv. 1; xx. 5; xxii. 33; xxiii. 17; Matt. xii. 36; Luke vi. 45; 1 Pet. iii. 10).

TONGUES, confusion of tongues at Babel (Gen. xi. 7, 9); the apostles and primitive Christians receive the gift of tongues (Acts ii. 4; x. 46; xix. 6); gift of tongues useless without that of interpretation (1 Cor. xiv. 13).

TO'PAZ, a precious stone (Ex. xxviii. 17; xxxix. 10; Job xxviii. 19; Ps. cxviii. 127; Ezec. xxviii. 13; Apoc. xxi. 20).

TO'PHETH, a place near Jerusalem, in the valley of the son of Ennom, where the Jews passed

SCHOOL OF THEOLOGY. (After Raphael.)

TIBERIAS.

their children through fire to Moloch (4 Kings xxiii. 10; Jerem. vii. 31); defiled by king Josias (4 Kings xxiii. 10); a place of burial (Jer. vii. 32; xix. 11); unclean (13); used as a figure of hell (Isai. xxx. 33); to be called the Valley of Slaughter (Jer. vii. 32; xix. 6).

TOR'MENTS, endured by the seven brethren (2 Mach. vii.); inflicted on the just (Wis. ii. 19); of the wicked (Wis. iv. 19; v.; xi. 10; Luke xvi. 23, 28; Apoc. xiv. 11; xviii. 7).

TOR'RENTS. The torrent of Arnon (Num. xxi. 14); torrent of Besor (1 Kings xxx. 9, 21); torrent Cadumim (Judg. v. 21); torrent of Carith near Socoth (3 Kings xvii. 3); torrent of Cedron (2 Kings xv. 23; 3 Kings xv. 13; 4 Kings xxiii. 12; Jerem. xxxi. 40; John xviii. 1); of Cison (Judg. iv. 7, 13); torrent of the Cluster (Num. xiii. 24, 25); torrent of Egypt (Num. xxxiv. 5; Jos. xv. 47); torrent of Ephraim (Jos. xvii. 9); torrent of Gaas (2 Kings xxiii. 30; 1 Paral. xi. 32); torrent of Gerara (Gen. xxvi. 17); torrent of Jeboc (Deut. ii. 37; iii. 16); torrent of Thorns (Joel iii. 18); torrent of Zared (Num. xxi. 12; Deut. ii. 13, 14).

TOR'RENT, or **GREAT WATERS,** taken figuratively to mean great joy or deep sorrow (2 Kings xxii. 5; Job xx. 17; Ps. xvii. 5; xxxv. 9; cix. 7; cxxiii. 5; cxxv. 4; Isai. viii. 7, 8).

TOR'TURERS (Matt. xviii. 34); leave St. Paul, finding him to be a citizen (Acts xxii. 29).

TOW'ER OF BABEL. The descendants of Noe attempt to erect it (Gen. xi. 4); the tower of Thebes and Sichem (Judg. ix. 49, 53); tower of the flock (Mich. iv. 8); tower of the watchmen (4 Kings xvii. 9); the tower that fell in Siloe (Luke xiii. 4).

TOW'ERS of the city of Jerusalem; tower of Hananeel (2 Esd. iii. 1; xii. 38); great tower (iii. 27); of the furnaces (xii. 37); of Emath (38).

TOWN-CLERK (Douay, Scribe), used by Challoner in Acts xix. 35 from the King James.

TRADIT'ION. We are to preserve the traditions of the apostles (2 Thess. ii. 14; iii. 6; 1 Cor. xi. 2; 2 Tim. i. 13; ii. 2; iii. 14); the apostles did not commit to writing all the instructions of our Lord (John xxi. 25).

TRANSFIGURA'TION. Our Lord took Peter, James and John into a high mountain apart to pray. They fell asleep, and on awaking he was transfigured before them; his face shone like the sun, and his garments became white as snow. Moses and Elias in glory appeared, speaking to him of his death to be accomplished in Jerusalem. St. Peter, in holy joy, wished to remain, and proposed erecting three tents, but a voice from a cloud declared, "This is my beloved Son, in whom I am well pleased; hear ye him." The disciples fell on their faces in terror, and

THE VALLEY OF TOPHETH.

when aroused by our Lord, saw no one but him (Matt. xvii. 1–9; Mark ix. 1–7; Luke ix. 28–36). St. John alludes to his transfiguration in John i. 14, and St. Peter in 2 Pet. i. 16, 17. According to the constant tradition, the scene was Mount Thabor.

TRANS'LA'TION, of Henoch (Gen. v. 24; Heb. xi. 5); of the prophet Elias (4 Kings ii. 11).

TRANS'MIGRA'TION OF BABYLON, the captivity so called in some Catholic Bibles (Matt. i. 11).

TRANS'SUBSTAN'TIATION. The real presence of our Lord in the Eucharist evident from Matt. xxvi. 26; Mark xiv. 22–24; Luke xxii. 19; John vi. 51; 1 Cor. x. 16; xi. 24–29.

TREACH'ERY, in Joseph's brethren (Gen. xxxvii. 17–36); in Simon, overseer of the temple (2

Mach. iii. 4; iv. 1); in Rhodocus (xiii. 21); in Judas Iscariot (Matt. xxvi. 48; xxvii. 5).

TREAS'URE. Where our treasure is, there is our heart (Matt. vi. 21; xix. 22).

TREASURY OF THE TEMPLE. Sesac carries away the treasures of the temple (2 Paral. xii. 9; 3 Kings xiv. 26); Asa took from the treasures of the temple to send to Benadad (2 Paral. xvi. 2); Joiada made a chest for the offerings of the people for the temple and set it by the altar (4 Kings xii. 9–11; 2 Paral. xxiv. 8–11); Ezechias gave all the silver in the house of the Lord to the Assyrians (4 Kings xviii. 15); Josias orders the treasure of the temple to be applied to its restoration (xxii. 4); the treasures of the temple carried off by Nabuchodonosor (xxiv. 13); our Lord approves the widow's contribution to it (Mark xii. 41; Luke xxi. 2); Jesus spoke in the treasury of the temple (John viii. 20).

TREE of the knowledge of good and evil in Paradise (Gen. ii. 17); prohibition against planting trees around the altar of the Lord (Deut. xvi. 21); Joatham's parable of the trees choosing a king (Judg. ix. 7–15).

TREMBLING. We are to work out our salvation with fear and trembling (Phil. ii. 12).

TRESPASS OF-FERINGS (Lev. v. 6).

TRI'ALS allowed by God to test the fidelity of the Israelites (Judg. iii. 1).

TRIBES. The twelve tribes of Israel descended from Ruben, Simeon, Juda, Issachar, Zabulon, Benjamin, Dan, Aser, Gad and Nephthali, sons of Jacob, and from Ephraim and Manasses, sons of Joseph, adopted by Jacob (Num. i. 5–15); first census of their numbers (20–46); second census (xxvi. 5–51); the tribes are blessed by Moses before his death with prophetic words as to each (Deut. xxxiii. 6–25); the Levites, or descendants of Levi, not numbered in the first census (Num. i. 47–49); counted in the second (xxvi. 62); the Promised Land allotted to the tribes (Num. xxxii. 33–42; Josue xiii.–xix.); the twelve tribes remain united under the Judges and Saul, Jos., Judges, 1 Kings, 2 Kings i.; David, king of Juda (2 Kings ii.); Isboseth for two years king of the other tribes (2 Kings ii. 8–11); David and Solomon, kings of the twelve tribes (2 Kings v.–3 Kings xii. 20); Roboam remains king of Juda and Benjamin only, forming the kingdom of Juda (3 Kings xii. 21); Jeroboam becomes king of the other ten tribes, known as the kingdom of Israel (3 Kings xii. 20); the kingdom of Israel overthrown, 730 B. C., by Salmanasar, king of Assyria, and the ten tribes carried

away into captivity (4 Kings xvii. 6); the kingdom of Juda overthrown by Nabuchodonosor and Juda, Benjamin and Levi carried away to Babylon (4 Kings xxv. 11).

TRIB'ULATION, God our refuge in (Gen. xxxv. 3; 2 Kings xxii. 7; 2 Paral. xx. 9; Ps. iv. 2; xvii. 7; xxxi. 7; xlv. 2; lxiii. 2; lxxvi. 3; xc. 15); to be gloried in (Rom. v. 3); work patience (ib.)

TRIBUNES at Herod's supper (Mark vi. 21; at our Saviour's mocking (John xviii. 12); Lysias, a tribune, arrests St. Paul (Acts xxi. 33); about to scourge him (xxii. 24); rescues him (xxiii. 10); provides for his safety (23).

TRIB'UTES paid to the kings of Egypt by their subjects (Gen. xlvii. 20); the obligation to pay tribute to the ruling powers (Matt. xvii. 24; xxii. 17; Rom. xiii. 7).

TRINITY. The mystery of the Holy Trinity prefigured (Gen. i. 26; xviii. 2; Ex. iii. 6, 15, 16; iv. 5; Ps. xxxii. 6; Ecclus. i. 9; xxiv. 5; Isai. vi. 3; xxxiv. 16; xlviii. 16; lxi. 1); declared explicitly (Matt. iii. 16; x. 20; xvii. 5; xxviii. 19; Luke iv. 18; John iii. 35; xiv.; xv. 26; xvi.; 1 John v. 7; 2 Cor. xiii. 13).

TRIP'OLIS, a city of Phœnicia, on the Mediterranean. Demetrius, son of Seleucus, enters the haven with a fleet and army, 162 B. C. (2 Mach. xiv. 1).

TRO'AS, a city of Phrygia or Mysia, on the Hellespont. St. Paul was in Troas in A. D. 52, when he had a vision of a man calling him to Macedonia (Acts xvi. 8); he preaches to the faithful assembled to break bread (xx. 6, 7); raises Eutychus to life (9, 10); another visit to Troas is alluded to (2 Cor. ii. 12); he left a cloak and books there (2 Tim. iv. 13).

TROG'LODYTES, cave-dwellers (2 Paral. xii. 3).

TROPH'IMUS, a disciple of St. Paul. He was a Gentile and a native of Ephesus. He accompanied him to Corinth and Jerusalem (Acts xx. 4); St. Paul was seized for having, as the Jews supposed, taken Trophimus into the temple (Acts xxi. 29); in his second epistle to Timothy, written from Rome not long before his death, St. Paul says he left Trophimus sick at Miletus (2 Tim. iv. 20).

TRUMPETS. God directed Moses to make two trumpets of beaten silver in order to call the people together when the camp was to be removed (Num. x. 1, 2); at one blast, the princes were to come to the tabernacle (4); at a long broken blast, the tribes on the east side were to march (5); at the second sound, those on the south (6); when the sound was plain, all the people were to gather (3, 7); they were to sound for a foreign war (9); at banquets and on festivals (10); none but the priests of the house of Aaron could sound them (8); they were to be sounded on the first day in the seventh month of the year of the feast of trumpets (Lev. xxiii. 24); and on the tenth day of the seventh month in the year of jubilee (xxv. 9); at Jericho the priests sounded the seven trumpets, as in the year of jubilee, going before the Ark of the Covenant seven times around the city each day for seven days (Jos. vi. 4–16); at the last blast of the trumpets and shout of the people the walls fell (20); the holy trumpets used by the Machabees in battle (1 Mach. xvi. 8); on the day of judgment the last trumpet shall sound and the dead shall rise again (1 Cor. xv. 52); in the Apocalypse seven angels sound trumpets—after the first to fifth, scourges came upon the earth (Apoc. viii. 6–13; ix. 1–21); when the seventh begins to sound the trumpet the mystery of God shall be finished (x. 7); the sounding of the seventh (xi. 15).

TRUTH. Isaias complains that it is forgotten (Isai. lix. 15); Jesus was full of grace and truth (John i. 14); grace come through Jesus (John i. 17); the truth will set us free (John viii. 32); Jesus Christ is the truth (xiv. 6); Pilate asks our Lord: "What is truth?" (John xviii. 38); the Holy Ghost to teach the apostles all truth (John xvi. 13); every one should speak according to the truth (Eph. iv. 25); if we say we have not sin, the truth is not in us (1 John i. 8).

TRYPHE'NA and **TRY-PHO'SA,** converts at Rome, whom St. Paul salutes as laboring in the Lord (Rom. xvi. 12).

TRY'PHON, king of Syria. He had been an adherent of Alexander Bales; finding the army murmur against Demetrius, he espoused the cause of young Antiochus (1 Mach. xi. 39, 40); crowns him and proclaims him king (54); defeats Demetrius and takes Antioch (56); Tryphon then aspired to the throne (xii. 39); he treacherously entraps Jonathan (40–48); sent an army into Galilee (49; xiii. 1); obtains money and hostages of Simon, but lied and did not let Jonathan go (19); slew Jonathan and his sons (23); slew young Antiochus while journeying with him (31); put the crown of Asia on his own head (32); ravaged the country (34); Antiochus, son of Demetrius, claims the throne, and the forces go over to him (xv. 10); Tryphon fled to Dora (11); besieged by Antiochus (13, 14, 25); he fled by ship to Orthosias (37); pursued by Antiochus (39).

TU'BALCAIN, son of Lamech and Sella (Gen. iv. 22); a hammerer and artificer in every kind of brass and iron (22).

TU'BIANITES, Jews of Characa so called (2 Mach. xii. 17).

TU'BIN, Jews mentioned as slain in the places of Tubin (1 Mach. v. 13).

TURPENTINE. Jacob buries idols under a turpentine tree (Gen. xxxv. 4); Jacob sends turpentine as a gift to Joseph (xliii. 11); a prophet under a turpentine tree (3 Kings xiii. 14); wisdom compared to one (Ecclus. xxiv. 22; Isai. vi. 13); heathen rites under (Osee iv. 13).

TURTLE' DOVE to be offered in sacrifice (Gen. xv. 9; Lev. i. 14; v. 7; xii., xiv., xv.; Luke ii. 24; Num. vi. 10); referred to (Ps. lxxxiii. 4; Cant. i. 9; ii. 12; Jer. viii. 8).

TYCH'ICUS, a disciple of St. Paul, often employed by the apostle to bear his letters. He was a native of the province of Asia, and accompanied St. Paul from Corinth to Jerusalem (Acts xx. 4); he was

the bearer of the Epistle to the Colossians, A. D. 61 (Coloss. iv. 7); that to the Ephesians, A. D. 65 (Ephes. vi. 21; 2 Tim. iv. 12); he calls him his dear brother, a faithful minister, and his companion in the service of God; he proposed to send him to Crete to replace Titus (Titus iii. 12).

TYRE, a famous commercial city of Phœnicia; a strong city (Jos. xix. 29); Hiram, king of Tyre, an ally of David (2 Kings v. 11; xxiv. 7); of Solomon (3 Kings v. 1; vii. 13; ix. 11; 1 Paral. xiv. 1; 2 Paral. ii.); mentioned (Ps. xliv.; lxxxii.;

THE TRANSFIGURATION OF OUR LORD.

lxxxvi.); her merchants princes, her traders the nobles of the earth (Isaias xxiii. 8); its luxury and commerce with different nations described eloquently (Ezech. xxvii. 1–34); the destruction foretold by Isaias, to come in seventy years (Isai. xxiii. 15); its proud king to be cast down, and to die by the hand of strangers (Ezech. xxviii.); its total destruction by Nabuchodonosor foretold (Ezech. xxvi.); to become like a naked rock, a drying place for nets (5, 14); never to be built up again (14; xxvii. 36); description of the fall (xxvi. 15–21; xxvii. 26–36; Amos i. 10;

Osee ix. 13; Joel iii. 4; Zach. ix. 2); games held at under Antiochus (2 Mach. iv. 18); Antiochus, there (44); our Lord alludes to the destruction of Tyre and Sidon (Matt. xi. 21, 22; Luke x. 13, 14); people from Tyre and Sidon came to hear him (Mark iii. 8; Luke vi. 17); he himself went into the coasts of Tyre and Sidon, and cured the possessed daughter of a Chanaanite or Syrophœnician woman (Matt. xv. 21–28; Mark vii. 24–30); St. Paul on his way to Jerusalem landed at Tyre, as the ship was to unlade there (Acts xxi. 3, 7).

UBIL, an Ismahelite, superintendent of David's camels (1 Paral. xxvii. 30).

U'LAI. Daniel had a vision when over the gate of Ulai, that is, the gate facing that river (Dan. viii. 2).

U'LAM, of the tribe of Manasses (1 Paral. vii. 16, 17).

UNBELIEF, sinfulness of (John iii. 18; xvi. 9; Rom. xi. 32; Heb. iii. 12; Tit. i. 15; 1 John v. 10).

UNCLEANNESS, legal purifications enjoined for (Lev. xi. 24, 25, 32–40; xv. 1–33; xvi. 16).

UNCLEAN ANIMALS, those that chew the cud, but divide not the hoof (Lev. xi. 4–7; Deut. xiv. 7); things bred in the waters that have not fins and scales (Lev. xi. 10–12; Deut. xiv. 10); unclean birds (Lev. xi. 13–19; Deut. xiv. 12–18); flying or hopping quadrupeds (Lev. xi. 20, 21); quadrumana (Lev. xi. 27); other unclean animals (Lev. xi. 30, 41, 42; Deut. xiv. 19).

UNC'TION, anointing, prescribed by law (Ex. xxix. 7, 21; xxx. 25, 31; xxxi. 11; xxxv. 15; xl. 9, 11; Lev. viii. 2, 10; x. 7; xxi. 10, 12; Num. iv. 16); the unction of the Holy Spirit (1 John ii. 20, 27); the sacrament of Extreme Unction, the anointing of the sick (James v. 14).

U'NITY OF THE CHURCH (Cant. vi. 8, 9; John x. 16; xvii. 12–14; Eph. iv. 4, 5); unity of Christians in the Eucharist (1 Cor. x. 17).

UN'KNOWN GOD. An altar in Athens erected to the Unknown God. St. Paul uses the fact in argument (Acts xvii. 23).

UNLEAV'ENED BREAD. See AZYMES.

UR, a city of the Chaldees, native place of Thare and Abraham. God orders Abraham to leave it, and proceed to the land of Chanaan (Gen. xi. 31; xv. 7).

UR, father of Eliphal, one of David's champions (1 Paral. xi. 35).

URBA'NUS, a convert whom St. Paul salutes as his helper in Christ Jesus (Rom. xvi. 9).

U'RI, father of Beseleel (Ex. xxxi. 2).

URI'AS, a Hethite, a brave and faithful soldier in

David's army, besieging Rabba (2 Kings xi. 1, 6); his wife, Bethsabee, seen and seduced by David (2–5); David sends for Urias, and endeavors to conceal

GREEK AND ROMAN BOXES.

his sinful act, but is baffled by the soldierly pride of Urias (7–13); sends him back to the army with a letter to Joab, directing him to put Urias in the post of danger (14, 15); he is killed (17); Bethsabee mourns for him (26).

URI'AS, high-priest of the Jews, builds an altar by order of King Achaz, like one at Damascus (4 Kings xvi. 10, 11); offers holocausts and libations on it by order of the king (15, 16).

URI'AS, a prophet of the Lord, son of Semei, of Cariathiarim (Jerem. xxvi. 20); prophesied at the same time as Jeremias, and predicted similar woes to Jerusalem and the country as that prophet (20); Joakim, king of Juda, sought to put him to death, but he fled to Egypt (21); the king sent to Egypt for him, and slew him with the sword, casting his dead body into the graves of the common people (23).

UR'IEL, of Gabaa, father of Michaia, wife of Roboam (2 Paral. xiii. 2).

US, son of Aram (Gen. x. 23).

US'URY forbidden (Ex. xxii. 25; Lev. xxv. 36; Deut. xxiii. 19; 2 Esd. v. 7; Ps. xiv. 5; Prov. xxii. 16; xxviii. 8; Jer. xv. 10; Ezech. xviii. 8, 13; xxii. 12; Luke vi. 34; xix. 8).

UZAL, sixth son of Jectan (Gen. x. 27); called Huzal (1 Paral. i. 21).

VAGA'O, eunuch of Holofernes, directed by him to summon Judith (Judith xii. 10, 12); closes the doors (xiii. 1); discovers his master's death, and Judith's flight (xiv. 13–16).

VALE, the Woodland Vale, which now is the Salt Sea (Gen. xiv. 3); vale of Mambre, where Abram dwelt (Gen. xiv. 13; xviii. 1); vale of Save, which is the king's vale (Gen. xiv. 17); the noble vale (Gen. xii. 6); vale of Gad (2 Kings xxiv. 5); vale of Sephata (2 Paral. xiv. 10); vale of Tabernacles (Ps. cvii. 8).

VALECASIS, a city (Josue xviii. 21).

VALLEY OF THE CLUSTER (Num. xxxii. 9); valley of Seboim (Gen. x.; 1 Kings xiii. 18);

valley of Achor (Jos. vii. 24, 26; Isai. lxv. 10; Osee ii. 15); valley of the Reeds (Jos. xvi. 8; xvii. 9); valley of Jephtahel or Jephthael (Jos. xix. 14, 27); valley of Sorec (Judg. xvi. 4); valley of Sennim (Judg. iv. 11); valley of Raphaim (2 Kings v. 18; xxiii. 13); valley of Terebinth (1 Kings xvii. 2); valley of Blessing (2 Paral. xx. 26); valley of the Salt Pits (2 Kings viii. 13; 4 Kings xiv. 7); valley of Josaphat (Joel iii. 12); valley of the Artificers (1 Paral. iv. 14; 2 Esd. xi. 35); valley of Tears (Ps. lxxxiii. 7); valley of Vision (Isai. xxii. 1); valley of Topheth, or of the Son of Ennon, or of Slaughter (Jerem. vii. 32), or of Dead Bodies (xxxi. 40); valley of the Passengers—valley of the Multitude of Gog (Ezech. xxxix. 11); valley of Cedron (4 Kings xxiii. 4); valley of Gihon (2 Paral. xxxiii. 14).

VAN'ITY OF EARTHLY THINGS (Eccles. i. 1).

VAP'SI, a Nephthalite (Num. xiii. 15).

VASH'TI, wife of Assuerus, refuses to obey his order to appear in the banquet to show her beauty to all the people and the princes (Esth. i. 10–12); had made a feast for the women (9); Assuerus consults what sentence should be passed upon her (12–15); by the advice of Mamuchan, Assuerus repudiates and deposes her, lest by her example wives of princes slight the commands of their husbands (16–22); Assuerus repents, remembering Vashti, what she had done, and what she had suffered (ii. 1).

VASSE'NI, eldest son of the prophet Samuel (1 Paral. vi. 28).

VEIL, separating the oracle, or holy of holies, from the rest of the tabernacle; its form, material and color (Ex. xxvi. 31, 32); how hung and fastened (33); it was under the care of the family of Gerson (Num. iii. 23, 25, 31; iv. 24–26); another veil in the entry that was before the tabernacle (Ex. xxxviii. 18; Num. iv. 25, 26); the veil before the oracle in Solomon's temple wrought with cherubim (2 Paral. iii. 14); Antiochus carried off the veil of the second temple (1 Mach. i. 23); Judas restores both veils (iv. 51); the veil of the temple rent at the death of our Lord (Matt. xxvii. 51; Mark xv. 38; Luke xxiii. 45).

VEIL, a sign of woman's dependence (Gen. xx. 16; xxiv. 65; xxxviii. 14; 1 Cor. xi. 10; Isai. iii. 23).

VEIL, Moses kept his face veiled at the request of the people, after descending from Sinai (Ex. xxxiv. 33).

VEN'GEANCE belongs to God alone, and his ministers, and is forbidden to others (Gen. xv. 14; Lev. xix. 18; Deut. xxxii. 35; Judg. viii. 19; xvi. 30; Ps. vii. 7; ix. 13; xciii. 1; Prov. xxiv. 29; xxix. 22; Ezech. xxv. 12, 14; Nah. i. 2; Matt. v. 39; Luke xvii.; ix. 54; 1 Thess. v. 15; 2 Tim. iv. 14; James v. 4; Apoc. vi. 10).

VERMIL'ION, a red coloring material (Wisd. xiii. 14).

VERSIONS OF THE SCRIPTURES. The Old Testament down to the time of the captivity was written in Hebrew; some portion was then written in Chaldaic, and after the conquests of Alexander the Great, all these portions were translated into Greek, and are known as the Septuagint. Later books were written in Greek; and, as is generally believed, the whole of the New Testament. In the early period of Christianity Greek was spoken from the mouth of the Rhone to the banks of the Jordan and the Nile. As the use of the language declined, the whole Bible was translated into Latin, and this version is known as the Vetus Itala. St. Jerome, a learned and holy priest, who had retired to the Holy Land, there with the aid of Jewish and other scholars, revised this old Latin translation by the Hebrew. His version or revision is known as the Vulgate, and it has ever since been in use in the Catholic church. The Psalms alone belong to the earlier version. See Introduction.

VES'SEL, parable of the potter's vessel broken (Jer. xix. 11).

VES'SELS of the temple of Jerusalem transported to Babylon (Jer. xxvii. 19–22; 4 Kings xxv. 13–16); put by Nabuchodonosor in the temple of his god (1 Esd. i. 7); profaned by Balthasar (Dan. v. 2); restored by Cyrus (1 Esd. i. 8–11); carried off by Antiochus (1 Mach. i. 23); new vessels made by Judas Machabeus (iv. 49).

VESTIBULE, the altar of holocausts, in the entry or vestibule of the tabernacle (Ex. xl. 27); victims immolated there (Lev. iii. 8).

VEST'MENTS of the Jewish priests (Ex. xxviii.; xxix. 5–9).

VETCHES, a legume (Isai. xxviii. 25; Ezech. iv. 9).

VIAL, Samuel took a little vial of oil to anoint

THE VEIL WORN IN THE EAST.

Saul (1 Kings x. 1); vials full of odors (Apoc. v. 8); vials of God's wrath (xv. 7; xvi.)

VICTIMS, qualities required in victims to be offered to God (Lev. xxii. 19.)

VIC′TORY comes from God (Ex. xvii. 9; Deut. vii. 18; Jos. xi. 6; Judg. vii. 7; 1 Kings xiv. 6; xvii. 45; 2 Paral. xiv. 11; xvi. 8; xxiv. 24; xxv. 8; Judith ix. 15; Ps. cxvii. 16; Prov. xxi. 31); God enables a few to overcome powerful armies (Gen. xiv. 14; Judg. vii. 2; 2 Paral. xiii. 14; 1 Mach. iii. 16, 22); rejoicings over victory (Num. xxxi. 54; Judg. xi. 34; 1 Kings xviii. 6); Christ's victory over death (1 Cor. xv. 54).

VIGILANCE. We are always to watch and to pray (Ps. lxii. 2; ci. 8; Prov. viii. 17; Cant. v. 2; Wis. vi. 15, 16; Ecclus. xiii. 17; xxxii. 18; xxxix. 6; Isai. xxix. 20; Jer. i. 11, 12; Matt. xxiv. 42; xxv. 13; xxvi. 38; Mark xiii. 13-37; xiv 38; Luke xii. 37; xxi. 36; Acts xx. 31; 1 Cor. xvi. 13; Eph. vi. 18; Col. iv. 2; 1 Thess. v. 6, 10; 1 Pet. iv. 7; Apoc. iii. 3).

VILLAGES (Jos. xiii. 17; xv. 32, 44-47, 51, 57, 59, 60, 62; xviii. 24, 28; Esth. ix. 19; Mark vi. 36, 56; Luke viii. 34; ix. 12).

VINE, planted by Noe (Gen. ix. 20, 21); generally cultivated in Egypt and Palestine (Gen. xl. 9; xlix. 11); vines with prodigious clusters (Num. xiii. 23); for every one to dwell under his own vine and fig-tree, a type of peace and happiness (3 Kings iv. 25; Mich. iv. 4); a wife compared to a fruitful vine (Ps. cxxvii. 3); choice vines (Isai. v. 2, 4); Israel a vine full of branches (Osec x. 1); our Lord compares himself to a vine, and his apostles to the branches (John xv. 1); the church compared to a vineyard (Ps. lxxix. 9; Cant. ii. 15; Isai. v. 2; Jer. ii. 21; xii. 10; Matt. xx. 1; Mark xii. 1; Luke xx. 9).

VIN′EGAR. Nazarites forbidden to drink (Num. vi. 3); Booz gives Ruth bread and vinegar (Ruth ii. 14); used as a type of sourness (Prov. x. 26); vinegar on nitre (xxv. 20); vinegar on a sponge given to our Lord on the cross (Matt. xxvii. 48; Mark xv. 36; Luke xxiii. 36; John xix. 29, 30).

VINE′YARD, the first mentioned is that planted by Noe (Gen. ix. 20); our Lord, in the person of Juda, represented in Jacob's blessing as "tying his foal to the vineyard, and his ass to the vine" (Gen. xlix. 11); law as to injury to vineyard (Ex. xxii. 5); grapes that fall in vineyard, or are left ungathered, not to be gathered, but left for poor (Deut. xxiv. 21; Lev. xix. 10); vineyard not to be pruned in the seventh year (xxv. 4); Nazarites to eat nothing coming from the vineyard (Num. vi. 4); Israelites promise not to touch the vineyards of the nations on their march (Num. xx., xxi.); vineyards enclosed by walls (xxii. 24); a person going into a neighbor's vineyard might eat but not carry away (Deut. xxiii. 24); vines of the vineyard of Sodom (xxxii. 32); God gave the Israelites vineyards they had not planted (Jos. xxiv. 13); Sichemites trample down vineyards (Judg. ix. 27); Samson destroys the vineyards of the Philistines (Judg. xv. 5); Achab kills Naboth to obtain his vineyard (3 Kings xxi. 1-16); vineyards referred to (Ps. lxxvii. 47; lxxix. 9; civ. 33; cvi. 37; Cant. i. 5; ii. 13; vi.–viii.); our Lord's parable of the vineyard (Matt. xx. 1); parable of the laborers in the

vineyard (Luke xx. 9; Matt. xxi. 34; Mark xii. 2); mysterious gathering of the vineyard of the earth by the son of man (Apoc. xiv. 18).

VI′PER, a venomous serpent (Job xx. 16; Isai. xxx. 6).

VIR′GIN. Isaias prophesies clearly that the Messias is to be born of a Virgin (Isai. vii. 14); the angel Gabriel announces to the Blessed Virgin Mary that she is to be the mother of the Messias (Luke i. 26); Elizabeth hails her as mother of her Lord (43).

VIRGIN′ITY recommended (Matt. xix. 12; 1 Cor. vii. 25; Apoc. xiv. 4); preferred by St. Paul to marriage (1 Cor. vii. 38, 40); vow of virginity evidently made by the Blessed Virgin (Luke i. 34); the

THE LAST COMMUNION OF ST. JEROME, WHO PREPARED THE VULGATE OR REVISED LATIN VERSION OF THE BIBLE.

violation of the vow of chastity draws down God's anger (1 Tim. v. 12).

VIR′GINS. In the slaughter of the Madianites only virgins are spared by God's order (Num. xxi. 18); the virgins of Jabes in Galaad and Silo carried off by the Benjamites (Judg. xxi. 21, 23; xxi.); some virgins shut up in the days of the Machabees (2 Mach. iii. 19); our Lord's parable of the wise and the foolish virgins (Matt. xxv. 1-13); virgins prophesying (Acts xxi. 9); virgins who follow the Lamb (Apoc. xiv. 4).

VIR′TUES, one of the choirs of angels (1 Pet. iii. 22).

VIR′TUES OF SOLOMON (2 Paral. ix. 5).
VIR′TUOUS WOMAN, Ruth declared to be (Ruth iii. 11).

VIS′ION, land of. Abraham is ordered to go into the Land of Vision to sacrifice Isaac (Gen. xxii. 2).

VIS′IONS, the most remarkable: Abraham's vision of the destiny of his posterity (Gen. xv. 12, 17); Jacob's vision of the ladder (Gen. xxviii. 12); vision of an angel with whom he wrestles (Gen. xxxii. 24); Joseph's vision of the sheaves of his brethren bowing to his sheaf (xxxvii. 5-9); Pharao's vision of the fat and lean kine, the full and blasted ears (xli.); Nabuchodonosor's vision of a statue of metals and clay (Dan. ii. 31-45); Nabuchodonosor's vision of a tree (iv. 7-14); its interpretation (16-24); Daniel's vision of the four beasts (vii. 1-28); his vision of the ram and the he-goat (viii. 3-27); his vision of an angel (x., xi.); Ezechiel's vision of the four living creatures (Ezech. i. 4-28); vision of the sins of Jerusalem (viii.); vision of the dry bones (xxxvii. 1-14).

VISIT, St. Paul desires to visit the saints (Rom. i. 11; xv. 23, 32; Gal. iv. 20; 1 Thess. ii. 17).

VOCA′TION of the Jewish people in Abraham (Gen. xii.); of the Gentiles instead of the ungrateful Jews (Acts xviii. 6); vocation of the twelve apostles (Matt. x. 2); we are to make our calling (2 Pet. i. 10).

VOICE OF GOD to be hearkened to (Ex. xv. 26; xix. 5; Num. xiv. 22; Deut. v. 25; viii. 20; xiii. 18; xxviii. 1; 1 Kings xii. 15; 4 Kings xviii. 12; Ps. lxxx.; Prov. v. 13; viii. 4; Isai. lxvi. 6-8; Jerem. iii. 13; vii. 29; xxvi. 13); the voice of many waters (Ps. xli. 8; xcii. 3; Apoc. i. 15); voice of one crying in the wilderness (Isai. xl. 3, 6; Matt. iii. 3; Mark i. 2, 3, 4; Luke iii. 4; John i. 23); the voice of ruins (Jer. xlix. 21).

VOW AND PROMISE to be made to God (Gen. xxviii. 20; Lev. xxvii. 2; Num. vi.; xxi. 2; xxx.; Deut. xxiii. 21; Judg. xi. 31; 1 Kings xiv.; 2 Kings xv. 8; Ps. lxxv. 12; Eccles. v. 4; Baruch vi. 34; Matt. xiv. 7; Acts xviii. 18; xxi. 23; xxiii. 12).

VULTURE, a bird of prey (Job xxviii. 7); forbidden as unclean (Lev. xi. 14; Deut. xiv. 13).

WA′FERS used in the divine worship (Ex. xxix. 2, 23); unleavened (Lev. ii. 4; vii. 12; Num. vi. 15).

WA′GES of the hired servants not to be detained (Deut. xxiv. 14; Tob. iv. 15); wages promised to the mother of Moses (Ex. ii. 9); wages of a hireling (Deut. xv. 18); illgotten wages not to be offered to God (xxiii. 18); the wages of iniquity (2 Pet. ii. 15).

WALL, St. Paul calls the high-priest a whited wall (Acts xxiii. 3).

WAN′DERING of the Israelites in the desert, its length (Ex. xiii. 17).

WAR, the penalty of sin (Lev. xxvi. 25; Deut. xxviii. 36; Judg. ii. 14; iii. 8; iv. 2; vi. 1; x. 7; xiii.; Isai. v. 25; Jer. v. 15); Abraham makes war in order to rescue Lot (Gen. xiv. 14); Israel makes war to avenge the wrong done a Levite (Judg. xx.);

Josue makes war by order of God (Jos. vi.; vii. 11–viii. 30; x.–xii.); David makes war on the Amalecites (1 Kings xxx.); conduct to be observed in war

A CITY TAKEN BY ASSAULT, AND THE INHABITANTS LED AWAY CAPTIVE. From Kouyunjik. (Layard's Nineveh, ii. 285.)

(Deut. xx. 1–20); prayer offered to God in battle by Moses (Ex. xvii. 8–12); David's trust in God before his combat against Goliath (1 Kings xvii. 45); Asa's prayer to God in war against the Ethiopians (2 Paral. xiv. 11); Josaphat's prayer (xx. 6–12; Ezechias' (xxxii. 20); Judith's prayer (Judith viii.–ix.); prayer of the Machabees (1 Mach. iii. 21; iv. 10; 2 Mach. viii. 16, 19); God fights in behalf of his own (Ex. xiv. 14; Deut. i. 30; iii. 22; 1 Kings xvii. 46; 2 Paral. xx. 15; Ps. xvii. 35; cxliii. 1; Isai. xxx. 15).

WARLIKE ENGINES, not to be made of fruit trees (Deut. xx. 19, 20); engines to shoot arrows and great stones (2 Paral. xxvi. 15; 1 Mach. vi. 20); engines to attack walls (1 Mach. v. 30; vi. 31; 2 Mach. xv. 15); on elephants (1 Mach. vi. 37); engines of war (2 Mach. xii. 27).

WARRIORS, names and exploits of the greatest warriors in David's army (2 Kings xxiii. 8–39; 1 Paral. xii. 1–37; xxvii. 2–15).

WASH. Our Lord washes his apostles' feet (John xiii. 5); washing of feet an oriental act of hospitality (Gen. xviii. 4; xix. 2; xxiv. 32; xliii. 24; Luke vii. 44; 1 Tim. v. 10).

WASH. Scruples of Pharisees in regard to washing the hands rebuked (Matt. xv. 2, 20; Mark vii.

2, 3); our Lord washes his disciples' feet (John xiii. 5); Pilate washes his hands to show that he took no part in the death of Christ (Matt. xxvii. 24).

WATCH. The night divided into watches (Ps. lxxxix. 4); the beginning of the watches (Judg. vii. 19; Lam. ii. 19); the second watch, third watch (Luke xii. 38); the fourth watch (Mark vi. 48); the morning watch (Ex. xiv. 24). The shepherds kept the night watch over their flocks (Luke ii. 8); watching vain without God's aid (Ps. cxxvi. 1).

WATCH, our Lord often enjoins on us to watch and pray (Matt. xxiv. 42, 43; xxv. 13; xxvi. 40, 41; Mark xiii. 33, 35; xiv. 37, 38; Luke xii. 37, 39; xxi. 36; 1 Cor. xvi. 13; 1 Pet. v. 8; Apoc. xvi. 15).

WATCHERS, angels so called (Dan. iv. 10, 14).

WATCHING, devotional (Ps. lxii. 2; ci. 8; 2 Cor. vi. 5; xi. 27); in the temple (1 Kings ii. 22; Luke ii. 37; Prov. viii. 34).

WA'TERS, their creation (Gen. i. 2); they are divided (6, 7); the lower waters gathered together and called seas (10); the waters bring forth the creeping creature having life, and the fowl that fly (20); the waters of the sea filled (22); God declares that he will bring the waters of a great flood upon the earth (vi. 17); they burst forth (vii. 11–24); they retire (viii. 3–13); water changed into blood in Egypt (Ex. vii. 17–22; Wis. xi. 7); waters of the Red Sea divided by Moses (xiv. 21–31); waters of the Jordan divided by Josue (Jos. iii. 13–17); by Eliseus (4 Kings ii. 13, 14); made sweet by Moses (Ex. xv. 25); by Eliseus (4 Kings ii. 19–22); Moses makes water flow from a rock (Ex. xvii. 6; Wis. xi. 4). Our Lord changes water into wine, at the wedding feast in Cana, of Galilee (John ii. 1–11); water that washes away the sins of the world (Matt. iii. 16; xxviii. 19; Luke iii. 21; John iii. 5; Ezech. xxxvi. 25; Zach. xiv. 8; Mark i. 4; Col. ii. 12; Heb. x. 22); water walked upon (Matt. xiv. 26; Mark vi. 48); inexhaustible (John iv. 14); many waters signify persecution (Ps. lxviii. 16; cxliii. 7; Cant. viii. 7; Matt. vii. 25; Apoc. xii. 15); water a figure of the knowledge of God, and of the gifts of the Holy Ghost (Isai. xi. 9; xii. 3; xxxiii. 16; xliii. 20; xliv. 3; Ezech. xlvii. 1–12; Zach. xiv. 8).

WAX formed by bees (Ps. xxi. 15; lxvii. 3; xcvi. 5; Mich. i. 4).

WAY. What should be the way of the true faithful (Ps. cxviii. 5; Prov. iii. 6, 17; xvi. 5, 17; Ecclus. v. 12; Isai. xxvi. 7; xxx. 21; xxxiii. 16; xxxv. 8; lx. 3; Jer. xxxi. 21; Osee xiv. 10; 1 Thess. iv. 1; Heb.

xii. 13); the Lord guides the way of the just (Tob. iv. 20; Ps. xvi. 5; xxiv. 4; cxviii. 35; Prov. iv. 12, 18; xiii. 6; xvi. 9; xx. 24; Isai. xlviii. 17; Jer. x. 23; Mich. iv. 2); what is the way of the wicked, and the end thereof (Job vi. 18; Ps. i. 6; cxviii. 3; Prov. iv. 19, 27; xii. 15; xiv. 12; xxi. 2; xxii. 5; xxviii. 18; Ecclus. ii. 16; xxi. 11; Isai. lvii. 10; Jer. ii. 36; iv. 18); there is a way which seemeth just to a man, but the end thereof leads to death (Prov. xiv. 12).

WEDDING. The riddle proposed at Samson's wedding (Judg. xiv. 14); wedding and marriage of Esther (Esth. ii. 18); description of a wedding (1 Mach. ix. 37, 39); we are to be like men who wait for their Lord when he shall return from the wedding (Luke xii. 36); we are not to take the first place at a wedding (xiv. 8). See MARRIAGE.

WEIGHTS. False weights and measures forbidden (Deut. xxv. 13, 14).

WEIGHTS AND MEASURES.

10 ghras	make	1 beka	5 dwts.
2 bekas		1 sicle	10 "
60 sicles		1 mna	2 lbs., 6 oz.
50 mnas		1 talent	125 lbs.

HEBREW MEASURE.			
4 digits		1 palm	3.6 inches.
3 palms		1 span	10.9 "
2 spans		1 cubit	1 ft. 9.8 "
4 cubits		1 fathom	7 ft. 3.5 "

LONG MEASURE.			
400 cubits		1 stadium or furlong	729.6 feet.
5 furlongs		1 Sabbath-day journ.	3648 "
2 Sabbath-day journ.		1 mile	1 mile, 2016 "
3 miles		1 parasang	4 " 768 "
8 parasangs		1 day's jour.	33 " 864 "

LIQUID MEASURE.			
1⅓ caphs		1 log or rebah	.833 pints.
4 logs		1 cabe	3.333 "
3 cabs		1 hin	1 gal., 1 qt.
2 hins		1 satum or measure	2 gal., 3 qts.
3 sata		1 bate or ephi	7 gal., 2 "
3 ephi		1 nebel	22 gal., 2 "
10 ephi		1 core	75 gal.

DRY MEASURE.			
20 gachals		1 cabe	2.83 pints.
36 gachals		1 omer	5.1 "
3⅓ gomor		1 satum	1 peck, 1 pt.
3 sata		1 ephi	3 pecks, 1 qt., 1 pt.
5 ephis		1 letech	2 bushels.
2 letech		1 core	4 "

THE VIPER.

COINS.			
20 obols		1 sicle	46.19 cents.
60 sicles		1 mna	$27.7
60 mnas		1 talent	$1663.02

WED'DING GARMENT. The man who had not on a wedding garment cast out into exterior darkness (Matt. xxii. 11–13).

WELL OF AGAR (Gen. xxi. 19), dug by Abraham (xxi. 25–30); called Well of Bersabee, or of the Oath (31); Well of the Living and Seeing, where Isaac dwelt (Gen. xxv. 11); Well of Bethlehem (1 Paral. xi. 17); Jacob's well near Samaria, where our Lord converted the Samaritan woman (John iv. 6–12).

WHALE, mentioned by Job (Job vii. 12); by Isaias (Isai. xxvii. 1); swallows the prophet Jonas (Jon. ii. 1–11; Matt. xii. 40).

WHEAT and **COCKLE,** our Lord's parable of the (Matt. xiii. 24).

WHELPS, parable of the lion's whelps (Ezech. xix. 2–9; Nah. ii. 11, 12).

WHIRL'WIND, the Lord answered Job out of a whirlwind (Job xxxviii. 1).

WICK'ED LIFE is worse than death (Ecclus. xxii. 12); the wicked court death (Wis. i. 16); the punishment of the wicked (Wis. v. xvi.; xix.); it is eternal (Matt. iii. 12; xxv. 41, 46; Mark ix. 43–48; Luke iii. 17; 2 Thess. i. 7–9; Jude 6, 7; Apoc. xiv. 10, 11; xx. 10; Isai. xxxiii. 14).

WID'OW of Sarephta entertains and lodges the prophet Elias (3 Kings xvii. 10); our Lord raises to life the son of the widow of Naim (Luke vii. 11–18); our Lord praises the charity of the widow who gave her mites to the temple (Mark xii. 42; Luke xxi. 2); under the law, a brother married the widow of a brother dying without issue (Gen. xxxviii. 8; Deut. xxv. 5, 10); the obligation of assisting widows (Ex. xxii. 22; Deut. xvi. 14; xxiv. 17, 19; xxvi. 12; xxvii. 19; Judith ix. 3; Job xxiv. 3; xxxi. 16; Ecclus. iv. 10; Isai. i. 17; Jer. xxii. 3; Zach. vii. 10; Mal. iii. 5; Matt. xxiii. 14; 1 Tim. v. 3, 16; James i. 27); God will not despise the prayer and complaint of a widow (Ecclus. xxxv. 17); the tears from her cheek go up even to heaven (18); how widows should live and employ their time (1 Tim. v. 3, 9, 16); examples of holy widows: the widow of Sarephta (3 Kings xvii. 10); Judith (Jud. viii. 4); the mother of the Machabees (2 Mach. vii.); Anna (Luke ii. 37); Tabitha or Dorcas (Acts ix. 36, 39).

WILL, the will of God should be the rule of ours (1 Kings iii. 18; 2 Kings x. 12; xv. 20; 1 Mach. iii. 60; Matt. vi. 10; xxvi. 39; Acts xxi. 14; 1 Cor. iv. 19; Heb. vi. 3; James iv. 15); we are to do the

WASHING OF HANDS IN THE EAST.

will of God in all things (Matt. vii. 21; xii. 50; Mark iii. 35; Rom. xii. 2; Eph. v. 17; Col. i. 19; 1 Thess. iv. 3; 1 John ii. 17); it is the will of God that all

men should be saved (Ezech. xviii. 23; John vi. 39; 1 Tim. ii. 4; 2 Pet. iii. 9); God accepts the sincere will for the act desired (2 Kings vii.; Gen. xxii. 16); free

EASTERN WINDOW AND CASEMENT.

will remained in man after and in spite of Adam's fall (Gen. iv. 7; Deut. xxx. 19; Jos. xxiv. 15; Ps. xxiv. 12; Wis. ix. 10; Ecclus. xv. 18; xxxi. 10; 1 Cor. iii. 8; vii. 37); the will of man co-operates with the grace of God (1 Kings vii. 3; 2 Paral. xii. 12; Ps. ix. 17; lxi. 13; Prov. xvi. 1, 5, 9; Ecclus. ii. 20; Isai. i. 16; xl. 3; xlvi. 8; lv. 6, 7; Jer. iii. 1–22; iv. 3–14; xxv. 5; xxvi. 13; Ezech. xviii. 21–32; Zach. i. 3; Mal. iii. 7; Matt. vi. 23; xi. 21; John vi. 37; Acts iii. 19; viii. 22; ix. 6; Rom. x. 13; 1 Cor. iii. 9; xv. 10; 2 Cor. vii. 1; Eph. v. 14; Phil. ii. 12, 13; iv. 13; Col. i. 29; iii. 10; 1 Tim. iv. 16; 2 Tim. ii. 21; Heb. iv. 16; xii. 12; James iv. 8; 1 Pet. i. 22; 1 John iii. 3; Apoc. iii. 20).

WIL'LOW, a tree; willows of the brook (Lev. xxiii. 40; Job xl. 17; Isai. xliv. 4); torrent of the willows (Isai. xv. 7); willows of Babylon (Ps. cxxxvi. 2).

WIN'DOWS (Cant. ii. 9; Judg. v. 28; Prov. vii. 6).

WINDS, the east wind (Job i. 19); the north wind (Ecclus. xliii. 22; Prov. xxv. 23); the east northeast wind (*Euro Aquilo*), (Acts xxvii. 14); the west wind (Ex. x. 19); the south wind (Ezech. xxvii. 26; Acts xxvii. 13); a burning wind (Gen. xli. 27; Ex. x. 13; Job xxvii. 21; Jer. iv. 11; xviii. 17; Ezech. xvii. 10; xix. 12; Osee xiii. 15; Agg. ii. 18); the four winds (Ez. xxxvii. 9; xlii. 20; Dan. vii. 2; viii. 8; xi. 4; Zach. ii. 6; vi. 5; Matt. xxiv. 31; Apoc. vii. 1); the wings of the wind (2 Kings xxii. 11); the winds and the sea obey our Lord (Matt. viii. 26, 27; Mark iv. 39, 40; Luke viii. 24, 25).

WINE, first recorded to have been made by Noe (Gen. ix. 21); Jewish priests forbidden to use (Lev. x. 9); Nazarites forbidden (Num. vi. 3); Rechabites forbidden by their founder, Jonadab (Jer. xxxv. 6); cautions as to the use of wine (Prov. xx. 1; xxi. 17; xxiii. 20, 31; Ecclus. xix. 2; xxxi. 38; Joel i. 5); the use of wine in moderation not forbidden (Ecclus. xxxi. 32, 35; 2 Mach. xv. 40; John ii. 3; 1 Tim. v. 13); use of wine in the worship of God (Ex. xxix. 40; Num. xv. 5); used in the institution of the holy Eucharist (Matt. xxvi. 27; Mark xiv. 23; Luke xxii. 20; 1 Cor. xi. 25); wine of the wrath of God (Jer. xxv. 15; Apoc. xiv. 10; xvi. 19; xix. 15); wine of Libanus (Osee xiv. 8); wine which maketh virgins to spring forth (Zach. ix. 17); water changed into wine by our Lord (John ii. 1–11).

WINE-PRESS, used in crushing the grapes to make wine (Num. xviii. 27; Deut. xv. 14; xvi. 13; Judg. vi. 11; vii. 25; 4 Kings vi. 27; 2 Esd. xiii. 15; Job xxiv. 11); the word is used in a figurative sense (Isai. lxiii. 3; Matt. xxi. 33; Apoc. xix. 15).

WIN'TER, one of the seasons (Gen. viii. 22); a season of rain (Job xxxvii. 6); its departure (Cant.

WINE-PRESS.

ii. 11); our Lord directs his disciples to pray that their flight from Jerusalem be not in winter (Matt. xxiv. 20; Mark xiii. 18).

WIS'DOM, one of the canonical books of the Old Testament, written by Jesus, the son of Sirach (Wis.)

WIS'DOM. Divine wisdom, its origin, properties (Deut. iv. 6; xxxiv. 9; Job xxviii. 20; xxxii. 7; Eccles. vii. 12; ix. 13; Wis. vi., vii., viii., ix., x., xi., xii.; Ecclus. i., iii.; iv. 12, 29; xxi. 13; xxiv.; xxxix. 1–14; Luke xxi. 15; Rom. x. 33; 1 Cor. i. 17; ii. 6, 10; iii. 19; Col. ii. 3; James i. 5; iii. 15); human wisdom rejected by God (1 Cor. i. 19); Jesus Christ our wisdom (1 Cor. i. 30); the wisdom of the philosophers exposed by St. Paul in the crimes they perpetrated (Rom. i. 21–24; iii.); wisdom granted to Solomon to other gifts (3 Kings iii.); our faith not to rest on human wisdom, but on the power of God (1 Cor. ii. 5); the foolishness of God is wiser than man (1 Cor. i. 25); the wisdom of the flesh is an enemy of God (Rom. viii. 7).

WISE MEN came from the East to Jerusalem when Jesus was born in Bethlehem (Matt. ii. 1); saying that they had seen his star in the East, and had come to adore him (2); Herod inquired the time of the appearing of the star (7); and sent them to Bethlehem, as the chief priests and scribes said that Christ was to be born there (3, 4); the star went before them till it stood over where the child was, they entered and adored him, offering gifts (9–11); warned in sleep they returned to their country by another way (12).

WITCH OF ENDOR, evokes Samuel by order of Saul (1 Kings xxviii. 15; Ecclus. xlvi. 23); a pythonical girl delivered from the devil by St. Paul (Acts xvi. 18).

WIT'NESS. False witness forbidden (Ex. xx. 16; Prov. vi. 16, 19; xix. 5, 9, 28; xxi. 28; xxv. 18).

WIT'NESSES. Two witnesses required (Num. xxxv. 30; Deut. xvii. 6; xix. 15; Matt. xviii. 16; 2 Cor. xiii. 1; 1 Tim. v. 19).

WIZ'ARD. The Jews forbidden to go aside after wizards (Lev. xix. 31).

WO. Why God menaces men and kingdoms with wo (Joel i. 15; Amos v. 18; Apoc. viii. 13; wo to Moab (Num. xxi. 29; Jer. xlviii.); wo to him that is alone (Eccles. iv. 10); wo to the land whose king is a child (Eccles. x. 16); wo to the Jews, the sinful nation (Ecclus. xli. 11; Isai. i. 4, 24; xvii. 12; xxiv. 16; xxix.–xxxi.; xlv. 10; Jer. xiii. 27; Ezech. ii. 9; xvi. 23; Osee vii. 13; Mich. ii. 1; Soph. ii. 5; iii. 1); wo to him who is hardened in evil (Isai. iii. 9, 11); to those who seek only to lay up goods (v. 8, 18; Amos vi. 1; Hab. ii. 6–12; Luke vi. 24); wo to him who speaks not when he should (Isai. vi. 5; 1 Cor. ix. 16); wo to unjust judges (Isai. x. 1; Jer. xxii. 13); wo to Ethiopia (Isai. xviii. 1); wo to the proud and the drunkard (xxviii. 1); wo to Sennacherib (xxxiii.); wo to pastors (Jer. xxiii.; Ezech. xxxiv. 2); to false prophets (Ezech. xiii. 3, 18; Jude 11); wo to Egypt (Ezech. xxx.); wo to Ninive (Nah. iii. 1); wo to the double heart (Ecclus. ii. 14); wo to impenitent cities (Matt. xi. 21); wo to him who gives scandal (xviii. 7); wo to the world on account of scandal (xviii. 7); wo to the scribes and Pharisees (xxiii. 13); wo to Babylon (Apoc. xviii. 10).

WOLF, its ferocity (Gen. xlix. 27; Ezech. xxii. 27; Hab. i. 8; Matt. vii. 15); its nocturnal habits (Jer. v. 6; Soph. iii. 3; Hab. i. 8); attacking sheep and lambs (Matt. x. 16; Luke x. 3; John x. 12); under the Messias the wolf shall lie down with the lamb (Isai. xi. 6; lxv. 25); cruel persecutors compared to wolves (Matt. x. 16; Acts xx. 29).

WOLF IN SHEEP'S CLOTHING, a well-known apologue, cited Matt. vii. 15.

WOM'AN. Eve, the first woman, formed from a rib taken from the side of Adam (Gen. ii. 22); created for him (1 Cor. xi. 9); subject to man (Gen. iii. 16; Eph. v. 22); seduced by the serpent (Gen. iii. 1–6); leads man to sin (6); under the Jewish law a woman could not make a vow without her husband's consent (Num. xxx. 13); forbidden to wear the dress of a man (Deut. xxii. 5); duties of a married woman (Tob. x. 13; 1 Cor. vii.; 1 Tim. iii. 11; v. 10; Tit. ii. 3, 4); her modesty elevates her in glory (Prov. xi. 16); vigilance renders her the crown of her husband (xii. 4); woman to have her head covered in prayer (1 Cor. xi. 5); to listen in silence (1 Tim. ii. 11); captive women and strange women sent away (1 Esd. x.)

WOM'AN (individuals), a woman condemned to have her hand cut off (Deut. xxv. 11); a wise woman saves Abela, and causes Seba to be beheaded (2 Kings xx. 16–22); Respha watches the bodies of her sons (2 Kings xxi. 8, 10); Debbora judges Israel and defeats Sisara (Judges iv.); Jahel, wife of Haber, kills Sisara with a nail (iv. 21); Abimelech killed by a woman (ix. 53); Judith slays Holofernes (Judith xiii. 10); Esther saves the Jewish nation (Esth.); women endowed with the spirit of prophecy: Mary, sister of Aaron (Ex. xv. 20); Holda (4 Kings xxii. 14); Anna (Luke ii. 36); the daughters of St. Philip (Acts xxi. 9); our Lord converts the Samaritan woman (John iv. 7); cures the daughter of the Syrophœnician woman (Mark vii. 26); the woman with the issue of blood (Matt. ix. 20); pardons the sinful woman (Luke vii. 48); the woman taken in adultery (John viii. 11). Woman in visions: woman seated in the midst of a vessel (Zach. v. 7); woman pursued by a dragon (Apoc. xii. 13); woman seated on a beast (xvii. 3).

WON'DERFUL WORKS OF GOD (Acts ii. 11; 1 Paral. xvi. 12; Tob. xii. 20, 22; Job xxxvii. 14; Ps. xxxix. 6; cxliv. 5).

WON'DERS, miracles (Ex. iii. 20; xv. 11; Jos. iii. 5; Judg. xiii. 19; 1 Paral. xvi. 9, 12, 24; 2 Esd. ix. 17; Ps. lxxxviii. 6, etc.; Dan. vi. 27; xiv. 42; Matt. xxi. 15; Luke v. 26; Mark xiii. 22; John iv. 48).

WORD. Jesus Christ, the Word of the Father, made flesh (John i. 14).

WORD OF GOD. We should always have it before our eyes (Deut. iv. 1; vi. 6, 17; xi. 18; Num. xv. 39; Ps. i. 2; Prov. iii. 1; iv. 1; vi. 20; vii. 1); we are not to depart from the Word of God (Deut. v. 32; xxviii. 1; Jos. i. 7; xxiii. 6; Prov. iv. 27; Isai. xxx. 21); the Word of God to be heard and practised (Deut. v. 1, 27; vi. 1; xxxi. 12; Isai. xxix. 13; Ezech. xxxiii. 31; Matt. v. 19; vii. 24; xv. 8; xix. 20; Luke vi. 47; xi. 28; xii. 47; John xiii. 17; Heb. iv. 2; James i. 22); contempt of the Word of God punished (3 Kings xiv. 10; 4 Kings xvii. 14, 19; 2 Paral. xxx. 6, 10; xxxvi. 15; Prov. i. 24, 28; xxviii. 9; Isai. xxviii. 14; xxx. 9, 14; lxv. 11; lxvi. 4; Jer. ii. 5; v. 12, 22; vii. 13; xvi. 9; xix.; xxv. 4; Ezech. xxxiii. 31; Matt. x. 14; xi. 20; Luke x. 10; Acts xiii. 45; xvii. 6; Rom. i. 20, 32; 2 Thess. ii. 10; Heb. ii. 3); the word of God remains forever (Num. xxiii. 19; Tob. xiv. 6; Ps. xxxii. 11; cxvi. 2; cxviii. 89; Isai. xl. 8; li. 6; liv. 10; Matt. v. 18; xxiv. 35; Mark xiii. 31; Luke xvi. 17; xxi. 32; 1 Pet. i. 25); its efficacy (Gen. i.; Ps. xxxii. 9; Job xxxviii. 11; Isai. xxvi. 12; lv. 11; Matt. viii. 13, 26; Mark i. 27; Luke v. 13, 24; viii. 24; xviii. 42); the word of God is the nourishment of the soul (Deut. viii. 3; Wis. xvi. 26; Jer. xv. 16; Ezech. iii. 3; Matt. iv. 4; Luke iv. 4); the word of God is precious (1 Kings

iii. 1; Ps. xviii. 11; Prov. iii. 15; Wis. vii. 9); compared to a sword (Isai. xi. 4; xxvii. 1; xxxi. 8; xlix. 2; lxvi. 16; Eph. vi. 17; Heb. iv. 12; Apoc. i. 16; xix. 15).

WORK'MEN, appointed by God himself for the construction of the tabernacle (Ex. xxxv. 30, 34); inspiration given them (31, 35); special laws for the payment of workmen (Deut. xxiv. 14; 3 Kings v. 6; Tob. iv. 15).

WORKS. Good works have merit, and will be rewarded (Gen. iv. 7; Ps. cxviii. 112; Prov. xi. 18; Ecclus. xxxvi. 18; li. 30, 38; Matt. v. 12; x. 42; xvi. 27; xxv. 34; Rom. ii. 6; 1 Cor. xv. 29; 2 Cor. v. 10; 2 Tim. iv. 8; Heb. vi. 10; x. 35; xi. 26; James ii. 24; Apoc. xx. 13; xxii. 7); good works agreeable to God and merit reward (Gen. iv. 4, 7; v. 24; vi. 8, 9; xix. 20, 21; xx. 7; xxii. 16; xxvi. 4, 5; xxix. 32; Ex. i. 20; xx., xxiii. 22, 25; Lev. xi. 43–45); it is not forbidden to do good works for the sake of the reward (Ps. cxviii. 112; Matt. v. 12; 2 Tim. iv. 8; Heb. xi. 26); man does not sin in all his works (2 Pet. i. 10; 1 John iii. 6, 9; v. 18); God regards as done to himself the good works done to our neighbor (Isai. xxxvii. 23; Jer. i. 19); evil works displease God, and deserve punishment (Gen. iii. 11; iv. 7; vi. 3–6; vii. 4; ix. 6; xi. 4; xvii. 14; xviii. 20; xix. 11, 24–26; xx. 3; xlii. 21; xliv. 16; Ex. iii. 9; vii., xii., xiv., xx., xxi., xxii.; xxxi. 13; xxxii.; Lev. xi. 44); men will be judged according to their works (Apoc. xx. 12).

WORLD created (Gen. i., ii.); overwhelmed by the deluge (vii. 21); condemned by Christ on account of its scandals (Matt. xviii. 7; John xii. 31; xv. 18; xvi. 8, 11); its end foretold by our Lord (Matt. xxiv. 29; Luke xxi. 9); the time hidden from us (Mark xiii. 32).

WORM. Manna kept over became full of worms (Ex. xvi. 20); vineyards wasted by worms as a punishment (Deut. xxviii. 39); bodies consumed by worms (Job xxi. 26; xxiv. 20; Isai. li. 8); the worm of the sinner shall not die (Is. lxvi. 24; Mark ix. 43–47; Ecclus. vii. 19); Herod devoured by worms (Acts xii. 23); worm used as a term of humility (Ps. xxi. 7; Isai. xli. 14).

WORM'WOOD. The harlot's end is as bitter as wormwood (Prov. v. 4); God threatens to feed his people with wormwood (Jerem. ix. 15; xxiii. 15; Lam. iii. 15, 19); a star called wormwood falls from heaven, and waters become wormwood (Apoc. viii. 10, 11).

WOR'SHIP OF GOD. Besides the exterior act, God requires the affection of the heart (Deut. v. 32; vi. 5; x. 12; xxvi. 16; xxviii. 47; xxx. 2; Jos. xxii. 5; 1 Kings xii. 20; Ecclus. vii. 31; Isai. xxix. 13; John iv. 23); God requires an exterior worship, adoration and service rendered to himself (Gen. iv. 3–5; viii. 20; Ex. xxiv. 5; xxv.–xxxi.; xxxvi.–xl.; Lev. i.–ix.); and forbids such adoration of false gods or idols (Ex. xx. 3–5; Deut. v. 9); or worship of himself in a form not appointed (John iv. 22).

WOR'SHIPPER. The city of Ephesus called a worshipper of Diana (Acts xix. 35).

WRANG'LING to be avoided as contrary to charity (2 Tim. ii. 24; Tit. iii. 9).

WRATH OF GOD on him that believeth not in the Son (John iii. 36).

WREST'LING, Jacob's mysterious wrestling with an angel (Gen. xxxii. 24).

WRITE, WRITING, Moses commanded to write in a book (Ex. xvii. 14); God writes the commandments on tables of stone (xxiv. 12; Deut. ix.

10); the law to be written on stone (xxvii. 8); writing on plates of lead (Job xix. 23, 24); on wood (Ez. xxxvii. 20); on writing table or tablet (Luke i. 63); an altar at Athens, on which was written: "To the Unknown God" (Acts xvii. 23); St. John commanded to write what he had seen (Apoc. i. 19); he wrote the gospel, and his testimony is true (John xxi. 24); he is commanded to write to the seven churches (Apoc. ii. 1–22); Jesus writes on the ground (John viii. 6, 8); the apostles did not write all things (John xxi. 25; 1 Cor. xi. 34; 2 Thess. ii. 14; 2 John 12; 3 John 13); the gospel written that you may believe that Jesus is the Christ, the Son of God (John xx. 31); written not with ink, but with the Spirit of the living God, on the fleshy tables of the heart (2 Cor. iii. 2).

XAN'THICUS, a month, referred to, 2 Mach. xi. 30–38.

XER'XES, king of Persia, not named, but is the fourth king spoken of in the prophecy of Daniel (Dan. xi. 2); his war against Greece (2).

YEA. Let your speech be: yea, yea (James v. 12).

YEAR, the beginning of the Jewish year (Ex. xii. 2; Lev. xxiii. 5); the months of the Jewish Ecclesiastical year, beginning in March: Nisan, Jiar, Sivan, Thammuz, Ab, Elul, Tizri, Marschebhon, Casleu, Thebet, Sebat or Sabat, Adar. Of the civil year, beginning in September: Tizri, Marschevan, Casleu, Thebet, Sebat, Adar, Nisan, Jiar, Sivan, Thammuz, Ab, Elul. Feasts of the Jewish year: Pasch, 14, 15 Nisan; Pentecost or Feast of Weeks, fifty days after the Pasch; Feast of Trumpets, 1 Tizri; Feast of Expiation, 10 Tizri; Feast of Tabernacles, 15 Tizri; Feast of Phurim or the Lots, 14, 15 Adar; Feast of the Dedication of the Temple or Encœnia, 25 Casleu.

YEAR OF JUBILEE (Lev. xxv. 10).

YES'TERDAY. A thousand years in God's sight are but as yesterday (Ps. lxxxix. 4); Jesus Christ yesterday, and to-day, and to-morrow (Heb. xiii. 8).

YOKE, used metaphorically. An iron yoke upon thy neck (Deut. xxviii. 48; Jer. xxviii. 14); used in this sense in 3 Kings xii. 4, 9–11; Isai. ix. 4; Jer. v. 5; xxviii. 11; yoke used on animals (Num. xix. 2; Deut. xxi. 3; 2 Kings xxiv. 22); in the sense of authority or law (Judg. xix. 22; 3 Kings xii. 4; 2 Paral. x.; Ecclus. li. 34; Lam. iii. 27); our Lord declares his yoke to be easy (Matt. xi. 29, 30; 1 John v. 3); in the sense of a pair of oxen (Job i. 3; xlii. 12; 1 Kings xiv. 14; Luke xiv. 19); metaphorically of marriage: Bear not the yoke with (2 Cor. vi. 14).

YOUTH. We are to serve God from our youth (Ps. lxx. 5, 17; Prov. xxii. 6; Eccles. xi. 9; xii. 1; Wis. viii. 2; Ecclus. vi. 18; xxx. 12; xlvii. 15; Matt. xix. 20; Luke xviii. 21; Lam. iii. 27; 1 Tim. iv. 14); the sins of youth (Job xiii. 26; xx. 11; Ps. xxiv. 7).

YOUNG. The young should cultivate silence (Ecclus. xxxii. 10); fortitude in young men (2 Mach. vi. 28; vii.); young men to be subject to the ancients (1 Pet. v. 5); St. John expressly addresses young men (1 John ii. 13).

ZABADI'A, son of Asael, grand-nephew of David, and one of his generals (1 Paral. xxvii. 7).

ZABADE'ANS, an Arabian tribe defeated by Jonathan Machabeus (1 Mach. xii. 31).

ZAB'DI, grandfather of Achan (Jos. vii. 17, 18). In many Catholic Bibles there is an omission here.

ZAB'DIEL, father of one of David's champions (1 Paral. xxvi. 2).

ZAB'DIEL, leads back some from the captivity (2 Esd. ii. 14).

ZAB'DIEL, the Arabian, killed Alexander Bales, who had fled to him for protection, and sent his head to Ptolemee Philometor, king of Egypt (1 Mach. xi. 17).

ZAB'UD, son of Nathan, an officer of king Solomon (3 Kings iv. 5).

ZAB'ULON, sixth son of Jacob and Lia, born 1748 B. C. (Gen. xxx. 20; 1 Paral. ii. 1); his sons were Sared, Elon, and Jahelel (Gen. xlvi. 14); Jacob blessing him before his death said: "Zabulon shall dwell on the sea-shore, and in the road of ships, reaching as far as Sidon (Gen. xlix. 13).

ZAB'ULON, tribe of, descended from Zabulon. When it left Egypt its prince was Eliab, son of Helon (Num. i. 9; ii. 7; x. 16); and it numbered 57,400 men able to go to war (i. 31); they formed part of the camp of Juda, on the east side (ii. 7, 8); their offerings for the tabernacle (vii. 24–29); its representative among those sent to view the Promised Land, was Geddiel, son of Sodi (xiii. 11); in the census at Settim they numbered 60,500 (xxvi. 26, 27); Elisaphan was chosen for Zabulon, to divide the land (xxxiv. 25); it was one of the tribes that stood on Hebal to curse (Deut. xxvii. 13); in blessing the tribes Moses said: "Rejoice, O Zabulon, in thy going out" (xxxiii. 18); in dividing the third lot fell to Zabulon (Jos. xix. 10–16); it destroyed not the inhabitants of Cetron and Naalol (Judg. i. 30); they, with the tribe of Nephthali, under Barac, defeated Sisara (iv. 6–22); it furnished leaders of the army (v. 14); respond to the call of Gedeon (vi. 35); Ahialon, one of the judges, was of Zabulon (xii. 11, 12); fifty thousand join David's army (1 Paral. xii. 33); revolt from Roboam to form kingdom of Israel (3 Kings xii. 20); a few only went to Jerusalem to celebrate the pasch under king Ezechias (2 Paral. xxx. 10, 11); carried away captive (4 Kings xv. 29; xvii. 6).

ZAB'ULON, a city (Jos. xix. 27); Ahialon was buried there (Judg. xii. 12).

ZACHARI'AS, son of Barachias, grandson of Iddo (1 Esd. v. 1; vi. 13), one of the twelve minor prophets. He was a priest, and with Aggeus labored to restore religion after the captivity (1 Esd. vi. 14); his vision of the four horns (Zach. i. 18, 19); on Jerusalem (ii. 2); of the two candlesticks (iv. 2); of the winged book (v. 2); of the four chariots (vi. 1); of the winged woman (vii. 9); of the Messias (the Orient) (iii. 8; vi. 12; ix. 9; xiv.).

ZACHARI'AS, one of the canonical books of the Old Testament (Zach.)

ZACHARI'AS, king of Israel, succeeded his father Jeroboam II., 772 B. C. (4 Kings xiv. 29); he continued the wicked career of his predecessors, but after six months was struck publicly and killed by Sellum, who conspired against him (xv. 9); with him ended the fourth generation prophesied to the house of Jehu (12).

ZACHARI'AS, the high-priest, the son of Joiada. When Joas fell into idolatry, the Spirit of the Lord came upon Zacharias, and he publicly rebuked the people (2 Paral. xxiv. 20); Joas, unmindful of what he owed to Joiada, ordered him to be put to death (22), and he was stoned in the court of the temple (21); his dying words were: "The Lord see and require it" (22).

ZACHARI'AS, one of the princes of Ruben (1 Paral. v. 7).

ZACHARI'AS, a prince sent by king Josaphat to teach in the cities of Juda (2 Paral. xvii. 7).

ZACHARI'AS understood and saw God (2 Paral. xxvi. 5).

ZACHARI'AS, a priest next to Helcias, in the days of Josias (2 Paral. xxxv. 8).

ZACHARI'AS, son of Barachias, called by Isaias as a faithful witness (Isai. viii. 2).

ZACHARI'AS, son of Barachias, killed by the Jews between the temple and the altar (Matt. xxiii. 35; Luke xi. 51). There is much uncertainty as to the person intended, whether the prophet or the one mentioned by Isaias, while many think him to be the son of Joiada.

ZACH'ARY, priest of the course of Abia, husband of St. Elizabeth, and father of St. John the Baptist (Luke i. 5); while offering incense in the temple, the angel Gabriel announced to him that he was to have a son, to be named John, who was to go before the Lord in the spirit of Elias (9–18); he was struck dumb for his incredulity (18–22); on writing his name John he recovered his speech (63, 64), and uttered the canticle *Benedictus* (68–79).

ZACH'EUS, a corrupt officer of Judas Machabeus (2 Mach. x. 19).

ZACH'EUS, a rich man, chief of the publicans at Jericho (Luke xix. 1, 2); being short, but anxious to see our Lord, he climbed a tree. Our Lord bade him come down, as he would abide with him (3–6); some murmured, but Zacheus promised half his goods to the poor, and full restitution to all whom he had wronged (8); our Lord declared that salvation had come to his house (9).

ZAM'BRI, son of Salu, and prince of the tribe of Simeon, slain by Phinees the priest, while sinning with Cozbi, a Madianite (Num. xxv. 14).

ZAM'BRI, captain of half the horsemen of Ela, king of Israel, killed that monarch while drunk in the house of Arsa, governor of Thersa, 930 B. C. (3 Kings xvi. 10; 4 Kings ix. 31); he reigned only seven days (3 Kings xvi. 15); the army at Gebbethon made Amri king, and Zambri, besieged in Thersa, burnt himself in the palace (16–18).

ZAM'BRI, a country mentioned by Jeremias in connexion with Persia and Media (Jer. xxv. 25).

ZAM'RAM, oldest son of Abraham by Cetura (Gen. xxv. 2).

ZANO'E, a city of Juda (Jos. xv.; 2 Esd. iii.)

ZA'RA, grandson of Esau (Gen. xxxvi. 13).

ZA'RA, son of Juda (Gen. xxxviii. 28, 30).

ZA'RA, son of Simeon (Num. xxvi. 13).

ZA'RA, king of Ethiopia (2 Paral. xiv. 9); he attacked Asa, king of Juda, with an army of a million men, but was utterly defeated in the vale of Sophata, near Maresa, 941 B. C. (2 Paral. xiv. 9–15).

ZA'RED, a torrent (Num. xxi. 12).

ZA'RES, wife of Aman, advised her husband to put Mardochai to death (Esth. v. 10, 14).

ZEAL of the sons of Jacob to avenge the deflowering of their sister Dina (Gen. xxxiv. 2, 25, 27); of Moses against the worshippers of the golden calf (Ex. xxxii. 19, 27); of Phinees, against immorality (Num. xxv. 7); of the tribes of Israel, occasioned by the wrong done the Levite (Judg. xx.); of Saul against the Ammonites (1 Kings xi. 6); of Samuel against Saul (xv. 32); of Elias against the prophets of Baal (3 Kings xviii. 40); of Elias against Israel (xix. 10); of Jehu against the house of Achab and the worshippers of Baal (4 Kings x.); of Mathathias (1 Mach. ii. 24); of our Lord against those who profaned the temple (Matt. xxi. 12).

ZEB and OREB, princes of Madian, taken by the tribe of Ephraim, and put to death, Zeb in the press of Zeb, and Oreb in the rock of Oreb (Judg. vii. 24, 25).

ZEB'EDEE, husband of Salome, and father of the apostle St. James and St. John (Matt. iv. 21; x. 3; xx. 20; xxvi. 37; xxvii. 56; Mark x. 35; Luke v. 10; John xxi. 2).

ZEB'EE, king of the Madianites. He and Salmana opposed Gedeon (Jos. viii. 5–10); fled and are pursued (12); they had slain Gedeon's brothers on Thabor (18); he slew them (21).

ZEB'IDA, mother of Joachim, king of Juda. She

ZEL'PHA, hand-maid of Lia, given to Jacob by Lia, and bears him Gad and Aser (Gen. xxx. 9–13; xlvi. 16–18).

ZE'NAS, a lawyer and disciple of St. Paul. The apostle asks Titus to send Zenas to him (Tit. iii. 13).

ZEPHRO'NA, a city north of the Promised Land (Num. xxxiv. 9).

ZETHU'A, leads back 940 Jews from the captivity (1 Esd. ii. 8).

ZI'O, second month of the Jewish Ecclesiastical year (3 Kings vi. 1).

ZORO'BABEL, son of Salathiel, of the royal race of David (2 Esd. xii. 1; Matt. i. 13; Luke iii. 27); or he may have been the son of Phadaia (1 Paral. iii. 19); and grandson of Salathiel. Cyrus delivered to him the sacred vessels of the temple (1 Esd. i. 11); and he was prince of those who returned (ii. 2; iii. 8; v. 2); he laid the foundations of the temple (1 Esd. iii. 8, 9; Zach. iv. 9); and restored the worship of God, and the accustomed sacrifices. After the interruption of the work the prophets Aggeus and Zacharius were inspired to encourage Zoro-

THE ANGELS OF THE APOCALYPSE WITH THE VIALS.

was daughter to Phadaia, of Ruma (4 Kings xxiii. 36).

ZE'BUL, made governor of Sichem, by Abimelech (Judges ix. 28); he informed Abimelech of Gaal's revolt (31) and drove Gaal out of the city (41).

ZECH'RI, a powerful man of the tribe of Ephraim, under Phacee, king of Israel, slew Maasias, son of Achaz, king of Juda, with Ezrica, governor of the palace, and Elcana, who was next to the king (2 Paral. xxviii. 7).

ZELO'TES or **CANANEUS,** a surname of the apostle St. Simon (Luke vi. 15; Acts i. 13).

ZIPH, a city in the tribe of Juda (Jos. xv. 24); apparently named after Ziph, son of Jalaleel (1 Paral. iv. 16).

ZI'ZA, son of Roboam, king of Juda, by Maacha (2 Paral. xi. 20).

ZO'HELETH. Adonias gave a banquet at the stone of Zoheleth, near the fountain Rogel (3 Kings i. 9).

ZOMZOMIM, ancient gigantic inhabitants of the country of the Ammonites (Deut. ii. 20).

ZO'OM, son of Roboam by Abihail, daughter of Eliab (2 Paral. xi. 19).

babel to continue the work (Agg. i. 1; ii. 3; Zach. iv. 6, 7; 1 Esd. v. 1–3); Zacharias had a vision of two olive trees by the golden candlestick, supplying the lamps with oil, and was told by the angel that they were Zorobabel and the high-priest Jesus (Zach. iv. 6–8). Zorobabel had seven sons, Mosollam, Hananias, Hasaba, Ohol, Barachias, Hasadias, and Josabhesed, and one daughter, Salomith (1 Paral. iii. 19); one of these sons is called by St. Matthew Abiud (Matt. i. 13); and by St. Luke, Resa (iii. 27).

ZU'ZIM, giants beyond the Jordan conquered by Chodorlahomor (Gen. xiv. 5).

A COMPREHENSIVE HISTORY

OF THE BOOKS OF

THE HOLY CATHOLIC BIBLE,

WRITTEN EXPRESSLY FOR THIS EDITION

BY

REV. BERNARD O'REILLY, L. D. (LAVAL.)

AUTHOR OF "HEROIC WOMEN OF THE BIBLE AND THE CHURCH," "A LIFE OF PIUS IX.," "THE MIRROR OF TRUE WOMANHOOD,"
"TRUE MEN AS WE NEED THEM," ETC., ETC.

The Whole Beautifully Illustrated with Appropriate and Select Scripture Subjects.

INTRODUCTORY.

MOST dear to the hearts of children in a family blessed with the best of parents and brought up to the practice of all that is most ennobling, is every monument of the dead or absent father's love.

Were it so to happen that such a father, whose whole life had been one of self-sacrifice and incomparable devotion to the interest of his dear ones, should bequeath them in dying, not only a share forever in his wealth and honor, but his last will and testament to be kept continually before their eyes in the home he had created for them—how would they not reverence this ever-present memorial of their worshipped parent's loving care? How would they not, in perusing every line and word of this last declaration of a father's tender forethought, find their own hearts moved by its undying eloquence—as if a hidden fire lived in each word to warn their own souls to gratitude, to generosity, and to all nobleness of life? This is precisely what we have in that Book of books, the BIBLE.* What we know of God's dealings with man proves Him to be much more of the parent than of the lord and master. Indeed when the Son came down in person to redeem and to teach the world, He taught us to call the Infinite God, with whom He is eternally one in the unity of the Godhead, by the sweet and endearing name of FATHER.

This was only restoring the supernatural relation which existed between God and man from the beginning of the latter's creation. For it is a doctrine of the Catholic faith, that Adam was raised by his all-bountiful Creator to the divine rank of adopted child of God. This rank with its privileges and prospective glory Adam forfeited by his sin; and this rank Christ, the Second Adam, restored to us, thus repairing the ruin caused by our first parent.

And because the Heavenly Father's purpose was, from the beginning, to raise us all up in Christ to the dignity from which we had fallen in Adam, therefore His wisdom provided means by which Adam and his descendants could still recover a claim to their lost rank and inheritance. A Saviour was promised them in Christ;

and they were required to believe in that Saviour, to hold fast to that promise, to profess that faith openly, and fulfil all the other conditions required by their Divine Benefactor as distinguishing those who were to have a share with the future Redeemer and Restorer.

This new covenant or testament, made by our merciful Father between Himself and Adam with his posterity, was preserved and cherished among the descendants of Seth, who were, in view of their living faith in the one true God and the promised Saviour, called ' the Sons of God " in the midst of a sinful world. It was this same living faith that saved Noe and his sons from the flood which swept their guilty brethren off the face of the earth. And when they came forth from the Ark, or ship, in which the hand of God had guarded them, their Preserver renewed His covenant with them, and once more enjoined, with increased solemnity, the duty of holding on invincibly to the Faith of Adam, of Abel, of Seth, and of Henoch.

When, in the course of time, the great bulk of mankind, now spread over the earth, forgot God and the faith in His most merciful Promise, Abraham was raised up as Noe had been to keep that faith alive in his family and descendants. To that family, become a people—God's own chosen people—the covenant was renewed more solemnly than ever before on Mount Sinai; and Moses, the deliverer and guide of that people, was inspired to write, for the instruction of all future time, the story of the creation of the world, of man's origin, of his elevation and fall, and of the Promise thus successively committed, like God's will and testament, to Adam, to Seth, to Noe, to Abraham, and to Moses in behalf of our fallen and disinherited race.

To the five books (Pentateuch) left us by Moses others were added age after age, completing the story of God's dealings with mankind, till God's own Son at length came down on earth, uniting our human nature with His Godhead, and to all who receive him as their Redeemer He giveth " power to be made the Sons of God."

Of Him—the Saviour, the Promised One—the Old Testament is full as well as the New. What wonder, then, seeing that God's faithful servants under the law of nature, and God's chosen people under the Mosaic law, were alike, upon earth, the Family of the Almighty Father—what wonder, if in that family, men and women, generation after generation, loved to make of the Sacred Scriptures the subject of devout and most profitable meditation?

Before the coming of Christ, how believing and yearning souls were wont to weigh the words of the oft-repeated Promise, and to

---

* The word "bible" is of Greek origin. The Egyptian reed papyrus (ancient Egyptian *papu*) was called βίβλος, *byblos*, by the Greeks, and from its innermost bark or cuticle, covering the pith, was made the papyrus or paper which, when written upon, was denominated βίβλος. A bundle of these scrolls was given the name of βιβλίον—and the nominative plural βιβλία, was adopted by the Latins, and employed to designate what we now call the BIBLE, that is, the collection of inspired books of both the Old and the New Testaments.

(1)

feed their hopes upon the study of the succession of events which, each as it happened, foreshadowed His redemption, and made the heart, sick with the spectacle of contemporary degeneracy, look forward to the establishment of the Kingdom of God, to His sweet sovereign sway over the spirits and lives of all men !

And since His coming and His return to Heaven, how earnestly do His followers the whole world over bathe their souls in the light of that everlasting glory into which He has entered to prepare us a place, and the ravishing perspectives of which lift man heavenward and enable him to bear every most bitter trial, to undertake the most arduous labor, and to fulfil the most painful sacrifices in view of the eternal reward and of the Infinite Love which bestows it !

In the immense Christian family, spread all over the earth, there is not a household in which "the words of eternal life" (St. John vi. 69) do not thus furnish sweetest food to the souls of young and old. For it is most sweet for enlightened and pious Christian parents to select from the Prophetical Books of the Old Testament the passages in which, so many centuries in advance, the Holy Spirit had prompted the inspired writers to describe the manner of Christ's coming, His sacred person, the labors, persecutions and death by which He was to redeem the world ; His miracles, His wisdom, and the immortal society He was to found. It is still, as it ever has been, most sweet to contemplate in the mighty events recorded in the Historical Books, the types of the great realities to be accomplished in the life of Christ, or in that of His church. Even the personages whose characters and deeds are recorded therein, when viewed with the eye of faith, all seem to point to Christ, whom they resemble in many wondrous ways, while still preserving their own identity, their own littlenesses and weaknesses.

Nor is it less delightful and refreshing to the soul to take up any one of the merely didactic or moral Books. Job still teaches the world and stirs the soul of every reader from amid the ruins of his home and the utter wreck of all his greatness and prosperity. Solomon still instructs princes and peoples, the highest and the lowliest, in the pregnant works which reflect his wisdom, and contain the manifold lessons of his long experience, of his days of innocence and wide-spread earthly dominion, and of his maturer years obscured by ingratitude to God, by boundless sensuality, and that worship of self which so easily leads to the worst forms of heathenish idolatry.

The author of Ecclesiasticus, Jesus, the son of Sirach, sings a hymn in praise of all the virtues, private and public, most dear to the heart of God, and sets before us, in succession, the images of the godlike men, who, since Adam, have glorified the Creator of mankind as well as human nature itself.

But sweeter than all the other inspired writers of the Old Law is the King-Prophet, David, the ancestor of Mary and her Divine Son, "the sweet singer of Israel." The church, spread all over the earth, uses his Psalms of prayer and praise in her solemn offices ; and her children, in their private devotions, ever find in these heart-cries of the much-tried David the very sentiments and words most suited to their needs in good and ill fortune, in trial and in temptation.

And so has the word of God, coming to us through the inspired books of the Old Testament, borne to every household, and to every soul within it, both during our darkest and during our sunniest days, comfort and peace, light, and warmth, and unfailing strength from the all-loving heart of our Father in Heaven !

But, oh, what shall we say of the books of the New Testament ? Of the Gospels, which set before us the simple and soul-stirring narrative of Christ's incarnation, birth, labors, miracles, sufferings and death ? Of the Acts of the Apostles, relating the birth of Christ's Church, and the struggles, sufferings, labors and triumphs of His two chief apostles, Peter and Paul ? And finally, of the other divinely beautiful instructions left to the Christian

world by these same Apostles, its glorious parents under God, the fathers of the new "people of God," to be made up of all the tribes of earth gathered together and held in the bonds of a true brotherhood by the one faith in Christ and the all-pervading love of the Father ?

Do not all remember, we children of Christian parents, how we hung in childhood and youth on the lips of father and mother as they read to us the sublime story of Christ's life and death ? how we fancied ourselves to be kneeling with the Shepherds around His crib, or travelling with Him and His parents across the desert to Egypt and back again to Nazareth ? How we loved to behold Him in imagination as He grew up in the carpenter's shop—the lovely child, the graceful and modest youth, the son lovingly obedient to Mary and Joseph during all these years of obscure toil and patient preparation for His great missionary work ? And then how we followed the Mighty Teacher, during the three years of His public life, as He ran His giant race—preaching, healing, enlightening the whole land as with the steady, but brief splendors of a heaven-sent meteor, till the young life was quenched amid the dark and shameful scenes of Calvary ?

Have we not, in our turn, read to our dear parents in their hour of darkness and trial—in poverty, or sickness, or when the shadow of death was over the home—some one sweet passage, more pregnant with heavenly light and consolation than the others, which made once more sunshine in their souls, which lifted up the fainting heart, which filled the spirit of our sorely-tried dear ones with renewed hopes and strength to do and to endure, which enabled them to bear the bitter pang of present losses in view of the eternal reward—or which made the passage from this life to the next bright, lightsome, joyous and exultant, like the blessed bridals of the children of God ?

And see how wonderfully that all-wise Providence, which clearly seeing things from end to end ordereth all things sweetly and surely, has taken means for preserving these sacred writings amid the rise and fall of kingdoms and empires, amid the revolutions, the destruction and the decay, which lift one hitherto obscure or barbarous race into power and long rule, while other races, till then prosperous, irresistible and enlightened, disappear forever from history.

Here we have, at this very moment, the same Hebrew descendants of Abraham, to whom Moses committed, with the Tables of the Law delivered on Sinai, the Pentateuch or five volumes written by himself, subsisting in our midst, clinging to their ancient faith with heroic tenacity, and cherishing not only the five books of Moses, but what they conceive to be the original Hebrew Scriptures with a religious fervor that will tolerate no change in substance or in letter.

Have we often reflected on the miraculous co-existence, side by side, and in every part of the globe, of the children of the Synagogue and of those of the Church—the former bearing undying testimony to the divinity of the Old Testament Scriptures—the latter vouching for the authority of the New ? Only think of the singular phenomenon which the presence of Abrahamite Hebrews amid the peoples of Christendom offers to the historian and philosopher ! They remain distinct from all other peoples while living among them ; mingling with Europeans, Africans, Asiatics and Americans in every walk of life and field of industry, and yet preserving their own national characteristics and physical type as clearly and persistently as they preserve their ancient religious faith and time-honored customs. In the tents of the Mohammedan Bedaween they protest against the monstrous reveries of the Coran and the pretensions of the Arabian visionary ; amid the crowded cities of China and India they uphold, as against idolatry, the doctrine of the one living God ; and in our midst, in the temple of Christian civilization, they bear witness unceasingly to the divinity of the Old Testament Scriptures.

and to the abiding faith of their ancestors and themselves in the promised Redeemer.

The conquering and widely dominating races of Babylon, Nineveh, Persia, and Egypt have utterly disappeared from the face of the earth. We can dig up from the Mesopotamian plains gigantic statues—the ornaments of palaces and temples contemporary with Heber and Abraham—and we discover far beneath the surface of the ruin-strewed earth whole chambers crowded with inscribed bricks and cylinders, the fragmentary annals of kingdoms grown old before Rome had been founded. But the wild nomadic tribes who aid the discoverer in his researches are not the descendants of the mighty races who ruled there upward of three thousand years ago. These have left upon earth no lineal heirs to the land, to its ruins, or to its glories.

So is it with Egypt. Modern curiosity and modern science have found their way into the very heart of the Pyramids, and rifled the tombs of the monarchs who built them; we have penetrated the deepest cave-sepulchres of the Valley of Kings at Thebes the Magnificent and Incomparable. But the sordid Arab and ignorant Fellah, who serve as guides and workmen to the explorer, have no thought of claiming descent from or kinship with the ancient people who inhabited the Nile Valley in its days of surpassing glory.

The descendants of Joseph and Aaron do, indeed, still live and thrive amid the modern cities along the shores of the great river; but of the warlike people who went forth under the Pharaohs to enslave the surrounding nations, no trace is left save in the tombs where the mummies of princes, priests, and warriors have slept for three thousand years beside the remains of the dumb animals they had, in life, worshiped in place of the living God!

Even so is it in the once imperial Rome. Not even the proudest of her living nobles, much less the lower and middle classes of her actual population, can establish any claim to direct descent from the families who dwelt there under the consuls or under the emperors.

Thus, in every civilized country beneath the sun, and every day on which that sun rises, we have these two immortal societies standing before us, side by side—the Jewish synagogue and the Catholic Church—and presenting to us the Old and the New Testaments as the Revealed Will of the one true and living God who is the Creator and the Judge of the whole race of man. For the divinity of the Old Testament Scriptures and the faith in the Promised Messiah the Jewish race has borne unfaltering and heroic witness for three thousand years; to the divinity of the New Testament and the fulfillment of all these promises in the person of Christ Jesus the Catholic Church has borne her witness during eighteen centuries. And this twofold testimony fills all historic time with a light as self-evident as the radiance of the noonday sun. What a spectacle to the religious mind! What a consolation to the Christian who sets more store on the promises of the eternal life and the glories of Christ's everlasting kingdom than on all the greatness and the glories, the possessions and the enjoyments of time!

THE OLD TESTAMENT.

Of the inspired writings thus committed to the care of the people of God before the birth of Christ the first in importance, as well as in the order of time, are five books of Moses, therefore called THE PENTATEUCH * or THE LAW. Then come the historical books, comprising: *Josue, Judges, Ruth*, the four *Books of Kings*, first and second *Paralipomenon*, first and second *Esdras*, first and second *Machabees*, together with *Tobias, Judith*, and *Esther*. Next in order are the doctrinal or didactic books: *Psalms, Job, Proverbs, Ecclesiastes, Canticle of Canticles, Wisdom*, and *Ecclesiasticus*. Lastly we have the prophetical books, which are subdivided into the greater and the lesser prophets.

---

* From the Greek word τεῦχος, a vessel. The designation arose, most probably, from the fact that the ancient manuscripts or rolls of writing were placed in cylinders or vessels when not in use.

Anciently the Jews divided these books into "the Law and the Prophets." Down to the time of our Lord the Jewish teachers had devised various arbitrary divisions of the Old Testament books. They were agreed in giving to the Pentateuch, or five books of Moses, the appellation of *Torah*, "the Law." But under the designation of "The Prophets" they included, together with the twelve lesser prophets and the three greater (Isaias, Jeremias, and Ezechiel), Josue, Judges, and the Four Books of Kings. Under the designation of *Hagiographa* (Hebrew, *Chetubim*, "writings") they classed all the other Scriptures of the Hebrew canon, whether historical, prophetical, didactic, or poetical.

The Jewish authors of the Greek or Septuagint version of the Old Testament deviated from this classification, giving the books of Scripture in the order which we have them both in the Latin Vulgate and in the Douay Bible.

However, as modern biblical scholars have agreed to treat of these venerable books in the more convenient order of

THE PENTATEUCH, THE HISTORICAL BOOKS, THE PROPHETS, THE POETICAL BOOKS,

We shall follow this classification in our remarks.

I. THE PENTATEUCH.

It is most probable that these "five books" formed in the original Hebrew only one volume or roll of manuscript. The present title—ἡ πεντάτευχος (βίβλος), "the fivefold book"—was bestowed on it by the Greek translators. To them also may be, in all likelihood, attributed the division of the books as each now stands, together with the Greek titles which distinguish them. In the Hebrew manuscripts the only division known was that into small sections called *parshiyoth* and *sedarim*, which had been adopted for the convenience of the public reader in the synagogue.

Of all books ever written, this fivefold book of Moses is the only one that enlightens us with infallible certainty on the origin of all things in this universe, visible and invisible; on the creation of mankind and their destinies; on their duties, during this life, toward their Almighty Creator and toward each other, and on the rewards and punishments of the eternal life hereafter.

In its first pages we see how our Divine Benefactor prepares this earth to become the blissful abode of our first parents and their descendants. We read of the compact or covenant which He makes with Adam and Eve; then comes the violation of that compact; and then the fall and banishment of the transgressors from their first delightful abode. We see the human race, divided into faithful servants of God, on the one hand, and despisers of his law, on the other, spreading themselves over the face of the globe, while wickedness goes on increasing to such a pitch that the offended Creator destroys the entire race, with the exception of one good man and his family.

With this man, Noe, and with his three sons, God once more renews the covenant made in the beginning. They are the parents of the human family as it now exists. But their descendants, counting, probably, on the long life of many centuries hitherto enjoyed by mankind as a privilege not to be taken away from themselves, soon fall into the old self-worship, the abominable sensuality, and the demon-worship begotten of pride, and following it as its sure chastisement. God, to preserve as a living faith the Promise in the Redeemer, and to secure a nation of faithful worshipers of his holy name, separates from the sinful crowd Abraham; and from his grandson, Jacob or Israel, spring the twelve patriarchs, the fathers of God's people. Of the history of this chosen race, their captivity in Egypt, their sufferings, their miraculous deliverance, the new covenant made with them by their divine Deliverer, down to the death of Moses and their arrival on the confines of the national territory reserved to them, the Pentateuch tells in detail.

It is a wonderful story. But let us glance rapidly at it, as we review in succession each of these five books.

GENESIS

THE BOOK OF GENESIS.—The Greek word which stands for title means "birth," just as the first word *bereschith* in the Hebrew text means "in the beginning." Genesis, therefore, gives us, in its first chapters, the brief and inspired history of the creation, of the birth and first beginning both of the world and of mankind. St. Paul, in his epistle to the infant church of the Colossians (i. 12–17), tells them that "the Father . . . hath made us worthy to be partakers of the lot of the saints in light. Who hath delivered us from the power of darkness, and hath translated us into the kingdom of the Son of his love, in whom we have redemption through His blood, the remission of sins; . . . for in Him were all things created in heaven and on earth, visible and invisible, whether Thrones, or Dominations, or Principalities or Powers: all things were created by Him and in Him: and He is before all, and by Him all things consist."

Before the coming of Christ the whole pagan world was plunged in darkness impenetrable concerning the origin of man and the world, and the sublime destinies appointed in Christ for Adam and his posterity in the very beginning. Christian teaching dispelled this midnight darkness and revealed to all believers both the secret of man's origin and the incomprehensible glory of his supernatural destinies. We, children of the nineteenth century of Christian civilization, being thus made "partakers of the lot of the saints in light," can find unspeakable pleasure in standing with the inspired penman at the very first beginning of God's ways, and in allowing our soul to dwell on the contemplation of his magnificence—of His infinite power and His infinite love.

According to the definition of the late general council of the Vatican, renewing the dogmatic decree of another general council also held in Rome, God in the beginning of time created—that is, brought from a state of absolute non-existence into full and complete existence—both the material universe and the world of angelic spirits. Man was only created after these.

Moreover, all things were created in and by the uncreated and eternal Son and Word of the Almighty Father, "all things . . . in heaven and on earth, visible and invisible, whether Thrones, or Dominations, or Principalities, or Powers." Thus together with the world of matter in all its inconceivable variety and magnificence was created the world of angelic spirits, in their own different orders of greatness goodness, wisdom, beauty, and loveliness—to be, in the design of their Creator and

King, associated afterward with man and his heavenly destinies. They, too—before man appeared on earth—had their own eventful history. They were created free—free to love their Divine Benefactor and to consecrate to Him in dutiful and devoted service the life and exalted powers He had given them—or free to refuse such service to the Highest.

Many chose to serve their own pride, and were forever separated from God and from the glorious abode of everlasting bliss, where He reveals His inmost being and shares His inmost life with His faithful ones. Many more yielded rapturous submission and lowly service to their most loving and magnificent Lord and Father, and they were forthwith exalted to the unchangeable possession of Himself and His Kingdom.

So, in these first verses and pages of Genesis—the Book of Origins—we are treading on abysses of revealed truth—of truth which explains to us both the world beneath and around us, and that unmeasured world which extends on all sides above and beyond our little globe, both the world we can see with the bodily eye and touch with this hand of flesh, and the unseen realities of that world far otherwise glorious, in which the Lord of Hosts Himself is the central Sun of spiritual beings innumerable, whose brightness and glory is shadowed forth dimly in the starry hosts of the firmament above our heads.

Man was made "a little less than the Angels" in natural excellence; but he was at the same time raised by the divine adoption to the supernatural rank and destiny of the Angels. He, too, was created free to choose between good and evil: between a loving submission and devoted service to his Maker, and obedience to his own weak will. Raised so high, surrounded with such lavish wealth of gifts and graces, "crowned with glory and honor, and set over the works" of God's hands here below, he too freely disobeyed and sinned, and was separated from the Most Holy God.

Not separated hopelessly and forever; for the merciful Son, whose work man was, took on Himself to expiate, in His own good time, the awful guilt of man's ingratitude and disobedience.

The promise that He would do so was deposited in the sorrowing hearts of our first parents, when they were justly banished from their beautiful abode in the earthly paradise. This is the Promise and the Hope kept alive in the long line of patriarchs extending from Abel and Seth to Abraham.

Genesis, from the end of the third chapter to its close, is but the history of this immortal Hope, and the other books of the Pentateuch do but describe the national institutions, political and religious, by and through which this Hope was to be preserved undimmed among the universal darkness of Heathendom, till the Star of Bethlehem warned Israel that the Light of the World was come.

THE BOOK OF EXODUS.—The title is a Greek word, meaning "a going out" or "departure," because its chief purpose is to describe the miraculous means by which God enabled Moses to lead the people of God out of Egypt in order that He might, in the wilderness of Mount Sinai, renew more solemnly His covenant with them, and give them such national laws and institutions as would distinguish them from all other peoples.

The sacred historian describes the wonderful increase of the descendants of Israel in the land of the Pharaohs, which had been saved from utter ruin by the genius of Joseph, Israel's youngest son. Then, after the death of the wise minister, the hatred of the idolatrous Egyptians against the worshipers of the one true God was aroused by the spectacle of the latter's wonderful increase in numbers. Egypt was full of enslaved foreign races whom their pitiless masters forced to work both in cultivating the land and in building the beautiful cities and stupendous monuments whose ruins survive to this day. To this slavery the Israelites were condemned one and all; and to check effectually their further increase—indeed, to extinguish the race altogether—the male children were ordered to be strangled at their birth.

Here comes in the story of Miriam or Mary, a little Hebrew maiden, who succeeds in saving from destruction her infant brother, ever afterward known as Moses, the most illustrious figure of our Lord, and the destined deliverer of his race. Adopted as her own son by Pharaoh's daughter, Moses is brought up amid the splendors of the Egyptian court and in all the varied learning of its schools, till he is old enough to prefer openly God's cause to the service of Pharaoh. He does not hesitate to cast his lot with his downtrodden brethren, but is repelled with unnatural ingratitude by them. After forty years of exile, he is commanded to return to "the House of Bondage," clothed with authority from on high and commissioned to lead his people forth free in spite of every obstacle.

The central fact and miracle in the book is the passage of the Red Sea—so strikingly typical of Christ's passion in Jerusalem, and of the manner in which the Cross wrought our redemption. The paschal lamb, whose blood on the Hebrew door-posts saved the believing households from the visit of the devastating angel, had its counterpart in the mystic oblation of Christ on the very eve of His death, and in the divine and ever-present reality of the commemorative sacrifice He then instituted for all coming time. "This is My Blood of the new testament which shall be shed for many unto remission of sins" (Matt. xxvi. 28), clearly points out the identity of the Victim, and of the redeeming Blood, both in the eucharistic celebration and in the fearful consummation of Calvary. The Cross was the instrument of victory used by the Redeemer in His supreme struggle; it was symbolical of the extremity of weakness and shame in the Sufferer—the Almighty Power thus shining forth in this very extremity. Even so did the aged Aaron's staff in the hand of Moses open a pathway through the waves for God's people in their dire need, and overwhelm in utter destruction Pharaoh and his pursuing hosts.

The fatal tree had been in the Garden the occasion of Adam's downfall and of the ruin of his posterity; a feeble staff in the hands of Moses works out the liberation of the chosen race and effects the destruction of their enemies: even so did our Divine Deliverer tread the Red Sea of His passion with all its abysses of shame and degradation, dividing the waves of the sanguinary multitude by His cross of ignominy, and allowing Himself to be nailed to the accursed Tree and to hang therefrom in death as the true fruit of saving Knowledge and eternal Life for the nations.

The Law afterward given to Israel on Mount Sinai, together with the detailed legislation concerning the chosen people's religion and government, all foreshadowed the more perfect Law to be given by Christ to His church and for the benefit of the whole world. Equally typical and prophetic of the sacraments and graces of the New Law were the manna, the water from the rock, the brazen serpent, and, indeed, all the incidents of the people's life during the forty years' wandering in the wilderness.

The whole of Exodus must be read in the light of the Christian revelation to be understood and appreciated.

THE BOOK OF LEVITICUS.—This book is so called because it chiefly treats of the ceremonies of divine worship to be performed under the direction of the Levites, the priestly order among the Jews. It is the detailed Ritual of the Jewish church.

It must never be forgotten, both in studying the solemn religious worship of the Jewish sanctuary and temple, and in assisting at the sacrificial service of the Christian church, that what God commanded to be done on earth is only the shadow, the preparation, and the foretaste of what takes place in the Heavenly City above, in that divinest of sanctuaries, where He receives unceasingly the worship of Angels and Saints, and in return eternally pours out on them the flood of His blissful love.

The Christian temple with its altar, its one sacrifice, its unchanging Victim, and its adorable and unfailing Presence, is but the lively image of that supernal Holy of Holies, in which the Lamb ever slain and ever immortal is the central object of praise and love and adoration (*Apocalypse*, chapters iv., v., and following). Thus the sweet and ever-abiding Presence in our tabernacles and the Communion in which in the Gift we receive the Giver, are but the foretaste and the pledge of the unchangeable union of eternity, and of that ineffable Possession destined to be the exceeding great reward of all the faithful children of God.

This blissful life of Angels and men, made perfect by charity in the City of God on high, being the END for which we are created, has, on earth, its nearest resemblance in the Church. But inasmuch as the Hebrew people of old were the forerunners of the Christian people, God so ordained it that the Jewish ritual and worship should be a preparation for the Christian liturgy.

Hence, the Mosaic sanctuary, first, and the Temple of Solomon, afterward, were, each in its turn, THE HOUSE OF GOD, in which He dwelt in the midst of His people—having, between the Cherubim of the Ark, His throne, on which He received their adorations, their hymns of praise, and their petitions, as well as His Mercy Seat for granting special favors in dire need.

Thus the Temple, the House of God, was also the house of the nation, who were God's family, just as every family dwelling in Israel was, in God's thought, and in the belief of the people, to be hallowed as God's own house and kept pure from moral evil. Wherefore, holiness in the heavenly as well as in the earthly temple, spotlessness and perfection in the principal sacrificial victims that typified the Lamb of God immaculate; purity in the pontiffs, priests, and inferior Levites who ministered at the altar, and purity also in the people who offered the victims for sacrifice or assisted at its celebration; all these are inseparably connected with the notion of worship; all these form the subject of the various ordinances of Leviticus; and all point most significantly to the far greater moral perfection and far higher purity of heart and hand required of the priests and people of the New Law, when they approach its altar.

THE BOOK OF NUMBERS.—It is so named from the double numbering or census of the Israelites mentioned, the first, in chapters i.-iv., and, the second, in chapter xxvi. It contains, moreover, the history of their wanderings in the desert, from their departure from Sinai till their arrival on the confines of their promised national territory, in the fortieth year of the Exodus. Both the census and the history are interspersed with various ordinances and prescriptions relating to the divine service and the moral purity of the nation.

Among the remarkable incidents which stand out in the narrative are: the sin and punishment of Aaron and his sister Mary (chap. xii.), and their death (chap. xx.); the prophecy of Balaam (chaps. xxii.-xxiv.); and the appointment of Josue as lieutenant to Moses.

THE BOOK OF DEUTERONOMY.—The title comes from a Greek word, meaning "a republication of the Law," because in it

Moses promulgates anew, with extraordinary solemnity, the law delivered on Mount Sinai. The adult people whom he had brought forth from "the house of bondage" had all died in the wilderness in punishment of their repeated sins and forgetfulness of the divine power and goodness shown in their deliverance. Of the "Three Deliverers," Aaron and Mary had been called to their rest; even Moses, because he had once publicly doubted the power of his good God, was not to set foot within the promised land.

The new people, who obeyed Moses as they came within sight of the beautiful country of Palestine, were nearly all born in the wilderness; they had not tasted of the bitterness of Egyptian servitude, nor had they witnessed the terrible display of Jehovah's power at the passage of the Red Sea. It was necessary, therefore, that he who, under God, had been the guide and parent of the nation in the crisis of its fate, should remind his followers of what God had done for them, and explain how truly the law which He gave them was a law of love—that the Covenant of the Most High with Israel was one pregnant with untold blessings to all who would faithfully observe it, while its violation was sure to be visited by the most awful chastisements.

Hence the Book is mainly taken up with the record of three discourses of the great Hebrew Lawgiver, delivered, all of them, in the plains of Moab, on the lofty eastern side of the Jordan, overlooking the Dead Sea. The country itself, the theatre of the most terrible vengeance of the outraged Majesty of Heaven on a favored but deeply sinning race, was eloquent of the suddenness and certainty of the divine retribution. Abraham, the father of the mighty multitude now assembled around Moses, had in his day witnessed the fate of the guilty "cities of the plain" of Jordan. A brackish sea now rolled its sullen waters where they had once stood in their beauty and pride amid all the fairest fruits of earth. Beyond and above toward the north, extended the fertile regions amid which Abraham and Sara had once tarried as pilgrims, and which had been promised as a lasting homestead to their posterity.

How well might Moses, himself about to close his earthy career, urge upon that posterity with all the fervor of a patriot and a parent the duty of being true to the God of Israel, of observing lovingly that Law which distinguished them from all the peoples of the earth, and fidelity to which should ensure them victory over every foe, with all the blessings of uninterrupted peace and prosperity!

1. The first discourse (chaps. i. to iv. 40) vividly recalls the causes for which their immediate ancestors were not allowed to take possession of the national territory. Then follows a most touching and eloquent exhortation to the perfect obedience in which their fathers had been so lamentably deficient. "And now, O Israel, hear the commandments and judgments which I teach thee: that doing them, thou mayst live, and entering in mayst possess the land which the Lord the God of your fathers will give you" (iv. 1).

There is nothing in the Old Testament more impressive or more fruitful in lessons of heroic generosity for parents and children and all who fear God, than these sublime pages, into which the dying Moses seems to have poured his great soul. "Behold, I die in this land (of Moab); I shall not pass over the Jordan: you shall pass and possess the goodly land. Beware lest thou ever forget the covenant of the Lord thy God which He hath made with thee!'' iv. 22, 23.

2. The second discourse, beginning with the fifth chapter, is, properly, the solemn and renewed promulgation of the Law. One feels the fire of divine inspiration glowing in every page of these soul-stirring chapters. "Hear, O Israel: the Lord our God is one Lord. Thou shalt love the Lord thy God with thy whole heart, and with thy whole soul, and with thy whole strength" (vi. 4, 5)! He reminds this singularly privileged people that God's severe dealings with themselves and their parents was the wise love of a father seeking to restrain the waywardness of an unruly child. "He afflicted thee with want, and gave thee manna for [thy] food, which neither thou nor thy fathers knew: to shew that not in bread alone doth man live, but in every word that proceedeth from the mouth of God. Thy raiment, with which thou wast covered, hath not decayed for age, and thy foot is not worn; lo! this is the fortieth year! That thou mayst consider in thy heart, that as a man traineth up his son, so the Lord God hath trained thee up" (viii. 3, 4, 5).

3. The third discourse (chaps. xxvii.–xxx. 20) enjoins on those who are to lead and govern the people after Moses the duty of binding the whole nation, when in possession of the land of Chanaan, to give themselves a solemn sanction to this covenant with God, by the alternate blessings on the obedient observers and curses on the transgressors, to be uttered near the grave of Joseph in the Valley of Sichem. The entire ceremonial to be observed in this memorable national solemnity is minutely detailed by the legislator.

God's grace, vouchsafed abundantly even then to His children in view of the future merits of His incarnate Son, will not fail the subjects of this law. "This commandment that I command thee this day, is not above thee, nor far off from thee. Nor is it in heaven, that thou shouldst say, 'Which of us can go up to heaven to bring it unto us, and we may hear and fulfill it in work?' Nor is it beyond the sea, that thou mayst excuse thyself and say, 'Which of us can cross the sea and bring it unto us, that we may hear and do that which is commanded?' But the word is very nigh unto thee, in thy mouth and in thy heart, that thou mayst do it. . . . I call heaven and earth to witness this day, that I have set before you life and death, blessing and cursing. Choose therefore life, that both thou and thy seed may live" (xxx. 11–19)!

There is not a family in which these inspired lessons should not still be repeated by parents to their children. The Spirit of God, who spoke by Moses, is ever near at hand to give efficacy to the dear voice of father or of mother, rehearsing these immortal teachings, and faithfully laboring to bring down on their loved ones the blessings promised by the Almighty Father, and to turn away from their homes the terrible curses sure to follow on the neglect of God and the contempt of His Law.

4. Most beautiful, too, and most touching is what is related in the concluding chapters of the parting of Moses with his people; of the sublime Canticle or hymn which he composed for them, and which is still one of the most triumphant songs of the Christian Church; of his going up to the summit of Mount Nebo to have a first and last look at the Promised Land, where it lay in all its beauty, across the Dead Sea and

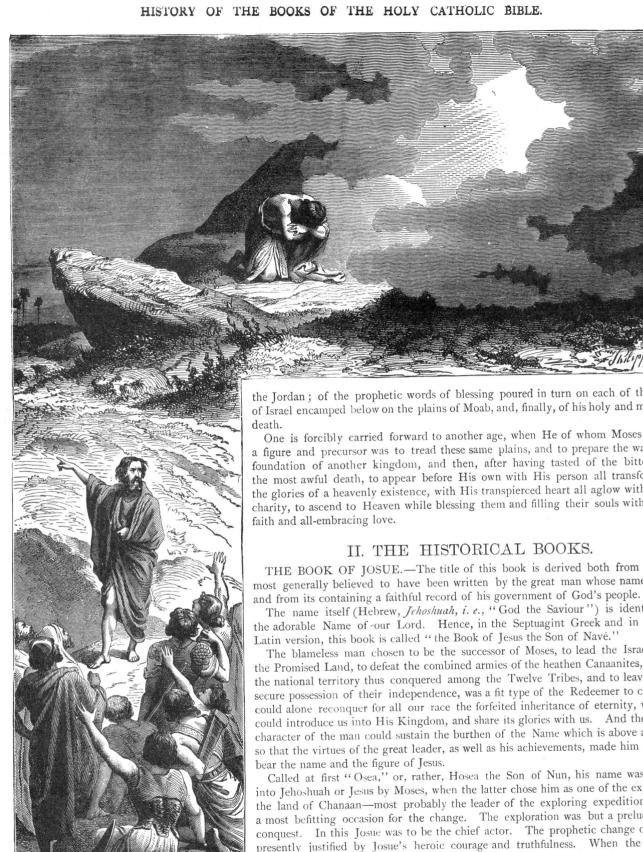

the Jordan ; of the prophetic words of blessing poured in turn on each of the Tribes of Israel encamped below on the plains of Moab, and, finally, of his holy and mysterious death.

One is forcibly carried forward to another age, when He of whom Moses was only a figure and precursor was to tread these same plains, and to prepare the way for the foundation of another kingdom, and then, after having tasted of the bitterness of the most awful death, to appear before His own with His person all transformed by the glories of a heavenly existence, with His transpierced heart all aglow with divinest charity, to ascend to Heaven while blessing them and filling their souls with undying faith and all-embracing love.

II. THE HISTORICAL BOOKS.

THE BOOK OF JOSUE.—The title of this book is derived both from its being most generally believed to have been written by the great man whose name it bears, and from its containing a faithful record of his government of God's people.

The name itself (Hebrew, *Jehoshuah*, *i. e.*, "God the Saviour") is identical with the adorable Name of our Lord. Hence, in the Septuagint Greek and in the early Latin version, this book is called "the Book of Jesus the Son of Navé."

The blameless man chosen to be the successor of Moses, to lead the Israelites into the Promised Land, to defeat the combined armies of the heathen Canaanites, to divide the national territory thus conquered among the Twelve Tribes, and to leave them in secure possession of their independence, was a fit type of the Redeemer to come, who could alone reconquer for all our race the forfeited inheritance of eternity, who alone could introduce us into His Kingdom, and share its glories with us. And the personal character of the man could sustain the burthen of the Name which is above all names, so that the virtues of the great leader, as well as his achievements, made him worthy to bear the name and the figure of Jesus.

Called at first "Osea," or, rather, Hosea the Son of Nun, his name was changed into Jehoshuah or Jesus by Moses, when the latter chose him as one of the explorers of the land of Chanaan—most probably the leader of the exploring expedition. It was a most befitting occasion for the change. The exploration was but a prelude to the conquest. In this Josue was to be the chief actor. The prophetic change of name is presently justified by Josue's heroic courage and truthfulness. When the explorers return and give the most discouraging accounts of the Chanaanites, who are to be dispossessed, of their giant stature and impregnable strongholds, the people revolt against Moses and murmur openly against the Lord Himself. Caleb and Josue, on the contrary, oppose the popular clamor and flatly contradict the exaggerations of their associates. "Be not rebellious against the Lord!" they say to the craven multitude. . . . "And fear ye not the people of this land . . . All aid is gone from them. The Lord is with us ; fear ye not !" The two heroic leaders would have been stoned on the spot had not God then and there saved them by a miracle.

Well worthy, therefore, of the attentive and devout perusal of all Christian families

are the inspired pages in which Josue relates how he crossed the Jordan at the head
of the embattled Tribes—God's Ark and the priestly bands leading the way, while th
waters of Jordan stood still.   Then the half-peaceful, half-military processions aroun
the walls of Jericho (chap. vi.); the terrible punishment of the avaricious and hypo
critical Achan (vii.); the utter extermination of a people given body and soul to th
abominable idolatry of which even modern science is ashamed, and the purification b
fire of the very site of the polluted cities; the sublime scene offered in the beautifu
vale of Sichem by the victorious Israelites, when they solemnly dedicate themselves t
Jehovah (viii.); the miraculous prolongation of daylight to enable Josue to comple
his victory over God's enemies:

"Move not, O Sun, toward Gabaon!
Nor thou, O Moon, toward the valley of Ajalon!"

In seven years Josue completed the work of conquest.   "And the land rested fro
the wars."   Then the venerable chief of God's people enters upon the more difficu
task of allotting to each tribe a portion of the national territory.   Here occurs a hero
incident deserving of everlasting remembrance.   Caleb demands that Hebron and i
territory be allotted to him in fulfillment of a previous promise made by God throug
Moses, and because the city itself and the mountainous district around it were then th
abode of a race of gigantic warriors (*Anakim* or *Enachim*), giants not only in statu
but in wickedness.   He takes on himself and his sons the task of driving out this ev
brood, three tribes or families of whom held the place and seemed to render it impre
nable.   "Give me therefore this mountain, which the Lord promised, in thy hearir
also, . . . if so be the Lord be with me.   And Josue blessed him and gave him Hebro
in possession.   And from that time Hebron belonged to Caleb, . . . until this prese
day: because he followed the Lord the God of Israel."

Josue himself emulated this splendid example of his friend: he asked and receive
from the nation another of these mountain-strongholds, situated on the confines of tl
hostile heathen nations who held the sea-coast, the possession of which must oblig
his posterity to be perpetually in arms for the defence of their country and the
religion.

His last solemn appearance before assembled Israel was in the Vale of Sichem, ne
the tomb of Joseph, on the spot hallowed so long before by Abraham and Jacob, looke
upon not only as the birthplace of the nation but as "the sanctuary of the Lord
(xxiv. 26).   To the people over whose welfare he has watched so long and so fait
fully the venerable leader, now one hundred and ten years old, delivers a prophet
message from the Most High, rehearsing briefly the History of His own providence ov
Abraham and his descendants, from the calling of the great patriarch in Chaldæa
the present hour of triumph and blissful security amid their predestined inheritanc
Again this most privileged race are challenged by their Divine Benefactor to use the
free will.   "Now therefore fear the Lord and serve Him with a perfect and most si
cere heart . . . But if it seem evil to you to serve the Lord, you have your choice . .

And the people answered and said: God forbid we should leave the Lord, and serve strange gods!"

"Josue therefore on that day made a covenant, and set before the people commandments and judgments in Sichem. And he wrote all these things in the volume of the law of the Lord: and he took a great stone, and set it under the oak that was in the sanctuary of the Lord" (xxiv. 14-26).

The power to serve the Lord freely or freely to turn their backs on Him, so clearly set forth in this striking passage of Holy Writ, was, as Josue foresaw and foretold, to be time and again most shockingly abused. How often was this same lovely vale to witness the dreadful retribution brought down on Israel by its incurable fickleness and ingratitude, till He whose Name Josue bore and honored by his glorious life came Himself to make another and an everlasting Covenant with mankind! On that same spot, seated, footsore and weary, at noontide by the side of Jacob's well, the Good Shepherd was one day to address to the Samaritan Woman—the type of erring humanity—the creative words that were to renew her soul and to renew the face of the earth as well.

THE BOOK OF JUDGES.—The engraving on page 10 is but too eloquent an illustration of the sad fate of those who, chosen to be God's children and His privileged instruments for good, forget Him, are shorn of all their glory, and become the thralls and playthings of His enemies. Behold one of the Judges of Israel, the mighty Samson, condemned to do the work of a brute beast and grind corn in a mill!

But what and who were the Judges of Israel? They were men raised up from time to time, during a period of about three hundred and forty years, to deliver the recreant Hebrews from the foreign oppression brought on them by their own sins, and to rule the land under the immediate direction of the Most High. Under Moses and Josue, and till the election of Saul, the Hebrew commonwealth was a theocracy, or a republic with God as its real head, and chosen leaders under Him to rule the people and secure the execution of His laws. Of these deliverers and rulers, called Judges, however, only a few are mentioned in Scripture. In ordinary times, and when no foreign yoke weighed on the whole people, they were governed by their tribal princes, elders, and chiefpriests.

Thus we see Josue before his death (xxiv. 1) calling together "the ancients, and the princes, and the judges, and the masters." He chose no one to succeed to his office; nor did God appoint any one to be his successor. Of the people, after his death, it is said (Judges ii. 7-14): . . . "They served the Lord all his (Josue's) days, and the days of the ancients that lived a long time after him, and who knew all the works of the Lord, which He had done for Israel . . . And all that generation was gathered to their fathers: and there arose others that knew not the Lord, and the works which He had done for Israel. And the children of Israel did evil in the sight of the Lord, and they served Baalim. . . . And the Lord being angry against Israel, delivered them into the hands of plunderers, who took them and sold them to their enemies that dwelt round about."

The first chapters in the book clearly account for this state of things. Thus, in chap. i., we see the joint efforts made by the neighboring tribes of Juda and Simeon, who held an extreme position in the south, to exterminate or expel the Chanaanites. Each of the two tribes acts as sovereign within its own territory, and invokes the aid of the other as that of a co-sovereign power. They gave no quarter to their foes and made no truce with them.

Not so with the other tribes mentioned in the sequel of the chapter. "The sons of Benjamin did not destroy the Jebusites that inhabited Jerusalem." "Manasses also . . . And the Chanaanites began to dwell with them." So with the other tribes on both sides of the Jordan. Even in Egypt the seductions of idolatry amid the splendors of a superior civilization had been too much for the early Hebrews, the immediate progeny of the twelve patriarchs. It required the hardships of slavery and all the wrongs of the most pitiless oppression to make the poor victims hate the gods as well as the persons of their oppressors.

But in the enchanted land of Palestine, with its lovely climate and its teeming soil, there were in the pleasant lives of the heathen population a thousand things capable of turning the brain and perverting the heart. God had made there the earth a paradise; and God's capital Enemy, the Devil, had turned it into a scene of perpetual riotousness and debauchery.

The bitter waters of the Dead Sea only covered up a few of the more guilty cities: others not less sinning against God and nature flaunted their iniquity all over the land. Even modern scholars do not dare to fathom the dark depths of this idolatry, or care to reveal the hateful mysteries of what they have fathomed. No wonder that He who is the Creator of man, and the lover of the soul and its purity, should have decreed the extermination of this gigantic wickedness and forbidden all intercourse with neighbors whose very breath was contamination.

Of the thirteen Judges whose names are mentioned in this book, the record is as follows: Othoniel, a younger brother of the great Caleb, chap. iii. 7-11; Aod and Samgar, iii. 12-31; Debbora and Barac, iv. and v.; Gedeon, vi.-ix; Abimelech, son of Gedeon, ix.; Thola and Jair, x. 1-5; Jephte, x. 6-18; xii 7; Abesan, Ahialon, and Abdon, xii. 8-15; finally, Samson, xiii.-xvi.

The remaining five chapters are a fearful story of the degeneracy of the tribe of Dan—the open practice of idolatry under the cover of the name of the true God beginning with one house and then adopted by the whole tribe; fast upon the heels of this apostasy comes a terrible outrage committed by the inhabitants of one Benjamite city, Gabaa, of which the entire tribe of Benjamin assume the responsibility, and which leads to a war of extermination waged against the offenders by the other tribes.

Some portions of this record of three centuries and a half are deserving of a close study. The deliverance wrought by Debbora, and the glorious hymn in which she pours forth her feelings of thanksgiving and triumph, recall the dark days of Egyptian servitude and the heroic part played by Mary, the sister and saviour of Moses. Then we come upon Gedeon and his chosen band of warriors—men who could refuse to drink even their fill of water from the brook; examples of heroic temperance in an age when unbridled sensuality reigned supreme over their own countrymen; men worthy to achieve the liberation of their people from the twofold slavery of vice and idol-worship; what a lesson for all future time!

More forcible still is the lesson taught by Samson in his incomparable strength and resistless prowess while faithful to his Nazarite vows and observant of the divine law, as well as by the extremity of his weakness when yielding to pleasure and preferring self-indulgence to the heroic abstemiousness and unwearying zeal demanded of God's representative and the champion of Israel. The lively image of Christ who fought single-handed the battle of our salvation and triumphed by his infinite self-abasement over Lucifer and all the hosts of pride—Samson, by his single arm, defeated the embattled Philistines, and, blind and degraded, brought down destruction on his oppressors, triumphing in death over the enemies of his God and of his people.

> "Samson hath quit himself
> Like Samson, and heroically hath finished
> A life heroic, . . .
>
> To Israel
> Honor hath left and freedom, . . .
> To himself and father's house eternal fame;
> And, which is best and happiest yet, all this
> With God not parted from him, as was feared
> But favoring and assisting to the end."

THE BOOK OF RUTH.—This book, received as canonical, by both Jews and Christians, formed, in early times, a portion of or an appendix to the preceding book of the Judges. The Talmud ascribes its authorship to Samuel. The Septuagint makes it a separate book; and in this, as well as in placing the Book of Ruth between Judges and the four Books of Kings, the Latin Vulgate and the English Version have followed the Septuagint.

It tells with exquisite and most touching simplicity the story of a young Moabite woman, the widow of a Jewish exile, who will not forsake her poor mother-in-law, Noemi, when the latter, having lost everything and every one dear to her, sets out on her return to her native city of Bethlehem. Ruth's devotion to her forlorn parent not only leads her to forsake country, relatives, and friends for Noemi's sake, but to support the latter by such labor as the very poorest had recourse to in an agricultural country. This heroic devotion, as well as the young woman's native grace and modesty, win the respect of Booz, a rich kinsman of her deceased husband's, who marries her.

From this auspicious union springs Obed, the father of Jesse, and the ancestor of King David and of the Redeemer Himself. Thus the purpose of the author was to point out clearly the genealogy of the Prophet-King and the descent from him of Mary and her Divine Babe. The Holy Spirit also intended to show how tenderly Providence watches over the souls of those who put their whole trust in Him, and give up for Him all earthly affections and possessions. The Holy Fathers have seen in Ruth the figure of the Church of the Gentiles whose heart was solely set upon faith and hope in Jesus, the blessed fruit of life and salvation borne by the stem of Jesse.

Moreover, the book itself is a sweet picture of rural home-life among the people of God. Our hearts, while reading it, are deeply touched by Noemi's yearning for Bethlehem, her native spot; for the religious atmosphere of her early home, and the companionship of her own kindred; by the single-mindedness of Ruth, her self-sacrificing attachment to her poor, lone kinswoman; her generous determination to support the latter by her own toil, and the docility, simplicity, and modesty which characterize her whole conduct in the most difficult and delicate circumstances; and by the manly piety and conscientious uprightness of Booz.

It is a lovely page of Holy Writ, full of precious teaching, from parents to children, when the former have applied both mind and heart to glean the precious ears of truth from a field that has given abundant harvest of edification to Jews and Christians for thousands of years. (See also the story of Ruth and Noemi in Heroic Women of the Bible and the Church, chap. x. p. 103.)

THE FOUR BOOKS OF KINGS.—This portion of the historical books of the Old Testament is so called, because it describes the rise of the kingly dignity in the person of Saul, and gives the history of all those who ruled as kings over God's people both while Israel formed one kingdom and after its division into two. In the Hebrew text the two first Books of Kings formed but one and was called the Book of Samuel, the third and fourth also forming one single volume called the Book of Kings or Kingdoms. In the Septuagint Greek all four were designated as the Books of Kings or Kingdoms; and this was adopted by the early Latin translators and is followed in the Vulgate—Protestants affecting and preferring in this as in other things to follow the Hebrew text and the Jewish authorities.

The first book contains the history of Samuel down to his death, in the beginning of chap. xxv. Hence the first twenty-four chapters are generally attributed to him; and as he had anointed both Saul and David to be kings over Israel, these two first books, which narrate the history of their reigns, may seem a continuation of the record begun by Samuel. The continuators are thought to be the Prophets Nathan and Gad, as one may gather from I Paralipomenon xxix. 29: "Now the acts of King David, first and last, are written in the book of Samuel the Seer, and in the book of Nathan the Prophet, and in the book of Gad the Seer."

FIRST AND SECOND KINGS.—As we travel down the road of history from the days of Samson and the other Judges, we come upon the grand figure of Samuel, one which arrests our attention and challenges our admiration equally with the sublime personages of Josue and Moses. Samson died gloriously, and by his heroic death expiated the sad weaknesses which marred his career and prevented him from effecting the complete independence of his people and reigning in undisputed power over a united and regenerated Israel.

There are no such weaknesses to dim the lustre of Samuel's saintly life. His birth is a boon granted to the prayers and tears of his pious mother, Anna. By her he is consecrated to God from the first instant of his existence, and placed from childhood in the sanctuary as a thing that exclusively belongs to the Most High and Most Holy. Even at that tender age, he is the privileged organ of the divine Will toward the aged and over-indulgent High Priest Heli, announcing to him, who was both the secular and religious head of the nation, the terrible judgments brought down on Israel by his sacrilegious and tyrannical sons.

There is no break in the beautiful life thus begun in the sanctuary. The soul nurtured and kept pure by the deep spirit of prayer, increases constantly in strength and holiness, till we find Samuel, now arrived at the age of manhood, delivering to guilty and oppressed Israel solemn exhortation couched almost in the last words of Josue: "If you turn to the Lord with all your heart, put away the strange gods from among you, Baalim and Astaroth; and prepare your hearts unto the Lord and serve Him only, and He will deliver you out of the hand of the Philistines " (1 vii. 3). Would you know the secret of that resistless energy with which the Son of Anna thenceforward to his dying day sought to promote the cause of God and the cause of His people? Listen to the adjuration which the Israelites in their despair, and surrounded by their cruel foes, address to Samuel: " Cease not to cry to the Lord our God for us, that He may save us out of the hand of the Philistines! . . . And Samuel cried to the Lord for Israel, and the Lord heard him." Then comes the great victory for Israel on the spot made memorable by former disastrous defeat; and there too a monument is set up called *Eben-ezer* or " The House of Help."

The man of prayer, of good counsel, and unsleeping energy, thus goes on from victory to victory: "And the hand of the Lord was against the Philistines all the days of Samuel."

It is most touching to read of the humility of this illustrious man, who, when his people reject him and demand a king to rule over them, submits like a little child to the divine will, anoints Saul for the kingly office, without ever ceasing to direct and counsel him, or to guide both prince and people in the faithful observance of the law of God. " Far from me be this sin against the Lord, that I should cease to pray for you; and I will teach you the good and right way. Therefore fear the Lord, and serve Him in truth and with your whole heart . . . But if you will still do wickedly, both you and your king shall perish together " (xii. 23–25).

Alas, both king and people do forget the " great works " done among them by their Divine Benefactor, and forget, as well, the fatherly counsels of Samuel, and go on from bad to worse till Saul and Jonathan and the strength of Israel go down together in one common ruin on the red field of Gilboe !

David, who had been anointed king in the life-time of Saul, does indeed profit by the terrible examples of the divine justice, bringing on himself and his people blessings in proportion with his fidelity. Most gifted himself—poet, musician, brave warrior and wise statesman, fitted by all these gifts to shine in peace as well as in war—David makes of Israel a united, prosperous, and mighty nation.

But he too forgets God in the intoxication of prosperity and power; he sins, sacrificing to the gross sensuality prevailing in the nations round about, and brings on his house, his people, and himself the terrible retribution which never fails to overtake the man who is placed on high to shine by his great virtues, and whose dark deeds are an incitement to evil in those beneath him.

But David, when guilty and visited with punishment for his guilt, differed from Saul in this: that, whereas the latter's proud self-will refused to bend beneath the chastising hand, or to confess his sin and make atonement for it, David put on sackcloth and ashes, invoked the spirit of repentance, sent up to the God of his heart continual cries for forgiveness, and watered his couch by night with the bitter tears wrung from him by his grief. David was a man after God's own heart, because, even in his fall, he forgot not the God of his youth; and the sense of his guilt only made him seek to serve the Divine Majesty with tenfold fervor and increased humility. Saul, guilty, turned his back on God and sought from demons the knowledge of his own future and of the fortunes of his house. David, guilty, prostrated himself in the dust and sent up his heart-cries to heaven for mercy on his people and on himself. "The Lord is my Rock, and my strength, and my Saviour; God is my strong One: in Him will I trust: my shield and the horn of my salvation. He lifteth me up and (is) my refuge: my Saviour! And thou wilt deliver me from iniquity" (2 Kings xxii. 2, 3).

THIRD AND FOURTH BOOKS OF KINGS.—More terrible even than the end of Saul is that of the wise and magnificent Solomon, David's son. God lavished on this prince the rarest gifts of mind and heart, together with the undisputed possession of his father's kingdom. To him whose reign was "established in peace," and who was the illustrious figure of the Prince of Peace, Christ, it was given to build the first glorious temple ever erected for the worship of the one true God. His reign forms a central point toward which all preceding events in Sacred History seemed to tend, and whose surpassing glories were to be reflected downward on succeeding ages till He appeared who was to fulfill all promises in His person, and to eclipse all glories in the divine achievements of His humility and His charity. And yet the student of the Bible is filled only with sadness, and something like discouragement, in seeing this most wise prince become the most besotted and depraved of sensualists—an object of contempt and loathing to all true manhood, while the early piety which impelled him to build the most magnificent of temples to the God of his fathers is forgotten in the disgusting and insatiable appetite for pleasure, which with pagan wives brings into the City of David the fearful scandal of the idol-worship of the Egyptians and Chanaanites.

To this most foolish and most guilty king succeeds a son who inherits some of his father's worst vices without any of his great

qualities. And then the curse of Heaven falls on Israel in the form of irremediable political division. Ten of the Twelve Tribes fall away from Roboam, and constitute an independent kingdom which is to have gods of its own. Thus, divided, Israel—divided in religious belief and political allegiance—goes on, reign after reign, with the consuming cancer of idolatry, and of the fearful immorality it begets, fastened on the majority of the nation, while the minority in the southern kingdom are ruled by a few good princes, whose reforms and examples are neutralized by the pagan vices of their successors. At length both kingdoms are blotted out and their people scattered abroad in captivity.

We see, during the period covered by these two last books—427 or 405 years—we see a people of brothers, instead of remaining united in the one religious faith and under one strong government, forming two rival and hostile nationalities, each of which, when the other prevails, calls in the aid of the stranger and the heathen to help restore the balance. A fatal mistake against sound policy—that is, against the laws of nature. But amid the gloom and the guilt of that long period grand figures loom up: the men of God, the prophets commissioned to keep alive the true faith among populations given over to doubt, to ignorance, to idolatry, and manifold corruption; or sent to save the national life from utter extinction: Elias, and Elisæus, and Jeremias, who wrote these same two last books of Kings, what names and what undying glory are theirs! No less illustrious and combining with the prophetic gifts of the others the glory of being, like Jeremias, an historical writer, Isaias has, moreover, the honor of being numbered among the martyrs of the Old Testament. But although living under several of the princes whose reigns are chronicled in the Books of Kings, this great Prophet-Martyr's name is not mentioned therein.

PARALIPOMENON OR CHRONICLES.—The original Hebrew title of these two books literally means "daily records," because they contain the substance of journals kept by the official annalists of the two kingdoms of Juda and Israel. In the Septuagint they are called "The First and Second Book of Paralipomenon," or of things overlooked in the Books of Kings. The books of Paralipomenon are therefore supplementary to the preceding historical works of the Bible. The title "Chronicles," adopted in the Protestant version, was suggested by St. Jerome. The books themselves are considered to be the work of Esdras, the restorer of the temple and of Jewish worship after the captivity. He evidently made use of documents prepared by others and dating from previous times.

One of his main objects, if not his chief purpose, seems to have been to place on record a series of genealogies which might assist the rulers of the restored remnants of tribes toward giving to each Jewish family the inheritance of its fathers, as allotted under Josue. As, moreover, the perfect regulation of divine worship in the Temple was in his eyes and those of the nation a matter of the most practical importance, he

drew up also genealogies of the priestly and levitic families, so that they might perform their functions in the order and with the regularity prescribed under David and Solomon. These families had to live on the tithes and offerings given them while discharging their sacred functions, each in their turn, in Jerusalem. It thus became imperative to have a public and authentic list of these families and their numbers, so as to secure perfect regularity and discipline in the successive bands of priests and levites called to minister in the sanctuary. This Esdras did, as may be seen in the books themselves.

As to the purely historical portion of the books, it contains what is the very heart of the national life—the detailed story of David's glorious reign, the great promise and performance of Solomon's youth, together with the incredible splendor and luxury that were to be his bane. Of his licentiousness and open encouragement of idolatry within his own capital and household, there is no mention here. The writer refers us back on this subject to the Second Book of Kings. The inspired Chronicler, however, is careful to describe Solomon's stolid and vicious son in such a way, that we are forced to behold in this precocious despot's conduct the natural result of the paternal training and examples.

Roboam had for mother an Ammonite princess, one of those women which God had so often and so solemnly forbidden his people to connect with themselves by marriage. What the influence of this idolatrous woman over the perverted and prematurely old monarch (he died at sixty) may have been, we know not from authentic history. The mere fact that her son became Solomon's successor allows us to suppose that she ruled supreme over the silly, pleasure-seeking king. Her son, as well as "the young men . . . brought up with him in pleasures," and his evil counselors from the beginning of his reign, had not more of faith than he had of kingly prudence. Even after the disruption of his kingdom, he refuses to profit by the terrible prophetic lessons delivered to Jeroboam during Solomon's lifetime (3 Kings xi. 29). "When the kingdom of Roboam was strengthened and fortified, he forsook the law of the Lord, and all Israel with him." And what is the consequence? "In the fifth year of the reign of Roboam, Sesac king of Egypt came up against Jerusalem (because they had sinned against the Lord." . . . There is terror and a show of that kind of repentance which is begotten of mortal fear. "The Lord is just!" both prince and people exclaim in their extremity. But the Lord, who is ever more merciful than just, will not allow the Egyptian to exterminate the guilty ones. They become vassals and tributaries of their old-time foes and oppressors. "So Sesac king of Egypt departed from Jerusalem, taking away the treasures of the house of the Lord, and of the king's house" (2 Paral. ii. 9).

The gold with which Solomon had so magnificently enriched the Sanctuary had been, every bit of it, the gift of David, the fruit of his conquests and pious economies. The lavish profusion of gold and silver with which Solomon had adorned and enriched his own palaces and harems, had been ground out of his impoverished and over-taxed people. All is now swept into the coffers of the Egyptian! Brass replaced gold in the

temple as well as in the palace. But the faith, the love, the heart-service which Jehovah solely prized, and which would have made Roboam and his people invincible against every enemy, neither the king nor his subjects thought of bringing to the house of God or to their own homes. "He did evil, and did not prepare his heart to seek the Lord!" But "even in Juda there were found good works;" and so God will keep to the promise made through Ahias (3 Kings xi. 36), "that there may remain a lamp for My servant David before Me always in Jerusalem, the city which I have chosen, that My Name might be there."

And so, through the gloom of the long succeeding centuries, this "lamp," the steady light of the Promise, shall continue to cheer faithful hearts both in Jerusalem and amid the sorrows and despair of exile, till our Day Star, our "Orient from on high," shines out above the hill-tops of Bethlehem.

THE FIRST BOOK OF ESDRAS.—Esdras, the author of this book, as well as the probable author of the preceding Chronicles, is justly revered as the second parent of the Hebrew nation. But before we speak of his personal merit or of his deeds, let us give one glance at the last chapter of Paralipomenon.

Here we have King Eliakim or Joakim placed on the throne of Jerusalem by the Egyptian conqueror who has deposed Joachaz. "Joakim was five and twenty years old," the sacred historian says, "when he began to reign, and he reigned eleven years in Jerusalem: and he did evil before the Lord his God. Against him came up Nabuchodonosor King of the Chaldeans, and led him bound in chains to Babylon."

On the throne of this unworthy prince is placed his son of nearly the same name. "Joachin was eight years old when he began to reign, and he reigned three months and ten days in Jerusalem, and he did evil in the sight of the Lord. And, at the return of the year, King Nabuchodonosor sent and brought him to Babylon." Sedecias, an uncle of this boy-king, and brother to the two deposed and exiled monarchs, now succeeds to this precarious sceptre. "Sedecias was one and twenty years old when he began to reign; and he reigned eleven years in Jerusalem. And he did evil in the sight of the Lord his God, and did not reverence the face of Jeremias the Prophet speaking to him from the mouth of the Lord . . . And he hardened his neck and his heart from returning to the Lord the God of Israel."

In the footsteps of this wicked prince walk the leading men of priests and people. Their patient God vainly warns them of the coming evils. "But they mocked the messengers of God, . . . until the wrath of the Lord arose against His people. For he brought upon them the King of the Chaldeans." . . . City, temple, everything strong and fair, all is swept from the face of the earth by the Babylonian conqueror, and the miserable remnants of Juda are driven away into captivity. Is it not terrible? and is not such blindness, such perseverance in evil, a something so incredible that one is staggered by the recital of such monstrous perverseness?

With regard to the Book of Esdras itself, it is, manifestly, a continuation of the preceding book of annals or chronicles. Cyrus the Great is moved to restore the Temple of Jerusalem and to revive thereby the Hebrew nationality. In captivity such holy priests as Esdras and Nehemias, and such prophets as Jeremias and Daniel, had shed on the Hebrew name and religion such extraordinary splendor, that the great and right-minded Cyrus was drawn toward the true faith and toward a people whose supernatural virtues formed such a contrast with the surrrounding corruption of heathendom. So, both priests and people had been chastened by the terrible trials of exile and bondage! And God would once more gather together His scattered ones! There is an accurate list of the exiles whom Cyrus permitted to accompany Zorobabel and Esdras on their touching patriotic mission. And what pregnant lessons for the most generous souls aspiring to build up anew the ruins of country and home are found in these monumental pages! How the story of patriotic self-sacrifice and religious faith belonging to these far-off times and countries apply literally to this our nineteenth century and the long-cherished aspirations of more than one struggling people! It would be so profitable to parents themselves in every Christian family to study, with their whole mind and heart, this and the following book, and then hold up to their dear ones the golden lessons gleaned from such attentive perusal!

THE BOOK OF NEHEMIAS, OR THE SECOND OF ESDRAS.—When Esdras had succeeded in building up the Temple and in restoring and reforming the remnants of his people, he returned to Mesopotamia to report on his accomplished mission. Alas, it required the eloquent voice, the strong hand, and conciliatory temper of the truest of priests and wisest of statesmen to keep the fickle people to their resolutions. Such of the Hebrews

as had been living in Judæa before the arrival of Esdras and his colony of exiles had either become as heathenish and corrupt as the neighboring Chanaanites, or had made of the little religion they retained a mixture of idolatrous practices and Hebrew superstitions. They were, at best, but poor auxiliaries to Esdras and his zealous band of restorers. But what shall we say of the non-Hebrew populations, the old enemies of God and of his people? They used every exertion and every artifice to prevent the restoration of Jerusalem and the rebuilding of the Temple. When force and fraud failed, they tried on the faithful Israelites the old fascination of their idolatrous customs, of their licentious celebrations, and pompous pagan festivals. And they succeeded.

Nehemias had to return with Esdras to Jerusalem to begin anew this unfinished labor of social and religious reform and material reconstruction. The story grows in interest from chapter to chapter, as the two great men, brother priests laboring together with one mind and one heart, rekindle by voice and example the faith and zeal of their fellow-countrymen. They proclaim the Law anew, and induce the people to celebrate with extraordinary fervor and solemnity the Feast of Tabernacles (2 Esdras viii. and ix.) With one voice priests, princes, and people confess God's infinite goodness in their behalf and their own inconceivable ingratitude. "Our kings, our princes, our priests, and our fathers have not kept Thy law . . . And they have not served Thee in their kingdoms, and in Thy manifold goodness, . . . and in the large and fat (wide and fruitful) land which Thou deliveredst before them . . . Behold, we ourselves this day are bondmen: and the land, which Thou gavest our fathers, . . . we ourselves are servants in it! . . . And because of all this we ourselves make a covenant, and write it, and our princes, our Levites, and our priests sign it" (Ibid. ix. 34–38).

THE BOOK OF TOBIAS.—We have, in the saintly man after whom this book is called, another illustrious instance of the living faith and heroic virtue displayed in exile by so many of God's people. No book in the Old Testament affords such touching examples of filial piety, domestic simplicity and purity, and that unflinching devotion to one's brethren in their darkest days of suffering and oppression. The virtues which shine forth in the life and home of Tobias are those which must be eternally the very soul of domestic happiness and public welfare. The morality of the whole book is a most beautiful commentary on the law of life delivered through Moses; a splendid mirror in which even Christians may see what they ought to be and are not, as compared with the saintly men and women of twenty-six hundred years ago.

Tobias was born in Cades (Kedesh)-Nephtali, in the northern part of Galilee. It was the native city of Barac, in which Debbora had organized the little army that was to prove victorious over the proud hosts of Jabin and Sisara. From time immemorial the place was a famous stronghold, one of the "cities of refuge" established by Josue. Near it Jonathan the Machabee fought against the treacherous generals of Demetrius, changing a disastrous defeat into a glorious victory. Beneath its very walls was shown the spot where the stout-hearted Jael completed Debbora's triumph by slaying with her own hand the cruel Sisara.

Tobias, nurtured in this eagles' nest, displayed from earliest boyhood qualities far superior to those of the soldier and conqueror. He learned even when a child in years, to do "no childish thing in his work," and when his fellow-countrymen and townsmen "all went to the golden calves" of Jeroboam in Samaria, "he alone fled the company of all, and went to Jerusalem to the temple of the Lord." He appears to have been a wealthy youth who delighted in devoting generously his wealth to the support of the true religion. What he had been in childhood and youth he continued to be in manhood and all through life. "He took to wife Anna of his own tribe, and had a son by her whom he called after his own name; and from his infancy he taught him to fear God and

to abstain from all sin." Carried with his wife and child into captivity by Salmanasar (Shalman-Ezor) IV., King of Assyria, Tobias shone so pre-eminently above his fellow-captives and the Assyrian nobles and courtiers at Niniveh that he attracted the notice and won the favor of the monarch himself, and was by him loaded with honor and wealth. For in the midst of this idolatrous and sensual race, when his Hebrew fellow-captives shared in the forbidden rites and pleasures of their captors, Tobias "kept his soul and never was defiled," being ever "mindful of the Lord with all his heart."

The book, from the first chapter to the end, reads like a glorious epic in praise of exalted piety and patriotism. Two kindred families, bound still more closely together by the same deep, practical faith, are the principal personages, while evil spirits and God's own archangel display respectively their baneful influences and healing power. What a picture is that household in the mighty Niniveh, in which the now poor and sightless Tobias is made the butt of his wife's unfeeling sarcasm and headlong temper! He had risked and spent everything on his persecuted countrymen; and now as he sits at home, blind and destitute of all earthly comfort, a woman's foolish tongue ceases not to lash him. "Where is thy hope, for which thou gavest alms, and buriedst the dead?" It was in vain that he replied, "We are the children of the saints, and look to that life which God will give to those that never change their faith from Him." The pitiless tongue ceased not for all that to scourge him with the reproof: "It is evident thy hope is come to nothing, and thy alms now appear!" And the poor, helpless sufferer, seeing no further aim in life, would lift his soul to God on high: "Thou art just, O Lord, and all Thy ways mercy and truth and judgment! . . . Command my spirit to be received in peace; for it is better for me to die than to live."

At the same hour, in the city of Northern Ecbatane, a dear friend and kinsman of Tobias, Raguel by name, was suffering deep affliction in the person of his only child, Sara. This man was both virtuous and wealthy. But, through some mysterious dispensation of Providence, evil spirits were allowed to persecute him and his. Every one who had till then sought the hand of his innocent and pious daughter had fallen a victim to the Evil One. This drew suspicion on Sara, so much so, indeed, that even her servant maid openly and bitterly taunted her with being a murderess. Prostrate before the Divine Majesty in the privacy of her own chamber, the distressed girl was sending up her heart-cry for help: "I beg, O Lord, that Thou loose me from the bond of this reproach, or else take me away from the earth." But Northern Ecbatane (the capital of Cyrus) is on the road to Rages (the modern *Rhey*, a few miles southeast of Teheran); and in this last city lived one of Tobias' tribesmen, Gabelus, to whom in the days of his great prosperity the former had lent a large sum of money. This sum, before dying and in the interest both of his wife and of his son, Tobias is now anxious to recover. And here comes in the sweet and loving providence of the Father. The succor needed by the two suffering families will not be delayed. Then is told the marvelous story of the Archangel Raphael's undertaking to guide the younger Tobias all the way to the distant home of his kinsman, where God was keeping in store for him the spotless soul of a true woman as well as part of the riches which were to raise his aged parents once more to affluence. To his father also the angelic guide, on their joyful return to Niniveh, restores the sight so long lost. How magnificent is the hymn of prophetic praise and exultation which goes up from this tried and grateful soul! "I and my soul will rejoice in Him. Bless ye the Lord all His elect; keep days of joy, and give glory to Him. Jerusalem, city of God, the Lord hath chastised thee for the works of thy hands. Give glory to the Lord for thy good things, and bless the God eternal; that He may rebuild His tabernacle in thee, and call back thy captives to thee, and thou mayst rejoice for ever and ever!"

THE BOOK OF JUDITH.—Here is another thrilling page of sacred history taken from the annals of that same epoch of partial restoration from captivity and exile. Moses had been saved from the waters of the Nile by the watchful love of his sister, Mary, who also continued to be the angel of his life in the court of Pharaoh, and till her great brother could openly choose between the service of the Egyptian oppressor and that of his own oppressed kinsmen. With him, when sent on his divine mission of liberation, was associated Mary, who thus deserved the name of Deliverer. Then came Debbora and Jael to work out the freedom of Israel during the period of the Judges; and now Judith stands forth to deliver the restored tribes from the threatened renewal of their subjugation and expulsion from their native land. No mere analysis of the story can give the reader a truthful idea of the condition of things in Palestine or of the desperate extremities from which a woman's inspired heroism freed her country and people. Even those who see in Judith's artifice a something exceedingly like criminal fraud, must remember that Sacred History records more than one deed of the most illustrious personages which the historian does not pretend to excuse or justify. But, to one who calmly considers the circumstances of the age and country— the brutal lust for conquest and plunder which animated the Nabuchodonosors and Holophernes of these pagan times—there can occur no valid reason for refusing to Judith the glorious praise due to a woman, who devotes her own life and imperils her honor in order to save the honor of her countrywomen and the independence of her own nation, then struggling to confirm its long-lost and scarcely recovered freedom. (See the Author's reasoning on this subject in HEROIC WOMEN OF THE BIBLE AND THE CHURCH, chap. xvii. pp. 180–81.)

THE BOOK OF ESTHER.—Just as the God, who watched so lovingly over the destinies of that race which was to give to the world Christ and His Apostles, showed again and again how easily and surely He could employ the hand of a single man to work out the salvation of an entire people, even so does He use again and again a weak and timid woman as His instrument, in order to render still more irresistible the demonstration of His almighty Power. Modern scholars judge it probable, that the Assuerus who raised Esther to the throne, was no other than the blindly proud and blundering Xerxes who attempted, at the head of the united armies and fleets of all Western Asia, to conquer and subjugate the little republics of Greece. The indescribable splendor and magnificence of this royal despot forms a kind of background for the picture of Esther's loveliness and piety, of the utter helplessness of her Hebrew fellow-exiles, and of the implacable animosity existing between them and their old Amalekite foes. The book, although affording us but a glimpse of that fairy-like luxury and incredible servility prevailing in these great eastern capitals, enables us, nevertheless, to see the fearful extent of the corruption from which God wished to preserve His people, by keeping them from intimate communication with their heathen

H. ANELAY.

neighbors, and binding them to his own service by inviolable fidelity within their own national territory.

Their existence as a free people in Palestine was to be the consequence of this fidelity to the law of Jehovah. His overshadowing protection secured them from disaster, defeat, and subjugation, so long as they served Him with their whole heart. And in their exile among the nations, while they were taking to heart the bitter lessons of experience, He ever showed Himself ready and prompt to assist them and to protect them from utter extinction, when the cry of their heart went up to Him.

Aman, the all-powerful favorite of Assuerus, has taken every means to annihilate the scattered remnants of the Hebrew race by one fell blow, and throughout the vast Persian empire. The young Hebrew Empress knows, as well as her uncle and foster-father, Mardochæus, that the hand of God alone can arrest the blow about to fall, and that united prayer to Him can make Him stretch forth His arm to save the innocent and strike down the guilty aggressor. Trusting in the intervention of that Power and Goodness which will have us entreat it in our direst need, Esther employs meanwhile all the means which human prudence suggests to enlighten the Emperor on his favorite's character and designs. Woman's wit comes to the aid of woman's loveliness and patriotism ; iniquity falls into the net it had itself spread for the guiltless, and cruelty perishes by its own devices. These are pages to be read again and again, as one reads the most enchanting tale of eastern romance. For here no romance can come up to the reality.

FIRST AND SECOND MACHABEES.—The two books bearing this title contain the history of a heroic family of priests who conquered the national independence under the Greek kings of Syria, and were also the successful champions of religious liberty. The surname of "Machabee," first borne by Judas, son of the priest Mathathias, arose, according to some, from a Hebrew word signifying "hammer"—both the father and his sons having been in the hand of God a hammer for shattering the might of their oppressors. Others, on the contrary, derive the appellation from the initial letters of the Hebrew sentence in Exodus xv. 11: "Who is like to Thee among the strong, O Lord?" These letters, it is said, were inscribed by Judas on his victorious banners : and hence the surname. The name is bestowed not only on Judas and his brethren, but on a generous widow and her seven sons most cruelly put to death in Antioch by the pitiless tyrant Antiochus Epiphanes.

The first book of Machabees—a manuscript copy of which in Hebrew, or, rather, in the popular Syro-Chaldaic of the Machabean age, was seen by St. Jerome—is the history of forty years, from the beginning of the reign of Antiochus Epiphanes to the death of the High Priest Simon Machabee. The second book is the abridged history of the persecutions under Antiochus Epiphanes and Ptolemy Eupator, his son, being compiled from a full and complete history of the same in five books, written by Jason, and now lost. This abridgment describes in detail many of the principal occurrences related in the first book. Both historians, however, seem to have written independently of each other, neither having seen the other's work.

No history, ancient or modern, contains a more vivid and thrilling story of living faith and heroic valor.

THE PROPHETS.

We must not, if we would form a correct conception of Sacred History, separate the Prophets and their utterances from their proper connection in the series of contemporary events. They, their prophecies, and their lives, form an integral portion of the annals of the epoch in which they lived. The very historical books we have been just passing in review are incomplete, and, in some parts, incomprehensible, if severed from the words and actions of such men as Isaias, Jeremias, Ezechiel, Haggæus, and other prophets, who acted such an important part under the Kings of Jerusalem and Samaria, while striving, under divine inspiration, to correct and convert bad sovereigns and their sinful people, or to direct and encourage the good.

The name of prophets is sometimes given in Scripture to persons who had no claim to prophetic inspiration. In classic Greek, the word προφήτης, "prophet," designates any person who speaks for another, especially one who speaks in the name of the Godhead, and thus declares or interprets His will to men. The primary meaning of the word prophet is, therefore, that of an interpreter. In the Bible the word has several significations : 1st. It applies to all persons of superior learning or uncommon intellectual gifts, whether their knowledge regards divine or human things. Thus in 1 Corinthians xiv. 6, "prophecy" means the supernatural knowledge of divine things bestowed as a gift on certain persons, and in the infancy of the Church, to enable them to teach others ; whereas, in Titus i. 12, "a prophet of their own," means a Cretan author who had accurately described his own countrymen as "always liars, evil beasts, etc." 2d. He is called a prophet who has either of things past or present a knowledge exceeding the power of nature. Thus Elisæus knew that his servant Giezi had secretly obtained rich presents from Naaman. Thus also when the soldiers buffeted our Lord the night before his death, they asked Him to "prophesy" who had struck Him. 3d. Again, a man is said to be a prophet when he is inspired to say what he does not understand, as Caiphas (St. John xi. 51) "prophesied that Jesus should die for the nation." 4th. In the proper and primitive sense of the word, Aaron is to be the "prophet;" that is, the interpreter, of his brother Moses (Exodus vii.) Hence both our Lord and St. Stephen upbraid the Jews with having persecuted all the prophets ; that is, all those who had been sent to declare to them the will of God. 5th. The designation of prophets was also given to all those who sang hymns or psalms with extraordinary enthusiasm, so as to seem beyond themselves. In 1 Kings x. 12, Saul meets a troop of these singers, joins them, is seized with their divine enthusiasm, and it is therefore said : "Is Saul also among the Prophets?" This same meaning applies on several occasions to David and Asaph and to the young men trained as singers for the temple, and who are therefore called "the sons of the prophets." 6th. The word "to prophesy," again, is understood of the power of working miracles. Hence (Ecclesiasticus xlviii. 14) it is said of Elisæus : "After death his body prophesied," because the contact with the holy man's corpse raised a dead man to life. 7th. But this gift of miracles was the seal which stamped with the divine authority the utterances of the Prophet properly so called ; that is, the man to whom God has revealed and enjoined to announce to the world future events which no created mind could of itself have foreseen. (See Bergier, *Dictionnaire de Théologie.*) Such are the divinely commissioned men whose books we are now to consider.

THE FOUR GREAT PROPHETS.

ISAIAS.—By the universal consent both of the Jewish Church and of the Christian, Isaias is given precedence in rank over the other prophets, though he cannot claim priority in time. He was of royal birth, and the elevation and beauty of his style are in keeping with his high rank and nobility of soul. He is by far the most eloquent of the Prophets. Besides, he describes so minutely the person of Christ and His sufferings, as well as the birth and destiny of the Christian Church, that one might think he was recording past events or describing what was present before his eyes, rather than announcing to the world what was still hidden in the night of ages, and could only be the secret of the divine mind and power. For this reason the book of Isaias has been called a fifth Gospel, so clearly does he perform the task of an evangelist.

The prophetic mission of this great man and great saint runs through the reigns of four kings of Juda—Ozias, Joathan, Achaz, and Ezechias, his life having been gloriously crowned with a cruel martyrdom under Manasses.　Like the Prophet Elias before him, and like John the Baptist long ages after him, Isaias in performing his sublime mission wore the penitential garb of the Nazarites, the long blackish-gray tunic of haircloth fastened round the loins with a rope or girdle of camel's hair.　Thus habited, the man of God would, most probably, go into one of the spacious courts of the Temple, while the people were flocking in to some solemn sacrifice, and from one of the lofty flights of steps leading up to the altar of burnt offerings, would pour forth the words of his divine message on the multitude beneath and around.　The very first words of these inspired oracles still thrill the coldest reader with emotion: "Hear, O ye Heavens! and give ear, O Earth!　For the Lord hath spoken.　I have brought up children and exalted them; but they have despised Me.　The ox knoweth his owner, and the ass his master's crib.　But Israel hath not known Me, and My people hath not understood!"

No words could more aptly state God's case as against His blind and ungrateful people under the Old Law, as well against the professed or nominal followers of Christ under the New Law of Grace.　We are, all of us who believe in Christ and through Him in the Father, the adopted children, the family of God.　How He has exalted the sons of Adam!　How tenderly He has provided for the bringing up of the human race to a God-like resemblance with their all-bountiful Parent and Benefactor!　And is not our life one long act of contempt of that Adorable Majesty?—one long and persistent ignoring and misunderstanding of that ever-present and patient Goodness?

To understand even the literal sense of these most pregnant chapters, it will be necessary to read not only the history of the four kings under whom Isaias preached and taught and performed miracles, but also the two preceding reigns of Amasias and his father Joas.　Joas, saved in infancy, and by a miracle, from the slaughter of all the male descendants of David, and brought up by his aunt Josabet in the very sanctuary of the Temple, would, one might think, be sure to be worthy of David and lovingly faithful to God his Protector.　And yet, in the very flower and pride of his manhood, he introduces among his people the abominable worship of Baal and Ashtarte—murders in the very sanctuary which had sheltered his infancy and childhood his cousin and foster-brother, the High Priest Zacharias, and runs, uncontrolled, his race of wickedness, till he is himself cut off by the hand of a murderer.　Not much better is his son Amasias. He was a cruel king: he caused 10,000 Edomite prisoners to be cast, in cold blood, headlong from the cliffs of Petra, while he hesitated not in the hour of victory to cause sacrifices to be offered in honor of the idols worshiped by his victims.　A cruel soldier is rarely a brave man; and a coward is always a vain one.　So Amasias provokes his father's namesake, Joas, King of Samaria, to war; is shamefully beaten, taken prisoner, brought in chains to Jerusalem, which is partially dismantled by the victor, and at length, like his father, is cut off by the red hand of murder.　There is no use in teaching or warning these purblind princes, in whose veins the heroic blood of David is changed into mud: they will neither be taught, nor enlightened, nor warned.　Such were the men who had ruled the Kingdom of Juda immediately before the birth of Isaias.

Now read in the first five chapters the prophetic denunciations and warnings which apply to the latter part of the long reign of Ozias. Like Solomon, he began his reign young—at the age of sixteen—and by his piety and his genius raised the Kingdom of Juda to a height of glory it had not known since Solomon. Though he did not end his long reign like this prince, so unwise with all his wisdom, Ozias forgot himself in his old age, and, like Saul, attempted to usurp the functions of the priestly office. He was stricken with leprosy at the very altar, and had thenceforward to yield his kingly functions to his son Joathan, and live in the rigorous seclusion imposed on lepers. That there was degeneracy in the body of the nation, as well as in the ruler himself, we may well believe. And in this light we can understand the denunciations of the first five chapters of Isaias. "O my people, they that call thee blessed, the same deceive thee, and destroy the way of thy steps (that is, 'lead thee along the way to destruction.'). The Lord standeth up to judge, and He standeth to judge the people." Listen to the fearful description, at the end of the fifth chapter, which he gives of the coming of the Babylonians and Assyrians to chastise the insolence and ingratitude of this wilfully blind people. The hostile armies coming on from the shores of the Persian Gulf are like a mighty tidal wave which rises and advances swiftly, bearing down all resistance. "And they shall make a noise against them that day like the roaring of the sea. We shall look towards the land, and behold darkness of tribulation, and the light is darkened with the mist thereof!"

2. With chapter vi. begins another series of prophetical teachings. "In the year that King Ozias died, I saw the Lord sitting upon a throne high and elevated; and His train filled the temple." The dead monarch had dimmed the glory of his long reign and splendid services to religion and country, by an obstinate attempt to thrust himself into the sanctuary and to offer with hands unanointed incense upon the altar. In contrast with this sacrilegious presumption stands out the shrinking humility of Isaias—called and chosen, as he knew himself to be, to the sublime and perilous functions of the prophetical office. "And I said, 'Woe is me . . . because I am a man of unclean lips, and I dwell in the midst of a people that hath unclean lips, and I have seen with my eyes the KING the Lord of Hosts.'"

Touched by the terrors of the prophet's humility, one of the attendant Seraphs takes a live coal from the altar of the heavenly temple, and touches therewith the lips which are to speak such mighty things to the world. The reign of Joathan was a continuation of the best traditions of the preceding reign. In one particular only did the son of Ozias fail in magnanimity and firmness of purpose. "The high places he took not away: the people still sacrificed and burnt incense in the high places" (4 Kings xv. 35). Had the people of Juda, then, become so addicted to these clandestine practices of idolatry that the very best princes dared not attempt their suppression? This was, therefore, the sin of the people, and argues to what extent the abominable idol-worship of Palestine and Syria had taken hold of the popular heart in Jehovah's special inheritance. This fact will furnish a key to the most terrible denunciations and predictions of the first chapters in the book, particularly to that uttered by the prophet after his lips had been purified by the sacred fire. "Go and say to this people, 'Hearing hear, and understand not! And see the vision and know it not!' . . . And I said: 'How long, O Lord?' And He said: 'Until the cities be wasted without inhabitant, and the houses without man, and the land shall be left desolate.'"

This brief and magnificent vision of the Heavenly Temple on high, and of the enthroned Majesty of the infinite God, was, doubtless, proclaimed in the temple of Jerusalem to the assembled multitude of tepid, half-hearted worshipers. It reminded them that the splendors of God's earthly house was but a faint image of the everlasting, and that the holiness demanded of both priests and people was only a preparation for the perfection of the beatified state. This sublime revelation, together with the clear and definite announcement of coming ruin to both temple and nation, hung over Juda and its rulers like a cloud big with coming storm during the entire reign of Joathan.

3. The prophecies in the three following chapters, vii., viii., and ix., were delivered during the reign of Joatham's successor, the weakminded and unprincipled Achaz. The league formed against Jerusalem by the Kings of Israel and Syria had always been baffled by the unflinching and prudent policy of Joathan. His son inherited none of his religious faith or statesmanship; and, threatened as he was by the allied armies, he bethought him of calling in to his aid the King of Assyria. Besides, one chief purpose of the King of Israel was to dethrone the descendants of David and set up a Syrian to rule in Jerusalem. This moved to its depths the patriotic soul of Isaias. He knew that the Kingdom of Juda had nothing to fear from the designs or power of the allied kings; and he scorned the idea of invoking the aid of the foreigner and the heathen to fight the battles of Jehovah and to protect the throne of David. The enemy is already in the neighborhood of Jerusalem, and it becomes a matter of life or death to prevent him from cutting off its supply of water. So Achaz marches out to protect the Upper Pool whence the chief supply was derived. Thereupon Isaias is bidden to take his son Sheas-Jashub ("Remnant shall Return") and to confront Achaz with these words: "See thou be quiet. Fear not, and let not thy heart be afraid! . . ." Speaking of the formidable league and its designs against the House of David, the divine oracle is most emphatic: "It (the league) shall not stand, and this shall not be!"

But the unbelieving and timid Achaz cannot set aside either his terrors at the sight of the hostile armies, or his doubts about the victory promised by Isaias. Here comes in the famous prophesy about the Deliverer to be born of a Virgin-Mother: "Hear ye, therefore, O house of David! Is it a small thing for you to be grievous to men, that you are grievous to my God also? Therefore the Lord Himself shall give you a sign. Behold a virgin shall conceive and bear a son, and his name shall be called EMMANUEL (God with us)." It was in vain that the prophet had assured Achaz that "within three score and five years Ephraim (that is, the Ten Schismatic Tribes forming the Kingdom of Israel under the leadership of the powerful tribe of Ephraim) shall cease to be a people." The young king will not believe and will not be dissuaded from calling in the Assyrians. Then comes the bitter reproof and the renewal of the glorious Promise made in the Garden to Eve and Adam guilty: "Behold a Virgin shall conceive," and God shall become Man, *Our God*, "God with us" for ever—the Son of David of whose Kingdom there shall be no end.

Let this unbelieving king, who will not trust to Jehovah's power and protection, call in the Heathen from the banks of the Tigris, and let his idol-worshiping people become the allies of the worst enemies of God. "The Lord shall bring upon thee (Achaz), and upon thy people, and upon the house of thy father, days that have not come since the time of the separation of Ephraim from Juda, with the King of the Assyrians." And all through the desolation and the long captivity of these coming years, there is for Juda a twofold consolation, like a twin beacon to light its path through the gloom: their "Remnant shall Return," and in the fulness of time Emmanuel shall be born to them. As for the prophet himself, with the clear foresight both of the devastation that is soon to come, and of the future Redemption of Israel and the entire race of man, he will put his sole trust in the Lord: "Behold, I and my children whom the Lord hath given me for a sign, and for a wonder in Israel from the Lord of hosts, who dwelleth in Mount Sion . . . I will wait for the Lord who hath hid His face from the house of

Jacob, and I will look for Him!" His two sons as they grow up and walk by his side in Jerusalem and through the land shall be "a sign," and a standing prodigy or "wonder" sent to Israel from the Lord of hosts. We have seen that the elder *Shear-Jashub*, or "Remnant shall Return," was an ever-present warning, by the very name he bore, both of the coming desolation and exile and of the restoration of a remnant of the race. The boy, therefore, was a sign of the Divine justice as well as of the Fatherly mercy soon to be displayed. In chapter viii. the birth of another son is described as attended with extraordinary solemnities. Isaias is commanded to set up a large scroll or tablet bearing the words, *Maher-Shalal-Hash-Baz;* that is, "Hasten, Booty, Speed, Spoil;" and when his younger son is born he is bidden to call him by this prophetic name so full of terrible significance to the kingdom of Juda. Already the King of Assyria had come down with an army on his allied enemies, the Kings of Damascus and Samaria, and had depopulated not only a portion of Syria but the valley of the Jordan around the Lake of Galilee, carrying the inhabitants away into exile. This does not make King Achaz heed any the more the warnings and exhortations of Isaias; this prince more than ever courts an alliance with the Assyrian. The people, however, without ceasing to cling to their vices and their idolatry, are frightened into favoring a league with Damascus and Samaria. This only hastens the coming of the Assyrian. It is in vain that the great prophet tries to fire the national heart with the only flame that should burn therein, the love of their fathers' God and the love of their fatherland. Vainly does he exhaust himself in repeating that no enemy can harm Juda and Jerusalem so long as they repose a loving trust in Jehovah. "Sanctify the Lord of hosts Himself; and let Him be your fear, and let Him be your dread. And He shall be a sanctification to you" (viii. 13, 14). . . . "By the wrath of the Lord of hosts the land is troubled, and the people shall be as fuel for the fire: no man shall spare his brother" (ix. 19). "What will you do in the day of visitation, and of the calamity which cometh from afar? to whom will ye flee for help? and where will ye leave your glory? . . . As my hand hath found the kingdoms of the idol, so also their idols of Jerusalem and of Samaria. Shall I not, as I have done to Samaria and her idols, so do to Jerusalem and her idols?" (ix. 3–11). Then will come the turn of the Assyrian empire itself. "Shall the axe boast itself against him that cutteth with it? . . . As if a rod should lift itself against him who taketh it up!" And again, after repeating for the twentieth time His promises of mercy and final restoration, the Lord adjures Jerusalem in these touching words: "Therefore, thus saith the Lord the God of hosts: O, my people, that dwellest in Sion, be not afraid of the Assyrian. He shall strike thee with his rod, and he shall lift up his staff over thee in the way of Egypt. For yet a little and a very little while, and My indignation shall cease, and My wrath shall be upon their wickedness. And the Lord shall raise up a scourge against him."

Meanwhile, in favor of the "true Israelites," the men of pure lives, unfaltering faith, and unshaken hope in the promises, the Prophet ever holds up their sure fulfillment. "And there shall come forth a rod out of the root of Jesse, and a flower shall rise up out of his root. And the Spirit of the Lord shall rest upon him" (xi. 1, 2).

Surely it was the same Spirit who rested upon the patriot prophet himself.

3. Chapters xi. and xii. form one of these exultant hymns which we conceive Faith to be wont to sing amid the darkness of the densest idolatry and the wrecks of home and country. "And it shall come to pass in that day, that the Lord shall set His hand the second time to possess the remnant of His people, which shall be left from the Assyrians. . . . And thou shalt say in that day: I will give thanks to Thee, O Lord, for Thou wast angry with me: Thy wrath is turned away, and Thou hast comforted me.

Behold, God is my Saviour, I will deal confidently and will not fear: because the Lord is my strength and my praise, and He is become my salvation."

Then come, under the designation of "burdens," the prediction of the terrible retribution which is to be dealt out on each of the enemies of God and His people—on Babylon, the Philistines, the Moabites, on Damascus, Samaria, the Assyrians and Egyptians. He pauses, in chapter xxii., while describing the devastation of Juda, to utter against Sobna, one of the blind and vicious counselors of blind and vicious princes and people, the divine judgment gone forth against him. "Thou hast hewed thee out carefully a monument in a high place, a dwelling for thyself in a rock. Behold the Lord will cause thee to be carried away, as a cock is carried away, and He will lift thee up as a garment. He will toss thee like a ball into a large and spacious country."

Nor shall the maritime powers of that age be spared by the scourge of divine justice. Tyre and Sidon shall fall. "The Lord of hosts hath designed it, to pull down the pride of all glory, and bring to disgrace all the mighty ones of the earth. . . . The earth is infected by the inhabitants thereof; because they have transgressed the laws, they have changed the ordinance, they have broken the everlasting covenant. Therefore shall a curse devour the earth, and the inhabitants thereof shall sin. . . . It shall be thus in the midst of the earth, in the midst of the people, as if a few olives that remain should be shaken out of the olive-tree, or grapes, when the vintage is ended. . . . With breaking shall the earth be broken, with crushing shall the earth be crushed, with trembling shall the earth be moved." This moral and social convulsion, like the mighty upheavals that are recorded in geology, is now a matter of history. And how very nearly its terrible teachings come home, at this hour, to the guilty Christendom of the nineteenth century, with the decline of faith, the weakening of all authority, human and divine, the spread of intellectual and moral corruption, and the breaking up of the whole order of society in opposition to the laws of nature and the solemn ordinances of nature's God!

Together with this breaking up of the old Pagan order there is present to the eye of the prophet the end of all things, the final judgment and doom; the wicked ones both of heaven and of earth "gathered together as in the gathering of one bundle into the Pit," and the eternal reign of God with His faithful servants in the heavenly Jerusalem. At this prospect the rapt soul of Isaias bursts forth into a shout of triumphant song: "O Lord, Thou art my God, I will exalt Thee, and give glory to Thy name; For Thou hast done wonderful things. Thy designs of old faithful, Amen! . . . Therefore shall a strong people praise Thee, the city of the mighty nations shall fear Thee. Because Thou hast been a strength to the poor, a strength to the needy in his distress: a refuge from the whirlwind, a shadow from the heat. . . . And they shall say in that day: Lo, this is our God; we have waited for Him, and He will save us: this is the Lord, we have patiently waited for Him, we shall rejoice and be joyful in His salvation."

From this vision of the Eternal Rest on high which thrills the soul of the prophet, he passes to the return of Israel from captivity, and the heart of the patriot bursts forth into a still more lofty strain, because with the vision of his restored people is mingled that of the glory of the Christian church. "Sion, the city of our strength—a Saviour! A wall and a bulwark shall be set therein. Open ye the gates, and let the just nation that keepeth the truth enter in! The old error is passed away: Thou wilt keep peace, peace, because we have hoped in Thee! You have hoped in the Lord for evermore, in the Lord God mighty for ever. . . . And in the way of Thy judgments, O Lord, we have patiently waited for Thee: Thy name and Thy remembrance (are) the desire of the soul!"

Full of divinest eloquence, most sublime poetry, of tender piety that stirs every pulse of the reader's heart, the stream of Isaias' inspiration flows onward in its rapid and majestic course, unlike anything else in sacred or profane literature,—the glory of the Hebrew intellect, the wonder and light of the Christian church.

The above beautiful canticle may have been written and uttered when Jerusalem, during the invasion of Salmanasar (Shalmanezer) IV., was preserved from capture and spoliation, while Samaria fell into the hands of the invader. This was during the reign of the incomparable Ezechias, the most perfect prince who ever sat on the throne of David, and who was of one mind and one heart with his kinsman, the great prophet of Juda. Ezechias had made a clean sweep of the "high places," and of every other relic of idolatry within his kingdom. Without positively neglecting what is called political prudence in his dealings with other sovereigns, he placed his whole trust in Jehovah alone, and spurned every alliance that might imperil the faith or weaken the proud self-reliance under God with which he inspired his people. There were, however, those among them, Sobna (Shebna), the high treasurer, for instance, who hankered for a close union with Egypt as a means of resisting Assyria. But neither the prophet nor the king showed any mercy to these politicians. We have seen above how Sobna was disgraced, and can judge from his case how it fared with all those of his class. "Woe to them that go down to Egypt for help, trusting in horses, and putting their confidence in chariots, because they are many; . . . and have not trusted in the Holy One of Israel! . . . Egypt is man, and not God, and their horses flesh, and not spirit: and the Lord shall put down (stretch out) his hand, and the helper shall fall, and he that is helped shall fall, and they shall be confounded together" (xxxi. 1–3). Formidable and resistless as then appeared the power of the Assyrians, their utter defeat is announced repeatedly and with such detailed circumstances as could not but challenge the attention of the whole people. "Behold the NAME of the Lord cometh from afar, His wrath burneth. . . . You shall have a song as in the night of the sanctified solemnity. . . . And the Lord shall make the glory of His voice to be heard. . . . For at the voice of the Lord the Assyrian shall fear being struck with the rod" (xxx. 27–31). But with these notions and predictions of deliverance from temporal evils and earthly foes are always mixed up visions of the Divine Liberator and of the long-delayed Redemption. "Behold a king shall reign in justice!" (xxxii. 1); and the Spirit is "poured upon us from on high" (xxxii. 15).

Meanwhile the flood-gates of the Assyrian invasion are opened, and the mighty hosts of Sennacherib inundate Syria and Palestine. Jerusalem, at length, is beset by the victorious host. To the faithful and brave-hearted King Isaias, in this extremity, utters messages of the most cheering import. "Thus saith the Lord: Be not afraid of the words that thou hast heard, with which the servants of the King of the Assyrians have blasphemed Me. . . . I will send a spirit upon him, . . . and I will cause him to fall by the sword in his own country." When the invader concentrates at length all his forces round the beleaguered city, Ezechias, in answer to his blasphemous insolence, challenges the fatherly love of Jehovah for His people: "O Lord our God, save us out of his hand, and let all the kingdoms of the earth know that Thou only art the Lord!" (xxxvii. 20). While still kneeling before the Mercy Seat, Ezechias receives through Isaias the answer to his prayer. It is Jehovah who speaks to the proud and blasphemous Assyrian: . . . "I will put a ring in thy nose and a bit between thy lips, and I will turn thee back by the way by which thou camest" (xxxvii. 29). That very night, . . . "The angel of the Lord went out, and slew in the camp of the Assyrians a hundred and eighty-five thousand."

This miraculous deliverance had been the great event toward which all the preceding prophecies, all the denunciations, and all the unceasing activity of Isaias pointed. From the very first page he knew what was to be the dreadful fate of the schismatic and idolatrous Ten Tribes forming the Northern Kingdom, that of Israel or Samaria. They were to be swept away by the hand of the Assyrian, and for them, as a nation or a body politic, there was to be no restoration. To avert from the Kingdom of Juda and Jerusalem, its capital, a similar fate, was the cherished purpose for which Isaias lived, labored, wrote, and prophesied. To inspire his people and their rulers with an absolute and unwavering trust in Jehovah,—in His love, His willingness and power to protect and shield them from all dangers, he bent all the resources of his genius and influence, and discharged most faithfully the duties of his recognized calling as a Seer and Prophet. When the epoch of the dreaded Assyrian invasion was near at hand, God sent to his people a perfect king in Ezechias, and to the Prophet a most zealous auxiliary in his mission of religious reformation and patriotic revival. Even the wretched remnants of the Ten Tribes which had escaped the sword or the greed of the Assyrian, understood the lesson which both Isaias and their own prophets Micheas, Osee, and Amos had vainly taught them throughout all these years of delusion and guilt. When they found the glory of Samaria gone, and their country wasted like a stubble-field over which the fire had passed, they turned their eyes and their hearts to Jerusalem and its God, and sought with them an asylum in their utter despair.

But history tells us that the turn of Juda and Jerusalem was yet to come. The Babylonian captivity awaited them. This God had revealed in advance to Isaias,—and this forms the subject of the last twenty-seven chapters of this book. Chapters xxxviii. and xxxix. are out of their place in the order of time; the sickness of Ezechias happened before the deliverance of Jerusalem and the flight of Sennacherib. But as the Prophet's soul was occupied with this central event in his life, he postponed what related to the illness and cure of the holy king to the thrilling recital of Jehovah's victory. This illness had occurred two years before the siege of Jerusalem by the Assyrians, and fifteen years before the close of the royal life. But connected with the King's restoration to health is an incident which had great influence on the events that were soon to follow on the flight of the Assyrian host.

Merodach-Baladan IV., King of Babylon, anxious to cultivate friendly relations with the enemies of the Assyrians, had sent ambassadors to compliment the King of Juda on his recovery. "Ezechias rejoiced at their coming, and he showed them the storehouse of his aromatical spices, and of the silver, and of the gold, . . . and all things that were found in his treasures. There was nothing in his house nor in all his dominion that Ezechias showed them not." It was a display prompted by a vanity unworthy of so great a character, and condemned by sound policy as well as by sound sense. Forthwith the divine messenger is at hand to question the imprudent sovereign, and to receive a frank answer. "And Isaias said to Ezechias: Hear the word of the Lord of hosts. Behold the days shall come, that all that is in thy house, and that thy fathers have laid up in store until this day, shall be carried away unto Babylon. There shall not be anything left, saith the Lord. And of thy children that shall issue from thee, . . . they shall take away, and they shall be eunuchs in the palace of the King of Babylon."

4. This Babylonian captivity and the means to be employed by Providence to restore Juda become henceforth to the prophet not only a subject of continual and absorbing interest, but one which he speaks of as present. Cyrus, the destroyer of the Babylonian power, though yet unborn, is mentioned by name again and again, and the providential mission that he is to fulfill is clearly sketched out. But the crimes which bring on Juda this visitation, and the manifold evils of exile and bondage which are the chastisement of these crimes,—only remind the Prophet of the sad condition of the entire race of man, miserably degraded by the captivity of sin and serving false gods in their degradation. Side by side with the restoration by Cyrus is described the Redemption by the Messiah ;

and together with the person of Cyrus we are made to behold the person of Christ. The birth, education, labors, sufferings, and death of the Redeemer are set forth in colors so vivid, minute, and life-like, that Isaias may be well said to be fulfilling the office of Evangelist rather than that of Prophet.

It is, however, to the book itself that you must go, dear Reader, to find in its inspired pages so much of light, and sweetness, and strength. For the Spirit who spoke by this great and holy man never fails to open the eyes and move the hearts of those who study his writings with humble and earnest faith.

THE BOOK OF JEREMIAS.—Two of the darkest reigns that ever disgraced any country, or saddened the hearts of men who believe in a Supreme Being and in the eternal laws of morality, separate Isaias from Jeremias. Manasses, born to the good King Ezechias after the latter's recovery from the mortal illness mentioned above, and about the very period of the siege and deliverance of Jerusalem, was as unlike his pious and public-spirited parent as a son could well be. The alliance which the former contracted with the Babylonians, and from which Isaias foretold the direst consequences, became a state necessity with his successor. Worse than that, however— worse indeed than any calamity which had ever before befallen the Kingdom of Juda —was the formal and open apostasy of Manasses. Not only did he forsake the faith of his father, but he introduced in its stead the foulest idol-worship of Babylon and Syria, banishing from the Temple every remnant of the worship of Jehovah, desecrating its precincts and the Holy of holies itself with the most odious heathen rites; blotting out, so far as he could, from the laws and institutions of his native country every trace of the Law of God, every memorial of His past mercies to Israel. Not content with this, he persecuted with the most unsparing cruelty all those who were faithful to their conscience, the priests and prophets, especially, and, among these, Isaias. This great man, the stay of religion and nationality, the glory of his race and age, was now past eighty. Of course, years had not diminished his zeal in the service of his God and his country. And the last chapters in his prophecies are there to tell us that the beautiful mind had lost none of its power, and the prophet's divine eloquence none of its inspiration. Had the Holy Spirit disclosed to him the secret of his own cruel death at the hands of the impious Manasses? We cannot say. But there is a touching appositeness in the last utterances recorded by Isaias. "For Sion's sake, I will not hold my peace; and for the sake of Jerusalem, I will not rest till her Just One come forth as brightness, and her Saviour be lighted as a lamp" (lxii. 1). "Who is this that cometh from Edom, with dyed garments from Bosra, this Beautiful One in His robe, walking in the greatness of His strength? Why then is Thy apparel red, and Thy garments like those that tread in the wine-press" (lxiii. 1, 2)? Are these the words of a martyr, conscious of his approaching fate, and gazing from afar on the form of the King of Martyrs, as He stands alone, with blood-stained garments and torn head and limbs on the wood of His cross, about to stretch forth His hands to the nails? For it is the constant tradition of both the Jewish and Christian churches

that Manasses caused the great-souled prophet to be inclosed in the trunk of a tree and sawn in the middle.

It was the privilege of Jeremias to be called to fulfill his prophetic mission during the reign of Josias, the grandson of Manasses and the son of a father who rivaled Manasses in impiety and wickedness. During the reign of the saintly Josias and till the destruction of Jerusalem by the Chaldæans—that is, during a period of forty years—Jeremias continued to discharge the duties of his sacred office with a heroism and eloquence that make him rank only after Isaias. Like St. John the Baptist, he was sanctified before his birth for the sublime mission to which he was destined. And he needed all the extraordinary graces of which this first one was a pledge. For to none of the prophets or of the saints of the Old Law was assigned a mission so barren in consolation, so full of that intense bitterness which arises from the spectacle of prolonged national degeneracy and apostasy, and from the utter ruin of the dearest hopes of the priest and the patriot. It was a life-long martyrdom. When he first heard the Divine Voice calling him to his long struggle with ignorance and iniquity—a woman Holda (Huldah) was the sole organ of the divine will in all Juda. Though afterward he was to have as his auxiliaries in the prophetic office not only Holda and his disciples, the brothers Baruch and Saraias, but Sophonias, Habacuc, and Urias, still, scattered as were the remnants of God's people both in Egypt and Mesopotamia, utterly desolate as was the land of Juda and Israel, and obstinately perverse as his countrymen and their leaders continued to be, Jeremias encountered nothing but contradiction, hatred, and persecution. He is imprisoned by his countrymen during the siege of Jerusalem, because he counsels them to make terms with the enemy, knowing supernaturally, as he does, that on a conditional surrender depends the preservation of the city and the Temple, as well as immunity from the frightful evils of a place carried by storm. He opposed, as did Isaias before him, every alliance with foreigners, and advocated as the only safeguards to national independence a total reform in manners and religion and unbounded loyalty to Jehovah. Even the good King Josias was continually hesitating between an alliance with Babylon and a league with Egypt. In spite of Jeremias' earnest remonstrances, the prince did attach himself to the Chaldæans, and perished by the hands of the Egyptians whom he persisted in attacking without cause. Thus the Prophet was assailed with equal hostility by both political parties in Jerusalem who happened to incline either for the Babylonian alliance or for the Egyptian. After the death of Josias began that succession of deplorable reigns each of which recalled the worst crimes of Manasses and Amon—princes and people continuing in exile and slavery what they had been in their own country, God-defying and God-forsaken.

As to the order in which these prophecies were given and consigned to writing, we are informed that, up to the fourth year of Joakim, King of Juda, Jeremias had not recorded his prophecies in writing. He, therefore, by divine command commits to writing "all the words" that he had spoken from the Lord "against Israel and Juda, and against all the nations." In this task his disciple Baruch fills the office of secretary. This first volume is destroyed in the wicked King's own chamber, and Jeremias is bidden to write another volume. This contains all that had been put down in the first "besides many more words than had been before" (chap. xxxvi. 1–32).

We can thus take these first thirty-six chapters as containing the first and principal portion of the prophecies of Jeremias, as well as the chief incidents of his own personal history as given by himself. Chapters xxxv. and xxxvi., however, interrupt the chronological order, the first to set forth the heroic fidelity of the Rechabites as a lesson to a sensual and faithless generation, and the other to give a history of the book itself, as well as to warn more solemnly both the nation and its King that the Babylonian captivity so long threatened was near at hand.

In chapter xxxvii. the prophet resumes the account of his mission under King Sedecias just where his narration ended in chapter xxxiv. At this point we find the Babylonians besieging Jerusalem, and the recreant King and his counselors send, in their terror, to consult Jeremias about the final issue. For the enemy had withdrawn his forces momentarily to meet the Egyptians advancing to the rescue. There is but one answer—the prediction so often repeated in vain: "The Chaldæans shall come again, and fight against this city, and take it, and burn it with fire." He cannot deliver to them a false message from the God of truth; and they will not bring themselves to believe in the destruction of Jerusalem as foretold. So, he is cast into prison, first, and then the Egyptian faction demand that he shall be put to death (xxxviii. 4). The King consents, and the prophet is cast into the worst of dungeons as a preliminary to his execution. Saved from this peril by an Ethiopian slave, he is pressed more vehemently by Sedecias to tell him, the King, the truth as he desires it. "And Jeremias said to Sedecias, Thus saith the Lord of hosts the God of Israel: If thou wilt take a resolution and go out to the princes of the King of Babylon, thy soul shall live, and this city shall not be burnt with fire; and thou shalt be safe and thy house." Of course the King would not assent.

And then the end came (xxxix). The remaining chapters, as far as xlv., recount the taking of Jerusalem and the evils which followed. The Prophet remains among the ruins of his country still bent on helping the miserable remnants of his people left behind by the conqueror to return sincerely to the God of their fathers. He knows what the Almighty can do with a few faithful, repentant, and resolute hearts to build up even a destroyed nationality. And so his crushing grief is lightened in the endeavor to make of the few who remain of Juda and Israel true worshipers and true citizens. But political division and party rivalries, the bane of falling commonwealths and the curse of such as strive to rise, set the Jews against each other; caused one faction to massacre the leaders of the other, and then to seek a refuge in Egypt against the vengeance of the Babylonians. The Prophet and his disciple, Baruch, are compelled to follow them thither. In vain did Jeremias announce that Egypt should not protect them; and equally in vain, during his captivity in that land, did he try to convert these men from their evil ways. The very accomplishment of the prophecies which they had so often derided before the event, only made them the more bitterly hostile to him, and only rendered more intolerable his denunciation of the crimes which his fellow-exiles in Egypt added to all their former wickedness. At length—so the most ancient and venerable traditions say—they put him to death, in order to silence forever the voice which no bribe could buy and no fear intimidate. But they could not thereby still the voice of their own conscience nor remove from above their own heads the Almighty Hand and the sword of the divine justice toward which Jeremias had so often directed their eyes in vain.

The remaining chapters of the book must be read in the light of contemporaneous history and with the aid of the most scholarly critics.

THE PROPHECY OF BARUCH.—All agree that the illustrious man, who has given his name to this book, was the disciple, secretary, and associate of Jeremias. His noble birth and powerful connections were so well known, as well as the esteem in which he was held by his master, that the court party under Joakim attributed to Baruch's persuasion the great prophet's constancy in proclaiming the certain destruction of Jerusalem by the Chaldæans. Both were imprisoned together, and both would have doubtless perished together had not the bad King's fears caused them to be reprieved; the taking of Jerusalem found them still in prison. The conquerors spared them. But their fate, according to the most ancient traditions, united them in life and death. They both died together in Egypt, witnessing to the end to the truth of Jehovah's prophecies. So must you, dear reader, study the writings and the lives of these two heroic men as one inseparable whole, full of elevating examples and divinest teachings.

EZECHIEL.

EZECHIEL, the son of Buzi, was of a priestly family, a contemporary of the two preceding prophets, and carried off a prisoner to Babylonia by Nabuchodonosor, together with King Jechonias, eleven years before the final capture and destruction of Jerusalem. He tells us that he was called to fulfill his prophetic mission "in the thirtieth year." And it has puzzled scholars not a little to find out from what event he reckons these years up to the "thirtieth." Be that event what it may, we know that the *thirtieth year* here mentioned coincided with the fifth of the captivity of Jechonias, as well as the fifth of the reign of his son, Sedecias. During the twenty years which followed Ezechiel did not cease to fill his sacred office. His chief purpose is to confirm in the faith his fellow-captives in Chaldæa. They despaired, in their bondage, of ever seeing their race restored to Palestine, many and clear as had been the declarations of Jeremias on this subject. What this great prophet had so often announced in his own country, what indeed he continued to predict in Jerusalem all through these first years of the captivity, Ezechiel was called to proclaim on the banks of the Euphrates. So that these two illustrious contemporaries were like two inspired singers taking up alternately the burden of the same song, the one in the far northeast amid the splendors of Babylonia, the other in the southwest and among the blindly-sinning multitudes of fore-doomed Jerusalem.

No other prophet has clothed his predictions and teachings under such varied and striking forms. Sometimes he gives his utterances the shape of distinct predictions (vi., vii., xx., etc.); sometimes they are proposed as allegories (xxiii., xxiv.); again as symbolical actions (iv., viii.), or similitudes (xii., xv.), or parables (xvii.); or as proverbs (xii. 22; xviii. 1 and following); or, finally, as visions (viii.–xi.) "The book," says Dr. Smith (*Dictionary of the Bible*, art. "Ezekiel"), "is divided into two great parts, of which the destruction of Jerusalem is the turning-point; chapters i.–xxiv. contain predictions delivered before that event, and xxv.–xlviii. after it, as we see from xxvi. 2. Again, chapters i.–xxxii. are mainly occupied with correction, denunciation and reproof, while the remainder deal chiefly in consolation and promise. A parenthetical section in the middle of the book (xxv.–xxxii.) contains a group of prophecies against seven foreign nations."

Another very convenient grouping of the prophecies, according to the same author, is that of Hävernick, who divides the book into nine sections, as follows: I. Ezechiel's call, i.–iii. 15. II. The general carrying out of the commission, iii. 16–vii. III. The rejection of the people because of their idolatry, viii.–xi. IV. The sins of the age rebuked in detail, xii.–xix. V. The nature of the judgment and the guilt which caused it, xx.–xxiii. VI. The meaning of the now commencing punishment, xxiv. VII. God's judgment denounced on seven heathen nations: Ammonites, xxv. 1–7; Moab, 8–14; the Philistines, 15–17; Tyre, xxvi.–xxviii. 19; Sidon, 20–24; Egypt, xxix.–xxxii. VIII. Prophecies after the destruction of Jerusalem concerning the future condition of Israel, xxxiii.–xxxix. IX. The glorious consummation, xl.–xlviii.

One most touching incident in the prophet's life deserves especial mention. During the ninth year of his captivity, his wife died at the very time that Jerusalem was sorely pressed by Nabuchodonosor. "Son of man, write thee the name of this day on which the King of Babylon hath set himself against Jerusalem. . . . Woe to the bloody city of which I shall make a great bonfire. . . . I will judge thee according to thy ways, and according to thy doings, saith the Lord. And the word of the Lord came to me, saying: I take

from thee the desire of thy eyes with a stroke; and thou shalt not lament, nor weep; neither shall thy tears run down. Sigh in silence, make no mourning for the dead: let the tire of thy head be upon thee, and thy shoes on thy feet, and cover not thy face, nor eat the meat of mourners. So I spoke to the people in the morning, and my wife died in the evening; and I did in the morning as He had commanded me. And the people said to me: Why dost thou not tell us what these things mean that thou doest? And I said, The word of the Lord came to me, saying, Speak to the house of Israel: Thus saith the Lord God, 'Behold, I will profane My sanctuary, the glory of your realm, and the thing that your eyes desire, and for which your soul feareth: your sons and your daughters shall fall by the sword.' And you shall do as I have done; you shall not cover your faces, nor shall you eat the meat of mourners. You shall have crowns on your head, and shoes on your feet" (xxiv. 1–23).

Alas, grievous as was the lot of these poor wrong-headed exiles in Babylonia at the moment of this particular prediction, it was to become incomparably worse after the return of Nabuchodonosor. They were to be separated and scattered through the length and breadth of the empire, most of them to perish through misery and hardship. This is the reason why the latter misfortune is so great as compared with the former, that even the loss of the nearest and dearest, and the annihilation of the most cherished national hopes are as nothing compared with the intolerable bitterness of their coming ills.

DANIEL.—While the Hebrews were enduring all the humiliations and hardships of captivity and exile under the yoke of their Assyrian masters, Providence was preparing avengers for all the impiety and cruelty displayed in Palestine and elsewhere by Sennacherib and his successors. The Chaldæans had ever borne with impatience the rule of Nineveh; and before this proud city fell forever Babylon began to reassert its own independence and superiority. Nabopolassar, the father of Nabuchodonosor, firmly established the Babylonian supremacy, and with the assistance of the Medes under Cyaxares effected the utter and final destruction of Nineveh.

For the exiled Hebrews the annihilation of the Assyrian power only meant a change of masters, not freedom from the yoke or restoration to their native land. The most extravagant despotism and the most repulsive forms of idolatry marked the new Chaldæan empire, as we may judge not only from the Book of Daniel, but from the very annals which are daily brought to light from the ruins of the Babylonian cities.

Daniel too, like Isaias, was of the royal race of David, was carried away into captivity in the third year of King Joakim, and with three young companions was brought up as a page in the royal palace. As the idolatrous practices of the Chaldæans demanded that all animal food served on the royal tables should have been previously offered to the gods, to partake of them implied a participation in this idol-worship. This to the worshipers of the true God was a defilement and an abomination. And such meats Daniel and his companions refused to touch, preferring to feed exclusively on vegetable food. On this fare they grew up to robust and comely manhood. And, as had long before happened to Joseph in the house of Putiphar, heroic temperance brought them supernatural wisdom. Though scarcely emerged from boyhood, Daniel, as the story of Susanna proves, was known among his fellow-captives to be possessed of a knowledge all divine. In the fourth year of the noble youth's exile happened the famous vision sent to the king of the statue made of divers metals, and the stern interpretation given of the monarch's dream by Daniel. The despot is awed for the moment into acknowledging the God of Israel as the only living God. But his subsequent career of con-

quest turns his head, and he, too, will have himself worshiped after the manner of his ancestor Bel or Baal. Then comes a second terrific dream (iv. 8–27) which Daniel also explains, and is followed by the proud king's salutary expiation. Finally, under Baltassar (Belshazzar), a third fearful vision is sent, prophetic of the impending doom of the empire itself. Daniel is again sent for to read "the hand-writing on the wall;" and that very night Babylon is taken by Cyrus and his Persians, and by Darius and his Medes.

The seven first chapters of the Book of Daniel are partly historical and partly prophetical, while the four following relate to the rise and fall of the great empires which are to rule the earth, and among which shall be cast the lot of the children of God till the end of time. In chapter ix. occurs the celebrated prophecy of the "seventy weeks of years" after the expiration of which Christ the Messiah was to consummate the work of redemption. In the last two chapters, xiii. and xiv., are found the story of Susanna and that of Bel and the Dragon.

THE TWELVE MINOR PROPHETS.

All the writers, who in the Old Testament are designated under the title of Prophets, lived within the period elapsed from the year before Christ, 784 to 445, the date of Nehemias' governorship over Judæa, a space, therefore, of about three hundred and forty years. Of the Four Greater Prophets we have already spoken. But, as the Twelve Lesser Prophets have lived at the same time with their more illustrious brethren in the prophetic office, giving to these, under God's inspiration and direction, the aid of their ministry, so it seems but rational to group them together in the order in which they lived. Thus we shall have four groups: 1st. Osee, Amos, Jonas, Michæas, and Nahum, who were contemporaries of Isaias. 2d. Sophonias, Joel, and Habacuc, who belong to the epoch of Jeremias. 3d. Abdias, who lived during the period of the captivity, thus is a contemporary of Daniel and Ezechiel. 4th. Aggias, Zacharias, and Malachias belong to the time of the Restoration, extending from Zorobabel in 546 to Nehemias in 445.

So, dear reader, it will help you not a little toward the understanding of what is most important in each prophecy, if you will go to the table on page oo, and then read a brief summary of the reigns of the contemporary kings whether of Israel or Juda. Thereby you will be better able to see the drift of the prophecy and to compare each prediction with what is contained in the book of the Greater Prophet, who lived at the same epoch, and for whose assistance God inspired and sent the Minor Prophets of his age.

Another advice we must here give parents or others who are desirous or accustomed to read for the young and innocent select passages from the Scripture, is—to be very careful not to allow their pure-minded and unsuspecting charge to read for themselves and without discrimination the books of the prophets. There are passages in them which might and would disedify or shock the sense of English readers.

Eastern nations, in the days of Isaias and Daniel, were anything rather than refined in their manners, their sentiments, or their language, although they were far advanced in the arts of mere material civilization. Even in Palestine, all through the centuries over which extended the lives and teachings of the prophets, there existed a sensuality in manners, derived from the too common practice of the abominable idolatry of their Chanaanite and Babylonian neighbors, and a corresponding coarseness of language, of which but few among us, happily, have any conception.

Hence it is, that the prophets sent to rouse men steeped in vice and almost brutified by the prevailing idol-worship from their deep sleep of forgetfulness or insensibility to divine things, use figures, comparisons, parables, allegories, expressions which to us are most shocking, but which conveyed the truth in the only form calculated to strike and startle the God-forgetting generations among whom they lived. Over these passages the guides of youth will pass to find what is edifying and beautiful and instructive in these inspired writings.

I. OSEE, AMOS, JONAS, MICHÆAS, AND NAHUM.—

1. Osee began his mission most probably in the last year of Jeroboam II., King of Israel (died B. C. 784), and continued his labors during sixty years down to the reign of Ezechias, King of Juda. He with his brother prophets in the northern kingdom did for the enlightenment and salvation of the Ten Tribes what Isaias was at the same time doing for the Kingdom of Juda. Jeroboam II. had been the most fortunate of all the rulers of the northern kingdom; had wrested from the surrounding Pagan nations not only the territories belonging to his own subject tribes, but also that which belonged to Juda and Benjamin and which had been long held by their enemies. This restoration of the entire patrimony of God's people had been the subject of more than one prophecy, and the restorer had even been designated as a deliverer in the inspired utterances. However Jeroboam II. was not the man to unite piety toward the true God with the courage of the soldier and the wisdom of the statesman. He could not or would not understand that unity of belief and worship was the great secret of national strength, prosperity, and invincibility. In religious matters he was the worthy successor of Jeroboam I. and of Jehu, favored idolatry to the exclusion of the worship of Jehovah, and allowed himself and his people to float unresistingly down the stream of drunkenness and licentiousness. As we shall see, Amos (vii. 9) predicted the utter overthrow of this prevaricating dynasty.

The first three chapters of Osee are filled by one terrible allegory full of light and menace for both kingdoms. God again and again in Scripture speaks of His love for this chosen race as that of a husband for the woman whom he has made his wife, choosing her from among all living women. The favors conferred on Israel He continually likens to the extraordinary proofs of affection, tenderness, and profuse liberality, which the most devoted of husbands never wearies in bestowing on the bride of his choice. It was the divine purpose to make of the privileged people a queen among nations. This purpose had been thwarted by the incurable perversity of the chosen one, and all the divine liberality and magnificence made the occasion of the foulest guilt. What reason would not favored Israel have of accusing the Most High of being untrue to His covenant, if He had neglected His own people despite their inviolable fidelity and heroic devotion, and lavished on the idolatrous nations round about the favors promised exclusively to His own? What if all the transgressions and the odium of faithlessness and inconstancy could be laid to His account? This is what is implied in the fearful allegory of these first chapters. Their thought, imagery, and expressions, are borrowed from the life and language of a people lost to all sense of guilt and shame, and accessible only to the terrible threats implied in the converse of the above supposition, and suggested by the awakened consciousness

of a nation that had so often in the past experienced the prodigies of Jehovah's love, and which is now threatened with the extremity of His vengeance. "The children of Israel shall sit many days without king, and without prince, and without sacrifice, and without altar. . . . And after this the children of Israel shall return, and shall seek the Lord their God, and David their King: and they shall fear the Lord and His goodness in the last days" (iii. 4, 5). This first portion may well apply to the close of Jeroboam's brilliant reign, while the troublous interregnum of eleven years which followed on his death may have filled the popular mind with serious apprehensions about the near fulfillment of the prophet's threat.

The succeeding chapters strike the reader of biblical history with the same feeling of singular aptness, when one remembers that the popular leaders in the northern, as well as in the southern kingdom were always hankering after an alliance with the Egyptian or the Mesopotamian kings, while they and the blind multitude they misled were plunging deeper every day into the criminal excesses reproved by the divine law. "Ephraim saw his sickness and Juda his band: and Ephraim went to the Assyrian, and sent to the avenging king. And he shall not be able to heal you, neither shall he be able to take off the band from you. For I will be like a lioness to Ephraim and like a lion's whelp to the house of Juda: I will catch, and go: I will take away, and there is none that can rescue" (v. 13–15). "Ephraim himself is mixed among the nations: Ephraim is become as bread baked under the ashes, that is not turned. . . . They called upon Egypt and went to the Assyrians" (vii. 8–11). . . . "Egypt shall gather them together, Memphis shall bury them: nettles shall inherit their beloved silver, the bur shall be in their tabernacles. The days of visitation are come, the days of repaying are come: Know ye, O Israel, that the prophet is foolish, the spiritual man was mad, for the multitude of thy iniquity, and the multitude of thy madness. . . . My God shall cast them away, because they hearkened not to him: and they shall be wanderers among the nations!" (ix. 6–17.)

So Osee in Samaria, as Isaias in Jerusalem, was looked upon by the scheming politicians as a madman, and by the pleasure-seeking populace as a fool, because he dared threaten the nation in the noonday of its prosperity and pride with defeat and dispersion. And yet the burthen is laid on them both to proclaim the coming doom to every prince who ascended the throne, and to the daily crowd who rushed to the groves and high places, to the altars of Ashtarte and haunts of forbidden pleasure.

But these incorruptible and fearless men, in whose hearts the love of country and race was inseparable from the love of their Master, ceased not to bear their witness in the midst of the sinful crowd. "Ephraim feedeth on the wind, and followeth the [changes of the] heat: all the day long he multiplied lies and desolation: and he hath made a covenant with the Assyrians, and carried oil into Egypt. Therefore there is a judgment of the Lord with Juda, and a visitation for Jacob: He will render to him according to his ways, and according to his devices. . . . Therefore turn thou to thy God: Keep mercy and judgment, and hope in thy God always" (xii. 1–6).

Would you, dear reader, understand both the purpose and the mission of such prophets as Osee, then go back to 2 Paralipomenon xviii., and peruse the entire chapter carefully. Few scenes in sacred or profane history are so full of salutary instruction, or so powerfully drawn as that in which the wily and impious Achab and the pious but inconsistent Joshaphat are placed, in presence of the population of Samaria, directly beneath the successive influence of the lying prophets of Baal and the cruelly-treated minister of Jehovah. Samaria is the capital of "Ephraim" or the Kingdom of Israel. From the perusal of that single chapter you can understand what enemies the worshipers of the true God found among their own brethren, the descendants of Jacob, the descendants even of Ephraim, the favored son of Joseph.

2. Amos.—This man of God had not been trained in the schools of the prophets, and, as we may judge from his style, knew little, if anything, of book-learning. He was by profession a dresser of sycamore or wild fig trees, and one of the numerous "herdsmen of Thecua," alternately pasturing his flocks or dressing his trees on the hills that stretch around his native town between Hebron and the Dead Sea. He was older than Osee, and exercised the prophetic office before him, about the middle of the reign of Jeroboam II.; that is, about the year 800 before Christ. If you have read, as we suggested, of the visit paid to the idolatrous Samaria and its dissolute court by the good King Josaphat, you may begin to have some conception of the dreadful apostasy of Ephraim or the Northern Kingdom. Not content with the Egyptian idols—the images of the ox worshiped on the banks of the Nile, and which Jeroboam I. had solemnly set up in the sanctuary of Bethel—Achab had filled Samaria with the abominable statues of Baal, and its palaces and temples with hundreds upon hundreds of priests, magicians, and prophets devoted to the service of the Sidonian god. These were the sights and this the worship with which Josaphat did not fear to defile his own soul and those of his followers in visiting the beautiful city where reigned Achab and Jezabel. But the power and splendor of Jezabel, Achab, and the First Jeroboam were cast into the shade by the military genius, the conquests, and the prudent administration of the Second. Israel (Ephraim) was then at the very highest point of glory, and with the prosperity of the Kingdom had increased the splendor of idolatry, the corruption of all classes, and the uncontrolled oppression of the poor by the rich.

Just when Samaria was thus steeped in sensual pleasure, and intoxicated with its recent greatness and glory, God sent the poor, illiterate herdsman of Thecua all the way to Samaria and Bethel to rebuke the prince, the priests, and the people for their crimes, and to announce the approach of the Assyrians with chains and a yoke . . . "Hear ye this word, ye fat kine that are in the mountains of Samaria—you that oppress the needy, and crush the poor. . . . Come ye to Bethel and do wickedly; to Galgal, and multiply transgressions; and bring in the morning your victims, your tithes in three days . . . I destroyed [some of] you, as God destroyed Sodom and Gomorrha, and you were as a firebrand plucked out of the burning: yet you returned not to Me, saith the Lord . . . Hear ye this word which I take up concerning you for a lamentation. *The House of Israel is fallen, and it shall rise no more*" (iv., v.)! "And the high places of the idol shall be thrown down, and the sanctuaries of Israel shall be laid waste: and I will rise up against the house of Jeroboam with the sword" (vii. 9).

Thereupon Amasias the High Priest of Bethel expels the prophet from the land. But the fearless Seer, ere he departs, declares to Israel one last vision, in which the terrible justice which strikes the unrepentant is blended with the tender mercy that will spare and not destroy utterly. "Behold, the eyes of the Lord God are upon the sinful kingdom, and I will destroy it from the face of the earth: but yet I will not utterly destroy the house of Jacob, saith the Lord. For behold I will command, and I will sift the house of Israel among all nations, as corn is sifted in a sieve: and there shall not a little stone fall to the ground" (ix. 8, 9).

3. Jonas.—It is a not improbable opinion among biblical scholars that Jonas was anterior in time to both Amos and Osee. He is generally thought to have exercised his ministry during the reigns of Joas, King of Israel, and of his son, Jeroboam II. He is the representative of our Lord both in His death and in His glorious resurrection. The mission on which the prophet was sent—that of procuring the conversion and the salvation of an entire people; his being cast into the sea during a storm to save the remaining ship's crew from perishing; the miracle by which his life is preserved amid the depths of the sea, and he is cast ashore the third

day to continue his journey and perform the errand on which he is divinely sent; all this is most wonderful, even in the history of that people whose life was a series of stupendous miracles, and whose existence down to the present day is a miracle that arrests the attention of all serious-minded persons. The resurrection of Christ—the basis of the Christian's faith and highest hopes—is the great central miracle in the history of Revealed Religion. The conversion of the pagan world hinged on a belief in it. The men who proclaimed it, and who had witnessed it, sealed their testimony both by miracles and their own blood. It was a supernatural fact, supernaturally proven to the world. The miracle of Jonas, which prefigured it, was also a supernatural fact to which God's people bore constant witness. The Divine Power which shone forth so transcendently on Calvary, shone also with surpassing evidence in the case of him who bore the figure of Christ buried in the sepulchre and arisen on the third day. To one who believes in the Living God and in His omnipotence, it is worse than folly to question the power of preserving life amid the most terrible dangers, and where no hope of escape appears to the eye of mere reason. If I believe in that Fatherly Hand which saved Daniel in the Lions' Den, and his three young companions amidst the flames of the Chaldæan furnace, why should I hesitate to believe that the same Hand could shield from harm in the deepest depths of ocean—the servant, albeit a momentarily recreant one—on whose mission a nation's welfare depended?

We cannot measure by the rule and square the power of Him who made the heavens and the earth, and with whom alone are the incommunicable secrets of life and death.

4. Micheas.—He was a native of Morasthi or Maresheth, a village in the southwestern part of the territory of Juda, and a contemporary of Isaias, whose phraseology he sometimes borrows (compare Micheas iv. 1–13; Isaias ii. 2, and xli. 15). During the reign of Ezechias, as we learn from Jeremias xxvi. 6–18, Micheas prophesied the chastisements about to befall both the northern and the southern kingdom. He foretells the coming of Salmanazar, the ruin of Samaria, which shall be made to resemble "a heap of stones in the field when a vineyard is planted." Then he predicts the evils which the invasion of Sennacherib will bring on Juda and Jerusalem. "I am filled with the strength of the Spirit of the Lord, with judgment and power, to declare unto Jacob his wickedness, and to Israel his sin. Hear this, ye princes of the house of Jacob, and ye judges of the house of Israel; you that abhor judgment, and pervert all that is right . . . Because of you, Sion shall be ploughed as a field, and Jerusalem shall be as a heap of stones, and the mountain of the Temple as the high places of the forests" (iii. 8–12). By the side of these clear and stern denunciations of coming woe and dispersion, are found no less clear and comforting promises of redemption from captivity, especially of the universal Redemption to be wrought by Christ. "And thou, Bethlehem Ephrata, art a little one among the thousands of Juda; out of thee shall He come forth unto Me that is to be the Ruler in Israel: and His going forth [is] from the beginning, from the days of eternity" (v. 2). Then come touching adjurations in which the Most High recalls to his ungrateful people the miracles performed of old for their deliverance, and the worthlessness of their present sacrificial worship, while they themselves lack all the virtues which are alone pleasing to the Deity. "I will show thee, O man, what is good, and what the Lord requireth of thee: Verily, to do judgment, and to love mercy, and to walk solicitous with thy God!" Such are the divine lessons of righteousness and piety which these inspired men ceased not to teach, not for their own generation only, but for all time.

5. Nahum.—He prophesied under Ezechias; and the desolation which had befallen the northern kingdom, as well as the destruction

which had been wrought in the Kingdom of Juda by the mighty and pitiless hosts of Sennacherib had fired the prophet's soul against the Assyrians. The downfall of their power and the utter ruin of Nineveh, their capital, form the subject of Nahum's three magnificent chapters. "The burden of Ninive!" he begins, one may imagine after the sudden and miraculous overthrow of Sennacherib's army before Jerusalem. The entire prophecy is colored by the spectacle of this terrible rout of the Assyrians. "The Lord is patient, and great in power, and will not cleanse and acquit [the guilty]. The Lord's ways [are] in the tempest and a whirlwind, and clouds [are] the dust of His feet. He rebuketh the sea and drieth it up: and bringeth all the rivers to be a desert." One may almost see the breath of the divine vengeance blowing on the countless army of horsemen, spearmen, and chariots that encompassed Jerusalem, like a surging tide which had hitherto overborne everything in its course. And lo! Jehovah blows upon it and it disappears with the morning light, living wave impelling living wave before it, and leaving the land covered far and wide with the wreck of chariots, horsemen, and infantry! "Who can stand before the face of his indignation? and who shall resist the fierceness of His anger?" Then comes the prophecy of the fall of Nineveh—the mistress and corruptor of all Asia, at the zenith of her glory and power when the Seer pronounced her doom. "Woe to thee, O city of blood, all full of lies and violence! Rapine shall not depart from thee. The noise of the whip, and the noise of the rattling of the wheels, and of the neighing horse, and of the running chariot, and of the horsemen coming up: and of the shining sword, and of the glittering spear, and of a multitude slain, and of grievous destruction! . . ."

Compare these pregnant chapters with the accounts given in our own days of the ruins of Nineveh and her palaces, and of the monuments and annals that had lain buried for thousands of years in this vast grave of a pitiless despotism.

II. SOPHONIAS, JOEL, AND HABACUC.—1. SOPHONIAS.—He lived in the reign of Josias, King of Juda, and was, it is thought, descended from the holy King Ezechias. He began his prophetic office some time before Jeremias entered on his, and also before Josias had seriously begun to reform the abuses and corruptions which Sophonias so bitterly denounces. There are but three chapters, the first of which sets forth the national sins and the certain retribution they shall bring on Juda. The Church has embodied in her liturgic hymns some of the sublime and terrible imagery of the prophet. "The great day of the Lord is near, it is near and exceeding swift: The voice of the day of the Lord is bitter . . . That day [is] a day of wrath, a day of tribulation and distress, a day of calamity and misery, a day of darkness and obscurity, a day of clouds and whirlwinds, a day of the trumpet and alarm against the fenced cities, and against the high bulwarks." The Chaldæans are to be the instrument of the divine wrath in chastising all Palestine; and then the hand of the Lord shall fall heavily on both Nineveh and Babylon. The remnants of Israel shall be gathered together and the Gentiles themselves shall find salvation.

2. JOEL.—Some weighty Jewish and Christian authorities make this prophet a con-

temporary of Joram, son of Achab, and King of Israel, who died in the year 889 B. C. For the mention by Joel of a great famine similar to that which occurred during the reign of that prince afforded a foundation for their opinion. If, however, this famine is identical with that mentioned by Jeremias (viii. 13), then this as well as other reasons allow us to make Joel a contemporary of the latter prophet. Jeremias says: "There is no grape on the vines, and there are no figs on the fig-tree, the leaf is fallen : and I have given them the things that are passed away." Joel, on the other hand, says : "That which the palmer-worm hath left, the locust hath eaten : and that which the locust hath left, the bruchus (cankerworm) hath eaten : and that which the bruchus hath left, the mildew hath destroyed." This plague, however, is only sent in mercy to rouse men to do penance for their sins. " Because the Day of the Lord is at hand, and it shall come like destruction from the mighty." The description of this dreadful day reminds one forcibly of that given in the prophecy of Sophonias, as quoted above. From this twofold picture of the temporal visitation of famine and the terrible judgment of the Last Day, Joel turns to the first coming of Christ—the " Teacher of Justice, and He will make the early and the latter rain to come down to you as in the beginning." Thus with the visions of judgment, and rigorous judgment, are always blended visions of mercy and reconciliation ; and with the calamities and miseries of the present are mixed the glorious perspectives of future redemption and everlasting peace.

3. HABACUC.—The Rabbinical traditions assign the reign of Manasses as the time of this prophet's mission. The latest researches, however, place him with Sophonias in the reign of Josias, thereby making him contemporary with the beginning of Jeremias' career. He and his two brother-prophets, Joel and Nahum, are looked upon by Hebrew scholars as classical models of diction. He predicts the downfall of the Chaldæan empire, brought on by the national vices, insatiable ambition, greed, cruelty, drunkenness, and manifold idolatry. How aptly the prophet's description and denunciation of all and each of these vices apply to the conquerors, statesmen, and politicians of our own day ! . . .

"The proud man . . . who hath enlarged his desire like hell [the grave]: and is himself like death, and he is never satisfied : but will gather together to him all nations, and heap together to him all people. Shall not all these take up a parable against him, and a dark speech concerning him : and it shall be said, Woe to him that heapeth together that which is not his own ? how long also doth he load himself with thick clay ? Shall they not rise up suddenly that shall bite thee ? and they be stirred up that shall tear thee, and thou shalt be a spoil to them? . . . Woe to him that buildeth a town with blood, and prepareth a city by iniquity " (ii. 5-12) ! The third and last chapter contains one of the most sublime hymns to be found in the Bible : the Church in her solemn office applies it to the triumph of the Redeemer.

III. ABDIAS.—It is quite uncertain when this prophet lived. Some scholars think that he lived at the same time with Elias. But others, with much more probability, say that he lived during the Babylonian captivity. He denounces the cruel persecutions got up against the exiled Jews by their traditional enemies the Edomites, of which we have an instance in the book of Esther. They followed in the wake of the Chaldæan conquerors, watching every road and by-way through which the fugitive Jews could escape, and cut them down mercilessly. The prophet predicts that Edom shall in its turn share the fate of its neighbors, without ever sharing their restoration to national independence and prosperity. On the contrary, they are to become the vassals of their restored Jewish brethren.

IV. AGGEUS, ZACHARIAS, AND MALACHIAS.—The first two of these prophets date their mission from the same year, "the second year of Darius." Both were probably born in exile and returned to Jerusalem with Zorobabel, in conformity with the edict of Cyrus. The building of the temple had been suspended during the space of fourteen years in consequence of the hostility of the neighboring Samaritans and Edomites (Moabites and Ammonites). Aggeus is sent to Zorobabel, the Governor of Judæa, and to Jesus the son of Josedec, the High Priest, to rouse their zeal for the completion of the sacred edifice, the very symbol and soul of Hebrew nationality. They and their countrymen are consoled for the inferiority of the second temple, as compared to the first, by the divine assurance that the former shall be glorified by the personal presence of the Messiah Himself. The resumption of this great national work was also the first object of Zacharias' prophetic labors. The first six chapters contain visions regarding the events which were then happening in Judæa, mingled with the prospective glories of the Christian Church and the conversion of the Gentiles. The completion of the Temple structure, as a thing essential to the national religion and a vital condition of the national existence, is insisted on in each of these successive visions. "Thus saith the Lord : I will return to Jerusalem in mercies : My house shall be built in it, saith the Lord of hosts " (i. 16). The nations which have dispersed and oppressed Juda shall see their power broken, and shall no longer oppose the restoration of Hebrew nationality. Jerusalem shall so increase in extent through the multitudes of returning exiles, that no wall can contain them. "I will be to it, saith the Lord, a

THE BOOK OF MALACHIAS

E.P.   W. J. LINTON

wall of fire round about" (ii. 4). The zealous priests who devote themselves to this great work of reconstruction shall be divinely protected against the calumnies of their enemies and the disfavor of the Chaldæan Kings. Jesus the son of Josedec, to whom this personally applies, brings, by his very name, the vision of the future JESUS before the prophet's mind. "Hear, O Jesus, thou High Priest, thou and thy friends that dwell before thee, . . . behold, I WILL BRING MY SERVANT THE ORIENT" (iii. 8). And so the prophetic visions continue, consoling and encouraging the toilers under Zorobabel, and strengthening their faith with the reiterated promise of His coming, who should reign over the whole earth. "Thou shalt take gold and silver, and shalt make crowns, and thou shalt set them on the head of Jesus the son of Josedec the High Priest. And thou shalt speak to him, saying: Thus saith the Lord of hosts, . . . BEHOLD A MAN, THE ORIENT IS HIS NAME . . . He shall build a temple to the Lord : and He shall bear the glory, and shall sit and rule upon His throne ; and He shall be a priest upon His throne " (vi. 11-13).

To the zealous men who desire to see the great ordained fasts kept solemnly as a means of propitiating the divine favor, Zacharias gives a reasonable answer. In the days of their former prosperity, the solemn fasts were kept in a narrow and selfish spirit. God had commanded them, while they fasted, "Judge ye true judgment, and show ye mercy and compassion every man to his brother. And oppress not the widow, and the fatherless, and the stranger and the poor ; and let not a man devise evil in his heart against his brother" (vii. 9, 10). Now that they and their fathers have paid so dearly for the violation of these divine precepts, the new generations must observe the spirit of the law while attending to the letter. "These then are the things which ye shall do. Speak ye truth every one to his neighbor : judge ye truth and judgment of peace in your gates. And let none of you imagine evil in his heart against his friend : and love not a false oath : for all these are the things that I hate, saith the Lord " (viii. 16, 17). Let true religion but shine forth in these godly virtues, "And many peoples and strong nations shall come to seek the Lord of hosts in Jerusalem. . . . In those days . . . ten men of all languages of the Gentiles shall take hold, and shall hold fast the skirt of one that is a Jew, saying : 'We will go with you ; for we have heard that God is with you ' " (viii. 22, 23). Are we not made to assist at the preaching of the Twelve Fishermen of Galilee among the proud nations of the Roman Empire ?

The three succeeding chapters, ix.-xi., are different in character from the preceding. They contain threatening prophecies against

the cities of Syria, Phœnicia, and the Philistine seaboard—threats which soon afterward found their realisation through the arms of Alexander the Great. Juda is comforted with the assurance that, meanwhile, no harm shall befall its children. These prophetic utterances, however, are in many cases only applicable to the epoch of the Messiah; for here we find the very words which the Evangelist St. Matthew applies to our Lord on his last entrance into Jerusalem: "Rejoice greatly, O daughter of Sion! shout for joy, O daughter of Jerusalem! BEHOLD THY KING will come to thee, the Just and Saviour: He is poor and riding upon an ass, and upon a colt the foal of an ass" (ix. 9)! There are menaces against guilty priests; a glowing description of the triumphs of Christianity; a distinct prediction of the final destruction of Jerusalem and the Temple under the Romans, and of the rejection of the Jews. The three last chapters, xii.–xiv., have for heading "The burden of the word of the Lord upon Israel." The events of the life of Christ, and the characters of His Person and sufferings, are portrayed with extraordinary vividness. A few pregnant sentences point out the trials of His church: xiii. 8, 9.

Zacharias is the most diffuse and obscure of all the Minor Prophets.

MALACHIAS, the last of these inspired men, has been thought by some scholars to be an angel in human form—the name itself meaning in Hebrew "a messenger of Jehovah," *Malachijah*. Some writers have identified him with Esdras. What, however, seems most probable is that he lived after Aggeus and Zacharias, and during the rule

of Esdras and Nehemias. In spite of the reformation which these great men labored so strenuously to effect in the morals and religious discipline of the restored people, Malachias, like his two elder brother-prophets, was offended by the scandals and abuses which were constantly occurring, and which inspired but little hope of a general and lasting improvement. The leading classes, whose example was to be the light of the nation, were themselves a prey to corruption even at this early stage of the Restoration. "To you, O Priests, that despise My Name, and have said, Wherein have we despised Thy Name? You offer polluted bread upon My altar, and you say, Wherein have we polluted Thee? In that you say, The table of the Lord is contemptible. . . . Who is there among you that will shut the doors, and will kindle the fire on My altar gratis? I nave no pleasure in you, saith the Lord of hosts" (i. 9, 10). And then comes the famous prophecy of "the clean oblation," to be offered in His Name "in every place from the rising of the sun even to the going down." Besides, the priests, who are the guardians and expounders of the law, were giving at that very time the fatal example of marrying Gentile wives, thereby renewing the sin which, more than any other in the past, had led to the national corruption, apostasy, and ruin. To this incurable inconstancy and unfaithfulness there remains but one remedy, the rejection of the Jewish dispensation and worship. "Presently the Lord whom you seek, and the Angel of the Testament whom you desire, shall come to His Temple. Behold, He cometh, saith the Lord of hosts" (iii. 1).

IV. POETICAL AND DIDACTIC BOOKS.

THE BOOK OF JOB.—This book—the authorship of which the most respectable Hebrew tradition, that of the Targum, attributes to Moses—is now acknowledged to resemble in style the Pentateuch and other most ancient Hebrew writings. It is generally believed among scholars that Job, whose name signifies "one persecuted or afflicted," lived in the northern part of Arabia. Indeed, St. Jerome, in his day, remarked that Job's diction bore a wonderful resemblance to the best Arabic compositions. Be that as it may, the great lesson taught by the life of Job is, that one who had "none like him in the earth, a simple and upright man, and fearing God, and avoiding evil," remains faithful to God and true to his own conscience, amid the most terrible afflictions. There is also that other sweet and consoling lesson taught at the same time, that the Father who permits His own to be most sorely tried,

never allows the trial to be too much for the sufferer. His own Divine Spirit is ever nigh flooding the soul with light from above, even when the night of suffering is darkest, and always warming the heart to love, to bear, to hope, when all human joys fail and all earthly affection is turned into bitterness. He who marks out for each star its fixed orbit in the heavens, and who sets to the ocean the limits beyond which its fury cannot prevail, also knows how to limit our misfortunes, to revisit us even here below with hours of sunshine and felicity that give us an earnest of the eternal joys. Read for yourselves, O children of God, and learn from Job how to bear, and how to hope in the Living God.

THE BOOK OF PSALMS.—David, "the sweet singer of Israel," is not only the great national poet of the chosen race, but the loved songster of the Christian church, whose words of prayer, praise, and triumph all true Christian homes and hearts have ever made their own. These inspired songs reflect the whole personal history of David from the time that he was secretly anointed King by Samuel, called to become the defender of the Kingdom against Goliath and his Philistines, obliged to charm with the sweet sounds of harp and voice the evil spirit of jealousy that possessed Saul, tried by persecution, exile, and treachery all through the remaining years of Saul's ill-starred reign, down to the dark days of Gilboe. The shepherd-lad of Bethlehem, the young conqueror of the Philistines, the son-in-law of Saul, the fugitive among the desert places of Israel, was still the man whose heart "thirsted after God," and whose frequent songs breathe the faith and hope and fervent love of these chequered years. How he delighted, when in possession of the throne, to form bodies of singers for the service of the Tabernacle, and to compose the most thrilling hymns for the solemn feasts of the nation! When he brought, at length, the Ark in triumph to the city of David, he would himself be foremost among the singers, casting aside the warrior's armor and the kingly robes, to sing and dance in a simple linen tunic before the Ark—the visible resting-place of his loved and adored Jehovah in the midst of the people. And when the Queen ridiculed her royal husband for what she thought so unseemly an exhibition, how David's indignation breaks forth! "Before the Lord who chose me rather than thy father (Saul) and than all his house, . . . I will both play, and make myself meaner than I have done: and I will be little in my own eyes." . . . David is still in heart the shepherd-lad of Bethlehem, whom God had so often protected against the assault of beasts of prey prowling in the night, and whose soul even then delighted in singing the praises of his Almighty Protector. So will he continue to the end. His one dreadful fall in the heyday of his power, only creates in his repentant soul a deeper humility, and calls forth those penitential psalms which are the comfort of all souls acquainted with sin and sorrow.

To the people whom he had made so great and so happy his psalms continued to be the cry of the national heart on all solemn festivals. Even in captivity they found in these inspired and prophetic strains incentives to sincere repentance for their past ingratitude, and the most cheering promises of future restoration to country and freedom. The Christian Church, ever since the day of Sion's final destruction, has continued to make of David's psalms her own book of praise and prayer. Around the altar of the Lamb in Jerusalem, as well as around every altar where He abides from the rising to the setting sun, we sing evermore the canticles of Sion's prophet-King. Other Hebrew poets, inspired like David himself, have added song after song to his immortal book; theirs, however, are only a few. David is still rightly called the PSALMIST.

THE BOOK OF PROVERBS.—This is the production of King Solomon. The first nine chapters excel the remainder of the book in poetic beauty of diction as well as in continuity of thought. The next twelve chapters are composed of separate and, apparently, independent maxims. Chapters xxv.–xxix. were composed under the reign of the best and greatest of Solomon's successors, the saintly King Ezechias, who collected the scattered maxims and utterances of his ancestor and added them to Solomon's book. The last two chapters are of uncertain authorship.

THE BOOK OF ECCLESIASTES.—This is also the work of Solomon, who throughout the book speaks of himself as the *Koheleth*, "preacher," *ecclesiastes* in Greek. We know from sacred history how wisely Solomon began his reign, and with what shameful folly and guilt he tarnished its premature close. This book is the composition of a man who has had his fill of worldly greatness and enjoyment, who has drunk to the dregs the cup of life, and found only bitterness and weariness at the bottom. It is as if the Spirit of God had forced the guilty King to confess that all is "vanity of vanities," save to fear God from one's youth and inviolably to keep His commandments. "And all things that are done God will bring to judgment!" What must have been, at its latest hour, the terrors of that soul so privileged and so guilty!

SOLOMON'S CANTICLE OF CANTICLES.—The God of Israel had designed that the chosen nation should be, under Solomon (Hebrew, *Shelōmōh*, peaceful, pacific), a living and ravishing picture of the state of the Christian people under the Redeemer,

the Prince of Peace. Solomon, on whom had descended in youth the spirit of supernatural wisdom as well as prophecy, afterward proved utterly unfaithful to the graces lavished on him. Still, just as the unworthy Balaam was forced by the Divine Spirit to prophesy the blessedness and final triumph of the Church, even so was the apostate soul of Solomon forced to sing in this Song the undying mutual love which binds the true Solomon to His Bride, the Church, and the Church to Him through all the struggles and persecutions of ages.

THE BOOK OF WISDOM.—The author of this book has for his chief object to teach rulers, statesmen, and judges. By many scholars the work is ascribed to Solomon. The authorship, however, remains uncertain. The first six chapters are a compendium of the first nine chapters of Proverbs. In vii., viii., ix., the writer describes the road by which he attained the possession of Wisdom, as well as her innate excellences. From the tenth chapter to the end a series of examples are quoted from sacred history to demonstrate the manifold utility of Wisdom, to show the wickedness of sin, the blissful reward of faithful souls, the undying punishment of the wicked.

THE BOOK OF ECCLESIASTICUS.—This book is also entitled "The Wisdom of Jesus the Son of Sirach," or "Ecclesiasticus," *i. e.*, preacher. Like the book of Ecclesiastes, the present work contains a body of moral precepts and exhortations tending to enforce the practice of all virtue and to exalt the excellence of wisdom. The author would appear to have aimed at following the plan of the three preceding books in composing his own. Hence we have first a body of maxims in imitation of the Proverbs, then a series of reflexions somewhat in the style of Ecclesiastes, and finally a long poetical panegyric of great and holy men, recalling the style of the Canticle of Canticles. It was written in the second century before Christ under the Asmonean or Machabean dynasty. It gives a very high idea of the culture of the Jewish schools of the period. Some passages recall the poetry and eloquence of Isaias.

THE NEW TESTAMENT.

MOST fittingly does the word "testament" apply to the body of inspired writings which contain the record of His death and last will, who is the great "Father of the world to come." From the lamb, the firstling of his flock, offered up in sacrifice by the martyred Abel in the first age of human history, and whose blood was mixed with the life-blood of the holy priest himself, all the victims offered to God by the patriarchs before Moses and by the sons of Aaron after him, only pointed to the one infinite and all-atoning Victim, CHRIST JESUS, "the Lamb of God who taketh away the sins of the world." He came as our true brother, flesh of our flesh and bone of our bone, to teach us how to sanctify the present life by labor and suffering and God-like charity, in order thereby to make ourselves worthy of the eternal life to come and the everlasting Kingdom that He reconquered for His own redeemed. From His blood sprang up an immortal and world-wide society, the Church, which He made the heir to His Kingdom, the unfailing depositary of His power, the infallible interpreter of His last Will and Testament for the sanctification and salvation of the nations.

So, then, as the Old Testament was the Will of God solemnly and repeatedly expressed to send us a Saviour and sanctifier, even so is the New Testament this same Will carried out in the death of the Saviour and in the ordinances by which the fruit of His redemption, the means of salvation and sanctification, are secured to the entire race of man in all coming ages. The Second Adam, the Father of the new life, has left us a Mother upon earth to hold His place, to love us, to teach us, to train us to walk in the royal road of generosity and holiness marked out for us by the precepts and examples of God made Man.

"The Old Testament," says Cardinal Erra, "shows God creating the universe by a word; the New, on the contrary, shows God repairing the world by His death. The former, by repeating the promises relating to a future Redeemer, kept alive, without satisfying them, the ardent hopes of mankind, while shadowing forth dimly the design of Redemption. But no sooner has Christ come into the world, and the new covenant taken the place of the old, than the former obscurities disappear in the light of His coming, and all the ancient figures, all the predictions of the Prophets are verified in His Person. The covenant made on Mount Sinai was only in favor of the single house of Israel; the covenant signed on Calvary regards all mankind. The one was sealed with the blood of goats and oxen, the other with the blood of God's own Son. The spirit of the Old Law was one of fear and bondage; the glory of the New is the Spirit of Love and adoption. The one was the covenant of a brief period of time; the other is to be everlasting. Christ's Gospel promises rewards that are to be perpetual, infinite, spiritual, and heavenly; the law of Moses only held out a perishable, limited, visible, and earthly recompense. The Jews did, indeed, hope for the life to come; but they could only attain to its unspeakable felicity through faith in Christ." (*Historia utriusque testamenti*, lib. xi., chap. i.)

The New Testament writings contain twenty-seven books, divided by biblical scholars as follows:

Five Historical Books; namely, the four Gospels and the Acts of the Apostles. *Fourteen Epistles of St. Paul. Seven Catholic or General Epistles. The Apocalypse or Revelation of St. John.*

THE GOSPEL ACCORDING TO
St MATTHEW

I. THE FIVE HISTORICAL BOOKS.

THE GOSPEL ACCORDING TO ST. MATTHEW.—Independent of all the curious learning which fill the books published in our day about the distinctive characters of each of the four Gospels, is the exquisite pleasure which the devout Christian mind never fails to find in reading and meditating the history of our dear Lord's life and death. The naked text of St. Matthew, or of any one of his brother Evangelists—take it up wherever you will—affords to the soul athirst for Him who is the Life of our life so much of sweet instruction, so much of consolation and strength, that one arises from the study of the chosen page with a great desire to return to it again. To all who sincerely and humbly seek to know Christ more and more, and to become more and more like to Him in thought and word and deed, God never fails to open, in every page of the Gospels, and sometimes in every verse, springs of thought so abundant, so unfailing, so refreshing, that one can scarcely tear one's lips away from these living waters. St. Ignatius Loyola was but a young and half-educated soldier, when he shut himself up behind the bushes and brambles of the Cavern of Manresa to study the mysteries of eternal life with only two books, the New Testament and the "Imitation of Christ." While there, as he afterward was impelled to declare for our edification, he learned more in a single hour spent alone with God in meditating on the life of our Lord, than years spent in listening to the most learned theologians could have taught him. And ever since his day, all who take up the Mysteries of Christ's life, passion, and resurrection, as laid down in the Saint's book of Spiritual Exercises, and meditate them reverently and humbly as he did, will learn more of Christ and of heavenly things than a lifetime of study could impart. "Was not our heart burning within us, whilst He spoke in the way, and opened to us the Scriptures?" said the two disciples of Emmaus to each other, when Christ had disappeared from their sight. To you, dear Reader, remembering our own sweet and frequent experience, we can only say: "Oh, taste and see that the Lord is sweet: blessed is the man that hopeth in Him!"

Let a modern writer, one—we would venture to affirm—who has drawn from this same source his deep knowledge of the Gospel and of its divine doctrines, instruct us on what distinguishes St. Matthew in particular. His Gospel, Father Coleridge says, "is penetrated from beginning to end with the thought that in our Lord were fulfilled all the types, all the anticipations, all the prophecies of the older dispensation. This and other features lie on the surface of St. Matthew's Gospel. It is not so obvious, but it seems equally true, to say that it is penned with a carefulness of design which makes it almost as much a treatise as a narrative: with a distinct

purpose of embodying our Lord's general teaching to an extent and with a complete
ness which can be asserted of no other of the Gospels. It alone contains the Serm
on the Mount, and it gives us a far greater number of the parables and of the teac
ings of our Lord as to the counsels of perfection than any other. To these purpos
St. Matthew has frequently, as might be expected in the writer of such a treatis
made the order of time subservient. . . . The plan of this Gospel is very simple a
very obvious, and explains in a manner quite sufficiently satisfactory that appare
neglect of order which is, in truth, the faithful adherence to an order of a high
kind than that of mere historical sequence.''

The sections into which St. Matthew's Gospel may be naturally divided are as f
lows: I. The birth, infancy, private life of Christ at Nazareth; the mission a
preaching of the Precursor; the baptism of our Lord, with His fasting and temptatio
chaps. i.–iv. 11. II. The first mission of our Lord in Galilee, together with t
pregnant summary of His doctrine, known as the Sermon on the Mount; chaps.
11–vii. III. The seal of our Lord's divine mission in the various displays of F
miraculous power; chaps. viii., ix. IV. The mission of the Apostles and the instr
tions delivered to them by the Master and destined for all future apostolic laborer
chap. x. V. St. John Baptist sends his disciples to Christ, and Christ's formal reco
nition of the Precursor's holiness, as well as the responsibility incurred by reject
both the Precursor and the Messiah; chap. xi. VI. The doubts and opposition whi
neutralized the effects of Christ's miracles and preaching; chap. xii. VII. Chris
teaching by parables; chap. xiii. VIII. The missionary work in Galilee described,
well as the miracles with which it was accompanied, and the opposition of Chris
enemies; chaps. xiv., xv., xvi. 12. IX. The confession of Peter in Northern Galil
and the solemn announcement of the Passion; xvi. 13. X. The Transfiguration a
the preaching of the mystery of the Cross; xvii.–xx. XI. Christ enters Jerusalem
the Day of Palms, and His teaching in that city till the beginning of His Passion; x
17; xxv. XII. The Passion; chaps. xxvi., xxvii. XIII. The Resurrection; chap. xxv

THE GOSPEL ACCORDING TO ST. MARK.—It is thought that Mark t
Evangelist is the same person as "John who was surnamed Mark" (Acts xii. 1
In this case his mother, Mary, is one of the most illustrious and blessed women
the early Church. For, beside being the sister of St. Barnabas, her son would th
have the twofold privilege of being an Evangelist and the associate of St. Paul in
apostolic labors. It is, moreover, a most venerable tradition, dating from the infan
of the Church, that St. Mark the Evangelist was even more closely bound to St. Pe
by constant companionship; and that the Gospel which bears his name was writt
in Rome under the direction of the Prince of the Apostles, and at the request of t
Roman Christians. Hence it is that St. Irenæus calls St. Mark "the interpreter a
disciple of Peter," *interpres et sectator Petri.* St. Mark was, therefore, the son of t
heroic and generous woman whose home in Jerusalem was not only that of Pe
and his fellow-laborers, the asylum of the faithful in the first persecution, but the ho
which was the very first temple of the Christian religion in the City of David.

THE GOSPEL ACCORDING TO St. LUKE

is no wonder that the son of such a mother should have been the loved and trusted companion of the two great Apostles.

The Gospel itself, as compared with that of St. Matthew, is more simple and elementary in its character. Some scholars have even considered it to be only an abridgment of the latter. Nevertheless, although St. Mark omits much of our Lord's teaching, whether discourses or parables, he dwells at greater length upon His miracles, as being more fitted to strike the pagan mind. "He drops the incidents and sayings which require special knowledge of the Jewish system or customs . . . The departures from the chronological order, which St. Matthew has made . . . are usually corrected by St. Mark" (Father Coleridge).

He begins with the missionary labors of John the Baptist, and his baptism of our Lord, the Temptation, and the first preaching in Galilee. At the close of the second chapter we have, in the controversy about the Sabbath, a key to the opposition which the Pharisees are getting up against the Master and His teaching. In the third chapter Christ's labors and miracles are at once introduced; then the selection of the Apostles. The multitude drawn by the new Teacher and His wondrous cures is such, and the labor of the little band of work-men is so unceasing and overwhelming, "that they could not so much as eat bread." The Scribes from Jerusalem declare the miracles to be the effect of Satanic power. There is a mighty fermentation of opinion and a pas-sionate contention among the masses. There is such danger, too, in the bold speeches of Jesus, that "when His friends heard of it, they went out to lay hold on Him. For they said, He is become mad." Presently His mother and His near relatives or "brethren" appear on the scene, anxious about His safety. But He, who knows that His time of suffering has not yet come, and who is solely anxious to impress upon His hearers the divine value of His own message to them, and the renovating virtue of the supernatural truth and grace He brings to His nation, only answers: "Who is My Mother and My brethren? . . . Whosoever shall do the will of God, he is My brother, and My sister, and Mother." With the fourth chapter begins the teaching by parables, which, however, is but briefly dwelt on, the Evangelist insisting chiefly in the four following chapters on Christ's labors and miracles in Galilee. The tenth chapter describes the Divine Master's work in Peræa or "Judæa beyond the Jordan." The remainder of the book, from the eleventh chapter inclusively, recounts our Lord's teaching, trials, and sufferings in Jerusalem down to His death, resurrection, and ascension.

THE GOSPEL ACCORDING TO ST. LUKE.—St. Luke wrote his Gospel at a time when the faith had spread, and several attempts had been made to compose a satisfactory history of its Author, its origin, and its progress. He had been the companion of St. Paul, as he relates himself in the Acts of the Apostles, which he also wrote. It has been the constant tradition, both of the eastern and the western churches, that St. Luke was by profession a physician. Another but less accepted tradition attributes

to him some skill as a painter. He remained the associate of St. Paul till after t
apostle's first imprisonment in Rome; and obtained himself the crown of martyrd
like his beloved master. St. Irenæus, Tertullian, Origen, and Eusebius bear witness
the general and early belief that he wrote his Gospel under the direction of St. Pa
as St. Mark had written his under that of St. Peter.

Being a native of Antioch, Luke was familiar with the Greek language and cultu
Hence the superior purity of his diction. "His work," says Father Coleridge,
more like a regular history than that of the other Evangelists. He covers the wh
ground from the Annunciation to the Ascension, and there is no prominent or
portant feature in the whole series of the mysteries and actions of our Lord's Life wh
he has left untouched. At the same time, his Gospel is to a great extent new—
either in the events which it relates or in the fresh incidents which it adds to
history of what has been already related, and he seems to make it his rule to sup
omissions, and to illustrate the method and principles of our Lord's conduct by an
dotes or discourses, which resemble very much those which others have inserted,
which are not the same . . . If we consider St. Matthew as addressing himself
marily to the Hebrew Christians, or rather to their teachers, and St. Mark as turn
upon the direct converts from heathenism, we may look upon St. Luke as the Ev
gelist of the Churches in which the Jewish element had been more or less absorbed
the larger influx of Gentiles . . . He dwells with particular care upon the sacerd
character of our Lord, upon the healing and compassionate aspect of His life, u
His love for penitents and sinners, and the like. . . ."

The first section, chaps. i., ii., supplies the omissions of the other Gospels, giv
the history of the conception and birth of our Lord and John Baptist, together w
His presentation in the Temple, His hidden life at Nazareth, and His appearing am
the Doctors in Jerusalem at the age of twelve. The incidents of this early portion
Christ's career mentioned by the two preceding Evangelists are passed over by
Luke. The second section comprises chaps. iii., iv. and v., bringing the narra
down to the first preaching in Galilee. Chaps. vi.–ix. 20 give the entire second per
of our Lord's life down to the Confession of St. Peter. From chap. ix. 21 to ch
xviii. 30 St. Luke relates what regards the doctrine of the Cross, the Transfigurat
and our Lord's labors in Judæa, a portion of his life—the last year—not mentio
in the other Gospels. From chap. xviii. 31 to chap. xix. 27 are detailed the occ
rences and sayings that took place between Christ's leaving Peræa and His arrival
Jerusalem. The remaining chapters are the history of His labors and sufferings in Je
salem, of His resurrection, His manifestation to His disciples, and His ascension.

THE GOSPEL ACCORDING TO ST. JOHN.—John, as well as James the E
or Greater, was by his mother, Mary-Salome, the first cousin of our Lord; Ja
the Less or Younger and Jude or Thadæus being the sons of another sister—all fo
on account of their near relationship, being designated in Jewish phrase as the broth
of our Lord. John was especially dear to Him; and this special affection has e
been attributed in the Church to John's virginal purity of heart. Of the life of t

Evangelist we shall speak more fully when we treat of his Epistles. At present it is very important that the reader should have a clear notion of what is distinctive in his Gospel.

St. Irenæus states that John published his Gospel while he was residing in Ephesus. St. Jerome says that he wrote it at the request of the Asiatic bishops, who besought him to treat in a special manner of the divinity of Christ. It is thought that this Gospel, although completed and published in Ephesus, was chiefly, if not wholly, written in the isle of Patmos, and, not improbably, after the destruction of Jerusalem.

In its contents and scope it is evidently supplementary to the three other Gospels. "In truth, St. John's Gospel touches the others only at one single point before he comes to the last few days of our Lord's Life, and even as to those, nine-tenths of what he relates are altogether supplementary. St. John is distinguished for the great length at which he relates the words of our Lord, and the large space which he spends upon single incidents or occasions. Thus no Gospel is so easily broken up into its component parts as this; its arrangement becomes perfectly simple as soon as its supplementary character is recognized." Such is the judgment of Father Coleridge.

The book may be divided into two very distinct parts; the first part embracing eleven chapters ending with the recalling Lazarus to life; and the second, ten chapters, the incidents and discourses pertaining to the Last Supper, the Passion, the Resurrection, and the Ascension. The first part comprises two sections: I. Chaps. i.–iv. describe incidents and events of which nothing is said by the other Evangelists. The time they cover extends from Christ's baptism to the beginning of his first missionary tour through Galilee. The occurrences take place alternately in Judæa—on the banks of the Jordan, in Jerusalem or the adjacent territory—and in Galilee. II. The scene of the next six chapters, v.–x., is mostly in Jerusalem. Chapter v. recounts the healing on the Sabbath of the man sick for thirty-eight years, and the assertion by Christ of His own divinity during the public discussion occasioned by this miracle. Chapter vi. describes the multiplication of the loaves and fishes in Galilee, just before the second Pasch of Christ's public ministry, together with the discussion relating to the Manna and the Bread of Life figured by the Manna. The next four chapters, vii.–x., relate our Lord's sayings and doings during the last year of His Life, at the Feast of Tabernacles in the beginning of October, and at the Feast of the Dedication of the Temple in the December following. III. This section, comprising the eleventh chapter, gives an account of the miracle performed in favor of Lazarus. The Second Part of this Gospel gives, chapter after chapter, the Evangelist's additions to what had been already recorded in the other Gospels.

To the attentive and devout student of the New Testament, St. John's Gospel will give much light to understand the Life of our Lord as a whole, and much food for pious contemplation. The Beloved Disciple has been called "the Theologian" by the early Church Fathers, because he alone affirms again and again the divinity of our Lord. He knew him to be true man, born of his own near kinswoman, reared in his own country among his own kinsfolk, and, during the last period of the life ended so tragically, admitted into the closest companionship and loving intimacy with Him who was the true Son of God as well as the true Son of the Virgin Mary. It is the Divine Sonship of the Master that John proclaims in the very preface to his Gospel, lifting our souls up to these eternal splendors amid which the Word dwells evermore in the bosom of the Father.

THE ACTS OF THE APOSTLES.—This book, which is also the work of the Evangelist St. Luke, is the only inspired history—even though a very partial one—of the infancy of the Christian Church. The events which it records cover a space of about thirty years. As the very title, "Acts," indicates, it is the record of an eye-witness. Still it is not, and does not purport to be, a full and complete history of the acts or labors of all the Apostles during that period. It relates, in the first part, principally the labors of St. Peter, and those of St. Paul in the second. Around these two great figures, indeed, are grouped subordinate laborers; these two, nevertheless, stand out in the narration as the central personages.

We see, in the very first chapter, the promise of Christ about the coming of the Holy Spirit fulfilled, and the timid Galilæan fishermen transformed into the dauntless and eloquent apostles of their crucified Master. Peter and John, the first in authority and the foremost in love, are also the boldest in confessing Him before the very people who had put Him to death. "Immediately after the Ascension," writes the Protestant Henry Alford, "St. Peter, the first of the Twelve, designated by our Lord as the Rock on which the Church was to be built, the holder of the Keys of the Kingdom, becomes the prime actor under God in the founding of the Church. He is the centre of the first group of sayings and doings. The opening of the door to the Jews (chap. ii.) and Gentiles (chap. x.) is his office, and by him, in good time, is accomplished." Let us listen to the great Bossuet as he resumes the belief of the Church on this point. "Peter appears as the first (among the apostles) in every way: the first to confess the faith (St. Matt. xvi. 16); the first in the obligation of exercising brotherly love (St. John xxi. 15 and following); the first of all the apostles who saw Christ risen from the dead (1 Cor. xv. 5), as he was to be the first to bear witness to the Resurrection in presence of the whole people (Acts ii. 14); the first to move in filling up the vacant place among the apostles (Acts i. 15); the first to confirm the faith by a miracle (Ib. iii. 6, 7); the first to convert the Jews (Ib. ii. 14); the first to admit the Gentiles (Ib. x.); the first in everything." Hear him again tracing out the design of Providence in the career of the two great Apostles. "Christ doth not speak in vain. Peter shall bear with him, whithersoever he goeth, in this open confession of the faith (St. Matt. xvi. 16), the foundation on which stand all the churches. And here is the road the Apostle has to follow. Through Jerusalem, the holy city in which Christ manifested Himself; in which the Church was to "begin" (St. Luke xxiv. 47), before continuing the succession of God's people; in which consequently Peter was to be for a long time the foremost in teaching and in directing; whence he was wont to go round about visiting the persecuted churches (Acts ix. 32), and confirming them in the faith; in which it was needful for the great Paul—Paul come back from the third heaven—to go "to see Peter" (Galat. i. 18), not James, though he, so great an apostle, the "brother of the Lord," the Bishop of Jerusalem, surnamed the Just, and equally revered by both Jews and Christians, was also there. But it was not James that Paul was bound to come "to see." He came to see Peter, and to see him, as the original text suggests, as a thing full of wonders and worthy of being sought after. He came to contemplate and study Peter, as St. John Chrysostom hath it (in Epist. ad Gal., c. i., n. 11): to see him as some one greater and older than himself: to see Peter, nevertheless, not to be instructed by him, for Christ instructed Paul by a special revelation; but in order to leave a model to future ages, and to establish, once for all, that no matter how learned a man might be, no matter how holy—were he even another Paul—he must go to see Peter. . . . Through this holy city, then, and through Antioch, the metropolitan city of the East, . . . far more than that, the most illustrious church on earth, since in it the Christian name arose; . . . through these two glorious cities, so dear to the Church, and distinguished by such opposite features, Peter had to come to Rome—Rome still more illustrious, the head of Paganism and of the Empire, and which, to seal the triumph of Christ over the world, is predestined to be the capital of religion, the head of the Church, Peter's own city Thither was he per force to come by Jerusalem and Antioch. But

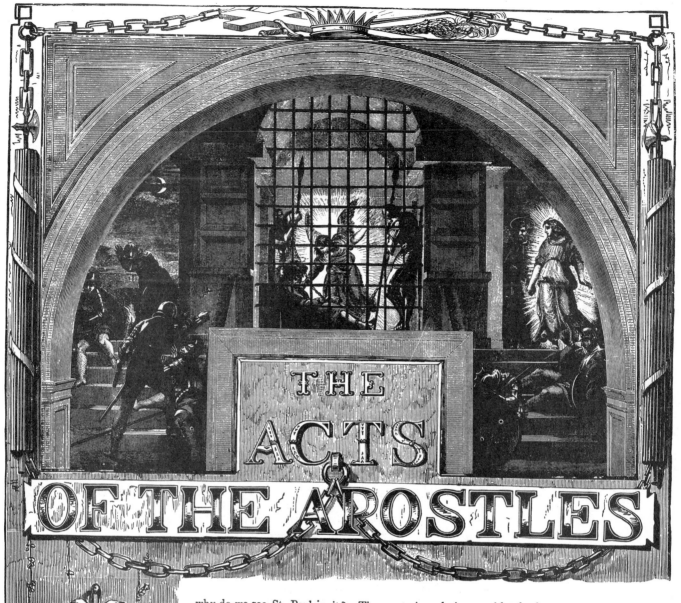

why do we see St. Paul in it? The mysterious design would take long to explain. Only bear in mind the great division of the world between Peter and Paul, in which Peter, though given the whole world in charge in consequence of his primacy, and charged by an express command (Acts x.) to have a care of the Gentiles whom he admitted in the person of Cornelius the Centurion, did, nevertheless, take on himself the special care of the Jews even as Paul took a special care of the Gentiles (Galat. ii. 7, 8, 9). As a division was necessary, it was fitting that the first of the apostles should have the first-born among the peoples (the Jews); that he who was the head, and to whom all the rest must be united, should have the nation on which the others must be grafted, and that the Vicar of Christ should have Christ's own share. That, however, is not enough: Rome itself must fall to Peter's share. For, although, as the capital of Paganism, Rome belonged in a special manner to Paul, the Apostle of the Gentiles, nevertheless, it was in Rome that Peter, the head of Christendom, was bound to found the Church. Nor is this all: the extraordinary commission of St. Paul must die there with him, and thus returning to the supreme Chair of Peter, to which it was subordinated, the power of Paul must raise the Roman church to the highest point of authority and splendor'' (Sermon on the Unity of the Church).

THE FOURTEEN EPISTLES OF ST. PAUL.

In the Acts of the Apostles St. Luke describes the first growth of the Church in Jerusalem and throughout Palestine, and, outside of Palestine, in various countries of Western Asia and Eastern Europe. A society arises and rapidly increases around the teaching and ruling body of Apostles so carefully chosen, trained, and instructed by our Lord Himself. They and their successors after them to the end of time were to teach the nations of earth "to observe all things whatsoever" the Master had revealed as the law of life for mankind (St. Matt. xxviii. 19, 20). This immortal society thus springing into existence beneath the shadow of the Cross of Calvary, was not only to teach with the fulness of Christ's own authority, but to baptize and administer to the faithful all Christ's saving and sanctifying ordinances; and on the human race who hear this preaching and this call to baptism and newness of life is imposed the necessity of complying under pain of eternal loss. "He that believeth and is baptized shall be saved: but he that believeth not, shall be condemned" (St. Mark xvi. 16). Baptism is but the door by which one enters into this Society: it is the indispensable initiatory rite and new birth in which the children of the fallen Adam are born again of the blood of the Second—the blood of a God. Other divine ordinances, sacraments of heavenly origin, and pregnant with divine virtue, are administered in due course, and according to the soul's needs, to maintain, renew, increase, and perfect the supernatural life bestowed in the new birth of Baptism.

And so this Society divinely commissioned to teach, to regenerate, and govern the race of man in all things pertaining to eternal salvation, stands forth in the full consciousness of its power, and speaks to Jerusalem and to the world by the mouth of Peter, its visible chief, on the day of the first Christian Pentecost. Three thousand men baptized and admitted forthwith into fellowship with the preacher and his associates, attest the might of the Spirit who moves both the speaker and his hearers. Thenceforward the mighty movement is propagated far and wide. They teach—these fathers of the new moral world which Christ came down to create—they baptize, they govern their flocks, with unquestioned authority, both the rulers and the subjects in the infant Church appreciating sensibly and to the full the last utterance of Christ: "Behold, I am with you all days even to the consummation of the world" (St. Matt. xxviii. 20).

In every one of the following epistles or letters addressed by St. Paul to the churches which he had founded or visited, or to the bishops he had set over them, the consciousness of this divinely-given authority is evident in the writer, and evidently supposed in the persons to whom they are written. He is in prison at Rome, and from there writes four of these touching letters, to Philemon, to the Colossians, the Philippians, and to the Ephesians. Just listen to some of the divine lessons of the imprisoned Apostle. To the noble Philemon whose forgiveness and brotherly charity he bespeaks for the fugitive slave Onesimus: "Though I have much confidence in Christ JESUS, to command thee that which is to the purpose, for charity sake I rather beseech, whereas thou art such an one, as Paul an old man, and now a prisoner also of Jesus Christ: I beseech thee for my son, whom I have begotten in my bands, Onesimus . . . Trusting in thy obedience, I have written to thee, knowing that thou wilt also do more than I say." Thus does apostolic charity address itself to the work of abolishing the inveterate evil of slavery along with the manifold corruptions of the Pagan world.—To the Colossians: "We (Timothy and Paul) . . . cease not to pray for you and to beg that you may be filled with the knowledge of His will, in all wisdom and spiritual understanding . . . If so ye continue in the faith, grounded, and settled, and immovable from the hope of the Gospel which ye have heard, which is preached in all the creation that is under heaven, whereof I Paul am made a minister. Who now rejoice in my sufferings for you, and fill up those things that are wanting of the sufferings of Christ, in my flesh for His body, which is the Church . . . If you be risen with Christ, seek the things that are above where Christ is sitting at the right hand of God. Mind the things that are above, not the things that are upon the earth. For you are dead, and your life is hid with Christ in God . . . Mortify therefore your members which are upon the earth . . . uncleanness, lust, evil concupiscence, and covetousness . . . Stripping yourselves of the old man with his deeds, and putting on the new, him who is renewed unto knowledge, according to the image of Him that created him." This God-like virtue was the new wine which could not be held in old vessels: all had to be divine in the Christian man.—To the

Philippians, who were especially dear to Paul: "My dearly beloved, my joy, and my crown: so stand fast in the Lord, my dearly beloved! . . . Let your modesty be known to all men . . . Whatsoever things are true, whatsoever modest, whatsoever just, whatsoever holy, whatsoever lovely, whatsoever of good fame—if there be any virtue, if any praise of discipline—think on these things. The things which you have both learned, and received, and heard, and seen in me, these do ye! and the God of peace shall be with you!"—Finally, to the Ephesians: "Blessed be the God and Father of our Lord Jesus Christ, who hath blessed us with spiritual blessings . . . in Christ. As He chose us in Him before the foundation of the world, that we should be holy and unspotted in His sight in charity . . . I bow my knees to the Father of our Lord Jesus Christ, . . . that He would grant you, . . . to be strengthened by His Spirit with might unto the inward man. That Christ may dwell by faith in your hearts: that being rooted and founded in charity, you may be able to comprehend with all the saints what is the breadth, and length, and height, and depth. To know also the charity of Christ, which surpasseth all knowledge, that you may be filled unto all the fulness of God."

"Any one, in reading the Epistles of St. Paul," says Bergier, "must see that they were written on the spur of some particular occurrence, to clear up some question put to the writer, to correct some dangerous abuse, to inculcate some special duties; that his purpose, in no one of these letters, was to draw up for the faithful a profession of faith, or an exposition of all the doctrines of Christian belief, or of all its moral duties; that, while writing to one Church, he never prescribes that his letter shall be communicated to all the others. It is, therefore, perverse obstinacy in Protestants to maintain that whenever St. Paul preached or taught by word of mouth, he confined himself to repeating the instructions contained in some one of his letters; and that no truth which is not laid down in writing can belong to the Christian doctrine." On the contrary, it is evident from a cursory glance at the Epistles themselves, that St. Paul refers to a previous body of truths delivered by oral teaching, and to the acknowledged fact that the members of each church had been thoroughly grounded by such teaching in the great truths of the new Revelation.

THE EPISTLE TO THE ROMANS.—This was, most probably, written from Corinth, in the 58th year after the birth of Christ, two years before St. Paul went to Rome, and twenty-four years after his conversion. During this quarter of a century the Christian faith had grown wonderfully in the capital of the Roman Empire. The church there, as in most other cities of the empire, was composed of Jewish and Gentile converts, among whom a discussion arose as to their relative claims to the esteem of the great body of believers throughout the world. The Jews prided themselves on their being the descendants of Abraham, on their ancestors having lived under a theocracy governed by a system of law and religion solemnly revealed to their own nation, while the rest of the human race remained in the darkness and horrid corruptions of idolatry. The converted Gentiles, on the other hand, nursed the belief that they had obtained the grace of conversion as a reward of their fidelity to the law of nature, and pointed out the many great and pure names of their philosophers, warriors, and statesmen. Thus the Jewish Christians seemed to think that their faithful observance of the Mosaic law had deserved the grace of the divine adoption and justification in Christ, while their Gentile brethren attributed their possessing a like privilege to their having followed the guidance of the natural light of reason. St. Paul, who had been specially chosen to teach the Gentile world, wrote this Epistle to convince both these classes of converts of their serious error, by showing that the supernatural grace of our adoption as children of God, and the whole subsequent train of graces which lead the soul to believe and to be justified, are bestowed on us

gratuitously, as the effect of God's pure mercy, without any previous merit of our own. To stop the vain boasting of both Jew and Gentile, St. Paul shows how both were the slaves of sin, and, therefore, unable to merit the gift of justification by their own good deeds. The condition of the people of God was, indeed, attended with many singular spiritual advantages and privileges, as compared with that of the pagan world. Nevertheless, neither Jew nor Pagan could by their own merits lift themselves up to the supernatural rank and regenerated condition of the Christian people. In order to convey a conviction of this truth to the minds of the faithful at Rome, St. Paul begins by exposing the horrible crimes committed among Pagans even by the most enlightened philosophers—chap. i. In chap. ii. he enumerates the transgressions of the Jews; and concludes, in chap. iii., that in as much as both were thus subject to sin, so the justification vouchsafed them in Christ must be absolutely gratuitous, the effect of grace and not of legal justice or natural virtue, and therefore to be attributed to supernatural faith, which is a gift of God. This position is confirmed and illustrated by the example of Abraham's heroic faith and justification, chap. iv. In chap. v. is set forth the excellence of this grace of Christ; in chap. vi. the Christian soul is urged to preserve, cherish, and increase this priceless gift. In chap. vii. he teaches that even in the Christian, after baptism and justification, the evil forces of nature still remain with the low animal appetites (concupiscence) that drag the soul down toward sensual gratification: this concupiscence is a force which rebels against the restraints of the Mosaic law or the law of nature, without being put down by them, the victory over it being reserved to the grace received through Christ. St. Paul then proceeds to enumerate the fruits of faith, chap. viii.; shows in chaps. ix., x., xi., that the grace of justification was bestowed on the Gentiles in preference to the Jews, because the former readily submitted to the preaching of the Gospel, while the latter rejected Christ; that, whereas the supernatural gift of faith was a thing not due to either Jews or Gentiles, the promises made to Abraham and his posterity do not therefore fail, nor can the divine justice be impugned. In chaps. xii.–xvi., the Apostle inculcates the cardinal precepts of morality so necessary to all who believe in the Gospel (see Picquigny's Commentary on the Epistle to the Romans).

Vainly have those who reject the infallible authority of the Catholic Church endeavored to build on the words of St. Paul a system of blind and fatal predestination, alike injurious to the divine goodness and destructive of man's free will under the action of divine grace. From the passage, chap. ix. 13, "Jacob I have loved, but Esau I have hated," we must not conclude that our good God, without any regard to the merits of men and independently of His foreknowledge of their good and evil deeds, predestines some to be the objects of His hate and others to be the objects of His love. On the contrary, we are to believe that this predestination in its twofold aspect is based on the foreknowledge God must needs have of the good or evil deeds of every human being. Even so the words, " I will have mercy on whom I will have mercy," etc. (Ibid. 15), are not to be construed into an absolute election of a certain class of persons destined to everlasting happiness, independently of all prevision of their good or evil deeds. They simply imply that the almighty

goodness is ever free to grant the grace of faith and justification to whomsoever it pleases. It is a supernatural gift, one not due to nature or natural merits. Hence St. Paul says (Ibid. 16): "So then it is not of him that willeth, nor of him that runneth, but of God that showeth mercy. . . . Therefore He hath mercy on whom He will; and, whom He will, He hardeneth;" that is, He allows the hard and rebellious heart to persist in its rejection of His graces, as He did in the case of Pharaoh and in that of the apostate Judas. So " to harden " is not to predestine to eternal damnation, any more than " to show mercy " or " to have mercy" is to predestine to eternal bliss.

Let us Catholics rest sweetly in the assurance that we have in the living voice of the Church an infallible interpreter of the dead letter of Scripture, whether it be the writings of St. Paul or any other book of the Old or New Testament.

I. AND II. TO THE CORINTHIANS.—Corinth, situated on a narrow neck of land that separated the Ægean from the Mediterranean Sea, was thus the central point on the very highway of commerce between Italy and Asia. The city was rich and beautiful, and the climate lovely. When it first fell beneath the arms of the Roman Republic, the seduction of its evil arts on that hitherto austere commonwealth was such, that from that time dates the decline of Roman virtue and liberty. The city had been visited by St. Peter before St. Paul came there, and the Christian faith had made such rapid conquests, and operated so extraordinary a change in the manners of the local Christian society, that it was the wonder of all Greece. Still, both because of the great mental activity which prevailed among Corinthians of all classes, and because of the concourse of strangers from the East and the West who met here like two adverse tides, there was a great diversity of opinion and sentiment among the faithful. St. Peter had left there as elsewhere the impress of his authority and the memory of his virtues. After him St. Paul had come, and the eloquence of the Apostle of the Gentiles had, not improbably, cast into the shade the preaching of the poor fisherman of Galilee; then had come from Alexandria Apollos, more eloquent even than Paul, and one who had the secret of all the philosophies of Egypt, Asia, and Greece. And so, as was the wont in the East, these cultured Christians would discuss the respective merits of their teachers, as the university students in Athens and Alexandria criticised the eloquence and doctrines of their rhetoricians and philosophers. This was one source of contention. Another came from their very imperfect acquaintance with the moral law of the Gospel—the Jewish converts, probably, contending for the maintenance of Jewish customs, while the Gentile proselytes refused to be governed by the prescriptions of the Mosaic law. The Corinthians themselves had, besides, written to St. Paul, begging to be instructed on several matters of doctrine and discipline. This letter is an answer to this prayer, as well as a general admonition to the church of Corinth to discountenance unwise and uncharitable discussions, and to cherish, above all things, union of souls by firm faith and inviolable charity. " Every one of you saith: I indeed am of Paul; and I am of Apollo; and I of Cephas; and I of Christ. Is Christ divided? Was Paul then crucified for you? or were you baptized in the name of Paul?" Such are the words of weighty remonstrance with which the Apostle begins his instruction, and they let us into the secret of these lamentable divisions. To the proud and vain Greeks, who sought and prized philosophical wisdom above all else, the Apostle declares that he knows but one wisdom: that by which God has redeemed and is converting the world through the mystery of the Cross, and the humiliations of the Crucified—a means of all the most inadequate according to the judgment of the worldly-wise. "But we have the mind of Christ," he declares, as the sole rule and measure of our judgments in things spiritual.

Wherefore, as the merits of their teachers did not bring about the change of heart wrought in the converts, but the hidden virtue of the Cross and the grace of the Crucified, so the labors of Apostolic men had been barren of all heavenly fruit without that same grace. "Let no man therefore glory in men. For all things are yours . . . And you are Christ's: and Christ is God's." It is worse than folly, then, to dispute about the personal qualities or merits of the Apostle through whom one has received the word of salvation, seeing that the Church and the whole body of the divine ordinances are God's gift to man in Christ, and that one ought to look to the Almighty Giver and the priceless gift rather than to the earthly channel through which it is communicated. Nevertheless, as the Apostles are the workmen and servants of the Master, to Him alone are they amenable in judgment. Hence, chap. iv., the severe reproof given to all who permit themselves to arraign the conduct of God's ministers.

To humble these vain-glorious and self-sufficient Corinthians, the Apostle, in chap. v., touches on the festering sore both of Pagan and Christian society in the beautiful city—unbridled licentiousness. A Christian man had forgotten himself so far as to marry his own stepmother. Him the Apostle excommunicates, and then comes the solemn admonition to the young Church of the place: "Your glorying is not good. Know ye not that a little leaven corrupteth the whole lump? Purge out the old leaven, that you may be a new paste . . . Put away the Evil One from among yourselves!"

Then follow authoritative admonitions against the unbrotherly practice of bringing their wrongs for judgment before the Pagan tribunals, and against those sins of impurity that are so opposed to the ideal of Christian holiness, chap. vi.; lessons on marriage, virginity, and celibacy, chap. vii.; on abstinence from meats offered to idols, chap. viii.; on his own voluntary poverty, his working at a trade, and his bodily austerities, chap. ix.; on the abstinence from certain meats to be observed by the faithful, x.; on the dress and functions of women in the church-services, and the celebration of the Holy Eucharist, xi.; on the divine economy in the distribution of extraordinary gifts and graces, xii.; on the incomparable excellence of charity as the great central virtue to be sought and practiced by all, xiii.; on the preference to be given to the gift or talent of prophesying; that is, of understanding and expounding divine things, xiv. In the xvth chapter he answers the last question put to him by the Corinthians on the final resurrection, concluding, in the last chapter, with directions about collecting alms for the needy churches, and various farewell words of admonition and blessing.

The Second Epistle, written a few months after the First, was penned by the Apostle to relieve the excommunicated Corinthian of his heavy censure, and to encourage the prompt good-will of all those who had profited by the reproofs and teachings detailed above. St. Paul once more reasserts his apostolic independence of all earthly praise and commendation. The Judaïzing faction, instead of yielding to Paul's appeal in favor of union and charity, still persisted in accusing him of undue leaning to the Gentiles and of defaming Moses and the law. They evidently went so far as to deny him the rank and quality of a true Apostle, thereby belittling his ministry and destroying his influence with a great number of people. These factious intrigues had, perhaps, induced the Corinthians to draw up letters commendatory of Paul and his labors. At any rate, he declines any such commendation, affirms the independence of the ministers of the New Testament, exalts the mission entrusted to himself and his associates (chap. iv.); urges them to be liberal in their charity toward the needy sister churches; and exhorts them to make a good use of God's liberality toward themselves. From chapter x. to the end he nobly defends himself and his labors against the detractors who had been so busy among the Corinthians.

EPISTLE TO THE GALATIANS.—This Epistle was written from Ephesus, according to the opinion of the best biblical scholars. The Galatians were the Gauls or Celts of Western Asia; they had been instructed in the faith by St. Paul, but, in his absence, had been, like the Corinthians, sadly disturbed by Judaïzing mischief-makers, who persuaded them of the necessity of conforming to the law of circumcision and to other Jewish observances, depreciating at the same time the apostolic rank and services of Paul. He therefore writes to undo what these false teachers and pernicious zealots had been doing among the fervent, hot-headed, and impulsive Galatians. He establishes his own claim to the Apostolate by relating the fact of his miraculous conversion and his special mission to the Gentiles, a mission received immediately from Christ, and expressly approved by the body of the Apostles and by Peter in particular. He shows, moreover, that Peter as well as his colleagues had sanctioned the stand that he (Paul) had taken on the questions arising about the Mosaic Law, and the free and sinless intercourse of converted Jews with their Gentile brethren and others. He solemnly rejects the obligation which Judaïzing Christians sought to impose on the Church of submitting to the prescriptions of the ceremonial law of Moses; and asserts the freedom from that law of servitude as the spiritual birthright of Christians. He, therefore, exhorts them to free themselves from the bondage of sensual superstitions to which both the modern Jews and the Gentiles were slaves, and to serve Christ in that lofty freedom of soul into which the apostolic teaching and the infallible guidance of the Church were sure to lead them. "Stand fast, and be not held again under the yoke of bondage. Behold, I Paul tell you, that if you be circumcised, Christ shall profit you nothing . . . You are made void of Christ, you who are justified in the law: you are fallen from grace . . . You did run well: who hath hindered you, that you should not obey the truth? This persuasion is not from Him that calleth you."

THE EPISTLE TO THE EPHESIANS.—The city of Ephesus has many claims on our veneration. It became, after the destruction of Jerusalem by Titus, the chief residence of the Apostle St. John, and the residence as well to the end of her life of the Blessed Virgin Mary. There, also, as tradition hath it, her blessed body was buried during the brief interval between her death and her assumption into heaven. Ephesus, moreover, was at that time not only the great stronghold of Pagan superstition—containing the incomparable Temple of Diana—but the great intellectual centre of Western Asia. Its schools rivaled in influence those of Alexandria and Athens, while its philosophers boasted of possessing

all the secrets of the most ancient philosophies of the East. During the first seven centuries of Christianity Ephesus held a commanding place among the Asiatic churches, and was the scene of events and discussions famous in ecclesiastical history. Even when it fell into the hands of the Mohammedans, its traditions and monuments secured to the remnants of its Catholic population unusual protection and privileges.

As St. Paul had repeatedly visited Ephesus and labored there with extraordinary zeal and success, he could not but feel a most fatherly interest in the prosperity of a church holding such a position, and destined to wield such a powerful influence on the sister-churches of Asia Minor. There is a most touching passage in Acts xx. 15–38, describing Paul's interview at Miletus with the clergy of the Church of Ephesus. The beautiful farewell discourse which the Apostle addresses to them ought to be read in conjunction with this Epistle, written during Paul's first imprisonment at Rome, in the year 62.

The Epistle itself is one of the most sublime productions of the Apostle of the Gentiles. To the infant and persecuted Church of Ephesus, surrounded by schools in which were taught all the systems of Grecian and Asiatic philosophy, all the seductive theories of Persian Gnosticism, St. Paul exposes in this letter the whole scheme of God's supernatural providence in the Incarnation, the Redemption, and the establishment of the Church, the great instrument by which the human race, through all succeeding generations, might become incorporated into one undying Society under Christ as Head, and thus be made sharers of all the temporal and eternal benefits of His redemption. The Christian family are thus "the adopted children of God," i. 5, under Christ, the God-Man, elevated in Heaven above all created beings, and being made "Head over all the Church, which is His body, and the fulness of Him, who is filled all in all," i. 20–23. In Him, in this blessed society which is His mystic Body, all the social barriers established by oriental castes and prejudices·are broken down ; there is neither Greek nor Barbarian, nor slave nor free, nor Jew nor Gentile : "the Gentiles" are "fellow-heirs and copartners of His promise in Christ Jesus by the Gospel," iii. 6 ; Paul hath been sent to preach "the unsearchable riches of Christ, and to enlighten all men," without distinction, on the merciful design of the eternal God, iii. 8–21. The remainder of the epistle is a most eloquent exhortation to the God-like virtues becoming such a divine rank.

THE EPISTLE TO THE PHILIPPIANS.—Of this sufficient mention was made in the section on the "Fourteen Epistles of St. Paul." It is the sweet and affectionate expression of the Apostle's gratitude and fatherly tenderness toward a church which sent him in his dire need substantial proofs of love, and which gave, amid continual persecutions, evidence of heroic constancy and piety.

THE EPISTLE TO THE COLOSSIANS.—Colossæ was a beautiful and flourishing city, situated inland from Ephesus, on the head-waters of the Mæander and near the high-road from Ephesus to the Euphrates. Colossæ was thus exposed to the same dangerous influences against which St. Paul wished to guard the Ephesians in the Epistle addressed to them. There is a striking resemblance both in the doctrinal lessons he gives to the Colossians and in the practical virtues which he recommends to them, and the substance of his great Epistle to the Ephesians. The letter to the Church of Colossæ was also written by the Apostle from his prison in Rome, and sent by Tychicus, Epaphras, and Onesimus, the two latter being themselves Colossians by birth, and Epaphras having been, moreover, the first to preach the Gospel in his native city. In the first, or doctrinal portion, St. Paul clearly warns the Colossians against the Gnostic theories, as well as the narrow exclusiveness of the Judaïzing preachers. We have been "translated (by God the Father) into the Kingdom of the Son of His love, . . . who is the first-born of every creature: for in Him were all things created in Heaven and on earth, visible and invisible," i. 13–16.

The whole "mystery" of the Christian dispensation, the whole purpose of Christ's work and government, is to present the Christian man "holy and unspotted and blameless before Him," i. 22. It is to attain this end that Paul labors and suffers: "We preach admonishing every man, and teaching every man in all wisdom, that we may present every man perfect in Christ Jesus," i. 28. They are to glory in Christ as being the infinite God and the infinite Wisdom. "As therefore you have received (been taught) Jesus Christ, walk ye in Him," ii. 6. They are not to go back to the imperfect and now empty forms and observances of Judaism, ii. 16–23. They are to shine forth in supernatural newness of life, iii., iv.

THE FIRST EPISTLE TO THE THESSALONIANS.—St. Paul had a special and well-merited affection for the churches of Thessalonica and Philippi. In both these cities the Gospel had been received willingly, and its professors there had shown themselves worthy followers of Paul and of his Master, Christ. There, however—throughout all Greece, indeed, as well as in Asia Minor—the Jews had shown themselves the bitter and unscrupulous opponents of the Apostles, and the unrelenting persecutors of all who embraced the Christian faith. Through their misrepresentations Paul had to fly from Philippi, and had been assailed in Thessalonica with still greater violence. Nevertheless, a flourishing church had sprung up there, composed principally of converts from Paganism. After St. Paul's departure, the Jewish Synagogue in Thessalonica—powerful even then, and comprising at present fully one-third of the entire population—employed its whole influence in shaking the fidelity of the new Christians, and in persecuting all those whose constancy remained proof against persecution. St. Timothy, Paul's indefatigable companion, had been sent to comfort the Thessalonians in their distress and to inquire carefully into their spiritual progress. On his return, he reported most favorably to his master. Thereupon St. Paul wrote to Thessalonica. It is the letter of a true fatherly, apostolic heart, written, most probably, from Corinth in the last months of the year 52. After expressing his devout gratitude for their progress and perseverance in virtue and piety, he replies to the personal abuse heaped on him by the Jews by recalling to the minds of his converts with what heroic zeal and disinterestedness he had labored among them, supporting himself the while by the work of his own hands. They have not, therefore, any cause to blush for their spiritual father. In the impossibility of returning to their city, he beseeches them to increase their fidelity and fervor; praises their extraordinary charity; urges them to attend, in all peacefulness and quietness, to their respective avocations, and to those steady habits of industry which secure independence. They are not to mourn hopelessly for their dead. They are destined to share in Christ's glorious resurrection. Being certain that this Great Day of awakening shall come for all, "Let us not sleep as others do; but let us watch and be sober . . . And we beseech you, brethren, rebuke the unquiet, comfort the feeble-minded, support the weak be patient towards all men."

THE SECOND EPISTLE TO THE THESSALONIANS.—This was also written from Corinth very soon after the First, and for a like purpose. He particularly instructs them not to be alarmed by the predictions of some false teachers who went about announcing that the end of the world was near at hand. "Therefore, brethren, stand fast! and hold the traditions which you have learned, whether by word, or by our epistle."

THE FIRST AND SECOND EPISTLE TO TIMOTHY.—This faithful companion and fellow-laborer of St. Paul was a native of Derbe or Lystra in Lycaonia, the son of a Greek father, and of a Jewish mother, Eunice, to whose careful training as well as to that of his grandmother, Lois, he owed not only his knowledge of the Old Testament writings, but his conversion to Christianity. From his first meeting with Paul at Lystra, the Apostle's soul was drawn to the heroic youth in whom he discovered all the great qualities that go to make the apostolic missionary and ruler of God's church. This was during St. Paul's first missionary tour, when Timothy was only a stripling. Seven years afterward, during Paul's second tour, Timothy was set apart and ordained for the apostolic ministry. Thenceforward he became Paul's right hand in his gigantic labors, going whithersoever the latter would, to confirm and console the faithful of Europe or Asia, following his master to Rome and sharing, it is thought, his first imprisonment there. After their liberation, Paul and his companion revisited Asia together, Timothy being placed in charge of the Church of Ephesus, while St. Paul went over to Macedonia.

The First Epistle, written at some uncertain date after the separation, is, manifestly, an instruction on the duties of the pastoral office, every line of which has been for eighteen centuries the delightful spiritual food of bishops and priests all over the world. The Second Epistle was written from St. Paul's prison in Rome, and most probably a very short time before his death. "I have a remembrance of thee in my prayers, night and day, desiring to see thee, being mindful of thy tears, that I may be filled with joy; calling to mind that faith which is in thee unfeigned, which also dwelt first in thy grandmother Lois, and in thy mother Eunice, and I am certain that in thee also" (i. 3–5). Thus does the fatherly heart of the aged Apostle go out to the young bishop, touching and moving powerfully every heroic fibre in it, before he lays before him the details of the high and holy duties which are incumbent on him. It is like the eagle encouraging its young to try the loftiest flights.

"Only Luke is with me," the imprisoned Apostle says in concluding; "take Mark and bring him with thee . . . The cloak that I left at Troas with Carpus, when thou comest, bring with thee, and the books, especially the parchments." Such is the poverty of this glorious apostle of Jesus of Nazareth! Would you see a further resemblance of Paul with his Master, listen to what the apostle says of his first appearance before the Roman magistrates, probably of his first trial by torture: "At my first answer no man stood with me, but all forsook me: may it not be laid to their charge! But the Lord stood by me and strengthened me," 2 Tim. iv. 16, 17.

THE EPISTLE TO TITUS.—Titus was the son of Greek parents, by birth a Gentile, consequently. He was a fellow-laborer of St. Paul and Barnabas at Antioch, and assisted with them at the Council of Jerusalem, in which it was decided that the Gentile converts should not be compelled to receive circumcision. He was employed by St. Paul on various missions to the churches, such as were intrusted to Timothy, and, like the latter, was appointed by the Apostle to discharge the episcopal functions. In the interval between St. Paul's first and second imprisonment at Rome, he visited Crete in company with Titus, and left the latter in the island after him to govern the church there. The Epistle addressed to Titus from Nicopolis (in Epirus, probably, where St. Paul was afterward arrested and carried a prisoner to Rome), after enumerating the chief virtues that should adorn a bishop, points out those which Titus is to insist on among the people he has to govern.

THE EPISTLE TO PHILEMON.—This is a touching plea for a fugitive slave, Onesimus, whom St. Paul had converted in Rome, whom he found a useful auxiliary in his ministrations, and whom he sends back to his native city, Colossæ, where he expects Philemon to receive him as a brother.

THE EPISTLE TO THE HEBREWS.—The constant belief of the Catholic Church ascribes the authorship of this most beautiful epistle to St. Paul. The doubts which modern critics have endeavored to cast on its authenticity are of too evanescent a nature to cloud the faith of the true Christian scholar. It was probably written from Rome, and in the year 63. It was addressed, not so much to the Hebrew race in general, as to the Hebrew Christians of Palestine, and, particularly, those of Jerusalem. For many years before this Jerusalem had been held in terror by an organized band of assassins (the *Sicarii*), and in the year 62 the new High Priest Annas, or Ananus II., a rigid Sadducee, began a formidable persecution against the Christians, and summoned before the Sanhedrim St. James, Bishop of Jerusalem, and other leading Christians. The other James had, several years before, been put to death by order of Herod Agrippa, and since then, as if in atonement of this innocent blood, the Sicarii, with the connivance of Felix, the Roman Governor, had killed the High Priest Jonathan at the altar and in the very act of sacrificing. Everything in Judæa portended the near accomplishment of our Lord's prediction—the utter destruction of Jerusalem and the Temple, and the final dispersion of the Jewish nation. It was thus a period of terrible and manifold trial for the Christian Hebrews of Palestine. What was to compensate them for the loss of their nationality, the destruction of the Holy City, the blotting out of the national sanctuary, and the cessation of the worship of their forefathers?

No one better than St. Paul could lift up the soul of these suffering Christians, confirm their faith by showing how the ancient promises were all fulfilled in Christ, how the trials of the Hebrews of old should animate their descendants to heroic constancy, and sustain their hopes by laying before them in the glorious spectacle of Christ's universal Kingdom and everlasting priesthood—the consummation of their most patriotic aspirations? To understand, therefore, both the purpose and the scope of this epistle, we must recall to mind the objections which non-believing Jews were continually making against the Christian religion and its Founder. Christ, they said, the author of this new faith, was a man put to the most shameful death by a solemn sentence of the magistrates and the people, whereas the Jewish religion could boast of a Law delivered to their nation by Angels acting in God's name, and promulgated by Moses, the holiest and most illustrious of men. Moreover, the Christians, instead of the glorious Temple of Jerusalem, the splendid sacrificial ritual ordained by Moses, the uninterrupted succession of priests and Levites descended from Aaron, and the sacred and solemn yearly festivals which assembled the Hebrew people around the altars of the living God, had only obscure and mysterious rites celebrated in holes and corners, without any hereditary priesthood or recognized public temple. Where could the Hebrew people go, as of old, in their manifold needs, in their consciousness of sin, to find the Mercy Seat on which Jehovah dwelt, or the altar of holocausts on which to offer the atoning victims of their guilt?

St. Paul purposes to show that the Christian Religion is incomparably above the Jewish, in this, that its Author and Lawgiver is Christ, the Son of God and very God Himself, as superior to the angels and to Moses as the Creator is to His creatures. Moses,

who stood as mediator between God and His people, was but a mortal man, whereas in our Mediator Christ, we have an infinite Person. The same transcendent excellence prevails in the rites and sacrifice of the New Law, and in the spiritual and eternal goods it bestows on its subjects.

In order to follow without confusion the course of St. Paul's demonstration, you have only to examine the natural divisions of this Epistle. I. From chap. i. to chap. iv., the Apostle shows the superiority of Christ's mediatorship above that intrusted either to the Angels or to Moses. He teaches (chap. i. 1–14) that Christ is above the Angels, although He has only spoken to us after the Prophets. For He is the Son of God, while they are only His messengers and ministers. Nor (ii. 6–8) does the fact of His being man argue His inferiority to the Angels, since even as Man, Christ hath been placed over all things. Besides, it was a necessary part of the divine plan of our redemption, that the Son should stoop to assume our human nature. "Because the children are partakers of flesh and blood, He also Himself in like manner hath been partaker of the same, that through death He might destroy him who had the empire of death, that is to say, the Devil."

Again (chaps. iii., iv.), Moses did not build the house in which he was a minister, whereas our Great High Priest is the builder and the master of God's House and Kingdom here below—a house and kingdom indeed which are only the figure of the heavenly and eternal. Moses, though faithful and true in his ministry, offended, and so did the people he guided, and they entered not into the rest of the Promised Land. Hence we Christians should take warning, and yearn for the eternal repose into which our Divine Leader hath already entered. "We have not a High Priest who cannot have compassion on our infirmities; but one tempted in all things, like as we are, without sin. Let us go therefore with confidence to the throne of grace: that we may obtain mercy, and find grace in seasonable aid" (iv. 15, 16). In these two last chapters the Apostle, with the art of a true orator, presses upon his afflicted and wavering brethren the danger and fearful consequences of apostasy or falling away from the faith. Those who followed Moses out of Egypt, who heard the word of the Lord in the wilderness and beheld His wonderful ways, wavered and failed in their faith; therefore did they not enter into the promised rest. How many perished in the desert! Even under Josue (*Jesus* iv. 8) they did not, in the land of Chanaan, obtain that divine and everlasting repose, which it belongs to the true Jesus, the only Saviour, to bestow. But firm faith in Him is already the beginning of possession, the anticipated enjoyment of that rest which gives God to the soul and the soul to God. Let us then give to Him through that living faith our whole heart and soul. "Having therefore a great High Priest that hath passed into the heavens, JESUS the Son of God, let us hold fast our confession."

II. St. Paul now proceeds to discuss the dignity and prerogatives of Christ's priesthood and the infinite virtue of His sacrifice, as the One Victim and oblation prefigured by the sacrificial offerings of the Old Law. In chap. v. 1–11, St. Paul proves that Christ performed the functions of the priestly office by offering up "gifts and sacrifices for sins." Moreover, He closed His earthly career by fulfilling in His own person and by His last acts the prophecy which likened Him to Melchisedech. "And being consummated, He became, to all that obey Him, the cause of eternal salvation, called by God a High Priest according to the order of Melchisedech."

As if the Reality prefigured in the sacrifice of Melchisedech, and consummated in the Bread and Wine offered up by Christ, recalled some formidable practical difficulties, the Apostle here turns aside (v. 11; vi. 20) to solve them for his readers. "Of whom (Melchisedech) we have much to say, and hard to be intelligibly uttered, because you are become weak to bear. . . . Strong meat is for the perfect, for them who by custom have their senses exercised to the discerning of good and evil." The Apostle is unwilling to rehearse for these vaccilating Christians the elementary truths delivered to catechumens. And then comes the terrible warning to those who allow their first fervor to cool during a time of persecution and their faith to waver, who have abused the most precious graces, and by this abuse placed themselves on the road to apostasy. "It is impossible for those who were once illuminated, have tasted also the heavenly Gift, and were made partakers of the Holy Ghost, have, moreover, tasted the good word of God, and the powers of the world to come, and are fallen away, to be renewed again to penance!" . . . Woe to "the earth that drinketh in the rain which cometh often upon it . . . but . . . . bringeth forth thorns and briars!" . . . "It is reprobate and very near to a curse . . ." Then come words of generous praise for their former noble deeds of piety and charity, and a most beautiful exhortation to constant and increasing carefulness under present trials. Theirs must be the invincible patience and living faith of Abraham, who was rewarded after so much suffering and waiting. Even so must they anchor their faith and hope in Heaven, "Where the fore-runner Jesus is entered for us."

Taking up the thread of his argument where he had left it at the mention of Christ's priesthood in connection with that of Melchisedech, the Apostle proceeds to show that even as the typical Melchisedech, the King-priest of Salem, was superior in dignity to Abraham, and to Levi descended from Abraham with his sacerdotal progeny, so and far more so He who is "a Priest forever according to the order of Melchisedech," transcends both the priest-King of Salem and the Levitical priesthood. "By so much is Jesus made a surety of a better testament," vii. 22. "We have such an High Priest, who is set on the right hand of the throne of majesty in the Heavens, a minister of the Holies and of the true tabernacle, which the Lord hath pitched, and not man," viii. 1, 2. This High Priest, this Priesthood, this Tabernacle, this sacrificial worship, are that most perfect and divine exemplar which all preceding types and systems copied and foreshadowed.

The blood which flowed in the manifold Mosaic sacrifices was figurative of the blood of the One Infinite Victim; the sacrifices were many and daily renewed because of themselves inefficacious toward atonement or sanctification, ix. 1–10. "But Christ being come an High Priest of the good things to come, . . . by His own blood entered once into the Holies, having obtained eternal redemption," ix. 11, 12.

The national Jewish religion with its gorgeous worship was thus only "a shadow of the good things to come, not the very image of the things," x. 1—could "never make the comers thereunto perfect." Now we have in the Lamb of God the victim of infinite price and merit; and, therefore, "we are sanctified by the oblation of the body of Jesus Christ once," x. 10. So, "this [great High Priest] offering one sacrifice for sins, for ever sitteth at the right hand of God . . . By one oblation He hath perfected for ever them that are sanctified," x. 12, 14. Thus by the application to us of the infinite atoning merits of this one bloody sacrifice of Calvary is the guilt of all sin remitted, and through that Blood applied to our souls in every sacrament and every individual grace, are we enabled to go on from degree to degree of spiritual perfection and holiness. O Jews, wherefore, then, do ye weep over the prospect of the near destruction of your Temple and the coming ruin of your Sion? Wherefore refuse to be comforted because with the Temple shall cease forever the sacrificial worship of your forefathers? Look up to Jesus promised by Moses and the Prophets, prefigured by Melchisedech and his oblation. He, the Great High Priest of the perfect and everlasting Covenant, hath fulfilled both the unbloody oblation of the King-Priest of Salem and the bloody expiation foreshown by the Levitic sacrifices. Our Divine Melchisedech sits forever at the right hand of the Father, offering evermore for all succeeding generations His Body and Blood as the price of their ransom and the source of all saving and sanctifying graces. And on earth, even when your Temple disappears, and not one drop of blood shall redden the spot where it now stands,

there shall continue all over the earth from the rising to the setting sun the Everlasting Commemoration of Christ's bloody sacrifice, the unbloody offering of Melchisedech. Thus heaven and earth shall ever unite in the divine and perfect offering of Him who is a Priest forever according to the order of Melchisedech.

Having thus established the superiority of the New Covenant over the Old, St. Paul once more appeals to his Hebrew coreligionists to continue steadfast in the faith, x. 19–30. "Let us consider one another to provoke unto charity and good works." The Christian Church may not punish with death apostates and transgressors, as was the wont of the Jewish (x. 28); but the spiritual and unseen punishment reserved to the apostate from Christianity is not the less terrible or uncertain, because unseen. "It is a fearful thing to fall into the hands of the living God!" The bitter trials which the Church has to endure will soon be ended. Meanwhile her sons must arm themselves with faith and the heroic patience faith begets.

III. The three remaining chapters are taken up with a description of that living faith—the mightiest of moral forces—and its wonderful effects, as exemplified in their own illustrious ancestors (chap. xi.); with a stirring exhortation to his Christian brethren to emulate such glorious examples (chap. xii.), and to devote themselves to the practice of brotherly charity and its kindred active virtues—the most efficacious preservative against human respect and loss of fervor (chap. xiii.)

III. THE SEVEN CATHOLIC EPISTLES.

THE EPISTLE OF ST. JAMES.—Although some writers have attributed the authorship of this Epistle to St. James the Elder, the brother of St. John, the great majority of biblical scholars ascribe it to St. James the Less or the Younger, Bishop of Jerusalem, and brother of St. Jude. The former was put to death by Herod Agrippa in the year 44, and the latter suffered martyrdom about 62 or 63 by order of the High Priest Annas or Ananus II. It is thought that he wrote this Epistle in the year 59, some three years before his death. This glorious relative of our Lord was one of those to whom He deigned to show Himself in a special manner after the resurrection (1 Cor. xv. 7). He had his residence in Jerusalem, where he was looked upon as a pillar of the Church, and where he was visited by St. Paul soon after the conversion of the latter (Galat. i. 18); and where also he assisted at the council held by the Apostles, and pronounced a discourse to which the others assented. From his coreligionists, fellow-citizens, and contemporaries he received the surname of "the Just," and was, besides, popularly designated as "Oblias" or "the bulwark of the people," on account of his extraordinary devotion to prayer and his influence with the Divine Majesty. St. Epiphanius says that he was appointed by our Lord Himself to govern the Church of Jerusalem.

In his Epistle, which he addressed to all the Christian Churches, St. James insists on the necessity of good works as the proper fruits of a soul filled with a living and active faith. He insisted on this in order to confute the erroneous interpretation given in many places to the doctrine of St. Paul, on the inadequacy of works performed in fulfillment either of the Law of Moses or the Law of Nature to merit or effect justification: this was to be the effect of divine grace alone. The false interpreters of St. Paul affirmed that the works performed by charity were not necessary to salvation; that faith alone sufficed. Hence the declaration of the Apostle: "Be ye doers of the word, and not hearers only, deceiving your own selves" (i. 22). "If then you fulfill the royal law, according to the Scriptures, *Thou shalt love thy neighbor as thyself,* you do well" (ii. 8). "What shall it profit, my brethren, if a man say he hath faith, but hath not works? Shall faith be able to save him?" (ii. 14). "For even as the body without the spirit is dead;

so also faith without works is dead" (ii. 26). Both St. Paul and St. James taught that in the Christian soul supernatural faith and charity should go hand in hand working out man's salvation under the guidance of the Spirit of God, and producing deeds worthy of an adopted child of God. Both the one and the other taught that supernatural faith and charity, and all the divine forces that lift the soul of the sinner or the natural man to the state of grace or justification, are the free gift of God through Jesus Christ. Man's part in the vital acts which enter into the process of justification consists in yielding a free assent to the light vouchsafed him and obeying the impulse of the Spirit who moves his heart.

In this Epistle St. James, as is the common opinion, promulgated the doctrine relating to Extreme Unction, which had been instituted by our Lord, and which He taught His disciples to practice as is hinted in St. Mark vi. 13.

THE FIRST AND SECOND EPISTLES OF ST. PETER.—These are also termed "Catholic," because addressed to the faithful at large. The First Epistle is dated from "Babylon;" that is, Rome, according to the common interpretation of Catholics. Its substance, form, and tone remind one forcibly of the doctrinal encyclicals of the Roman Pontiffs, Peter's successors. Its purpose evidently is to instruct the Hebrew converts of Asia Minor, while edifying also those of other nationalities. He bids them adorn their Christian profession by holiness of life. Like St. Paul, Peter lifts the souls of his readers to the contemplation of the unchangeable Kingdom which is to be their inheritance in heaven, as the adopted children of the Father in Christ. This, however, is only the prize to be won by long-suffering patience here. This glorious and fruitful trial of their faith, as well as its unspeakable reward, has been the subject of the Prophecies so familiar to the Jews and now not unknown to their Gentile fellow-believers; for this trial they have been also prepared by the ministers of the Gospel (i. 1-12). Purchased from sin by an infinite price, "the precious blood of Christ, as of a Lamb unspotted and undefiled," let them be holy even as He is holy (13-25). In chap. ii. the Apostle continues to describe in fuller detail the means by which Christian humanity, regenerated or born anew of the blood of a God, may form a society of God-like brothers. Laying aside all the passions that are born of pride and selfishness, they are to be "as new-born babes" desiring earnestly the milk of this heavenly truth which feeds and elevates their rational nature, that thereby they may "grow unto salvation." Nay, more than that, the members of this society are likened to "living stones built up, a spiritual house" (ii. 5), the "chief corner-stone" of which is Christ. Anxious to see this glorious edifice brought to perfection and filling the earth, Peter, who is, under Christ, the Rock and foundation on which the whole structure reposes, addresses the faithful on the virtues that are most conducive to edification. "Dearly beloved, I beseech you as strangers and pilgrims, to refrain yourselves from carnal desires which war against the soul, having your conversation (manner of living) good among the Gentiles: that, whereas they speak against you as evil doers, they may, by the good works which they shall behold in you, glorify God in the day of visitation" (11, 12). And so, throughout the remainder of the Epistle, he continues to inculcate the practice of the private and public virtues that are ever sure to win Christians the love and reverence of mankind.

In the Second Epistle, written, most probably, from prison and shortly before his death, St. Peter insists on the divine rank to which regenerated man is lifted in Jesus Christ. This great and fundamental truth must be, for converted Jews and Gentiles, like a beacon-light placed on high above the road of life and guiding all the followers of Christ to the loftiest aims and the noblest deeds. "All things of His divine power, which appertain to life and godliness, are given us through the knowledge of Him who hath called us by His own proper glory and virtue. By whom He

hath given us most great and precious promises; that by these you may be made PARTAKERS OF THE DIVINE NATURE, flying the corruption of that concupiscence which is in the world" (i. 3, 4).

The supernatural knowledge of Christ, and of the Christian's sublime destinies in Him, is not only light in the mind but fire in the heart, purging it from the dross of all earthly and impure affections. This sacred fire cannot be concealed within the soul, but must needs break forth in one's whole outward life, enlightening all who come within its reach, and communicating to them the ardor of that heavenly charity which is as inseparable from the words and deeds of the true Christian as the sun's radiance and warmth are from the sun itself. Ponder every line and word throughout these too short chapters, and see how the inspired admonitions of the first Roman Pontiff are fitted to the needs of our own nineteenth century, warning us against the apostate Christians who put away Revealed Truth from them, because they, too, have "eyes full of adultery and of sin that ceaseth not" (ii. 14); . . . "Speaking proud words of vanity, they allure by the desires of fleshly riotousness those who for a little while escape, such as converse in error: promising them liberty, whereas they themselves are the slaves of corruption" (18, 19).

And how touching is the allusion to the Apostle's own death, so near at hand and so clearly revealed to himself! "I think it meet as long as I am in this tabernacle, to stir you up by putting you in remembrance, being assured that the laying away of my tabernacle is at hand, according as our Lord Jesus Christ also hath signified to me" (ii. 13, 14). The truth which this man, who is already in chains for his faith, and who is about to crown his apostleship by martyrdom and thus to seal his witness by his own blood, has preached throughout the Roman Empire and planted in Rome itself, is neither fiction nor imposture. "For we have not followed cunningly devised fables, when we made known to you the power and presence of our Lord Jesus Christ: but having been made eye-witness of His majesty . . . And we have the more firm prophetical word, whereunto you do well to attend, as to a light that shineth in a dark place, until the day dawn, and the Day-Star arise in your hearts: understanding this first, that no prophecy of Scripture is made by private interpretation. For prophecy came not by the will of man at any time: but the holy men of God spoke, inspired by the Holy Ghost. But there were also false prophets among the [Jewish] people, even as there shall be among you lying teachers, who shall bring in sects of perdition, and deny the Lord who bought them . . . And many shall follow their riotousnesses, through whom the WAY OF TRUTH shall be evil spoken of" (ii. 16-21; iii. 1, 2).

THE THREE EPISTLES OF ST. JOHN THE APOSTLE.—The first of these bore anciently the title of "Epistle to the Parthians," and was therefore supposed to have been addressed to such Jewish Christians as resided within the Parthian Empire. It is directed against the followers of Simon Magus, Cerinthus, and of Gnosticism. Simon maintained that Christ was not the Messiah, and claimed for himself the glory which he denied to Jesus, affirming that He only bore the semblance of our humanity, and that the body nailed to the Cross was not a substantial body. This was also, to a certain extent, the error of the Gnostics and the Docetæ, who denied the reality of Christ's birth and death. Finally, Cerinthus taught that Jesus was nothing but an ordinary man, the real son of Joseph, on whom, at His baptism by John, the Holy Ghost or Christ descended in the form of a dove, forsaking Him during His death agony. Thus, all of these agreed in denying the divinity of Christ. Against them all, and in favor of the One true Messiah whom he knew to be both very God and very man, John wrote. "That which was from the beginning, which we have heard, which we have seen with our eyes, which we have looked upon and our hands have handled, of the word of life: for the

THE FIRST EPISTLE GENERAL OF St. JOHN.

life was manifested; and we have seen and do bear witness, and declare unto you the life eternal, which was with the Father, and hath appeared unto us " (i. 1, 2). "Every spirit which confesseth that Jesus Christ is come in the flesh, is of God: and every spirit that dissolveth Jesus, is not of God" (iv. 2, 3). On the necessity of good work, especially of brotherly charity and its fruits, St. John insists with the other Apostles, Peter, Paul, and James, while inculcating a firm faith, invincible patience and spotless purity of life.

The authenticity of the Second and Third Epistles was denied by some scholars. They belong, however, to the canon received by the Church, and bear intrinsic evidence of St. John's authorship, besides the external weight of authority which ascribes these two letters to him.

THE EPISTLE OF ST. JUDE THE APOSTLE.—Jude was the brother of St. James the Younger or the Just, Bishop of Jerusalem. He was, consequently, a son of Alpheus or Cleophas, and a near relative of our Lord. It is not known when and where this epistle was written. It warns the faithful against following certain false teachers and sharing their awful doom. The reader will perceive, on an attentive perusal, how closely it resembles the Second Epistle of St. Peter.

THE APOCALYPSE OF ST. JOHN THE APOSTLE.—The Greek word *Apocalypsis* means "an unveiling;" hence the Protestant translators have called it *The Revelation* of St. John. It is thought to have been written about the year of our Lord 95 or 97, and, most likely, in the Island of Patmos. It is the only prophetic book among the New Testament Scriptures, and its inherent obscurity has exercised, during more than eighteen hundred years, the ingenuity of the most eminent biblical scholars and theologians.

It may suffice, however, to take up the text of the Apocalypse, and to find in the natural sequence of the chapters themselves the light which will enable one to understand more clearly the history of the Christian Church in the past, to appreciate her struggles in the present, and to look forward with the eye of exultant hope to her certain victories in the future, as well as to that Supreme Day of Judgment which will vindicate the whole mysterious order of God's providence.

We can divide the whole matter of this sublime book into two parts. In the first, embracing the first three chapters, St. John addresses himself in particular to the faithful of Proconsular Asia, who were his special charge, and reproves what he finds censurable in the seven dioceses or churches within the Proconsulate. This portion, therefore, is strictly ethical and historical. The second and prophetical portion embraces the remainder of the book from chap. iv. to the end, and describes, under various allegorical and mystical forms, the stages through which the Church has to pass, especially the last period of her existence, the times of Antichrist. Such is the view presented by the learned and saintly Cornelius à Lapide. The purpose of the Apostle, according to this author, is to animate the faithful of the apostolic age and of all future times to invincible constancy in the faith, to the highest forms of holiness, and more particularly to strengthen the martyrs in the days of persecution to bear their witness with unflinching firmness. Let me add here to the learned Jesuit's thought, that St. John regarded in a special manner the condition and the needs of the numerous Jewish Christians at the close of the first century. St. Paul, in almost every one of his epistles, shows them in the magnificent realities promised in the Gospel a compensation for their loss of caste among their non-Christian countrymen, and a sublime consolation for the dispersion of their race, the destruction of Jerusalem, and the annihilation of their national worship. The spectacle disclosed to the Apostle of the Eternal Temple on high, the Throne with its ineffable splendors, the seventy Elders on their royal seats, the twelve times twelve thousand from the Tribes of Israel forming the glorious nucleus of the beatified multitude which no man could

number, and the Altar with its Lamb ever sacrificed and ever immortal—a
that went home to the hearts of the poor down-trodden Jewish exiles; all th
was calculated to make them find in the daily *Agapæ* or celebrations of t
Eucharistic sacrifice a significance, a divine and blissful Reality that cou
well make them feel that Heaven was not far from earth, and that the earth
house of God, though but a corner in the Catacombs, had some of the inten
and unspeakable enjoyments of the Eternal Home. And so the seed o
Abraham continued to be, among the Gentiles, the fruitful seed of Christianit
thanks to the skilful and loving husbandry of Peter and Paul and John an
James and Jude.

Besides, all throughout Asia Minor, during the age of St. John and lo
afterward, such heretics as Cerinthus and Ebion denied openly, and in Ephes
itself, the divinity of Christ, although they persisted in calling themselves H
followers, as do to this day among ourselves Sects that we need not nam
They also taught that Christ, even as the Son of God, had no existence befo
the Blessed Virgin Mary. As it was to prepare an antidote to this heretic
poison that St. John wrote his Gospel, and proclaimed "In the beginning w
the Word, etc., ..." so in the Apocalypse he makes Christ Himself declar
"I am Alpha and Omega, the beginning and the end, . . . who is, and wh
was, and who is to come, the Almighty" (i. 8). Others, again, never ceas
to say, amid the horrible and unceasing persecutions with which the you
Christian Church was assailed, that she must of a necessity be crushed
the irresistible might of the hostile powers, and that there could be no rewa
for the Confessors and martyrs of Christ. John shows, on the contrary, th
the tree of the Church waxes strong amid all the fury of the tempest, a
that for those who struggle here for the good cause there is laid up an etern
reward. It is this triumph of the just which he describes in chaps. xx
and xxii.